Jacob and Wilhelm
Grimm

Complete Fairy Tales

With an introduction by Padraic Colum

and a folkloristic commentary by Joseph Campbell

With illustrations by Josef Scharl

London and New York

First published in the United Kingdom 1948
by Routledge & Kegan Paul

First published in Routledge Classics 2002
by Routledge
2 Park Square, Milton Park, Abingdon, Oxon OX14 4RN

Reprinted 2004 (twice), 2005, 2006 (twice), 2007

Routledge is an imprint of the Taylor & Francis Group, an informa business

© 1944 Pantheon Inc
© 1972 Random House Inc
This edition © 2002 Routledge

Typeset in Joanna by RefineCatch Limited, Bungay, Suffolk
Printed and bound in Great Britain by TJ International Ltd,
Padstow, Cornwall

British Library Cataloguing in Publication Data
A catalogue record for this book is available from the British Library

ISBN10: 0–415–28595–X (hbk)
ISBN10: 0–415–28596–8 (pbk)

ISBN13: 978–0–415–28595–7 (hbk)
ISBN13: 978–0–415–28596–4 (pbk)

Contents

THE CHILDREN'S LEGENDS

INTRODUCTION

In the place where the storyteller was the coming of night was marked as it was not in towns nor in modern houses. It was so marked that it created in the mind a different rhythm. There had been a rhythm of the day and now there was a rhythm of the night. . . . The storyteller seated on a roughly made chair on a clay floor did not look unusually intelligent or sensitive. He certainly did not look histrionic. What was in his face showed that he was ready to respond to and make articulate the rhythm of the night. He was a storyteller because he was attuned to this rhythm and had in his memory the often repeated incidents that would fit it. . . . These notions were in the present writer's mind once upon a time when he sat in a cottage where the tradition of storytelling was still in being.

A rhythm that was compulsive, fitted to daily tasks, waned, and a rhythm that was acquiescent, fitted to wishes, took its place. But when the distinction between day and night could be passed over as it could be in towns and in modern houses the change of rhythm that came with the passing of day into night ceased to be marked. This happened when light was prolonged until it was time to turn to sleep.

The prolongation of light meant the cessation of traditional stories in European cottages. And when the cottages took in American kerosene or paraffin there was prolongation. Then came lamps with full and steady light, lamps that gave real illumination. Told under this illumination the traditional stories ceased to be appropriate because the rhythm that gave them meaning was weakened.

Other things happened to put traditional stories out of date. Young people went to schools and learned to read. The world reached into the villages; wars and the doings of parliaments interested country people more and more. Claiming attention for the happenings of the day before, the newspaper reader took the place of the traditional story-teller, the man of memories.

A real culture, we know, is all of a piece and all its parts fit together. Household stories imply work done in a household and work done in a household implies household stories. In western Ireland today a loom or a spinning-wheel is a sign that one can find a traditional storyteller in the cottage or in the neighbourhood. The present writer has heard from his elders that in times when the girls of the neighbourhood came to a cottage to do the spinning a storyteller was fetched to entertain them. Men and women coming in from factories would not be entertained by household stories but people who worked in the house would. The prolongation of light, the introduction of books and newspapers, the cessation of the household arts all went together to make an end of traditional stories in European cottages.

There were other reasons. A widespread language took the place of dialects and the language of the traditional stories became obscure. The meaning of the stories could only be put baldy into the widespread language; the current language was not traditional enough to relate the traditions in. In High German, the Brothers Grimm noted, a story gained in clearness (that is, clearness for the reader), but it "lost in flavor, and no longer had such a firm hold of the kernel of the thing signified." They were wise enough not to put all their collection in High German; frequently they retained the dialect of the district where they heard the stories.

Today we can hear traditional stories but in very out-of-the-way parts of Europe. A writer who lived in such places gives us a sense of distance from the modern world when he puts a storytelling session before us. "He is so blind that I can gaze at him without discourtesy, and after a while the expression of his face made me forget to listen. . . . The glow of childish transport that came over him when he reached the nonsense ending—so common in these tales—recalled me to myself, and I listened attentively while he gabbled with delighted haste: "They found the path and I found the puddle. They were drowned and I was found. If it's all one to me to-night, it wasn't all one to them the next night. Yet, if it wasn't myself, not a thing did they lose but an old back tooth."*

The Brothers Grimm tell us about one who at the beginning of the nineteenth century gave them their best stories, a woman from near Kassel. "Her memory kept a firm grip on all the sagas. She herself knew that this gift was not granted to everyone, and that there were many who could remember nothing connectedly. She told her stories thoughtfully, accurately, with wonderful vividness, and evidently had delight in doing it. First, she related them from beginning to end, and then, if required, repeated them more slowly, so that after some practice, it was perfectly easy to write from her dictation." Very likely, because they had to write down her words, the Brothers Grimm laid stress upon this storyteller's verbal memory; others in listening to her might have thought that her real gift was perception of pattern, and her real accomplishment making it, the pattern, evident.

"There were those who could remember nothing connectedly." We might say that they were the mediocre storytellers who confused the pattern by putting incidents in the wrong place, by using unfitting metaphors, by making a hurried beginning or a hurried end, by being unable to use the chiming words that made special—or, as we would say now, that featured some passage: 'puddle' with 'path', 'tooth' with 'lose', for example.

The rhythm of night, marked in the place where it was told, set the mood without which the traditional story would have diminished appeal. The household arts there were unvarying from generation to generation, and so were the patterns of the stories. One did not introduce new designs into weaving or cart-building, and one did not introduce new designs into storytelling. We have been told that the hearers of traditional stories wanted to have remembered incidents, remembered sentences, repeated. But the unvarying content of a story was not altogether due to a liking for the same thing over again. The

* J. M. Synge: *The Aran Islands.*

good traditional storyteller had a sense of pattern and prided himself or herself on knowing and keeping to it.

Because they had few possessions and these transmitted to them, or made by their own hands or the hands of people they knew, the tellers and hearers of these stories valued things, visible, tangible, usable things. They put a thing in the centre of the story and it gave a pattern. What an advantage it is to a storyteller to have a feeling for the value, for the uniqueness of a thing! Things remain real while mental states become doubtful to us.

The golden slipper on the stairway is what the incidents in "Cinderella" lead up to and lead away from. And the gold of the slipper puts into greater obscurity the drably dressed girl crouched by the ashes. In "Snow White" there is the looking glass of the wicked queen which is doubled in the glass coffin in which Snow White is laid by the kindly dwarfs. In "Briar Rose" there is the spindle that is doubled in the thorns that hedge the castle. In "The Goose Girl" the horse's head that speaks is doubled in the hat the wind blows away, and in "King Trushbeard" the crockery which the king's daughter has to sell is doubled in the jars which, as the kitchen maid, she uses to bring the dinner leavings home, and which break, too. These correspondences are like rhymes which chance gives a poet and which, duly set down, gives his poem a happy completeness. Another kind of correspondence is in "Rapunzel:" the maiden has long hair and the witch confines her in a tower, and we do not know whether the tower makes it proper she should have long hair, or whether her long hair makes the tower part of the story.

It is this achievement of pattern so much more fundamental than that achieved by the conscious writer that makes the best of these stories so memorable. In "The Water of Life" the flowing of the fountain (not a still well, mark!) is set against the rigid lines of the ravine that the narrow-minded brothers find themselves in and the iron wand and the iron doors that close at twelve o'clock. The flowing water, the unconsumable loaf, the sword that ends the waste of war are things proper for the generous-minded younger brother to gain. And there is the golden road that leads to the princess's castle. Narrow-minded as before the elder brothers can only take one side of it while the younger brother can take its whole expanse.

The primary stories—leaving out of account fables and anecdotes—are concerned with subjection, the subjection of the hero or heroine, and this has to be made striking or pathetic; with wisdom from within or without that provides release, and this has to be made transcendent, with compensation that means a return to a human life that is greatly enhanced. In some of the stories the subjection, the release, the compensation have to come over again as in the case of the girl whose wisdom released the hero and who is displaced by the false bride. The incidents have to be marvellous but the human situation has to be recognizable.

Recall "One-Eye, Two-Eyes and Three-Eyes." The incidents apart from the characters with one eye and three eyes are marvellous: her goat provides meals for a hungry girl and when it is killed its entrails planted in the yard grow into a tree with golden and silver fruit. But how recognizable is the situation of Little Two-Eyes between her jealous sisters and her inimical mother. Being different from the others she is spied upon and talked about and no gentleness on her part can save her from that excess of ill-will which unfeeling people can always find in themselves. A sentence reveals how poignant her situation is: "Then Two-Eyes said the shortest prayer she knew, 'Lord God, be with us always. Amen', and helped herself to some food and enjoyed it." We know that the girl was really hungry.

Told by generation after generation, the traditional stories projected the deepest wishes of the folk, generalized diverse characters into a few types, selected the incidents that would most strikingly illustrate what heroes and heroines, witches, enchanters, giants and dwarfs, the haughty, the envious and the unfaithful were capable of. As in work long thought about and lived with, the stories have something which the most brilliant improvisations are without—depth, fullness, a mysterious relation of parts. We can think upon them, reflect over them. How it can come about that a king's daughter can be made to marry a beggarly fiddler, sit at a street corner selling crockery, be sent back as a kitchen maid to her father's castle to remain there unknown until the man she rejected in her haughtiness comes to claim her, and how it all can be intelligible, we do not know. But we believe in the movement to the king's castle and back to the king's castle through the hut in the forest and the crockery stall in the street and admit that her adversity has made the king's daughter a more human person.

We go to our writers for distraction or relaxation while still keeping hold on our daily affairs, but the people who listened to him or to her went to the storyteller for release, leaving their daily affairs outside the house door. They felt, as we do not feel, the rhythm that succeeds the rhythm of the day. Compulsiveness gave place to acquiescence. Outside, the geese, the goats, the sheep and the cattle were folded; within, the cat purred, the dog lay in a corner, and on a beam at the opening of the roof the hens roosted. Elders and youngsters sat round the fire or beside the stove; the candle or dim oil lamp made shadows on the walls; a woman spun a thread. Out of the reverie such settled and familiar things held came the storyteller's utterance, familiar, too, in repetition of traditions that were the people's own like the table, the bench, the grandmother's chair. What was told was news of persons they knew—the queen's daughter who herded geese, the king's son whose quest was for nothing less than the Water of Life, the miller's youngest son who would show he had deeper wisdom than his elder, clever brothers.

Heroes and heroines moved towards and gained an absolute worth in life; after subjection they became wise kings and beloved queens and lived happy ever afterwards. Elders and youngsters heard about people who were as beautiful, wise and fortunate as human beings could be, who had envious, unfaithful, unworthily privileged fellows, who knew giants and dwarfs who threatened or helped them, who had birds or animals for friends.

They had belief in magic, witchcraft, transformation; they had no doubt about the efficacy of spells, charms, incantations; many incidents in what they related came from savage conceptions. But in their stories human behaviour is always in accordance with a fine ideal. A real faith in human powers is present. Happiness is possible and compensation is due to those who have been wronged. Envy and unfaithfulness are condemned and punished. There is no concern with what is negative. Wicked people keep on their course of badness but they are not bored. Decent people may be lonely but they are never despondent. In the traditional stories—at least in the stories the Brothers Grimm brought us—revenge and cruelty for its own sake have no place.

For stories in which a character may be put in a barrel studded with nails and hauled by a horse through a town until she is dead, it is odd to claim a humane quality. But notice that such punishments are infrequent; that those condemned have broken trust and have been unfaithful and oppressive. Even so, the storytellers are troubled about it and have the criminal herself pronounce the doom. We hear of queens unjustly accused being condemned to be burned to death. But the burning never eventuates. In the world that is opened to us by the Brothers Grimm good-will predominates: the hero is characterized by courtesy as the heroine by gentleness.

We have mentioned a name that is august in the world of traditional stories: the Brothers Grimm. Their "Household Tales," almost the first, have remained the most popular of the collections of European folk-tales. To the great German pioneers and to the many who followed them in various European countries, all imaginative and studious men, we owe a deep debt of gratitude. They brought us lore that will always be an entertainment for us; they brought us, too, an account of our forefathers' ways which we should be mindful of. The people who told and who listened to the traditional stories lived under emperors, monarchs, viceroys; they spoke diverse languages; they lived on mountains and in valleys, in forests and dales. But they were at one in their love for certain things—for human good nature, for enterprise, wisdom and devotion, for the genius through which men are drawn to the far-off and the superior—the Golden Tree, the Water of Life, the Matchless Maiden.

We have another past besides the past that history tells us about, a past which is in us, in individuals, more livingly than the recorded past. It is a past in which men slowly arrived at self-consciousness while building up the community, the arts and the laws. Today we have advanced poets and novelists who are trying to find means to suggest the unrecorded past in our memories and in our attitudes and so give their work another dimension. Well, it is this long past, the past that merges with the time when men were comradely with the animals and personalized the powers of nature, that comes over to us in these and in other traditional stories. With it certain things are restored to our imagination. Wilhelm Grimm who knew much more about the inwardness of these stories than the philologists and the historians of culture who were to comment on them was aware of "fragments of belief dating back to most ancient times, in which spiritual things are expressed in a figurative manner." "The mythic element," he told us, "resembles small pieces of a shattered jewel which are lying strewn on the ground all overgrown with grass and flowers, and can only be discovered by the most far-seeing eye." "Their signification has long been lost, but it is still felt," he says, "and imparts value to the story." It is this felt but hidden value that makes a connection between certain subtle modern works and these old-world fairy tales.

PADRAIC COLUM

The Fairy Tales

THE FROG-KING, OR IRON HENRY

In olden times when wishing still helped one, there lived a king whose daughters were all beautiful, but the youngest was so beautiful that the sun itself, which has seen so much, was astonished whenever it shone in her face. Close by the King's castle lay a great dark forest, and under an old lime-tree in the forest was a well, and when the day was very warm, the King's child went out into the forest and sat down by the side of the cool fountain; and when she was bored she took a golden ball, and threw it up on high and caught it; and this ball was her favourite plaything.

Now it so happened that on one occasion the princess's golden ball did not fall into the little hand which she was holding up for it, but on to the ground beyond, and rolled straight into the water. The King's daughter followed it with her eyes, but it vanished, and the well was deep, so deep that the bottom could not be seen. At this she began to cry, and cried louder and louder, and could not be comforted. And as she thus lamented, someone said to her: "What ails you, King's daughter? You weep so that even a stone would show pity." She looked round to the side from whence the voice came, and saw a frog stretching forth its big, ugly head from the water. "Ah! old water-splasher, is it you?" said she; "I am weeping for my golden ball, which has fallen into the well."

"Be quiet, and do not weep," answered the frog, "I can help you, but what will you give me if I bring your plaything up again?" "Whatever you will have, dear frog," said she—"my clothes, my pearls and jewels, and even the golden crown which I am wearing."

The frog answered: "I do not care for your clothes, your pearls and jewels, nor for your golden crown; but if you will love me and let me be your companion and play-fellow, and sit by you at your little table, and eat off your little golden plate, and drink out of your little cup, and sleep in your little bed—if you will promise me this I will go down below, and bring you your golden ball up again."

"Oh, yes," said she, "I promise you all you wish, if you will but bring me my ball back again." But she thought: "How the silly frog does talk! All he does is to sit in the water with the other frogs, and croak! He can be no companion to any human being!"

But the frog when he had received this promise, put his head into the water and sank down, and in a short while came swimming up again with the ball in his mouth, and threw it on the grass. The King's daughter was delighted to see her pretty plaything once more, and picked it up, and ran away with it. "Wait, wait," said the frog. "Take me with you. I can't run as you can." But what did it avail him to scream his croak, croak, after her, as loudly as he could? She did not listen to it, but ran home and soon forgot the poor frog, who was forced to go back into his well again.

The next day when she had seated herself at table with the King and all the courtiers, and was eating from her little golden plate, something came creeping splish splash, splish splash, up the marble staircase, and when it had got to the top, it knocked at the door and cried: "Princess, youngest princess, open the door for me." She ran to see who was outside, but when she opened the door, there sat the frog in front of it. Then she slammed the door to, in great haste, sat down to dinner again, and was quite frightened. The King saw plainly that her heart was beating violently, and said: "My child, what are you so afraid of? Is there perchance a giant outside who wants to carry you away?" "Ah, no," replied she, "it is no giant, but a disgusting frog."

"What does the frog want with you?" "Ah, dear father, yesterday as I was in the forest sitting by the well, playing, my golden ball fell into the water. And because I cried so, the frog brought it out again for me; and because he so insisted, I promised him he should be my companion, but I never thought he would be able to come out of his water! And now he is outside there, and wants to come in to me."

In the meantime it knocked a second time, and cried:

"Princess! youngest princess!
Open the door for me!
Do you not know what you said to me
Yesterday by the cool waters of the well?
Princess, youngest princess!
Open the door for me!"

Then said the King: "That which you have promised must you perform. Go and let him in." She went and opened the door, and the frog
hopped in and followed her, step by step, to her chair. There he sat and
cried: "Lift me up beside you." She delayed, until at last the King
commanded her to do it. Once the frog was on the chair he wanted to
be on the table, and when he was on the table he said: "Now, push your
little golden plate nearer to me that we may eat together." She did this,
but it was easy to see that she did not do it willingly. The frog enjoyed
what he ate, but almost every mouthful she took choked her. At length
he said: "I have eaten and am satisfied; now I am tired, carry me into
your little room and make your little silken bed ready, and we will both
lie down and go to sleep."

The King's daughter began to cry, for she was afraid of the cold frog
which she did not like to touch, and which was now to sleep in her
pretty, clean little bed. But the King grew angry and said: "He who
helped you when you were in trouble ought not afterwards to be
despised by you." So she took hold of the frog with two fingers,
carried him upstairs, and put him in a corner. But when she was in bed
he crept to her and said: "I am tired, I want to sleep as well as you, lift
me up or I will tell your father." At this she was terribly angry, and
took him up and threw him with all her might against the wall. "Now,
will you be quiet, odious frog," said she. But when he fell down he was
no frog but a king's son with kind and beautiful eyes. He by her
father's will was now her dear companion and husband. Then he told
her how he had been bewitched by a wicked witch, and how no one
could have delivered him from the well but herself, and that to-
morrow they would go together into his kingdom. Then they went to
sleep, and next morning when the sun awoke them, a carriage came
driving up with eight white horses, which had white ostrich feathers
on their heads, and were harnessed with golden chains, and behind

stood the young King's servant, faithful Henry. Faithful Henry had been so unhappy when his master was changed into a frog, that he had caused three iron bands to be laid round his heart, lest it should burst with grief and sadness. The carriage was to conduct the young King into his kingdom. Faithful Henry helped them both in, and placed himself behind again, and was full of joy because of this deliverance. And when they had driven a part of the way, the King's son heard a cracking behind him as if something had broken. So he turned round and cried: "Henry, the carriage is breaking."

"No, master, it is not the carriage. It is a band from my heart, which was put there in my great pain when you were a frog and imprisoned in the well." Again and once again while they were on their way something cracked, and each time the King's son thought the carriage was breaking; but it was only the bands which were springing from the heart of faithful Henry because his master was set free and was happy.

CAT AND MOUSE IN PARTNERSHIP

A certain cat had made the acquaintance of a mouse, and had said so much to her about the great love and friendship she felt for her, that at length the mouse agreed that they should live and keep house together. "But we must make a provision for winter, or else we shall suffer from hunger," said the cat; "and you, little mouse, cannot venture everywhere, or you will be caught in a trap some day." The good advice was followed, and a pot of fat was bought, but they did not know where to put it. At length, after much consideration, the cat said: "I know no place where it will be better stored up than in the church, for no one dares take anything away from there. We will set it beneath the altar, and not touch it until we are really in need of it." So the pot was placed in safety, but it was not long before the cat had a great yearning for it, and said to the mouse: "I want to tell you something, little mouse; my cousin has brought a little son into the world, and has asked me to be godmother; he is white with brown spots, and I am to hold him over the font at the christening. Let me go out to-day, and you look after the house by yourself." "Yes, yes," answered the mouse, "by all means go, and if you get anything very good to eat, think of me, I should like a drop of sweet red christening wine myself." All this, however, was untrue; the cat had no cousin, and had not been asked to be godmother. She went straight to the church, stole to the pot of fat, began to lick at it, and licked the top of the fat off. Then she took a walk upon the roofs of the town, looked out for opportunities, and then stretched herself in the sun, and licked her lips whenever she thought of the pot of fat, and not until it was evening did she return home. "Well, here you are again," said the mouse, "no doubt you have had a merry day." "All went off well," answered the cat. "What name did they give the child?" "Top off!" said the cat quite coolly. "Top off!" cried the mouse, "that is a very odd and uncommon name, is it a usual one in your family?" "What does that matter," said the cat, "it is no worse than Crumb-stealer, as your god-children are called."

Before long the cat was seized by another fit of yearning. She said to the mouse: "You must do me a favour, and once more manage the house for a day alone. I am again asked to be godmother, and, as the child has a white ring round its neck, I cannot refuse." The good mouse consented, but the cat crept behind the town walls to the church, and devoured half the pot of fat. "Nothing ever seems so good as what one keeps to oneself," said she, and was quite satisfied with her day's work. When she went home the mouse inquired: "And what was this child christened?" "Half-done," answered the cat. "Half-done! What are you saying? I never heard the name in my life, I'll wager anything it is not in the calendar!"

The cat's mouth soon began to water for some more licking. "All good things go in threes," said she, "I am asked to stand godmother again. The child is quite black, only it has white paws, but with that exception, it has not a single white hair on its whole body; this only happens once every few years, you will let me go, won't you?" "Top-off! Half-done!" answered the mouse, "they are such odd names, they make me very thoughtful." "You sit at home," said the cat, "in your dark-grey fur coat and long tail, and are filled with fancies, that's because you do not go out in the daytime." During the cat's absence the mouse cleaned the house, and put it in order, but the greedy cat entirely emptied the pot of fat. "When everything is eaten up one has some peace," said she to herself, and well filled and fat she did not return home till night. The mouse at once asked what name had been given to the third child. "It will not please you more than the others," said the cat. "He is called All-gone." "All-gone," cried the mouse, "that is the most suspicious name of all! I have never seen it in print. All-gone; what can that mean?" and she shook her head, curled herself up, and lay down to sleep.

From this time forth no one invited the cat to be godmother, but when the winter had come and there was no longer anything to be found outside, the mouse thought of their provision, and said: "Come, cat, we will go to our pot of fat which we have stored up for ourselves—we shall enjoy that." "Yes," answered the cat, "you will enjoy it as much as you would enjoy sticking that dainty tongue of yours out of the window." They set out on their way, but when they arrived, the pot of fat certainly was still in its place, but it was empty. "Alas!" said the mouse, "now I see what has happened, now it comes to light! You a true friend! You have devoured all when you were standing godmother. First top off, then half done, then—" "Will you hold your tongue," cried the cat, "one word more, and I will eat you too." "All gone" was already on the poor mouse's lips; scarcely had she spoken it before the cat sprang on her, seized her, and swallowed her down. Verily, that is the way of the world.

OUR LADY'S CHILD

Hard by a great forest dwelt a wood-cutter with his wife, who had an only child, a little girl three years old. They were so poor, however, that they no longer had daily bread, and did not know how to get food for her. One morning the wood-cutter went out sorrowfully to his work in the forest, and while he was cutting wood, suddenly there stood before him a tall and beautiful woman with a crown of shining stars on her head, who said to him: "I am the Virgin Mary, mother of the child Jesus. You are poor and needy, bring your child to me, I will take her with me and be her mother, and care for her." The wood-cutter obeyed, brought his child, and gave her to the Virgin Mary, who took her up to heaven with her. There the child fared well, ate sugar-cakes, and drank sweet milk, and her clothes were of gold, and the little angels played with her. And when she was fourteen years of age, the Virgin Mary called her one day and said: "Dear child, I am about to make a long journey, so take into your keeping the keys of the thirteen doors of heaven. Twelve of these you may open, and behold the glory which is within them, but the thirteenth, to which this little key belongs, is forbidden you. Take care not to open it, or you will be unhappy." The girl promised to be obedient, and when the Virgin Mary was gone, she began to examine the dwellings of the kingdom of heaven. Each day she opened one of them, until she had made the round of the twelve. In each of them sat one of the Apostles in the midst of a great light, and she rejoiced in all the magnificence and splendour, and the little angels who always accompanied her rejoiced with her. Then the forbidden door alone remained, and she felt a great desire to know what could be hidden behind it, and said to the angels: "I will not open it entirely, and I will not go inside, but I will unlock it so that we can see just a little through the opening." "Oh, no," said the little angels, "that would be a sin. The Virgin Mary has forbidden it, and it might easily cause your unhappiness." Then she was silent, but the desire in her heart was not stilled, but gnawed there and tormented her, and let her have no rest. And once when the angels had all gone out, she thought: "Now I am quite alone, and I could peep in. If I do, no one will ever know." She sought out the key, and when she had got it in her hand, she put it in the lock, and when she had put it in, she turned it round as well. Then the door sprang open, and she saw there the Trinity sitting in fire and splendour. She stayed there awhile, and looked at everything in amazement; then she touched the light a little with her finger, and her finger became quite golden. Immediately a great fear fell on her. She shut the door violently, and ran away. But her terror would not quit her, let her do what she might, and her heart beat continually and would not be still; the gold too stayed on her finger, and would not go away, let her rub it and wash it never so much.

It was not long before the Virgin Mary came back from her journey. She called the girl before her, and asked to have the keys of heaven back. When the maiden gave her the bunch, the Virgin looked into her eyes and said: "Have you not opened the thirteenth door also?" "No," she replied. Then she laid her hand on the girl's heart, and felt how it beat and beat, and saw right well that she had disobeyed her order and had opened the door. Then she said once again: "Are you certain that you have not done it?" "Yes," said the girl, for the second time. Then she perceived the finger which had become golden from touching the fire of heaven, and saw well that the child had sinned, and said for the third time: "Have you not done it?" "No," said the girl for the third time. Then said the Virgin Mary: "You have not obeyed me, and besides that you have lied, you are no longer worthy to be in heaven."

Then the girl fell into a deep sleep, and when she awoke she lay on the earth below, and in the midst of a wilderness. She wanted to cry out, but she could bring forth no sound. She sprang up and wanted to run away, but whithersoever she turned herself, she was continually held back by thick hedges of thorns through which she could not break. In the desert, in which she was imprisoned, there stood an old hollow tree, and this had to be her dwelling-place. Into this she crept when night came, and here she slept. Here, too, she found a shelter from storm and rain, but it was a miserable life, and bitterly did she weep when she remembered how happy she had been in heaven, and how the angels had played with her. Roots and wild berries were her only food, and for these she sought as far as she could go. In the autumn she picked up the fallen nuts and leaves, and carried them into the hole. The nuts were her food in winter, and when snow and ice came, she crept amongst the leaves like a poor little animal that she

might not freeze. Before long her clothes were all torn, and one bit of them after another fell off her. As soon, however, as the sun shone warm again, she went out and sat in front of the tree, and her long hair covered her on all sides like a mantle. Thus she sat year after year, and felt the pain and the misery of the world.

One day, when the trees were once more clothed in fresh green, the King of the country was hunting in the forest, and followed a roe, and as it had fled into the thicket which shut in this part of the forest, he got off his horse, tore the bushes asunder, and cut himself a path with his sword. When he had at last forced his way through, he saw a wonderfully beautiful maiden sitting under the tree; and she sat there and was entirely covered with her golden hair down to her very feet. He stood still and looked at her full of surprise, then he spoke to her and said: "Who are you? Why are you sitting here in the wilderness?" But she gave no answer, for she could not open her mouth. The King continued: "Will you go with me to my castle?" Then she just nodded her head a little. The King took her in his arms, carried her to his horse, and rode home with her, and when he reached the royal castle he caused her to be dressed in beautiful garments, and gave her all things in abundance. Although she could not speak, she was still so beautiful and charming that he began to love her with all his heart, and it was not long before he married her.

After a year or so had passed, the Queen brought a son into the world. Thereupon the Virgin Mary appeared to her in the night when she lay in her bed alone, and said: "If you will tell the truth and confess that you did unlock the forbidden door, I will open your mouth and give you back your speech, but if you persevere in your sin, and deny obstinately, I will take your new-born child away with me." Then the Queen was permitted to answer, but she remained hard, and said, "No, I did not open the forbidden door"; and the Virgin Mary took the new-born child from her arms, and vanished with it. Next morning, when the child was not to be found, it was whispered among the people that the Queen was a man-eater, and had put her own child to death. She heard all this and could say nothing to the contrary, but the King would not believe it, for he loved her so much.

When a year had gone by the Queen again bore a son, and in the night the Virgin Mary again came to her, and said: "If you will confess that you opened the forbidden door, I will give you your child back and untie your tongue; but if you continue in sin and deny it, I will take away with me this new child also." Then the Queen again said: "No, I did not open the forbidden door"; and the Virgin took the child out of her arms, and away with her to heaven. Next morning, when this child also had disappeared, the people declared quite loudly that the Queen had devoured it, and the King's councillors demanded that she should be brought to justice. The King, however, loved her so dearly that he would not believe it, and commanded the councillors under pain of death not to say any more about it.

The following year the Queen gave birth to a beautiful little daughter, and for the third time the Virgin Mary appeared to her in the night and said: "Follow me." She took the Queen by the hand and led her to heaven, and showed her there her two eldest children, who smiled at her, and were playing with the ball of the world. When the Queen rejoiced thereat, the Virgin Mary said: "Is your heart not yet softened? If you will own that you opened the forbidden door, I will give you back your two little sons." But for the third time the Queen answered: "No, I did not open the forbidden door." Then the Virgin let her sink down to earth once more, and took from her likewise her third child.

Next morning, when the loss was reported abroad, all the people cried loudly: "The Queen is a man-eater! She must be judged," and the King was no longer able to restrain his councillors. Thereupon a trial was held, and as she could not answer, and defend herself, she was condemned to be burnt at the stake. The wood was got together, and when she was fast bound to the stake, and the fire began to burn round about her, the hard ice of pride melted, her heart was moved by repentance, and she thought: "If I could but confess before my death that I opened the door." Then her voice came back to her, and she cried out loudly: "Yes, Mary, I did it"; and straight-way rain fell from the sky and extinguished the flames of fire, and a light broke forth above her, and the Virgin Mary descended with the two little sons by her side, and the new-born daughter in her arms. She spoke kindly to her, and said: "He who repents his sin and acknowledges it, is forgiven." Then she gave her the three children, untied her tongue, and granted her happiness for her whole life.

THE STORY OF THE YOUTH WHO WENT FORTH TO LEARN WHAT FEAR WAS

A certain father had two sons, the elder of whom was smart and sensible, and could do everything, but the younger was stupid and could neither learn nor understand anything, and when people saw him they said: "There's a fellow who will give his father some trouble!" When anything had to be done, it was always the elder who was forced to do it; but if his father bade him fetch anything when it was late, or in the night-time, and the way led through the churchyard, or any other dismal place, he answered: "Oh, no, father, I'll not go there, it makes me shudder!" for he was afraid. Or when stories were told by the fire at night which made the flesh creep, the listeners sometimes said: "Oh, it makes us shudder!" The younger sat in a corner and listened with the rest of them, and could not imagine what they could mean. "They are always saying: 'It makes me shudder, it makes me shudder!' It does not make me shudder," thought he. "That, too, must be an art of which I understand nothing!"

Now it came to pass that his father said to him one day: "Hearken to me, you fellow in the corner there, you are growing tall and strong, and you too must learn something by which you can earn your bread. Look how your brother works, but you do not even earn your salt." "Well, father," he replied, "I am quite willing to learn something— indeed, if it could but be managed, I should like to learn how to shudder. I don't understand that at all yet." The elder brother smiled when he heard that, and thought to himself: "Goodness, what a blockhead that brother of mine is! He will never be good for anything as long as he lives! He who wants to be a sickle must bend himself betimes."

The father sighed, and answered him: "You shall soon learn what it is to shudder, but you will not earn your bread by that."

Soon after this the sexton came to the house on a visit, and the father bewailed his trouble, and told him how his younger son was so backward in every respect that he knew nothing and learnt nothing. "Just think," said he, "when I asked him how he was going to earn his bread, he actually wanted to learn to shudder." "If that be all," replied the sexton, "he can learn that with me. Send him to me, and I will soon polish him." The father was glad to do it, for he thought: "It will train the boy a little." The sexton therefore took him into his house, and he had to ring the church bell. After a day or two, the sexton awoke him at midnight, and bade him arise and go up into the church tower and ring the bell. "You shall soon learn what shuddering is," thought he, and secretly went there before him; and when the boy was at the top of the tower and turned round, and was just going to take hold of the bell rope, he saw a white figure standing on the stairs opposite the sounding hole. "Who is there?" cried he, but the figure made no reply, and did not move or stir. "Give an answer," cried the boy, "or take yourself off, you have no business here at night."

The sexton, however, remained standing motionless that the boy might think he was a ghost. The boy cried a second time: "What do you want here?—speak if you are an honest fellow, or I will throw you down the steps!" The sexton thought: "He can't mean to be as bad as his words," uttered no sound and stood as if he were made of stone. Then the boy called to him for the third time, and as that was also to no purpose, he ran against him and pushed the ghost down the stairs, so that it fell down ten steps and remained lying there in a corner. Thereupon he rang the bell, went home, and without saying a word went to bed, and fell asleep. The sexton's wife waited a long time for her husband, but he did not come back. At length she became uneasy, and wakened the boy, and asked: "Do you not know where my husband is? He climbed up the tower before you did." "No, I don't know," replied the boy, "but someone was standing by the sounding hole on the other side of the steps, and as he would neither give an answer nor go away, I took him for a scoundrel, and threw him downstairs. Just go there and you will see if it was he. I should be sorry if it were." The woman ran away and found her husband, who was lying moaning in the corner, and had broken his leg.

She carried him down, and then with loud screams she hastened to the boy's father. "Your boy," cried she, "has been the cause of a great misfortune! He has thrown my husband down the steps so that he broke his leg. Take the good-for-nothing fellow out of our house." The father was terrified, and ran thither and scolded the boy. "What wicked tricks are these?" said he, "the devil must have put them into your head." "Father," he replied, "do listen to me. I am quite innocent. He was standing there by night like one intent on doing evil. I did not know who it was, and I entreated him three times either to speak or to go away." "Ah," said the father, "I have nothing but unhappiness with you. Go out of my sight. I will see you no more."

"Yes, father, right willingly, wait only until it is day. Then will I go forth and learn how to shudder, and then I shall, at any rate, understand one art which will support me." "Learn what you will," spoke the father, "it is all the same to me. Here are fifty talers for you. Take these and go into the wide world, and tell no one from whence you come, and who is your father, for I have reason to be ashamed of you." "Yes, father, it shall be as you will. If you desire nothing more than that, I can easily keep it in mind."

When day dawned, therefore, the boy put his fifty talers into his pocket, and went forth on the great highway, and continually said to himself: "If I could but shudder! If I could but shudder!" Then a man approached who heard this conversation which the youth was holding with himself, and when they had walked a little farther to where they could see the gallows, the man said to him: "Look, there is the tree where seven men have married the ropemaker's daughter, and are now learning how to fly. Sit down beneath it, and wait till night comes, and you will soon learn how to shudder." "If that is all that is wanted," answered the youth, "it is easily done; but if I learn how to shudder as fast as that, you shall have my fifty talers. Just come back to me early in the morning." Then the youth went to the gallows, sat down beneath it, and waited till evening came. And as he was cold, he lighted himself a fire, but at midnight the wind blew so sharply that in spite of his fire, he could not get warm. And as the wind knocked the hanged men against each other, and they moved backwards and forwards, he thought to himself: "If you shiver below by the fire, how those up above must freeze and suffer!" And as he felt pity for them, he raised the ladder, and climbed up, unbound one of them after the other, and brought down all seven. Then he stoked the fire, blew it, and set them all round it to warm themselves. But they sat there and did not stir, and the fire caught their clothes. So he said: "Take care, or I will hang you up again." The dead men, however, did not hear, but were quite silent, and let their rags go on burning. At this he grew angry, and said: "If you will not take care, I cannot help you, I will not be burnt with you," and he hung them up again each in his turn. Then he sat down by his fire and fell asleep, and the next morning the man came to him and wanted to have the fifty talers, and said: "Well, do you know how to shudder?" "No," answered he, "how should I know? Those fellows up there did not open their mouths, and were so stupid that they let the few old rags which they had on their bodies get burnt." Then the man saw that he would not get the fifty talers that day, and went away saying: "Such a youth has never come my way before."

The youth likewise went his way, and once more began to mutter to himself: "Ah, if I could but shudder! Ah, if I could but shudder!" A waggoner who was striding behind him heard this and asked: "Who are you?" "I don't know," answered the youth. Then the waggoner asked: "From whence do you come?" "I know not." "Who is your father?" "That I may not tell you." "What is it that you are always muttering between your teeth?" "Ah," replied the youth, "I do so wish I could shudder, but no one can teach me how." "Enough of your foolish chatter," said the waggoner. "Come, go with me, I will see about a place for you." The youth went with the waggoner, and in the evening they arrived at an inn where they wished to pass the night. Then at the entrance of the parlour the youth again said quite loudly: "If I could but shudder! If I could but shudder!" The host who heard this, laughed and said: "If that is your desire, there ought to be a good opportunity for you here." "Ah, be silent," said the hostess, "so many prying persons have already lost their lives, it would be a pity and a shame if such beautiful eyes as these should never see the daylight again."

But the youth said: "However difficult it may be, I will learn it. For this purpose indeed have I journeyed forth." He let the host have no rest, until the latter told him, that not far from thence stood a haunted castle where any one could very easily learn what shuddering was, if he would but watch in it for three nights. The King had promised that he who would venture should have his daughter to wife, and she was the most beautiful maiden the sun shone on. Likewise in the castle lay great treasures, which were guarded by evil spirits, and these treasures would then be freed, and would make a poor man rich enough. Already many men had gone into the castle, but as yet none had come out again. Then the youth went next morning to the King, and said: "If it be allowed, I will willingly watch three nights in the haunted castle." The King looked at him, and as the youth pleased him, he said: "You may ask for three things to take into the castle with you, but they must be things without life." Then he answered: "Then I ask for a fire, a turning lathe, and a cutting-board with the knife."

The King had these things carried into the castle for him during the day. When night was drawing near, the youth went up and made himself a bright fire in one of the rooms, placed the cutting-board and knife beside it, and seated himself by the turning-lathe. "Ah, if I could but shudder!" said he, "but I shall not learn it here either." Towards midnight he was about to poke his fire, and as he was blowing it, something cried suddenly from one corner: "Au, miau! how cold we are!" "You fools!" cried he, "what are you crying about? If you are cold, come and take a seat by the fire and warm yourselves." And when he had said that, two great black cats came with one tremendous leap and sat down on each side of him, and looked savagely at him with their fiery eyes. After a short time, when they had warmed themselves, they said: "Comrade, shall we have a game of cards?" "Why not?" he replied, "but just show me your paws." Then they stretched out their claws. "Oh," said he, "what long nails you have! Wait, I must first cut them for you." Thereupon he seized them by the throats, put them on the cutting-board and screwed their feet fast. "I have looked at your fingers," said he, "and my fancy for card-playing has gone," and he struck them dead and threw them out into the water. But when he had made away with these two, and was about to sit down again by his fire, out from every hole and corner came black cats and black dogs with red-hot chains, and more and more of them came until he could no longer move, and they yelled horribly, and got on his fire, pulled it to pieces, and tried to put it out. He watched them for a while quietly, but at last when they were going too far, he seized his cutting-knife, and cried: "Away with you, vermin," and began to cut them down. Some of them ran away, the others he killed, and threw out into the fish-pond. When he came back he fanned the embers of his fire again and warmed himself. And as he thus sat, his eyes would keep open no longer, and he felt a desire to sleep. Then he looked round and saw a great bed in the corner. "That is the very thing for me," said he, and got

into it. When he was just going to shut his eyes, however, the bed began to move of its own accord, and went over the whole of the castle. "That's right," said he, "but go faster." Then the bed rolled on as if six horses were harnessed to it, up and down, over thresholds and stairs, but suddenly hop, hop, it turned over upside down, and lay on him like a mountain. But he threw quilts and pillows up in the air, got out and said: "Now any one who likes, may drive," and lay down by his fire, and slept till it was day. In the morning the King came, and when he saw him lying there on the ground, he thought the evil spirits had killed him and he was dead. Then said he: "After all it is a pity,—for so handsome a man." The youth heard it, got up, and said: "It has not come to that yet." Then the King was astonished, but very glad, and asked how he had fared. "Very well indeed," answered he; "one night is past, the two others will pass likewise." Then he went to the inn-keeper, who opened his eyes very wide, and said: "I never expected to see you alive again! Have you learnt how to shudder yet?" "No," said he, "it is all in vain. If some one would but tell me!"

The second night he again went up into the old castle, sat down by the fire, and once more began his old song: "If I could but shudder!" When midnight came, an uproar and noise of tumbling about was heard; at first it was low, but it grew louder and louder. Then it was quiet for a while, and at length with a loud scream, half a man came down the chimney and fell before him. "Hullo!" cried he, "another half belongs to this. This is not enough!" Then the uproar began again, there was a roaring and howling, and the other half fell down likewise. "Wait," said he, "I will just stoke up the fire a little for you." When he had done that and looked round again, the two pieces were joined together, and a hideous man was sitting in his place. "That is no part of our bargain," said the youth, "the bench is mine." The man wanted to push him away; the youth, however, would not allow that, but thrust him off with all his strength, and seated himself again in his own place. Then still more men fell down, one after the other; they brought nine dead men's legs and two skulls, and set them up and played at nine-pins with them. The youth also wanted to play and said: "Listen you, can I join you?" "Yes, if you have any money." "Money enough," replied he, "but your balls are not quite round." Then he took the skulls and put them in the lathe and turned them till they were round.

"There, now they will roll better!" said he. "Hurrah! now we'll have fun!" He played with them and lost some of his money, but when it struck twelve, everything vanished from his sight. He lay down and quietly fell asleep. Next morning the King came to inquire after him. "How has if fared with you this time?" asked he. "I have been playing at nine-pins," he answered, "and have lost a couple of farthings." "Have you not shuddered then?" "What?" said he, "I have had a wonderful time! If I did but know what it was to shudder!"

The third night he sat down again on his bench and said quite sadly: "If I could but shudder." When it grew late, six tall men came in and brought a coffin. Then said he: "Ha, ha, that is certainly my little cousin, who died only a few days ago," and he beckoned with his finger, and cried: "Come, little cousin, come." They placed the coffin on the ground, but he went to it and took the lid off, and a dead man lay therein. He felt his face, but it was cold as ice. "Wait," said he, "I will warm you a little," and went to the fire and warmed his hand and laid it on the dead man's face, but he remained cold. Then he took him out, and sat down by the fire and laid him on his breast and rubbed his arms that the blood might circulate again. As this also did no good, he thought to himself: "When two people lie in bed together, they warm each other," and carried him to the bed, covered him over and lay down by him. After a short time the dead man became warm too, and began to move. Then said the youth, "See, little cousin, have I not warmed you?" The dead man, however, got up and cried: "Now will I strangle you."

"What!" said he, "is that the way you thank me? You shall at once go into your coffin again," and he took him up, threw him into it, and shut the lid. Then came the six men and carried him away again. "I cannot manage to shudder," said he. "I shall never learn it here as long as I live."

Then a man entered who was taller than all others, and looked terrible. He was old, however, and had a long white beard. "You wretch," cried he, "you shall soon learn what it is to shudder, for you shall die." "Not so fast," replied the youth. "If I am to die, I shall have to have a say in it." "I will soon seize you," said the fiend. "Softly, softly, do not talk so big. I am as strong as you are, and perhaps even stronger." "We shall see," said the old man. "If you are stronger, I will let you go—come, we will try." Then he led him by dark passages to a smith's forge, took an axe, and with one blow struck an anvil into the ground. "I can do better than that," said the youth, and went to the other anvil. The old man placed himself near and wanted to look on, and his white beard hung down. Then the youth seized the axe, split the anvil with one blow, and in it caught the old man's beard. "Now I have you," said the youth. "Now it is your turn to die." Then he seized an iron bar and beat the old man till he moaned and entreated him to stop, when he would give him great riches. The youth drew out the axe and let him go. The old man led him back into the castle, and in a cellar showed him three chests full of gold. "Of these," said he, "one part is for the poor, the other for the king, the third yours." In the meantime it struck twelve, and the spirit disappeared, so that the youth stood in darkness. "I shall still be able to find my way out," said he, and felt about, found the way into the room, and slept there by his fire. Next morning the King came and said: "Now you must have learnt what shuddering is?" "No," he answered; "what can it be? My dead cousin was here, and a bearded man came and showed me a great deal of money down below, but no one told me what it was to shudder." "Then," said the King, "you have saved the castle, and shall marry my daughter." "That is all very well," said he, "but still I do not know what it is to shudder!"

Then the gold was brought up and the wedding celebrated; but howsoever much the young King loved his wife, and however happy he was, he still said always: "If I could but shudder—if I could but shudder." And this at last angered her. Her waiting-maid said: "I will find a cure for him; he shall soon learn what it is to shudder." She went out to the stream which flowed through the garden, and had a whole bucketful of gudgeons brought to her. At night when the young King was sleeping, his wife was to draw the clothes off him and empty the bucketful of cold water with the gudgeons in it over him, so that the little fishes would sprawl about him. Then he woke up and cried: "Oh, what makes me shudder so?—what makes me shudder so, dear wife? Ah! now I know what it is to shudder!"

THE WOLF AND THE SEVEN LITTLE KIDS

There was once upon a time an old goat who had seven little kids, and loved them with all the love of a mother for her children. One day she wanted to go into the forest and fetch some food. So she called all seven to her and said: "Dear children, I have to go into the forest, be on your guard against the wolf; if he comes in, he will devour you all—skin, hair, and everything. The wretch often disguises himself, but you will know him at once by his rough voice and his black feet." The kids said: "Dear mother, we will take good care of ourselves; you may go away without any anxiety." Then the old one bleated, and went on her way with an easy mind.

It was not long before some one knocked at the house-door and called: "Open the door, dear children; your mother is here, and has brought something back with her for each of you." But the little kids knew that it was the wolf, by the rough voice. "We will not open the door," cried they, "you are not our mother. She has a soft, pleasant voice, but your voice is rough; you are the wolf!" Then the wolf went away to a shopkeeper and bought himself a great lump of chalk, ate this and made his voice soft with it. Then he came back, knocked at the door of the house, and called: "Open the door, dear children, your mother is here and has brought something back with her for each of you." But the wolf had laid his black paws against the window, and the children saw them and cried: "We will not open the door, our mother has not black feet like you: you are the wolf!" Then the wolf ran to a baker and said: "I have hurt my feet, rub some dough over them for me." And when the baker had rubbed his feet over, he ran to the miller and said: "Strew some white meal over my feet for me." The miller thought to himself: "The wolf wants to deceive someone," and refused; but the wolf said: "If you will not do it, I will devour you." Then the miller was afraid, and made his paws white for him. Truly, this is the way of mankind.

So now the wretch went for the third time to the house-door, knocked at it and said: "Open the door for me, children, your dear little mother has come home, and has brought every one of you something back from the forest with her." The little kids cried: "First show us your paws that we may know if you are our dear little mother." Then he put his paws in through the window, and when the kids saw that they were white, they believed that all he said was true, and opened the door. But who should come in but the wolf! They were terrified and wanted to hide themselves. One sprang under the table, the second into the bed, the third into the stove, the fourth into the kitchen, the fifth into the cupboard, the sixth under the washing-bowl, and the seventh into the clock-case. But the wolf found them all, and used no great ceremony; one after the other he swallowed them down his throat. The youngest, who was in the clock-case, was the only one he did not find. When the wolf had satisfied his appetite he took himself off, laid himself down under a tree in the green meadow outside, and began to sleep. Soon afterwards the old goat came home again from the forest. Ah! what a sight she saw there! The house-door stood wide open. The table, chairs, and benches were thrown down, the washing-bowl lay broken to pieces, and the quilts and pillows were pulled off the bed. She sought her children, but they were nowhere to be found. She called them one after another by name, but no one answered. At last, when she came to the youngest, a soft voice cried: "Dear mother, I am in the clock-case." She took the kid out, and it told her that the wolf had come and had eaten all the others. Then you may imagine how she wept over her poor children.

At length in her grief she went out, and the youngest kid ran with her. When they came to the meadow, there lay the wolf by the tree and snored so loud that the branches shook. She looked at him on every side and saw that something was moving and struggling in his gorged belly. "Ah, heavens," she said, "is it possible that my poor children whom he has swallowed down for his supper, can be still alive?" Then the kid had to run home and fetch scissors, and a needle and thread, and the goat cut open the monster's stomach, and hardly had she made one cut, than one little kid thrust its head out, and when she had cut farther, all six sprang out one after another, and were all still alive, and had suffered no injury whatever, for in his greediness the monster had swallowed them down whole. What rejoicing there was! They embraced their dear mother, and jumped like a tailor at his wedding. The mother, however, said: "Now go and look for some big stones, and we will fill the wicked beast's stomach with them while he is still

asleep." Then the seven kids dragged the stones thither with all speed, and put as many of them into his stomach as they could get in; and the mother sewed him up again in the greatest haste, so that he was not aware of anything and never once stirred.

When the wolf at length had had his fill of sleep, he got on his legs, and as the stones in his stomach made him very thirsty, he wanted to go to a well to drink. But when he began to walk and to move about, the stones in his stomach knocked against each other and rattled. Then cried he:

"What rumbles and tumbles
Against my poor bones?
I thought 'twas six kids,
But it feels like big stones."

And when he got to the well and stooped over the water to drink, the heavy stones made him fall in, and he had to drown miserably. When the seven kids saw that, they came running to the spot and cried aloud: "The wolf is dead! The wolf is dead!" and danced for joy round about the well with their mother.

FAITHFUL JOHN

There was once upon a time an old king who was ill, and thought to himself: "I am lying on what must be my deathbed." Then said he: "Tell Faithful John to come to me." Faithful John was his favourite servant, and was so called, because he had for his whole life long been so true to him. When therefore he came beside the bed, the King said to him: "Most faithful John, I feel my end approaching, and have no anxiety except about my son. He is still of tender age, and cannot always know how to guide himself. If you do not promise me to teach him everything that he ought to know, and to be his foster-father, I cannot close my eyes in peace." Then answered Faithful John: "I will not forsake him, and will serve him with fidelity, even if it should cost me my life." At this, the old King said: "Now I die in comfort and peace." Then he added: "After my death, you shall show him the whole castle: all the chambers, halls, and vaults, and all the treasures which lie therein, but the last chamber in the long gallery, in which is the picture of the princess of the Golden Dwelling, shall you not show. If he sees that picture, he will fall violently in love with her, and will drop down in a swoon, and go through great danger for her sake, therefore you must protect him from that." And when Faithful John had once more given his promise to the old King about this, the King said no more, but laid his head on his pillow, and died.

When the old King had been carried to his grave, Faithful John told the young King all that he had promised his father on his deathbed, and said: "This will I assuredly keep, and will be faithful to you as I have been faithful to him, even if it should cost me my life." When the mourning was over, Faithful John said to him: "It is now time that you should see your inheritance. I will show you your father's palace." Then he took him about everywhere, up and down, and let him see all the riches, and the magnificent apartments, only there was one room which he did not open, that in which hung the dangerous picture. The picture, however, was so placed that when the door was opened you looked straight on it, and it was so admirably painted that it seemed to breathe and live, and there was nothing more charming or more beautiful in the whole world. The young king noticed, however, that Faithful John always walked past this one door, and said: "Why do you never open this one for me?" "There is something within it," he replied, "which would terrify you." But the King answered: "I have seen all the palace, and I want to know what is in this room also," and he went and tried to break open the door by force. Then Faithful John held him back and said: "I promised your father before his death that you should not see that which is in this chamber, it might bring the greatest misfortune on you and on me." "Ah, no," replied the young King, "if I do not go in, it will be my certain destruction. I should have no rest day or night until I had seen it with my own eyes. I shall not leave the place now until you have unlocked the door."

Then Faithful John saw that there was no help for it now, and with a heavy heart and many sighs, sought out the key from the great bunch. When he had opened the door, he went in first, and thought by standing before him he could hide the portrait so that the King should not see it in front of him. But what good was this? The King stood on tiptoe and saw it over his shoulder. And when he saw the portrait of the maiden, which was so magnificent and shone with gold and precious stones, he fell fainting to the ground. Faithful John took him up, carried him to his bed, and sorrowfully thought: "The misfortune has befallen us, Lord God, what will be the end of it?" Then he strengthened him with wine, until he came to himself again. The first words the King said were: "Ah, the beautiful portrait! whose is it?" "That is the princess of the Golden Dwelling," answered Faithful John. Then the King continued: "My love for her is so great, that if all the leaves on all the trees were tongues, they could not declare it. I will give my life to win her. You are my most faithful John, you must help me."

The faithful servant considered within himself for a long time how to set about the matter, for it was difficult even to obtain a sight of the King's daughter. At length he thought of a way, and said to the King: "Everything which she has about her is of gold—tables, chairs, dishes, glasses, bowls, and household furniture. Among your treasures are five tons of gold; let one of the goldsmiths of the kingdom fashion these into all manner of vessels and utensils, into all kinds of birds, wild beasts and strange animals, such as may please her, and we will go there with them and try our luck."

The King ordered all the goldsmiths to be brought to him, and they had to work night and day until at last the most splendid things were prepared. When everything was stowed on board a ship, Faithful John put on the dress of a merchant, and the King was forced to do the same in order to make himself quite unrecognizable. Then they sailed across the sea, and sailed on until they came to the town wherein dwelt the princess of the Golden Dwelling.

Faithful John bade the King stay behind on the ship, and wait for him. "Perhaps I shall bring the princess with me," said he, "therefore see that everything is in order; have the golden vessels set out and the whole ship decorated." Then he gathered together in his apron all kinds of golden things, went on shore and walked straight to the royal palace. When he entered the courtyard of the palace, a beautiful girl was standing there by the well with two golden buckets in her hand, drawing water with them. And when she was just turning round to carry away the sparkling water she saw the stranger, and asked who he was. So he answered: "I am a merchant," and opened his apron, and let her look in. Then she cried: "Oh, what beautiful golden things!" and put her pails down and looked at the golden wares one after the other. Then said the girl: "The princess must see these, she has such great pleasure in golden things, that she will buy all you have." She took him by the hand and led him upstairs, for she was the waiting-maid. When the King's daughter saw the wares, she was quite delighted and said: "They are so beautifully worked, that I will buy them all from you." But Faithful John said: "I am only the servant of a rich merchant. The things I have here are not to be compared with those my master has in his ship. They are the most beautiful and valuable things that have ever been made in gold." When she wanted to have everything brought up to her, he said: "There are so many of them that it would take a great many days to do that, and so many rooms would be required to exhibit them, that your house is not big enough." Then her curiosity and longing were still more excited, until at last she said: "Conduct me to the ship, I will go there myself, and behold the treasures of your master."

At this Faithful John was quite delighted, and led her to the ship, and when the King saw her, he perceived that her beauty was even greater than the picture had represented it to be, and thought no other than that his heart would burst in twain. Then she boarded the ship, and the King led her within. Faithful John, however, remained with the helmsman, and ordered the ship to be pushed off, saying: "Set all sail, till it fly like a bird in the air." Within, the King showed her the golden vessels, every one of them, also the wild beasts and strange animals. Many hours went by whilst she was seeing everything, and in her delight she did not observe that the ship was sailing away. After she had looked at the last, she thanked the merchant and wanted to go home, but when she came to the side of the ship, she saw that it was on the high seas far from land, and hurrying onwards with all sail set. "Ah," cried she in her alarm, "I am betrayed! I am carried away and have fallen into the power of a merchant—I would rather die!" The King, however, seized her hand, and said: "I am not a merchant. I am a king, and of no meaner origin than you are, and if I have carried you away with subtlety, that has come to pass because of my exceeding great love for you. The first time that I looked on your portrait, I fell fainting to the ground." When the princess of the Golden Dwelling heard this, she was comforted, and her heart was drawn to him, so that she willingly consented to be his wife.

It so happened, while they were sailing onwards over the deep sea, that Faithful John, who was sitting on the fore part of the vessel, making music, saw three ravens in the air, which came flying towards

them. At this he stopped playing and listened to what they were saying to each other, for that he well understood. One cried: "Oh, there he is carrying home the princess of the Golden Dwelling." "Yes," replied the second, "but he has not got her yet." Said the third: "But he has got her, she is sitting beside him in the ship." Then the first began again, and cried: "What good will that do him? When they reach land a chestnut horse will leap forward to meet him, and the prince will want to mount it, but if he does that, it will run away with him, and rise up into the air, and he will never see his maiden more." Spoke the second: "But is there no escape?"

"Oh, yes, if someone else mounts it swiftly, and takes out the pistol which he will find in its holster, and shoots the horse dead, the young King is saved. But who knows that? And whosoever does know it, and tells it to him, will be turned to stone from the toe to the knee." Then said the second: "I know more than that; even if the horse be killed, the young King will still not keep his bride. When they go into the castle together, a wrought bridal garment will be lying there in a dish, and looking as if it were woven of gold and silver; it is, however, nothing but sulphur and pitch, and if he put it on, it will burn him to the very bone and marrow." Said the third: "Is there no escape at all?"

"Oh, yes," replied the second, "if any one with gloves on seizes the garment and throws it into the fire and burns it, the young King will be saved. But what good will that do? Whosoever knows it and tells it to him, half his body will become stone from the knee to the heart."

Then said the third: "I know still more; even if the bridal garment be burnt, the young King will still not have his bride. After the wedding, when the dancing begins and the young Queen is dancing, she will suddenly turn pale and fall down as if dead, and if some one does not lift her up and draw three drops of blood from her right breast and spit them out again, she will die. But if any one who knows that were to declare it, he would become stone from the crown of his head to the sole of his foot." When the ravens had spoken of this together, they flew onwards, and Faithful John had well understood everything, but from that time forth he became quiet and sad, for if he concealed what he had heard from his master, the latter would be unfortunate, and if he disclosed it to him, he himself must sacrifice his life. At length, however, he said to himself: "I will save my master, even if it bring destruction on myself."

When therefore they came to shore, all happened as had been foretold by the ravens, and a magnificent chestnut horse sprang forward. "Good," said the King, "he shall carry me to my palace," and was about to mount it when Faithful John got before him, jumped quickly on it, drew the pistol out of the holster, and shot the horse. Then the other attendants of the King, who were not very fond of Faithful John, cried: "How shameful to kill the beautiful animal, that was to have carried the King to his palace!" But the King said: "Hold your peace and leave him alone, he is my most faithful John. Who knows what good may come of this!" They went into the palace, and in the hall there stood a dish, and therein lay the bridal garment looking no otherwise than as if it were made of gold and silver. The young King went towards it and was about to take hold of it, but Faithful John pushed him away, seized it with gloves on, carried it quickly to the fire and burnt it. The other attendants again began to murmur, and said: "Behold, now he is even burning the King's bridal garment!" But the young King said: "Who knows what good he may have done, leave him alone, he is my most faithful John."

And now the wedding was solemnized: the dance began, and the bride also took part in it; then Faithful John was watchful and looked into her face, and suddenly she turned pale and fell to the ground as if she were dead. On this he ran hastily to her, lifted her up and bore her into a chamber—then he laid her down, and knelt and sucked the three drops of blood from her right breast, and spat them out. Immediately she breathed again and recovered herself, but the young King had seen this, and being ignorant why Faithful John had done it, was angry and cried: "Throw him into a dungeon." Next morning Faithful John was condemned, and led to the gallows, and when he stood on high, and was about to be executed, he said: "Every one who has to die is permitted before his end to make one last speech; may I too claim the right?" "Yes," answered the King, "it shall be granted unto you." Then said Faithful John: "I am unjustly condemned, and have always been true to you," and he related how he had hearkened to the conversation of the ravens when on the sea, and how he had been obliged to do all these things in order to save his master. Then cried the King: "Oh, my most faithful John. Pardon, pardon—bring him down." But as Faithful John spoke the last word he had fallen down lifeless and become a stone.

Thereupon the King and the Queen suffered great anguish, and the King said: "Ah, how ill I have requited great fidelity!" and ordered the stone figure to be taken up and placed in his bedroom beside his bed. And as often as he looked on it he wept and said: "Ah, if I could bring you to life again, my most faithful John."

Some time passed and the Queen bore twins, two sons who grew fast and were her delight. Once when the Queen was at church and the father was sitting with his two children playing beside him, he looked at the stone figure again, sighed, and full of grief he said: "Ah, if I could but bring you to life again, my most faithful John." Then the stone began to speak and said: "You can bring me to life again if you will use for that purpose what is dearest to you." Then cried the King: "I will give everything I have in the world for you." The stone continued: "If you will cut off the heads of your two children with your own hand, and sprinkle me with their blood, I shall be restored to life."

The King was terrified when he heard that he himself must kill his dearest children, but he thought of Faithful John's great fidelity, and how he had died for him, drew his sword, and with his own hand cut off the children's heads. And when he had smeared the stone with their blood, life returned to it, and Faithful John stood once more safe and healthy before him. He said to the King: "Your truth shall not go unrewarded," and took the heads of the children, put them on again, and rubbed the wounds with their blood, at which they became whole again immediately, and jumped about, and went on playing as if nothing had happened. Then the King was full of joy, and when he saw the Queen coming he hid Faithful John and the two children in a great cupboard. When she entered, he said to her: "Have you been praying in the church?" "Yes," answered she, "but I have constantly been thinking of Faithful John and what misfortune has befallen him through us." Then said he: "Dear wife, we can give him his life again, but it will cost us our two little sons, whom we must sacrifice." The Queen turned pale, and her heart was full of terror, but she said: "We owe it to him, for his great fidelity." Then the King was rejoiced that she thought as he had thought, and went and opened the cupboard, and brought forth Faithful John and the children, and said: "God be praised, he is delivered, and we have our little sons again also," and told her how everything had occurred. Then they dwelt together in much happiness until their death.

THE GOOD BARGAIN

There was once a peasant who had driven his cow to the fair, and sold her for seven talers. On the way home he had to pass a pond, and already from afar he heard the frogs crying: "Aik, aik, aik, aik." "Well," said he to himself, "they are talking without rhyme or reason, it is seven that I have received, not eight." When he got to the water, he cried to them: "Stupid animals that you are! Don't you know better than that? It is seven talers and not eight." The frogs, however, stuck to their "aik, aik, aik, aik." "Come, then, if you won't believe it, I can count it out to you," and he took his money out of his pocket and counted out the seven talers, always reckoning four and twenty groschen to a taler. The frogs, however, paid no attention to his reckoning, but still cried: "aik, aik, aik, aik." "What," cried the peasant quite angry, "if you know better than I, count it yourselves," and threw all the money at them into the water. He stood still and wanted to wait until they were through and had returned to him what was his, but the frogs maintained their opinion and cried continually "aik, aik, aik, aik," and besides that, did not throw the money out again. He still waited a long while until evening came on and he was forced to go home. Then he abused the frogs and cried: "You water-splashers, you thick-heads, you goggle-eyes, you have great mouths and can screech till you hurt one's ears, but you cannot count seven talers! Do you think I'm going to stand here till you get through?" And with that he went away, but the frogs still cried: "aik, aik, aik, aik," after him till he went home sorely vexed.

After a while he bought another cow, which he slaughtered, and he made the calculation that if he sold the meat well he might gain as much as the two cows were worth, and have the hide into the bargain. When therefore he got to the town with the meat, a great pack of dogs were gathered together in front of the gate, with a large greyhound at the head of them, which jumped at the meat, sniffed at it, and barked: "Wow, wow, wow." As there was no stopping him, the peasant said to him: "Yes, yes, I know quite well that you are saying 'wow, wow, wow', because you want some of the meat; but I should be in a fine state if I were to give it to you." The dog, however, answered nothing but "wow, wow." "Will you promise not to devour it all then, and will you go bail for your companions?" "Wow, wow, wow," said the dog. "Well, if you insist on it, I will leave it for you; I know you well, and know whom you serve; but this I tell you, I must have my money in three days or else it will go ill with you; you can just bring it out to me." Thereupon he unloaded the meat and turned back again. The dogs fell upon it and loudly barked: "wow, wow."

The countryman, who heard them from afar, said to himself: "Hark, now they all want some, but the big one is responsible to me for it."

When three days had passed, the countryman thought: "To-night my money will be in my pocket," and was quite delighted. But no one would come and pay it. "There is no trusting any one now," said he; and at last he lost patience, and went into the town to the butcher and demanded his money. The butcher thought it was a joke, but the peasant said: "Jesting apart, I will have my money! Did not the big dog bring you the whole of the slaughtered cow three days ago?" Then the butcher grew angry, snatched a broom-stick and drove him out. "Wait," said the peasant, "there is still some justice in the world!" and went to the royal palace and begged for an audience. He was led before the King, who

sat there with his daughter, and asked him what injury he had suffered. "Alas!" said he, "the frogs and the dogs have taken from me what is mine, and the butcher has paid me for it with the stick," and he related at full length what had happened. Thereupon the King's daughter began to laugh heartily, and the King said to him: "I cannot give you justice in this, but you shall have my daughter to wife for it,—in her whole life she has never yet laughed as she has just done at you, and I have promised her to him who could make her laugh. You may thank God for your good fortune!"

"Oh," answered the peasant, "I do not want her at all. I have a wife already, and she is one too many for me; when I go home, it is just as if I had a wife standing in every corner." Then the King grew angry, and said: "You are a boor." "Ah, Lord King," replied the peasant, "what can you expect from an ox, but beef?" "Stop," answered the King, "you shall have another reward. Be off now, but come back in three days, and then you shall have five hundred counted out in full."

When the peasant went out by the gate, the sentry said: "You have made the King's daughter laugh, so you will certainly receive something good." "Yes, that is what I think," answered the peasant; "five hundred are to be counted out to me." "Listen," said the soldier, "give me some of it. What can you do with all that money?" "As it is you," said the peasant, "you shall have two hundred; present yourself in three days' time before the King, and let it be paid to you." A Jew, who was standing by and had heard the conversation, ran after the peasant, held him by the coat, and said: "Oh, wonder of God! what a child of fortune you are! I will change it for you, I will change it for you into small coins, what do you want with the great talers?" "Jew," said the countryman, "three hundred can you still have; give it to me at once in coin, in three days from this, you will be paid for it by the King." The Jew was delighted with the small profit, and brought the sum in bad groschen, three of which were worth two good ones. After three days had passed, according to the King's command, the peasant went before the King. "Pull his coat off," said the latter, "and he shall have his five hundred." "Ah!" said the peasant, "they no longer belong to me; I presented two hundred of them to the sentry, and three hundred the Jew has changed for me, so by right nothing at all belongs to me." In the meantime the soldier and the Jew entered and claimed what they had gained from the peasant, and they received the blows strictly counted out. The soldier bore it patiently and knew already how it tasted; but the Jew said sorrowfully: "Alas, alas, are these the heavy talers?" The King could not help laughing at the peasant, and when all his anger was spent, he said: "As you have already lost your reward before it fell to your lot, I will give you compensation. Go into my treasure chamber and get some money for yourself, as much as you will." The peasant did not need to be told twice, and stuffed into his big pockets whatsoever would go in. Afterwards he went to an inn and counted out his money. The Jew had crept after him and heard how he muttered to himself: "That rogue of a king has cheated me after all, why could he not have given me the money himself, and then I should have known what I had? How can I tell now if what I have had the luck to put in my pockets is right or not?" "Good heavens!" said the Jew to himself, "that man is speaking disrespectfully of our lord the King, I will run and inform, and then I shall get a reward, and he will be punished as well."

When the King heard of the peasant's words he fell into a passion, and commanded the Jew to go and bring the offender to him. The Jew ran to the peasant: "You are to go at once to the lord King in the very clothes you have on." "I know what's right better than that," answered the peasant, "I shall have a new coat made first. Do you think that a man with so much money in his pocket should go there in his ragged old coat?" The Jew, as he saw that the peasant would not stir without another coat, and as he feared that if the King's anger cooled, he himself would lose his reward, and the peasant his punishment, said: "I will out of pure friendship lend you a coat for the short time. What will people not do for love!" The peasant was contented with this, put the Jew's coat on, and went off with him.

The King reproached the countryman because of the evil speaking of which the Jew had informed him. "Ah," said the peasant, "what a Jew says is always false—no true word ever comes out of his mouth! That rascal there is capable of maintaining that I have his coat on."

"What is that?" shrieked the Jew. "Is the coat not mine? Have I not lent it to you out of pure friendship, in order that you might appear before the lord King?" When the King heard that, he said: "The Jew has assuredly deceived one or the other of us, either myself or the peasant," and again he ordered something to be counted out to him in hard talers. The peasant, however, went home in the good coat, with the good money in his pocket, and said to himself: "This time I have done it!"

THE STRANGE MUSICIAN

There was once a wonderful musician, who went quite forlorn through a forest and thought of all manner of things, and when nothing was left for him to think about, he said to himself: "Time is beginning to pass heavily with me here in the forest, I will fetch hither a good companion for myself." Then he took his fiddle from his back, and played so that it echoed through the trees. It was not long before a wolf came trotting through the thicket towards him. "Ah, here is a wolf coming! I have no desire for him!" said the musician; but the wolf came nearer and said to him: "Ah, dear musician, how beautifully you play! I should like to learn that, too." "It is soon learnt," the musician replied, "you have only to do all that I bid you." "Oh, musician," said the wolf, "I will obey you as a scholar obeys his master." The musician bade him follow, and when they had gone part of the way together, they came to an old oak-tree which was hollow inside, and cleft in the middle. "Look," said the musician, "if you will learn to fiddle, put your fore paws into this crevice." The wolf obeyed, but the musician quickly picked up a stone and with one blow wedged his two paws so fast that he was forced to stay there like a prisoner. "Wait there until I come back again," said the musician, and went his way.

After a while he again said to himself: "Time is beginning to pass heavily with me here in the forest, I will fetch hither another companion," and took his fiddle and again played in the forest. It was not long before a fox came creeping through the trees towards him. "Ah, there's a fox coming!" said the musician. "I have no desire for him." The fox came up to him and said: "Oh, dear musician, how beautifully you play! I should like to learn that, too." "That is soon learnt," said the musician. "You have only to do everything that I bid you." "Oh, musician," then said the fox, "I will obey you as a scholar obeys his master." "Follow me," said the musician; and when they had walked a part of the way, they came to a footpath, with high bushes on both sides of it. There the musician stood still, and from one side bent a young hazel-bush down to the ground, and put his foot on the end of it. Then he bent down a young tree from the other side as well, and said: "Now, little fox, if you will learn something, give me your left front paw." The fox obeyed, and the musician fastened his paw to the left bough. "Little fox," said he, "now reach me your right paw," and he tied it to the right bough. When he had examined whether the knots were firm enough, he let go, and the bushes sprang up again, and jerked up the little fox, so that it hung struggling in the air. "Wait there till I come back again," said the musician, and went his way.

Again he said to himself: "Time is beginning to pass heavily with me here in the forest, I will fetch hither another companion," so he took his fiddle, and the sound echoed through the forest. Then a little hare came springing towards him. "Ah, a hare is coming," said the musician, "I do not want him." "Ah, dear musician," said the hare, "how beautifully you fiddle; I, too, should like to learn that." "That is soon learnt," said the musician, "you have only to do everything that I bid you."

"Oh, musician," replied the little hare, "I will obey you as a scholar obeys his master." They went a part of the way together until they came to an open space in the forest, where stood an aspentree. The musician tied a long string round the little hare's neck, the other end of which he fastened to the tree. "Now briskly, little hare, run twenty times round the tree!" cried the musician, and the little hare obeyed, and when it had run round twenty times, it had twisted the string twenty times round the trunk of the tree, and the little hare was caught, and let it pull and tug as it liked, it only made the string cut into its tender neck. "Wait there till I come back," said the musician, and went onwards.

The wolf, in the meantime, had pushed and pulled and bitten at the stone, and had worked so long that he had set his feet at liberty and had drawn them once more out of the cleft. Full of anger and rage he hurried after the musician and wanted to tear him to pieces. When the fox saw him running, he began to lament, and cried with all his might: "Brother wolf, come to my help, the musician has betrayed me!" The wolf drew down the little tree, bit the cord in two, and freed the fox, who went with him to take revenge on the musician. They found the tied-up hare, whom likewise they rescued, and then they all sought the enemy together.

The musician had once more played his fiddle as he went on his way, and this time he had been more fortunate. The sound reached the ears of a poor wood-cutter, who instantly, whether he would or not, gave up his work and came with his hatchet under his arm to listen to the music. "At last comes the right companion," said the musician, "for I was seeking a human being, and no wild beast." And he began and played so beautifully and delightfully that the poor man stood there as if bewitched, and his heart leaped with gladness. And as he thus stood, the wolf, the fox, and the hare came up, and he saw well that they had some evil design. So he raised his glittering axe and placed himself before the musician, as if to say: "Whoso wishes to touch him let him beware, for he will have to deal with me!" Then the beasts were terrified and ran back into the forest. The musician, however, played once more to the man out of gratitude, and then went onwards.

THE TWELVE BROTHERS

There were once upon a time a King and a Queen who lived happily together and had twelve children, but they were all boys. Then said the King to his wife: "If the thirteenth child which you are about to bring into the world, is a girl, the twelve boys shall die, in order that her possessions may be great, and that the kingdom may fall to her alone." He even caused twelve coffins to be made, which were already filled with shavings, and in each lay the little death pillow, and he had them taken into a locked-up room, and then he gave the Queen the key of it, and bade her not to speak of this to anyone.

The mother, however, now sat and lamented all day long, until the youngest son, who was always with her, and whom she had named

Benjamin, from the Bible, said to her: "Dear mother, why are you so sad?"

"Dearest child," she answered, "I may not tell you." But he let her have no rest until she went and unlocked the room, and showed him the twelve coffins ready filled with shavings. Then she said: "My dearest Benjamin, your father has had these coffins made for you and for your eleven brothers, for if I bring a little girl into the world, you are all to be killed and buried in them." And as she wept while she was saying this, the son comforted her and said: "Weep not, dear mother, we will save ourselves, and go hence." But she said: "Go forth into the forest with your eleven brothers, and let one sit constantly on the highest tree which can be found, and keep watch, looking towards the tower here in the castle. If I give birth to a little son, I will put up a white flag, and then you may venture to come back. But if I bear a daughter, I will hoist a red flag, and then fly hence as quickly as you are able, and may the good God protect you. And every night I will rise up and pray for you—in winter that you may be able to warm yourself at a fire, and in summer that you may not faint away in the heat."

After she had blessed her sons therefore, they went forth into the forest. They each kept watch in turn, and sat on the highest oak and looked towards the tower. When eleven days had passed and the turn came to Benjamin, he saw that a flag was being raised. It was, however, not the white, but the blood-red flag which announced that they were all to die. When the brothers heard that, they were very angry and said: "Are we all to suffer death for the sake of a girl? We swear that we will avenge ourselves—wheresoever we find a girl, her red blood shall flow."

Thereupon they went deeper into the forest, and in the midst of it, where it was the darkest, they found a little bewitched hut, which was standing empty. Then said they: "Here we will dwell, and you Benjamin, who are the youngest and weakest, you shall stay at home and keep house, we others will go out and fetch food." Then they went into the forest and shot hares, wild deer, birds and pigeons, and whatsoever there was to eat; this they took to Benjamin, who had to dress it for them in order that they might appease their hunger. They lived together ten years in the little hut, and the time did not appear long to them.

The little daughter which their mother the Queen had given birth to, was now grown up; she was good of heart, and fair of face, and had a golden star on her forehead. Once, on a great washing, she saw twelve men's shirts among the things, and asked her mother: "To whom do these twelve shirts belong, for they are far too small for father?" Then the Queen answered with a heavy heart: "Dear child, these belong to your twelve brothers." Said the maiden: "Where are my twelve brothers, I have never yet heard of them?" She replied: "God knows where they are, they are wandering about the world." Then she took the maiden and opened the chamber for her, and showed her the twelve coffins with the shavings, and the death pillows. "These coffins," said she, "were destined for your brothers, who went away secretly before you were born," and she related to her how everything had happened; then said the maiden: "Dear mother, weep not, I will go and seek my brothers."

So she took the twelve shirts and went forth, and straight into the great forest. She walked the whole day, and in the evening she came to the bewitched hut. Then she entered it and found a young boy, who asked: "From whence do you come, and whither are you bound?" and was astonished that she was so beautiful, and wore royal garments, and had a star on her forehead. And she answered: "I am a king's daughter, and am seeking my twelve brothers, and I will walk as far as the sky is blue until I find them." And she showed him the twelve shirts which belonged to them. Then Benjamin saw that she was his sister, and said: "I am Benjamin, your youngest brother." And she began to weep for joy, and Benjamin wept also, and they kissed and embraced each other with the greatest love. But after this he said: "Dear sister, there is still one difficulty. We have agreed that every maiden whom we meet shall die, because we have been obliged to leave our kingdom on account of a girl." Then said she: "I will willingly die, if by so doing I can save my twelve brothers."

"No," answered he, "you shall not die. Seat yourself beneath this tub until our eleven brothers come, and then I will soon come to an agreement with them."

She did so, and when it was night the others came from hunting, and their dinner was ready. And as they were sitting at table, and eating, they asked: "What news is there?" Said Benjamin: "Don't you know anything?" "No," they answered. He continued: "You have been in the forest and I have stayed at home, and yet I know more than you do." "Tell us then," they cried. He answered: "But promise me that the first maiden who meets us shall not be killed." "Yes," they all cried, "she shall have mercy, only do tell us."

Then said he: "Our sister is here," and he lifted up the tub, and the King's daughter came forth in her royal garments with the golden star on her forehead, and she was beautiful, delicate, and fair. Then they were all rejoiced, and fell on her neck, and kissed and loved her with all their hearts.

Now she stayed at home with Benjamin and helped him with the work. The eleven went into the forest and caught game, and deer, and birds, and wood-pigeons that they might have food, and the little sister and Benjamin took care to make it ready for them. She sought for the wood for cooking and herbs for vegetables, and put the pans on the fire so that the dinner was always ready when the eleven came. She likewise kept order in the little house, and put beautifully white clean coverings on the little beds, and the brothers were always contented and lived in great harmony with her.

Once upon a time the two at home had prepared a wonderful feast, and when they were all together, they sat down and ate and drank and were full of gladness. There was, however, a little garden belonging to the bewitched house wherein stood twelve lily flowers, which are likewise called student-lilies. She wished to give her brothers pleasure, and plucked the twelve flowers, and thought she would present each brother with one while at dinner. But at the self-same moment that she plucked the flowers the twelve brothers were changed into twelve ravens, and flew away over the forest, and the house and garden vanished likewise. And now the poor maiden was alone in the wild forest, and when she looked around, an old woman was standing near her who said: "My child, what have you done? Why did you not leave the twelve white flowers growing? They were your brothers, who are now for evermore changed into ravens." The maiden said, weeping: "Is there no way of saving them?"

"No," said the woman, "there is but one in the whole world, and that is so hard that you will not save them by it, for you must be dumb for seven years, and may not speak or laugh, and if you speak one

single word, and only an hour of the seven years is wanting, all is in vain, and your brothers will be killed by the one word."

Then said the maiden in her heart: "I know with certainty that I shall set my brothers free," and went and sought a high tree and seated herself in it and spun, and neither spoke nor laughed. Now it so happened that a King was hunting in the forest, who had a great greyhound which ran to the tree on which the maiden was sitting, and sprang about it, whining, and barking at her. Then the King came by and saw the beautiful King's daughter with the golden star on her brow, and was so charmed with her beauty that he called to ask her if she would be his wife. She made no answer, but nodded a little with her head. So he climbed up the tree himself, carried her down, placed her on his horse, and bore her home. Then the wedding was solemnized with great magnificence and rejoicing, but the bride neither spoke nor smiled. When they had lived happily together for a few years, the King's mother, who was a wicked woman, began to slander the young Queen, and said to the King: "This is a common beggar girl whom you have brought back with you. Who knows what wicked tricks she practises secretly! Even if she be dumb, and not able to speak, she still might laugh for once; but those who do not laugh have bad consciences." At first the King would not believe it, but the old woman urged this so long, and accused her of so many evil things, that at last the King let himself be persuaded and sentenced her to death.

And now a great fire was lighted in the courtyard in which she was to be burnt, and the King stood above at the window and looked on with tearful eyes, because he still loved her so much. And when she was bound fast to the stake, and the fire was licking at her clothes with its red tongue, the last instant of the seven years expired. Then a whirring sound was heard in the air, and twelve ravens came flying towards the place, and sank downwards, and when they touched the earth they were her twelve brothers, whom she had saved. They tore the fire asunder, extinguished the flames, set their dear sister free, and kissed and embraced her. And now as she dared to open her mouth and speak, she told the King why she had been dumb, and had never laughed. The King rejoiced when he heard that she was innocent, and they all lived in great unity until their death. The wicked step-mother was taken before the judge, and put into a barrel filled with boiling oil and venomous snakes, and died an evil death.

THE PACK OF RAGAMUFFINS

The cock once said to the hen: "It is now the time when the nuts are ripe, so let us go to the hill together and for once eat our fill before the squirrel takes them all away." "Yes," replied the hen, "come, we will have some fun together." Then they went away to the hill, and as it was a bright day they stayed till evening. Now I do not know whether it was that they had eaten till they were too fat, or whether they had become too proud, but they would not go home on foot, and the cock had to build a little carriage of nut-shells. When it was ready, the little hen seated herself in it and said to the cock: "You can just harness yourself to it." "I like that!" said the cock, "I would rather go home on foot than let myself be harnessed to it; no, that is not our bargain. I do not mind being coachman and sitting on the box, but drag it myself I will not."

As they were thus disputing, a duck quacked at them: "You thieving folks, who bade you go to my nut-hill? Wait, you shall suffer for it!" and ran with open beak at the cock. But the cock also was not idle, and fell boldly on the duck, and at last wounded her so with his spurs that she begged for mercy, and willingly let herself be harnessed to the carriage as a punishment. The little cock now seated himself on the box and was coachman, and thereupon they went off at a gallop, with the cock crying: "Duck, go as fast as you can." When they had driven a part of the way they met two foot-passengers, a pin and a needle. They cried "Stop! stop!" and said that it would soon be as dark as pitch, and then they could not go a step further, and that it was so dirty on the road, and asked if they could not get into the carriage for a while. They had been at the tailor's public-house by the gate, and had stayed too long over the beer. As they were thin people, who did not take up much room, the cock let them both get in, but they had to promise him and his little hen not to step on their feet. Late in the evening they came to an inn, and as they did not like to go further by night, and as the duck also was not strong on her feet, and fell from one side to the other, they went in. The host at first made many objections, his house was already full, besides he thought they could not be very distinguished persons; but at last, as they made pleasant speeches, and told him that he should have the egg which the little hen had laid on the way, and should likewise keep the duck, which laid one every day, he at length said that they might stay the night. And now they had themselves well served, and feasted and had a high good time. Early in the morning, when day was breaking, and every one was asleep, the cock awoke the hen, brought the egg, pecked it open, and they ate it together, but they threw the shell on the hearth. Then they went to the needle which was still asleep, took it by the head and stuck it into the cushion of the landlord's chair, and put the pin in his towel, and at last without more ado they fled away over the heath. The duck who liked to sleep in the open air and had stayed in the yard, heard them going away, made herself merry and found a stream, down which she swam, which was a much quicker way of travelling than being harnessed to a carriage. The host did not get out of bed until a couple of hours later; he washed himself and was about to dry himself, when the pin went over his face and made a red scratch from one ear to the other. After this he went into the kitchen and wanted to light a pipe, but when he came to the hearth the egg-shell darted into his eyes. "This morning everything attacks my head," said he, and angrily sat down on his grandfather's chair, but he quickly started up again and cried: "Ow!" for the needle had pricked him still worse than the pin, and not in the head. Now he was thoroughly angry, and suspected the guests who had come so late the night before; and when he went in search of them, they were gone. Then he made a vow to take no more ragamuffins into his house, for they consume much, pay for nothing, and play mischievous tricks into the bargain by way of gratitude.

BROTHER AND SISTER

Little brother took his little sister by the hand and said: "Since our mother died we have had no happiness; our step-mother beats us every day, and if we come near her she kicks us away with her foot. Our meals are the hard crusts of bread that are left over; and the little dog under the table is better off, for she often throws it a choice morsel. God pity us, if our mother only knew! Come, we will go forth together into the wide world."

They walked the whole day over meadows, fields, and stony places; and when it rained the little sister said: "Heaven and our hearts are weeping together." In the evening they came to a large forest, and they were so weary with sorrow and hunger and the long walk, that they lay down in a hollow tree and fell asleep.

The next day when they awoke, the sun was already high in the sky, and shone down hot into the tree. Then the brother said: "Sister, I am thirsty; if I knew of a little brook I would go and just take a drink; I think I hear one running." The brother got up and took the little sister by the hand, and they set off to find the brook. But the wicked step-mother was a witch, and had seen how the two children had gone away, and had crept after them secretly, as witches creep, and had bewitched all the brooks in the forest.

Now when they found a little brook leaping brightly over the stones, the brother was going to drink out of it, but the sister heard how it said as it ran: "Who drinks of me will be a tiger; who drinks of me will be a tiger." Then the sister cried: "Pray, dear brother, do not drink, or you will become a wild beast, and tear me to pieces." The brother did not drink, although he was so thirsty, but said: "I will wait for the next spring."

When they came to the next brook the sister heard this also say: "Who drinks of me will be a wolf; who drinks of me will be a wolf." Then the sister cried out: "Pray, dear brother, do not drink, or you will become a wolf, and devour me." The brother did not drink, and said: "I will wait until we come to the next spring, but then I must drink, say what you like; for my thirst is too great."

And when they came to the third brook the sister heard how it said as it ran: "Who drinks of me will be a roebuck; who drinks of me will be a roebuck." The sister said: "Oh, I pray you, dear brother, do not drink, or you will become a roebuck, and run away from me." But the brother had knelt down at once by the brook, and had bent down and drunk some of the water, and as soon as the first drops touched his lips he lay there in the form of a young roebuck.

And now the sister wept over her poor bewitched brother, and the little roe wept also, and sat sorrowfully near to her. But at last the girl said: "Be quiet, dear little roe, I will never, never leave you."

Then she untied her golden garter and put it round the roebuck's neck, and she plucked rushes and wove them into a soft cord. This she tied to the little animal and led it on, and she walked deeper and deeper into the forest.

And when they had gone a very long way they came at last to a little house, and the girl looked in; and as it was empty, she thought: "We can stay here and live." Then she sought for leaves and moss to make a soft bed for the roe; and every morning she went out and gathered roots and berries and nuts for herself, and brought tender grass for the roe, who ate out of her hand, and was content and played round about her. In the evening, when the sister was tired, and had said her prayer, she laid her head upon the roebuck's back: that was her pillow, and she slept softly on it. And if only the brother had had his human form it would have been a delightful life.

For some time they were alone like this in the wilderness. But it happened that the King of the country held a great hunt in the forest. Then the blasts of the horns, the barking of dogs, and the merry shouts of the huntsmen rang through the trees, and the roebuck heard all, and was only too anxious to be there. "Oh," said he to his sister, "let me be off to the hunt, I cannot bear it any longer"; and he begged so much that at last she agreed. "But," said she to him, "come back to me in the evening; I must shut my door for fear of the rough huntsmen, so knock and say: 'My little sister, let me in!' that I may know you; and if you do not say that, I shall not open the door." Then the young roebuck sprang away; so happy was he and so merry in the open air.

The King and the huntsmen saw the lovely animal, and started after him, but they could not catch him, and when they thought that they surely had him, away he sprang through the bushes and vanished. When it was dark he ran to the cottage, knocked, and said: "My little sister, let me in." Then the door was opened for him, and he jumped in, and rested himself the whole night through upon his soft bed.

The next day the hunt began again, and when the roebuck once more heard the bugle-horn, and the ho! ho! of the huntsmen, he had no peace, but said: "Sister, let me out, I must be off." His sister opened the door for him, and said: "But you must be here again in the evening and say your pass-word."

When the King and his huntsmen again saw the young roebuck with the golden collar, they all chased him, but he was too quick and nimble for them. This lasted the whole day, but by the evening the huntsmen had surrounded him, and one of them wounded him a little in the foot, so that he limped and ran slowly. Then a hunter crept after him to the cottage and heard how he said: "My little sister, let me in," and saw that the door was opened for him, and was shut again at once. The huntsman took notice of it all, and went to the King and told him what he had seen and heard. Then the King said: "To-morrow we will hunt once more."

The little sister, however, was dreadfully frightened when she saw that her fawn was hurt. She washed the blood off him, laid herbs on the wound, and said: "Go to your bed, dear roe, that you may get well again." But the wound was so slight that the roebuck, next morning, did not feel it any more. And when he again heard the sport outside, he said: "I cannot bear it, I must be there; they shall not find it so easy to catch me." The sister cried, and said: "This time they will kill you, and here am I alone in the forest and forsaken by all the world. I will not let you out." "Then you will have me die of grief," answered the roe;

"when I hear the buglehorns I feel as if I must jump out of my skin."
Then the sister could not do otherwise, but opened the door for him
with a heavy heart, and the roebuck, full of health and joy, bounded
into the forest.

When the King saw him, he said to his huntsmen: "Now chase him
all day long till night-fall, but take care that no one does him any
harm."

As soon as the sun had set, the King said to the huntsman: "Now
come and show me the cottage in the wood"; and when he was at the
door, he knocked and called out: "Dear little sister, let me in." Then the
door opened, and the King walked in, and there stood a maiden more
lovely than any he had ever seen. The maiden was frightened when she
saw, not her little roe, but a man come in who wore a golden crown
upon his head. But the King looked kindly at her, stretched out his
hand, and said: "Will you go with me to my palace and be my dear
wife?" "Yes, indeed," answered the maiden, "but the little roe must go
with me, I cannot leave him." The King said: "It shall stay with you as
long as you live, and shall want nothing." Just then he came running
in, and the sister again tied him with the cord of rushes, took it in her
own hand, and went away with the King from the cottage.

The King took the lovely maiden upon his horse and carried her to
his palace, where the wedding was held with great pomp. She was now
the Queen, and they lived for a long time happily together; the roebuck
was tended and cherished, and ran about in the palace-garden.

But the wicked step-mother, because of whom the children had
gone out into the world, had never thought but that the sister had been
torn to pieces by the wild beasts in the wood, and that the brother had
been shot for a roebuck by the huntsmen. Now when she heard that
they were so happy, and so well off, envy and jealousy rose in her heart
and left her no peace, and she thought of nothing but how she could
bring them again to misfortune. Her own daughter, who was as ugly as
night, and had only one eye, reproached her and said: "A Queen! that
ought to have been my luck." "Just be quiet," answered the old
woman, and comforted her by saying: "when the time comes I shall be
ready."

As time went on, the Queen had a pretty little boy, and it happened
that the King was out hunting; so the old witch took the form of the

chamber-maid, went into the room where the Queen lay, and said to her: "Come, the bath is ready; it will do you good, and give you fresh strength; make haste before it gets cold."

Her daughter also was close by; so they carried the weakly Queen into the bath-room, and put her into the bath; then they shut the door and ran away. But in the bath-room they had made a fire of such terrible heat that the beautiful young Queen was soon suffocated.

When this was done the old woman took her daughter, put a night-cap on her head, and laid her in bed in place of the Queen. She gave her too the shape and the look of the Queen, only she could not make good the lost eye. But in order that the King might not see it, she was to lie on the side on which she had no eye.

In the evening when he came home and heard that he had a son he was heartily glad, and was going to the bed of his dear wife to see how she was. But the old woman quickly called out: "For your life leave the curtains closed; the Queen ought not to see the light yet, and must have rest." The King went away, and did not find out that a false Queen was lying in the bed.

But at midnight, when all slept, the nurse, who was sitting in the nursery by the cradle, and who was the only person awake, saw the door open and the true Queen walk in. She took the child out of the cradle, laid it on her arm, and suckled it. Then she shook up it pillow, laid the child down again, and covered it with the little quilt. And she did not forget the roebuck, but went into the corner where it lay, and stroked it back. Then she went quite silently out of the door again. The next morning the nurse asked the guards whether anyone had come into the palace during the night, but they answered: "No, we have seen no one."

She came thus many nights and never spoke a word: the nurse always saw her, but she did not dare to tell anyone about it.

When some time had passed in this manner, the Queen began to speak in the night, and said:

"How fares my child, how fares my roe?
Twice shall I come, then never more."

The nurse did not answer, but when the Queen had gone again, went to the King and told him all. The King said: "Ah, God! what is this? To-morrow night I will watch by the child." In the evening he went into the nursery, and at midnight the Queen again appeared and said:

"How fares my child, how fares my roe?
Once will I come, then never more."

And she nursed the child as she was wont to do before she disappeared. The King dared not speak to her, but on the next night he watched again. Then she said:

"How fares my child, how fares my roe?
This time I come, then never more."

Then the King could not restrain himself; he sprang towards her, and said: "You can be none other than my dear wife." She answered: "Yes, I am your dear wife," and at the same moment she received life again, and by God's grace became fresh, rosy, and full of health.

Then she told the King the evil deed which the wicked witch and her daughter had been guilty of towards her. The King ordered both to be led before the judge, and judgment was delivered against them. The daughter was taken into the forest where she was torn to pieces by wild beasts, but the witch was cast into the fire and miserably burnt. And as soon as she was burnt to ashes, the roebuck changed his shape, and received his human form again, so the sister and brother lived happily together all their lives.

RAPUNZEL*

There were once a man and a woman who had long in vain wished for a child. At length the woman hoped that God was about to grant her desire. These people had a little window at the back of their house from which a splendid garden could be seen, which was full of the most

* Rampion.

beautiful flowers and herbs. It was, however, surrounded by a high wall, and no one dared to go into it because it belonged to an enchantress, who had great power and was dreaded by all the world. One day the woman was standing by this window and looking down into the garden, when she saw a bed which was planted with the most beautiful rampion (rapunzel), and it looked so fresh and green that she longed for it, and had the greatest desire to eat some. This desire increased every day, and as she knew that she could not get any of it, she quite pined away, and began to look pale and miserable. Then her husband was alarmed, and asked: "What ails you, dear wife?" "Ah," she replied, "if I can't eat some of the rampion, which is in the garden behind our house, I shall die." The man, who loved her, thought: "Sooner than let your wife die, bring her some of the rampion yourself, let it cost what it will." At twilight, he clambered down over the wall into the garden of the enchantress, hastily clutched a handful of rampion, and took it to his wife. She at once made herself a salad of it, and ate it greedily. It tasted so good to her—so very good, that the next day she longed for it three times as much as before. If he was to have any rest, her husband must once more descend into the garden. In the gloom of evening, therefore, he let himself down again; but when he had clambered down the wall he was terribly afraid, for he saw the enchantress standing before him. "How can you dare," said she with angry look, "descend into my garden and steal my rampion like a thief? You shall suffer for it!" "Ah," answered he, "let mercy take the place of justice, I only made up my mind to do it out of necessity. My wife saw your rampion from the window, and felt such a longing for it that she would have died if she had not got some to eat." Then the enchantress allowed her anger to be softened, and said to him: "If the case be as you say, I will allow you to take away with you as much rampion as you will, only I make one condition, you must give me the child which your wife will bring into the world; it shall be well treated, and I will care for it like a mother." The man in his terror consented to everything, and when the woman was brought to bed, the enchantress appeared at once, gave the child the name of Rapunzel, and took it away with her.

Rapunzel grew into the most beautiful child under the sun. When she was twelve years old, the enchantress shut her into a tower, which lay in a forest, and had neither stairs nor door, but quite at the top was a little window. When the enchantress wanted to go in, she placed herself beneath it and cried:

"Rapunzel, Rapunzel,
Let down your hair to me."

Rapunzel had magnificent long hair, fine as spun gold, and when she heard the voice of the enchantress she unfastened her braided tresses, wound them round one of the hooks of the window above, and then the hair fell twenty ells down, and the enchantress climbed up by it.

After a year or two, it came to pass that the King's son rode through the forest and passed by the tower. Then he heard a song, which was so charming that he stood still and listened. This was Rapunzel, who in her solitude passed her time in letting her sweet voice resound. The King's son wanted to climb up to her, and looked for the door of the tower, but none was to be found. He rode home, but the singing had so deeply touched his heart, that every day he went out into the forest and listened to it. Once when he was thus standing behind a tree, he saw that an enchantress came there, and he heard how she cried:

"Rapunzel, Rapunzel,
Let down your hair."

Then Rapunzel let down the braids of her hair, and the enchantress climbed up to her. "If that is the ladder by which one mounts, I too will try my fortune," said he, and the next day when it began to grow dark, he went to the tower and cried:

"Rapunzel, Rapunzel,
Let down your hair."

Immediately the hair fell down and the King's son climbed up.

At first Rapunzel was terribly frightened when a man, such as her eyes had never yet beheld, came to her; but the King's son began to talk to her quite like a friend, and told her that his heart had been so stirred that it had let him have no rest, and he had been forced to see her. Then Rapunzel lost her fear, and when he asked her if she would take him for her husband, and she saw that he was young and handsome, she thought: "He will love me more than old Dame Gothel does"; and she said yes, and laid her hand in his. She said: "I will willingly go away with you, but I do not know how to get down. Bring with you a skein of silk every time that you come, and I will weave a ladder with it, and when that is ready I will descend, and you will take me on your horse." They agreed that until that time he should come to her every evening, for the old woman came by day. The enchantress remarked nothing of this, until once Rapunzel said to her: "Tell me, Dame Gothel, how it happens that you are so much heavier for me to draw up than the young King's son—he is with me in a moment." "Ah! you wicked child," cried the enchantress. "What do I hear you say! I thought I had separated you from all the world, and yet you have deceived me!" In her anger she clutched Rapunzel's beautiful tresses, wrapped them twice round her left hand, seized a pair of scissors with the right, and snip, snap, they were cut off, and the lovely braids lay on the ground. And she was so pitiless that she took poor Rapunzel into a desert where she had to live in great grief and misery.

On the same day that she cast out Rapunzel, however, the enchantress fastened the braids of hair, which she had cut off, to the hook of the window, and when the King's son came and cried:

"Rapunzel, Rapunzel,
Let down your hair,"

she let the hair down. The King's son ascended, but instead of finding his dearest Rapunzel, he found the enchantress, who gazed at him with wicked and venomous looks. "Aha!" she cried mockingly, "you would fetch your dearest, but the beautiful bird sits no longer singing in the nest; the cat has got it, and will scratch out your eyes as well. Rapunzel is lost to you; you will never see her again." The King's son was beside himself with pain, and in his despair he leapt down from the tower. He escaped with his life, but the thorns into which he fell pierced his eyes. Then he wandered quite blind about the forest, ate nothing but roots and berries, and did naught but lament and weep over the loss of his dearest wife. Thus he roamed about in misery for some years, and at length came to the desert where Rapunzel, with the twins to which she

had given birth, a boy and a girl, lived in wretchedness. He heard a voice, and it seemed so familiar to him that he went towards it, and when he approached, Rapunzel knew him and fell on his neck and wept. Two of her tears wetted his eyes and they grew clear again, and he could see with them as before. He led her to his kingdom where he was joyfully received, and they lived for a long time afterwards, happy and contented.

THE THREE LITTLE MEN IN THE WOOD

There was once a man whose wife died, and a woman whose husband died, and the man had a daughter, and the woman also had a daughter. The girls were acquainted with each other, and went out walking together, and afterwards came to the woman in her house. Then said she to the man's daughter: "Listen, tell your father that I would like to marry him, and then you shall wash yourself in milk every morning, and drink wine, but my own daughter shall wash herself in water and drink water." The girl went home, and told her father what the woman had said. The man said: "What shall I do? Marriage is a joy and also a torment." At length as he could come to no decision, he pulled off his boot, and said: "Take this boot, it has a hole in the sole of it. Go with it up to the loft, hang it on the big nail, and then pour water into it. If it hold the water, then I will again take a wife, but if it run through, I will not." The girl did as she was bid, but the water drew the hole together and the boot became full to the top. She informed her father how it had turned out. Then he himself went up, and when he saw that she was right, he went to the widow and wooed her, and the wedding was celebrated.

The next morning, when the two girls got up, there stood before the man's daughter milk for her to wash in and wine for her to drink, but before the woman's daughter stood water to wash herself with and water for drinking. On the second morning, stood water for washing and water for drinking before the man's daughter as well as before the woman's daughter. And on the third morning stood water for washing and water for drinking before the man's daughter, and milk for washing and wine for drinking, before the woman's daughter, and so it continued. The woman became her step-daughter's bitterest enemy, and day by day did her best to treat her still worse. She was also envious because her step-daughter was beautiful and lovable, and her own daughter ugly and repulsive.

Once, in winter, when everything was frozen as hard as a stone, and hill and vale lay covered with snow, the woman made a frock of paper, called her step-daughter, and said: "Here, put on this dress and go out into the wood, and fetch me a little basketful of strawberries,—I have a fancy for some." "Good heavens!" said the girl, "no strawberries grow in winter! The ground is frozen, and besides the snow has covered everything. And why am I to go in this paper frock? It is so cold outside that one's very breath freezes! The wind will blow through the frock, and the thorns tear it off my body." "Will you contradict me?" said the step-mother. "See that you go, and do not show your face again until you have the basketful of strawberries!" Then she gave her a little piece of hard bread, and said: "This will last you the day," and thought: "You will die of cold and hunger outside, and will never be seen again by me."

Then the maiden was obedient, and put on the paper frock, and went out with the basket. Far and wide there was nothing but snow, and not a green blade to be seen. When she got into the wood she saw a small house out of which peeped three little men. She wished them good day, and knocked modestly at the door. They cried: "Come in," and she entered the room and seated herself on the bench by the stove, where she began to warm herself and eat her breakfast. The little men said: "Give us some of it, too." "Willingly," she said, and divided her piece of bread in two, and gave them the half. They asked: "What do you here in the forest in the winter time, in your thin dress?" "Ah," she answered, "I am to look for a basketful of strawberries, and am not to go home until I can take them with me." When she had eaten her bread, they gave her a broom and said: "Sweep away the snow at the back door." But when she was outside, the three little men said to each other: "What shall we give her as she is so good, and has shared her bread with us?" Then said the first: "My gift is, that she shall every day grow more beautiful." The second said: "My gift is, that gold pieces shall fall out of her mouth every time she speaks." The third said: "My gift is, that a king shall come and take her to wife."

The girl, however, did as the little men had bidden her, swept away the snow behind the little house with the broom, and what did she find but real ripe strawberries, which came up quite dark-red out of the snow! In her joy she hastily gathered her basket full, thanked the little men, shook hands with each of them, and ran home to take her step-mother what she had longed for so much. When she went in and said good-evening, a piece of gold at once fell out of her mouth. Thereupon she related what had happened to her in the wood, but with every word she spoke, gold pieces fell from her mouth, until very soon the whole room was covered with them. "Now look at her arrogance," cried the step-sister, "to throw about gold in that way!" But she was secretly envious of it, and wanted to go into the forest also to seek strawberries. The mother said: "No, my dear little daughter, it is too cold, you might freeze to death." However, as her daughter let her have no peace, the mother at last yielded, made her a magnificent coat of fur, which she was obliged to put on, and gave her bread-and-butter and cake for her journey.

The girl went into the forest and straight up to the little house. The three little men peeped out again, but she did not greet them, and without looking round at them and without speaking to them, she went awkwardly into the room, seated herself by the stove, and began to eat her bread-and-butter and cake. "Give us some of it," cried the little men; but she replied: "There is not enough for myself, so how can I give it away to other people?" When she had finished eating, they said: "There is a broom for you, sweep it all clean in front of the back-door." "Sweep for yourselves," she answered, "I am not your servant."

When she saw that they were not going to give her anything, she went out by the door. Then the little men said to each other: "What shall we give her as she is so naughty, and has a wicked envious heart, that will never let her do a good turn to any one?" The first said: "I grant that she may grow uglier every day." The second said: "I grant that at every word she says, a toad shall spring out of her mouth." The third said: "I grant that she may die a miserable death." The maiden looked for strawberries outside, but as she found none, she went angrily home. And when she opened her mouth, and was about to tell her mother what had happened to her in the wood, with every word she said, a toad sprang out of her mouth, so that everyone was seized with horror of her.

Then the step-mother was still more enraged, and thought of nothing but how to do every possible injury to the man's daughter, whose beauty, however, grew daily greater. At length she took a cauldron, set it on the fire, and boiled yarn in it. When it was boiled, she flung it on the poor girl's shoulder, and gave her an axe in order that she might go on the frozen river, cut a hole in the ice, and rinse the yarn. She was obedient, went thither and cut a hole in the ice; and while she was in the midst of her cutting, a splendid carriage came driving up, in which sat the King. The carriage stopped, and the King asked: "My child, who are you, and what are you doing here?" "I am a poor girl, and I am rinsing yarn." Then the King felt compassion, and when he saw that she was so very beautiful, he said to her: "Will you go away with me?" "Ah, yes, with all my heart," she answered, for she was glad to get away from the mother and sister.

So she got into the carriage and drove away with the King, and when they arrived at his palace, the wedding was celebrated with great pomp, as the little men had granted to the maiden. When a year was over, the young Queen bore a son, and as the step-mother had heard of her great good-fortune, she came with her daughter to the palace and pretended that she wanted to pay her a visit. But, when the King had gone out, and no one else was present, the wicked woman seized the Queen by the head, and her daughter seized her by the feet, and they lifted her out of the bed, and threw her out of the window into the stream which flowed by. Then the ugly daughter laid herself in the bed, and the old woman covered her up over her head. When the King came home again and wanted to speak to his wife, the old woman cried: "Hush, hush, that can't be now, she is lying in a violent sweat; you must let her rest to-day." The King suspected no evil, and did not come back again till next morning; and as he talked with his wife and she answered him, with every word a toad leaped out, whereas formerly a piece of gold had fallen. Then he asked what that could be, but the old woman said that she had got that from the violent sweat, and would soon lose it again. During the night, however, the scullion saw a duck come swimming up the gutter, and it said:

"King, what art thou doing now?
Sleepest thou, or wakest thou?"

And as he returned no answer, it said:

"And my guests, What may they do?"

The scullion said:

"They are sleeping soundly, too."

Then it asked again:

"What does little baby mine?"

He answered:

"Sleepeth in her cradle fine."

Then she went upstairs in the form of the Queen, nursed the baby, shook up its little bed, covered it over, and then swam away again down the gutter in the shape of a duck. She came thus for two nights; on the third, she said to the scullion: "Go and tell the King to take his sword and swing it three times over me on the threshold." Then the scullion ran and told this to the King, who came with his sword and swung it thrice over the spirit, and at the third time, his wife stood before him strong, living, and healthy as she had been before. Thereupon the King was full of great joy, but he kept the Queen hidden in a chamber until the Sunday, when the baby was to be christened. And when it was christened he said: "What does a person deserve who drags another out of bed and throws him in the water?" "The wretch deserves nothing better," answered the old woman, "than to be taken and put in a barrel stuck full of nails, and rolled down hill into the water." "Then," said the King, "you have pronounced your own sentence"; and he ordered such a barrel to be brought, and the old woman to be put into it with her daughter, and then the top was hammered on, and the barrel rolled down hill until it went into the river.

THE THREE SPINNERS

There was once a girl who was idle and would not spin, and let her mother say what she would, she could not bring her to it. At last the mother was once so overcome with anger and impatience, that she beat her, at which the girl began to weep loudly. Now at this very moment the Queen drove by, and when she heard the weeping she stopped her carriage, went into the house and asked the mother why she was beating her daughter so that the cries could be heard out on the road? Then the woman was ashamed to reveal the laziness of her daughter and said: "I cannot get her to leave off spinning. She insists on spinning for ever and ever, and I am poor, and cannot procure the flax." Then answered the Queen: "There is nothing that I like better to hear than spinning, and I am never happier than when the wheels are humming. Let me have your daughter with me in the palace. I have flax enough, and there she shall spin as much as she likes." The mother was heartily satisfied with this, and the Queen took the girl with her. When they had arrived at the palace, she led her up into three rooms which were filled from the bottom to the top with the finest flax. "Now spin me this flax," said she, "and when you have done it, you shall have my eldest son for a husband, even if you are poor. I care not for that, your untiring industry is dowry enough." The girl was secretly terrified, for she could not have spun the flax, no, not if she had lived till she was three hundred years old, and had sat at it every day from morning till night. When therefore she was alone, she began to weep, and sat thus for three days without moving a finger. On the third day came the Queen, and when she saw that nothing had yet been spun, she was surprised; but the girl excused herself by saying that she had not been able to begin because of her great distress at leaving her mother's house. The Queen was satisfied with this, but said when she was going away: "Tomorrow you must begin to work."

When the girl was alone again, she did not know what to do, and in her distress went to the window. Then she saw three women coming towards her, the first of whom had a broad flat foot, the second had such a great underlip that it hung down over her chin, and the third had a broad thumb. They remained standing before the window, looked up, and asked the girl what was amiss with her. She complained of her trouble, and then they offered her their help and said: "If you will invite us to the wedding, not be ashamed of us, and will call us your aunts, and likewise will place us at your table, we will spin up the flax for you, and that in a very short time." "With all my heart," she replied, "do but come in and begin the work at once." Then she let in the three strange women, and cleared a place in the first room, where they seated themselves and began their spinning. The one drew the thread and trod the wheel, the other wetted the thread, the third twisted it, and struck the table with her finger, and as often as she struck it, a skein of thread fell to the ground that was spun in the finest manner possible. The girl concealed the three spinners from the Queen, and showed her whenever she came the great quantity of spun thread, until the latter could not praise her enough. When the first room was empty she went to the second, and at last to the third, and that too was quickly cleared. Then the three women took leave and said to the girl: "Do not forget what you have promised us,—it will make your fortune."

When the maiden showed the Queen the empty rooms, and the great heap of yarn, she gave orders for the wedding, and the bridegroom rejoiced that he was to have such a clever and industrious wife, and praised her mightily. "I have three aunts," said the girl, "and as they have been very kind to me, I should not like to forget them in my good fortune; allow me to invite them to the wedding, and let them sit with us at table." The Queen and the bridegroom said: "Why should

we not allow that?" Therefore when the feast began, the three women entered in strange apparel, and the bride said: "Welcome, dear aunts." "Ah," said the bridegroom, "how do you come by these odious friends?" Thereupon he went to the one with the broad flat foot, and said: "How do you come by such a broad foot?" "By treading," she answered, "by treading." Then the bridegroom went to the second, and said: "How do you come by your falling lip?" "By licking," she answered, "by licking." Then he asked the third: "How do you come by your broad thumb?" "By twisting the thread," she answered, "by twisting the thread." On this the King's son was alarmed and said: "Neither now nor ever shall my beautiful bride touch a spinning-wheel." And thus she got rid of the hateful flax-spinning.

HÄNSEL AND GRETEL

Hard by a great forest dwelt a poor wood-cutter with his wife and his two children. The boy was called Hänsel and the girl Gretel. He had little to bite and to break, and once when great dearth fell on the land, he could no longer procure even daily bread. Now when he thought over this by night in his bed, and tossed about in his anxiety, he groaned and said to his wife: "What is to become of us? How are we to feed our poor children, when we no longer have anything even for ourselves?" "I'll tell you what, husband," answered the woman, "early to-morrow morning we will take the children out into the forest to where it is the thickest; there we will light a fire for them, and give each of them one more piece of bread, and then we will go to our work and leave them alone. They will not find the way home again, and we shall be rid of them." "No, wife," said the man, "I will not do that; how can I bear to leave my children alone in the forest?—the wild animals would soon come and tear them to pieces." "O, you fool!" said she, "then we must all four die of hunger, you may as well plane the planks for our coffins," and she left him no peace until he consented. "But I feel very sorry for the poor children, all the same," said the man.

The two children had also not been able to sleep for hunger, and had heard what their step-mother had said to their father. Gretel wept bitter tears, and said to Hänsel: "Now all is over with us." "Be quiet, Gretel," said Hänsel, "do not distress yourself, I will soon find a way to help us." And when the old folks had fallen asleep, he got up, put on his little coat, opened the door below, and crept outside. The moon shone brightly, and the white pebbles which lay in front of the house glittered like real silver pennies. Hänsel stooped and stuffed the little pocket of his coat with as many as he could get in. Then he went back and said to Gretel: "Be comforted, dear little sister, and sleep in peace, God will not forsake us," and he lay down again in his bed. When day dawned, but before the sun had risen, the woman came and awoke the two children, saying: "Get up, you sluggards! we are going into the forest to fetch wood." She gave each a little piece of bread, and said: "There is something for your dinner, but do not eat it up before then, for you will get nothing else." Gretel took the bread under her apron, as Hänsel had the pebbles in his pocket. Then they all set out together on the way to the forest. When they had walked a short time, Hänsel stood still and peeped back at the house, and did so again and again. His father said: "Hänsel, what are you looking at there and staying behind for? Pay attention, and do not forget how to use your legs." "Ah, father," said Hänsel, "I am looking at my little white cat, which is sitting up on the roof, and wants to say good-bye to me." The wife said: "Fool, that is not your little cat, that is the morning sun which is shining on the chimneys." Hänsel, however, had not been looking back at the cat, but had been constantly throwing one of the white pebble-stones out of his pocket on the road.

When they had reached the middle of the forest, the father said: "Now, children, pile up some wood, and I will light a fire that you may not be cold." Hänsel and Gretel gathered brushwood together, as high as a little hill. The brushwood was lighted, and when the flames were burning very high, the woman said: "Now, children, lay yourselves down by the fire and rest, we will go into the forest and cut some wood. When we have done, we will come back and fetch you away."

Hänsel and Gretel sat by the fire, and when noon came, each ate a little piece of bread, and as they heard the strokes of the wood-axe they believed that their father was near. It was not the axe, however, but a branch which he had fastened to a withered tree which the wind was blowing backwards and forwards. And as they had been sitting such a long time, their eyes closed with fatigue, and they fell fast asleep. When at last they awoke, it was already dark night. Gretel began to cry and said: "How are we to get out of the forest now?" But Hänsel comforted her and said: "Just wait a little, until the moon has risen, and then we will soon find the way." And when the full moon had risen, Hänsel took his little sister by the hand, and followed the pebbles which shone like newly-coined silver pieces, and showed them the way.

They walked the whole night long, and by break of day came once more to their father's house. They knocked at the door, and when the woman opened it and saw that it was Hänsel and Gretel, she said: "You naughty children, why have you slept so long in the forest?—we thought you were never coming back at all!" The father, however, rejoiced, for it had cut him to the heart to leave them behind alone.

Not long afterwards, there was once more great dearth throughout the land, and the children heard their mother saying at night to their father: "Everything is eaten again, we have one half loaf left, and that is the end. The children must go, we will take them farther into the wood, so that they will not find their way out again; there is no other means of saving ourselves!" The man's heart was heavy, and he thought: "It would be better for you to share the last mouthful with your children." The woman, however, would listen to nothing that he had to say, but scolded and reproached him. He who says A must say B, likewise, and as he had yielded the first time, he had to do so a second time also.

The children, however, were still awake and had heard the conversation. When the old folks were asleep, Hänsel again got up, and wanted to go out and pick up pebbles as he had done before, but the woman had locked the door, and Hänsel could not get out. Nevertheless he comforted his little sister, and said: "Do not cry, Gretel, go to sleep quietly, the good God will help us."

Early in the morning came the woman, and took the children out of their beds. Their piece of bread was given to them, but it was still smaller than the time before. On the way into the forest Hänsel crumbled his in his pocket, and often stood still and threw a morsel on the ground. "Hänsel, why do you stop and look round?" said the father, "go on." "I am looking back at my little pigeon which is sitting on the roof, and wants to say good-bye to me," answered Hänsel. "Fool!" said the woman, "that is not your little pigeon, that is the morning sun that is shining on the chimney." Hänsel, however, little by little, threw all the crumbs on the path.

The woman led the children still deeper into the forest, where they had never in their lives been before. Then a great fire was again made, and the mother said: "Just sit there, you children, and when you are tired you may sleep a little; we are going into the forest to cut wood, and in the evening when we are done, we will come and fetch you away." When it was noon, Gretel shared her piece of bread with Hänsel, who had scattered his by the way. Then they fell asleep and evening passed, but no one came to the poor children. They did not awake until it was dark night, and Hänsel comforted his little sister and said: "Just wait, Gretel, until the moon rises, and then we shall see the crumbs of bread which I have strewn about, they will show us our way home again." When the moon came they set out, but they found no crumbs, for the many thousands of birds which fly about in the woods and fields had picked them all up. Hänsel said to Gretel: "We shall soon find the way," but they did not find it. They walked the whole night and all the next day too from morning till evening, but they did not get out of the forest, and were very hungry, for they had nothing to eat but two or three berries, which grew on the ground. And as they were so weary that their legs would carry them no longer, they lay down beneath a tree and fell asleep.

It was now three mornings since they had left their father's house. They began to walk again, but they always came deeper into the forest, and if help did not come soon, they must die of hunger and weariness. When it was mid-day, they saw a beautiful snow-white bird sitting on a bough, which sang so delightfully that they stood still and listened to it. And when its song was over, it spread its wings and flew away before them, and they followed it until they reached a little house, on the roof of which it alighted; and when they approached the little house they saw that it was built of bread and covered with cakes, but that the windows were of clear sugar. "We will set to work on that," said Hänsel, "and have a good meal. I will eat a bit of the roof, and you Gretel, can eat some of the window, it will taste sweet." Hänsel reached up above, and broke off a little of the roof to try how it tasted, and Gretel leant against the window and nibbled at the panes. Then a soft voice cried from the parlor:

"Nibble, nibble, gnaw,
Who is nibbling at my little house?"

The children answered:

"The wind, the wind,
The heaven-born wind,"

and went on eating without disturbing themselves. Hänsel, who liked the taste of the roof, tore down a great piece of it, and Gretel pushed out the whole of one round window-pane, sat down, and enjoyed herself with it. Suddenly the door opened, and a woman as old as the

hills, who supported herself on crutches, came creeping out. Hänsel and Gretel were so terribly frightened that they let fall what they had in their hands. The old woman, however, nodded her head, and said: "Oh, you dear children, who has brought you here? Do come in, and stay with me. No harm shall happen to you." She took them both by the hand, and led them into her little house. Then good food was set before them, milk and pancakes, with sugar, apples, and nuts. Afterwards two pretty little beds were covered with clean white linen, and Hänsel and Gretel lay down in them, and thought they were in heaven.

The old woman had only pretended to be so kind; she was in reality a wicked witch, who lay in wait for children, and had only built the little house of bread in order to entice them there. When a child fell into her power, she killed it, cooked and ate it, and that was a feast day with her. Witches have red eyes, and cannot see far, but they have a keen scent like the beasts, and are aware when human beings draw near. When Hänsel and Gretel came into her neighborhood, she laughed with malice, and said mockingly: "I have them, they shall not escape me again!" Early in the morning before the children were awake, she was already up, and when she saw both of them sleeping and looking so pretty, with their plump and rosy cheeks, she muttered to herself: "That will be a dainty mouthful!" Then she seized Hänsel with her shrivelled hand, carried him into a little stable, and locked him in behind a grated door. Scream as he might, it would not help him. Then she went to Gretel, shook her till she awoke, and cried: "Get up, lazy thing, fetch some water, and cook something good for your brother, he is in the stable outside, and is to be made fat. When he is fat, I will eat him." Gretel began to weep bitterly, but it was all in vain, for she was forced to do what the wicked witch commanded.

And now the best food was cooked for poor Hänsel, but Gretel got nothing but crab-shells. Every morning the woman crept to the little stable, and cried: "Hänsel, stretch out your finger that I may feel if you will soon be fat." Hänsel, however, stretched out a little bone to her, and the old woman, who had dim eyes, could not see it, and thought it was Hänsel's finger, and was astonished that there was no way of fattening him. When four weeks had gone by, and Hänsel still remained thin, she was seized with impatience and would not wait any longer. "Now, then, Gretel," she cried to the girl, "stir yourself, and bring some water. Let Hänsel be fat or lean, to-morrow I will kill him, and cook him." Ah, how the poor little sister did lament when she had to fetch the water, and how her tears did flow down her cheeks! "Dear God, do help us," she cried. "If the wild beasts in the forest had but devoured us, we should at any rate have died together." "Just keep your noise to yourself," said the old woman, "it won't help you at all."

Early in the morning, Gretel had to go out and hang up the cauldron with the water, and light the fire. "We will bake first," said the old woman, "I have already heated the oven, and kneaded the dough." She pushed poor Gretel out to the oven, from which flames of fire were already darting. "Creep in," said the witch, "and see if it is properly heated, so that we can put the bread in." And once Gretel was inside, she intended to shut the oven and let her bake in it, and then she would eat her, too. But Gretel saw what she had in mind, and said: "I do not know how I am to do it; how do I get in?" "Silly goose," said the old woman. "The door is big enough; just look, I can get in myself!" and she crept up and thrust her head into the oven. Then Gretel gave her a push that drove her far into it, and shut the iron door, and fastened the bolt. Oh! then she began to howl quite horribly, but Gretel ran away, and the godless witch was miserably burnt to death.

Gretel, however, ran like lightning to Hänsel, opened his little stable, and cried: "Hänsel, we are saved! The old witch is dead!" Then Hänsel sprang like a bird from its cage when the door is opened. How they did rejoice and embrace each other, and dance about and kiss each other! And as they had no longer any need to fear her, they went into the witch's house, and in every corner there stood chests full of pearls and jewels. "These are far better than pebbles!" said Hänsel, and thrust into his pockets whatever could be got in, and Gretel said: "I, too, will take something home with me," and filled her pinafore full. "But now we must be off," said Hänsel, "that we may get out of the witch's forest."

When they had walked for two hours, they came to a great stretch of water. "We cannot cross," said Hänsel, "I see no footplank, and no bridge." "And there is also no ferry," answered Gretel, "but a white duck is swimming there; if I ask her, she will help us over." Then she cried:

> "Little duck, little duck, dost thou see,
> Hänsel and Gretel are waiting for thee?
> There's never a plank, or bridge in sight,
> Take us across on thy back so white."

The duck came to them, and Hänsel seated himself on its back, and told his sister to sit by him. "No," replied Gretel, "that will be too heavy for the little duck; she shall take us across, one after the other." The good little duck did so, and when they were once safely across and had walked for a short time, the forest seemed to be more and more familiar to them, and at length they saw from afar their father's house. Then they began to run, rushed into the parlour, and threw themselves round their father's neck. The man had not known one happy hour since he had left the children in the forest; the woman, however, was dead. Gretel emptied her pinafore until pearls and precious stones ran about the room, and Hänsel threw one handful after another out of his pocket to add to them. Then all anxiety was at an end, and they lived together in perfect happiness. My tale is done, there runs a mouse, whosoever catches it, may make himself a big fur cap out of it.

THE THREE SNAKE-LEAVES

There was once upon a time a poor man, who could no longer support his only son. Then said the son: "Dear father, things go so badly with us that I am a burden to you. I would rather go away and see how I can earn my bread." So the father gave him his blessing, and with great sorrow took leave of him. At this time the King of a mighty empire was at war, and the youth took service with him, and went out to fight. And when he came before the enemy, there was a battle, and great danger, and it rained shot until his comrades fell on all sides, and when the leader also was killed, those left were about to take flight, but the youth stepped forth, spoke boldly to them, and cried: "We will not let our fatherland be ruined!" Then the others followed him, and he pressed on and conquered the enemy. When the King heard that he owed the victory to him alone, he raised him above all the others, gave him great treasures, and made him the first in the kingdom.

The King had a daughter who was very beautiful, but she was also very strange. She had made a vow to take no one as her lord and husband who did not promise to let himself be buried alive with her if she died first. "If he loves me with all his heart," said she, "of what use will life be to him afterwards?" On her side she would do the same, and if he died first, would go down to the grave with him. This strange oath had up to this time frightened away all wooers, but the youth became so charmed with her beauty that he cared for nothing, but asked her father for her. "But do you know what you must promise?" said the King. "I must be buried with her," he replied, "if I outlive her, but my love is so great that I do not mind the danger." Then the King consented, and the wedding was solemnized with great splendour.

They lived now for a while happy and contented with each other, and then it befell that the young Queen was attacked by a severe illness, and no physician could save her. And as she lay there dead, the young King remembered what he had been obliged to promise, and was horrified at having to lie down alive in the grave, but there was no escape. The King had placed sentries at all the gates, and it was not possible to avoid his fate. As the day came when the corpse was to be buried, he was taken down with it into the royal vault and then the door was shut and bolted.

Near the coffin stood a table on which were four candles, four loaves of bread, and four bottles of wine, and when this provision came to an end, he would have to die of hunger. And now he sat there full of pain and grief, ate every day only a little piece of bread, drank only a mouthful of wine, and nevertheless saw death daily drawing nearer. Whilst he thus gazed before him, he saw a snake creep out of a corner of the vault and approach the dead body. And as he thought it came to gnaw at it, he drew his sword and said: "As long as I live, you shall not touch her," and hewed the snake in three pieces. After a time a second snake crept out of the hole, and when it saw the other lying dead and cut in pieces, it went back, but soon came again with three green leaves in its mouth. Then it took the three pieces of the snake, laid them together, as they fitted, and placed one of the leaves on each wound. Immediately the severed parts joined themselves together, the snake moved, and became alive again, and both of them hastened away together. The leaves were left lying on the ground, and a desire came into the mind of the unhappy man who had been watching all this, to know if the wondrous power of the leaves which had brought the snake to life again, could not likewise be of service to a human being. So he picked up the leaves and laid one of them on the mouth of his dead wife, and the two others on her eyes. And hardly had he done this than the blood stirred in her veins, rose into her pale face, and coloured it again. Then she drew breath, opened her eyes, and said: "Ah, God, where am I?" "You are with me, dear wife," he answered, and told her how everything had happened, and how he had brought her back again to life. Then he gave her some wine and bread, and when she had regained her strength, he raised her up and they went to the door and knocked, and called so loudly that the sentries heard it, and told the King. The King came down himself and opened the door, and there he found both strong and well, and rejoiced with them that now all sorrow was over. The young King, however, took the three snake-leaves with him, gave them to a servant and said: "Keep them for me carefully, and carry them constantly about you; who knows in what trouble they may yet be of service to us!"

But a change had taken place in his wife; after she had been restored to life, it seemed as if all love for her husband had gone out of her heart. After some time, when he wanted to make a voyage over the sea, to visit his old father, and they had gone on board a ship, she forgot the great love and fidelity which he had shown her, and which had been the means of rescuing her from death, and conceived a wicked inclination for the captain. And once when the young King lay there asleep, she called in the captain and seized the sleeper by the head, and the captain took him by the feet, and thus they threw him down into the sea. When the shameful deed was done, she said: "Now let us return home, and say that he died on the way. I will extol and praise you so to my father that he will marry me to you, and make you the heir to his crown." But the faithful servant who had seen all that they did, unseen by them, unfastened a little boat from the ship, got into it, sailed after his master, and let the traitors go on their way. He fished up the dead body, and by the help of the three snake-leaves which he carried about with him, and laid on the eyes and mouth, he fortunately brought the young King back to life.

They both rowed with all their strength day and night, and their little boat sailed so swiftly that they reached the old King before the others. He was astonished when he saw them come alone, and asked what had happened to them. When he learnt the wickedness of his daughter he said: "I cannot believe that she has behaved so ill, but the truth will soon come to light," and bade both go into a secret chamber and keep themselves hidden from everyone. Soon afterwards the great ship came sailing in, and the godless woman appeared before her father with a troubled countenance. He said: "Why do you come back alone? Where is your husband?" "Ah, dear father," she replied, "I come home again in great grief; during the voyage, my husband became suddenly ill and died, and if the good captain had not given me his help, it would have gone ill with me. He was present at his death, and can tell you all." The King said: "I will make the dead alive again," and opened the chamber, and bade the two come out. When the woman saw her husband, she was thunderstruck, and fell on her knees and begged for mercy. The King said: "There is no mercy. He was ready to die with you and restored you to life again, but you have murdered him in his sleep, and shall receive the reward that you deserve." Then she was placed with her accomplice in a ship which had been pierced with holes, and sent out to sea, where they soon sank amid the waves.

THE WHITE SNAKE

A long time ago there lived a king who was famed for his wisdom through all the land. Nothing was hidden from him, and it seemed as if news of the most secret things was brought to him through the air. But he had a strange custom; every day after dinner, when the table was cleared, and no one else was present, a trusty servant had to bring him one more dish. It was covered, however, and even the servant did not know what was in it, neither did anyone know, for the King never took off the cover to eat of it until he was quite alone.

This had gone on for a long time, when one day the servant, who took away the dish, was overcome with such curiosity that he could not help carrying the dish into his room. When he had carefully locked the door, he lifted up the cover, and saw a white snake lying on the dish. But when he saw it he could not deny himself the pleasure of tasting it, so he cut off a little bit and put it into his mouth. No sooner had it touched his tongue than he heard a strange whispering of little voices outside his window. He went and listened, and then noticed that it was the sparrows who were chattering together, and telling one another of all kinds of things which they had seen in the fields and woods. Eating the snake had given him power of understanding the language of animals.

Now it so happened that on this very day the Queen lost her most beautiful ring, and suspicion of having stolen it fell upon this trusty servant, who was allowed to go everywhere. The King ordered the man to be brought before him, and threatened with angry words that unless he could before the morrow point out the thief, he himself should be looked upon as guilty and executed. In vain he declared his innocence; he was dismissed with no better answer.

In his trouble and fear he went down into the courtyard and took thought how to help himself out of his trouble. Now some ducks were sitting together quietly by a brook and taking their rest; and, whilst they were making their feathers smooth with their bills, they were having a confidential conversation together. The servant stood by and listened. They were telling one another of all the places where they had been waddling about all the morning, and what good food they had found; and one said in a pitiful tone: "Something lies heavy on my stomach; as I was eating in haste I swallowed a ring which lay under the Queen's window." The servant at once seized her by the neck, carried her to the kitchen, and said to the cook: "Here is a fine duck; pray, kill her." "Yes," said the cook, and weighed her in his hand; "she has spared no trouble to fatten herself, and has been waiting to be roasted long enough." So he cut off her head, and as she was being dressed for the spit, the Queen's ring was found inside her.

The servant could now easily prove his innocence; and the King, to make amends for the wrong, allowed him to ask a favour, and promised him the best place in the court that he could wish for. The servant refused everything, and only asked for a horse and some money for travelling, as he had a mind to see the world and go about a little. When his request was granted he set out on his way, and one day came to a pond, where he saw three fishes caught in the reeds and gasping for water. Now, though it is said that fishes are dumb, he heard them lamenting that they must perish so miserably, and, as he had a kind heart, he got off his horse and put the three prisoners back into the water. They leapt with delight, put out their heads, and cried to him: "We will remember you and repay you for saving us!"

He rode on, and after a while it seemed to him that he heard a voice in the sand at his feet. He listened, and heard an ant-king complain: "Why cannot folks, with their clumsy beasts, keep off our bodies? That stupid horse, with his heavy hoofs, has been treading down my people without mercy!" So he turned on to a side path and the ant-king cried out to him: "We will remember you—one good turn deserves another!"

The path led him into a wood, and there he saw two old ravens standing by their nest, and throwing out their young ones. "Out with you, you idle, good-for-nothing creatures!" cried they; "we cannot find food for you any longer; you are big enough, and can provide for yourselves." But the poor young ravens lay upon the ground, flapping their wings, and crying: "Oh, what helpless chicks we are! We must shift for ourselves, and yet we cannot fly! What can we do, but lie here and starve?" So the good young fellow alighted and killed his horse with his sword, and gave it to them for food. Then they came hopping up to it, satisfied their hunger, and cried: "We will remember you— one good turn deserves another!"

And now he had to use his own legs, and when he had walked a long way, he came to a large city. There was a great noise and crowd in the streets, and a man rode up on horseback, crying aloud: "The King's daughter wants a husband; but whoever seeks her hand must perform a hard task, and if he does not succeed he will forfeit his life." Many had already made the attempt, but in vain; nevertheless when the youth saw the King's daughter he was so overcome by her great beauty that he forgot all danger, went before the King, and declared himself a suitor.

So he was led out to the sea, and a gold ring was thrown into it, before his eyes; then the King ordered him to fetch this ring up from the bottom of the sea, and added: "If you come up again without it you will be thrown in again and again until you perish amid the waves." All the people grieved for the handsome youth; then they went away, leaving him alone by the sea.

He stood on the shore and considered what he should do, when suddenly he saw three fishes come swimming towards him, and they were the very fishes whose lives he had saved. The one in the middle held a mussel in its mouth, which it laid on the shore at the youth's feet, and when he had taken it up and opened it, there lay the gold ring in the shell. Full of joy he took it to the King, and expected that he would grant him the promised reward.

But when the proud princess perceived that he was not her equal in birth, she scorned him, and required him first to perform another task.

She went down into the garden and strewed with her own hands ten sacks-full of millet-seed on the grass; then she said: "To-morrow morning before sunrise these must be picked up, and not a single grain be wanting."

The youth sat down in the garden and considered how it might be possible to perform this task, but he could think of nothing, and there he sat sorrowfully awaiting the break of day, when he should be led to death. But as soon as the first rays of the sun shone into the garden he saw all the ten sacks standing side by side, quite full, and not a single grain was missing. The ant-king had come in the night with thousands and thousands of ants, and the grateful creatures had by great industry picked up all the millet-seed and gathered them into the sacks.

Presently the King's daughter herself came down into the garden, and was amazed to see that the young man had done the task she had given him. But she could not yet conquer her proud heart, and said: "Although he has performed both the tasks, he shall not be my husband until he has brought me an apple from the Tree of Life." The youth did not know where the Tree of Life stood, but he set out, and would have gone on for ever, as long as his legs would carry him, though he had no hope of finding it. After he had wandered through three kingdoms, he came one evening to a wood, and lay down under a tree to sleep. But he heard a rustling in the branches, and a golden apple fell into his hand. At the same time three ravens flew down to him, perched themselves upon his knee, and said: "We are the three young ravens whom you saved from starving; when we had grown big, and heard that you were seeking the Golden Apple, we flew over the sea to the end of the world, where the Tree of Life stands, and have brought you the apple." The youth, full of joy, set out homewards, and took the Golden Apple to the King's beautiful daughter, who had now no more excuses left to make. They cut the Apple of Life in two and ate it together; and then her heart became full of love for him, and they lived in undisturbed happiness to a great age.

THE STRAW, THE COAL, AND THE BEAN

In a village dwelt a poor old woman, who had gathered together a dish of beans and wanted to cook them. So she made a fire on her hearth, and that it might burn the quicker, she lighted it with a handful of straw. When she was emptying the beans into the pan, one dropped without her observing it, and lay on the ground beside a straw, and soon afterwards a burning coal from the fire leapt down to the two. Then the straw began and said: "Dear friends, from whence do you come here?" The coal replied: "I fortunately sprang out of the fire, and if I had not escaped by sheer force, my death would have been certain,—I should have been burnt to ashes." The bean said: "I too have escaped with a whole skin, but if the old woman had got me into the pan, I should have been made into broth without any mercy, like my comrades." "And would a better fate have fallen to my lot?" said the straw. "The old woman has destroyed all my brethren in fire and smoke; she seized sixty of them at once, and took their lives. I luckily slipped through her fingers."

"But what are we to do now?" said the coal.

"I think," answered the bean, "that as we have so fortunately escaped death, we should keep together like good companions, and lest a new mischance should overtake us here, we should go away together, and repair to a foreign country."

The proposition pleased the two others, and they set out on their way together. Soon, however, they came to a little brook, and as there was no bridge or foot-plank, they did not know how they were to get over it. The straw hit on a good idea, and said: "I will lay myself straight across, and then you can walk over on me as on a bridge." The straw therefore stretched itself from one bank to the other, and the coal, who was of an impetuous disposition, tripped quite boldly on to the newly-built bridge. But when she had reached the middle, and heard the water rushing beneath her, she was, after all, afraid, and stood still, and ventured no farther. The straw, however, began to burn, broke in two pieces, and fell into the stream. The coal slipped after her, hissed when she got into the water, and breathed her last. The bean, who had prudently stayed behind on the shore, could not but laugh at the event, was unable to stop, and laughed so heartily that she burst. It would have been all over with her, likewise, if, by good fortune, a tailor who was travelling in search of work, had not sat down to rest by the brook. As he had a compassionate heart he pulled out his needle and thread, and sewed her together. The bean thanked him most prettily, but as the tailor used black thread, all beans since then have a black seam.

THE FISHERMAN AND HIS WIFE

There was once upon a time a Fisherman who lived with his wife in a pigsty close by the sea, and every day he went out fishing; and he fished, and he fished. And once he was sitting with his rod, looking at the clear water, and he sat and he sat. Then his line suddenly went down, far down below, and when he drew it up again, he brought out a large Flounder. Then the Flounder said to him: "Hark, you Fisherman, I pray you, let me live, I am no Flounder really, but an enchanted prince. What good will it do you to kill me? I should not be good to eat, put me in the water again, and let me go." "Come," said the Fisherman, "there is no need for so many words about it—a fish that can talk I should certainly let go, anyhow." And with that he put him back again into the clear water, and the Flounder went to the bottom, leaving a long streak of blood behind him. Then the Fisherman got up and went home to his wife in the pigsty.

"Husband," said the woman, "have you caught nothing to-day?" "No," said the man, "I did catch a Flounder, who said he was an enchanted prince, so I let him go again." "Did you not wish for anything first?" said the woman. "No," said the man; "what should I wish for?" "Ah," said the woman, "it is surely hard to have to live always in this pigsty which stinks and is so disgusting; you might have wished for a little hut for us. Go back and call him. Tell him we want to have a little hut, he will certainly give us that." "Ah," said the man, "why should I go there again?" "Why," said the woman, "you did catch him, and you let him go again; he is sure to do it. Go at once." The man still did not quite like to go, but did not like to oppose his wife either, and went to the sea.

When he got there the sea was all green and yellow, and no longer so smooth; so he stood and said:

> "Flounder, flounder in the sea,
> Come, I pray thee, here to me;
> For my wife, good Ilsabil,
> Wills not as I'd have her will."

Then the Flounder came swimming to him and said: "Well, what does she want, then?" "Ah," said the man, "I did catch you, and my wife says I really ought to have wished for something. She does not like to live in a pigsty any longer; she would like to have a hut." "Go, then," said the Flounder, "she has it already."

When the man went home, his wife was no longer in the sty, but instead of it there stood a hut, and she was sitting on a bench before the door. Then she took him by the hand and said to him: "Just come inside. Look, now isn't this a great deal better?" So they went in, and there was a small porch, and a pretty little parlor and bedroom, and a kitchen and pantry, with the best of furniture, and fitted up with the most beautiful things made of tin and brass, whatsoever was wanted. And behind the hut there was a small yard, with hens and ducks, and a little garden with flowers and fruit. "Look," said the wife, "is not that nice!" "Yes," said the husband, "and so it shall remain—now we will live quite contented." "We will think about that," said the wife. With that they ate something and went to bed.

Everything went well for a week or a fortnight, and then the woman said: "Hark you, husband, this hut is far too small for us, and the garden and yard are little; the Flounder might just as well have given us a larger house. I should like to live in a great stone castle; go to the Flounder, and tell him to give us a castle." "Ah, wife," said the man, "the hut is quite good enough; why should we live in a castle?" "What!" said the woman; "just go there, the Flounder can always do that." "No, wife," said the man, "the Flounder has just given us the hut, I do not like to go back so soon, it might make him angry." "Go," said the woman, "he can do it quite easily, and will be glad to do it; just you go to him."

The man's heart grew heavy, and he would not go. He said to himself: "It is not right," and yet he went. And when he came to the sea the water was quite purple and dark-blue, and grey and thick, and no longer so green and yellow, but it was still quiet. And he stood there and said:

"Flounder, flounder in the sea,
Come, I pray thee, here to me;
For my wife, good Ilsabil,
Wills not as I'd have her will."

"Well, what does she want, now?" said the Flounder. "Alas," said the man, half scared, "she wants to live in a great stone castle." "Go back, then, she is standing before the door," said the Flounder.

Then the man went away, intending to go home, but when he got there, he found a great stone palace, and his wife was just standing on the steps going in, and she took him by the hand and said: "Come in." So he went in with her, and in the castle was a great hall paved with marble, and many servants, who flung wide the doors; and the walls were all bright with beautiful hangings, and in the rooms were chairs and tables of pure gold, and crystal chandeliers hung from the ceiling, and all the rooms and bedrooms had carpets, and food and wine of the very best were standing on all the tables, so that they nearly broke down beneath it. Behind the house, too, there was a great court-yard, with stables for horses and cows, and the very best of carriages; there was a magnificent large garden, too, with the most beautiful flowers and fruit-trees, and a park quite half a mile long, in which were stags, deer, and hares, and everything that could be desired. "Come," said the woman, "isn't that beautiful?" "Yes, indeed," said the man, "now let it be; and we will live in this beautiful castle and be content." "We will consider about that," said the woman, "and sleep upon it"; thereupon they went to bed.

Next morning the wife awoke first, and it was just daybreak, and from her bed she saw the beautiful country lying before her. Her husband was still stretching himself, so she poked him in the side with her elbow, and said: "Get up, husband, and just peep out of the window. Look you, couldn't we be the King over all that land? Go to the Flounder, we will be the King." "Ah, wife," said the man, "why should we be King? I do not want to be King." "Well," said the wife, "if you won't be King, I will; go to the Flounder, for I will be King." "Ah, wife," said the man, "why do you want to be King? I do not like to say that to him." "Why not?" said the woman; "go to him this instant; I must be King!" So the man went, and was quite unhappy because his wife

wished to be King. "It is not right; it is not right," thought he. He did not wish to go, but yet he went.

And when he came to the sea, it was quite dark-grey, and the water heaved up from below, and smelt putrid. Then he went and stood by it, and said:

> "Flounder, flounder in the sea,
> Come, I pray thee, here to me;
> For my wife, good Ilsabil,
> Wills not as I'd have her will."

"Well, what does she want, now?" said the Flounder. "Alas," said the man, "she wants to be King." "Go to her; she is King already."

So the man went, and when he came to the palace, the castle had become much larger, and had a great tower and magnificent ornaments, and the sentinel was standing before the door, and there were numbers of soldiers with kettle-drums and trumpets. And when he went inside the house, everything was of real marble and gold, with velvet covers and great golden tassels. Then the doors of the hall were opened, and there was the court in all its splendour, and his wife was sitting on a high throne of gold and diamonds, with a great crown of gold on her head, and a sceptre of pure gold and jewels in her hand, and on both sides of her stood her maids-in-waiting in a row, each of them always one head shorter than the last.

Then he went and stood before her, and said: "Ah, wife, and now you are King." "Yes," said the woman, "now I am King." So he stood and looked at her, and when he had looked at her thus for some time, he said: "And now that you are King, let all else be, now we will wish for nothing more." "No, husband," said the woman, quite anxiously, "I find time passes very heavily, I can bear it no longer; go to the Flounder—I am King, but I must be Emperor, too." "Oh, wife, why do you wish to be Emperor?" "Husband," said she, "go to the Flounder. I will be Emperor." "Alas, wife," said the man, "he cannot make you Emperor; I may not say that to the fish. There is only one Emperor in the land. An Emperor the Flounder cannot make you! I assure you he cannot."

"What!" said the woman, "I am the King, and you are nothing but my husband; will you go this moment? go at once! If he can make a king he can make an emperor. I will be Emperor; go instantly." So he was forced to go. As the man went, however, he was troubled in mind, and thought to himself: "It will not end well; it will not end well! Emperor is too shameless! The Flounder will at last be tired out."

With that he reached the sea, and the sea was quite black and thick, and began to boil up from below, so that it threw up bubbles, and such a sharp wind blew over it that it curdled, and the man was afraid. Then he went and stood by it, and said:

"Flounder, flounder in the sea,
Come, I pray thee, here to me;
For my wife, good Ilsabil,
Wills not as I'd have her will."

"Well, what does she want, now?" said the Flounder. "Alas, Flounder," said he, "my wife wants to be Emperor." "Go to her," said the Flounder; "she is Emperor already."

So the man went, and when he got there the whole palace was made of polished marble with alabaster figures and golden ornaments, and soldiers were marching before the door blowing trumpets, and beating cymbals and drums; and in the house, barons, and counts, and dukes were going about as servants. Then they opened the doors to him, which were of pure gold. And when he entered, there sat his wife on a throne, which was made of one piece of gold, and was quite two miles high; and she wore a great golden crown that was three yards high, and set with diamonds and carbuncles, and in one hand she had the sceptre, and in the other the imperial orb; and on both sides of her stood the yeomen of the guard in two rows, each being smaller than the one before him, from the biggest giant, who was two miles high, to the very smallest dwarf, just as big as my little finger. And before it stood a number of princes and dukes.

Then the man went and stood among them, and said: "Wife, are you Emperor now?" "Yes," said she, "now I am Emperor." Then he stood and looked at her well, and when he had looked at her thus for some time, he said: "Ah, wife, be content, now that you are Emperor." "Husband," said she, "why are you standing there? Now, I am Emperor, but

I will be Pope too; go to the Flounder." "Oh, wife," said the man, "what will you not wish for? You cannot be Pope; there is but one in Christendom; he cannot make you Pope." "Husband," said she, "I will be Pope; go immediately, I must be Pope this very day." "No, wife," said the man, "I do not like to say that to him; that would not do, it is too much; the Flounder can't make you Pope." "Husband," said she, "what nonsense! if he can make an emperor he can make a pope. Go to him directly. I am Emperor, and you are nothing but my husband; will you go at once?"

Then he was afraid and went; but he was quite faint, and shivered and shook, and his knees and legs trembled. And a high wind blew over the land, and the clouds flew, and towards evening all grew dark, and the leaves fell from the trees, and the water rose and roared as if it were boiling, and splashed upon the shore; and in the distance he saw ships which were firing guns in their sore need, pitching and tossing on the waves. And yet in the midst of the sky there was still a small patch of blue, though on every side it was as red as in a heavy storm. So, full of despair, he went and stood in much fear and said:

"Flounder, flounder in the sea,
Come, I pray thee, here to me;
For my wife, good Ilsabil,
Wills not as I'd have her will."

"Well, what does she want, now?" said the Flounder. "Alas," said the man, "she wants to be Pope." "Go to her then," said the Flounder; "she is Pope already."

So he went, and when he got there, he saw what seemed to be a large church surrounded by palaces. He pushed his way through the crowd. Inside, however, everything was lighted up with thousands and thousands of candles, and his wife was clad in gold, and she was sitting on a much higher throne, and had three great golden crowns on, and round about her there was much ecclesiastical splendour; and on both sides of her was a row of candles the largest of which was as tall as the very tallest tower, down to the very smallest kitchen candle, and all the emperors and kings were on their knees before her, kissing her shoe. "Wife," said the man, and looked attentively at her, "are you now

Pope?" "Yes," said she, "I am Pope." So he stood and looked at her, and it was just as if he was looking at the bright sun. When he had stood looking at her thus for a short time, he said: "Ah, wife, if you are Pope, do let well alone!" But she looked as stiff as a post, and did not move or show any signs of life. Then said he: "Wife, now that you are Pope, be satisfied, you cannot become anything greater now." "I will consider about that," said the woman. Thereupon they both went to bed, but she was not satisfied, and greediness let her have no sleep, for she was continually thinking what there was left for her to be.

The man slept well and soundly, for he had run about a great deal during the day; but the woman could not fall asleep at all, and flung herself from one side to the other the whole night through, thinking always what more was left for her to be, but unable to call to mind anything else. At length the sun began to rise, and when the woman saw the red of dawn, she sat up in bed and looked at it. And when, through the window, she saw the sun thus rising, she said: "Cannot I, too, order the sun and moon to rise?" "Husband," she said, poking him in the ribs with her elbows, "wake up! go to the Flounder, for I wish to be even as God is." The man was still half asleep, but he was so horrified that he fell out of bed. He thought he must have heard amiss, and rubbed his eyes, and said: "Wife, what are you saying?" "Husband," said she, "if I can't order the sun and moon to rise, and have to look on and see the sun and moon rising, I can't bear it. I shall not know what it is to have another happy hour, unless I can make them rise myself." Then she looked at him so terribly that a shudder ran over him, and said: "Go at once; I wish to be like unto God." "Alas, wife," said the man, falling on his knees before her, "the Flounder cannot do that; he can make an emperor and a pope; I beseech you, go on as you are, and be Pope." Then she fell into a rage, and her hair flew wildly about her head, she tore open her bodice, kicked him with her foot, and screamed: "I can't stand it, I can't stand it any longer! will you go this instant?" Then he put on his trousers and ran away like a madman. But outside a great storm was raging, and blowing so hard that he could scarcely keep his feet; houses and trees toppled over, the mountains trembled, rocks rolled into the sea, the sky was pitch black, and it thundered and lightened, and the sea came in with black waves as high as church-towers and mountains, and all with crests of white foam at the top. Then he cried, but could not hear his own words:

"Flounder, flounder in the sea,
Come, I pray thee, here to me;
For my wife, good Ilsabil,
Wills not as I'd have her will."

"Well, what does she want, now?" said the Flounder. "Alas," said he, "she wants to be like unto God." "Go to her, and you will find her back again in the pigsty." And there they are still living to this day.

THE VALIANT LITTLE TAILOR

One summer's morning a little tailor was sitting on his table by the window; he was in good spirits, and sewed with all his might. Then came a peasant woman down the street crying: "Good jams, cheap! Good jams, cheap!" This rang pleasantly in the tailor's ears; he stretched his delicate head out of the window, and called: "Come up here, dear woman; here you will get rid of your goods." The woman came up the three steps to the tailor with her heavy basket, and he made her unpack all the pots for him. He inspected each one, lifted it up, put his nose to it, and at length said: "The jam seems to me to be good, so weigh me out four ounces, dear woman, and if it is a quarter of a pound that is of no consequence." The woman who had hoped to find a good sale, gave him what he desired, but went away quite angry and grumbling. "Now, this jam shall be blessed by God," cried the little tailor, "and give me health and strength"; so he brought the bread out of the cupboard, cut himself a piece right across the loaf and spread the jam over it. "This won't taste bitter," said he, "but I will just finish the jacket before I take a bite." He laid the bread near him, sewed on, and in his joy, made bigger and bigger stitches. In the meantime the smell of the sweet jam rose to where the flies were sitting in great numbers, and they were attracted and descended on it in hosts. "Hi! who invited you?" said the little tailor, and drove the unbidden guests away. The flies, however, who understood no German, would not be turned away, but came back again in ever-increasing companies. The little tailor at last lost all patience, and drew a piece of cloth from the hole under his work-table, and saying: "Wait, and I will give it to you," struck it mercilessly on them. When he drew it away and counted, there lay before him no fewer than seven, dead and with legs stretched out. "Are you a fellow of that sort?" said he, and could not help admiring his own bravery. "The whole town shall know of this!" And the little tailor hastened to cut himself a girdle, stitched it, and embroidered on it in large letters: "Seven at one stroke!" "What, the town!" he continued, "the whole world shall hear of it!" and his heart wagged with joy like a lamb's tail. The tailor put on the girdle, and resolved to go forth into the world, because he thought his workshop was too small for his valour. Before he went away, he sought about in the house to see if there was anything which he could take with him; however, he found nothing but an old cheese, and that he put in his pocket. In front of the door he observed a bird which had caught itself in the thicket. It had to go into his pocket with the cheese. Now he took to the road boldly, and as he was light and nimble, he felt no fatigue. The road led him up a mountain, and when he had reached the highest point of it, there sat a powerful giant looking peacefully about him. The little tailor went bravely up, spoke to him, and said: "Good day, comrade, so you are sitting there overlooking the wide-spread world! I am just on my way thither, and want to try my luck. Have you any inclination to go with me?" The giant looked contemptuously at the tailor, and said: "You ragamuffin! You miserable creature!"

"Oh, indeed?" answered the little tailor, and unbuttoned his coat, and showed the giant the girdle, "there may you read what kind of a man I am!" The giant read: "Seven at one stroke," and thought that they had been men whom the tailor had killed, and began to feel a little respect for the tiny fellow. Nevertheless, he wished to try him first, and took a stone in his hand and squeezed it together so that water dropped out of it. "Do that likewise," said the giant, "if you have strength." "Is that all?" said the tailor, "that is child's play with us!" and put his hand into his pocket, brought out the soft cheese, and pressed it until the liquid ran out of it. "Faith," said he, "that was a little better, wasn't it?" The giant did not know what to say, and could not believe it of the little man. Then the giant picked up a stone and threw it so high that the eye could scarcely follow it. "Now, little mite of a man, do that likewise." "Well thrown," said the tailor, "but after all the stone came down to earth again; I will throw you one which shall never come back at all," and he put his hand into his pocket, took out the bird, and threw it into the air. The bird, delighted with its liberty, rose, flew away and did not come back. "How does that shot please you, comrade?" asked the tailor. "You can certainly throw," said the giant, "but now we will see if you are able to carry anything properly." He took the little tailor to a mighty oak tree which lay there felled on the ground, and said: "If you are strong enough, help me to carry the tree out of the forest." "Readily," answered the little man; "take you the trunk on your shoulders, and I will raise up the branches and twigs; after all, they are the heaviest." The giant took the trunk on his shoulder, but the tailor seated himself on a branch, and the giant who could not look round, had to carry away the whole tree, and the little tailor into the bargain: he behind, was quite merry and happy, and whistled the song: "Three tailors rode forth from the gate," as if carrying the tree were child's play. The giant, after he had dragged the heavy burden part of the way, could go no further, and cried: "Hark you, I shall have to let the tree fall!" The tailor sprang nimbly down, seized the tree with both arms as if he had been carrying it, and said to the giant: "You are such a great fellow, and yet can not even carry the tree!"

They went on together, and as they passed a cherry-tree, the giant laid hold of the top of the tree where the ripest fruit was hanging, bent it down, gave it into the tailor's hand, and bade him eat. But the little tailor was much too weak to hold the tree, and when the giant let it go, it sprang back again, and the tailor was tossed into the air with it. When he had fallen down again without injury, the giant said: "What is this? Have you not strength enough to hold the weak twig?" "There is no lack of strength," answered the little tailor. "Do you think that could be anything to a man who has struck down seven at one blow? I leapt over the tree because the huntsmen are shooting down there in the thicket. Jump as I did, if you can do it." The giant made the attempt, but could not get over the tree, and remained hanging in the branches, so that in this also the tailor kept the upper hand.

The giant said: "If you are such a valiant fellow, come with me into our cavern and spend the night with us." The little tailor was willing, and followed him. When they went into the cave, other giants were sitting there by the fire, and each of them had a roasted sheep in his hand and was eating it. The little tailor looked round and thought: "It is much more spacious here than in my workshop." The giant showed him a bed, and said he was to lie down in it and sleep. The bed, however, was too big for the little tailor; he did not lie down in it, but crept into a corner. When it was mid-night, and the giant thought that the little tailor was lying in a sound sleep, he got up, took a great iron bar, cut through the bed with one blow, and thought he had finished off the grasshopper for good. With the earliest dawn the giants went into the forest, and had quite forgotten the little tailor, when all at once he walked up to them quite merrily and boldly. The giants were terrified, they were afraid that he would strike them all dead, and ran away in a great hurry.

The little tailor went onwards, always following his own pointed nose. After he had walked for a long time, he came to the courtyard of a royal palace, and as he felt weary, he lay down on the grass and fell asleep. Whilst he lay there, the people came and inspected him on all sides, and read on his girdle: "Seven at one stroke." "Ah!" said they, "what does the great warrior here in the midst of peace? He must be a mighty lord." They went and announced him to the King, and gave it as their opinion that if war should break out, this would be a weighty and useful man who ought on no account to be allowed to depart. The counsel pleased the King, and he sent one of his courtiers to the little tailor to offer him military service when he awoke. The ambassador remained standing by the sleeper, waited until he stretched his limbs and opened his eyes, and then conveyed to him this proposal. "For this very reason have I come here," the tailor replied, "I am ready to enter the King's service." He was therefore honourably received, and a special dwelling was assigned him.

The soldiers, however, were set against the little tailor, and wished him a thousand miles away. "What is to be the end of this?" they said among themselves. "If we quarrel with him, and he strikes about him, seven of us will fall at every blow; not one of us can stand against him." They came therefore to a decision, betook themselves in a body to the King, and begged for their dismissal. "We are not prepared," said they, "to stay with a man who kills seven at one stroke." The King was sorry that for the sake of one he should lose all his faithful servants, wished that he had never set eyes on the tailor, and would willingly have been rid of him again. But he did not venture to give him his dismissal, for he dreaded lest he should strike him and all his people dead, and place himself on the royal throne. He thought about it for a long time, and at last found good counsel. He sent to the little tailor and caused him to be informed that as he was such a great warrior, he had one request to make to him. In a forest of his country lived two giants, who caused great mischief with their robbing, murdering, ravaging, and burning, and no one could approach them without putting himself in danger of death. If the tailor conquered and killed these two giants, he would give him his only daughter to wife, and half of his kingdom as a dowry, likewise one hundred horsemen should go with him to assist him. "That would indeed be a fine thing for a man like me!" thought the little tailor. "One is not offered a beautiful princess and half a kingdom every day of one's life!" "Oh, yes," he replied, "I will soon subdue the giants, and do not require the help of the hundred horsemen to do it; he who can hit seven with one blow has no need to be afraid of two."

The little tailor went forth, and the hundred horsemen followed him. When he came to the outskirts of the forest, he said to his followers: "Just stay waiting here, I alone will soon finish off the giants." Then he bounded into the forest and looked about right and left. After a while he perceived both giants. They lay sleeping under a tree, and snored so that the branches waved up and down. The little tailor, not idle, gathered two pocketsful of stones, and with these climbed up the tree. When he was half-way up, he slipped down by a branch, until he sat just above the sleepers, and then let one stone after another fall on the breast of one of the giants. For a long time the giant felt nothing, but at last he awoke, pushed his comrade, and said: "Why are you knocking me?" "You must be dreaming," said the other, "I am not knocking you." They laid themselves down to sleep again, and then the tailor threw a stone down on the second. "What is the meaning of this?" cried the other. "Why are you pelting me?" "I am not pelting you," answered the first, growling. They disputed about it for a time, but as they were weary they let the matter rest, and their eyes closed

once more. The little tailor began his game again, picked out the biggest stone, and threw it with all his might on the breast of the first giant. "That is too bad!" cried he, and sprang up like a madman, and pushed his companion against the tree until it shook. The other paid him back in the same coin, and they got into such a rage that they tore up trees and belaboured each other so long, that at last they both fell down dead on the ground at he same time. Then the little tailor leapt down. "It is a lucky thing," said he, "that they did not tear up the tree on which I was sitting, or I should have had to spring on to another like a squirrel; but we tailors are nimble." He drew out his sword and gave each of them a couple of thrusts in the breast, and then went out to the horsemen and said: "The work is done; I have finished both of them off, but it was hard work! They tore up trees in their sore need, and defended themselves with them, but all that is to no purpose when a man like myself comes, who can kill seven at one blow." "But are you not wounded?" asked the horsemen. "You need not concern yourself about that," answered the tailor, "they have not bent one hair of mine." The horsemen would not believe him, and rode into the forest; there they found the giants swimming in their blood, and all round about lay the torn-up trees.

The little tailor demanded of the King the promised reward; he, however, repented of his promise, and again bethought himself how he could get rid of the hero. "Before you receive my daughter, and the half of my kingdom," siad he to him, "you must perform one more heroic deed. In the forest roams a unicorn which does great harm, and you must catch it first." "I fear one unicorn still less than two giants. Seven at one blow, is my kind of affair." He took a rope and an axe with him, went forth into the forest, and again bade those who were sent with him to wait outside. He had not long to seek. The unicorn soon came towards him, and rushed directly on the tailor, as if it would gore him with its horn without more ado. "Softly, softly; it can't be done as quickly as that," said he, and stood still and waited until the animal was quite close, and then sprang nimbly behind the tree. The unicorn ran against the tree with all its strength, and struck its horn so fast in the trunk that it had not strength enough to draw it out again, and thus it was caught. "Now, I have got the bird," said the tailor, and came out from behind the tree and put the rope round its neck, and then with his axe he hewed the horn out of the tree, and when all was ready he led the beast away and took it to the King.

The King still would not give him the promised reward, and made a third demand. Before the wedding the tailor was to catch him a wild boar that made great havoc in the forest, and the huntsmen should give him their help. "Willingly," said the tailor, "that is child's play!" He did not take the huntsmen with him into the forest, and they were well pleased that he did not, for the wild boar had several times received them in such a manner that they had no inclination to lie in wait for him. When the boar perceived the tailor, it ran on him with foaming mouth and whetted tusks, and was about to throw him to the ground, but the hero fled and sprang into a chapel which was near, and up to the window at once, and in one bound out again. The boar ran in after him, but the tailor ran round outside and shut the door behind it, and then the raging beast, which was much too heavy and awkward to leap out of the window, was caught. The little tailor called the huntsmen thither that they might see the prisoner with their own eyes. The hero, however, went to the King, who was now, whether he liked it or not, obliged to keep his promise, and gave him his daughter and the half of his kingdom. Had he known that it was no warlike hero, but a little tailor who was standing before him, it would have gone to his heart still more than it did. The wedding was held with great magnificence and small joy, and out of a tailor a king was made.

After some time the young Queen heard her husband say in his dreams at night: "Boy, make me the doublet, and patch the pantaloons, or else I will rap the yard-measure over your ears." Then she discovered in what state of life the young lord had been born, and next morning complained of her wrongs to her father, and begged him to help her to get rid of her husband, who was nothing else but a tailor. The King comforted her and said: "Leave your bedroom door open this night, and my servants shall stand outside, and when he has fallen asleep shall go in, bind him, and take him on board a ship which shall carry him into the wide world." The woman was satisfied with this; but the King's armour-bearer, who had heard all, was friendly with the young lord, and informed him of the whole plot. "I'll put a screw into that business," said the little tailor. At night he went to bed with his wife at the usual time, and when she thought that he had fallen asleep, she got up, opened the door, and then lay down again. The little tailor, who was only pretending to be asleep, began to cry out in a clear voice: "Boy, make me the doublet and patch me the pantaloons, or I will rap the yard-measure over your ears. I smote seven at one blow. I killed two giants, I brought away one unicorn, and caught a wild boar, and am I to fear those who are standing outside the room." When these men heard the tailor speaking thus, they were overcome by a great dread, and ran as if the wild huntsmen were behind them, and none of them would venture anything further against him. So the little tailor was and remained a king to the end of his life.

CINDERELLA

The wife of a rich man fell sick, and as she felt that her end was drawing near, she called her only daughter to her bedside and said: "Dear child, be good and pious, and then the good God will always protect you, and I will look down on you from heaven and be near you." Thereupon she closed her eyes and departed. Every day the maiden went out to her mother's grave and wept, and she remained pious and good. When winter came the snow spread a white sheet over the grave, and by the time the spring sun had drawn it off again, the man had taken another wife.

The woman had brought with her into the house two daughters, who were beautiful and fair of face, but vile and black of heart. Now began a bad time for the poor step-child. "Is the stupid goose to sit in the parlour with us?" they said. "He who wants to eat bread must earn it; out with the kitchen-wench." They took her pretty clothes away from her, put an old grey bedgown on her, and gave her wooden shoes. "Just look at the proud princess, how decked out she is!" they cried, and laughed, and led her into the kitchen. There she had to do hard work from morning till night, get up before daybreak, carry water, light fires, cook and wash. Besides this, the sisters did her every imaginable injury—they mocked her and emptied her peas and lentils into the ashes, so that she was forced to sit and pick them out again. In the evening when she had worked till she was weary she had no bed to go to, but had to sleep by the hearth in the cinders. And as on that account she always looked dusty and dirty, they called her Cinderella.

It happened that the father was once going to the fair, and he asked his two step-daughters what he should bring back for them. "Beautiful dresses," said one, "pearls and jewels," said the second. "And you, Cinderella," said he, "what will you have?" "Father, break off for me the first branch which knocks against your hat on your way home." So he bought beautiful dresses, pearls and jewels for his two step-daughters, and on his way home, as he was riding through a green thicket, a hazel twig brushed against him and knocked off his hat. Then he broke off the branch and took it with him. When he reached home he gave his step-daughters the things which they had wished for, and to Cinderella he gave the branch from the hazel-bush. Cinderella thanked him, went to her mother's grave and planted the branch on it, and wept so much that the tears fell down on it and watered it. And it grew and became a handsome tree. Thrice a day Cinderella went and sat beneath it, and wept and prayed, and a little white bird always came on the tree, and if Cinderella expressed a wish, the bird threw down to her what she had wished for.

It happened, however, that the King gave orders for a festival which was to last three days, and to which all the beautiful young girls in the country were invited, in order that his son might choose himself a bride. When the two step-sisters heard that they too were to appear among the number, they were delighted, called Cinderella and said: "Comb our hair for us, brush our shoes and fasten our buckles, for we are going to the wedding at the King's palace." Cinderella obeyed, but wept, because she too would have liked to go with them to the dance, and begged her step-mother to allow her to do so. "You go, Cinderella!" said she; "covered in dust and dirt as you are, and would go to the festival? You have no clothes and shoes, and yet would dance!" As, however, Cinderella went on asking, the step-mother said at last: "I have emptied a dish of lentils into the ashes for you, if you have picked them out again in two hours, you shall go with us." The maiden went through the back-door into the garden, and called: "You tame pigeons, you turtle-doves, and all you birds beneath the sky, come and help me to pick

> The good into the pot,
> The bad into the crop."

Then two white pigeons came in by the kitchen-window, and afterwards the turtle-doves, and at last all the birds beneath the sky, came whirring and crowding in, and alighted amongst the ashes. And the pigeons nodded with their heads and began pick, pick, pick, pick, and the rest began also pick, pick, pick, pick, and gathered all the good grains into the dish. Hardly had one hour passed before they had finished, and all flew out again. Then the girl took the dish to her step-mother, and was glad, and believed that now she would be allowed to go with them to the festival. But the step-mother said: "No, Cinderella, you have no clothes and you cannot dance; you would only be laughed at." And as Cinderella wept at this, the step-mother said: "If you can pick two dishes of lentils out of the ashes for me in one hour, you shall go with us." And she thought to herself: "That she most certainly cannot do again." When the step-mother had emptied the two dishes of lentils amongst the ashes, the maiden went through the back-door into the garden and cried: "You tame pigeons, you turtle-doves, and all you birds beneath the sky, come and help me to pick

> The good into the pot,
> The bad into the crop."

Then two white pigeons came in by the kitchen-window, and afterwards the turtle-doves, and at length all the birds beneath the sky, came whirring and crowding in, and alighted amongst the ashes. And the doves nodded with their heads and began pick, pick, pick, pick, and the others began also pick, pick, pick, pick, and gathered all the good seeds into the dishes, and before half an hour was over they had already finished, and all flew out again. Then the maiden carried the dishes to the step-mother and was delighted, and believed that she might now go with them to the wedding. But the step-mother said: "All this will not help; you cannot go with us, for you have no clothes and cannot dance; we should be ashamed of you!" On this she turned her back on Cinderella, and hurried away with her two proud daughters.

As no one was now at home, Cinderella went to her mother's grave beneath the hazel-tree, and cried:

"Shiver and quiver, little tree,
Silver and gold throw down over me."

Then the bird threw a gold and silver dress down to her, and slippers embroidered with silk and silver. She put on the dress with all speed, and went to the wedding. Her step-sisters and the step-mother however did not know her, and thought she must be a foreign princess, for she looked so beautiful in the golden dress. They never once thought of Cinderella, and believed that she was sitting at home in the dirt, picking lentils out of the ashes. The prince approached her, took her by the hand and danced with her. He would dance with no other maiden, and never let loose of her hand, and if any one else came to invite her, he said: "This is my partner."

She danced till it was evening, and then she wanted to go home. But the King's son said: "I will go with you and bear you company," for he wished to see to whom the beautiful maiden belonged. She escaped from him, however, and sprang into the pigeon-house. The King's son waited until her father came, and then he told him that the unknown maiden had leapt into the pigeon-house. The old man thought: "Can it be Cinderella?" and they had to bring him an axe and a pickaxe that he might hew the pigeon-house to pieces, but no one was inside it. And when they got home Cinderella lay in her dirty clothes among the ashes, and a dim little oil-lamp was burning on the mantle-piece, for Cinderella had jumped quickly down from the back of the pigeon-house and had run to the little hazel-tree, and there she had taken off her beautiful clothes and laid them on the grave, and the bird had taken them away again, and then she had seated herself in the kitchen amongst the ashes in her grey gown.

Next day when the festival began afresh, and her parents and the step-sisters had gone once more, Cinderella went to the hazel-tree and said:

"Shiver and quiver, my little tree,
Silver and gold throw down over me."

Then the bird threw down a much more beautiful dress than on the preceding day. And when Cinderella appeared at the wedding in this dress, every one was astonished at her beauty. The King's son had waited until she came, and instantly took her by the hand and danced with no one but her. When others came and invited her, he said: "This is my partner." When evening came she wished to leave, and the King's son followed her and wanted to see into which house she went. But she sprang away from him, and into the garden behind the house. Therein stood a beautiful tall tree on which hung the most magnificent pears. She clambered so nimbly between the branches like a squirrel that the King's son did not know where she was gone. He waited until her father came, and said to him: "The unknown maiden has escaped from me, and I believe she has climbed up the pear-tree." The father thought: "Can it be Cinderella?" and had an axe brought and cut the tree down, but no one was on it. And when they got into the kitchen, Cinderella lay there among the ashes, as usual, for she had jumped down on the other side of the tree, had taken the beautiful dress to the bird on the little hazel-tree, and put on her grey gown.

On the third day, when the parents and sisters had gone away, Cinderella went once more to her mother's grave and said to the little tree:

"Shiver and quiver, my little tree,
Silver and gold throw down over me."

And now the bird threw down to her a dress which was more splendid and magnificent than any she had yet had, and the slippers were golden. And when she went to the festival in the dress, no one knew how to speak for astonishment. The King's son danced with her only and if any one invited her to dance, he said: "This is my partner."

When evening came, Cinderella wished to leave, and the King's son was anxious to go with her, but she escaped from him so quickly that he could not follow her. The King's son, however, had employed a ruse, and had caused the whole staircase to be smeared with pitch, and there, when she ran down, had the maiden's left slipper remained stuck. The King's son picked it up, and it was small and dainty, and all golden. Next morning, he went with it to the father, and said to him: "No one shall be my wife but she whose foot this golden slipper fits." Then were the two sisters glad, for they had pretty feet. The eldest went with the shoe into her room and wanted to try it on, and her mother stood by. But she could not get her big toe into it, and the shoe was too small for her. Then her mother gave her a knife and said: "Cut the toe off; when you are Queen you will have no more need to go on foot." The maiden cut the toe off, forced the foot into the shoe, swallowed the pain, and went out to the King's son. Then he took her on his horse as his bride and rode away with her. They were obliged, however, to pass the grave, and there, on the hazel-tree, sat the two pigeons and cried:

"Turn and peep, turn and peep,
There's blood within the shoe,
The shoe it is too small for her,
The true bride waits for you."

Then he looked at her foot and saw how the blood was trickling from it. He turned his horse round and took the false bride home again, and said she was not the true one, and that the other sister was to put the shoe on. Then this one went into her chamber and got her toes safely into the shoe, but her heel was too large. So her mother gave her a knife and said: "Cut a bit off your heel; when you are Queen you will have no more need to go on foot." The maiden cut a bit off her heel, forced her foot into the shoe, swallowed the pain, and went out to the King's son. He took her on his horse as his bride, and rode away with her, but when they passed by the hazel-tree, the two little pigeons sat on it and cried:

"Turn and peep, turn and peep,
There's blood within the shoe,
The shoe it is too small for her,
The true bride waits for you."

He looked down at her foot and saw how the blood was running out of her shoe, and how it had stained her white stocking quite red. Then he turned his horse and took the false bride home again. "This also is not the right one," said he, "have you no other daughter?" "No," said the

man, "there is still a little stunted kitchen-wench which my late wife
left behind her, but she cannot possibly be the bride." The King's son
said he was to send her up to him; but the mother answered: "Oh no,
she is much too dirty, she cannot show herself!" But he absolutely
insisted on it, and Cinderella had to be called. She first washed her
hands and face clean, and then went and bowed down before the
King's son, who gave her the golden shoe. Then she seated herself on a
stool, drew her foot out of the heavy wooden shoe, and put it into the
slipper, which fitted like a glove. And when she rose up and the King's
son looked at her face he recognized the beautiful maiden who had
danced with him and cried: "That is the true bride!" The step-mother
and the two sisters were horrified and became pale with rage; he,
however, took Cinderella on his horse and rode away with her. As they
passed by the hazel-tree, the two white doves cried:

> "Turn and peep, turn and peep,
> No blood is in the shoe,
> The shoe is not too small for her,
> The true bride rides with you,"

and when they had cried that, the two came flying down and placed
themselves on Cinderella's shoulders, one on the right, the other on
the left, and remained sitting there.

When the wedding with the King's son was to be celebrated, the two
false sisters came and wanted to get into favour with Cinderella and
share her good fortune. When the betrothed couple went to church,
the elder was at the right side and the younger at the left, and the
pigeons pecked out one eye from each of them. Afterwards as they

came back, the elder was at the left, and the younger at the right, and then the pigeons pecked out the other eye from each. And thus, for their wickedness and falsehood, they were punished with blindness all their days.

THE RIDDLE

There was once a King's son who was seized with a desire to travel about the world, and took no one with him but a faithful servant. One day he came to a great forest, and when darkness overtook him he could find no shelter, and knew not where to pass the night. Then he saw a girl who was going towards a small house, and when he came nearer, he saw that the maiden was young and beautiful. He spoke to her, and said: "Dear child, can I and my servant find shelter for the night in the little house?" "Oh, yes," said the girl, in a sad voice, "that you certainly can, but I do not advise you to venture it. Do not go in." "Why not?" asked the King's son. The maiden sighed and said: "My step-mother practises wicked arts; she is ill-disposed toward strangers." Then he saw very well that he had come to the house of a witch, but as it was dark, and he could not go farther, and also was not afraid, he entered. The old woman was sitting in an armchair by the fire, and looked at the stranger with her red eyes. "Good evening," growled she, and pretended to be quite friendly. "Take a seat and rest yourselves." She fanned the fire on which she was cooking something in a small pot. The daughter warned the two to be prudent, to eat nothing, and drink nothing, for the old woman brewed evil drinks. They slept quietly until early morning. When they were making ready for their departure, and the King's son was already seated on his horse, the old woman said: "Stop a moment, I will first hand you a parting draught." Whilst she fetched it, the King's son rode away, and the servant who had to buckle his saddle tight, was the only one present when the wicked witch came with the drink. "Take that to your master," said she; but at that instant the glass broke and the poison spirted on the horse, and it was so strong that the animal immediately fell down dead. The servant ran after his master and told him what had happened, but as he did not want to leave his saddle behind, he ran back to fetch it. When he came to the dead horse, however, a raven was already sitting on it devouring it. "Who knows whether we shall find anything better to-day?" said the servant; so he killed the raven, and took it with him. And now they journeyed onwards into the forest the whole day, but could not get out of it. By nightfall they found an inn and entered it. The servant gave the raven to the innkeeper to prepare for supper. They had stumbled, however, on a den of murderers, and during the darkness twelve of these came, intending to kill the strangers and rob them. But before they set about this work, they sat down to supper, and the innkeeper and the witch sat down with them, and together they ate a dish of soup in which was cut up the flesh of the raven. Hardly had they swallowed a couple of mouthfuls, before they all fell down dead, for the raven had communicated to them the poison from the horse-flesh. There was now no one else left in the house but the innkeeper's daughter, who was honest, and had taken no part in their godless deeds. She opened all doors to the stranger and showed him the store of treasures. But the King's son said she might keep everything, he would have none of it, and rode onwards with his servant.

After they had travelled about for a long time, they came to a town in which was a beautiful but proud princess, who had made it known that whosoever should set her a riddle which she could not guess, that man should be her husband; but if she guessed it, his head must be cut off. She had three days to guess it in, but was so clever that she always found the answer to the riddle given her before the appointed time. Nine suitors had already perished in this manner, when the King's son arrived, and, blinded by her great beauty, was willing to stake his life for it. Then he went to her and laid his riddle before her. "What is this?" said he: "One slew none, and yet slew twelve." She did not know what that was; she thought and thought, but she could not solve it. She opened her riddle-books, but it was not in them—in short, her wisdom was at an end. As she did not know how to help herself, she ordered her maid to creep into the lord's sleeping-chamber, and listen to his dreams, and thought that he would perhaps speak in his sleep and reveal the riddle. But the clever servant had placed himself in the bed instead of his master, and when the maid came there, he tore off from her the mantle in which she had wrapped herself, and chased her out with rods. The second night the King's daughter sent her maid-in-waiting, who was to see if she could succeed better in listening, but the servant took her mantle also away from her, and hunted her out with rods. Now the master believed himself safe for the third night, and lay down in his own bed. Then came the princess herself, and she had put on a misty-grey mantle, and she seated herself near him. And when she thought that he was asleep and dreaming, she spoke to him, and hoped that he would answer in his sleep, as many do, but he was awake, and understood and heard everything quite well. Then she asked: "One slew none, what is that?" He replied: "A raven, which ate of a dead and poisoned horse, and died of it." She inquired further: "And yet slew twelve, what is that?" He answered: "That means twelve murderers, who ate the raven and died of it."

When she knew the answer to the riddle she wanted to steal away, but he held her mantle so fast that she was forced to leave it behind her. Next morning, the King's daughter announced that she had guessed the riddle, and sent for the twelve judges and expounded it before them. But the youth begged for a hearing, and said: "She stole into my room in the night and questioned me, otherwise she could not have discovered it." The judges said: "Bring us a proof of this." Then were the three mantles brought thither by the servant, and when the judges saw the misty-grey one which the King's daughter usually wore, they said: "Let the mantle be embroidered with gold and silver, and then it will be your wedding-mantle."

THE MOUSE, THE BIRD, AND THE SAUSAGE

Once upon a time a mouse, a bird, and a sausage became companions, kept house together, lived well and happily in peace, and wonderfully increased their possessions. The bird's work was to fly every day into the forest and bring back wood. The mouse had to carry water, light the fire, and lay the table, but the sausage had to cook.

He who is too well off is always longing for something new. One day the bird met with another bird, to whom it related its excellent circumstances and boasted of them. The other bird, however, called it a poor simpleton for its hard work, but said that the two at home had good times. For when the mouse had made her fire and carried her water, she went into her little room to rest until they called her to lay the table. The sausage stayed by the pot, saw that the food was cooking well, and, when it was nearly time for dinner, it rolled itself once or twice through the broth or vegetables and then they were buttered, salted, and ready. When the bird came home and laid his burden down, they sat down to dinner, and after they had had their meal, they slept their fill till next morning, and that was a splendid life.

Next day the bird, prompted by the other bird, would go no more into the wood, saying that he had been servant long enough, and had been made a fool of by them, and that they must change about for once, and try to arrange it in another way. And, though the mouse and the sausage also begged most earnestly, the bird would have his way, and said it must be tried. They cast lots about it, and the lot fell on the sausage who was to carry wood, the mouse became cook, and the bird was to fetch water.

What happened? The little sausage went out towards the wood, the little bird lighted the fire, the mouse stayed by the pot and waited alone until little sausage came home and brought wood for next day. But the little sausage stayed so long on the road that they both feared something was amiss, and the bird flew out a little way in the air to meet it. Not far off, however, it met a dog on the road who had fallen on the poor sausage as lawful booty, and had seized and swallowed it. The bird charged the dog with an act of barefaced robbery, but words were useless, for the dog said he had found forged letters on the sausage, on which account its life was forfeited to him.

The bird sadly took up the wood, flew home, and related what he had seen and heard. They were much troubled, but agreed to do their best and remain together. The bird therefore laid the table, and the mouse made ready the food, and wanted to dress it, and to get into the pot as the sausage used to do, and roll and creep amongst the vegetables to mix them; but before she got into the midst of them she was stopped, and lost her skin and hair and life in the attempt.

When the bird came to carry in the dinner, no cook was there. In its distress the bird threw the wood here and there, called and searched, but no cook was to be found! Owing to his carelessness the wood caught fire, so that a conflagration broke out; the bird hastened to fetch water, but the bucket dropped into the well, and he fell in with it, and could not recover himself, but had to drown there.

MOTHER HOLLE

There was once a widow who had two daughters—one of whom was pretty and industrious, whilst the other was ugly and idle. But she was much fonder of the ugly and idle one, because she was her own daughter; and the other, who was a step-daughter, was obliged to do all the work, and be the Cinderella of the house. Every day the poor girl had to sit by a well, in the highway, and spin and spin till her fingers bled.

Now it happened that one day the shuttle was marked with her blood, so she dipped it in the well, to wash the mark off; but it dropped out of her hand and fell to the bottom. She began to weep, and ran to her step-mother and told her of the mishap. But she scolded her sharply, and was so merciless as to say: "Since you have let the shuttle fall in, you must fetch it out again."

So the girl went back to the well, and did not know what to do; and in the sorrow of her heart she jumped into the well to get the shuttle. She lost her senses; and when she awoke and came to herself again, she was in a lovely meadow where the sun was shining and many thousands of flowers were growing. Across this meadow she went, and at last came to a baker's oven full of bread, and the bread cried out: "Oh, take me out! take me out! or I shall burn; I have been baked a long time!" So she went up to it, and took out all the loaves one after another with the bread-shovel. After that she went on till she came to a tree covered with apples, which called out to her: "Oh, shake me! shake me! we apples are all ripe!" So she shook the tree till the apples fell like rain, and went on shaking till they were all down, and

when she had gathered them into a heap, she went on her way.

At last she came to a little house, out of which an old woman peeped; but she had such large teeth that the girl was frightened, and was about to run away. But the old woman called out to her: "What are you afraid of, dear child? Stay with me; if you will do all the work in the house properly, you shall be the better for it. Only you must take care to make my bed well, and to shake it thoroughly till the feathers fly—for then there is snow on the earth. I am Mother Holle."

As the old woman spoke so kindly to her, the girl took courage and agreed to enter her service. She attended to everything to the satisfaction of her mistress, and always shook her bed so vigorously that the feathers flew about like snow-flakes. So she had a pleasant life with her; never an angry word; and to eat she had boiled or roast meat every day.

She stayed some time with Mother Holle, before she became sad. At first she did not know what was the matter with her, but found at length that it was home-sickness: although she was many thousand times better off here than at home, still she had a longing to be there. At last she said to the old woman: "I have a longing for home; and however well off I am down here, I cannot stay any longer; I must go up again to my own people." Mother Holle said: "I am pleased that you long for your home again, and as you have served me so truly, I myself will take you up again." Thereupon she took her by the hand, and led her to a large door. The door was opened, and just as the maiden was standing beneath the doorway, a heavy shower of golden rain fell, and all the gold clung to her, so that she was completely covered over with it.

"You shall have that because you have been so industrious," said Mother Holle; and at the same time she gave her back the shuttle which she had let fall into the well. Thereupon the door closed, and the maiden found herself up above upon the earth, not far from her mother's house.

And as she went into the yard the cock was sitting on the well, and cried:

"Cock-a-doodle-doo!
Your golden girl's come back to you!"

So she went in to her mother, and as she arrived thus covered with gold, she was well received, both by her and her sister.

The girl told all that had happened to her; and as soon as the mother heard how she had come by so much wealth, she was very anxious to obtain the same good luck for the ugly and lazy daughter. She had to seat herself by the well and spin; and in order that her shuttle might be stained with blood, she stuck her hand into a thorn bush and pricked her finger. Then she threw her shuttle into the well, and jumped in after it.

She came, like the other, to the beautiful meadow and walked along the very same path. When she got to the oven the bread again cried: "Oh, take me out! take me out! or I shall burn; I have been baked a long time!" But the lazy thing answered: "As if I had any wish to make myself dirty!" and on she went. Soon she came to the apple-tree, which cried: "Oh, shake me! shake me! we apples are all ripe!" But she answered: "I like that! one of you might fall on my head," and so went on. When she came to Mother Holle's house she was not afraid, for she had already heard of her big teeth, and she hired herself to her immediately.

The first day she forced herself to work diligently, and obeyed Mother Holle when she told her to do anything, for she was thinking of all the gold that she would give her. But on the second day she began to be lazy, and on the third day still more so, and then she would not get up in the morning at all. Neither did she make Mother Holle's bed as she ought, and did not shake it so as to make the feathers fly up. Mother Holle was soon tired of this, and gave her notice to leave. The lazy girl was willing enough to go, and thought that now the golden rain would come. Mother Holle led her also to the great door; but while she was standing beneath it, instead of the gold a big kettleful of pitch was emptied over her. "That is the reward for your service," said Mother Holle, and shut the door.

So the lazy girl went home; but she was quite covered with pitch, and the cock on the well, as soon as he saw her, cried out:

"Cock-a-doodle-doo!
Your dirty girl's come back to you!"

But the pitch clung fast to her, and could not be got off as long as she lived.

THE SEVEN RAVENS

There was once a man who had seven sons, and still he had no daughter, however much he wished for one. At length his wife again gave him hope of a child, and when it came into the world it was a girl. The joy was great, but the child was sickly and small, and had to be privately baptized on account of its weakness. The father sent one of the boys in haste to the spring to fetch water for the baptism. The other six went with him, and as each of them wanted to be first to fill it, the jug fell into the well. There they stood and did not know what to do, and none of them dared to go home. As they still did not return, the father grew impatient, and said: "They have certainly forgotten it while playing some game, the wicked boys!" He became afraid that the girl would have to die without being baptized, and in his anger cried: "I wish the boys were all turned into ravens." Hardly was the word spoken before he heard a whirring of wings over his head, looked up and saw seven coal-black ravens flying away.

The parents could not withdraw the curse, and however sad they were at the loss of their seven sons, they still to some extent comforted themselves with their dear little daughter, who soon grew strong and every day became more beautiful. For a long time she did not know that she had had brothers, for her parents were careful not to mention them before her, but one day she accidentally heard some people saying of herself, that the girl was certainly beautiful, but that in reality she was to blame for the misfortune which had befallen her seven brothers. Then she was much troubled, and went to her father and mother and asked if it was true that she had brothers, and what had become of them. The parents now dared keep the secret no longer, but said that what had befallen her brothers was the will of Heaven, and that her birth had only been the innocent cause. But the maiden took it to heart daily, and thought she must save her brothers. She had no rest or peace until she set out secretly, and went forth into the wide world to search for her brothers and set them free, let it cost what it might. She took nothing with her but a little ring belonging to her parents as a keepsake, a loaf of bread against hunger, a little pitcher of water against thirst, and a little chair as a provision against weariness.

And now she went continually onwards, far, far, to the very end of the world. Then she came to the sun, but it was too hot and terrible, and devoured little children. Hastily she ran away, and ran to the moon, but it was far too cold, and also awful and malicious, and when it saw the child, it said: "I smell, I smell the flesh of men." At this she ran swiftly away, and came to the stars, which were kind and good to her, and each of them sat on its own particular little chair. But the morning star arose, and gave her the drumstick of a chicken, and said: "If you have not that drumstick you can not open the Glass mountain, and in the Glass mountain are your brothers."

The maiden took the drumstick, wrapped it carefully in a cloth, and went onwards again until she came to the Glass mountain. The door was shut, and she thought she would take out the drumstick; but when she undid the cloth, it was empty, and she had lost the good star's present. What was she now to do? She wished to rescue her brothers, and had no key to the Glass mountain. The good sister took a knife, cut off one of her little fingers, put it in the door, and succeeded in opening it. When she had gone inside, a little dwarf came to meet her, who said: "My child, what are you looking for?" "I am looking for my brothers, the seven ravens," she replied. The dwarf said: "The lord ravens are not at home, but if you will wait here until they come, step in." Thereupon the little dwarf carried the ravens' dinner in, on seven little plates, and in seven little glasses, and the little sister ate a morsel from each plate, and from each little glass she took a sip, but in the last little glass she dropped the ring which she had brought away with her.

Suddenly she heard a whirring of wings and a rushing through the air, and then the little dwarf said: "Now the lord ravens are flying home." Then they came, and wanted to eat and drink, and looked for their little plates and glasses. Then said one after the other: "Who has eaten something from my plate? Who has drunk out of my little glass? It was a human mouth." And when the seventh came to the bottom of the glass, the ring rolled against his mouth. Then he looked at it, and saw that it was a ring belonging to his father and mother, and said:

"God grant that our sister may be here, and then we shall be free." When the maiden, who was standing behind the door watching, heard that wish, she came forth, and on this all the ravens were restored to their human form again. And they embraced and kissed each other, and went joyfully home.

LITTLE RED-CAP

Once upon a time there was a dear little girl who was loved by every one who looked at her, but most of all by her grandmother, and there was nothing that she would not have given to the child. Once she gave her a little cap of red velvet, which suited her so well that she would never wear anything else; so she was always called 'Little Red-Cap'.

One day her mother said to her: "Come, Little Red-Cap, here is a piece of cake and a bottle of wine; take them to your grandmother, she is ill and weak, and they will do her good. Set out before it gets hot, and when you are going, walk nicely and quietly and do not run off the path, or you may fall and break the bottle, and then your grandmother will get nothing; and when you go into her room, don't forget to say, 'Good-morning', and don't peep into every corner before you do it."

"I will take great care," said Little Red-Cap to her mother, and gave her hand on it.

The grandmother lived out in the wood, half a league from the village, and just as Little Red-Cap entered the wood, a wolf met her. Red-Cap did not know what a wicked creature he was, and was not at all afraid of him.

"Good-day, Little Red-Cap," said he.

"Thank you kindly, wolf."

"Whither away so early, Little Red-Cap?"

"To my grandmother's."

"What have you got in your apron?"

"Cake and wine; yesterday was baking-day, so poor sick grandmother is to have something good, to make her stronger."

"Where does your grandmother live, Little Red-Cap?"

"A good quarter of a league farther on in the wood; her house stands under the three large oak-trees, the nut-trees are just below; you surely must know it," replied Little Red-Cap.

The wolf thought to himself: "What a tender young creature! what a nice plump mouthful—she will be better to eat than the old woman. I must act craftily, so as to catch both." So he walked for a short time by the side of Little Red-Cap, and then he said: "See, Little Red-Cap, how pretty the flowers are about here—why do you not look round? I believe, too, that you do not hear how sweetly the little birds are singing; you walk gravely along as if you were going to school, while everything else out here in the wood is merry."

Little Red-Cap raised her eyes, and when she saw the sunbeams dancing here and there through the trees, and pretty flowers growing everywhere, she thought: "Suppose I take grandmother a fresh nosegay; that would please her too. It is so early in the day that I shall still get there in good time"; and so she ran from the path into the wood to look for flowers. And whenever she had picked one, she fancied that she saw a still prettier one farther on, and ran after it, and so got deeper and deeper into the wood.

Meanwhile the wolf ran straight to the grandmother's house and knocked at the door.

"Who is there?"

"Little Red-Cap," replied the wolf. "She is bringing cake and wine; open the door."

"Lift the latch," called out the grandmother, "I am too weak, and cannot get up."

The wolf lifted the latch, the door sprang open, and without saying a word he went straight to the grandmother's bed, and devoured her. Then he put on her clothes, dressed himself in her cap, laid himself in bed and drew the curtains.

Little Red-Cap, however, had been running about picking flowers, and when she had gathered so many that she could carry no more, she remembered her grandmother, and set out on the way to her.

She was surprised to find the cottage-door standing open, and when she went into the room, she had such a strange feeling that she said to herself: "Oh dear! how uneasy I feel to-day, and at other times I like being with grandmother so much. She called out: "Good morning," but received no answer; so she went to the bed and drew back the

curtains. There lay her grandmother with her cap pulled far over her face, and looking very strange.

"Oh! grandmother," she said, "what big ears you have!"

"The better to hear you with, my child," was the reply.

"But, grandmother, what big eyes you have!" she said.

"The better to see you with, my dear."

"But, grandmother, what large hands you have!"

"The better to hug you with."

"Oh! but, grandmother, what a terrible big mouth you have!"

"The better to eat you with!"

And scarcely had the wolf said this, than with one bound he was out of bed and swallowed up Red-Cap.

When the wolf had appeased his appetite, he lay down again in the bed, fell asleep and began to snore very loud. The huntsman was just passing the house, and thought to himself: "How the old woman is snoring! I must just see if she wants anything." So he went into the room, and when he came to the bed, he saw that the wolf was lying in it. "Do I find you here, you old sinner!" said he. "I have long sought you!" Then just as he was going to fire at him, it occurred to him that the wolf might have devoured the grandmother, and that she might still be saved, so he did not fire, but took a pair of scissors, and began to cut open the stomach of the sleeping wolf. When he had made two snips, he saw the little Red-Cap shining, and then he made two snips more, and the little girl sprang out, crying: "Ah, how frightened I have been! How dark it was inside the wolf"; and after that the aged grandmother came out alive also, but scarcely able to breathe. Red-Cap, however, quickly fetched great stones with which they filled the wolf's belly, and when he awoke, he wanted to run away, but the stones were so heavy that he collapsed at once, and fell dead.

Then all three were delighted. The huntsman drew off the wolf's skin and went home with it; the grandmother ate the cake and drank the wine which Red-Cap had brought, and revived, but Red-Cap thought to herself: "As long as I live, I will never by myself leave the path, to run into the wood, when my mother has forbidden me to do so."

It is also related that once when Red-Cap was again taking cakes to the old grandmother, another wolf spoke to her, and tried to entice her from the path. Red-Cap, however, was on her guard, and went straight forward on her way, and told her grandmother that she had met the wolf, and that he had said "good-morning" to her, but with such a wicked look in his eyes, that if they had not been on the public road she was certain he would have eaten her up. "Well," said the grandmother, "we will shut the door, that he may not come in." Soon afterwards the wolf knocked, and cried: "Open the door, grandmother, I am little Red-Cap, and am bringing you some cakes." But they did not speak, or open the door, so the grey-beard stole twice or thrice round the house, and at last jumped on the roof, intending to wait until Red-Cap went home in the evening, and then to steal after her and devour her in the darkness. But the grandmother saw what was in his thoughts. In front of the house was a great stone trough, so she said to the child: "Take the pail, Red-Cap; I made some sausages yesterday, so carry the water in which I boiled them to the trough." Red-Cap carried until the great trough was quite full. Then the smell of the sausages reached the wolf, and he sniffed and peeped down, and at last stretched out his neck so far that he could no longer keep his footing and began to slip, and slipped down from the roof straight into the great trough, and was drowned. But Red-Cap went joyously home, and no one ever did anything to harm her again.

THE BREMEN TOWN-MUSICIANS

A certain man had a donkey, which had carried the corn-sacks to the mill indefatigably for many a long year; but his strength was going, and he was growing more and more unfit for work. Then his master began to consider how he might best save his keep; but the donkey, seeing that no good wind was blowing, ran away and set out on the road to Bremen. "There," he thought, "I can surely be town-musician." When he had walked some distance, he found a hound lying on the road, gasping like one who had run till he was tired. "What are you gasping so for, you big fellow?" asked the donkey.

"Ah," replied the hound, "as I am old, and daily grow weaker, and no longer can hunt, my master wanted to kill me, so I took to flight; but now how am I to earn my bread?"

"I tell you what," said the donkey, "I am going to Bremen, and shall be town-musician there; go with me and engage yourself also as a musician. I will play the lute, and you shall beat the kettle-drum."

The hound agreed, and on they went.

Before long they came to a cat, sitting on the path, with a face like three rainy days! "Now then, old shaver, what has gone askew with you?" asked the donkey.

"Who can be merry when his neck is in danger?" answered the cat. "Because I am now getting old, and my teeth are worn to stumps, and I prefer to sit by the fire and spin, rather than hunt about after mice, my

mistress wanted to drown me, so I ran away. But now good advice is scarce. Where am I to go?"

"Go with us to Bremen. You understand night-music. So you can be a town-musician."

The cat thought well of it, and went with them. After this the three fugitives came to a farm-yard, where the cock was sitting upon the gate, crowing with all his might. "Your crow goes through and through one," said the donkey. "What is the matter?"

"I have been foretelling fine weather, because it is the day on which Our Lady washes the Christ-child's little shirts, and wants to dry them," said the cock; "but guests are coming for Sunday, so the housewife has no pity, and has told the cook that she intends to eat me in the soup to-morrow, and this evening I am to have my head cut off. Now I am crowing at the top of my lungs while still I can."

"Ah, but red-comb," said the donkey, "you had better come away with us. We are going to Bremen; you can find something better than death everywhere: you have a good voice, and if we make music together it must have some quality!"

The cock agreed to this plan, and all four went on together. They could not reach the city of Bremen in one day, however, and in the evening they came to a forest where they meant to pass the night. The donkey and the hound laid themselves down under a large tree, the cat and the cock settled themselves in the branches; but the cock flew right to the top, where he was most safe. Before he went to sleep he looked round on all four sides, and thought he saw in the distance a little spark burning; so he called out to his companions that there must be a house not far off, for he saw a light. The donkey said: "If so, we had better get up and go on, for the shelter here is bad." The hound thought too that a few bones with some meat on would do him good!

So they made their way to the place where the light was, and soon saw it shine brighter and grow larger, until they came to a well-lighted robbers' house. The donkey, as the biggest, went to the window and looked in.

"What do you see, my grey-horse?" asked the cock. "What do I see?" answered the donkey; "a table covered with good things to eat and drink, and robbers sitting at it enjoying themselves." "That would be the sort of thing for us," said the cock. "Yes, yes; ah, if only we were there!" said the donkey.

Then the animals took counsel together how they should manage to drive away the robbers, and at last they thought of a plan. The donkey was to place himself with his fore-feet upon the window-ledge, the hound was to jump on the donkey's back, the cat was to climb upon the dog, and lastly the cock was to fly up and perch upon the head of the cat.

When this was done, at a given signal, they began to perform their music together: the donkey brayed, the hound barked, the cat mewed, and the cock crowed; then they burst through the window into the room, shattering the glass! At this horrible din, the robbers sprang up, thinking no otherwise than that a ghost had come in, and fled in a great fright out into the forest. The four companions now sat down at the table, well content with what was left, and ate as if they were going to fast for a month.

As soon as the four minstrels had done, they put out the light, and each sought for himself a sleeping-place according to his nature and to what suited him. The donkey laid himself down upon some straw in the yard, the hound behind the door, the cat upon the hearth near the warm ashes, and the cock perched himself upon a beam of the roof; and being tired from their long walk, they soon went to sleep.

When it was past midnight, and the robbers saw from afar that the light was no longer burning in their house, and all appeared quiet, the captain said: "We ought not to have let ourselves be frightened out of our wits"; and ordered one of them to go and examine the house.

The messenger finding all still, went into the kitchen to light a candle, and, taking the glistening fiery eyes of the cat for live coals, he held a lucifer-match to them to light it. But the cat did not understand the joke, and flew in his face, spitting and scratching. He was dreadfully frightened, and ran to the back-door, but the dog, who lay there, sprang up and bit his leg; and as he ran across the yard by the dunghill, the donkey gave him a smart kick with its hind foot. The cock, too, who had been awakened by the noise, and had become lively, cried down from the beam: "Cock-a-doodle-doo!"

Then the robber ran back as fast as he could to his captain, and said: "Ah, there is a horrible witch sitting in the house, who spat on me and scratched my face with her long claws; and by the door stands a man with a knife, who stabbed me in the leg; and in the yard there lies a black monster, who beat me with a wooden club; and above, upon the roof, sits the judge, who called out, 'Bring the rogue here to me!' so I got away as well as I could."

After this the robbers never again dared enter the house; but it suited the four musicians of Bremen so well that they did not care to leave it any more. And the mouth of him who last told this story is still warm.

THE SINGING BONE

In a certain country there was once great lamentation over a wild boar that laid waste the farmers' fields, killed the cattle, and ripped up people's bodies with his tusks. The King promised a large reward to anyone who would free the land from this plague; but the beast was so big and strong that no one dared to go near the forest in which it lived. At last the King gave notice that whosoever should capture or kill the wild boar should have his only daughter to wife.

Now there lived in the country two brothers, sons of a poor man, who declared themselves willing to undertake the hazardous enterprise; the elder, who was crafty and shrewd, out of pride; the younger, who was innocent and simple, from a kind heart. The King said: "In order that you may be the more sure of finding the beast, you must go into the forest from opposite sides." So the elder went in on the west side, and the younger on the east.

When the younger had gone a short way, a little man stepped up to him. He held in his hand a black spear and said: "I give you this spear because your heart is pure and good; with this you can boldly attack the wild boar, and it will do you no harm."

He thanked the little man, shouldered the spear, and went on fearlessly.

Before long he saw the beast, which rushed at him; but he held the spear towards it, and in its blind fury it ran so swiftly against it that its heart was cloven in twain. Then he took the monster on his back and went homewards with it to the King.

As he came out at the other side of the wood, there stood at the entrance a house where people were making merry with wine and dancing. His elder brother had gone in here, and, thinking that after all the boar would not run away from him, was going to drink until he felt brave. But when he saw his young brother coming out of the wood laden with his booty, his envious, evil heart gave him no peace. He called out to him: "Come in, dear brother, rest and refresh yourself with a cup of wine."

The youth, who suspected no evil, went in and told him about the good little man who had given him the spear where with he had slain the boar.

The elder brother kept him there until the evening, and then they went away together, and when in the darkness they came to a bridge over a brook, the elder brother let the other go first; and when he was half-way across he gave him such a blow from behind that he fell down dead. He buried him beneath the bridge, took the boar, and carried it to the King, pretending that he had killed it; whereupon he obtained the King's daughter in marriage. And when his younger brother did not come back he said: "The boar must have ripped up his body," and every one believed it.

But as nothing remains hidden from God, so this black deed also was to come to light.

Years afterwards a shepherd was driving his herd across the bridge, and saw lying in the sand beneath, a snow-white little bone. He thought that it would make a good mouth-piece, so he clambered down, picked it up, and cut out of it a mouth-piece for his horn. But when he blew through it for the first time, to his great astonishment, the bone began of its own accord to sing:

"Ah, friend, thou blowest upon my bone!
Long have I lain beside the water;
My brother slew me for the boar,
And took for his wife the King's young daughter."

"What a wonderful horn!" said the shepherd; "it sings by itself; I must take it to my lord the King." And when he came with it to the King the horn again began to sing its little song. The King understood it

all, and caused the ground below the bridge to be dug up, and then the whole skeleton of the murdered man came to light. The wicked brother could not deny the deed, and was sewn up in a sack and drowned. But the bones of the murdered man were laid to rest in a beautiful tomb in the churchyard.

THE DEVIL WITH THE THREE GOLDEN HAIRS

There was once a poor woman who gave birth to a little son; and as he came into the world with a caul on, it was predicted that in his four-teenth year he would have the King's daughter for his wife. It happened that soon afterwards the King came into the village, and no one knew that he was the King, and when he asked the people what news there was, they answered: "A child has just been born with a caul on; whatever anyone so born undertakes turns out well. It is prophesied, too, that in his fourteenth year he will have the King's daughter for his wife."

The King, who had a bad heart, and was angry about the prophecy, went to the parents, and, seeming quite friendly, said: "You poor people, let me have your child, and I will take care of it." At first they refused, but when the stranger offered them a large amount of gold for it, and they thought: "It is a child of good fortune, and everything must turn out well for it," they at last consented, and gave him the child.

The King put it in a box and rode away with it until he came to a deep piece of water; then he threw the box into it and thought: "I have freed my daughter from her undesired suitor."

The box, however, did not sink, but floated like a boat, and not a drop of water made its way into it. And it floated to within two miles of the King's chief city, where there was a mill, and it came to a halt at the mill-dam. A miller's boy, who by good luck was standing there, noticed it and pulled it out with a hook, thinking that he had found a great treasure, but when he opened it there lay a pretty boy inside, quite fresh and lively. He took him to the miller and his wife, and as they had no children they were glad, and said: "God has given him to us." They took great care of the foundling, and he grew up in all goodness.

It happened that once in a storm, the King went into the mill, and he asked the mill-folk if the tall youth were their son. "No," answered they, "he's a foundling. Fourteen years ago he floated down to the mill-dam in a box, and the mill-boy pulled him out of the water."

Then the King knew that it was none other than the child of good fortune which he had thrown into the water, and he said: "My good people, could not the youth take a letter to the Queen; I will give him two gold pieces as a reward." "Just as the King commands," answered they, and they told the boy to hold himself in readiness. Then the King wrote a letter to the Queen, wherein he said: "As soon as the boy arrives with this letter, let him be killed and buried, and all must be done before I come home."

The boy set out with this letter; but he lost his way, and in the evening came to a large forest. In the darkness he saw a small light; he went towards it and reached a cottage. When he went in, an old woman was sitting by the fire quite alone. She started when she saw the boy, and said: "Whence do you come, and whither are you going?" "I come from the mill," he answered, "and wish to go to the Queen, to whom I am taking a letter; but as I have lost my way in the forest I should like to stay here over night." "You poor boy," said the woman, "you have come into a den of thieves, and when they come home they will kill you." "Let them come," said the boy, "I am not afraid; but I am so tired that I cannot go any farther." And he stretched himself upon a bench and fell asleep.

Soon afterwards the robbers came, and angrily asked what strange boy was lying there. "Ah," said the old woman, "it is an innocent child who has lost himself in the forest, and out of pity I have let him come in; he has to take a letter to the Queen." The robbers opened the letter and read it, and in it was written that the boy as soon as he arrived should be put to death. Then the hard-hearted robbers felt pity, and their leader tore up the letter and wrote another, saying, that as soon as the boy came, he should be married at once to the King's daughter. Then they let him lie quietly on the bench until the next morning, and when he awoke they gave him the letter, and showed him the right way.

And the Queen, when she had received the letter and read it, did as was written in it, and had a splendid wedding-feast prepared, and the King's daughter was married to the child of good fortune; and as the youth was handsome and friendly she lived with him in joy and contentment.

After some time the King returned to his palace and saw that the prophecy was fulfilled, and the child married to his daughter. "How has that come to pass?" said he; "I gave quite another order in my letter."

So the Queen gave him the letter, and said that he might see for himself what was written in it. The King read the letter and saw quite well that it had been exchanged for the other. He asked the youth what had become of the letter entrusted to him, and why he had brought another instead of it. "I know nothing about it," answered he; "it must

have been changed in the night, when I slept in the forest." The King said in a passion: "You shall not have everything quite so much your own way; whosoever marries my daughter must fetch me from hell three golden hairs from the head of the Devil; bring me what I want, and you shall keep my daughter." In this way the King hoped to be rid of him for ever. But the child of good fortune answered: "I will fetch the golden hairs, I am not afraid of the Devil." Whereupon he took leave of them and began his journey.

The road led him to a large town, where the watchman by the gates asked him what his trade was, and what he knew. "I know everything," answered the child of good fortune. "Then you can do us a favour," said the watchman, "if you will tell us why our market-fountain, which once flowed with wine has become dry, and no longer gives even water?" "That you shall know," answered he; "only wait until I come back."

Then he went farther and came to another town, and there also the gatekeeper asked him what was his trade, and what he knew. "I know everything," answered he. "Then you can do us a favour and tell us why a tree in our town which once bore golden apples now does not even put forth leaves?" "You shall know that," answered he; "only wait until I come back."

Then he went on and came to a wide river over which he must cross. The ferryman asked him what his trade was, and what he knew. "I know everything," answered he. "Then you can do me a favour," said the ferryman, "and tell me why I must always be rowing backwards and forwards, and am never set free?" "You shall know that," answered he; "only wait until I come back."

When he had crossed the water he found the entrance to Hell. It was black and sooty within, and the Devil was not at home, but his grandmother was sitting in a large arm-chair. "What do you want?" said she to him, but she did not look so very wicked. "I should like to have three golden hairs from the Devil's head," answered he, "else I cannot keep my wife." "That is a good deal to ask for," said she; "if the devil comes home and finds you, it will cost you your life; but as I pity you, I will see if I cannot help you."

She changed him into an ant and said: "Creep into the folds of my dress, you will be safe there." "Yes," answered he, "so far, so good; but there are three things besides that I want to know: why a fountain which once flowed with wine has become dry, and no longer gives even water; why a tree which once bore golden apples does not even put forth leaves; and why a ferryman must always be going backwards and forwards, and is never set free?"

"Those are difficult questions," answered she, "but just be silent and quiet and pay attention to what the Devil says when I pull out the three golden hairs."

As the evening came on, the Devil returned home. No sooner had he entered than he noticed that the air was not pure. "I smell man's flesh," said he; "all is not right here." Then he pried into every corner, and searched, but could not find anything. His grandmother scolded him. "It has just been swept," said she, "and everything put in order, and now you are upsetting it again; you have always got man's flesh in your nose. Sit down and eat your supper."

When he had eaten and drunk he was tired, and laid his head in his grandmother's lap, and told her she should louse him a little. It was not long before he was fast asleep, snoring and breathing heavily. Then the old woman took hold of a golden hair, pulled it out, and laid it down beside her. "Oh!" cried the Devil, "what are you doing?" "I have had a bad dream," answered the grandmother, "so I seized hold of your hair." "What did you dream then?" said the Devil. "I dreamt that a fountain in a market-place from which wine once flowed was dried up, and not even water would flow out of it; what is the cause of it?" "Oh, ho! if they did but know it," answered the Devil; "there is a toad sitting under a stone in the well; if they killed it, the wine would flow again."

The grandmother loused him again until he went to sleep and snored so that the windows shook. Then she pulled the second hair out. "Ha! what are you doing?" cried the Devil angrily. "Do not take it ill," said she, "I did it in a dream." "What have you dreamt this time?" asked he. "I dreamt that in a certain kingdom there stood an apple-tree which had once borne golden apples, but now would not even bear leaves. What, think you, was the reason?" "Oh! if they did but know," answered the Devil. "A mouse is gnawing at the root; if they killed it they would have golden apples again, but if it gnaws much longer the tree will wither altogether. But I have had enough of your dreams; if you disturb me in my sleep again you will get a box on the ear."

The grandmother spoke gently to him and picked his lice once more until he fell asleep and snored. Then she took hold of the third golden hair and pulled it out. The Devil jumped up, roared out, and would have treated her ill if she had not quieted him again and said: "Who can help bad dreams?" "What was the dream, then?" asked he, and was quite curious. "I dreamt of a ferryman who complained that he must always ferry from one side to the other, and was never released. What is the cause of it?" "Ah! the fool," answered the Devil; "when anyone comes and wants to go across he must put the oar in his hand, and the other man will have to ferry and he will be free." As the grandmother had plucked out the three golden hairs, and the three questions were answered, she let the old Devil alone, and he slept until daybreak.

When the Devil had gone out again the old woman took the ant out of the folds of her dress, and gave the child of good fortune his human shape again. "There are the three golden hairs for you," said she. "What the Devil said to your three questions, I suppose you heard?" "Yes," answered he, "I heard, and will take care to remember." "You have what you want," said she, "and now you can go your way." He thanked the old woman for helping him in his need, and left Hell well content that everything had turned out so fortunately.

When he came to the ferryman he was expected to give the promised answer. "Ferry me across first," said the child of good fortune, "and then I will tell you how you can be set free," and when he had reached the opposite shore he gave him the Devil's advice: "Next time anyone comes, who wants to be ferried over, just put the oar in his hand."

He went on and came to the town wherein stood the unfruitful tree, and there too the watchman wanted an answer. So he told him what he had heard from the Devil: "Kill the mouse which is gnawing at its root, and it will again bear golden apples." Then the watchman thanked him, and gave him as a reward two asses laden with gold, which followed him.

Finally, he came to the town whose well was dry. He told the watchman what the Devil had said: "A toad is in the well beneath a stone; you must find it and kill it, and the well will again give wine in plenty." The watchman thanked him, and also gave him two asses laden with gold.

At last the child of good fortune got home to his wife, who was heartily glad to see him again, and to hear how well he had prospered in everything. To the King he took what he had asked for, the Devil's three golden hairs, and when the King saw the four asses laden with gold he was quite content, and said: "Now all the conditions are fulfilled, and you can keep my daughter. But tell me, dear son-in-law, where did all that gold come from? this is tremendous wealth!" "I was rowed across a river," answered he, "and got it there; it lies on the shore instead of sand." "Can I too fetch some of it?" said the King; and he was quite eager about it. "As much as you like," answered he. "There is a ferryman on the river; let him ferry you over, and you can fill your sacks on the other side." The greedy King set out in all haste, and when he came to the river he beckoned to the ferryman to put him across. The ferryman came and bade him get in, and when they got to the other shore he put the oar in his hand and sprang out. But from this time forth the King had to ferry, as a punishment for his sins. Perhaps he is ferrying still? If he is, it is because no one has taken the oar from him.

THE LOUSE AND THE FLEA

A louse and a flea kept house together and were brewing beer in an egg-shell. Then the little louse fell in and burnt herself. At this the little flea began to scream loudly. Then said the little room-door: "Little flea, why are you screaming?" "Because the louse has burnt herself."

Then the little door began to creak. At this a little broom in the corner said: "Why are you creaking, little door?" "Have I not reason to creak?

> The little louse has burnt herself,
> The little flea is weeping."

So the little broom began to sweep frantically. Then a little cart passed by and said: "Why are you sweeping, little broom?" "Have I not reason to sweep?

> The little louse has burnt herself,
> The little flea is weeping,
> The little door is creaking."

So the little cart said: "Then I will run," and began to run like mad. Then said the ash-heap by which it ran: "Why are you running so, little cart?" "Have I not reason to run?

> The little louse has burnt herself,
> The little flea is weeping,
> The little door is creaking,
> The little broom is sweeping."

The ash-heap said: "Then I will burn furiously," and began to burn in clear flames. A little tree stood near the ash-heap and said: "Ash-heap, why are you burning?" "Have I not reason to burn?

> The little louse has burnt herself,
> The little flea is weeping,
> The little door is creaking,
> The little broom is sweeping,
> The little cart is running."

The little tree said: "Then I will shake myself," and began to shake herself so that all her leaves fell off; a girl who came up with her water-pitcher saw that, and said: "Little tree, why are you shaking yourself?" "Have I not reason to shake myself?

> The little louse has burnt herself,
> The little flea is weeping,
> The little door is creaking,
> The little broom is sweeping,
> The little cart is running,
> The little ash-heap is burning."

At this the girl said: "Then I will break my little water-pitcher," and she broke her little water-pitcher. Then said the little spring from

which ran the water: "Girl, why are you breaking your water-pitcher?"
"Have I not reason to break my water-pitcher?

> The little louse has burnt herself,
> The little flea is weeping,
> The little door is creaking,
> The little broom is sweeping,
> The little cart is running,
> The little ash-heap is burning,
> The little tree is shaking itself."

"Oh, ho!" said the spring, "then I will begin to flow," and began to
flow violently. And in the water everything was drowned, the girl, the
little tree, the little ash-heap, the little cart, the broom, the little door,
the little flea, the little louse, all together.

THE GIRL WITHOUT HANDS

A certain miller had little by little fallen into poverty, and had nothing
left but his mill and a large apple-tree behind it. Once when he had
gone into the forest to fetch wood, an old man stepped up to him
whom he had never seen before, and said: "Why do you plague yourself with cutting wood, I will make you rich, if you will promise me
what is standing behind your mill." "What can that be but my apple-
tree?" thought the miller, and said: "Yes," and gave a written promise
to the stranger. He, however, laughed mockingly and said: "When three
years have passed, I will come and carry away what belongs to me,"
and then he went. When the miller got home, his wife came to meet
him and said: "Tell me, miller, from whence comes this sudden wealth
into our house? All at once every box and chest was filled; no one
brought it in, and I know not how it happened." He answered: "It
comes from a stranger who met me in the forest, and promised me
great treasure. I, in return, have promised him what stands behind the
mill; we can very well give him the big apple-tree for it." "Ah, husband," said the terrified wife, "that must have been the Devil! He did

not mean the apple-tree, but our daughter, who was standing behind the mill sweeping the yard."

The miller's daughter was a beautiful, pious girl, and lived through the three years in the fear of God and without sin. When therefore the time was over, and the day came when the Evil One was to fetch her, she washed herself clean, and made a circle round herself with chalk. The Devil appeared quite early, but he could not come near to her. Angrily, he said to the miller: "Take all water away from her, that she may no longer be able to wash herself, for otherwise I have no power over her." The miller was afraid, and did so. The next morning the Devil came again, but she had wept on her hands, and they were quite clean. Again he could not get near her, and furiously said to the miller: "Cut her hands off, or else I have no power over her." The miller was shocked and answered: "How could I cut off my own child's hands?" Then the Evil One threatened him and said: "If you do not do it you are mine, and I will take you yourself." The father became alarmed, and promised to obey him. So he went to the girl and said: "My child, if I do not cut off both your hands, the Devil will carry me away, and in my terror I have promised to do it. Help me in my need, and forgive me the harm I do you." She replied: "Dear father, do with me what you will, I am your child." Thereupon she laid down both her hands, and let them be cut off. The Devil came for the third time, but she had wept so long and so much on the stumps, that after all they were quite clean. Then he had to give in, and had lost all right over her.

The miller said to her: "I have by means of you received such great wealth that I will keep you most handsomely as long as you live." But she replied: "Here I cannot stay, I will go forth, compassionate people will give me as much as I require." Thereupon she caused her maimed arms to be bound to her back, and by sunrise she set out on her way, and walked the whole day until night fell. Then she came to a royal garden, and by the shimmering of the moon she saw that trees covered with beautiful fruits grew in it, but she could not enter, for it was surrounded by water. And as she had walked the whole day and not eaten one mouthful, and hunger tormented her, she thought: "Ah, if I were but inside, that I might eat of the fruit, else must I die of hunger!" Then she knelt down, called on God the Lord, and prayed. And suddenly an angel came towards her, who made a dam in the water, so that the moat became dry and she could walk through it. And now she went into the garden and the angel went with her. She saw a tree covered with beautiful pears, but they were all counted. Then she went to them, and to still her hunger, ate one with her mouth from the tree, but no more. The gardener was watching; but as the angel was standing by, he was afraid and thought the maiden was a spirit, and was silent, neither did he dare to cry out, or to speak to the spirit. When she had eaten the pear, she was satisfied, and went and concealed herself among the bushes. The King to whom the garden belonged, came down to it next morning, and counted, and saw that one of the pears was missing, and asked the gardener what had become of it, as it was not lying beneath the tree, but was gone. Then answered the gardener: "Last night, a spirit came in, who had no hands, and ate off one of the pears with its mouth." The King said: "How did the spirit get over the water, and where did it go after it had eaten the pear?" The gardener answered: "Someone came in a snow-white garment from heaven who made a dam, and kept back the water, that the spirit might walk through the moat. And as it must have been an angel, I was afraid, and asked no questions, and did not cry out. When the spirit had eaten the pear, it went back again." The King said: "If it be as you say, I will watch with you to-night."

When it grew dark the King came into the garden and brought a priest with him, who was to speak to the spirit. All three seated themselves beneath the tree and watched. At midnight the maiden came creeping out of the thicket, went to the tree, and again ate one pear off it with her mouth, and beside her stood the angel in white garments. Then the priest went out to them and said: "Do you come from heaven or from earth? Are you a spirit, or a human being?" She replied: "I am no spirit, but an unhappy mortal deserted by all but God." The King said: "If you are forsaken by all the world, yet will I not forsake you." He took her with him into his royal palace, and as she was so beautiful and good, he loved her with all his heart, had silver hands made for her, and took her to wife.

After a year the King had to go on a journey, so he commended his young Queen to the care of his mother and said: "If she is brought to child-bed take care of her, nurse her well, and tell me of it at once in a letter." Then she gave birth to a fine boy. So the old mother made haste

to write and announce the joyful news to him. But the messenger rested by a brook on the way, and as he was fatigued by the great distance, he fell asleep. Then came the Devil, who was always seeking to injure the good Queen, and exchanged the letter for another, in which was written that the Queen had brought a monster into the world. When the King read the letter he was shocked and much troubled, but he wrote in answer that they were to take great care of the Queen and nurse her well until his arrival. The messenger went back with the letter, but rested at the same place and again fell asleep. Then came the Devil once more, and put a different letter in his pocket, in which it was written that they were to put the Queen and her child to death. The old mother was terribly shocked when she received the letter, and could not believe it. She wrote back again to the King, but received no other answer, because each time the Devil substituted a false letter, and in the last letter it was also written that she was to preserve the Queen's tongue and eyes as a token that she had obeyed.

But the old mother wept to think such innocent blood was to be shed, and had a hind brought by night and cut out her tongue and eyes, and kept them. Then said she to the Queen: "I cannot have you killed as the King commands, but here you may stay no longer. Go forth into the wide world with your child, and never come here again." The poor woman tied her child on her back, and went away with eyes full of tears. She came into a great wild forest, and then she fell on her knees and prayed to God, and the angel of the Lord appeared to her and led her to a little house on which was a sign with the words: "Here all dwell free." A snow-white maiden came out of the little house and said: "Welcome, Lady Queen," and conducted her inside. Then she unbound the little boy from her back, and held him to her breast that he might feed, and laid him in a beautifully-made little bed. Then said the poor woman: "From whence do you know that I was a queen?" The white maiden answered: "I am an angel sent by God, to watch over you and your child." The Queen stayed seven years in the little house, and was well cared for, and by God's grace, because of her piety, her hands which had been cut off, grew once more.

At last the King came home again from his journey, and his first wish was to see his wife and the child. Then his aged mother began to weep and said: "You wicked man, why did you write to me that I was to take those two innocent lives?" and she showed him the two letters which the Evil One had forged, and then continued: "I did as you bade me," and she showed the tokens, the tongue and eyes. Then the King began to weep for his poor wife and his little son so much more bitterly than she was doing, that the aged mother had compassion on him and said: "Be at peace, she still lives; I secretly caused a hind to be killed, and took these tokens from it; but I bound the child to your wife's back and bade her go forth into the wide world, and made her promise never to come back here again, because you were so angry with her." Then spoke the King: "I will go as far as the sky is blue, and will neither eat nor drink until I have found again my dear wife and my child, if in the meantime they have not been killed, or died of hunger."

Thereupon the King travelled about for seven long years and sought her in every cleft of the rocks and in every cave, but he found her not, and thought she had died of want. During the whole of this time he neither ate nor drank, but God supported him. At length he came into a great forest, and found therein the little house whose sign was, "Here all dwell free." Then forth came the white maiden, took him by the hand, led him in, and said: "Welcome, Lord King," and asked him from whence he came. He answered: "Soon shall I have travelled about for the space of seven years, and I seek my wife and her child, but cannot find them." The angel offered him meat and drink, but he did not take anything, and only wished to rest a little. Then he lay down to sleep, and laid a handkerchief over his face.

Thereupon the angel went into the chamber where the Queen sat with her son, whom she usually called "Sorrowful," and said to her: "Go out with your child, your husband has come." So she went to the place where he lay, and the handkerchief fell from his face. Then said she: "Sorrowful, pick up your father's handkerchief, and cover his face again." The child picked it up, and put it over his face again. The King in his sleep heard what passed, and had pleasure in letting the handkerchief fall once more. But the child grew impatient, and said: "Dear mother, how can I cover my father's face when I have no father in this world? I have learnt to say the prayer, 'Our Father, which art in Heaven', you have told me that my father was in Heaven, and was the good God, and how can I know a wild man like this? He is not my father." When the King heard that, he got up, and asked who they were. Then said she: "I am your wife, and that is your son, Sorrowful." And he saw her living hands, and said: "My wife had silver hands." She answered: "The good God has caused my natural hands to grow again"; and the angel went into the inner room, and brought the silver hands, and showed them to him. Here upon he knew for a certainty that it was his dear wife and his dear child, and he kissed them, and was glad, and said: "A heavy stone has fallen off my heart." Then the angel of God ate with them once again, and after that they went home to the King's aged mother. There were great rejoicings everywhere, and the King and Queen were married again, and lived contentedly to their happy end.

CLEVER HANS

The mother of Hans said: "Whither away, Hans?" Hans answered: "To Gretel." "Behave well, Hans." "Oh, I'll behave well. Good-bye, mother." "Good-bye, Hans." Hans comes to Gretel. "Good day, Gretel." "Good day, Hans. What do you bring that is good?" "I bring nothing, I want to have something given me." Gretel presents Hans with a needle. Hans says: "Good-bye, Gretel." "Good-bye, Hans."

Hans takes the needle, sticks it into a hay-cart, and follows the cart home. "Good evening, mother." "Good evening, Hans. Where have you been?" "With Gretel." "What did you take her?" "Took nothing; had something given me." "What did Gretel give you?" "Gave me a needle." "Where is the needle, Hans?" "Stuck in the hay-cart." "That was ill done, Hans. You should have stuck the needle in your sleeve." "Never mind, I'll do better next time."

"Whither away, Hans?" "To Gretel, mother." "Behave well, Hans." "Oh, I'll behave well. Good-bye, mother." "Good-bye, Hans." Hans comes to Gretel. "Good day, Gretel." "Good day, Hans. What do you bring that is good?" "I bring nothing, I want to have something given me." Gretel presents Hans with a knife. "Good-bye, Gretel." "Good-bye, Hans." Hans takes the knife, sticks it in his sleeve, and goes home. "Good evening, mother." "Good evening, Hans. Where have you been?" "With Gretel." "What did you take her?" "Took her nothing, she gave me something." "What did Gretel give you?" "Gave me a knife." "Where is the knife, Hans?" "Stuck in my sleeve." "That's ill done, Hans, you should have put the knife in your pocket." "Never mind, will do better next time."

"Whither away, Hans?" "To Gretel, mother." "Behave well, Hans." "Oh, I'll behave well. Good-bye, mother." "Good-bye, Hans." Hans comes to Gretel. "Good day, Gretel." "Good day, Hans. What good thing do you bring?" "I bring nothing, I want something given me." Gretel presents Hans with a young goat. "Good-bye, Gretel." "Good-bye, Hans." Hans takes the goat, ties its legs, and puts it in his pocket. When he gets home it is suffocated. "Good evening, mother." "Good evening, Hans. Where have you been?" "With Gretel." "What did you take her?" "Took nothing, she gave me something." "What did Gretel give you?" "She gave me a goat." "Where is the goat, Hans?" "Put it in my pocket." "That was ill done, Hans, you should have put a rope round the goat's neck." "Never mind, will do better next time."

"Whither away, Hans?" "To Gretel, mother." "Behave well, Hans." "Oh, I'll behave well. Good-bye, mother." "Good-bye, Hans." Hans comes to Gretel. "Good day, Gretel." "Good day, Hans. What good thing do you bring?" "I bring nothing, I want something given me." Gretel presents Hans with a piece of bacon. "Good-bye, Gretel." "Good-bye, Hans."

Hans takes the bacon, ties it to a rope, and drags it away behind him. The dogs come and devour the bacon. When he gets home, he has the rope in his hand, and there is no longer anything hanging to it. "Good evening, mother." "Good evening, Hans. Where have you been?" "With Gretel." "What did you take her?" "I took her nothing, she gave me something." "What did Gretel give you?" "Gave me a bit of bacon." "Where is the bacon, Hans?" "I tied it to a rope, brought it home, dogs took it." "That was ill done, Hans, you should have carried the bacon on your head." "Never mind, will do better next time."

"Whither away, Hans?" "To Gretel, mother." "Behave well, Hans." "I'll behave well. Good-bye, mother." "Good-bye, Hans." Hans comes to Gretel. "Good day, Gretel." "Good day, Hans. What good thing do you bring?" "I bring nothing, but would have something given." Gretel presents Hans with a calf. "Good-bye, Gretel." "Good-bye, Hans."

Hans takes the calf, puts it on his head, and the calf kicks his face. "Good evening, mother." "Good evening, Hans. Where have you been?" "With Gretel." "What did you take her?" "I took nothing, but had something given me." "What did Gretel give you?" "A calf." "Where have you the calf, Hans?" "I set it on my head and it kicked my face." "That was ill done, Hans, you should have led the calf, and put it in the stall." "Never mind, will do better next time."

"Whither away, Hans?" "To Gretel, mother." "Behave well, Hans." "I'll behave well. Good-bye, mother." "Good-bye, Hans."

Hans comes to Gretel. "Good day, Gretel." "Good day, Hans. What good thing do you bring?" "I bring nothing, but would have something given." Gretel says to Hans: "I will go with you."

Hans takes Gretel, ties her to a rope, leads her to the rack, and binds her fast. Then Hans goes to his mother. "Good evening, mother." "Good evening, Hans. Where have you been?" "With Gretel." "What did you take her?" "I took her nothing." "What did Gretel give you?" "She gave me nothing, she came with me." "Where have you left Gretel?" "I led her by the rope, tied her to the rack, and scattered some grass for her." "That was ill done, Hans, you should have cast friendly eyes on her." "Never mind, will do better."

Hans went into the stable, cut out all the calves' and sheep's eyes, and threw them in Gretel's face. Then Gretel became angry, tore herself loose and ran away, and was no longer the bride of Hans.

THE THREE LANGUAGES

An aged count once lived in Switzerland, who had an only son, but he was stupid, and could learn nothing. Then said the father: "Hark you, my son, try as I will I can get nothing into your head. You must go from hence, I will give you into the care of a celebrated master, who shall see what he can do with you." The youth was sent into a strange town, and remained a whole year with the master. At the end of this time, he came home again, and his father asked: "Now, my son, what have you learnt?" "Father, I have learnt what the dogs say when they bark." "Lord have mercy on us!" cried the father; "is that all you have learnt? I will send you into another town, to another master." The youth was taken thither, and stayed a year with this master likewise. When he came back the father again asked: "My son, what have you learnt?" He answered: "Father, I have learnt what the birds say." Then the father fell into a rage and said: "Oh, you lost man, you have spent the precious time and learnt nothing; are you not ashamed to appear before my eyes? I will send you to a third master, but if you learn nothing this time also, I will no longer be your father." The youth remained a whole year with the third master also, and when he came home again, and his father inquired: "My son, what have you learnt?" he answered: "Dear father, I have this year learnt what the frogs croak." Then the father fell into the most furious anger, sprang up, called his people thither, and said: "This man is no longer my son, I drive him forth, and command you to take him out into the forest, and kill him." They took him forth, but when they should have killed him, they could not do it for pity, and let him go, and they cut the eyes and the tongue out of a deer that they might carry them to the old man as a token.

The youth wandered on, and after some time came to a fortress where he begged for a night's lodging. "Yes," said the lord of the castle, "if you will pass the night down there in the old tower, go thither; but I warn you, it is at the peril of your life, for it is full of wild dogs, which bark and howl without stopping, and at certain hours a man has to be given to them, whom they at once devour." The whole district was in sorrow and dismay because of them, and yet no one could do anything to stop this. The youth, however, was without fear, and said: "Just let me go down to the barking dogs, and give me something that I can throw to them; they will do nothing to harm me." As he himself would have it so, they gave him some food for the wild animals, and led him down to the tower. When he went inside, the dogs did not bark at him, but wagged their tails quite amicably around him, ate what he set before them, and did not hurt one hair of his head. Next morning, to the astonishment of everyone, he came out again safe and unharmed, and said to the lord of the castle: "The dogs have revealed to me, in their own language, why they dwell there, and bring evil on the land. They are bewitched, and are obliged to watch over a great treasure which is below in the tower, and they can have no rest until it is taken away, and I have likewise learnt, from their discourse, how that is to be done." Then all who heard this rejoiced, and the lord of the castle said he would adopt him as a son if he accomplished it successfully. He went down again, and as he knew what he had to do, he did it thoroughly, and brought a chest full of gold out with him. The howling of the wild dogs was henceforth heard no more; they had disappeared, and the country was freed from the trouble.

After some time he took it into his head that he would travel to Rome. On the way he passed by a marsh, in which a number of frogs were sitting croaking. He listened to them, and when he became aware of what they were saying, he grew very thoughtful and sad. At last he arrived in Rome, where the Pope had just died, and there was great doubt among the Cardinals as to whom they should appoint as his successor. They at length agreed that the person should be chosen as pope who should be distinguished by some divine and miraculous token. And just as that was decided on, the young count entered into the church, and suddenly two snow-white doves flew on his shoulders and remained sitting there. The ecclesiastics recognized therein the token from above, and asked him on the spot if he would be pope. He was undecided, and knew not if he were worthy of this, but the doves counselled him to do it, and at length he said yes. Then was he anointed and consecrated, and thus was fulfilled what he had heard from the frogs on his way, which had so affected him, that he was to be his Holiness the Pope. Then he had to sing a mass, and did not know one word of it, but the two doves sat continually on his shoulders, and said it all in his ear.

CLEVER ELSIE

There was once a man who had a daughter who was called Clever Elsie. And when she had grown up her father said: "We will get her married." "Yes," said the mother, "if only someone would come who would have her." At length a man came from a distance and wooed her, who was called Hans; but he stipulated that Clever Elsie should be really smart. "Oh," said the father, "she has plenty of good sense"; and the mother said: "Oh, she can see the wind coming up the street, and hear the flies coughing." "Well," said Hans, "if she is not really smart, I won't have her." When they were sitting at dinner and had eaten, the mother said: "Elsie, go into the cellar and fetch some beer." Then Clever Elsie took the pitcher from the wall, went into the cellar, and tapped the lid briskly as she went, so that the time might not appear long. When she was below she fetched herself a chair, and set it before the barrel so that she had no need to stoop, and did not hurt her back or do herself any unexpected injury. Then she placed the can before her, and turned the tap, and while the beer was running she would not let her eyes be idle, but looked up at the wall, and after much peering here and there, saw a pick-axe exactly above her, which the masons had accidentally left there.

Then Clever Elsie began to weep and said: "If I get Hans, and we have a child, and he grows big, and we send him into the cellar here to draw beer, then the pick-axe will fall on his head and kill him." Then she sat and wept and screamed with all the strength of her body, over the misfortune which lay before her. Those upstairs waited for the drink, but Clever Elsie still did not come. Then the woman said to the servant: "Just go down into the cellar and see where Elsie is." The maid went and found her sitting in front of the barrel, screaming loudly. "Elsie, why do you weep?" asked the maid. "Ah," she answered, "have I not reason to weep? If I get Hans, and we have a child, and he grows big, and has to draw beer here, the pick-axe will perhaps fall on his head, and kill him." Then said the maid: "What a clever Elsie we have!" and sat down beside her and began loudly to weep over the misfortune. After a while, as the maid did not come back, and those upstairs were thirsty for the beer, the man said to the boy: "Just go down into the cellar and see where Elsie and the girl are." The boy went down, and there sat Clever Elsie and the girl both weeping together. Then he asked: "Why are you weeping?" "Ah," said Elsie, "have I not reason to weep? If I get Hans, and we have a child, and he grows big, and has to draw beer here, the pick-axe will fall on his head and kill him." Then said the boy: "What a clever Elsie we have!" and sat down by her, and likewise began to howl loudly. Upstairs they waited for the boy, but as he still did not return, the man said to the woman: "Just go down into the cellar and see where Elsie is!" The woman went down, and found all three in the midst of their lamentations, and inquired what was the cause; then Elsie told her also that her future child was to be killed by the pick-axe, when it grew big and had to draw beer, and the pick-axe fell down. Then said the mother likewise: "What a clever Elsie we have!" and sat down and wept with them. The man upstairs waited a short time, but as his wife did not come back and his thirst grew ever greater, he said: "I must go into the cellar myself and see where Elsie is." But when he got into the cellar, and they were all sitting together crying, and he heard the reason, and that Elsie's child was the cause, and that Elsie might perhaps bring one into the world some day, and that he might be killed by the pick-axe, if he should happen to be sitting beneath it, drawing beer just at the very time when it fell down, he cried: "Oh, what a clever Elsie!" and sat down, and likewise wept with them. The bridegroom stayed upstairs alone for a long time; then as no one would come back he thought: "They must be waiting for me below: I too must go there and see what they are about." When he got down, the five of them were sitting screaming and lamenting quite piteously, each out-doing the other. "What misfortune has happened then?" asked he. "Ah, dear Hans," said Elsie, "if we marry each other and have a child, and he is big, and we perhaps send him here to draw something to drink, then the pick-axe which has been left up there might dash his brains out if it were to fall down, so have we not reason to weep?" "Come," said Hans, "more understanding than that is not needed for my household, as you are such a clever Elsie, I will have you," and he seized her hand, took her upstairs with him, and married her.

After Hans had had her some time, he said: "Wife, I am going out to work and earn some money for us; go into the field and cut the corn that we may have some bread." "Yes, dear Hans, I will do that." After Hans had gone away, she cooked herself some good broth and took it into the field with her. When she came to the field she said to herself: "What shall I do; shall I cut first, or shall I eat first? Oh, I will eat first." Then she drank her cup of broth, and when she was fully satisfied, she once more said: "What shall I do? Shall I cut first, or shall I sleep first? I will sleep first." Then she lay down among the corn and fell asleep. Hans had been at home for a long time, but Elsie did not come; then said he: "What a clever Elsie I have; she is so industrious that she does not even come home to eat." But when evening came and she still stayed away, Hans went out to see what she had cut, but nothing was cut, and she was lying among the corn asleep. Then Hans hastened home and brought a fowler's net with little bells and hung it round about her, and she still went on sleeping. Then he ran home, shut the house-door, and sat down in his chair and worked. At length, when it was quite dark, Clever Elsie awoke and when she got up there was a jingling all round about her, and the bells rang at each step which she took. Then she was alarmed, and became uncertain whether she really was Clever Elsie or not, and said: "Is it I, or is it not I?" But she knew not what answer to make to this, and stood for a time in doubt; at length she thought: "I will go home and ask if it be I, or if it be not I, they will be sure to know." She ran to the door of her own house, but it was shut; then she knocked at the window and cried: "Hans, is Elsie within?" "Yes," answered Hans, "she is within." Hereupon she was terrified, and said: "Ah, heavens! Then it is not I," and went to another door; but when the people heard the jingling of the bells they would not open it, and she could get in nowhere. Then she ran out of the village, and no one has seen her since.

THE TAILOR IN HEAVEN

One very fine day it came to pass that the good God wished to enjoy himself in the heavenly garden, and took all the apostles and saints with him, so that no one stayed in Heaven but Saint Peter. The Lord had commanded him to let no one in during his absence, so Peter stood by the door and kept watch. Before long someone knocked. Peter asked who was there, and what he wanted? "I am a poor, honest tailor who prays for admission," replied a smooth voice. "Honest indeed," said Peter, "like the thief on the gallows! You have been light-fingered and have snipped folks' clothes away. You will not get into Heaven. The Lord has forbidden me to let anyone in while he is out." "Come, do be merciful," cried the tailor. "Little scraps which fall off the table of their own accord are not stolen, and are not worth speaking about. Look, I am lame, and have blisters on my feet from walking here, I cannot possibly turn back again. Just let me in, and I will do all the dirty work. I will carry the children, and wash their clothes, and scrub and clean the benches on which they have been playing, and patch all their torn frocks." Saint Peter let himself be moved by pity, and opened the door of Heaven just wide enough for the lame tailor to slip his lean body in. He was forced to sit down in a corner behind the door, and told to stay quietly and peaceably there, in order that the Lord, when he returned, might not observe him and be angry. The tailor obeyed, but once when Saint Peter went outside the door, he got up, and full of curiosity, peeped into every corner of Heaven, and inspected the arrangement of the whole place. At length he came to a spot where many beautiful and precious chairs were standing, and in the midst was a seat all of gold which was set with shining jewels. Likewise it was much higher than the other chairs, and a footstool of gold was before it. It was the seat, however, on which the Lord

sat when he was at home, and from which he could see all that happened on earth. The tailor stood still, and looked at the seat for a long time, for it pleased him better than all else. At last he could master his curiosity no longer, and climbed up and seated himself in the chair. Then he saw everything which was happening on earth, and observed an ugly old woman who was standing washing by the side of a stream, secretly laying two veils on one side for herself. The sight of this made the tailor so angry that he laid hold of the golden footstool, and threw it down to earth through Heaven, at the old thief. But since he could not bring the stool back again, he slipped quietly out of the chair, seated himself in his place behind the door, and behaved as if the had never stirred from the spot.

When the Lord and master returned again with his heavenly companions, he did not see the tailor behind the door, but when he seated himself on his chair the footstool was missing. He asked Saint Peter what had become of the stool, but he did not know. Then he asked if he had let anyone come in. "I know of no one who has been here," answered Peter, "but a lame tailor, who is still sitting behind the door." Then the Lord had the tailor brought before him, and asked him if he had taken away the stool, and where he had put it. "Oh, Lord," answered the tailor joyously, "I threw it in my anger down to earth at an old woman whom I saw stealing two veils at the washing." "Oh, you knave," said the Lord, "were I to judge as you judge, how do you think you could have escaped so long? I should long ago have had no chairs, benches, seats, nay, not even an oven-fork, but should have thrown everything down at the sinners. Henceforth you can stay no longer in Heaven, but must go outside the door again. Then go where you will. No one shall give punishment here, but I alone, the Lord."

Peter was obliged to take the tailor out of heaven again, and as he had torn shoes, and feet covered with blisters, he took a stick in his hand, and went to "Wait-a-while," where the good soldiers sit and make merry.

THE WISHING-TABLE, THE GOLD-ASS, AND THE CUDGEL IN THE SACK

There was once upon a time a tailor who had three sons, and only one goat. But as the goat supported all of them with her milk, she was obliged to have good food, and to be taken every day to pasture. The sons did this, in turn. Once the eldest took her to the churchyard, where the finest herbs were to be found, and let her eat and run about there. At night when it was time to go home he asked: "Goat, have you had enough?" The goat answered:

"I have eaten so much,
Not a leaf more I'll touch, meh! meh!"

"Come home, then," said the youth, and took hold of the cord round her neck, led her into the stable and tied her up securely. "Well," said the old tailor, "has the goat had as much food as she ought?" "Oh," answered the son, "she has eaten so much, not a leaf more she'll touch." But the father wished to satisfy himself, and went down to the stable, stroked the dear animal and asked: "Goat, are you satisfied?" The goat answered:

> "How should I be satisfied?
> Among the ditches I leapt about,
> Found no leaf, so went without, meh! meh!"

"What do I hear?" cried the tailor, and ran upstairs and said to the youth: "Hi, you liar; you said the goat had had enough, and have let her hunger!" and in his anger he took the yard-measure from the wall, and drove him out with blows.

Next day it was the turn of the second son, who sought a place in the fence of the garden, where nothing but good herbs grew, and the goat gobbled them all up. At night when he wanted to go home, he asked: "Goat, are you satisfied?" The goat answered:

> "I have eaten so much,
> Not a leaf more I'll touch, meh! meh!"

"Come home, then," said the youth, and led her home, and tied her up in the stable. "Well," said the old tailor, "has the goat had as much food as she ought?" "Oh," answered the son, "she has eaten so much, not a leaf more she'll touch." The tailor would not rely on this, but went down to the stable and said: "Goat, have you had enough?" The goat answered:

> "How should I be satisfied?
> Among the ditches I leapt about,
> Found no leaf, so went without, meh! meh!"

"The godless wretch!" cried the tailor, "to let such a good animal hunger," and he ran up and drove the youth out of doors with the yard-measure.

Now came the turn of the third son, who wanted to do his duty well, and sought out some bushes with the finest leaves, and let the goat devour them. In the evening when he wanted to go home, he asked: "Goat, have you had enough?" The goat answered:

"I have eaten so much,
Not a leaf more I'll touch, meh! meh!"

"Come home, then," said the youth, and led her into the stable, and tied her up. "Well," said the old tailor, "has the goat had her full share of food?" "She has eaten so much, not a leaf more she'll touch." The tailor was distrustful, went down and asked: "Goat, have you had enough?" The wicked beast answered:

"How should I be satisfied?
Among the ditches I leapt about,
Found no leaf, so went without, meh! meh!"

"Oh, the brood of liars!" cried the tailor, "each as wicked and forgetful of his duty as the other! You shall no longer make a fool of me," and, quite beside himself with anger, he ran upstairs and belaboured the poor young fellow so vigorously with the yard-measure that he sprang out of the house.

The old tailor was now alone with his goat. Next morning he went down into the stable, stroked the goat and said: "Come, my dear little animal, I myself will take you to feed." He took her by the rope and conducted her to green hedges, and amongst milfoil, and whatever else goats like to eat. "There you may for once eat to your heart's content," said he to her, and let her browse till evening. Then he asked: "Goat, are you satisfied?" she replied:

"I have eaten so much,
Not a leaf more I'll touch, meh! meh!"

"Come home, then," said the tailor, and led her into the stable, and tied her fast. When he was going away, he turned round again and said: "Well, are you satisfied for once?" But the goat behaved no better to him, and cried:

"How should I be satisfied?
Among the ditches I leapt about,
Found no leaf, so went without, meh! meh!"

When the tailor heard that, he was shocked, and saw clearly that he had driven away his three sons without cause. "Wait, you ungrateful creature," cried he, "it is not enough to drive you forth, I will brand you so that you will no more dare to show yourself amongst honest tailors." In great haste he ran upstairs, fetched his razor, lathered the goat's head, and shaved her as clean as the palm of his hand. And as the yard-measure would have been too good for her, he brought the horsewhip, and gave her such cuts with it that she bounded away with tremendous leaps.

When the tailor was thus left quite alone in his house he fell into great grief, and would gladly have had his sons back again, but no one knew whither they were gone. The eldest had apprenticed himself to a joiner, and learnt industriously and indefatigably, and when the time came for him to go travelling, his master presented him with a little table which was not particularly beautiful, and was made of common wood, but which had one good property; if anyone set it out, and said: "Little table, spread yourself," the good little table was at once covered with a clean little cloth, and a plate was there, and a knife and fork beside it, and dishes with boiled meats and roasted meats, as many as there was room for, and a great glass of red wine shone so that it made the heart glad. The young journeyman thought: "With this you have enough for your whole life," and went joyously about the world and never troubled himself at all whether an inn was good or bad, or if anything was to be found in it or not. When it suited him he did not enter an inn at all, but either on the plain, in a wood, a meadow, or wherever he fancied, he took his little table off his back, set it down before him, and said: "Spread yourself," and then everything appeared that his heart desired. At length he took it into his head to go back to his father, whose anger would now be appeased, and who would now willingly receive him with his magic table. It came to pass that on his way home, he came one evening to an inn which was filled with guests. They bade him welcome, and invited him to sit and eat with them, for otherwise he would have difficulty in getting anything.

"No," answered the joiner, "I will not take the few morsels out of your mouths; rather than that, you shall be my guests." They laughed, and thought he was jesting with them; he but placed his wooden table in the middle of the room, and said, "Little table, spread yourself." Instantly it was covered with food, so good that the host could never have procured it, and the smell of it ascended pleasantly to the nostrils of the guests. "Fall to, dear friends," said the joiner; and the guests when they saw that he meant it, did not need to be asked twice, but drew near, pulled out their knives and attacked it valiantly. And what surprised them the most was that when a dish became empty, a full one instantly took its place of its own accord. The innkeeper stood in one corner and watched the affair; he did not at all know what to say, but thought: "You could easily find a use for such a cook as that in your household." The joiner and his comrades made merry until late into the night; at length they lay down to sleep, and the young apprentice also went to bed, and set his magic table against the wall. The host's thoughts, however, let him have no rest; it occurred to him that there was a little old table in his lumber-room, which looked just like the apprentice's, and he brought it out, and carefully exchanged it for the wishing table. Next morning, the joiner paid for his bed, took up his table, never thinking that he had got a false one, and went his way. At mid-day he reached his father, who received him with great joy. "Well, my dear son, what have you learnt?" said he to him. "Father, I have become a joiner."

"A good trade," replied the old man; "but what have you brought back with you from your apprenticeship?" "Father, the best thing which I have brought back with me is this little table." The tailor inspected it on all sides and said: "You did not make a masterpiece when you made that; it is a bad old table." "But it is a table which furnishes itself," replied the son. "When I set it out, and tell it to spread itself, the most beautiful dishes stand on it, and a wine also, which gladdens the heart. Just invite all our relations and friends, they shall refresh and enjoy themselves for once, for the table will give them all they require." When the company was assembled, he put his table in the middle of the room and said: "Little table, spread yourself," but the little table did not bestir itself, and remained just as bare as any other table which does not understand language. Then the poor apprentice became aware that his table had been changed, and was ashamed at having to stand there like a liar. The relations, however, mocked him, and were forced to go home without having eaten or drunk. The father brought out his patches again, and went on tailoring, but the son went to a master in the craft.

The second son had gone to a miller and had apprenticed himself to him. When his years were over, the master said: "As you have conducted yourself so well, I give you an ass of a peculiar kind, which neither draws a cart nor carries a sack." "What good is he, then?" asked the young apprentice. "He spews forth gold," answered the miller. "If you set him on a cloth and say 'Bricklebrit', the good animal will spew forth gold pieces for you from back and front." "That is a fine thing," said the apprentice, and thanked the master, and went out into the world. When he had need of gold, he had only to say "Bricklebrit" to his ass, and it rained gold pieces, and he had nothing to do but pick them off the ground. Wheresoever he went, the best of everything was good enough for him, and the dearer the better, for he had always a full purse. When he had looked about the world for some time, he thought: "You must seek out your father. If you go to him with the gold-ass he will forget his anger, and receive you well." It came to pass that he came to the same inn in which his brother's table had been exchanged. He led his ass by the bridle, and the host was about to take the animal from him and tie him up, but the young apprentice said: "Don't trouble yourself, I will take my grey horse into the stable, and tie him up myself too, for I must know where he stands." This struck the host as odd, and he thought that a man who was forced to look after his ass himself, could not have much to spend; but when the stranger put his hand in his pocket and brought out two gold pieces, and said he was to provide something good for him, the host opened his eyes wide, and ran and sought out the best he could muster. After dinner the guest asked what he owed. The host did not see why he should not double the reckoning, and said the apprentice must give two more gold pieces. He felt in his pocket, but his gold was just at an end. "Wait an instant, sir host," said he, "I will go and fetch some money"; but he took the table-cloth with him. The host could not imagine what this could mean, and being curious, stole after him, and as the guest bolted the stable door, he peeped through a hole left by a knot in the wood. The stranger spread out the cloth under the animal and cried: "Bricklebrit," and immediately the beast began to let gold pieces fall from back and front, so that it fairly rained down money on the ground. "Eh, my word," said the host, "ducats are quickly coined there! A purse like that is not to be sniffed at!" The guest paid his score, and went to bed, but in the night the host stole down into the stable, led away the master of the mint, and tied up another ass in his place.

Early next morning the apprentice travelled away with his ass, and thought that he had his gold-ass. At mid-day he reached his father, who rejoiced to see him again, and gladly took him in. "What have you made of yourself, my son?" asked the old man. "A miller, dear father," he answered. "What have you brought back with you from your travels?" "Nothing else but an ass." "There are asses enough here," said the father, "I would rather have had a good goat." "Yes," replied the son, "but it is no common ass, but a gold-ass, when I say 'Bricklebrit', the good beast spews forth a whole sheetful of gold pieces. Just summon all our relations hither, and I will make them rich folks." "That suits me well," said the tailor, "for then I shall have no need to torment myself any longer with the needle," and ran out himself and called the relations together. As soon as they were assembled, the miller bade them make way, spread out his cloth, and brought the ass into the room. "Now watch," said he, and cried: "Bricklebrit," but what fell were not gold pieces, and it was clear that the animal knew nothing of the art, for every ass does not attain such perfection. Then the poor miller pulled a long face, saw that he was betrayed, and begged pardon of the relatives, who went home as poor as they came. There was no help for it, the old man had to betake him to his needle once more, and the youth hired himself to a miller.

The third brother had apprenticed himself to a turner, and as that is skilled labor, he was the longest in learning. His brothers, however, told him in a letter how badly things had gone with them, and how the innkeeper had cheated them of their beautiful wishing-gifts on the last evening before they reached home. When the turner had served his time, and had to set out on his travels, as he had conducted himself so well, his master presented him with a sack and said: "There is a cudgel in it." "I can put on the sack," said he, "and it may be of good service to me, but why should the cudgel be in it? It only makes it heavy." "I will tell you why," replied the master; "if anyone has done anything to injure you, do but say 'Out of the sack, Cudgel!' and the cudgel will leap forth among the people, and play such a dance on their backs that they will not be able to stir or move for a week, and it will not leave off until you say, 'Into the sack, Cudgel!'" The apprentice thanked him, put the sack on his back, and when anyone came too near him, and wished to attack him, he said: "Out of the sack, Cudgel!" and instantly the cudgel sprang out, and dusted the coat or jacket of one after the other on their backs, and never stopped until it had stripped it off them, and it was done so quickly, that before anyone was aware, it was already his own turn. In the evening the young turner reached the inn where his brothers had been cheated. He laid his sack on the table before him, and began to talk of all the wonderful things which he had seen in the world. "Yes," said he, "people may easily find a table which

will spread itself, a gold-ass, and things of that kind—extremely good things which I by no means despise—but these are nothing in comparison with the treasure which I have won for myself, and am carrying about with me in my sack there." The innkeeper pricked up his ears. "What in the world can that be?" thought he; "the sack must be filled with nothing but jewels; I ought to get them cheap too, for all good things go in threes." When it was time for sleep, the guest stretched himself on the bench, and laid his sack beneath him for a pillow. When the innkeeper thought his guest was lying in a sound sleep, he went to him and pushed and pulled quite gently and carefully at the sack to see if he could possibly draw it away and lay another in its place. The turner, however, had been waiting for this for a long time, and now just as the innkeeper was about to give a hearty tug, he cried: "Out of the sack, Cudgel!" Instantly the little cudgel came forth, and fell on the innkeeper, and gave him a sound thrashing.

The host cried for mercy; but the louder he cried, the harder the cudgel beat the time on his back, until at length he fell to the ground exhausted. Then the turner said: "If you do not give back the table which spreads itself, and the gold-ass, the dance shall begin afresh." "Oh, no," cried the host, quite humbly, "I will gladly produce everything, only make the accursed kobold creep back into the sack." Then said the apprentice: "I will let mercy take the place of justice, but beware of getting into mischief again!" So he cried: "Into the sack, Cudgel!" and let him have rest.

Next morning the turner went home to his father with the wishing-table, and the gold-ass. The tailor rejoiced when he saw him once more, and asked him likewise what he had learned in foreign parts. "Dear father," said he, "I have become a turner." "A skilled trade," said the father. "What have you brought back with you from your travels?"

"A precious thing, dear father," replied the son, "a cudgel in the sack."

"What!" cried the father, "a cudgel! That's certainly worth your trouble! From every tree you can cut yourself one." "But not one like this, dear father. If I say 'Out of the sack, Cudgel!' the cudgel springs out and leads anyone ill-disposed toward me a weary dance, and never stops until he lies on the ground and prays for fair weather. Look you, with this cudgel have I rescued the wishing-table and the gold-ass which the thievish innkeeper took away from my brothers. Now let them both be sent for, and invite all our kinsmen. I will give them to eat and to drink, and will fill their pockets with gold into the bargain." The old tailor had not much confidence; nevertheless he summoned the relatives together. Then the turner spread a cloth in the room and led in the gold-ass, and said to his brother: "Now, dear brother, speak to him." The miller said: "Bricklebrit," and instantly the gold pieces rained down on the cloth like a thunder-shower, and the ass did not stop until every one of them had so much that he could carry no more. (I can see by your face that you also would have liked to be there.)

Then the turner brought the little table, and said: "Now, dear brother, speak to it." And scarcely had the carpenter said: "Table, spread yourself," than it was spread and amply covered with the most exquisite dishes. Then such a meal took place as the good tailor had never yet known in his house, and the whole party of kinsmen stayed together till far in the night, and were all merry and glad. The tailor locked away needle and thread, yard-measure and goose, in a closet, and lived with his three sons in joy and splendour.

What, however, happened to the goat who was to blame for the tailor driving out his three sons? That I will tell you. She was ashamed that she had a bald head, and ran to a fox's hole and crept into it. When the fox came home, he was met by two great eyes shining out of the darkness, and was terrified and ran away. A bear met him, and as the fox looked quite disturbed, he said: "What is the matter with you, brother Fox, why do you look like that?" "Ah," answered Redskin, "a fierce beast is in my cave and stared at me with its fiery eyes." "We will soon drive him out," said the bear, and went with him to the cave and looked in, but when he saw the fiery eyes, fear seized on him likewise; he would have nothing to do with the furious beast, and took to his heels. The bee met him, and as she saw that he was ill at ease, she said: "Bear, you are really pulling a very pitiful face; what has become of all your gaiety?" "It is all very well for you to talk," replied the bear, "a furious beast with staring eyes is in Redskin's house, and we can't drive him out." The bee said: "Bear, I pity you, I am a poor weak creature whom you would not turn aside to look at, but still, I believe, I can help you." She flew into the fox's cave, lighted on the goat's smoothly-shorn head, and stung her so violently, that she sprang up, crying

"Meh, meh," and ran forth into the world as if mad, and to this hour no one knows where she has gone.

THUMBLING

There was once a poor peasant who sat in the evening by the hearth and poked the fire, and his wife sat and spun. Then said he: "How sad it is that we have no children! With us all is so quiet, and in other houses it is noisy and lively."

"Yes," replied the wife, and sighed, "even if we had only one, and it were quite small, and only as big as a thumb, I should be quite satisfied, and we would still love it with all our hearts." Now it so happened that the woman fell ill, and after seven months, gave birth to a child, that was perfect in all its limbs, but no longer than a thumb. Then said they; "It is as we wished it to be, and it shall be our dear child"; and because of its size, they called it Thumbling. Though they did not let it want for food, the child did not grow taller, but remained as it had been at the first. Nevertheless it looked sensibly out of its eyes, and soon showed itself to be a wise and nimble creature, for everything it did turned out well.

One day the peasant was getting ready to go into the forest to cut wood, when he said as if to himself: "How I wish that there was someone who would bring the cart to me!" "Oh, father," cried Thumbling, "I will soon bring the cart, rely on that; it shall be in the forest at the appointed time." The man smiled and said: "How can that be done, you are far too small to lead the horse by the reins?" "That's of no consequence, father, if my mother will only harness it, I will sit in the horse's ear, and call out to him how he is to go." "Well," answered the man, "for once we will try it."

When the time came, the mother harnessed the horse, and placed Thumbling in its ear, and then the little creature cried "Gee up, gee up!"

Then it went quite properly as if with its master, and the cart went the right way into the forest. It so happened that just as he was turning a corner, and the little one was crying "Gee up," two strange men came towards him. "My word!" said one of them. "What is this? There is a cart coming, and a driver is calling to the horse, and still he is not to be seen!" "That can't be right," said the other, "we will follow the cart and see where it stops." The cart, however, drove right into the forest, and exactly to the place where the wood had been cut. When Thumbling saw his father, he cried to him: "Do you see, father, here I am with the cart; now take me down." The

father got hold of the horse with his left hand, and with the right took his little son out of the ear. Thumbling sat down quite merrily on a straw, but when the two strange men saw him, they did not know what to say for astonishment. Then one of them took the other aside and said: "Listen, the little fellow would make our fortune if we exhibited him in a large town, for money. We will buy him." They went to the peasant and said: "Sell us the little man. He shall be well treated with us." "No," replied the father, "he is the apple of my eye, and all the money in the world cannot buy him from me." Thumbling, however, when he heard of the bargain, had crept up the folds of his father's coat, placed himself on his shoulder, and whispered in his ear: "Father, do give me away, I will soon come back again." Then the father parted with him to the two men for a handsome sum of money. "Where will you sit?" they said to him. "Oh, just set me on the rim of your hat, and then I can walk backwards and forwards and look at the country, and still not fall down." They did as he wished, and when Thumbling had taken leave of his father, they went away with him. They walked until it was dusk, and then the little fellow said: "Do take me down, it is necessary." "Just stay up there," said the man on whose hat he sat, "it makes no difference to me. The birds sometimes let things fall on me." "No," said Thumbling, "I know what's manners; take me quickly down." The man took his hat off, and put the little fellow on the ground by the wayside, and he leapt and crept about a little between the sods, and then he suddenly slipped into a mousehole which he had sought out. "Good evening, gentlemen, just go home without me," he cried to them, and mocked them. They ran thither and stuck their sticks into the mouse-hole, but it was all in vain. Thumbling crept still farther in, and as it soon became quite dark, they were forced to go home with their vexation and their empty purses.

When Thumbling saw that they were gone, he crept back out of the subterranean passage. "It is so dangerous to walk on the ground in the dark," said he; "how easily a neck or a leg is broken!" Fortunately he stumbled against an empty snail-shell. "Thank God!" said he. "In that I can pass the night in safety," and got into it. Not long afterwards, when he was just going to sleep, he heard two men go by, and one of them was saying: "How shall we set about getting hold of the rich pastor's silver and gold?" "I could tell you that," cried Thumbling, interrupting them. "What was that?" said one of the thieves in a fright, "I heard someone speaking." They stood still listening, and Thumbling spoke again, and said: "Take me with you, and I'll help you."

"But where are you?" "Just look on the ground, and observe from whence my voice comes," he replied. There the thieves at length found him, and lifted him up. "You little imp, how will you help us?" they said. "Listen," said he, "I will creep into the pastor's room through the iron bars, and will reach out to you whatever you want to have." "Come then," they said, "and we will see what you can do." When they got to the pastor's house, Thumbling crept into the room, but instantly cried out with all his might: "Do you want to have everything that is here?" The thieves were alarmed, and said: "But do speak softly, so as not to waken any one!" Thumbling, however, behaved as if he had not understood this, and cried again: "What do you want? Do you want to have everything that is here?" The cook, who slept in the next room, heard this and sat up in bed, and listened. The thieves, however, had in their fright run some distance away, but at last they took courage, and thought: "The little rascal wants to mock us." They came back and whispered to him: "Come, be serious, and reach something out to us." Then Thumbling again cried as loudly as he could: "I really will give you everything, just put your hands in." The maid who was listening, heard this quite distinctly, and jumped out of bed and rushed to the door. The thieves took flight, and ran as if the Wild Huntsman were behind them, but as the maid could not see anything, she went to strike a light. When she came to the place with it, Thumbling, unperceived, betook himself to the granary, and the maid, after she had examined every corner and found nothing, lay down in her bed again, and believed that, after all, she had only been dreaming with open eyes and ears.

Thumbling had climbed up among the hay and found a beautiful place to sleep in; there he intended to rest until day, and then go home again to his parents. But there were other things in store for him. Truly, there is much worry and affliction in this world! When day dawned, the maid arose from her bed to feed the cows. Her first walk was into the barn, where she laid hold of an armful of hay, and precisely that very one in which poor Thumbling was lying asleep. He, however, was sleeping so soundly that he was aware of nothing, and did not awake until he was in the mouth of the cow, who had picked him up with the hay. "Ah, heavens!" cried he, "how have I got into the fulling mill?" but he soon discovered where he was. Then he had to take care not to let himself go between the teeth and be dismembered, but he was subsequently forced to slip down into the stomach with the hay. "In this little room the windows are forgotten," said he, "and no sun shines in, neither will a candle be brought." His quarters were especially unpleasing to him, and the worst was that more and more hay was always coming in by the door, and the space grew less and less. Then, at length in his anguish, he cried as loud as he could: "Bring me no more fodder, bring me no more fodder." The maid was just milking the cow, and when she heard some one speaking, and saw no one, and perceived that it was the same voice that she had heard in the night, she was so terrified that she slipped off her stool, and spilt the milk. She ran in the greatest haste to her master, and said: "Oh, heavens, pastor, the cow has been speaking!" "You are mad," replied the pastor; but he went himself to the byre to see what was there. Hardly, however, had he set his foot inside when Thumbling again cried: "Bring me no more fodder, bring me no more fodder." Then the pastor himself was alarmed, and thought that an evil spirit had gone into the cow, and ordered her to be killed. She was killed, but the stomach, in which

Thumbling was, thrown on the dunghill. Thumbling had great difficulty in working his way out; however, he succeeded so far as to get some room, but, just as he was going to thrust his head out, a new misfortune occurred. A hungry wolf ran thither, and swallowed the whole stomach at one gulp. Thumbling did not lose courage. "Perhaps," thought he, "the wolf will listen to what I have got to say," and he called to him from out of his belly: "Dear wolf, I know of a magnificent feast for you."

"Where is it to be had?" said the wolf.

"In such and such a house; you must creep into it through the kitchen-sink, and will find cakes, and bacon, and sausages, and as much of them as you can eat," and he described to him exactly his father's house. The wolf did not require to be told this twice, squeezed himself in at night through the sink, and ate to his heart's content in the larder. When he had eaten his fill, he wanted to go out again, but he had become so big that he could not go out by the same way. Thumbling had reckoned on this, and now began to make a violent noise in the wolf's body, and raged and screamed as loudly as he could. "Will you be quiet," said the wolf, "you will waken up the people!" "What do I care!" replied the little fellow, "you have eaten your fill, and I will make merry likewise," and began once more to scream with all his strength. At last his father and mother were aroused by it, and ran to the room and looked in through the opening in the door. When they saw that a wolf was inside, they ran away, and the husband fetched his axe, and the wife the scythe. "Stay behind," said the man, when they entered the room. "When I have given him a blow, if he is not killed by it, you must cut him down and hew his body to pieces." Then Thumbling heard his parents' voices, and cried: "Dear father, I am here; I am in the wolf's body." Said the father, full of joy: "Thank God, our dear child has found us again," and bade the woman take away her scythe, that Thumbling might not be hurt with it. After that he raised his arm, and struck the wolf such a blow on his head that he fell down dead, and then they got knives and scissors and cut his body open, and drew the little fellow forth. "Ah," said the father, "what sorrow we have gone through for your sake." "Yes, father, I have gone about the world a great deal, Thank heaven, I breathe fresh air again!" "Where have you been, then?" "Ah, father, I have been in a mouse's hole, in a cow's belly, and then in a wolf's paunch; now I will stay with you." "And we will not sell you again, no, not for all the riches in the world," said his parents, and they embraced and kissed their dear Thumbling. They gave him to eat and to drink, and had some new clothes made for him, for his own had been spoiled on his journey.

THE WEDDING OF MRS. FOX

FIRST STORY

There was once upon a time an old fox with nine tails, who believed that his wife was not faithful to him, and wished to put her to the test. He stretched himself out under the bench, did not move a limb, and behaved as if he were stone dead. Mrs. Fox went up to her room, shut herself in, and her maid, Miss Cat, sat by the fire, and did the cooking. When it became known that the old fox was dead, suitors presented themselves. The maid heard someone standing at the house-door, knocking. She went and opened it, and it was a young fox, who said:

> "What may you be about, Miss Cat?
> Do you sleep or do you wake?"

She answered:

> "I am not sleeping, I am waking,
> Would you know what I am making?
> I am boiling warm beer with butter,
> Will you be my guest for supper?"

"No, thank you, miss," said the fox, "what is Mrs. Fox doing?" The maid replied:

> "She is sitting in her room,
> Moaning in her gloom,
> Weeping her little eyes quite red,
> Because old Mr. Fox is dead."

"Do just tell her, miss, that a young fox is here, who would like to woo her." "Certainly, young sir."

> The cat goes up the stairs trip, trap,
> The door she knocks at tap, tap, tap,
> "Mistress Fox, are you inside?"
> "Oh, yes, my little cat," she cried.
> "A wooer he stands at the door out there."
> "What does he look like, my dear?"

"Has he nine as beautiful tails as the late Mr. Fox?" "Oh, no," answered the cat, "he has only one." "Then I will not have him."

Miss Cat went downstairs and sent the wooer away. Soon afterwards there was another knock, and another fox was at the door who wished to woo Mrs. Fox. He had two tails, but he did not fare better than the first. After this still more came, each with one tail more than the other, but they were all turned away, until at last one came who had nine tails, like old Mr. Fox. When the widow heard that, she said joyfully to the cat:

> "Now open the gates and doors all wide,
> And carry old Mr. Fox outside."

But just as the wedding was going to be solemnized, old Mr. Fox stirred under the bench, and cudgeled all the rabble, and drove them and Mrs. Fox out of the house.

SECOND STORY

When old Mr. Fox was dead, the wolf came as a suitor, and knocked at the door, and the cat who was servant to Mrs. Fox, opened it for him. The wolf greeted her, and said:

"Good day, Mrs. Cat of Kehrewit,
How comes it that alone you sit?
What are you making good?"

The cat replied:

"In milk I'm breaking bread so sweet,
Will you be my guest, and eat?"

"No, thank you, Mrs. Cat," answered the wolf. "Is Mrs. Fox not at home?"

The cat said:

"She sits upstairs in her room,
Bewailing her sorrowful doom,
Bewailing her trouble so sore,
For old Mr. Fox is no more."

The wolf answered:

"If she's in want of a husband now,
Then will it please her to step below?"
The cat runs quickly up the stair,
And lets her tail fly here and there,
Until she comes to the parlour door.
With her five gold rings at the door she knocks:
"Are you within, good Mistress Fox?
If you're in want of a husband now,
Then will it please you to step below?"

Mrs. Fox asked: "Has the gentleman red stockings on, and has he a pointed mouth?" "No," answered the cat. "Then he won't do for me."

When the wolf was gone, came a dog, a stag, a hare, a bear, a lion, and all the beasts of the forest, one after the other. But one of the good qualities which old Mr. Fox had possessed, was always lacking, and the cat had continually to send the suitors away. At length came a young fox. Then Mrs. Fox said: "Has the gentleman red stockings on, and has he a little pointed mouth?" "Yes," said the cat, "he has." "Then let him come upstairs," said Mrs. Fox, and ordered the servant to prepare the wedding feast.

> "Sweep me the room as clean as you can,
> Up with the window, fling out my old man!
> For many a fine fat mouse he brought,
> Yet of his wife he never thought,
> But ate up every one he caught."

Then the wedding was solemnized with young Mr. Fox, and there was much rejoicing and dancing; and if they have not left off, they are dancing still.

THE ELVES

FIRST STORY

A shoemaker, by no fault of his own, had become so poor that at last he had nothing left but leather for one pair of shoes. So in the evening, he cut out the shoes which he wished to begin to make the next morning, and as he had a good conscience, he lay down quietly in his bed, commended himself to God, and fell asleep. In the morning, after he had said his prayers, and was just going to sit down to work, the two shoes stood quite finished on his table. He was astounded, and knew not what to think. He took the shoes in his hands to observe them closer, and they were so neatly made, with not one bad stitch in them, that it was just as if they were intended as a masterpiece. Before long, a buyer came in, and as the shoes pleased him so well, he paid more for them than was customary, and, with the money, the shoemaker was able to purchase leather for two pairs of shoes. He cut them out at night, and next morning was about to set to work with fresh courage; but he had no need to do so, for, when he got up, they were already made, and buyers also were not wanting, who gave him money enough to buy leather for four pairs of shoes. Again the following morning he found the four pairs made; and so it went on constantly, what he cut out in the evening was finished by the morning, so that he soon had his honest independence again, and at last became a wealthy man.

Now it befell that one evening not long before Christmas, when the man had been cutting out, he said to his wife, before going to bed: "What think you if we were to stay up to-night to see who it is that lends us this helping hand?" The woman liked the idea, and lighted a candle, and then they hid themselves in a corner of the room, behind some clothes which were hanging up there, and watched. When it was midnight, two pretty little naked men came, sat down by the shoe-maker's table, took all the work which was cut out before them and began to stitch, and sew, and hammer so skilfully and so quickly with their little fingers that the shoemaker could not avert his eyes for aston-ishment. They did not stop until all was done, and stood finished on the table, and then they ran quickly away.

Next morning the woman said: "The little men have made us rich, and we really must show that we are grateful for it. They run about so, and have nothing on, and must be cold. I'll tell you what I'll do: I will make them little shirts, and coats, and vests, and trousers, and knit both of them a pair of stockings, and you make them two little pairs of shoes." The man said: "I shall be very glad to do it"; and one night, when everything was ready, they laid their presents all together on the table instead of the cut-out work, and then concealed themselves to see how the little men would behave. At midnight they came bound-ing in, and wanted to get to work at once, but as they did not find any leather cut out, but only the pretty little articles of clothing, they were at first astonished, and then they showed intense delight. They dressed themselves with the greatest rapidity, put on the beautiful clothes, and sang:

"Now we are boys so fine to see,
Why should we longer cobblers be?"

Then they danced and skipped and leapt over chairs and benches. At last they danced out of doors. From that time forth they came no more, but as long as the shoemaker lived all went well with him, and all his efforts prospered.

SECOND STORY

There was once a poor servant-girl, who was industrious and cleanly, and swept the house every day, and emptied her sweepings on the great heap in front of the door. One morning when she was just going back to her work, she found a letter on this heap, and as she could not read, she put her broom in the corner, and took the letter to her employers, and behold it was an invitation from the elves, who asked the girl to hold a child for them at its christening. The girl did not know what to do, but at length, after much persuasion, and as they told her that it was not right to refuse an invitation of this kind, she consented. Then three elves came and conducted her to a hollow mountain, where the little folks lived. Everything there was small, but more elegant and beautiful than can be described. The baby's mother lay in a bed of black ebony ornamented with pearls, the covers were embroidered with gold, the cradle was of ivory, the bath-tub of gold. The girl stood as godmother, and then wanted to go home again, but the little elves urgently entreated her to stay three days with them. So she stayed, and passed the time in pleasure and gaiety, and the little folks did all they could to make her happy. At last she set out on her way home. But first they filled her pockets quite full of money, and then they led her out of the mountain again. When she got home, she wanted to begin her work, and took the broom, which was still standing in the corner, in her hand and began to sweep. Then some strangers came out of the house, who asked her who she was, and what business she had there. And she had not, as she thought, been three days with the little men in the mountains, but seven years, and in the meantime her former masters had died.

THIRD STORY

A certain mother had her child taken out of its cradle by the elves, and a changeling with a large head and staring eyes, which would do nothing but eat and drink, lay in its place. In her trouble she went to her neighbour, and asked her advice. The neighbour said that she was to carry the changeling into the kitchen, set it down on the hearth, light a fire, and boil some water in two egg-shells, which would make the changeling laugh, and if he laughed, all would be over with him. The woman did everything that her neighbour bade her. When she put the eggshells with water on the fire, goggle-eyes said: "I am as old now as the Wester Forest, but never yet have I seen anyone boil anything in an egg-shell!" And he began to laugh at it. Whilst he was laughing, suddenly came a host of little elves, who brought the right child, set it down on the hearth, and took the changeling away with them.

THE ROBBER BRIDEGROOM

There was once upon a time a miller, who had a beautiful daughter, and as she was grown up, he wished that she was provided for, and well married. He thought: "If any good suitor comes and asks for her, I will give her to him." Not long afterwards, a suitor came, who appeared to be very rich, and as the miller had no fault to find with him, he promised his daughter to him. The maiden, however, did not like him quite so much as a girl should like the man to whom she is engaged, and had no confidence in him. Whenever she saw, or thought of him, she felt a secret horror. Once he said to her: "You are my betrothed, and yet you have never once paid me a visit." The maiden replied: "I know not where your house is." Then said the bridegroom: "My house is out there in the dark forest." She tried to excuse herself, and said she could not find the way there. The bridegroom said: "Next Sunday you must come out there to me; I have already invited the guests, and I will strew ashes in order that you may find your way through the forest." When Sunday came, and the maiden had to set out on her way, she became very uneasy, she herself knew not exactly why, and to mark her way she filled both her pockets full of peas and lentils. Ashes were strewn at the entrance of the forest, and these she followed, but at every step she threw a couple of peas on the ground. She walked almost the whole day until she reached the middle of the forest, where it was the darkest, and there stood a solitary house, which she did not like, for it looked so dark and dismal. She went inside it, but no one was within, and the most absolute stillness reigned. Suddenly a voice cried:

"Turn back, turn back, young maiden dear,
'Tis a murderer's house you enter here."

The maiden looked up, and saw that the voice came from a bird, which was hanging in a cage on the wall. Again it cried:

"Turn back, turn back, young maiden dear,
'Tis a murderer's house you enter here."

Then the young maiden went on farther from one room to another, and walked through the whole house, but it was entirely empty and not one human being was to be found. At last she came to the cellar, and there sat an extremely aged woman, whose head shook constantly. "Can you not tell me," said the maiden, "if my betrothed lives here?"

"Alas, poor child," replied the old woman, "whither have you come? You are in a murderer's den. You think you are a bride soon to be married, but you will keep your wedding with death. Look, I have been forced to put a great kettle on there, with water in it, and when they have you in their power, they will cut you to pieces without mercy, will cook you, and eat you, for they are eaters of human flesh. If I do not have compassion on you, and save you, you are lost."

Thereupon the old woman led her behind a great hogshead where she could not be seen. "Be as still as a mouse," said she, "do not make a sound, or move, or all will be over with you. At night, when the robbers are asleep, we will escape; I have long waited for an opportunity." Hardly was this done, than the godless crew came home. They dragged with them another young girl. They were drunk, and paid no heed to her screams and lamentations. They gave her wine to drink, three glasses full, one glass of white wine, one glass of red, and a glass of yellow, and with this her heart burst in twain. Thereupon they tore off her delicate raiment, laid her on a table, cut her beautiful body in pieces, and strewed salt thereon. The poor bride behind the cask trembled and shook, for she saw right well what fate the robbers had destined for her. One of them noticed a gold ring on the little finger of the murdered girl, and as it would not come off at once, he took an axe and cut the finger off, but it sprang up in the air, away over the cask and fell straight into the bride's bosom. The robber took a candle and wanted to look for it, but could not find it. Then another of them said: "Have you looked behind the great hogshead?" But the old woman cried: "Come and get something to eat, and leave off looking till the morning, the finger won't run away from you."

Then the robbers said: "The old woman is right," and gave up their search, and sat down to eat, and the old woman poured a sleeping-draught in their wine, so that they soon lay down in the cellar, and slept and snored. When the bride heard that, she came out from behind the hogshead, and had to step over the sleepers, for they lay in rows on the ground, and great was her terror lest she should waken one of them. But God helped her, and she got safely over. The old woman went up with her, opened the doors, and they hurried out of the murderers' den with all the speed in their power. The wind had blown away the strewn ashes, but the peas and lentils had sprouted and grown up, and showed them the way in the moonlight. They walked the whole night, until in the morning they arrived at the mill, and then the maiden told her father everything exactly as it had happened.

When the day came for the wedding to be celebrated, the bridegroom appeared, and the miller had invited all his relations and friends.

As they sat at table, each was bidden to relate something. The bride sat still, and said nothing. Then said the bridegroom to the bride: "Come, my darling, do you know nothing? Relate something to us like the rest." She replied: "Then I will relate a dream. I was walking alone through a wood, and at last I came to a house, in which no living soul was, but on the wall there was a bird in a cage which cried:

'Turn back, turn back, young maiden dear,
'Tis a murderer's house you enter here.'

And this it cried once more. My darling, I only dreamt this. Then I went through all the rooms, and they were all empty, and there was something so horrible about them! At last I went down into the cellar, and there sat a very very old woman, whose head shook; I asked her: 'Does my bridegroom live in this house?' She answered: 'Alas, poor child, you have got into a murderer's den, your bridegroom does live here, but he will hew you in pieces, and kill you, and then he will cook you, and eat you.' My darling, I only dreamt this. But the old woman hid me behind a great hogshead, and scarcely was I hidden, when the robbers came home, dragging a maiden with them, to whom they gave three kinds of wines to drink, white, red, and yellow, with which her heart broke in twain. My darling, I only dreamt this. Thereupon they pulled off her pretty clothes, and hewed her fair body in pieces on a table, and sprinkled them with salt. My darling, I only dreamt this. And one of the robbers saw that there was still a ring on her little finger, and as it was hard to draw off, he took an axe and cut it off, but the finger sprang up in the air, and sprang behind the great hogshead, and fell in my bosom. And there is the finger with the ring!" And with these words she drew it forth, and showed it to those present.

The robber, who had during this story become as pale as ashes, leapt up and wanted to escape, but the guests held him fast, and delivered him over to justice. Then he and his whole troop were executed for their infamous deeds.

HERR KORBES

There were once a cock and a hen who wanted to take a journey together. So the cock built a beautiful carriage, which had four red wheels, and harnessed four mice to it. The hen seated herself in it with the cock, and they drove away together. Not long afterwards they met a cat who said: "Where are you going?" The cock replied: "We are going to the house of Herr Korbes." "Take me with you," said the cat. The cock answered: "Most willingly, get up behind, lest you fall off in front. Take great care not to dirty my little red wheels. And you little wheels, roll on, and you little mice pipe out, as we go forth on our way to the house of Herr Korbes."

After this came a millstone, then an egg, then a duck, then a pin, and at last a needle, who all seated themselves in the carriage, and drove with them. When they reached the house of Herr Korbes, however, Herr Korbes was not there. The mice drew the carriage into the barn, the hen flew with the cock upon a perch. The cat sat down by the hearth, the duck on the well-pole. The egg rolled itself into a towel, the pin stuck itself into the chair-cushion, the needle jumped on to the bed in the middle of the pillow, and the millstone laid itself over the door. Then Herr Korbes came home, went to the hearth, and was about to light the fire, when the cat threw a quantity of ashes in his face. He ran into the kitchen in a great hurry to wash it off, and the duck splashed some water in his face. He wanted to dry it with the towel, but the egg rolled up against him, broke, and glued up his eyes. He wanted to rest, and sat down in the chair, and then the pin pricked him. He fell in a passion, and threw himself on his bed, but as soon as he laid his head on the pillow, the needle pricked him, so that he screamed aloud, and was just going to run out into the wide world in his rage, but when he came to the house-door, the millstone fell down and struck him dead. Herr Korbes must have been a very wicked man!

THE GODFATHER

A poor man had so many children that he had already asked everyone in the world to be godfather, and when still another child was born, no one else was left whom he could invite. He knew not what to do, and, in his perplexity, he lay down and fell asleep. Then he dreamt that he was to go outside the gate, and ask the first person he met to be godfather. When he awoke, he determined to obey his dream, and went outside the gate, and asked the first person who came up to him to be godfather. The stranger presented him with a little glass of water, and said: "This is a wonderful water, with it you can heal the sick, only you must see where Death is standing. If he is standing by the patient's head, give the patient some of the water and he will be healed, but if Death is standing by his feet, all trouble will be in vain, for the sick man must die." From this time forth, the man could always say whether a patient could be saved or not, and became famous for his skill, and earned a great deal of money. Once he was called in to the child of the King, and when he entered, he saw Death standing by the child's head and cured it with the water, and he did the same a second time, but the third time Death was standing by its feet, and then he knew the child had to die.

Once the man thought he would visit the godfather, and tell him how he had succeeded with the water. But when he entered the house, the strangest things were going on within! On the first flight of stairs, the broom and shovel were disputing, and knocking each other about violently. He asked them: "Where does the godfather live?" The broom replied: "One flight of stairs higher up." When he came to the second flight, he saw a heap of dead fingers lying. He asked: "Where does the godfather live?" One of the fingers replied: "One flight of stairs higher." On the third flight lay a heap of dead heads, which again directed him to a flight beyond. On the fourth flight, he saw fishes on the fire, which frizzled in the pans and baked themselves. They, too, said: "One flight of stairs higher." And when he had ascended the fifth, he came to the door of a room and peeped through the keyhole, and there he saw the godfather who had a pair of long horns. When he opened the door and went in, the godfather got into bed in a great hurry and covered himself up. Then said the man: "Sir godfather, what a strange household you have! When I came to your first flight of stairs, the shovel and broom were quarreling, and beating each other violently."

"How stupid you are!" said the godfather. "That was the boy and the maid talking to each other." "But on the second flight I saw dead fingers lying." "Oh, how silly you are! Those were some roots of scorzonera." "On the third flight lay a heap of dead men's heads." "Foolish man, those were cabbages." "On the fourth flight, I saw fishes in a pan, which were hissing and baking themselves." When he had said that, the fishes came and served themselves up. "And when I got to the fifth flight, I peeped through the keyhole of a door, and there, godfather, I saw you, and you had long, long horns." "Oh, that is not true!" The man became alarmed, and ran out, and if he had not, who knows what the godfather would have done to him.

FRAU TRUDE

There was once a little girl who was obstinate and inquisitive, and when her parents told her to do anything, she did not obey them, so how could she fare well? One day she said to her parents: "I have heard so much of Frau Trude, I will go to her some day. People say that everything about her does look so strange, and that there are such odd things in her house, that I have become quite curious!" Her parents absolutely forbade her, and said: "Frau Trude is a bad woman, who does wicked things, and if you go to her, you are no longer our child." But the maiden did not let herself be turned aside by her parents' prohibition, and still went to Frau Trude, And when she got to her, Frau Trude said: "Why are you so pale?" "Ah," she replied, and her whole body trembled, "I have been so terrified at what I have seen." "What have you seen?" "I saw a black man on your steps." "That was a collier." "Then I saw a green man." "That was a huntsman." "After that I saw a blood-red man." "That was a butcher." "Ah, Frau Trude, I was terrified; I looked through the window and saw not you, but, as I verily believe, the Devil himself with a head of fire." "Oho!" said she, "then you have seen the witch in her proper costume. I have been waiting for you, and wanting you a long time already; you shall give me some light." Then she changed the girl into a block of wood, and threw it into the fire. And when it was in full blaze she sat down close to it, and warmed herself by it, and said: "That shines bright for once in a way."

GODFATHER DEATH

A poor man had twelve children and was forced to work night and day to give them even bread. When therefore the thirteenth came into the world, he knew not what to do in his trouble, but ran out into the great highway, and resolved to ask the first person whom he met to be godfather. The first to meet him was the good God who already knew what filled his heart, and said to him: "Poor man, I pity you. I will hold your child at its christening, and will take charge of it and make it happy on earth." The man said: "Who are you?" "I am God." Then I do not desire to have you for a godfather," said the man; "you give to the rich, and leave the poor to hunger." Thus spoke the man, for he did not know how wisely God apportions riches and poverty. He turned therefore away from the Lord, and went farther. Then the Devil came to him and said: "What do you seek? If you will take me as a godfather for your child, I will give him gold in plenty and all the joys of the world as well." The man asked: "Who are you?" "I am the Devil." "Then I do not desire to have you for godfather," said the man; "you deceive men and lead them astray." He went onwards, and then came Death striding up to him with withered legs, and said: "Take me as godfather." The man asked: "Who are you?" "I am Death, and I make all equal." Then said the man, "You are the right one, you take the rich as well as the poor, without distinction; you shall be godfather." Death answered: "I will make your child rich and famous, for he who has me for a friend can lack nothing." The man said: "Next Sunday is the christening; be there at the right time." Death appeared as he had promised, and stood godfather quite in the usual way.

When the boy had grown up, his godfather one day appeared and bade him go with him. He led him forth into a forest, and showed him a herb which grew there, and said: "Now you shall receive your god-father's present. I make you a celebrated physician. When you are called to a patient, I will always appear to you. If I stand by the head of the sick man, you may say with confidence that you will make him well again, and if you give him of this herb he will recover; but if I stand by the patient's feet, he is mine, and you must say that all remedies are in vain, and that no physician in the world could save him. But beware of using the herb against my will, or it might fare ill with you."

It was not long before the youth was the most famous physician in the whole world. "He had only to look at the patient and he knew his condition at once, whether he would recover, or must needs die." So they said of him, and from far and wide people came to him, sent for him when they had anyone ill, and gave him so much money that he soon became a rich man. Now it so befell that the King became ill, and the physician was summoned, and was to say if recovery were possible. But when he came to the bed, Death was standing by the feet of the sick man, and the herb did not grow which could save him. "If I could but cheat Death for once," thought the physician, "he is sure to take it ill if I do but, as I am his godson, he will shut one eye; I will risk it." He therefore took up the sick man, and laid him the other way, so that now Death was standing by his head. Then he gave the King some of the herb, and he recovered and grew healthy again. But Death came to the physician, looking very black and angry, threatened him with his finger, and said: "You have betrayed me; this time I will pardon it, as you are my godson; but if you venture it again, it will cost you your neck, for I will take you yourself away with me."

Soon afterwards the King's daughter fell into a severe illness. She was his only child, and he wept day and night, so that he began to lose the sight of his eyes, and he caused it to be made known that whosoever rescued her from death should be her husband and inherit the crown. When the physician came to the sick girl's bed, he saw Death by her feet. He ought to have remembered the warning given by his godfather, but he was so infatuated by the great beauty of the King's daughter, and the happiness of becoming her husband, that he flung all thought to the winds. He did not see that Death was casting angry glances on him, that he was raising his hand in the air, and threatening him with his withered fist. He raised up the sick girl, and placed her head where her feet had lain. Then he gave her some of the herb, and instantly her cheeks flushed red, and life stirred afresh in her.

When Death saw that for a second time his own property had been misused, he walked up to the physician with long strides, and said: "All is over with you, and now the lot falls on you," and seized him so firmly with his ice-cold hand, that he could not resist, and led him into a cave below the earth. There he saw how thousands and thousands of candles were burning in countless rows, some large, some medium-sized, others small. Every instant some were extinguished, and others again burnt up, so that the flames seemed to leap hither and thither in perpetual change. "See," said Death, "these are the lights of men's lives. The large ones belong to children, the medium-sized ones to married people in their prime, the little ones belong to old people; but children and young folks likewise have often only a tiny candle." "Show me the light of my life," said the physician, and he thought that it would be still very tall. Death pointed to a little end which was just threatening to go out, and said: "Behold, it is there." "Ah, dear godfather," said the horrified physician, "light a new one for me, do it for love of me, that I may enjoy my life, be King, and the husband of the King's beautiful daughter." "I cannot," answered Death, "one must go out before a new one is lighted." "Then place the old one on a new one, that will go on burning at once when the old one has come to an end," pleaded the physician. Death behaved as if he were going to fulfill his wish, and took hold of a tall new candle; but as he desired to revenge himself, he purposely made a mistake in fixing it, and the little piece fell down and was extinguished. Immediately the physician fell on the ground, and now he himself was in the hands of Death.

THUMBLING'S TRAVELS

A certain tailor had a son, who happened to be small, and no bigger than a thumb, and on this account he was always called Thumbling. He had, however, some courage in him, and said to his father: "Father, I must and will go out into the world." "That's right, my son," said the old man, and took a long darning-needle and made a knob of sealing-wax on it at the handle, "and there is a sword for you to take with you on the way." Then the little tailor wanted to have one more meal with them, and hopped into the kitchen to see what his mother had cooked for the last time. But it was already served, and the dish stood on the hearth. Then he said: "Mother, what is there to eat to-day?" "See for yourself," said his mother. So Thumbling jumped on to the hearth, and peeped into the dish, but as he stretched his neck in too far the steam from the food caught hold of him, and carried him up the chimney. He rode about in the air on the steam for a while, until at length he sank down to the ground again. Now the little tailor was outside in the wide world, and he travelled about, and went to a master in his craft, but the food was not good enough for him. "Mistress, if you give us no better food," said Thumbling, "I will go away, and early to-morrow morning I will write with chalk on the door of your house: 'Too many potatoes, too little meat! Farewell, Mr. Potato-King'." "What would you have forsooth, grasshopper?" said the mistress, and grew angry, and seized a dishcloth, and was just going to strike him; but my little tailor crept nimbly under a thimble, peeped out from beneath it, and put his tongue out at the mistress. She took up the thimble, and wanted to get hold of him, but little Thumbling hopped into the cloth, and while the mistress was opening it out and looking for him, he got into a crevice in the table. "Ho, ho, lady mistress," cried he, and thrust his head out, and when she began to strike him he leapt down into the drawer. At last, however, she caught him and drove him out of the house.

The little tailor journeyed on and came to a great forest, and there he fell in with a band of robbers who had a design to steal the King's treasure. When they saw the little tailor, they thought: "A little fellow like that can creep through a key-hole and serve as picklock to us." "Hi, there!" cried one of them, "you giant Goliath, will you go to the treasure-chamber with us? You can slip yourself in and throw out the money." Thumbling reflected a while, and at length he said "yes," and went with them to the treasure-chamber. Then he looked at the doors above and below, to see if there was any crack in them. It was not long before he espied one which was broad enough to let him in. He was therefore about to get in at once, but one of the two sentries who stood before the door, observed him, and said to the other: "What an ugly spider is creeping there; I will kill it." "Let the poor creature alone," said the other, "it has done you no harm." Then Thumbling got safely through the crevice into the treasure-chamber, opened the window beneath which the robbers were standing, and threw out to them one taler after another. When the little tailor was in the full swing of his work, he heard the King coming to inspect his treasure-chamber, and crept hastily into a hiding-place. The King noticed that several solid talers were missing, but could not conceive who could have stolen them, for locks and bolts were in good condition, and all seemed well guarded. Then he went away again, and said to the sentries: "Be on the watch, someone is after the money." When therefore Thumbling recommenced his labours, they heard the money moving, and a sound of klink, klink, klink. They ran swiftly in to seize the thief, but the little tailor, who heard them coming, was still swifter, and leapt into a corner and covered himself with a taler, so that nothing could be seen of him, and at the same time he mocked the sentries and cried: "Here am I!" The sentries ran thither, but as they got there, he had already hopped into another corner under a taler, and was crying: "Ho, ho, here am I!"

The watchmen sprang there in haste, but Thumbling had long ago got into a third corner, and was crying: "Ho, ho, here am I!" And thus he made fools of them, and drove them so long round about the treasure-chamber that they were weary and went away. Then by degrees he threw all the talers out, despatching the last with all his might, then hopped nimbly upon it, and flew down with it through the window. The robbers paid him great compliments. "You are a valiant hero," said they; "will you be our captain?"

Thumbling, however, declined, and said he wanted to see the world first. They now divided the booty, but the little tailor only asked for a kreuzer because he could not carry more.

Then he once more buckled on his sword, bade the robbers good-bye, and took to the road. First, he went to work with some masters, but he had no liking for that, and at last he hired himself as man-servant in an inn. The maids, however, could not endure him, for he saw all that they did secretly, without their seeing him, and he told their employers what they had taken off the plates, and carried away out of the cellar, for themselves. Then said they: "Wait, and we will pay you out!" and arranged with each other to play him a trick. Soon afterwards when one of the maids was mowing in the garden, and saw Thumbling jumping about and creeping up and down the plants, she mowed him up quickly with the grass, tied all in a great cloth, and secretly threw it to the cows. Now amongst them there was a great black one, who swallowed him down without hurting him. Down below, however, it did not suit him, for it was quite dark, neither was any candle burning. When the cow was being milked he cried:

"Strip, strap, strull,
When will the pail be full?"

But the noise of the milking prevented his being understood. After this the master of the house came into the stall and said: "That cow shall be killed to-morrow." Then Thumbling was so alarmed that he cried out in a clear voice: "Let me out first, I am sitting inside her." The master heard that quite well, but did not know from whence the voice came. "Where are you?" asked he. "In the black one," answered

Thumbling, but the master did not understand what that meant, and went out.

Next morning the cow was killed. Happily Thumbling did not meet with one blow at the cutting up and chopping; he got among the sausage-meat. And when the butcher came in and began his work, he cried out with all his might: "Don't chop too deep, don't chop too deep, I am amongst it." No one heard this because of the noise of the chopping-knife. Now poor Thumbling was in trouble, but trouble sharpens the wits, and he sprang out so adroitly between the blows that none of them touched him, and he escaped with a whole skin. But still he could not get away, there was nothing for it but to let himself be thrust into a black-pudding with the bits of bacon. His quarters there were rather confined, and besides that he was hung up in the chimney to be smoked, and there time did hang terribly heavy on his hands.

At length in winter he was taken down again, as the black-pudding had to be set before a guest. When the hostess was cutting it in slices, he took care not to stretch out his head too far lest a bit of it should be cut off; at last he saw his opportunity, cleared a passage for himself, and jumped out.

The little tailor, however, would not stay any longer in a house where he fared so ill, so at once set out on his journey again. But his liberty did not last long. In the open country he met with a fox who snapped him up without thinking. "Hi, there, Mr. Fox," cried the little tailor, "it is I who am sticking in your throat, set me at liberty again." "You are right," answered the fox. "You are next to nothing for me, but if you will promise me the fowls in your father's yard I will let you go." "With all my heart," replied Thumbling. "You shall have all the cocks and hens, that I promise you." Then the fox let him go again, and himself carried him home. When the father once more saw his dear son, he willingly gave the fox all the fowls which he had. "For this I likewise bring you a handsome bit of money," said Thumbling, and gave his father the kreuzer which he had earned on his travels.

"But why did the fox get the poor chickens to eat?" "Oh, you silly, your father would surely love his child far more than the fowls in the yard!"

FITCHER'S BIRD

There was once a wizard who used to take the form of a poor man, and went to houses and begged, and caught pretty girls. No one knew whither he carried them, for they were never seen again. One day he appeared before the door of a man who had three pretty daughters; he looked like a poor weak beggar, and carried a basket on his back, as if he meant to collect charitable gifts in it. He begged for a little food, and when the eldest daughter came out and was just handing him a piece of bread, he did but touch her, and she was forced to jump into his basket. Thereupon he hurried off with long strides, and carried her away into a dark forest to his house, which stood in the midst of it. Everything in the house was magnificent; he gave her whatsoever she could possibly desire, and said: "My darling, you will certainly be happy with me, for you have everything your heart can wish for." This lasted a few days, and then he said: "I must journey forth, and leave you alone for a short time; here are the keys of the house; you may go everywhere and look at everything except into one room, which this little key opens, and there I forbid you to go on pain of death." He likewise gave her an egg and said: "Preserve the egg carefully for me, and carry it continually about with you, for a great misfortune would arise from the loss of it."

She took the keys and the egg, and promised to obey him in everything. When he was gone, she went all round the house from the bottom to the top, and examined everything. The rooms shone with silver and gold, and she thought she had never seen such great splendour. At length she came to the forbidden door; she wished to pass it by, but curiosity let her have no rest. She examined the key, it looked just like any other; she put it in the keyhole and turned it a little, and the door sprang open. But what did she see when she went in? A great bloody basin stood in the middle of the room, and therein lay human beings, dead and hewn to pieces, and hard by was a block of wood, and a gleaming axe lay upon it. She was so terribly alarmed that the egg which she held in her hand fell into the basin. She got it out and wiped the blood off, but in vain, it appeared again in a moment. She washed and scrubbed, but she could not get it off.

It was not long before the man came back from his journey, and the first things which he asked for were the key and the egg. She gave them to him, but she trembled as she did so, and he saw at once by the red spots that she had been in the bloody chamber. "Since you have gone into the room against my will," said he, "you shall go back into it against your own. Your life is ended." He threw her down, dragged her along by her hair, cut her head off on the block, and hewed her in pieces so that her blood ran on the ground. Then he threw her into the basin with the rest.

"Now I will fetch myself the second," said the wizard, and again he went to the house in the shape of a poor man, and begged. Then the second daughter brought him a piece of bread; he caught her like the first, by simply touching her, and carried her away. She did not fare better than her sister. She allowed herself to be led away by her curiosity, opened the door of the bloody chamber, looked in, and had to atone for it with her life on the wizard's return. Then he went and brought the third sister, but she was clever and wily. When he had given her the keys and the egg, and had left her, she first put the egg away with great care, and then she examined the house, and at last went into the forbidden room. Alas, what did she behold! Both her dear sisters lay there in the basin, cruelly murdered, and cut in pieces. But she began to gather their limbs together and put them in order, head, body, arms and legs. And when nothing further was wanting the limbs began to move and unite themselves together, and both the maidens opened their eyes and were once more alive. Then they rejoiced and kissed and caressed each other.

On his arrival, the man at once demanded the keys and the egg, and as he could perceive no trace of any blood on it, he said: "You have stood the test, you shall be my bride." He now had no longer any power over her, and was forced to do whatsoever she desired. "Oh, very well," said she, "you shall first take a basketful of gold to my father and mother, and carry it yourself on your back; in the meantime I will prepare for the wedding. Then she ran to her sisters, whom she had hidden in a little chamber, and said: "The moment has come when I can save you. The wretch shall himself carry you home again, but as soon as you are at home send help to me." She put both of them in a basket and covered them quite over with gold, so that nothing of them was to be seen. Then she called in the wizard and said to him: "Now carry the basket away, but I shall look through my little window and watch to see if you stop on the way to stand or to rest."

The wizard raised the basket on his back and went away with it, but it weighed him down so heavily that the sweat streamed from his face. Then he sat down and wanted to rest awhile, but immediately one of the girls in the basket cried: "I am looking through my little window, and I see that you are resting. Will you go on at once?" He thought it was his bride who was talking to him; and got up on his legs again. Once more he was going to sit down, but instantly she cried: "I am looking through my little window, and I see that you are resting. Will you go on directly?" And whenever he stood still, she cried this, and then he was forced to go onwards, until at last, groaning and out of breath, he took the basket with the gold and the two maidens into their parents' house. At home, however, the bride prepared the marriage-feast, and sent invitations to the friends of the wizard. Then she took a skull with grinning teeth, put some ornaments on it and a wreath of flowers, carried it upstairs to the garret-window, and let it look out from thence. When all was ready, she got into a barrel of honey, and then cut the feather-bed open and rolled herself in it, until she looked like a wondrous bird, and no one could recognize her. Then she went

out of the house, and on her way she met some of the wedding-guests, who asked:

> "O, Fitcher's bird, how com'st thou here?"
> "I come from Fitcher's house quite near."
> "And what may the young bride be doing?"
> "From cellar to garret she's swept all clean,
> And now from the window she's peeping, I ween."

At last she met the bridegroom, who was coming slowly back. He, like the others, asked:

> "O, Fitcher's bird, how com'st thou here?"
> "I come from Fitcher's house quite near."
> "And what may the young bride be doing?"
> "From cellar to garret she's swept all clean,
> And now from the window she's peeping, I ween."

The bridegroom looked up, saw the decked-out skull, thought it was his bride, and nodded to her, greeting her kindly. But when he and his guests had all gone into the house, the brothers and kinsmen of the bride, who had been sent to rescue her, arrived. They locked all the doors of the house, that no one might escape, set fire to it, and the wizard and all his crew had to burn.

THE JUNIPER TREE

It is now long ago, quite two thousand years, since there was a rich man who had a beautiful and pious wife, and they loved each other dearly. They had, however, no children, though they wished for them very much, and the woman prayed for them day and night, but still they had none. Now there was a court-yard in front of their house in which was a juniper tree, and one day in winter the woman was standing beneath it, paring herself an apple, and while she was paring herself the apple she cut her finger, and the blood fell on the snow.

"Ah," said the woman, and sighed right heavily, and looked at the blood before her, and was most unhappy, "ah, if I had but a child as red as blood and as white as snow!" And while she thus spoke, she became quite happy in her mind, and felt just as if that were going to happen. Then she went into the house, and a month went by and the snow was gone, and two months, and then everything was green, and three months, and then all the flowers came out of the earth, and four months, and then all the trees in the wood grew thicker, and the green branches were all closely entwined, and the birds sang until the wood resounded and the blossoms fell from the trees, then the fifth month passed away and she stood under the juniper tree, which smelt so sweetly that her heart leapt, and she fell on her knees and was beside herself with joy, and when the sixth month was over the fruit was large and fine, and then she was quite still, and the seventh month she snatched at the juniper-berries and ate them greedily, then she grew sick and sorrowful, then the eighth month passed, and she called her husband to her, and wept and said: "If I die, then bury me beneath the juniper tree." Then she was quite comforted and happy until the next month was over, and then she had a child as white as snow and as red as blood, and when she beheld it she was so delighted that she died.

Then her husband buried her beneath the juniper tree, and he began to weep sore; after some time he was more at ease, and though he still wept he could bear it, and after some time longer he took another wife.

By the second wife he had a daughter, but the first wife's child was a little son, and he was as red as blood and as white as snow. When the woman looked at her daughter she loved her very much, but then she looked at the little boy and it seemed to cut her to the heart, for the thought came into her mind that he would always stand in her way, and she was for ever thinking how she could get all the fortune for her daughter, and the Evil One filled her mind with this till she was quite wroth with the little boy and she pushed him from one corner to the other and slapped him here and cuffed him there, until the poor child was in continual terror, for when he came out of school he had no peace in any place.

One day the woman had gone upstairs to her room, and her little daughter went up too, and said: "Mother, give me an apple." "Yes, my child," said the woman, and gave her a fine apple out of the chest, but the chest had a great heavy lid with a great sharp iron lock. "Mother," said the little daughter, "is brother not to have one too?" This made the woman angry, but she said: "Yes, when he comes out of school." And when she saw from the window that he was coming, it was just as if the Devil entered into her, and she snatched at the apple and took it away again from her daughter, and said: "You shall not have one before your brother." Then she threw the apple into the chest, and shut it. Then the little boy came in at the door, and the Devil made her say to him kindly: "My son, will you have an apple?" and she looked wickedly at him. "Mother," said the little boy, "how dreadful you look! Yes, give me an apple." Then it seemed to her as if she were forced to say to him: "Come with me," and she opened the lid of the chest and said: "Take out an apple for yourself," and while the little boy was stooping inside, the Devil prompted her, and crash! she shut the lid down, and his head flew off and fell among the red apples. Then she was overwhelmed with terror, and thought: "If I could but make them think that it was not done by me!" So she went upstairs to her room to her chest of drawers, and took a white handkerchief out of the top drawer, and set the head on the neck again, and folded the handkerchief so that nothing could be seen, and she set him on a chair in front of the door, and put the apple in his hand.

After this Marlinchen came into the kitchen to her mother, who was standing by the fire with a pan of hot water before her which she was constantly stirring round. "Mother," said Marlinchen, "brother is sitting at the door, and he looks quite white, and has an apple in his hand. I asked him to give me the apple, but he did not answer me, and I was quite frightened." "Go back to him," said her mother, "and if he will not answer you, give him a box on the ear." So Marlinchen went to him and said: "Brother, give me the apple." But he was silent, and she gave him a box on the ear, where-upon his head fell off. Marlinchen was terrified, and began crying and screaming, and ran to her mother, and said: "Alas, mother, I have knocked my brother's head off!" and she wept and wept and could not be comforted. "Marlinchen," said the mother, "what have you done? but be quiet and let no one know it; it cannot be helped now, we will make him into black-puddings." Then the mother took the little boy and chopped him in pieces, put him into the pan and made him into black-puddings; but Marlinchen stood by

weeping and weeping, and all her tears fell into the pan and there was no need of any salt.

Then the father came home, and sat down to dinner and said: "But where is my son?" And the mother served up a great dish of black-puddings, and Marlinchen wept and could not leave off. Then the father again said: "But where is my son?" "Ah," said the mother, "he has gone across the country to his mother's great uncle; he will stay there awhile." "And what is he going to do there? He did not even say good-bye to me."

"Oh, he wanted to go, and asked me if he might stay six weeks, he is well taken care of there." "Ah," said the man, "I feel so unhappy lest all should not be right. He ought to have said good-bye to me." With that he began to eat and said: "Marlinchen, why are you crying? Your brother will certainly come back." Then he said: "Ah, wife, how delicious this food is, give me some more." And the more he ate the more he wanted to have, and he said: "Give me some more, you shall have none of it. It seems to me as if it were all mine." And he ate and ate and threw all the bones under the table, until he had finished the whole. But Marlinchen went away to her chest of drawers, and took her best silk handkerchief out of the bottom drawer, and got all the bones from beneath the table, and tied them up in her silk handkerchief, and carried them outside the door, weeping tears of blood. Then she lay down under the juniper tree on the green grass, and after she had lain down there, she suddenly felt light-hearted and did not cry any more. Then the juniper tree began to stir itself, and the branches parted asunder, and moved together again, just as if someone were rejoicing and clapping his hands. At the same time a mist seemed to arise from the tree, and in the centre of this mist it burned like a fire, and a beautiful bird flew out of the fire singing magnificently, and he flew high up in the air, and when he was gone, the juniper tree was just as it had been before, and the handkerchief with the bones was no longer there. Marlinchen, however, was as gay and happy as if her brother were still alive. And she went merrily into the house, and sat down to dinner and ate.

But the bird flew away and lighted on a goldsmith's house, and began to sing:

> "My mother she killed me,
> My father he ate me,
> My sister, little Marlinchen,
> Gathered together all my bones,
> Tied them in a silken handkerchief,
> Laid them beneath the juniper tree,
> Kywitt, kywitt, what a beautiful bird am I!"

The goldsmith was sitting in his workshop making a golden chain, when he heard the bird which was sitting singing on his roof, and very beautiful the song seemed to him. He stood up, but as he crossed the threshold he lost one of his slippers. But he went away right up the middle of the street with one shoe on and one sock; he had his apron on, and in one hand he had the golden chain and in the other the pincers, and the sun was shining brightly on the street. Then he went right on and stood still, and said to the bird: "Bird," said he then, "how beautifully you can sing! Sing me that piece again." "No," said the bird, "I'll not sing it twice for nothing! Give me the golden chain, and then I will sing it again for you." "There," said the goldsmith, "there is the golden chain for you, now sing me that song again." Then the bird came and took the golden chain in his right claw, and went and sat in front of the goldsmith, and sang:

"My mother she killed me,
My father he ate me,
My sister, little Marlinchen,
Gathered together all my bones,
Tied them in a silken handkerchief,
Laid them beneath the juniper tree,
Kywitt, kywitt, what a beautiful bird am I!"

Then the bird flew away to a shoemaker, and lighted on his roof, and sang:

"My mother she killed me,
My father he ate me,
My sister, little Marlinchen,
Gathered together all my bones,
Tied them in a silken handkerchief,
Laid them beneath the juniper tree,
Kywitt, kywitt, what a beautiful bird am I!"

The shoemaker heard that and ran out of doors in his shirt sleeves, and looked up at his roof, and was forced to hold his hand before his eyes lest the sun should blind him. "Bird," said he, "how beautifully you can sing!" Then he called in at his door: "Wife, just come outside, there is a bird, look at that bird, he certainly can sing." Then he called his daughter and children, and apprentices, boys and girls, and they all came up the street and looked at the bird and saw how beautiful he was, and what fine red and green feathers he had, and how like real gold his neck was, and how the eyes in his head shone like stars. "Bird," said the shoemaker, "now sing me that song again." "Nay," said the bird, "I do not sing twice for nothing; you must give me something." "Wife," said the man, "go to the garret, upon the top shelf there stands a pair of red shoes, bring them down." Then the wife went and brought the shoes. "There, bird," said the man, "now sing me that piece again." Then the bird came and took the shoes in his left claw, and flew back on the roof, and sang:

"My mother she killed me,
My father he ate me,
My sister; little Marlinchen,
Gathered together all my bones,
Tied them in a silken handkerchief,
Laid them beneath the juniper tree,
Kywitt, kywitt, what a beautiful bird am I!"

And when he had finished his song he flew away. In his right claw he had the chain and in his left the shoes, and he flew far away to a mill, and the mill went "klipp klapp, klipp klapp, klipp klapp," and in the mill sat twenty miller's men hewing a stone, and cutting, hick hack, hick hack, hick hack, and the mill went klipp klapp, klipp klapp, klipp klapp. Then the bird went and sat on a lime-tree which stood in front of the mill, and sang:

"My mother she killed me,"

Then one of them stopped working,

"My father he ate me,"

Then two more stopped working and listened to that,

"My sister, little Marlinchen,"

Then four more stopped,

"Gathered together all my bones,
Tied them in a silken handkerchief,"

Now eight only were hewing,

"Laid them beneath"

Now only five,

"The juniper tree,"

And now only one,

"Kywitt, kywitt, what a beautiful bird am I!"

Then the last stopped also, and heard the last words. "Bird," said he, "how beautifully you sing! Let me, too, hear that. Sing that once more for me."

"Nay," said the bird, "I will not sing twice for nothing. Give me the millstone, and then I will sing it again."

"Yes," said he, "if it belonged to me only, you should have it."

"Yes," said the others, "if he sings again he shall have it." Then the bird came down, and the twenty millers all set to work with a beam and raised the stone up. And the bird stuck his neck through the hole, and put the stone on as if it were a collar, and flew on to the tree again, and sang:

"My mother she killed me,
My father he ate me,
My sister, little Marlinchen,
Gathered together all my bones,
Tied them in a silken handkerchief,
Laid them beneath the juniper tree,
Kywitt, kywitt, what a beautiful bird am I!"

And when he had done singing, he spread his wings, and in his right claw he had the chain, and in his left the shoes, and round his neck the millstone, and he flew far away to his father's house.

In the room sat the father, the mother, and Marlinchen at dinner, and the father said: "How light-hearted I feel, how happy I am!" "Nay," said the mother, "I feel so uneasy, just as if a heavy storm were coming." Marlinchen, however, sat weeping and weeping, and then came the bird flying, and as it seated itself on the roof the father said: "Ah, I feel so truly happy, and the sun is shining so beautifully outside, I feel just as if I were about to see some old friend again." "Nay," said the woman, "I feel so anxious, my teeth chatter, and I seem to have fire in my veins." And she tore her stays open, but Marlinchen sat in a corner crying, and held her plate before her eyes and cried till it was quite wet. Then the bird sat on the juniper tree, and sang:

"My mother she killed me,"

Then the mother stopped her ears, and shut her eyes, and would not see or hear, but there was a roaring in her ears like the most violent storm, and her eyes burnt and flashed like lightning:

"My father he ate me,"

"Ah, mother," says the man, "that is a beautiful bird! He sings so splendidly, and the sun shines so warm, and there is a smell just like cinnamon."

"My sister, little Marlinchen,"

Then Marlinchen laid her head on her knees and wept without ceasing, but the man said: "I am going out, I must see the bird quite close." "Oh, don't go," said the woman, "I feel as if the whole house were shaking and on fire." But the man went out and looked at the bird:

"Gathered together all my bones,
Tied them in a silken handkerchief,
Laid them beneath the juniper tree,
Kywitt, kywitt, what a beautiful bird am I!"

On this the bird let the golden chain fall, and it fell exactly round the man's neck, and so exactly round it that it fitted beautifully. Then he went in and said: "Just look what a fine bird that is, and what a handsome golden chain he has given me, and how pretty he is!" But the woman was terrified, and fell down on the floor in the room, and her cap fell off her head. Then sang the bird once more:

"My mother she killed me,"

"Would that I were a thousand feet beneath the earth so as not to hear that!"

"My father he ate me,"

Then the woman fell down again as if dead.

"My sister, little Marlinchen,"

"Ah," said Marlinchen, "I too will go out and see if the bird will give me anything," and she went out.

"Gathered together all my bones,
Tied them in a silken handkerchief,"

Then he threw down the shoes to her.

"Laid them beneath the juniper tree,
Kywitt, kywitt, what a beautiful bird am I!"

Then she was light-hearted and joyous, and she put on the new red shoes, and danced and leaped into the house. "Ah," said she, "I was so sad when I went out and now I am so light-hearted; that is a splendid bird, he has given me a pair of red shoes!" "Well," said the woman, and sprang to her feet and her hair stood up like flames of fire, "I feel as if the world were coming to an end! I, too, will go out and see if my heart feels lighter." And as she went out at the door, crash! the bird threw down the millstone on her head, and she was entirely crushed by it. The father and Marlinchen heard what had happened and went out, and smoke, flames and fire were rising from the place, and when that was over, there stood the little brother, and he took his father and Marlinchen by the hand, and all three were right glad, and they went into the house to dinner, and ate.

OLD SULTAN

A farmer once had a faithful dog called Sultan, who had grown old, and lost all his teeth, so that he could no longer hold on to anything. One day the farmer was standing with his wife before the house-door, and said: "To-morrow I intend to shoot Old Sultan, he is no longer of any use."

His wife, who felt pity for the faithful beast, answered, "He has served us so long, and been so faithful, that we might well give him his keep."

"What?" said the man. "You are not very bright. He has not a tooth left in his head, and not a thief is afraid of him; now he can go. If he has served us, he has had good feeding for it."

The poor dog, who was lying stretched out in the sun not far off, had heard everything, and was sorry that the morrow was to be his last day. He had a good friend, the wolf, and he crept out in the evening into the forest to him, and complained of the fate that awaited him. "Listen, gossip," said the wolf, "be of good cheer, I will help you out of your trouble. I have thought of something. To-morrow, early in the morning, your master is going with his wife to make hay, and they will take their little child with them, for no one will be left behind in the house. They are wont, during work-time, to lay the child under the hedge in the shade; you lay yourself there too, just as if you wished to guard it. Then I will come out of the wood, and carry off the child. You must rush swiftly after me, as if you would seize it again from me. I will let it fall, and you will take it back to its parents, who will think that you have saved it, and will be far too grateful to do you any harm; on the contrary, you will be in high favour, and they will never let you want for anything again."

The plan pleased the dog, and it was carried out just as it was arranged. The father screamed when he saw the wolf running across the field with his child, but when Old Sultan brought it back, then he was full of joy, and stroked him and said: "Not a hair of yours shall be hurt, you shall eat my bread free as long as you live." And to his wife he said: "Go home at once and make Old Sultan some bread-sop that he will not have to bite, and bring the pillow out of my bed, I will give him that to lie upon."

Henceforth Old Sultan was as well off as he could wish to be.

Soon afterwards the wolf visited him, and was pleased that everything had succeeded so well. "But, gossip," said he, "you will just wink an eye if, when I have a chance, I carry off one of your master's fat sheep." "Do not reckon upon that," answered the dog; "I will remain true to my master; I cannot agree to that." The wolf, who thought that this could not be spoken in earnest, came creeping about in the night and was going to take away the sheep. But the farmer, to whom the faithful Sultan had told the wolf's plan, caught him and dressed his hide soundly with the flail. The wolf had to make himself scarce, but he cried out to the dog: "Wait a bit, you scoundrel, you shall pay for this."

The next morning the wolf sent the boar to challenge the dog to come out into the forest so that they might settle the affair. Old Sultan could find no one to stand by him but a cat with only three legs, and as they went out together the poor cat limped along, and at the same time stretched out her tail into the air with pain.

The wolf and his friend were already at the appointed place, but when they saw their enemy coming they thought that he was bringing a sabre with him, for they mistook the outstretched tail of the cat for one. And when the poor beast hopped on its three legs, they could only think every time that it was picking up a stone to throw at them. So they were both afraid; the wild boar crept into the under-wood and the wolf jumped up a tree.

The dog and the cat, when they came up, wondered that there was no one to be seen. The wild boar, however, had not been able to hide himself altogether; one of his ears was sticking out. Whilst the cat was looking carefully about, the boar moved his ear; the cat, who thought it was a mouse moving there, jumped upon it and bit it hard. The boar made a fearful noise and ran away, crying out: "The guilty one is up in the tree." The dog and cat looked up and saw the wolf, who was ashamed of having shown himself so timid, and made friends with the dog.

THE SIX SWANS

Once upon a time, a certain King was hunting in a great forest, and he chased a wild beast so eagerly that none of his attendants could follow him. When evening drew near he stopped and looked around him, and then he saw that he had lost his way. He sought a way out, but could find none. Then he perceived an aged woman with a head which nodded perpetually, who came towards him, but she was a witch. "Good woman," said he to her, "can you not show me the way through the forest?" "Oh, yes, Lord King," she answered, "that I certainly can, but on one condition, and if you do not fulfil that, you will never get out of the forest, and will die of hunger in it."

"What kind of condition is it?" asked the King.

"I have a daughter," said the old woman, "who is as beautiful as anyone in the world, and well deserves to be your consort, and if you will make her your Queen, I will show you the way out of the forest." In the anguish of his heart the King consented, and the old woman led him to her little hut, where her daughter was sitting by the fire. She received the King as if she had been expecting him, and he saw that she was very beautiful, but still she did not please him, and he could not look at her without secret horror. After he had taken the maiden up on his horse, the old woman showed him the way, and the King reached his royal palace again, where the wedding was celebrated.

The King had already been married once, and had by his first wife, seven children, six boys and a girl, whom he loved better than anything else in the world. As he now feared that the step-mother might not treat them well, and even do them some injury, he took them to a lonely castle which stood in the midst of a forest. It lay so concealed, and the way was so difficult to find, that he himself would not have found it, if a wise woman had not given him a ball of yarn with wonderful properties. When he threw it down before him, it unrolled itself and showed him his path. The King, however, went so frequently away to his dear children that the Queen observed his absence; she was curious and wanted to know what he did when he was quite alone in the forest. She gave a great deal of money to his servants, and they betrayed the secret to her, and told her likewise of the ball which alone could point out the way. And now she knew no rest until she had learnt where the King kept the ball of yarn, and then she made little shirts of white silk, and as she had learnt the art of witchcraft from her mother, she sewed a charm inside them. And once when the King had ridden forth to hunt, she took the little shirts and went into the forest, and the ball showed her the way. The children, who saw from a distance that someone was approaching, thought that their dear father was coming to them, and full of joy, ran to meet him. Then she threw one of the little shirts over each of them, and no sooner had the shirts touched their bodies than they were changed into swans, and flew away over the forest. The Queen went home quite delighted, and thought she had got rid of her step-children, but the girl had not run out with her brothers, and the Queen knew nothing about her. Next day the King went to visit his children, but he found no one but the little girl. "Where are your brothers?" asked the King. "Alas, dear father," she answered, "they have gone away and left me alone!" and she told him that she had seen from her little window how her brothers had flown away over the forest in the shape of swans, and she showed him the feathers, which they had let fall in the courtyard, and which she had picked up. The King mourned, but he did not think that the Queen had done this wicked deed, and as he feared that the girl would also be stolen away from him, he wanted to take her away with him. But she was afraid of her step-mother, and entreated the King to let her stay just this one night more in the forest castle.

The poor girl thought: "I can no longer stay here. I will go and seek my brothers." And when night came, she ran away, and went straight into the forest. She walked the whole night long, and next day also without stopping, until she could go no farther for weariness. Then she saw a forest-hut, and went into it, and found a room with six little beds, but she did not venture to get into one of them, but crept under one, and lay down on the hard ground, intending to pass the night there. Just before sunset, however, she heard a rustling, and saw six swans come flying in at the window. They alighted on the ground and blew at each other, and blew all the feathers off, and their swans' skins stripped off like a shirt. Then the maiden looked at them and recognized her brothers, was glad and crept forth from beneath the bed. The brothers were not less delighted to see their little sister, but their joy was of short duration. "Here you cannot abide," they said to her. "This is a shelter for robbers, if they come home and find you, they will kill you." "But can you not protect me?" asked the little sister. "No," they replied, "only for one quarter of an hour each evening can we lay aside our swans' skins and have during that time our human form, after that, we are once more turned into swans." The little sister wept and said: "Can you not be set free?" "Alas, no," they answered, "the conditions are too hard! For six years you may neither speak nor laugh, and in that time you must sew together six little shirts of starwort for us. And if one single word falls from your lips, all your work will be lost." And when the brothers had said this, the quarter of an hour was over, and they flew out of the window again as swans.

The maiden, however, firmly resolved to deliver her brothers, even if it should cost her her life. She left the hut, went into the midst of the forest, seated herself on a tree, and there passed the night. Next morning she went out and gathered starwort and began to sew. She could not speak to anyone, and she had no inclination to laugh; she sat there and looked at nothing but her work. When she had already spent a long time there it came to pass that the King of the country was hunting in the forest, and his huntsmen came to the tree on which the maiden was sitting. They called to her and said: "Who are you?" But she made no answer. "Come down to us," said they. "We will not do you any harm." She only shook her head. As they pressed her further with questions she threw her golden necklace down to them, and thought to content them thus. They, however, did not cease, and then she threw her girdle down to them, and as this also was to no purpose, her garters, and by degrees everything that she had on that she could do without until she had nothing left but her shirt. The huntsmen, however, did not let themselves be turned aside by that, but climbed the tree and fetched the maiden down and led her before the King. The King asked: "Who are you? What are you doing on the tree?" But she did not answer. He put the question in every language that he knew, but she remained as mute as a fish. As she was so beautiful, the King's heart was touched, and he was smitten with a great love for her. He put his mantle on her, took her before him on his horse, and carried her to his castle. Then he caused her to be dressed in rich garments, and she shone in her beauty like bright daylight, but no word could be drawn from her. He placed her by his side at table, and her modest bearing and courtesy pleased him so much that he said: "She is the one whom I wish to marry, and no other woman in the world." And after some days he united himself to her.

The King, however, had a wicked mother who was dissatisfied with this marriage and spoke ill of the young Queen. "Who knows," said she, "from whence the creature who can't speak, comes? She is not worthy of a king!" After a year had passed, when the Queen brought her first child into the world, the old woman took it away from her, and smeared her mouth with blood as she slept. Then she went to the King and accused the Queen of being a man-eater. The King would not believe it, and would not suffer anyone to do her any injury. She, however, sat continually sewing at the shirts, and cared for nothing else. The next time, when she again bore a beautiful boy, the false mother-in-law used the same treachery, but the King could not bring himself to give credit to her words. He said: "She is too pious and good to do anything of that kind; if she were not dumb, and could defend herself, her innocence would come to light." But when the old woman stole away the newly-born child for the third time, and accused the Queen, who did not utter one word of defence, the King could do no other-wise than deliver her over to justice, and she was sentenced to suffer death by fire.

When the day came for the sentence to be carried out, it was the last day of the six years during which she was not to speak or laugh, and she had delivered her dear brothers from the power of the enchant-ment. The six shirts were ready, only the left sleeve of the sixth was wanting. When, therefore, she was led to the stake, she laid the shirts on her arm, and when she stood on high and the fire was just going to be lighted, she looked around and six swans came flying through the air towards her. Then she saw that her deliverance was near, and her heart leapt with joy. The swans swept towards her and sank down so that she could throw the shirts over them, and as they were touched by them, their swans' skins fell off, and her brothers stood in their own bodily form before her, and were vigorous and handsome. The young-est only lacked his left arm, and had in the place of it a swan's wing on his shoulder. They embraced and kissed each other, and the Queen went to the King, who was greatly moved, and she began to speak and said: "Dearest husband, now I may speak and declare to you that I am innocent, and falsely accused." And she told him of the treachery of the old woman who had taken away her three children and hidden them. Then to the great joy of the King they were brought thither, and as a punishment, the wicked mother-in-law was bound to the stake, and burnt to ashes. But the King and the Queen with her six brothers lived many years in happiness and peace.

LITTLE BRIAR ROSE

A long time ago there were a King and Queen who said every day: "Ah, if only we had a child!" but they never had one. But it happened that once when the Queen was bathing, a frog crept out of the water on to the land, and said to her: "Your wish shall be fulfilled; before a year has gone by, you shall have a daughter."

What the frog had said came true, and the Queen had a little girl who was so pretty that the King could not contain himself for joy, and ordered a great feast. He invited not only his kindred, friends and acquaintances, but also the Wise Women, in order that they might be kind and well-disposed towards the child. There were thirteen of them in his kingdom, but, as he had only twelve golden plates for them to eat out of, one of them had to be left at home.

The feast was held with all manner of splendor, and when it came to an end the Wise Women bestowed their magic gifts upon the baby: one gave virtue, another beauty, a third riches, and so on with everything in the world that one can wish for.

When eleven of them had made their promises, suddenly the thirteenth came in. She wished to avenge herself for not having been invited, and without greeting, or even looking at anyone, she cried with a loud voice: "The King's daughter shall in her fifteenth year prick herself with a spindle, and fall down dead." And, without saying a word more, she turned round and left the room.

They were all shocked; but the twelfth, whose good wish still remained unspoken, came forward, and as she could not undo the evil sentence, but only soften it, she said: "It shall not be death, but a deep sleep of a hundred years, into which the princess shall fall."

The King, who would fain keep his dear child from the misfortune, gave orders that every spindle in the whole kingdom should be burnt. Meanwhile the gifts of the Wise Women were plenteously fulfilled on the young girl, for she was so beautiful, modest, good-natured, and wise, that everyone who saw her was bound to love her.

It happened that on the very day when she was fifteen years old, the King and Queen were not at home, and the maiden was left in the palace quite alone. So she went round into all sorts of places, looked into rooms and bed-chambers just as she liked, and at last came to an old tower. She climbed up the narrow winding-staircase, and reached a little door. A rusty key was in the lock, and when she turned it the door sprang open, and there in a little room sat an old woman with a spindle, busily spinning her flax.

"Good day, old mother," said the King's daughter; "what are you doing there?" "I am spinning," said the old woman, and nodded her head. "What sort of thing is that, that rattles round so merrily?" said the girl, and she took the spindle and wanted to spin too. But scarcely had she touched the spindle when the magic decree was fulfilled, and she pricked her finger with it.

And, in the very moment when she felt the prick, she fell down upon the bed that stood there, and lay in a deep sleep. And this sleep extended over the whole palace; the King and Queen who had just come home, and had entered the great hall, began to go to sleep, and the whole of the court with them. The horses, too, went to sleep in the stable, the dogs in the yard, the pigeons upon the roof, the flies on the wall; even the fire that was flaming on the hearth became quiet and slept, the roast meat left off frizzling, and the cook, who was just going to pull the hair of the scullery boy, because he had forgotten something, let him go, and went to sleep. And the wind fell, and on the trees before the castle not a leaf moved again.

But round about the castle there began to grow a hedge of thorns, which every year became higher, and at last grew close up round the castle and all over it, so that there was nothing of it to be seen, not even the flag upon the roof. But the story of the beautiful sleeping "Briar Rose," for so the princess was named, went about the country, so that

from time to time Kings' sons came and tried to get through the thorny hedge into the castle.

But they found it impossible, for the thorns held fast together, as if they had hands, and the youths were caught in them, could not get loose again, and died a miserable death.

After long, long years a King's son came again to that country, and heard an old man talking about the thorn-hedge, and that a castle was said to stand behind it in which a wonderfully beautiful princess, named Briar Rose, had been asleep for a hundred years; and that the King and Queen and the whole court were asleep likewise. He had heard, too, from his grandfather, that many kings' sons had already come, and had tried to get through the thorny hedge, but they had remained sticking fast in it, and had died a pitiful death. Then the youth said: "I am not afraid, I will go and see the beautiful Briar Rose." The good old man might dissuade him as he would, he did not listen to his words.

But by this time the hundred years had just passed, and the day had come when Briar Rose was to awake again. When the King's son came near to the thorn-hedge, it was nothing but large and beautiful flowers, which parted from each other of their own accord, and let him pass unhurt, then they closed again behind him like a hedge. In the castle yard he saw the horses and the spotted hounds lying asleep; on the roof sat the pigeons with their heads under their wings. And when he entered the house, the flies were asleep upon the wall, the cook in the kitchen was still holding out his hand to seize the boy, and the maid was sitting by the black hen which she was going to pluck.

He went on farther, and in the great hall he saw the whole of the court lying asleep, and up by the throne lay the King and Queen.

Then he went on still farther, and all was so quiet that a breath could be heard, and at last he came to the tower, and opened the door into the little room where Briar Rose was sleeping. There she lay, so beautiful that he could not turn his eyes away; and he stooped down and gave her a kiss. But as soon as he kissed her, Briar Rose opened her eyes and awoke, and looked at him quite sweetly.

Then they went down together, and the King awoke, and the Queen, and the whole court, and looked at each other in great astonishment. And the horses in the courtyard stood up and shook themselves; the hounds jumped up and wagged their tails; the pigeons upon the roof pulled out their heads from under their wings, looked round, and flew into the open country; the flies on the wall crept again; the fire in the kitchen burned up and flickered and cooked the meat; the joint began to turn and sizzle again, and the cook gave the boy such a box on the ear that he screamed, and the maid finished plucking the fowl.

And then the marriage of the King's son with Briar Rose was celebrated with all splendour, and they lived contented to the end of their days.

FUNDEVOGEL*

There was once a forester who went into the forest to hunt, and as he entered it he heard a sound of screaming as if a little child were there. He followed the sound, and at last came to a high tree, and at the top of this a little child was sitting, for the mother had fallen asleep under the tree with the child, and a bird of prey had seen it in her arms, had flown down, snatched it away, and set it on the high tree.

The forester climbed up, brought the child down, and thought to himself: "You will take him home with you, and bring him up with your Lina." He took it home, therefore, and the two children grew up together. And the one, which he had found on a tree was called Fundevogel, because a bird had carried it away. Fundevogel and Lina loved each other so dearly that when they did not see each other they were sad.

Now the forester had an old cook, who one evening took two pails and began to fetch water, and did not go once only, but many times, out to the spring. Lina saw this and said, "Listen, old Sanna, why are you fetching so much water?" "If you will never repeat it to anyone, I will tell you why." So Lina said, no, she would never repeat it to anyone, and then the cook said: "Early to-morrow morning, when the forester is out hunting, I will heat the water, and when it is boiling in the kettle, I will throw in Fundevogel, and will boil him in it."

* Bird-foundling.

Early next morning the forester got up and went out hunting, and when he was gone the children were still in bed. Then Lina said to Fundevogel: "If you will never leave me, I too will never leave you." Fundevogel said: "Neither now, nor ever will I leave you." Then said Lina: "Then will I tell you. Last night, old Sanna carried so many buckets of water into the house that I asked her why she was doing that, and she said that if I would promise not to tell anyone she would tell me, and I said I would be sure not to tell anyone, and she said that early to-morrow morning when father was out hunting, she would set the kettle full of water, throw you into it and boil you; but we will get up quickly, dress ourselves, and go away together."

The two children therefore got up, dressed themselves quickly, and went away. When the water in the kettle was boiling, the cook went into the bed-room to fetch Fundevogel and throw him into it. But when she came in, and went to the beds, both the children were gone. Then she was terribly alarmed, and she said to herself: "What shall I say now when the forester comes home and sees that the children are gone? They must be followed instantly to get them back again."

Then the cook sent three servants after them, who were to run and overtake the children. The children, however, were sitting outside the forest, and when they saw from afar the three servants running, Lina said to Fundevogel: "Never leave me, and I will never leave you." Fundevogel said: "Neither now, nor ever." Then said Lina: "Do you become a rose-tree, and I the rose upon it." When the three servants came to the forest, nothing was there but a rose-tree and one rose on it, but the children were nowhere. Then said they: "There is nothing to be done here," and they went home and told the cook that they had seen nothing in the forest but a little rose-bush with one rose on it. Then the old cook scolded and said: "You simpletons, you should have cut the rose-bush in two, and have broken off the rose and brought it home with you; go, and do it at once." They had therefore to go out and look for the second time. The children, however, saw them coming from a distance. Then Lina said: "Fundevogel, never leave me, and I will never leave you." Fundevogel said: "Neither now, nor ever." Said Lina: "Then do you become a church, and I'll be the chandelier in it." So when the three servants came, nothing was there but a church, with a chandelier in it. They said therefore to each other: "What can we do here, let us go home." When they got home, the cook asked if they had not found them; so they said no, they had found nothing but a church, and that there was chandelier in it. And the cook scolded them and said: "You fools! why did you not pull the church to pieces, and bring the chandelier home with you?" And now the old cook herself got on her legs, and went with the three servants in pursuit of the children. The children, however, saw from afar that the three servants were coming, and the cook waddling after them. Then said Lina: "Fundevogel, never leave me, and I will never leave you." Then said Fundevogel: "Neither now, nor ever." Said Lina: "Be a fishpond, and I will be the duck upon it." The cook, however, came up to them, and when she saw the pond she lay down by it, and was about to drink it up. But the duck swam quickly to her, seized her head in its beak and drew her into the water, and there the old witch had to drown. Then the children went home together, and were heartily delighted, and if they have not died, they are living still.

KING THRUSHBEARD

A King had a daughter who was beautiful beyond all measure, but so proud and haughty withal that no suitor was good enough for her. She sent away one after the other, and ridiculed them as well.

Once the King made a great feast and invited thereto, from far and near, all the young men likely to marry. They were all marshalled in a row according to their rank and standing; first came the kings, then the grand-dukes, then the princes, the earls, the barons, and the gentry. Then the King's daughter was led through the ranks, but to each one she had some objection to make; one was too fat, "The wine-barrel," she said. Another was too tall, "Long and thin has little in." The third was too short, "Short and thick is never quick." The fourth was too pale, "As pale as death." The fifth too red, "A fighting-cock." The sixth was not straight enough, "A green log dried behind the stove."

So she had something to say against each one, but she made herself especially merry over a good king who stood quite high up in the row, and whose chin had grown a little crooked. "Look," she cried and laughed, "he has a chin like a thrush's beak!" and from that time he got the name of King Thrushbeard.

But the old King, when he saw that his daughter did nothing but mock the people, and despised all the suitors who were gathered there, was very angry, and swore that she should have for her husband the very first beggar that came to his doors.

A few days afterwards a fiddler came and sang beneath the windows, trying to earn a few pennies. When the King heard him he said: "Let him come up." So the fiddler came in, in his dirty, ragged clothes, and sang before the King and his daughter, and when he had ended he asked for a trifling gift. The King said: "Your song has pleased me so well that I will give you my daughter there, to wife."

The King's daughter shuddered, but the King said: "I have taken an oath to give you to the very first beggar-man, and I will keep it." All she could say was in vain; the priest was brought, and she had to let herself be wedded to the fiddler on the spot. When that was done the King said: "Now it is not proper for you, a beggar-woman, to stay any longer in my palace, you may just go away with your husband."

The beggar-man led her out by the hand, and she was obliged to walk away on foot with him. When they came to a large forest she asked: "To whom does that beautiful forest belong?" "It belongs to King Thrushbeard; if you had taken him, it would have been yours." "Ah, unhappy girl that I am, if I had but taken King Thrushbeard!"

Afterwards they came to a meadow, and she asked again: "To whom does this beautiful green meadow belong?" "It belongs to King Thrushbeard; if you had taken him, it would have been yours." "Ah, unhappy girl that I am, if I had but taken King Thrushbeard!"

Then they came to a large town, and she asked again: "To whom does this fine large town belong?" "It belongs to King Thrushbeard; if you had taken him, it would have been yours." "Ah, unhappy girl that I am, if I had but taken King Thrushbeard!"

"It does not please me," said the fiddler, "to hear you always wishing for another husband; am I not good enough for you?" At last they came to a very little hut, and she said: "Oh, goodness! what a small house; to whom does this miserable, tiny hovel belong?" The fiddler answered: "That is my house and yours, where we shall live together."

She had to stoop in order to go in at the low door. "Where are the servants?" said the King's daughter. "What servants?" answered the beggar-man; "you must yourself do what you wish to have done. Just make a fire at once, and set on water to cook my supper, I am quite tired." But the King's daughter knew nothing about lighting fires or cooking, and the beggar-man had to lend a hand himself to get anything fairly done. When they had finished their scanty meal they went to bed; but he forced her to get up quite early in the morning in order to look after the house.

For a few days they lived in this way as well as might be, and came to the end of all their provisions. Then the man said: "Wife, we cannot go on any longer eating and drinking here and earning nothing. You must make baskets." He went out, cut some willows, and brought them home. Then she began to make baskets, but the tough willows wounded her delicate hands.

"I see that this will not do," said the man; "you had better spin, perhaps you can do that better." She sat down and tried to spin, but the hard thread soon cut her soft fingers so that the blood ran down. "See," said the man, "you are fit for no sort of work; I have made a bad bargain with you. Now I will try to make a business with pots and earthenware; you must sit in the market-place and sell the ware." "Alas," thought she, "if any of the people from my father's kingdom come to the market and see me sitting there, selling, how they will mock me!" But it was of no use, she had to yield unless she chose to die of hunger.

For the first time she succeeded well, for the people were glad to buy the woman's wares because she was good-looking, and they paid her what she asked; many even gave her the money and left the pots with her as well. So they lived on what she had earned as long as it lasted, then the husband bought a lot of new crockery. With this she sat down at the corner of the market-place, and set it out round about her ready for sale. But suddenly there came a drunken hussar galloping along, and he rode right amongst the pots so that they were all broken into a thousand bits. She began to weep, and did not know what to do for fear. "Alas! what will happen to me?" cried she; "what will my husband say to this?"

She ran home and told him of the misfortune. "Who would seat herself at a corner of the market-place with crockery?" said the man;

"leave off crying, I see very well that you cannot do any ordinary work, so I have been to our King's palace and have asked whether they cannot find a place for a kitchen-maid, and they have promised me to take you; in that way you will get your food for nothing."

The King's daughter was now a kitchen-maid, and had to be at the cook's beck and call, and do the dirtiest work. In both her pockets she fastened a little jar, in which she took home her share of the leavings, and upon this they lived.

It happened that the wedding of the King's eldest son was to be celebrated, so the poor woman went up and placed herself by the door of the hall to look on. When all the candles were lit, and people, each more beautiful than the other, entered, and all was full of pomp and splendour, she thought of her lot with a sad heart, and cursed the pride and haughtiness which had humbled her and brought her to so great poverty.

The smell of the delicious dishes which were being taken in and out reached her, and now and then the servants threw her a few morsels of them: these she put in her jars to take home.

All at once the King's son entered, clothed in velvet and silk, with gold chains about his neck. And when he saw the beautiful woman standing by the door he seized her by the hand, and would have danced with her; but she refused and shrank with fear, for she saw that it was King Thrushbeard, her suitor whom she had driven away with scorn.

Her struggles were of no avail, he drew her into the hall; but the string by which her pockets were hung broke, the pots fell down, the soup ran out, and the scraps were scattered all about. And when the people saw it, there arose general laughter and derision, and she was so ashamed that she would rather have been a thousand fathoms below the ground. She sprang to the door and would have run away, but on the stairs a man caught her and brought her back; and when she looked at him it was King Thrushbeard again. He said to her kindly: "Do not be afraid, I and the fiddler who has been living with you in that wretched hovel are one. For love of you I disguised myself so; and I also was the hussar who rode through your crockery. This was all done to humble your proud spirit, and to punish you for the insolence with which you mocked me."

Then she wept bitterly and said: "I have done great wrong, and am not worthy to be your wife." But he said: "Be comforted, the evil days are past; now we will celebrate our wedding." Then the maids-in-waiting came and put on her the most splendid clothing, and her father and his whole court came and wished her happiness in her marriage with King Thrushbeard, and the joy now began in earnest. I wish you and I had been there too.

LITTLE SNOW WHITE

Once upon a time in the middle of winter, when the flakes of snow were falling like feathers from the sky, a Queen sat at a window sewing, and the frame of the window was made of black ebony. And whilst she was sewing and looking out of the window at the snow, she pricked her finger with the needle, and three drops of blood fell upon the snow. And the red looked pretty upon the white snow, and she thought to herself: "Would that I had a child as white as snow, as red as blood, and as black as the wood of the window-frame."

Soon after that she had a little daughter, who was as white as snow, and as red as blood, and her hair was as black as ebony; and she was therefore called Little Snow White. And when the child was born, the Queen died.

After a year had passed the King took to himself another wife. She was a beautiful woman, but proud and haughty, and she could not bear that anyone else should surpass her in beauty. She had a wonderful looking-glass, and when she stood in front of it and looked at herself in it, and said:

> "Looking-glass, Looking-glass, on the wall,
> Who in this land is the fairest of all?"

the looking-glass answered:

> "Thou, O Queen, art the fairest of all!"

Then she was satisfied, for she knew that the looking-glass spoke the truth.

But Snow White was growing up, and grew more and more beautiful; and when she was seven years old she was as beautiful as the day, and more beautiful than the Queen herself. And once when the Queen asked her looking-glass:

> "Looking-glass, Looking-glass, on the wall,
> Who in this land is the fairest of all?"

it answered:

> "Thou art fairer than all who are here, Lady Queen.
> But more beautiful still is Snow White, as I ween."

Then the Queen was shocked, and turned yellow and green with envy. From that hour, whenever she looked at Snow White, her heart heaved in her breast, she hated the girl so much.

And envy and pride grew higher and higher in her heart like a weed, so that she had no peace day or night. She called a huntsman, and said: "Take the child away into the forest; I will no longer have her in my sight. Kill her, and bring me back her lung and liver as a token." The huntsman obeyed, and took her away; but when he had drawn his knife, and was about to pierce Snow White's innocent heart, she began to weep, and said: "Ah, dear huntsman, leave me my life! I will run away into the wild forest, and never come home again."

And as she was so beautiful the huntsman had pity on her and said: "Run away, then, you poor child." "The wild beasts will soon have devoured you," thought he, and yet it seemed as if a stone had been rolled from his heart since it was no longer needful for him to kill her. And as a young boar just then came running by he stabbed it, and cut out its lung and liver and took them to the Queen as proof that the child was dead. The cook had to salt them, and the wicked Queen ate them, and thought she had eaten the lung and liver of Snow White.

But now the poor child was all alone in the great forest, and so terrified that she looked at all the leaves on the trees, and did not know what to do. Then she began to run, and ran over sharp stones and through thorns, and the wild beasts ran past her, but did her no harm.

She ran as long as her feet would go until it was almost evening; then she saw a little cottage and went into it to rest herself. Everything in the cottage was small, but neater and cleaner than can be told. There was a table on which was a white cover, and seven little plates, and on each plate a little spoon; moreover, there were seven little knives and forks, and seven little mugs. Against the wall stood seven little beds side by side, and covered with snow-white counterpanes.

Little Snow White was so hungry and thirsty that she ate some vegetables and bread from each plate and drank a drop of wine out of each mug, for she did not wish to take all from one only. Then, as she was so tired, she laid herself down on one of the little beds, but none of them suited her; one was too long, another too short, but at last she found that the seventh one was right, and so she remained in it, said a prayer and went to sleep.

When it was quite dark the owners of the cottage came back; they were seven dwarfs who dug and delved in the mountains for ore. They lit their seven candles, and as it was now light within the cottage they saw that someone had been there, for everything was not in the same order in which they had left it.

The first said: "Who has been sitting on my chair?"

The second: "Who has been eating off my plate?"

The third: "Who has been taking some of my bread?"

The fourth: "Who has been eating my vegetables?"

The fifth: "Who has been using my fork?"

The sixth: "Who has been cutting with my knife?"

The seventh: "Who has been drinking out of my mug?"

Then the first looked round and saw that there was a little hollow on his bed, and he said: "Who has been getting into my bed?" The others came up and each called out: "Somebody has been lying in my bed too." But the seventh when he looked at his bed saw little Snow White, who was lying asleep therein. And he called the others, who came running up, and they cried out with astonishment, and brought their seven little candles and let the light fall on little Snow White. "Oh, heavens! oh, heavens!" cried they, "what a lovely child!" and they were so glad that they did not wake her up, but let her sleep on in the bed. And the seventh dwarf slept with his companions, one hour with each, and so passed the night.

When it was morning little Snow White awoke, and was frightened when she saw the seven dwarfs. But they were friendly and asked her what her name was. "My name is Snow White," she answered. "How have you come to our house?" said the dwarfs. Then she told them that her step-mother had wished to have her killed, but that the huntsman had spared her life, and that she had run for the whole day, until at last she had found their dwelling. The dwarfs said: "If you will take care of our house, cook, make the beds, wash, sew, and knit, and if you will keep everything neat and clean, you can stay with us and you shall want for nothing." "Yes," said Snow White, "with all my heart," and she stayed with them. She kept the house in order for them; in the mornings they went to the mountains and looked for copper and gold, in the evenings they came back, and then their supper had to be ready. The girl was alone the whole day, so the good dwarfs warned her and said:

"Beware of your step-mother, she will soon know that you are here; be sure to let no one come in."

But the Queen, believing that she had eaten Snow White's lung and liver, could not but think that she was again the first and most beautiful of all; and she went to her looking-glass and said:

"Looking-glass, Looking-glass, on the wall,
who in this land is the fairest of all?"

and the glass answered:

"Oh, Queen, thou art fairest of all I see,
But over the hills, where the seven dwarfs dwell,
Snow White is still alive and well,
And none is so fair as she."

Then she was astounded, for she knew that the looking-glass never spoke falsely, and she knew that the huntsman had betrayed her, and that little Snow White was still alive.

And so she thought and thought again how she might kill her, for so long as she was not the fairest in the whole land, envy let her have no rest. And when she had at last thought of something to do, she painted her face, and dressed herself like an old pedlar-woman, and no one could have known her. In this disguise she went over the seven mountains to the seven dwarfs, and knocked at the door and cried: "Pretty things to sell, very cheap, very cheap." Little Snow White looked out of the window and called out: "Goodday, my good woman, what have you to sell?" "Good things, pretty things," she answered; "stay-laces of all colours," and she pulled out one which was woven of bright-coloured silk. "I may let the worthy old woman in," thought Snow White, and she unbolted the door and bought the pretty laces. "Child," said the old woman, "what a fright you look; come, I will lace you properly for once." Snow White had no suspicion, but stood before her, and let herself be laced with the new laces. But the old woman laced so quickly and laced so tightly that Snow White lost her breath and fell down as if dead. "Now I am the most beautiful," said the Queen to herself, and ran away.

Not long afterwards, in the evening, the seven dwarfs came home, but how shocked they were when they saw their dear little Snow White lying on the ground, and that she neither stirred nor moved, and seemed to be dead. They lifted her up, and, as they saw that she was laced too tightly, they cut the laces; then she began to breathe a little, and after a while came to life again. When the dwarfs heard what had happened they said: "The old pedlar-woman was no one else than the wicked Queen; take care and let no one come in when we are not with you."

But the wicked woman when she had reached home went in front of the glass and asked:

> "Looking-glass, Looking-glass, on the wall,
> Who in this land is the fairest of all?"

and it answered as before:

> "Oh, Queen, thou art fairest of all I see,
> But over the hills, where the seven dwarfs dwell,
> Snow White is still alive and well,
> And none is so fair as she."

When she heard that, all her blood rushed to her heart with fear, for she saw plainly that little Snow White was again alive. "But now," she said, "I will think of something that shall really put an end to you," and by the help of witchcraft, which she understood, she made a poisonous comb. Then she disguised herself and took the shape of another old woman. So she went over the seven mountains to the seven dwarfs, knocked at the door, and cried: "Good things to sell, cheap, cheap!" Little Snow White looked out and said: "Go away; I cannot let anyone come in." "I suppose you can look," said the old woman, and pulled the poisonous comb out and held it up. It pleased the girl so well that she let herself be beguiled, and opened the door. When they had made a bargain the old woman said: "Now I will comb you properly for once." Poor little Snow White had no suspicion, and let the old woman do as she pleased, but hardly had she put the comb in her hair than the poison in it took effect, and the girl fell down senseless. "You paragon of beauty," said the wicked woman, "you are finished now," and she went away.

But fortunately it was almost evening, when the seven dwarfs came home. When they saw Snow White lying as if dead upon the ground they at once suspected the step-mother, and they looked and found the poisoned comb. Scarcely had they taken it out when Snow White came to herself, and told them what had happened. Then they warned her once more to be upon her guard and to open the door to no one.

The Queen, at home, went in front of the glass and said:

"Looking-glass, Looking-glass, on the wall,
Who in this land is the fairest of all?"

then it answered as before:

"Oh, Queen, thou art fairest of all I see,
But over the hills, where the seven dwarfs dwell,
Snow White is still alive and well,
And none is so fair as she."

When she heard the glass speak thus she trembled and shook with rage. "Snow White shall die," she cried, "even if it costs me my life!"

Thereupon she went into a quite secret, lonely room, where no one ever came, and there she made a very poisonous apple. Outside it looked pretty, white with a red cheek, so that everyone who saw it longed for it; but whoever ate a piece of it must surely die.

When the apple was ready she painted her face, and dressed herself up as a farmer's wife, and so she went over the seven mountains to the seven dwarfs. She knocked at the door. Snow White put her head out of the window and said: "I cannot let anyone in; the seven dwarfs have forbidden me." "It is all the same to me," answered the woman, "I shall soon get rid of my apples. There, I will give you one."

"No," said Snow White, "I dare not take anything." "Are you afraid of poison?" said the old woman; "look, I will cut the apple in two pieces; you eat the red cheek, and I will eat the white." The apple was so cunningly made that only the red cheek was poisoned. Snow White longed for the fine apple, and when she saw that the woman ate part of it she could resist no longer, and stretched out her hand and took the poisonous half. But hardly had she a bit of it in her mouth than she fell down dead. Then the Queen looked at her with a dreadful look, and laughed aloud and said: "White as snow, red as blood, black as ebony-wood! this time the dwarfs cannot wake you up again."

And when she asked of the looking-glass at home:

"Looking-glass, Looking-glass, on the wall,
Who in this land is the fairest of all?"

it answered at last:

"Oh, Queen, in this land thou art fairest of all."

Then her envious heart had rest, so far as an envious heart can have rest.

The dwarfs, when they came home in the evening, found Snow White lying upon the ground; she breathed no longer and was dead. They lifted her up, looked to see whether they could find anything poisonous, unlaced her, combed her hair, washed her with water and wine, but it was all of no use; the poor child was dead, and remained dead. They laid her upon a bier, and all seven of them sat round it and wept for her, and wept three days long.

Then they were going to bury her, but she still looked as if she were living, and still had her pretty red cheeks. They said: "We could not bury her in the dark ground," and they had a transparent coffin of glass made, so that she could be seen from all sides, and they laid her in it, and wrote her name upon it in golden letters, and that she was a king's daughter. Then they put the coffin out upon the mountain, and one of them always stayed by it and watched it. And birds came too, and wept for Snow White; first an owl, then a raven, and last a dove.

And now Snow White lay a long, long time in the coffin, and she did not change, but looked as if she were asleep; for she was as white as snow, as red as blood, and her hair was as black as ebony.

It happened, however, that a king's son came into the forest, and went to the dwarfs' house to spend the night. He saw the coffin on the mountain, and the beautiful Snow White within it, and read what was

written upon it in golden letters. Then he said to the dwarfs: "Let me have the coffin, I will give you whatever you want for it." But the dwarfs answered: "We will not part with it for all the gold in the world." Then he said: "Let me have it as a gift, for I cannot live without seeing Snow White. I will honour and prize her as my dearest possession." As he spoke in this way the good dwarfs took pity upon him, and gave him the coffin.

And now the King's son had it carried away by his servants on their shoulders. And it happened that they stumbled over a tree-stump, and with the shock the poisonous piece of apple which Snow White had bitten off came out of her throat. And before long she opened her eyes, lifted up the lid of the coffin, sat up, and was once more alive. "Oh, heavens, where am I?" she cried. The King's son, full of joy, said: "You are with me," and told her what had happened, and said: "I love you more than everything in the world; come with me to my father's palace, you shall be my wife."

And Snow White was willing, and went with him, and their wedding was held with great show and splendour. But Snow White's wicked step-mother was also bidden to the feast. When she had arrayed herself in beautiful clothes she went before the Looking-glass, and said:

"Looking-glass, Looking-glass, on the wall,
Who in this land is the fairest of all?"

the glass answered:

"Oh, Queen, of all here the fairest art thou,
But the young Queen is fairer by far as I trow."

Then the wicked woman uttered a curse, and was so wretched, so utterly wretched, that she knew not what to do. At first she would not go to the wedding at all, but she had no peace, and had to go to see the young Queen. And when she went in she recognized Snow White; and she stood still with rage and fear, and could not stir. But iron slippers had already been put upon the fire, and they were brought in with tongs, and set before her. Then she was forced to put on the red-hot shoes, and dance until she dropped down dead.

THE KNAPSACK, THE HAT, AND THE HORN

There were once three brothers who had fallen deeper and deeper into poverty, and at last their need was so great that they had to endure hunger, and had nothing to eat or drink. Then said they: "It cannot go on like this, we had better go into the world and seek our fortune." They therefore set out, and had already walked over many a long road and many a blade of grass, but had not yet met with good luck. One day they arrived in a great forest, and in the midst of it was a hill, and when they came nearer they saw that the hill was all silver. Then spoke the eldest: "Now I have found the good luck I wished for, and I desire nothing more." He took as much of the silver as he could possibly carry, and then turned back and went home again. But the two others said: "We want something more from good luck than mere silver," and did not touch it, but went onwards. After they had walked for two days longer without stopping, they came to a hill which was all gold. The second brother stopped, took thought with himself, and was undecided. "What shall I do?" said he; "shall I take for myself so much of this gold, that I have sufficient for all the rest of my life, or shall I go farther?" At length he made a decision, and putting as much into his pockets as would go in, said farewell to his brother, and went home. But the third said: "Silver and gold do not move me, I will not renounce my chance of fortune, perhaps something better still will be given me." He journeyed onwards, and when he had walked for three days, he came to a forest which was still larger than the one before, and never would come to an end, and as he found nothing to eat or to drink, he was all but exhausted. Then he climbed up a high tree to find out if up there he could see the end of the forest, but so far as his eye could pierce he saw nothing but the tops of trees. Then he began to descend the tree again, but hunger tormented him, and he thought to himself: "If I could but eat my fill once more!" When he got down he saw with astonishment a table beneath the tree richly spread with food, the steam of which rose up to meet him. "This time," said he, "my wish has been fulfilled at the right moment." And without inquiring who had brought the food, or who had cooked it, he approached the table, and ate with enjoyment until he had appeased his hunger. When he was done, he thought: "It would after all be a pity if the pretty little table-cloth were to be spoilt in the forest here," and folded it up tidily and put it in his pocket. Then he went onwards, and in the evening, when hunger once more returned to him, he wanted to make a trial of his little cloth, and spread it out and said: "I wish you to be covered with good cheer again," and scarcely had the wish crossed his lips than as many dishes with the most exquisite food on them stood on the table as there was room for. "Now I perceive," said he, "in what kitchen my cooking is done. You shall be dearer to me than the mountains of silver and gold." For he saw plainly that it was a wishing-cloth. The cloth, however, was still not enough to enable him to sit down quietly at home; he preferred to wander about the world and pursue his fortune farther.

One night he met, in a lonely wood, a dusty, black charcoal-burner, who was burning charcoal there, and had some potatoes by the fire, on which he was going to make a meal. "Good evening, blackbird!" said the youth. "How do you get on in your solitude?"

"One day is like another," replied the charcoal-burner, "and every night potatoes! Have you a mind to have some, and will you be my guest?" "Many thanks," replied the traveller, "I won't rob you of your supper; you did not reckon on a visitor, but if you will put up with what I have, you shall have an invitation."

"Who is to prepare it for you?" said the charcoal-burner. "I see that you have nothing with you, and there is no one within a two hours' walk who could give you anything." "And yet there shall be a meal," answered the youth, "and better than any you have ever tasted." Thereupon he brought his cloth out of his knapsack, spread it on the ground, and said: "Little cloth, cover yourself," and instantly boiled meat and baked meat stood there, and as hot as if it had just come out of the kitchen. The charcoal-burner stared with wide-open eyes, but did not require much pressing; he fell to, and thrust larger and larger mouthfuls into his black mouth. When they had eaten everything, the charcoal-burner smiled contentedly, and said: "Listen, your table-cloth has my approval; it would be a fine thing for me in this forest, where no one ever cooks me anything good. I will propose an exchange to you; there in the corner hangs a soldier's knapsack, which is certainly old and shabby, but in it lie concealed wonderful powers; but, as I no longer use it, I will give it to you for the table-cloth."

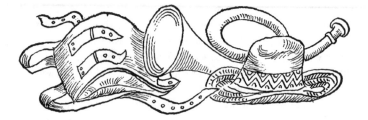

"I must first know what these wonderful powers are," answered the youth.

"That will I tell you," replied the charcoal-burner; "every time you tap it with your hand, a corporal comes with six men armed from head to foot, and they do whatsoever you command them." "So far as I am concerned," said the youth, "if nothing else can be done, we will exchange," and he gave the charcoal-burner the cloth, took the knapsack from the hook, put it on, and bade farewell. When he had walked a while, he wished to make a trial of the magical powers of his knapsack and tapped it. Immediately the seven warriors stepped up to him, and the corporal said: "What does my lord and ruler wish for?"

"March with all speed to the charcoal-burner, and demand my wishing-cloth back." They faced to the left, and it was not long before they brought what he required, and had taken it from the charcoal-burner without asking many questions. The young man bade them retire, went onwards, and hoped fortune would shine yet more brightly on him. By sunset he came to another charcoal-burner, who was making his supper ready by the fire. "If you will eat some potatoes with salt, but with no dripping, come and sit down with me," said the sooty fellow.

"No," he replied, "this time you shall be my guest," and he spread out his cloth, which was instantly covered with the most beautiful dishes. They ate and drank together, and enjoyed themselves heartily. After the meal was over, the charcoal-burner said: "Up there on that shelf lies a little old worn-out hat which has strange properties: the moment someone puts it on, and turns it round on his head, the cannons go off as if twelve were fired all together, and they demolish everything so that no one can withstand them. The hat is of no use to me, and I will willingly give it for your table-cloth."

"That suits me very well," he answered, took the hat, put it on, and left his table-cloth behind him. But hardly had he walked away than he tapped on his knapsack, and his soldiers had to fetch the cloth back again. "One thing comes on the top of another," thought he, "and I feel as if my luck had not yet come to an end." Neither had his thoughts deceived him. After he had walked on for the whole of one day, he came to a third charcoal-burner, who like the previous ones, invited him to potatoes without dripping. But he let him also dine with him from his wishing-cloth, and the charcoal-burner liked it so well, that at last he offered him a horn for it, which had very different properties from those of the hat. The moment someone blew it all the walls and fortifications fell down, and all towns and villages became ruins. For this he immediately gave the charcoal-burner the cloth, but he afterwards sent his soldiers to demand it back again, so that at length he had the knapsack, hat and horn, all three. "Now," said he, "I am a made man, and it is time for me to go home and see how my brothers are getting on."

When he reached home, his brothers had built themselves a handsome house with their silver and gold, and were living in clover. He went to see them, but as he came in a ragged coat, with his shabby hat on his head, and his old knapsack on his back, they would not acknowledge him as their brother. They mocked and said: "You give out that you are our brother who despised silver and gold, and craved for something still better for himself. Such a person arrives in his carriage in full splendor like a mighty king, not like a beggar," and they drove him out of doors. Then he fell into a rage, and tapped his knapsack until a hundred and fifty men stood before him armed from head to foot. He commanded them to surround his brothers' house, and two of them were to take hazel-sticks with them, and beat the two insolent men until they knew who he was. A violent disturbance broke out, people ran together, and wanted to lend the two some help in their need, but against the soldiers they could do nothing. News of this at length came to the King, who was very angry, and ordered a captain to march out with his troop, and drive this disturber of the peace out of the town; but the man with the knapsack soon got a greater body of men together, who repulsed the captain and his men, so that they were forced to retire with bloody noses. The King said: "This vagabond is not brought to order yet," and next day sent a still larger troop against him, but they could do even less. The youth set still more men against them, and in order to be done the sooner, he turned his hat twice round on his head, and heavy guns began to play, and the king's men were beaten and put to flight. "And now," said he, "I will not make peace until the King gives me his daughter to wife, and I govern the whole kingdom in his name." He caused this to be announced to the King, and the latter said to his daughter: "Necessity is a hard nut to crack—what else is there for me to do but what he desires? If I want peace and to keep the crown on my head, I must give you away."

So the wedding was celebrated, but the King's daughter was vexed that her husband should be a common man, who wore a shabby hat, and put on an old knapsack. She longed to get rid of him, and night and day studied how she could accomplish this. Then she thought to herself: "Is it possible that his wonderful powers lie in the knapsack?" and she feigned affection and caressed him, and when his heart was softened, she said: "If you would but lay aside that horrid knapsack, it makes you look so ugly, that I can't help being ashamed of you." "Dear child," said he, "this knapsack is my greatest treasure; as long as I have it, there is no power on earth that I am afraid of." And he revealed to her the wonderful virtue with which it was endowed. Then she threw herself in his arms as if she were going to kiss him, but cleverly took the knapsack off his shoulders, and ran away with it. As soon as she was alone she tapped it, and commanded the warriors to seize their former master, and take him out of the royal palace. They obeyed, and the false wife sent still more men after him, who were to drive him quite out of the country. Then he would have been ruined if he had not had the little hat. And hardly were his hands free before he turned it twice. Immediately the cannon began to thunder, and demolished everything, and the King's daughter herself was forced to come and beg for mercy. As she entreated in such moving terms, and promised to better her ways, he allowed himself to be persuaded and granted her peace. She behaved in a friendly manner to him, and acted as if she loved him very much, and after some time managed so to befool him, that he confided to her that even if someone got the knapsack into his power, he could do nothing against him so long as the old hat was still his. When she knew the secret, she waited until he was asleep, and then she took the hat away from him, and had it thrown out into the street. But the horn still remained to him, and in great anger he blew it with all his strength. Instantly all walls, fortifications, towns, and villages, toppled down, and crushed the King and his daughter to death. And had he not put down the horn and had blown just a little longer, everything would have been in ruins, and not one stone would have been left standing on another. Then no one opposed him any longer, and he made himself King of the whole country.

RUMPELSTILTSKIN

Once there was a miller who was poor, but who had a beautiful daughter. Now it happened that he had to go and speak to the King, and in order to make himself appear important he said to him: "I have a daughter who can spin straw into gold." The King said to the miller: "That is an art which pleases me well; if your daughter is as clever as you say, bring her to-morrow to my palace, and I will put her to the test."

And when the girl was brought to him he took her into a room which was quite full of straw, gave her a spinning-wheel and a reel, and said: "Now set to work, and if by to-morrow morning early you have not spun this straw into gold during the night, you must die." Thereupon he himself locked up the room, and left her in it alone. So there sat the poor miller's daughter, and for the life of her could not tell what to do; she had no idea how straw could be spun into gold, and she grew more and more frightened, until at last she began to weep.

But all at once the door opened, and in came a little man, and said: "Good evening, Mistress Miller; why are you crying so?" "Alas!" answered the girl, "I have to spin straw into gold, and I do not know how to do it." "What will you give me," said the manikin, "if I do it for you?" "My necklace," said the girl. The little man took the necklace, seated himself in front of the wheel, and whirr, whirr, whirr, three turns, and the reel was full; then he put another on, and whirr, whirr, whirr, three times round, and the second was full too. And so it went on until the morning, when all the straw was spun, and all the reels were full of gold. By daybreak the King was already there, and when he saw the gold he was astonished and delighted, but his heart became only more greedy. He had the miller's daughter taken into another room full of straw, which was much larger, and commanded her to spin that also in one night if she valued her life. The girl knew not how to help herself, and was crying, when the door opened again, and the little man appeared, and said: "What will you give me if I spin that straw into gold for you?" "The ring on my finger," answered the girl. The little man took the ring, again began to turn the wheel, and by morning had spun all the straw into glittering gold.

The King rejoiced beyond measure at the sight, but still he had not gold enough; and he had the miller's daughter taken into a still larger room full of straw, and said: "You must spin this, too, in the course of this night; but if you succeed, you shall be my wife." "Even if she be a miller's daughter," thought he, "I could not find a richer wife in the whole world."

When the girl was alone the manikin came again for the third time, and said: "What will you give me if I spin the straw for you this time also?" "I have nothing left that I could give," answered the girl. "Then promise me, if you should become Queen, to give me your first child." "Who knows whether that will ever happen?" thought the miller's daughter; and, not knowing how else to help herself in this strait, she promised the manikin what he wanted, and for that he once more spun the straw into gold.

And when the King came in the morning, and found all as he had wished, he took her in marriage, and the pretty miller's daughter became a Queen.

A year after, she brought a beautiful child into the world, and she never gave a thought to the manikin. But suddenly he came into her room, and said: "Now give me what you promised." The Queen was horror-struck, and offered the manikin all the riches of the kingdom if he would leave her the child. But the manikin said: "No, something alive is dearer to me than all the treasures in the world." Then the Queen began to lament and cry, so that the manikin pitied her. "I will give you three days' time," said he; "if by that time you find out my name, then shall you keep your child."

So the Queen thought the whole night of all the names that she had ever heard, and she sent a messenger over the country to inquire, far and wide, for any other names that there might be. When the manikin came the next day, she began with Caspar, Melchior, Balthazar, and said all the names she knew, one after another; but to every one the little man said: "That is not my name." On the second day she had inquiries made in the neighborhood as to the names of the people there, and she repeated to the manikin the most uncommon and curious. "Perhaps your name is Shortribs, or Sheepshanks, or Laceleg?" but he always answered: "That is not my name."

On the third day the messenger came back again, and said: "I have not been able to find a single new name, but as I came to a high mountain at the end of the forest, where the fox and the hare bid each other good night, there I saw a little house, and before the house a fire was burning, and round about the fire quite a ridiculous little man was jumping: he hopped upon one leg, and shouted:

" 'To-day I bake, to-morrow brew,
The next I'll have the young Queen's child.
Ha! glad am I that no one knew
That Rumpelstiltskin I am styled.' "

You may imagine how glad the Queen was when she heard the name! And when soon afterwards the little man came in, and asked:

"Now, Mistress Queen, what is my name?" at first she said, "Is your name Conrad?" "No." "Is your name Harry?" "No."

"Perhaps your name is Rumpelstiltskin?"

"The devil has told you that! the devil has told you that!" cried the little man, and in his anger he plunged his right foot so deep into the earth that his whole leg went in; and then in rage he pulled at his left leg so hard with both hands that he tore himself in two.

SWEETHEART ROLAND

There was once upon a time a woman who was a real witch and had two daughters, one ugly and wicked, and this one she loved because she was her own daughter, and one beautiful and good, and this one she hated, because she was her step-daughter. The step-daughter once had a pretty apron, which the other fancied so much that she became envious, and told her mother that she must and would have that apron. "Be quiet, my child," said the old woman, "and you shall have it. Your step-sister has long deserved death, to-night when she is asleep I will come and cut her head off. Only be careful that you are at the far-side of the bed, and push her well to the front." It would have been all over with the poor girl if she had not just then been standing in a corner, and heard everything. All day long she dared not go out of doors, and when bed-time had come, the witch's daughter got into bed first, so as to lie at the far side, but when she was asleep, the other pushed her gently to the front, and took for herself the place at the back, close by the wall. In the night, the old woman came creeping in, she held an axe in her right hand, and felt with her left to see if anyone were lying at the outside, and then she grasped the axe with both hands, and cut her own child's head off.

When she had gone away, the girl got up and went to her sweetheart, who was called Roland, and knocked at his door. When he came out, she said to him: "Listen, dearest Roland, we must fly in all haste; my step-mother wanted to kill me, but has struck her own child. When daylight comes, and she sees what she has done, we shall be lost." "But," said Roland, "I counsel you first to take away her magic wand, or we cannot escape if she pursues us." The maiden fetched the magic wand, and she took the dead girl's head and dropped three drops of blood on the ground, one in front of the bed, one in the kitchen, and one on the stairs. Then she hurried away with her lover.

When the old witch got up next morning, she called her daughter, and wanted to give her the apron, but she did not come. Then the witch cried: "Where are you?" "Here, on the stairs, I am sweeping," answered the first drop of blood. The old woman went out, but saw no one on the stairs, and cried again: "Where are you?" "Here in the kitchen, I am warming myself," cried the second drop of blood. She went into the kitchen, but found no one. Then she cried again: "Where are you?" "Ah, here in the bed, I am sleeping." cried the third drop of blood. She went into the room to the bed. What did she see there? Her own child, whose head she had cut off, bathed in her blood. The witch fell into a passion, sprang to the window, and as she could look forth quite far into the world, she perceived her step-daughter hurrying away with her sweet-heart Roland. "That shall not help you," cried she, "even if you have got a long way off, you shall still not escape me." She put on her many league boots, in which she covered an hour's walk at every step, and it was not long before she overtook them. The girl, however, when she saw the old woman striding towards her, changed, with her magic wand, her sweetheart Roland into a lake, and herself into a duck swimming in the middle of it. The witch placed herself on the shore, threw bread-crumbs in, and went to endless trouble to entice the duck; but the duck did not let herself be enticed, and the old woman had to go home at night as she had come. At this the girl and her sweetheart Roland resumed their natural shapes again, and they walked on the whole night until daybreak. Then the maiden changed herself into a beautiful flower which stood in the midst of a briar hedge, and her sweetheart Roland into a fiddler. It was not long before the witch came striding up towards them, and said to the musician: "Dear musician, may I pluck that beautiful flower for myself?" "Oh, yes," he replied, "I will play to you while you do it." As she was hastily creeping into the hedge and was just going to pluck the flower, knowing perfectly well who the flower was, he began to play, and whether she would or not, she was forced to dance, for it was a magical dance. The faster he played, the more violent springs was she forced to make, and the thorns tore her clothes from her body, and pricked her and wounded her till she bled, and as he did not stop, she had to dance till she lay dead on the ground.

As they were now set free, Roland said: "Now I will go to my father and arrange for the wedding." "Then in the meantime I will stay here and wait for you," said the girl, "and that no one may recognize me, I will change myself into a red stone land-mark." Then Roland went away, and the girl stood like a red land-mark in the field and waited for her beloved. But when Roland got home, he fell into the snares of another, who so fascinated him that he forgot the maiden. The poor girl remained there a long time, but at length, as he did not return at all, she was sad, and changed herself into a flower, and thought: "Someone will surely come this way, and trample me down."

It befell, however, that a shepherd kept his sheep in the field, and saw the flower, and as it was so pretty, plucked it, took it with him, and laid it away in his chest. From that time forth, strange things happened in the shepherd's house. When he arose in the morning, all the work was already done, the room was swept, the table and benches cleaned, the fire on the hearth was lighted, and the water was fetched, and at noon, when he came home, the table was laid, and a good dinner served. He could not conceive how this came to pass, for he never saw a human being in his house, and no one could have concealed himself in it. He was certainly pleased with this good attendance, but still at last he was so afraid that he went to a wise woman and asked for her advice. The wise woman said: "There is some enchantment behind it, listen very early some morning if anything is moving in the room, and if you see anything, no matter what it is, throw a white cloth over it, and then the magic will be stopped."

The shepherd did as she bade him, and next morning just as day dawned, he saw the chest open, and the flower come out. Swiftly he sprang towards it, and threw a white cloth over it. Instantly the transformation came to an end, and a beautiful girl stood before him, who admitted to him that she had been the flower, and that up to this time she had attended to his housekeeping. She told him her story, and as she pleased him he asked her if she would marry him, but she answered: "No," for she wanted to remain faithful to her sweetheart

Roland, although he had deserted her. Nevertheless, she promised not to go away, but to continue keeping house for the shepherd.

And now the time drew near when Roland's wedding was to be celebrated, and then, according to an old custom in the country, it was announced that all the girls were to be present at it, and sing in honor of the bridal pair. When the faithful maiden heard of this, she grew so sad that she thought her heart would break, and she would not go thither, but the other girls came and took her. When it came to her turn to sing, she stepped back, until at last she was the only one left, and then she could not refuse. But when she began her song, and it reached Roland's ears, he sprang up and cried: "I know the voice, that is the true bride, I will have no other!" Everything he had forgotten, and which had vanished from his mind, had suddenly come home again to his heart. Then the faithful maiden held her wedding with her sweetheart Roland, and grief came to an end and joy began.

THE GOLDEN BIRD

In olden times there was a King, who had behind his palace a beautiful pleasure-garden in which there was a tree that bore golden apples. When the apples were getting ripe they were counted, but on the very next morning one was missing. This was told to the King, and he ordered that a watch should be kept every night beneath the tree.

The King had three sons, the eldest of whom he sent, as soon as night came on, into the garden; but when midnight came he could not keep himself from sleeping, and next morning again an apple was gone.

The following night the second son had to keep watch, but it fared no better with him; as soon as twelve o'clock had struck he fell asleep, and in the morning an apple was gone.

Now it came to the turn of the third son to watch; and he was quite ready, but the King had not much trust in him, and thought that he would be of less use even than his brothers: but at last he let him go. The youth lay down beneath the tree, but kept awake, and did not let sleep master him. When it struck twelve, something rustled through the air, and in the moonlight he saw a bird coming whose feathers were all shining with gold. The bird alighted on the tree, and had just plucked off an apple, when the youth shot an arrow at him. The bird flew off, but the arrow had struck his plumage, and one of his golden feathers fell down. The youth picked it up, and the next morning took it to the King and told him what he had seen in the night. The King called his council together, and everyone declared that a feather like this was worth more than the whole kingdom. "If the feather is so precious," declared the King, "one alone will not do for me; I must and will have the whole bird!"

The eldest son set out, and trusting to his cleverness, thought that he would easily find the Golden Bird. When he had gone some distance he saw a Fox sitting at the edge of a wood, so he cocked his gun and took aim at him. The Fox cried: "Do not shoot me! and in return I will give you some good counsel. You are on the way to the Golden Bird; and this evening you will come to a village in which stand two inns opposite to one another. One of them is lighted up brightly, and all goes on merrily within, but do not go into it; go rather into the other, even though it looks like a bad one." "How can such a silly beast give wise advice?" thought the King's son, and he pulled the trigger. But he missed the Fox, who stretched out his tail and ran quickly into the wood.

So he pursued his way, and by evening came to the village where the two inns were; in one they were singing and dancing; the other had a poor, miserable look. "I should be a fool, indeed," he thought, "if I were to go into the shabby tavern, and pass by the good one." So he went into the cheerful one, lived there in riot and revel, and forgot the bird and his father, and all good counsels.

When many months had passed, and the eldest son did not come back home, the second set out, wishing to find the Golden Bird. The Fox met him as he had met the eldest, and gave him the good advice of which he took no heed. He came to the two inns, and his brother was standing at the window of the one from which came the music, and called out to him. He could not resist, but went inside and lived only for pleasure.

Again some time passed, and then the King's youngest son wanted to set off and try his luck, but his father would not allow it. "It is of no use," said he, "he will find the Golden Bird still less than his brothers, and if a mishap were to befall him he knows not how to help himself; he's not too bright at the best." But at last, as he had no peace, he let him go.

Again the Fox was sitting outside the wood, and begged for his life, and offered his good advice. The youth was good-natured, and said: "Be easy, little Fox, I will do you no harm." "You shall not repent it," answered the Fox; "and that you may get on more quickly, get up behind on my tail." And scarcely had he seated himself when the Fox began to run, and away he went over stock and stone till his hair whistled in the wind. When they came to the village the youth got off; he followed the good advice, and without looking round turned into the little inn, where he spent the night quietly.

The next morning, as soon as he got into the open country, there sat the Fox already, and said: "I will tell you further what you have to do. Go on quite straight, and at last you will come to a castle, in front of which a whole regiment of soldiers is lying, but do not trouble yourself about them, for they will all be asleep and snoring. Go through the midst of them straight into the castle, and go through all the rooms, till at last you will come to a chamber where a Golden Bird is hanging in a wooden cage. Close by, there stands an empty gold cage for show, but beware of taking the bird out of the common cage and putting it into the fine one, or it may go badly with you." With these words the Fox again stretched out his tail, and the King's son seated himself upon it, and away he went over stock and stone till his hair whistled in the wind.

When he came to the castle he found everything as the Fox had said. The King's son went into the chamber where the Golden Bird was shut up in a wooden cage, whilst a golden one stood hard by; and the three golden apples lay about the room. "But," thought he, "it would be absurd if I were to leave the beautiful bird in the common and ugly cage," so he opened the door, laid hold of it, and put it into the golden cage. But at the same moment the bird uttered a shrill cry. The soldiers awoke, rushed in, and took him off to prison. The next morning he was taken before a court of justice, and as he confessed everything, was sentenced to death.

The King, however, said that he would grant him his life on one condition—namely, if he brought him the Golden Horse which ran faster than the wind; and in that case he should receive, over and above, as a reward, the Golden Bird.

The King's son set off, but he sighed and was sorrowful, for how was he to find the Golden Horse? But all at once he saw his old friend the Fox sitting on the road. "Look you," said the Fox, "this has happened because you did not give heed to me. However, be of good courage. I will give you my help, and tell you how to get to the Golden Horse. You must go straight on, and you will come to a castle, where in the stable stands the horse. The grooms will be lying in front of the stable; but they will be asleep and snoring, and you can quietly lead out the Golden Horse. But of one thing you must take heed; put on him the common saddle of wood and leather, and not the golden one, which hangs close by, else it will go ill with you." Then the Fox stretched out

his tail, the King's son seated himself upon it, and away he went over stock and stone until his hair whistled in the wind.

Everything happened just as the Fox had said; the prince came to the stable in which the Golden Horse was standing, but just as he was going to put the common saddle upon him, he thought: "Such a beautiful beast will be shamed if I do not give him the good saddle which belongs to him by right." But scarcely had the golden saddle touched the horse than he began to neigh loudly. The grooms awoke, seized the youth, and threw him into prison. The next morning he was sentenced by the court to death; but the King promised to grant him his life, and the Golden Horse as well, if he could bring back the beautiful princess from the Golden Castle.

With a heavy heart the youth set out; yet luckily for him he soon found the trusty Fox. "I ought only to leave you to your ill-luck," said the Fox, "but I pity you, and will help you once more out of your trouble. This road takes you straight to the Golden Castle, you will reach it by eventide; and at night when everything is quiet the beautiful princess goes to the bathing-house to bathe. When she enters it, run up to her and give her a kiss, then she will follow you, and you can take her away with you; only do not allow her to take leave of her parents first, or it will go ill with you."

Then the Fox stretched out his tail, the King's son seated himself upon it, and away went the Fox, over stock and stone, till his hair whistled in the wind.

When he reached the Golden Castle it was just as the Fox had said. He waited until midnight, when everything lay in deep sleep, and the beautiful princess was going to the bathing-house. Then he sprang out and gave her a kiss. She said that she would like to go with him, but she asked him pitifully, and with tears, to allow her first to take leave of her parents. At first he withstood her prayer, but when she wept more and more, and fell at his feet, he at last gave in. But no sooner had the maiden reached the beside of her father than he and all the rest in the castle awoke, and the youth was laid hold of and put into prison.

The next morning the King said to him: "Your life is forfeited, and you can only find mercy if you take away the hill which stands in front of my windows, and prevents my seeing beyond it; and you must finish it all within eight days. If you do that you shall have my daughter as your reward."

The King's son began, and dug and shoveled without stopping, but when after seven days he saw how little he had done, and how all his work was as good as nothing, he fell into great sorrow and gave up all hope. But on the evening of the seventh day the Fox appeared and said: "You do not deserve that I should take any trouble about you; but just go away and lie down to sleep, and I will do the work for you."

The next morning when he awoke and looked out of the window the hill had gone. The youth ran, full of joy, to the King, and told him that the task was fulfilled, and whether he liked it or not, the King had to hold to his word and give him his daughter.

So the two set forth together, and it was not long before the trusty Fox came up with them. "You have certainly got what is best," said he, "but the Golden Horse also belongs to the maiden of the Golden Castle." "How shall I get it?" asked the youth. "That I will tell you," answered the Fox; "first take the beautiful maiden to the King who sent you to the Golden Castle. There will be unheard-of rejoicing; they will gladly give you the Golden Horse, and will bring it out to you. Mount it as soon as possible, and offer your hand to all in farewell; last of all to the beautiful maiden. And as soon as you have taken her hand swing her up on to the horse, and gallop away, and no one will be able to bring you back, for the horse runs faster than the wind."

All was carried out successfully, and the King's son carried off the beautiful princess on the Golden Horse.

The Fox did not remain behind, and he said to the youth: "Now I will help you to get the Golden Bird. When you come near to the castle where the Golden Bird is to be found, let the maiden get down, and I will take her into my care. Then ride with the Golden Horse into the castle-yard; there will be great rejoicing at the sight, and they will bring out the Golden Bird for you. As soon as you have the cage in your hand gallop back to us, and take the maiden away again."

When the plan had succeeded, and the King's son was about to ride home with his treasures, the Fox said: "Now you shall reward me for my help." "What do you require for it?" asked the youth. "When you get into the wood yonder, shoot me dead, and chop off my head and feet."

"That would be fine gratitude," said the King's son. "I cannot possibly do that for you."

The Fox said: "If you will not do it I must leave you, but before I go away I will give you a piece of good advice. Be careful about two things. Buy no gallows'-flesh, and do not sit at the edge of any well." And then he ran into the wood.

The youth thought: "That is a wonderful beast, he has strange whims; who on earth would want to buy gallows'-flesh. As for the desire to sit at the edge of a well it has never yet occurred to me."

He rode on with the beautiful maiden, and his road took him again through the village in which his two brothers had remained. There was a great stir and noise, and, when he asked what was going on, he was told that two men were going to be hanged. As he came nearer to the place he saw that they were his brothers, who had been playing all kinds of wicked pranks, and had squandered all their wealth. He inquired whether they could not be set free. "If you will pay for them," answered the people; "but why should you waste your money on wicked men, and buy them free." He did not think twice about it, but paid for them, and when they were set free they all went on their way together.

They came to the wood where the Fox had first met them, and as it was a hot day, but cool and pleasant within the wood, the two brothers said: "Let us rest a little by the well, and eat and drink." He agreed, and whilst they were talking he forgot himself, and sat down upon the edge of the well without thinking of any evil. But the two brothers threw him backwards into the well, took the maiden, the Horse, and the Bird, and went home to their father. "Here we bring you not only the Golden Bird," said they; "we have won the Golden Horse also, and the maiden from the Golden Castle." Then was there great joy; but the Horse would not eat, the Bird would not sing, and the maiden sat and wept.

But the youngest brother was not dead. By good fortune the well was dry, and he fell upon soft moss without being hurt, but he could not get out again. Even in this strait the faithful Fox did not leave him: it came and leapt down to him, and upbraided him for having forgotten its advice. "But yet I cannot give up," he said; "I will help you up again into daylight." He bade him grasp his tail and keep tight hold of it; and then he pulled him up.

"You are not out of all danger yet," said the Fox. "Your brothers were not sure of your death, and have surrounded the wood with watchers, who are to kill you if you let yourself be seen." But a poor man was sitting upon the road, with whom the youth changed clothes, and in this way he got to the King's palace.

No one knew him, but the Bird began to sing, the Horse began to eat, and the beautiful maiden left off weeping. The King, astonished, asked: "What does this mean?" Then the maiden said: "I do not know, but I have been so sorrowful and now I am so happy! I feel as if my true bridegroom had come." She told him all that had happened, although the other brothers had threatened her with death if she were to betray anything.

The King commanded that all people who were in his castle should be brought before him; and amongst them came the youth in his ragged clothes; but the maiden knew him at once and fell upon his neck. The wicked brothers were seized and put to death, but he was married to the beautiful maiden and declared heir to the King.

But what happened to the poor Fox? Long afterwards the King's son was once again walking in the wood, when the Fox met him and said: "You have everything now that you can wish for, but there is never an end to my misery, and yet it is in your power to free me," and again he asked him with tears to shoot him dead and to chop off his head and feet. So he did it, and scarcely was it done when the Fox was changed into a man, and was no other than the brother of the beautiful princess, who at last was freed from the magic charm which had been laid upon him. And now they had all the happiness they wanted as long as they lived.

THE DOG AND THE SPARROW

A sheep-dog had not a good master, but, on the contrary, one who let him suffer hunger. As he could stay no longer with him, he went quite sadly away. On the road he met a sparrow who said: "Brother dog, why are you so sad?" The dog replied: "I am hungry, and have nothing to eat." Then said the sparrow: "Dear brother, come into the town with me, and I will satisfy your hunger." So they went into the town together, and when they came in front of a butcher's shop the sparrow said to the dog: "Stay there, and I will pick a bit of meat down for you," and he alighted on the stall, looked about him to see that no one was observing him, and pecked and pulled and tore so long at a piece which lay on the edge, that it slipped down. Then the dog seized it, ran into a corner, and devoured it. The sparrow said: "Now come with me to another shop, and then I will get you one more piece that you may be satisfied." When the dog had devoured the second piece as well, the sparrow asked: "Brother dog, have you now had enough?" "Yes, I have had meat enough," he answered, "but I have had no bread yet." Said the sparrow: "You shall have that also, come with me." Then he took him to a baker's shop, and pecked at a couple of little buns till they rolled down, and as the dog wanted still more, he led him to another stall, and again got bread for him. When that was consumed, the sparrow said: "Brother dog, have you now had enough?" "Yes," he replied, "now we will walk awhile outside the town."

Then they both went out on to the highway. The weather was warm, however, and when they had walked a little way the dog said: "I am tired, and would like to sleep." "Well, do sleep," answered the sparrow, "and in the meantime I will seat myself on a branch." So the dog lay down on the road, and fell fast asleep. Whilst he lay sleeping there, a waggoner came driving by, who had a cart with three horses, laden with two barrels of wine. The sparrow, however, saw that he was not going to turn aside, but was staying in the wheel track in which the dog was lying, so it cried: "Waggoner, don't do it, or I will make you poor." But the waggoner growled to himself: "You will not make me poor," and cracked his whip and drove the cart over the dog, and the wheels killed him. Then the sparrow cried: "You have run over my brother dog and killed him, it shall cost you your cart and horses." "Cart and horses indeed!" said the waggoner. "What harm can you do me?" and drove onwards. Then the sparrow crept under the cover of the cart, and pecked so long at the same bung-hole that he got the bung out, and then all the wine ran out without the driver noticing it. But once when he was looking behind him he saw that the cart was dripping, and looked at the barrels and saw that one of them was empty. "Unfortunate fellow that am I," cried he. "Not unfortunate enough yet," said the sparrow, and flew on to the head of one of the horses and pecked his eyes out. When the driver saw that, he drew out his axe and wanted to hit the sparrow, but the sparrow flew into the air, and he hit his horse on the head, and it fell down dead. "Oh, what an unfortunate man am I," cried he. "Not unfortunate enough yet," said the sparrow, and when the driver drove on with the two horses, the sparrow again crept under the cover, and pecked the bung out of the second cask, so all the wine was spilt. When the driver became aware of it, he again cried: "Oh, what an unfortunate man am I," but the sparrow replied: "Not unfortunate enough yet," and seated himself on the head of the second horse, and pecked his eyes out. The driver ran up to it and raised his axe to strike, but the sparrow flew in the air and the blow struck the horse, which fell. "Oh, what an unfortunate man am I." "Not unfortunate enough yet," said the sparrow, and lighted on the third horse's head, and pecked out his eyes. The driver, in his rage, struck at the sparrow without looking round, and did not hit him, but killed his third horse likewise. "Oh, what an unfortunate man am I," cried he. "Not unfortunate enough yet," answered the sparrow. "Now will I make you unfortunate in your home," and flew away.

The driver had to leave the waggon standing, and full of anger and vexation went home. "Ah," said he to his wife, "what misfortunes I have had! My wine has run out, and the horses are all three dead!" "Alas, husband," she answered, "what a malicious bird has come into the house! It has gathered together every bird there is in the world, and they have fallen on our corn up there, and are devouring it." Then he went upstairs, and thousands and thousands of birds were sitting in the loft and had eaten up all the corn, and the sparrow was sitting in the midst of them. Then the driver cried: "Oh, what an unfortunate man am I?"

"Not unfortunate enough yet!" answered the sparrow; "waggoner, it shall cost you your life as well," and flew out.

Then the waggoner had lost all his property, and he went downstairs into the room, sat down behind the stove and was quite furious and bitter. But the sparrow sat outside in front of the window, and cried: "Waggoner, it shall cost you your life." Then the waggoner snatched the axe and threw it at the sparrow, but it only broke the window, and did not hit the bird. The sparrow now hopped in, placed itself on the stove and cried: "Waggoner, it shall cost you your life." The latter, quite mad and blind with rage, smote the stove in twain, and as the sparrow flew from one place to another so it fared with all his household furniture, looking-glass, benches, table, and at last the walls of his house, and yet he could not hit the bird. At length, however, he caught it with his hand. Then his wife said: "Shall I kill it?" "No," cried he, "that would be too merciful. It shall die much more cruelly," and he took it and swallowed it whole. The sparrow, however, began to flutter about in his body, and fluttered up again into the man's mouth; then it stretched out its head, and cried: "Waggoner, it shall still cost you your life." The driver gave the axe to his wife, and said: "Wife, kill the bird in my mouth for me." The woman struck, but missed her blow, and hit the waggoner square on his head, so that he fell dead. But the sparrow flew up and away.

FREDERICK AND CATHERINE

There was once upon a time a man who was called Frederick and a woman called Catherine, who had married each other and lived together as young married folks. One day Frederick said: "I will now go and plough, Catherine; when I come back, there must be some roast meat on the table for hunger, and a fresh draught for thirst." "Just go, Frederick," answered Kate, "just go, I will have all ready for you." So when dinner-time drew near she got a sausage out of the chimney, put it in the frying-pan, put some butter to it, and set it on the fire. The sausage began to fry and to hiss, Catherine stood beside it and held the handle of the pan, and had her own thoughts as she was doing it. Then it occurred to her: "While the sausage is getting done you could go into the cellar and draw beer." So she set the frying-pan safely on the fire, took a can, and went down into the cellar to draw beer. The beer ran into the can and Kate watched it, and then she thought: "Oh, dear! The dog upstairs is not fastened up, it might get the sausage out of the pan. Lucky I thought of it." And in a trice she was up the cellar-steps again, but the Spitz had the sausage in its mouth already, and trailed it away on the ground. But Catherine, who was not idle, set out after it, and chased it a long way into the field; the dog, however, was swifter than Catherine and did not let the sausage go, but skipped over the furrows with it. "What's gone is gone!" said Kate, and turned round, and as she had run till she was weary, she walked quietly and comfortably, and cooled herself. During this time the beer was still running out of the cask, for Kate had not turned the tap. And when the can was full and there was no other place for it, it ran into the cellar and did not stop until the whole cask was empty. As soon as Kate was on the steps she saw the accident. "Good gracious!" she cried. "What shall I do now to stop Frederick finding out?" She thought for a while, and at last she remembered that up in the garret was still standing a sack of the finest wheat flour from the last fair, and she would fetch that down and strew it over the beer. "Yes," said she, "he who saves a thing when he ought, has it afterwards when he needs it," and she climbed up to the garret and carried the sack below, and threw it straight down on the can of beer, which she knocked over, and Frederick's draught swam also in the cellar. "It is all right," said Kate, "where the one is the other ought to be also," and she strewed the meal over the whole cellar. When it was done she was heartily delighted with her work, and said: "How clean and wholesome it does look here!" At midday home came Frederick: "Now, wife, what have you ready for me?" "Ah, Freddy," she answered, "I was frying a sausage for you, but whilst I was drawing the beer to drink with it, the dog took it away out of the pan, and whilst I was running after the dog, all the beer ran out, and whilst I was drying up the beer with the flour, I knocked over the can as well, but be easy, the cellar is quite dry again." Said Frederick: "Kate, Kate, you should not have done that! to let the sausage be carried off and the beer run out of the cask, and throw out all our flour into the bargain!" "Well, Frederick, I did not know that, you should have told me." The man thought: "If this is the kind of wife I have, I had better take more care of things." Now he had saved up a good number of talers which he changed into gold, and said to Catherine: "Look, these are yellow counters for playing games; I will put them in a pot and bury them in the stable under the cow's manger, but mind you keep away from them, or it will be the worse for you." Said she: "Oh, no, Frederick, I certainly will not go near them." And when Frederick was gone some pedlars came into the village who had cheap earthen bowls and pots, and asked the young woman if there was nothing she wanted to bargain with them for. "Oh, dear people," said Catherine, "I have no money and can buy nothing, but if you have any use for yellow counters I will buy of you." "Yellow counters, why not? But just let us see them." "Then go into the stable and dig under the cow's manger, and you will find the yellow counters. I am not allowed to go there." The rogues went thither, dug and found pure gold. Then they laid hold of it, ran away, and left their pots and bowls behind in the house. Catherine thought she must use her new things, and as she had no lack in the kitchen already without these, she knocked the bottom out of every pot, and set them all as ornaments on the paling which went round about the house. When Frederick came and saw the new decorations, he said: "Catherine, what have you been about?" "I have bought them, Frederick, for the counters which were under the cow's manger. I did not go there myself, the pedlars had to dig them out for themselves." "Ah, wife," said Frederick, "what have you done? Those were not counters, but pure gold, and all our wealth; you should not have done that." "Indeed, Frederick," said she, "I did not know that, you should have forewarned me."

Catherine stood for a while and wondered; then she said: "Listen, Frederick, we will soon get the gold back again, we will run after the thieves." "Come, then," said Frederick, "we will try it; but take with you some butter and cheese that we may have something to eat on the way." "Yes, Frederick, I will take them." They set out, and as Frederick was the better walker, Catherine followed him. "It is to my advantage," thought she, "when we turn back I shall be a little way in advance." Then she came to a hill where there were deep ruts on both sides of the road. "There one can see," said Catherine, "how they have torn and skinned and galled the poor earth, it will never be whole again as long as it lives," and in her heart's compassion she took her butter and smeared the ruts right and left, that they might not be so hurt by the wheels, and as she was thus bending down in her charity, one of the cheeses rolled out of her pocket down the hill. Said Catherine: "I have made my way once up here, I will not go down again; another may run and fetch it back." So she took another cheese and rolled it down. But the cheeses did not come back, so she let a third run down, thinking: "Perhaps they are waiting for company, and do not like to walk alone."

As all three stayed away she said: "I do not know what that can mean, but it may perhaps be that the third has not found the way, and has gone wrong, I will just send the fourth to call it." But the fourth did no better than the third. Then Catherine was angry, and threw down the fifth and sixth as well, and these were her last. She remained standing for some time watching for their coming, but when they still did not come, she said: "Oh, you are good folks to send in search of death, you stay a fine long time away! Do you think I will wait any longer for you? I shall go my way, you may run after me; you have younger legs than I." Catherine went on and found Frederick, who was standing waiting for her because he wanted something to eat. "Now just let us have what you have brought with you," said he. She gave him the dry bread. "Where have you the butter and the cheeses?" asked the man. "Ah, Freddy," said Catherine, "I smeared the cart-ruts with the butter and the cheese will come soon; one ran away from me, so I sent the others after to call it." Said Frederick: "You should not have done that, Catherine, to smear the butter on the road, and let the cheeses run down the hill!" "Really, Frederick, you should have told me."

Then they ate the dry bread together, and Frederick said: "Catherine, did you make the house safe when you came away?" "No, Frederick, you should have told me to do it before." "Then go home again, and make the house safe before we go any farther, and bring with you something else to eat. I will wait here for you." Catherine went back and thought: "Frederick wants something more to eat, he does not like butter and cheese, so I will take with me a handkerchief full of dried pears and a pitcher of vinegar for him to drink." Then she bolted the upper half of the door fast, but unhinged the lower door, and took it on her back, believing that when she had placed the door in security the house must be well taken care of. Catherine took her time on the way, and thought: "Frederick will rest himself so much the longer." When she had once more reached him she said: "Here is the house-door for you, Frederick, and now you can take care of the house yourself." "Oh, heavens," said he, "what a wise wife I have! She takes the underdoor off the hinges that everything may run in, and bolts the upper one. It is now too late to go back home again, but since you have brought the door here, you shall just carry it farther." "I will carry the door,

Frederick, but the dried pears and the vinegar-jug will be too heavy for me; I will hang them on the door, it may carry them."

And now they went into the forest, and sought the rogues, but did not find them. At length as it grew dark they climbed into a tree and resolved to spend the night there. Scarcely, however, had they sat down at the top of it than the rascals came thither who carry away with them what does not want to go, and find things before they are lost. They sat down under the very tree in which Frederick and Catherine were sitting, lighted a fire, and were about to share their booty. Frederick got down on the other side and collected some stones together. Then he climbed up again with them, and wished to throw them at the thieves and kill them. The stones, however, did not hit them, and the knaves cried: "It will soon be morning, the wind is shaking down the fir-cones." Catherine still had the door on her back, and as it pressed so heavily on her, she thought it was the fault of the dried pears, and said: "Frederick, I must throw the pears down." "No, Catherine, not now," he replied, "they might betray us." "Oh, but, Frederick, I must! They weigh me down far too much." "Do it, then, and be hanged!" Then the dried pears rolled down between the branches, and the rascals below said: "Those are birds' droppings."

A short time afterwards, as the door was still heavy, Catherine said: "Ah, Frederick, I must pour out the vinegar." "No, Catherine, you must not, it might betray us." "Ah, but, Frederick, I must, it weighs me down far too much." "Then do it and be hanged!" So she emptied out the vinegar, and it spattered over the robbers. They said amongst themselves: "The dew is already falling." At length Catherine thought: "Can it really be the door which weighs me down so?" and said: "Frederick, I must throw the door down." "No, not now, Catherine, it might betray us." "Oh, but, Frederick, I must. It weighs me down far too much." "Oh, no, Catherine, do hold it fast." "Ah, Frederick, I am letting it fall!" "Let it go, then, in the devil's name." Then it fell down with a violent clatter, and the rascals below cried: "The devil is coming down the tree!" and they ran away and left everything behind them. Early next morning, when the two came down they found all their gold again, and carried it home.

When they were once more at home, Frederick said: "And now, Catherine, you, too, must be industrious and work." "Yes, Frederick, I will soon do that, I will go into the field and cut corn." When Catherine got into the field, she said to herself: "Shall I eat before I cut, or shall I sleep before I cut? Oh, I will eat first." Then Catherine ate and eating made her sleepy, and she began to cut, and half in a dream cut all her clothes to pieces, her apron, her gown, and her shift. When Catherine awoke again after a long sleep she was standing there half-naked, and said to herself: "Is it I, or is it not I? Alas, it is not I." In the meantime night came, and Catherine ran into the village, knocked at her husband's window, and cried: "Frederick."

"What is the matter?" "I should very much like to know if Catherine is in?" "Yes, yes," replied Frederick, "she must be in and asleep."

Said she, "That's all right, then I am certainly at home already," and ran away.

Outside Catherine found some vagabonds who were going to steal. Then she went to them and said: "I will help you to steal." The rascals thought that she knew what opportunities the place offered, and were willing. Catherine went in front of the houses, and cried: "Good folks, have you anything? We want to steal." The thieves thought to themselves: "That's a fine way of doing things," and wished themselves once more rid of Catherine. Then they said to her: "Outside the village the pastor has some turnips in the field. Go there and pull up some turnips for us." Catherine went to the ground, and began to pull them up, but was so lazy that she never stood up straight. Then a man came by, saw her, and stood still and thought that it was the devil who was thus rooting amongst the turnips. He ran away into the village to the pastor, and said: "Mr. Pastor, the devil is in your turnip-ground, rooting up turnips." "Ah, heavens," answered the pastor, "I have a lame foot, I cannot go out and drive him away." Said the man: "Then I will carry you on my back," and he carried him out on his back. And when they came to the ground, Catherine arose and stood up her full height. "Ah, the devil!" cried the pastor, and both hurried away, and in his great fright the pastor could run better with his lame foot than the man had carried him on his back could do on his sound legs.

THE TWO BROTHERS

There were once upon a time two brothers, one rich and the other poor. The rich one was a goldsmith and evil-hearted. The poor one supported himself by making brooms, and was good and honourable. He had two children, who were twin brothers and as like each other as two drops of water. The two boys went in and out of the rich house, and often got some of the scraps to eat. It happened once when the poor man was going into the forest to fetch brush-wood, that he saw a bird which was quite golden and more beautiful than any he had ever chanced to meet with. He picked up a small stone, threw it at it, and was lucky enough to hit it, but one golden feather only fell down, and the bird flew away. The man took the feather and carried it to his brother, who looked at it and said: "It is pure gold!" and gave him a great deal of money for it. Next day the man climbed into a birch-tree, and was about to cut off a couple of branches when the same bird flew out, and when the man searched he found a nest, and an egg lay inside it, which was of gold. He took the egg home with him, and carried it to his brother, who again said: "It is pure gold," and gave him what it was worth. At last the goldsmith said: "I should indeed like to have the bird itself." The poor man went into the forest for the third time, and again saw the golden bird sitting on the tree, so he took a stone and brought it down and carried it to his brother, who gave him a great heap of gold for it. "Now I can get on," thought he, and went contentedly home.

The goldsmith was crafty and cunning, and knew very well what kind of a bird it was. He called his wife and said: "Roast me the gold bird, and take care that none of it is lost. I have a fancy to eat it all myself." The bird, however, was no common one, but of so wondrous a kind that whosoever ate its heart and liver found every morning a piece of gold beneath his pillow. The woman prepared the bird, put it on the spit, and let it roast. Now it happened that while it was on the fire, and the woman was forced to go out of the kitchen on account of some other work, the two children of the poor broom-maker ran in, stood by the spit and turned it round once or twice. And as at that very moment two little bits of the bird fell down into the pan, one of the boys said: "We will eat these two little bits; I am so hungry, and no one will ever miss them." Then the two ate the pieces, but the woman came into the kitchen and saw that they were eating something and said: "What have you been eating?" "Two little morsels which feel out of the bird," answered they. "That must have been the heart and the liver," said the woman, quite frightened, and in order that her husband might not miss them and be angry, she quickly killed a young cock, took out his heart and liver, and put them beside the golden bird. When it was ready, she carried it to the goldsmith, who consumed it all alone, and left none of it. Next morning, however, when he felt beneath his pillow, and expected to bring out the piece of gold, no more gold pieces were there than there had always been.

The two children did not know what a piece of good-fortune had fallen to their lot. Next morning when they arose, something fell rattling to the ground, and when they picked it up there were two gold pieces! They took them to their father, who was astonished and said: "How can that have happened?" When next morning they again found two, and so on daily, he went to his brother and told him the strange story. The goldsmith at once knew how it had happened, and that the children had eaten the heart and liver of the golden bird, and in order to revenge himself, and because he was envious and hard-hearted, he said to the father: "Your children are in league with the Evil One, do not take the gold, and do not suffer them to stay any longer in your house, for he has them in his power, and may ruin you likewise." The father feared the Evil One, and painful as it was to him, he nevertheless led the twins forth into the forest, and with a sad heart left them there.

And now the two children ran about the forest, and sought the way home again, but could not find it, and only lost themselves more and more. At length they met with a huntsman, who asked: "To whom do you children belong?" "We are the poor broom-maker's boys," they replied, and they told him that their father would not keep them any longer in the house because a piece of gold lay every morning under their pillows. "Come," said the huntsman, "that is nothing so very bad, if at the same time you remain honest, and are not idle." As the good man liked the children, and had none of his own, he took them home with him and said: "I will be your father, and bring you up till you are big." They learnt huntsmanship from him, and the piece of gold which each of them found when he awoke, was kept for them by him in case they should need it in the future.

When they were grown up, their foster-father one day took them into the forest with him, and said: "To-day shall you make your trial shot, so that I may release you from your apprenticeship, and make you huntsmen." They went with him to lie in wait and stayed there a long time, but no game appeared. The huntsman, however, looked above him, and saw a covey of wild geese flying in the form of a triangle, and said to one of them: "Shoot me down one from each corner." He did it, and thus accomplished his trial shot. Soon after another covey came flying by in the form of the figure two, and the huntsman bade the other also bring down one from each corner, and his trial shot was likewise successful. "Now," said the foster-father, "I pronounce you out of your apprenticeship; you are skilled huntsmen." Thereupon the two brothers went forth together into the forest, and took counsel with each other and planned something. And in the evening when they had sat down to supper, they said to their foster-father: "We will not touch food, or take one mouthful, until you have granted us a request." Said he: "What, then, is your request?" They replied: "We have now finished learning, and we must prove ourselves in the world, so allow us to go away and travel." Then spoke the old man joyfully: "You talk like brave huntsmen, that which you desire has been my wish; go forth, all will go well with you." Thereupon they ate and drank joyously together.

When the appointed day came, their foster-father presented each of them with a good gun and a dog, and let each of them take as many of his saved-up gold pieces as he chose. Then he accompanied them a part of the way, and when taking leave, he gave them a bright knife, and said: "If ever you separate, stick this knife into a tree at the place where you part, and when one of you returns, he will be able to see how his absent brother is faring, for the side of the knife which is turned in the direction by which he went, will rust if he dies, but will remain bright as long as he is alive." The two brothers went still farther onwards, and came to a forest which was so large that it was impossible for them to get out of it in one day. So they passed the night in it, and ate what they had put in their hunting-pouches, but they walked all the second day likewise, and still did not get out. As they had nothing to eat, one of them said: "We must shoot something for ourselves or we shall suffer from hunger," and loaded his gun, and looked about him. And when an old hare came running up towards them, he laid his gun on his shoulder, but the hare cried:

"Dear huntsman, do but let me live,
Two little ones to thee I'll give,"

and sprang instantly into the thicket, and brought two young ones. But the little creatures played so merrily, and were so pretty, that the huntsmen could not find it in their hearts to kill them. They therefore kept them with them, and the little hares followed on foot. Soon after this, a fox crept past; they were just going to shoot it, but the fox cried:

"Dear huntsman, do but let me live,
Two little ones to thee I'll give."

He, too, brought two little foxes, and the huntsmen did not like to kill them either, but gave them to the hares for company, and they followed behind. It was not long before a wolf strode out of the thicket; the huntsmen made ready to shoot him, but the wolf cried:

"Dear huntsman, do but let me live,
Two little ones to thee I'll give."

The huntsmen put the two wolves beside the other animals, and they followed behind them. Then a bear came who wanted to trot about a little longer, and cried:

"Dear huntsman, do but let me live,
Two little ones to thee I'll give."

They two young bears were added to the others, and there were already eight of them. Then who should come? A lion came, and tossed his mane. But the huntsmen did not let themselves be frightened and aimed at him likewise, but the lion also said:

"Dear huntsman, do but let me live,
Two little ones to thee I'll give."

And he brought his little ones to them, and now the hunstmen had two lions, two bears, two wolves, two foxes, and two hares, who followed them and served them. In the meantime their hunger was not appeased by this, and they said to the foxes: "Listen you sneakers, provide us with something to eat. You are crafty and cunning." They replied: "Not far from here lies a village, from which we have already brought many a fowl; we well show you the way there." So they went into the village, bought themselves something to eat, had some food given to their beasts, and then travelled onwards. The foxes knew their way very well about the district and where the poultry-yards were, and were able to guide the huntsmen.

Now they travelled about for a while but could find no situations where they could remain together, so they said: "There is nothing else for it, we must part. They divided the animals, so that each of them had a lion, a bear, a wolf, a fox, and a hare, then they took leave of each other, promised to love each other like brothers till their death, and stuck the knife which their foster-father had given them, into a tree, after which one went east, and the other west.

The younger, however, arrived with his beasts in a town which was all hung with black craps. He went into an inn, and asked the host if he could accommodate his animals. The innkeeper gave him a stable, where there was a hole in the wall, and the hare crept out and fetched himself the head of a cabbage, and the fox fetched himself a hen, and when he had devoured it got the cock as well, but the wolf, the bear, and the lion could not get out because they were too big. Then the innkeeper let them be taken to a place where a cow happened to be lying on the grass, that they might eat till they were satisfied. And when the huntsman had taken care of his animals, he asked the innkeeper why the town was thus hung with black crape? Said the host: "Because our King's only daughter is to die to-morrow." The huntsman inquired: "Is she sick unto death?" "No," answered the host, "she is vigorous and healthy, nevertheless she must die!" "How is that?" asked the huntsman. "There is a high hill without the town, whereon dwells a dragon who every year mut have pure virgin, or he lays the whole country waste, and now all the maidens have already been given to him, and there is no longer anyone left but the King's daughter, yet there is no mercy for her; she must be given up to him, and that is to be done to-morrow." Said the huntsman: 'Why is the dragon not killed?" "Ah," replied the host, "so many knights have tried it, but it has cost all of them their lives. The King has promised that he who conquers the dragon shall have his daughter to wife, and shall likewise govern the kingdom after his own death.

The huntsman said nothing more to this, but next morning took his animals, and with them ascended the dragon's hill. A little church stood at the top of it, and on the altar three full cups were standing, with the inscription: "Whosoever empties the cups will become the strongest man on earth, and will be able to wield the sword which is buried before the threshold of the door," The huntsman did not drink,

but went out and sought for the sword in the ground, but was unable to move it from its place. Then he went in and emptied the cups, and now he was strong enough to take up the sword, and his hand could quite easily wield it. As the hour came when the maiden was to be delivered over to the dragon, the King, the marshal, and courtiers accompanied her. From after she saw the huntsman on the dragon's hill, and thought it was the dragon standing there waiting for her, and did not want to go up to him, but at last, because otherwise the whole town would have been destroyed, she was forced to take the fatal journey. The King and courtiers returned home full of grief; the King's marshal, however, was to stand still, and see all from a distance.

When the King's daughter got to the top of the hill, it was not the dragon which stood there, but the young huntsman, who comforted her, and said he would save her, led her into the church, and locked her in. It was not long before the seven-headed dragon came thither with loud roaring. When he perceived the huntsman, he was astonished and said: "What business have you here on the hill?" The huntsman answered: "I want to fight with you." Said the dragon: "Many knights have left their lives here, I shall soon have made an end of you too," and he breathed fire out of seven jaws. The fire was to have lighted the dry grass, and the huntsman was to have been suffocated in the heat and smoke, but the animals came running up and trampled out the fire. Then the dragon rushed upon the huntsman, but he swung his sword until it sang through the air, and struck off three of his heads. Then the dragon grew really furious, and rose up in the air, and spat out flames of fire over the huntsman, and was about to plunge down on him, but the huntsman once more drew out his sword, and again cut off three of his heads. The monster became faint and sank down; nevertheless it was just able to rush upon the huntsman, when he with his last strength smote its tail off, and as he could fight no longer, called up his animals who tore it in pieces. When the struggle was ended, the huntsman unlocked the church, and found the King's daughter lying on the floor, as she had lost her senses with anguish and terror during the contest. He carried her out, and when she came to herself once more, and opened her eyes, he showed her the dragon all cut to pieces, and told her that she was now set free. She rejoiced and said: "Now you will be my dearest husband, for my father has promised me to him who kills the dragon." Thereupon she took off her necklace of coral, and divided it amongst the animals in order to reward them, and the lion received the golden clasp. Her pocket-handkerchief, however, on which was her name, she gave to the huntsman, who went and cut the tongues out of the dragon's seven heads, wrapped them in the handkerchief, and preserved them carefully.

That done, as he was so faint and weary with the fire and the battle, he said to the maiden: "We are both faint and weary, we will sleep awhile." Then she said "Yes," and they lay down on the ground, and the huntsman said to the lion: "You shall keep watch, that no one surprises us in our sleep," and both fell asleep. The lion lay down beside them to watch, but he also was so weary with the fight, that he called to the bear and said: "Lie down near me, I must sleep a little; if anything comes, waken me." Then the bear lay down beside him, but he also was tired, and called the wolf and said: "Lie down by me, I must sleep a little, but if anything comes, waken me." Then the wolf lay down by him, but he was tired likewise, and called the fox and said: "Lie down by me, I must sleep a little; if anything comes, waken me." Then the fox lay down beside him, but he too was weary, and called the hare and said: "Lie down near me, I must sleep a little, and if anything should come, waken me." Then the hare sat down by him, but the poor hare was tired too, and had no one whom he could call there to keep watch, and fell asleep. And now the King's daughter, the huntsman, the lion, the bear, the wolf, the fox, and the hare, were all sleeping a sound sleep. The marshal, however, who was to look on from a distance, took courage when he did not see the dragon flying away with the maiden, and finding that all the hill had become quiet, ascended it. There lay the dragon hacked and hewn to pieces on the ground, and not far from it were the King's daughter and a huntsman with his animals, and all of them were sunk in a sound sleep. And as he was wicked and godless he took his sword, cut off the huntsman's head, and seized the maiden in his arms, and carried her down the hill. Then she awoke and was terrified, but the marshal said: "You are in my hands, you shall say that it was I who killed the dragon." "I cannot do that," she replied, for it was a huntsman with his animals who did it." Then he drew his sword, and threatened to kill her if she did not obey him, and so compelled her that she promised it. Then he took her to the King, who did not know how to contain himself for joy when he once more looked on his dear child in life, whom he had believed to have been torn to pieces by the monster. The marshal said to him: "I have killed the dragon, and delivered the maiden and the whole kingdom as well, therefore I demand her as my wife, as was promised." The King said to the maiden: "Is what he says true?" "Ah, yes," she answered, "it must indeed by true, but I will not consent to have the wedding celebrated until after a year and day," for she thought in that time she should hear something of her dear huntsman.

The animals, however, were still lying sleeping beside their dead master on the dragon's hill, and there came a great bumble-bee and lighted on the hare's nose, but the hare wiped it off with his paw, and went on sleeping. The bumble-bee came a second time, but the hare again rubbed it off and slept on. Then it came for the third time, and stung his nose so that he awoke. As soon as the hare was awake, he roused the fox, and the fox the wolf, and the wolf the bear, and the bear the lion. And when the lion awoke and saw that the maiden was gone, and his master was dead, he began to roar frightfully and cried: "Who has done that? Bear, why did you not waken me?" The bear asked the wolf: "Why did you not waken me?" and the wolf the fox: "Why did you not waken me?" and the fox the hare: "Why did you not waken me?" The poor hare alone did not know what answer to make, and the blame rested with him. Then they were just going to fall upon him, but he entreated them and said: "Kill me not, I will bring our master to life again. I know a mountain on which a root grows which, when placed in the mouth of anyone, cures him of all illness and every wound. But the mountain lies two hundred hours' journey from here." The lion said: "In four-and-twenty hours must you have run thither and have come back, and have brought the root with you." Then the hare sprang away, and in four-and-twenty hours he was back, and brought the root with him. The lion put the huntsman's head on again, and the hare placed the root in his mouth, and immediately everything united together again, and his heart beat, and life came back. Then the huntsman awoke, and was alarmed when he did not see the maiden, and thought: "She must have gone away whilst I was sleeping, in order to get rid of me." The lion in his greater haste had put his master's head on the wrong way round, but the huntsman did not observe it because of his melancholy thoughts about the King's daughter. But at noon, when he was going to eat something, he saw that his head was turned backwards and could not understand it, and asked the animals what had happened to him in his sleep. Then the lion told him that they, too, had all fallen asleep from weariness, and on awaking, had found him dead with his head cut off, that the hare had brought the life-giving root, and that he, in his haste, had laid hold of the head the wrong way, but that he would repair his mistake. Then he tore the huntsman's head off again, turned it round, and the hare healed it with the root.

The huntsman, however, was sad at heart and travelled about the world, and made his animals dance before people. It came to pass that precisely at the end of one year he came back to the same town where he had rescued the King's daughter from the dragon, and this time the town was gaily hung with red cloth. Then he said to the host: "What does this mean? Last year the town was all hung with black crape, what means the red cloth to-day?" The host answered: "Last year our King's daughter was to have been delivered over to the dragon, but the marshal fought with it and killed it, and so to-morrow their wedding is to be solemnized, and that is why the town was then hung with black crape for mourning, and is to-day covered with red cloth for joy."

Next day when the wedding was to take place, the huntsman said at mid-day to the inn-keeper: "Do you believe, sir host, that I while with you here to-day shall eat bread from the King's own table?" "Nay," said the host, "I would bet a hundred pieces of gold that that will not come true." The huntsman accepted the wager, and set against it a purse with just the same number of gold pieces. Then he called the hare and said: "Go, my dear runner, and fetch me some of the bread which the King is eating." Now the little hare was the lowest of the animals, and could not transfer this order to any of the others, but had to get on his legs himself. "Alas!" thought he, "if I bound through the streets thus alone, the butchers' dogs will all be after me." It happened as he expected, and the dogs came after him and wanted to make holes in his good skin. But he sprang away, you have never seen the like, and sheltered himself in a sentrybox without the soldier being aware of it. Then the dogs came and wanted to have him out, but the soldier did not understand a jest, and struck them with the butt-end of his gun, till they ran away yelling and howling. As soon as the hare saw that the way was clear, he ran into the palace and straight to the King's daughter, sat down under her chair, and scratched at her foot. Then she said: "Will you get away?" and thought it was her dog. The hare scratched her foot for the second time, and she again said: "Will you get away?" and thought it was her dog. But the hare did not let itself be turned from its purpose, and scratched her for the third time. Then she peeped down, and knew the hare by its collar. She took him on her lap, carried him into her chamber, and said: "Dear Hare, what do you want?" He answered: "My master, who killed the dragon, is here, and has sent me to ask for a loaf of bread like that which the King eats." Then she was full of joy and had the baker summoned, and ordered him to bring a loaf such as was eaten by the King. The little hare said: "But the baker must likewise carry it thither for me, that the butchers' dogs may do no harm to me." The baker carried it for him as far as the door of the inn, and then the hare got on his hind legs, took the loaf in his front paws, and carried it to his master. Then said the huntsman: "Behold, sir host, the hundred pieces of gold are mine." The host was astonished, but the huntsman went on to say: "Yes, sir host, I have the bread, but now I will likewise have some of the King's roast meat."

The host said: "I should indeed like to see that," but he would make no more waters. The huntsman called the fox and said: "My little fox, go and fetch me some roast meat, such as the King eats." The red fox knew the byways better, and went by holes and corners without any dog seeing him, seated himself under the chair of the King's daughter, and scratched her foot. Then she looked down and recognized the fox by its collar, took him into her chamber with her, and said: "Dear Fox, what do you want?" He answered: "My master, who killed the dragon, is here, and has sent me. I am to ask for some roast meat such as the King is eating." Then she made the cook come, who was obliged to prepare a roast joint, the same as was eaten by the King, and to carry it for the fox as far as the door. Then the fox took the dish, waved away with his tail the flies which had settled on the meat, and then carried it to his master. "Behold, sir host," said the huntsman, "bread and meat are here, but now I will also have proper vegetables with it, such as are eaten by the King." Then he called the wolf, and said: "Dear Wolf, go thither and fetch me vegetables such as the King eats." Then the wolf went straight to the palace, as he feared no one, and when he got to the

King's daughter's parlour he tugged at the back of her dress, so that she was forced to look round. She recognized him by his collar, and took him into her chamber with her, and said: "Dear Wolf, what do you want?" He answered: "My master, who killed the dragon, is here, I am to ask for some vegetables, such as the King eats." Then she made the cook come, and he had to make ready a dish of vegetables, such as the King ate, and had to carry it for the wolf as far as the door, and then the wolf took the dish from him, and carried it to his master. "Behold, sir host," said the huntsman, "now I have bread and meat and vegetables, but I will also have some pastry to eat like that which the King eats." He called the bear, and said: "Dear Bear, you are fond of licking anything sweet; go and bring me some confectionery, such as the King eats." Then the bear trotted to the palace, and everyone got out of his way, but when he went to the guard, they presented their muskets, and would not let him go into the royal palace. But he got up on his hind legs, and gave them a few boxes on the ears, right and left, with his paws, so that the whole watch broke up, and then he went straight to the King's daughter, placed himself behind her, and growled a little. Then she looked behind her, knew the bear, and bade him go into her room with her, and said: "Dear Bear, what do you want?" He answered: "My master, who killed the dragon, is here, and I am to ask for some confectionery such as the King eats." Then she summoned her confectioner, who had to bake confectionery such as the King ate, and carry it to the door for the bear; then the bear first licked up the comfits which had rolled down, and then he stood upright, took the dish, and carried it to his master. "Behold, sir host," said the huntsman, "now I have bread, meat, vegetables and confectionery, but I will drink wine also, and such as the King drinks." He called his lion to him and said: "Dear Lion, you yourself like to drink till you are tipsy, go and fetch me some wine, such as is drunk by the King." Then the lion strode through the streets, and the people fled from him, and when he came to the watch, they wanted to bar the way against him, but he did but roar once, and they all ran away. Then the lion went to the royal apartment, and knocked at the door with his tail. Then the King's daughter came forth, and was almost afraid of the lion, but she knew him by the golden clasp of her necklace, and bade him go with her into her chamber, and said: "Dear Lion, what will you have?" He answered:

"My master, who killed the dragon, is here, and I am to ask for some wine such as is drunk by the King." Then she bade the cup-bearer be called, who was to give the lion some wine like that which was drunk by the King. The lion said: "I will go with him, and see that I get the right wine." Then he went down with the cup-bearer, and when they were below, the cup-bearer wanted to draw him some of the common wine that was drunk by the King's servants; but the lion said: "Stop, I will taste the wine first," and he drew half a measure, and swallowed it down at one draught. "No," said he, "that is not right." The cup-bearer looked at him askance, but went on, and was about to give him some out of another barrel which was for the King's marshal. The lion said: "Stop, let me taste the wine first," and drew half a measure and drank it. "That is better, but still not right," said he. Then the cup-bearer grew angry and said: "How can a stupid animal like you understand wine?" But the lion gave him a blow behind the ears, which made him fall down by no means gently, and when he had got up again, he conducted the lion quite silently into a little cellar apart, where the King's wine lay, from which no one ever drank. The lion first drew half a measure and tried the wine, and then he said: "That may possibly be the right sort," and bade the cup-bearer fill six bottles of it. And now they went upstairs again, but when the lion came out of the cellar into the open air, he reeled here and there, and was rather drunk, and the cup-bearer was forced to carry the wine as far as the door for him, and then the lion took the handle of the basket in his mouth, and took it to his master. The huntsman said: "Behold, sir host, here have I bread, meat, vegetables, confectionery and wine such as the King has, and now I will dine with my animals," and he sat down and ate and drank, and gave the hare, the fox, the wolf, the bear, and the lion also to eat and to drink, and was joyful, for he saw that the King's daughter still loved him. And when he had finished his dinner, he said: "Sir host, now have I eaten and drunk, as the King eats and drinks, and now I will go to the King's court and marry the King's daughter." Said the host: "How can that be, when she already has a betrothed husband, and when the wedding is to be solemnized to-day?" Then the huntsman drew forth the handkerchief which the King's daughter had given him on the dragon's hill, and in which were folded the monster's seven tongues, and said: "That which I hold in my hand shall help me to do it." Then the innkeeper looked at the handkerchief, and said: "Whatever I believe, I do not believe that, and I am willing to stake my house and courtyard on it." The huntsman, however, took a bag with a thousand gold pieces, put it on the table, and said: "I stake that on it."

Now the King said to his daughter, at the royal table: "What did all the wild animals want, which have been coming to you, and going in and out of my palace?" She replied: "I may not tell you, but send and have the master of these animals brought, and you will do well." The King sent a servant to the inn, and invited the stranger, and the servant came just as the huntsman had laid his wager with the innkeeper. Then said he: "Behold, sir host, now the King sends his servant and invites me, but I do not go in this way." And he said to the servant: "I request the Lord King to send me royal clothing, and a carriage with six horses, and servants to attend me." When the King heard the answer, he said to his daughter: "What shall I do?" She said: "Cause him to be fetched as he desires to be, and you will do well." Then the King sent royal apparel, a carriage with six horses, and servants to wait on him. When the huntsman saw them coming, he said: "Behold, sir host, now I am fetched as I desired to be," and he put on the royal garments, took the handkerchief with the dragon's tongues with him, and drove off to the King. When the King saw him coming, he said to his daughter: "How shall I receive him?" She answered: "Go to meet him and you will do well." Then the King went to meet him and led him in, and his animals followed. The King gave him a seat near himself and his daughter, and the marshal, as bridegroom, sat on the other side, but no longer knew the huntsman. And now at this very moment, the seven heads of the dragon were brought in as a spectacle, and the King said: "The seven heads were cut off the dragon by the marshal, wherefore to-day I give him my daughter to wife." Then the huntsman stood up, opened the seven mouths, and said: "Where are the seven tongues of the dragon?" Then was the marshal terrified, and grew pale and knew not what answer he should make, and at length in his anguish he said: "Dragons have no tongues." The huntsman said: "Liars ought to have none, but the dragon's tongues are the tokens of the victor," and he unfolded the handkerchief, and there lay all seven inside it. And he put each tongue in the mouth to which it belonged, and it fitted exactly. Then he took the handkerchief on which the name of the princess was embroidered, and showed it to the maiden, and asked to whom she had given it, and she replied: "To him who killed the dragon." And then he called his animals, and took the collar off each of them and the golden clasp from the lion, and showed them to the maiden and asked to whom they belonged. She answered: "The necklace and golden clasp were mine, but I divided them among the animals who helped to conquer the dragon." Then spoke the huntsman: "When I, tired of the fight, was resting and sleeping, the marshal came and cut off my head. Then he carried away the King's daughter, and gave out that it was he who had killed the dragon, but that he lied I prove with the tongues, the handkerchief, and the necklace."

And then he related how his animals had healed him by means of a wonderful root, and how he had travelled about with them for one year, and had at length again come there and had learnt the treachery of the marshal by the inn-keeper's story. Then the King asked his daughter: "Is it true that this man killed the dragon?" And she answered: "Yes, it is true. Now can I reveal the wicked deed of the marshal, as it has come to light without my connivance, for he wrung from me a promise to be silent. For this reason, however, did I make the condition that the marriage should not be solemnized for a year and a day." Then the King bade twelve councillors be summoned who were to pronounce judgment on the marshal, and they sentenced him to be torn to pieces by four bulls. The marshal was therefore executed, but the King gave his daughter to the huntsman, and named him his viceroy over the whole kingdom. The wedding was celebrated with great joy, and the young King caused his father and his foster-father to be brought, and loaded them with treasures. Neither did he forget the innkeeper, but sent for him and said: "Behold, sir host, I have married the King's daughter, and your house and yard are mine." The host said: "Yes, according to justice it is so." But the young King said: "It shall be done according to mercy," and told him that he should keep his house and yard, and gave him the thousand pieces of gold as well.

And now the young King and Queen were thoroughly happy, and lived in gladness together. He often went out hunting because it was a delight to him, and the faithful animals had to accompany him. In the neighbourhood, however, there was a forest of which it was reported that it was haunted, and that whosoever did but enter it did not easily get out again. But the young King had a great inclination to hunt in it, and let the old King have no peace until he allowed him to do so. So he rode forth with a great following, and when he came to the forest, he saw a snow-white hind, and said to his men: "Wait here until I return, I want to hunt that beautiful creature," and he rode into the forest after it, followed only by his animals. The attendants halted and waited until evening, but he did not return, so they rode home, and told the young Queen that the young King had followed a white hind into the enchanted forest, and had not come back again. Then she was in the greatest concern about him. He, however, had still continued to ride on and on after the beautiful wild animal, and had never been able to overtake it; when he thought he was near enough to aim, he instantly saw it bound away into the far distance, and at length it vanished altogether. And now he perceived that he had penetrated deep into the forest, and blew his horn but he received no answer, for his attendants could not hear it. And as night was falling, he saw that he could not get home that day, so he dismounted from his horse, lighted himself a fire near a tree, and resolved to spend the night by it. While he was sitting by the fire, and his animals also were lying down beside him, it seemed to him that he heard a human voice. He looked round, but could perceive nothing. Soon afterwards, he again heard a groan as if from above, and then he looked up, and saw an old woman sitting in the tree, who wailed unceasingly: "Oh, oh, oh, how cold I am!" Said he: "Come down, and warm yourself if you are cold." But she said: "No, your animals will bite me." He answered: "They will do you no harm, old mother, do come down." She however, was a witch, and said: "I will throw down a wand from the tree, and if you strike them on the back with it, they will do me no harm." Then she threw him a small wand, and he struck them with it, and instantly they lay still and were turned into stone. And when the witch was safe from the animals, she leapt down and touched him also with a wand, and changed him to stone. Thereupon she laughed, and dragged him and the animals into a vault, where many more such stones already lay.

As the young King did not come back at all, the Queen's anguish and care grew constantly greater. And it so happened that at this very time the other brother who had turned to the east when they separated, came into the kingdom. He had sought a situation, and had found none, and had then travelled about here and there, and had made his animals dance. Then it came into his mind that he would just go and look at the knife that they had thrust in the trunk of a tree at their parting, that he might learn how his brother was. When he got there his brother's side of the knife was half rusted, and half bright. Then he was alarmed and thought: "A great misfortune must have befallen my brother, but perhaps I can still save him, for half the knife is still bright." He and his animals travelled towards the west, and when he entered the gate of the town, the guard came to meet him, and asked if he was to announce him to his consort the young Queen, who had for a couple of days been in the greatest sorrow about his staying away, and was afraid he had been killed in the enchanted forest. The sentries, indeed, thought no otherwise than that he was the young King himself, for he looked so like him, and had wild animals running behind him. Then he saw that they were speaking of his brother, and thought: "It will be better if I pass myself off for him, and then I can rescue him more easily." So he allowed himself to be escorted into the castle by the guard, and was received with the greatest joy. The young Queen indeed thought that he was her husband, and asked him why he had stayed away so long. He answered: "I had lost myself in a forest, and could not find my way out again any sooner." At night he was taken to the royal bed, but he laid a two-edged sword between him and the young Queen; she did not know what that could mean, but did not venture to ask.

He remained in the palace a couple of days, and in the meantime inquired into everything which related to the enchanted forest, and at last he said: "I must hunt there once more." The King and the young Queen wanted to persuade him not to do it, but he stood out against them, and went forth with a larger following. When he had got into the forest, it fared with him as with his brother; he saw a white hind and said to his men: "Stay here, and wait until I return, I want to chase the lovely wild beast," and then he rode into the forest and his animals ran after him. But he could not overtake the hind, and got so deep into the forest that he was forced to pass the night there. And when he had lighted a fire, he heard someone wailing above him: "Oh, oh, oh, how cold I am!" Then he looked up, and the self-same witch was sitting in the tree. Said he: "If you are cold, come down, little old mother, and warm yourself." She answered: "No, your animals will bite me." But he said: "They will not hurt you." Then she cried: "I will throw down a wand to you, and if you smite them with it they will do me no harm." When the huntsman heard that, he had no confidence in the old woman, and said: "I will not strike my animals. Come down, or I will fetch you." Then she cried: "What do you want? You shall not touch me." But he replied: "If you do not come, I will shoot you." Said she: "Shoot away, I do not fear your bullets!" Then he aimed, and fired at her, but the witch was proof against all leaden bullets, and laughed shrilly and cried: "You shall not hit me." The huntsman knew what to do, tore three silver buttons off his coat, and loaded his gun with them, for against them her arts were useless, and when he fired she fell down at once with a scream. Then he set his foot on her and said: "Old witch, if you do not instantly confess where my brother is, I will seize you with both my hands and throw you into the fire." She was in a great fright, begged for mercy, and said: "He and his animals lie in a vault, turned to stone." Then he compelled her to go thither with him, threatened her, and said: "Old sea-cat, now you shall make my brother and all the human beings lying here, alive again, or you shall go into the fire!" She took a wand and touched the stones, and then his brother with his animals came to life again, and many others, merchants, artisans, and shepherds, arose, thanked him for their deliverance, and went to their homes. But when the twin brothers saw each other again, they kissed each other and rejoiced with all their hearts. Then they seized the witch, bound her and laid her on the fire, and when she was burnt the forest opened of its own accord, and was light and clear, and the King's palace could be seen at about the distance of a three hours' walk.

Thereupon the two brothers went home together, and on the way told each other their histories. And when the younger said that he was ruler of the whole country in the King's stead, the other observed: "That I remarked very well, for when I came to the town, and was taken for you, all royal honours were paid me; the young Queen looked on me as her husband, and I had to eat at her side, and sleep in your bed." When the other heard that, he became so jealous and angry that he drew his sword, and struck off his brother's head. But when he saw him lying there dead, and saw his red blood flowing, he repented most violently: "My brother delivered me," cried he, "and I have killed him for it," and he bewailed him aloud. Then his hare came and offered to go and bring some of the root of life, and bounded away and brought it while yet there was time, and the dead man was brought to life again, and knew nothing about the wound.

After this they journeyed onwards, and the younger said: "You look like me, you have royal apparel on as I have, and the animals follow you as they do me; we will go in by opposite gates, and arrive at the same time from the two sides in the aged King's presence." So they separated, and at the same time came the watchmen from the one door and from the other, and announced that the young King and the animals had returned from the chase. The King said: "It is not possible, the gates lie quite a mile apart." In the meantime, however, the two brothers entered the courtyard of the palace from opposite sides, and both mounted the steps. Then the King said to the daughter: "Say which is your husband. Each of them looks exactly like the other, I cannot tell." Then she was in great distress, and could not tell; but at last she remembered the necklace which she had given to the animals, and she sought for and found her little golden clasp on the lion, and she cried in her delight: "He who is followed by this lion is my true husband. Then the young King laughed and said: "Yes, he is the right one," and they sat down together to table, and ate and drank, and were merry. At night when the young King went to bed, his wife said: "Why have you for these last nights always laid a two-edged sword in our bed? I thought you had a wish to kill me." Then he knew how true his brother had been.

THE LITTLE PEASANT

There was a certain village wherein no one lived but really rich peasants, and just one poor one, whom they called the little peasant. He had not even so much as a cow, and still less money to buy one, and yet he and his wife did so wish to have one. One day he said to her: "Listen, I have a good idea, there is our gossip the carpenter, he shall make us a wooden calf, and paint it brown, so that it looks like any other, and in time it will certainly get big and be a cow." The woman also liked the idea, and their gossip the carpenter cut and planed the calf, and painted it as it ought to be, and made it with its head hanging down as if it were eating.

Next morning when the cows were being driven out, the little peasant called the cow-herd in and said: "Look, I have a little calf there, but it is still small and has to be carried." The cow-herd said: "All right," and took it in his arms and carried it to the pasture, and set it among the grass. The little calf always remained standing like one which was eating, and the cow-herd said: "It will soon run by itself, just look how it eats already!" At night when he was going to drive the herd home again, he said to the calf: "If you can stand there and eat your fill, you can also go on your four legs; I don't care to drag you home again in my arms." But the little peasant stood at his door, and waited for his little calf, and when the cow-herd drove the cows through the village, and the calf was missing, he inquired where it was. The cow-herd answered: "It is still standing out there eating. It would not stop and come with us." But the little peasant said: "Oh, but I must have my beast back again." Then they went back to the meadow together, but someone had stolen the calf, and it was gone. The cow-herd said: "It must have run away." The peasant, however, said: "Don't tell me that," and led the cow-herd before the Mayor, who for his carelessness condemned him to give the peasant a cow for the calf which had run away.

And now the little peasant and his wife had the cow for which they had so long wished, and they were heartily glad, but they had no food for it, and could give it nothing to eat, so it soon had to be killed. They salted the flesh, and the peasant went into the town and wanted to sell the skin there, so that he might buy a new calf with the proceeds. On the way he passed by a mill, and there sat a raven with broken wings, and out of pity he took him and wrapped him in the skin. But as the weather grew so bad and there was a storm of rain and wind, he could go no farther, and turned back to the mill and begged for shelter. The miller's wife was alone in the house, and said to the peasant: "Lay yourself on the straw there," and gave him a slice of bread and cheese. The peasant ate it, and lay down with his skin beside him, and the woman thought: "He is tired and has gone to sleep." In the meantime came the parson; the miller's wife received him well, and said: "My husband is out, so we will have a feast." The peasant listened, and when he heard them talk about feasting he was vexed that he had been forced to make shift with a slice of bread and cheese. Then the woman served up four different things, roast meat, salad, cakes, and wine.

Just as they were about to sit down and eat, there was a knocking outside. The woman said: "Oh, heavens! It is my husband!" She quickly hid the roast meat inside the tiled stove, the wine under the pillow, the salad on the bed, the cakes under it, and the parson in the closet on the porch. Then she opened the door for her husband, and said: "Thank heaven, you are back again! There is such a storm, it looks as if the world were coming to an end." The miller saw the peasant lying on the straw, and asked: "What is that fellow doing there?" "Ah," said the wife, "the poor knave came in the storm and rain, and begged for shelter, so I gave him a bit of bread and cheese, and showed him where the straw was." The man said: "I have no objection, but be quick and get me something to eat." The woman said: "But I have nothing but bread and cheese." "I am contented with anything," replied the husband, "so far as I am concerned, bread and cheese will do," and looked at the peasant and said: "Come and eat some more with me." The peasant did not require to be invited twice, but got up and ate. After this the miller saw the skin in which the raven was, lying on the ground, and asked: "What have you there?" The peasant answered: "I have a soothsayer inside it." "Can he foretell anything to me?" said the miller. "Why not?" answered the peasant: "but he only says four things, and the fifth he keeps to himself." The miller was curious, and said: "Let him foretell something for once." Then the peasant pinched the raven's head, so that he croaked and made a noise like krr, krr. The miller said: "What did he say?" The peasant answered: "In the first place, he says that there is some wine hidden under the pillow." "Bless me!" cried the miller, and went there and found the wine. "Now go on," said he. The peasant made the raven croak again, and said: "In the second place, he says that there is some roast meat in the tiled stove." "Upon my word!" cried the miller, and went thither, and found the roast meat. The peasant made the raven prophesy still more, and said: "Thirdly, he says that there is some salad on the bed." "That would be a fine thing!" cried the miller, and went there and found the salad. At last the peasant pinched the raven once more till he croaked, and said:

"Fourthly, he says that there are some cakes under the bed." "That would be a fine thing!" cried the miller, and looked there, and found the cakes.

And now the two sat down to the table together, but the miller's wife was frightened to death, and went to bed and took all the keys with her. The miller would have liked much to know the fifth, but the little peasant said: "First, we will quickly eat the four things, for the fifth is something bad." So they ate, and after that they bargained how much the miller was to give for the fifth prophesy, until they agreed on three hundred talers. Then the peasant once more pinched the raven's head

till he croaked loudly. The miller asked: "What did he say?" The peasant replied: "He says that the Devil is hiding outside there in the closet on the porch." The miller said: "The Devil must go out," and opened the house-door; then the woman was forced to give up the keys, and the peasant unlocked the closet. The parson ran out as fast as he could, and the miller said: "It was true; I saw the black rascal with my own eyes." The peasant, however, made off next morning by daybreak with the three hundred talers.

At home the small peasant gradually launched out; he built a beautiful house, and the peasants said: "The small peasant has certainly been to the place where golden snow falls, and people carry the gold home in shovels."

Then the small peasant was brought before the Mayor, and bidden to say from whence his wealth came. He answered: "I sold my cow's skin in the town, for three hundred talers." When the peasants heard that, they too wished to enjoy this great profit, and ran home, killed all their cows, and stripped off their skins in order to sell them in the town to the greatest advantage. The Mayor, however, said: "But my servant must go first." When she came to the merchant in the town, he did not give her more than two talers for a skin, and when the others came, he did not give them so much, and said: "What can I do with all these skins?"

Then the peasants were vexed that the small peasant should have thus outwitted them, wanted to take vengeance on him, and accused him of this treachery before the Mayor. The innocent little peasant was unanimously sentenced to death, and was to be rolled into the water, in a barrel pierced full of holes. He was led forth, and a priest was brought who was to say a mass for his soul. The others were all obliged to retire to a distance, and when the peasant looked at the priest, he recognized the man who had been with the miller's wife. He said to him: "I set you free from the closet, set me free from the barrel." At this same moment up came, with a flock of sheep, the very shepherd whom the peasant knew had long been wishing to be Mayor, so he cried with all his might: "No, I will not do it; if the whole world insists on it, I will not do it!" The shepherd hearing that, came up to him, and asked: "What are you about? What is it that you will not do?" The peasant said: "They want to make me Mayor, if I will but put myself in the barrel, but I will not do it." The shepherd said: "If nothing more than that is needful in order to be Mayor, I would get into the barrel at once." The peasant said: "If you will get in, you will be Mayor." The shepherd was willing, and got in, and the peasant shut the top down on him; then he took the shepherd's flock for himself, and drove it away. The parson went to the crowd, and declared that the mass had been said. Then they came and rolled the barrel towards the water. When the barrel began to roll, the shepherd cried: "I am quite willing to be Mayor." They believed no otherwise than that it was the peasant who was saying this, and answered: "That is what we intend, but first you shall look about you a little down below there," and they rolled the barrel down into the water.

After that the peasants went home, and as they were entering the village, the small peasant also came quietly in, driving a flock of sheep and looking quite contented. Then the peasants were astonished, and said: "Peasant, from whence do you come? Have you come out of the water?" "Yes, truly," replied the peasant, "I sank deep, deep down, until at last I got to the bottom; I pushed the bottom out of the barrel, and crept out, and there were pretty meadows on which a number of lambs were feeding, and from thence I brought this flock away with me." Said the peasants: "Are there any more there?" "Oh, yes," said he, "more than I could want." Then the peasants made up their minds that they too would fetch some sheep for themselves, a flock apiece, but the Mayor said: "I come first." So they went to the water together, and just then there were some of the small fleecy clouds in the blue sky, which are called little lambs, and they were reflected in the water, whereupon the peasants cried: "We already see the sheep down below!" The Mayor pressed forward and said: "I will go down first, and look about me, and if things promise well I'll call you." So he jumped in; splash! went the water; it sounded as if he were calling them, and the whole crowd plunged in after him as one man. Then the entire village was dead, and the small peasant, as sole heir, became a rich man.

THE QUEEN BEE

Two kings' sons once went out in search of adventures, and fell into a wild, disorderly way of living, so that they never came home again. The youngest, who was called Simpleton, set out to seek his brothers, but when at length he found them they mocked him for thinking that he with his simplicity could get through the world, when they two could not make their way, and yet were so much cleverer. They all three travelled away together, and came to an ant-hill. The two elder wanted to destroy it, to see the little ants creeping about in their terror, and carrying their eggs away, but Simpleton said: "Leave the creatures in peace; I will not allow you to disturb them." Then they went onwards and came to a lake, on which a great number of ducks were swimming. The two brothers wanted to catch a couple and roast them, but Simpleton would not permit it, and said: "Leave the creatures in peace, I will not suffer you to kill them." At length they came to a bee's nest, in which there was so much honey that it ran out of the trunk of the tree where it was. The two wanted to make a fire beneath the tree, and suffocate the bees in order to take away the honey, but Simpleton again stopped them and said: "Leave the creatures in peace, I will not allow you to burn them." At length the two brothers arrived at a castle where stone horses were standing in the stables, and no human being was to be seen, and they went through all the halls until, quite at the end, they came to a door in which were three locks. In the middle of the door, however, there was a little pane, through which they could see into the room. There they saw a little grey man, who was sitting at a table. They called him, once, twice, but he did not hear; at last they called him for the third time, when he got up, opened the locks, and came out. He said nothing, however, but conducted them to a handsomely-spread table, and when they had eaten and drunk, he took each of them to a bedroom. Next morning the little grey man came to the eldest, beckoned to him, and conducted him to a stone table, on which were inscribed three tasks, by the performance of which the castle could be delivered from enchantment. The first was that in the forest, beneath the moss, lay the princess's pearls, a thousand in number, which must be picked up, and if by sunset one single pearl was missing, he who had looked for them would be turned to stone. The eldest went thither, and sought the whole day, but when it came to an end, he had only found one hundred, and what was written on the table came true, and he was turned into stone. Next day, the second brother undertook the adventure; but it did not fare much better with him than with the eldest; he did not find more than two hundred pearls, and was changed to stone. At last it was Simpleton's turn to seek in the moss; but it was so difficult for him to find the pearls, and he got on so slowly, that he seated himself on a stone, and wept. And while he was thus sitting, the King of the ants whose life he had once saved, came with five thousand ants, and before long the little creatures had got all the pearls together, and laid them in a heap. The second task, however, was to fetch out of the lake the key of the King's daughter's bed-chamber. When Simpleton came to the lake, the ducks which he had saved, swam up to him, dived down, and brought the key out of the water. But the third task was the most difficult; from amongst the three sleeping daughters of the King was the youngest and dearest to be sought out. They, however, resembled each other exactly, and were only to be distinguished by their having eaten different sweetmeats before they fell asleep: the eldest a bit of sugar; the second a little syrup; and the youngest a spoonful of honey. Then the Queen of the bees, whom Simpleton had protected from the fire, came and tasted the lips of all three, and at last she remained sitting on the mouth which had eaten honey, and thus the King's son recognized the right princess. Then the enchantment was at an end; everything was delivered from sleep, and those who had been turned to stone received once more their natural forms. Simpleton married the youngest and sweetest princess, and after her father's death became King, and his two brothers received the two other sisters.

THE THREE FEATHERS

There was once upon a time a King who had three sons, of whom two were clever and wise, but the third did not speak much, and was simple, and was called the Simpleton. When the King had become old and weak, and was thinking of his end, he did not know which of his sons should inherit the kingdom after him. Then he said to them: "Go forth, and he who brings me the most beautiful carpet shall be King after my death." And that there should be no dispute amongst them, he took them outside his castle, blew three feathers in the air, and said: "You shall go as they fly." One feather flew to the east, the other to the west, but the third flew straight up and did not fly far, but soon fell to the ground. And now one brother went to the right, and the other to the left, and they mocked Simpleton, who was forced to stay where the third feather had fallen. He sat down and was sad. Then all at once he saw that there was a trap-door close by the feather. He raised it up, found some steps, and went down them. Then he came to another door, knocked at it, and heard somebody inside calling:

"Little green waiting-maid,
Waiting-maid with the limping leg,
Little dog of the limping leg,
Hop hither and thither,
And quickly see who is without."

The door opened, and he saw a great, fat toad sitting, and round about her a crowd of little toads. The fat toad asked what he wanted. He answered: "I should like to have the prettiest and finest carpet in the world." Then she called a young one and said:

"Little green waiting-maid,
Waiting-maid with the limping leg,
Little dog of the limping leg,
Hop hither and thither,
And bring me the great box."

The young toad brought the box, and the fat toad opened it, and gave Simpleton a carpet out of it, so beautiful and so fine, that on the earth above, none could have been woven like it. Then he thanked her, and climbed out again. The two others, however, had looked on their youngest brother as so stupid that they believed he would find and bring nothing at all. "Why should we give ourselves a great deal of trouble searching?" said they, and got some coarse handkerchiefs from the first shepherds' wives whom they met, and carried them home to the King. At the same time Simpleton also came back, and brought his beautiful carpet, and when the King saw it he was astonished, and said: "If justice be done, the kingdom belongs to the youngest." But the two others let their father have no peace, and said that it was impossible that Simpleton, who in everything lacked understanding, should be King, and entreated him to make a new agreement with them. Then the father said: "He who brings me the most beautiful ring shall inherit the kingdom," and led the three brothers out, and blew into the air three feathers, which they were to follow. Those of the two eldest again went east and west, and Simpleton's feather flew straight up, and fell down near the door into the earth. Then he went down again to the fat toad, and told her that he wanted the most beautiful ring. She at once ordered her big box to be brought, and gave him a ring out of it, which sparkled with jewels, and was so beautiful that no goldsmith on earth would have been able to make it. The two eldest laughed at Simpleton for going to seek a golden ring. They gave themselves no trouble, but knocked the nails out of an old carriage-ring, and took it to the King; but when Simpleton produced his golden ring, his father again said: "The kingdom belongs to him." The two eldest did not cease from

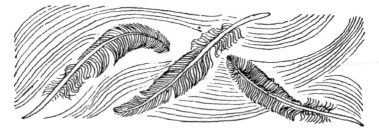

tormenting the King until he made a third condition, and declared that the one who brought the most beautiful woman home, should have the kingdom. He again blew the three feathers into the air, and they flew as before.

Then Simpleton without more ado went down to the fat toad, and said: "I am to take home the most beautiful woman!" "Oh," answered the toad, "the most beautiful woman! She is not at hand at the moment, but still you shall have her." She gave him a yellow turnip which had been hollowed out, to which six mice were harnessed. Then Simpleton said quite mournfully: "What am I to do with that?" The toad answered: "Just put one of my little toads into it." Then he seized one at random out of the circle, and put her into the yellow coach, but hardly was she seated inside it than she turned into a wonderfully beautiful maiden, and the turnip into a coach, and the six mice into horses. So he kissed her, and drove off quickly with the horses, and took her to the King. His brothers, who came afterwards, had given themselves no trouble at all looking for beautiful girls, but had brought with them the first peasant women they chanced to meet. When the King saw them he said: "After my death the Kingdom belongs to my youngest son." But the two eldest deafened the King's ears afresh with their clamour: "We cannot consent to Simpleton's being King," and demanded that the one whose wife could leap through a ring which hung in the centre of the hall should have the preference. They thought: "The peasant women can do that easily; they are strong enough, but the delicate maiden will jump herself to death." The aged King agreed likewise to this. Then the two peasant women jumped, and jumped through the ring, but were so clumsy that they fell, and their coarse arms and legs broke in two. And then the pretty maiden whom Simpleton had brought with him, sprang, and sprang through as lightly as a deer, and all opposition had to cease. So he received the crown, and has ruled wisely for a length of time.

THE GOLDEN GOOSE

There was a man who had three sons, the youngest of whom was called Dummling,* and was despised, mocked, and sneered at on every occasion.

It happened that the eldest wanted to go into the forest to hew wood, and before he went his mother gave him a beautiful sweet cake

* Simpleton.

and a bottle of wine in order that he might not suffer from hunger or thirst.

When he entered the forest he met a little grey-haired old man who bade him good-day, and said: "Do give me a piece of cake out of your pocket, and let me have a draught of your wine; I am so hungry and thirsty." But the clever son answered: "If I give you my cake and wine, I shall have none for myself; be off with you," and he left the little man standing and went on.

But when he began to hew down a tree, it was not long before he made a false stroke, and the axe cut him in the arm, so that he had to go home and have it bound up. And this was the little grey man's doing.

After this the second son went into the forest, and his mother gave him, like the eldest, a cake and a bottle of wine. The little old grey man met him likewise, and asked him for a piece of cake and a drink of wine. But the second son, too, said sensibly enough: "What I give you will be taken away from myself; be off!" and he left the little man standing and went on. His punishment, however, was not delayed; when he had made a few blows at the tree he struck himself in the leg, so that he had to be carried home.

Then Dummling said: "Father, do let me go and cut wood." The father answered: "Your brothers have hurt themselves with it, leave it alone, you do not understand anything about it." But Dummling begged so long that at last he said: "Just go then, you will get wiser by hurting yourself." His mother gave him a cake made with water and baked in the cinders, and with it a bottle of sour beer.

When he came to the forest the little old grey man met him likewise, and greeting him, said: "Give me a piece of your cake and a drink out of your bottle; I am so hungry and thirsty." Dummling answered: "I have only cinder-cake and sour beer; if that pleases you, we will sit down and eat." So they sat down, and when Dummling pulled out his cinder-cake, it was a fine sweet cake, and the sour beer had become good wine. So they ate and drank, and after that the little man said: "Since you have a good heart, and are willing to divide what you have, I will give you good luck. There stands an old tree, cut it down, and you will find something at the roots." Then the little man took leave of him.

Dummling went and cut down the tree, and when it fell there was a goose sitting in the roots with feathers of pure gold. He lifted her up, and taking her with him, went to an inn where he thought he would stay the night. Now the host had three daughters, who saw the goose and were curious to know what such a wonderful bird might be, and would have liked to have one of its golden feathers.

The eldest thought: "I shall soon find an opportunity of pulling out a feather," and as soon as Dummling had gone out she seized the goose by the wing, but her finger and hand remained sticking fast to it.

The second came soon afterwards, thinking only of how she might get a feather for herself, but she had scarcely touched her sister than she was held fast.

At last the third also came with the like intent, and the others screamed out: "Keep away; for goodness' sake keep away!" But she did not understand why she was to keep away. "The others are there," she thought, "I may as well be there too," and ran to them; but as soon as she had touched her sister, she remained sticking fast to her. So they had to spend the night with the goose.

The next morning Dummling took the goose under his arm and set out, without troubling himself about the three girls who were hanging on to it. They were obliged to run after him continually, now left, now right, wherever his legs took him.

In the middle of the fields the parson met them, and when he saw the procession he said: "For shame, you good-for-nothing girls, why are you running across the fields after this young man? Is that seemly?" At the same time he seized the youngest by the hand in order to pull her away, but as soon as he touched her he likewise stuck fast, and was himself obliged to run behind.

Before long the sexton came by and saw his master, the parson, running behind three girls. He was astonished at this and called out: "Hi! your reverence, whither away so quickly? Do not forget that we have a christening to-day!" and running after him he took him by the sleeve, but was also held fast to it.

Whilst the five were trotting thus one behind the other, two labourers came with their hoes from the fields; the parson called out to them and begged that they would set him and the sexton free. But they had scarcely touched the sexton when they were held fast, and now there were seven of them running behind Dummling and the goose.

Soon afterwards he came to a city, where a king ruled who had a daughter who was so serious that no one could make her laugh. So he had put forth a decree that whosoever should be able to make her laugh should marry her. When Dummling heard this, he went with his goose and all her train before the King's daughter, and as soon as she saw the seven people running on and on, one behind the other, she began to laugh quite loudly, and as if she would never stop. Thereupon Dummling asked to have her for his wife; but the King did not like the son-in-law, and made all manner of excuses and said he must first produce a man who could drink a cellarful of wine. Dummling thought of the little grey man, who could certainly help him; so he went into the forest, and in the same place where he had felled the tree, he saw a man sitting, who had a very sorrowful face. Dummling asked him what he was taking to heart so sorely, and he answered: "I have such a great thirst and cannot quench it; cold water I cannot stand, a barrel of wine I have just emptied, but that to me is like a drop on a hot stone!"

"There, I can help you," said Dummling, "just come with me and you shall be satisfied."

He led him into the King's cellar, and the man bent over the huge barrels, and drank and drank till his loins hurt, and before the day was out he had emptied all the barrels. Then Dummling asked once more for his bride, but the king was vexed that such an ugly fellow, whom everyone called Dummling, should take away his daughter, and he made a new condition; he must first find a man who could eat a whole mountain of bread. Dummling did not think long, but went straight into the forest, where in the same place there sat a man who was tying up his body with a strap, and making an awful face, and saying: "I have eaten a whole ovenful of rolls, but what good is that when one has such a hunger as I? My stomach remains empty, and I must tie myself up if I am not to die of hunger."

At this Dummling was glad, and said: "Get up and come with me; you shall eat yourself full." He led him to the King's palace, where all the flour in the whole Kingdom was collected, and from it he caused a huge mountain of bread to be baked. The man from the forest stood before it, began to eat, and by the end of one day the whole mountain had vanished. Then Dummling for the third time asked for his bride;

but the King again sought a way out, and ordered a ship which could sail on land and on water. "As soon as you come sailing back in it," said he, "you shall have my daughter for wife."

Dummling went straight into the forest, and there sat the little grey man to whom he had given his cake. When he heard what Dummling wanted, he said: "Since you have given me to eat and to drink, I will give you the ship; and I do all this because you once were kind to me." Then he gave him the ship which could sail on land and water, and when the king saw that, he could no longer prevent him from having his daughter. The wedding was celebrated, and after the King's death, Dummling inherited his Kingdom and lived for a long time contentedly with his wife.

ALLERLEIRAUH*

There was once upon a time a King who had a wife with golden hair, and she was so beautiful that her equal was not to be found on earth. It came to pass that she lay ill, and as she felt that she must soon die, she called the King and said: "If you wish to marry again after my death, take no one who is not quite as beautiful as I am, and who has not just such golden hair as I have: this you must promise me." And after the King had promised her this she closed her eyes and died.

For a long time the King could not be comforted, and had no thought of taking another wife. At length his councillors said: "This cannot go on. The King must marry again, that we may have a Queen." And now messengers were sent about far and wide, to seek a bride who equalled the late Queen in beauty. In the whole world, however, none was to be found, and even if one had been found, still there would have been no one who had such golden hair. So the messengers came home as they went.

Now the King had a daughter, who was just as beautiful as her dead mother, and had the same golden hair. When she was grown up the King looked at her one day, and saw that in every respect she was like

* Of many different kinds of fur.

his late wife, and suddenly felt a violent love for her. Then he spoke to his councillors: "I will marry my daughter, for she is the counterpart of my late wife, otherwise I can find no bride who resembles her." When the councillors heard that, they were shocked, and said: "God has forbidden a father to marry his daughter. No good can come from such a crime, and the kingdom will be involved in the ruin."

The daughter was still more shocked when she became aware of her father's resolution, but hoped to turn him from his design. Then she said to him: "Before I fulfil your wish, I must have three dresses, one as golden as the sun, one as silvery as the moon, and one as bright as the stars; besides this, I wish for a mantle of a thousand different kinds of fur and peltry joined together, and one of every kind of animal in your kingdom must give a piece of his skin for it." For she thought: "To get that will be quite impossible, and thus I shall divert my father from his wicked intentions." The King, however, did not give it up, and the cleverest maidens in his kingdom had to weave the three dresses, one as golden as the sun, one as silvery as the moon, and one as bright as the stars, and his huntsmen had to catch one of every kind of animal in the whole of his kingdom, and take from it a piece of its skin, and out of these was made a mantle of a thousand different kinds of fur. At length, when all was ready, the King caused the mantle to be brought, spread it out before her, and said: "The wedding shall be to-morrow."

When, therefore, the King's daughter saw that there was no longer any hope of turning her father's heart, she resolved to run away. In the night whilst every one was asleep, she got up, and took three different things from her treasures, a golden ring, a golden spinning-wheel, and a golden reel. The three dresses of the sun, moon, and stars she placed into a nutshell, put on her mantle of all kinds of fur, and blackened her face and hands with soot. Then she commended herself to God, and went away, and walked the whole night until she reached a great forest. And as she was tired, she got into a hollow tree, and fell asleep.

The sun rose, and she slept on, and she was still sleeping when it was full day. Then it so happened that the King to whom this forest belonged, was hunting in it. When his dogs came to the tree, they sniffed, and ran barking round about it. The King said to the huntsmen: "Just see what kind of wild beast has hidden itself in there." The huntsmen obeyed his order, and when they came back they said: "A wondrous beast is lying in the hollow tree; we have never before seen one like it. Its skin is fur of a thousand different kinds, but it is lying asleep." Said the King: "See if you can catch it alive, and then fasten it to the carriage, and we will take it with us." When the huntsmen laid hold of the maiden, she awoke full of terror, and cried to them: "I am a poor child, deserted by father and mother; have pity on me, and take me with you." Then said they: "Allerleirauh, you will be useful in the kitchen, come with us, and you can sweep up the ashes." So they put her in the carriage, and took her home to the royal palace. There they pointed out to her a closet under the stairs, where no daylight entered, and said: "Hairy animal, there you can live and sleep." Then she was sent into the kitchen, and there she carried wood and water, swept the hearth, plucked the fowls, picked the vegetables, raked the ashes, and did all the dirty work.

Allerleirauh lived there for a long time in great wretchedness. Alas, fair princess, what is to become of you now! It happened, however, that one day a feast was held in the palace, and she said to the cook: "May I go upstairs for a while, and look on? I will place myself outside the door." The cook answered: "Yes, go, but you must be back here in half-an-hour to sweep the hearth." Then she took her oil-lamp, went into her den, put off her dress of fur, and washed the soot off her face and hands, so that her full beauty once more came to light. And she opened the nut, and took out her dress which shone like the sun, and when she had done that she went up to the festival, and every one made way for her, for no one knew her, and thought no otherwise than that she was a king's daughter. The King came to meet her, gave his hand to her, and danced with her, and thought in his heart: "My eyes have never yet seen any one so beautiful!" When the dance was over she curtsied, and when the King looked round again she had vanished, and none knew whither. The guards who stood outside the palace were called and questioned, but no one had seen her.

She had run into her little den, however, there quickly taken off her dress, made her face and hands black again, put on the mantle of fur, and again was Allerleirauh. And now when she went into the kitchen, and was about to get to her work and sweep up the ashes, the cook said: "Leave that alone till morning, and make me the soup for the King; I, too, will go upstairs awhile, and take a look; but let no hairs fall in, or in future you shall have nothing to eat." So the cook went away, and Allerleirauh made the soup for the King, and made bread soup and the best she could, and when it was ready she fetched her golden ring from her little den, and put it in the bowl in which the soup was served. When the dancing was over, the King had his soup brought and ate it, and he liked it so much that it seemed to him he had never tasted better. But when he came to the bottom of the bowl, he saw a golden ring lying, and could not conceive how it could have got there. Then he ordered the cook to appear before him. The cook was terrified when he heard the order, and said to Allerleirauh: "You have certainly let a hair fall into the soup, and if you have, you shall be beaten for it." When he came before the King the latter asked who had made the soup? The cook replied: "I made it." But the King said: "That is not true, for it was much better than usual, and cooked differently." He answered: "I must acknowledge that I did not make it, it was made by the hairy animal." The King said: "Go and bid it come up here."

When Allerleirauh came, the King said: "Who are you?" "I am a poor girl who no longer has any father or mother." He asked further: "Of what use are you in my palace?" She answered: "I am good for nothing but to have boots thrown at my head." He continued: "Where did you get the ring which was in the soup?" She answered: "I know nothing about the ring." So the King could learn nothing, and had to send her away again.

After a while, there was another festival, and then, as before, Allerleirauh begged the cook for leave to go and look on. He answered: "Yes, but come back again in half-an-hour, and make the King the bread soup which he so much likes." Then she ran into her den, washed herself quickly, and took out of the nut the dress which was as silvery as the moon, and put it on. Then she went up and was like a princess, and the King stepped forward to meet her, and rejoiced to see her once more, and as the dance was just beginning they danced it together. But when it was ended, she again disappeared so quickly that the King could not observe where she went. She, however, sprang into her den, and once more made herself a hairy animal, and went into the kitchen to prepare the bread soup. When the cook had gone upstairs, she fetched the little golden spinning-wheel, and put it in the bowl so that the soup covered it. Then it was taken to the King, who ate it, and liked it as much as before, and had the cook brought, who this time likewise was forced to confess that Allerleirauh had prepared the soup. Allerleirauh again came before the King, but she answered that she was good for nothing else but to have boots thrown at her head, and that she knew nothing at all about the little golden spinning-wheel.

When, for the third time, the King held a festival, all happened just as it had done before. The cook said: "Fur-skin, you are a witch, and always put something in the soup which makes it so good that the King likes it better than that which I cook," but as she begged so hard, he let her go up at the appointed time. And now she put on the dress which shone like the stars, and thus entered the hall. Again the King danced with the beautiful maiden, and thought that she never yet had been so beautiful. And whilst she was dancing, he contrived, without her noticing it, to slip a golden ring on her finger, and he had given orders that the dance should last a very long time. When it was ended, he wanted to hold her fast by her hands, but she tore herself loose, and sprang away so quickly through the crowd that she vanished from his sight. She ran as fast as she could into her den beneath the stairs, but as she had been too long, and had stayed more than half-an-hour she could not take off her pretty dress, but only threw over it her mantle of fur, and in her haste she did not make herself quite black, but one finger remained white. Then Allerleirauh ran into the kitchen, and cooked the bread soup for the King, and as the cook was away, put her golden reel into it. When the King found the reel at the bottom of it, he caused Allerleirauh to be summoned, and then he espied the white finger, and saw the ring which he had put on it during the dance. Then he grasped her by the hand, and held her fast, and when she wanted to release herself and run away, her mantle of fur opened a little, and the star-dress shone forth. The King clutched the mantle and tore it off. Then her golden hair shone forth, and she stood there in full splendour, and could no longer hide herself. And when she had washed the soot and ashes from her face, she was more beautiful than anyone who had ever been seen on earth. But the King said: "You are my dear bride, and we will never more part from each other." Thereupon the marriage was solemnized, and they lived happily until their death.

THE HARE'S BRIDE

There was once a woman and her daughter who lived in a pretty garden with cabbages; and a little hare came into it, and during the winter time ate all the cabbages. Then says the mother to the daughter: "Go into the garden, and chase the hare away." The girl says to the little hare: "Sh-sh, hare, you will be eating all our cabbages." Says the hare: "Come, maiden, and seat yourself on my little hare's tail, and come with me into my little hare's hut." The girl will not do it. Next day the hare comes again and eats the cabbages, then says the mother to the daughter: "Go into the garden, and drive the hare away." The girl says to the hare: "Sh-sh, little hare, you will be eating all the cabbages." The little hare says: "Maiden, seat yourself on my little hare's tail, and come with me into my little hare's hut." The maiden refuses. The third day the hare comes again, and eats the cabbages. On this the mother says to the daughter: "Go into the garden, and hunt the hare away." Says the maiden: "Sh-sh, little hare, you will be eating all our cabbages." Says the little hare: "Come, maiden, seat yourself on my little hare's tail, and come with me into my little hare's hut." The girl seats herself on the little hare's tail, and then the hare takes her far away to his little hut, and says: "Now cook green cabbage and millet-seed, and I will invite the wedding-guests." Then all the wedding-guests assembled. (Who were the wedding-guests? That I can tell you as another told it to me. They were all hares, and the crow was there as parson to marry the bride and bridegroom, and the fox as clerk, and the altar was under the rainbow.)

The girl, however, was sad, for she was all alone. The little hare comes and says: "Open the doors, open the doors, the wedding-guests are merry." The bride says nothing, but weeps. The little hare goes away. The little hare comes back and says: "Take off the lid, take off the lid, the wedding-guests are hungry." The bride again says nothing, and weeps. The little hare goes away. The little hare comes back and says: "Take off the lid, take off the lid, the wedding-guests are waiting." Then the bride says nothing, and the hare goes away, but she dresses a straw-doll in her clothes, and gives her a spoon to stir with, and sets her by the pan with the millet-seed, and goes back to her mother. The little hare comes once more and says: "Take off the lid, take off the lid," and gets up, and strikes the doll on the head so that her cap falls off.

Then the little hare sees that it is not his bride, and goes away and is sorrowful.

THE TWELVE HUNTSMEN

There was once a King's son who had a bride whom he loved very much. And when he was sitting beside her and very happy, news came that his father lay sick unto death, and desired to see him once again before his end. Then he said to his beloved: "I must now go and leave you, I give you a ring as a remembrance of me. When I am King, I will return and fetch you." So he rode away, and when he reached his father, the latter was dangerously ill, and near his death. He said to him: "Dear son, I wished to see you once again before my end, promise me to marry as I wish," and he named a certain King's daughter who was to be his wife. The son was in such trouble that he did not think what he was doing, and said: "Yes, dear father, your will shall be done," and thereupon the King shut his eyes, and died.

When therefore the son had been proclaimed King, and the time of mourning was over, he was forced to keep the promise which he had given his father, and caused the King's daughter to be asked in marriage, and she was promised to him. His first betrothed heard of this, and fretted so much about his faithlessness that she nearly died. Then her father said to her: "Dearest child, why are you so sad? You shall have whatsoever you will." She thought for a moment and said: "Dear father, I wish for eleven girls exactly like myself in face, figure, and size." The father said: "If it be possible, your desire shall be fulfilled," and he caused a search to be made in his whole kingdom, until eleven young maidens were found who exactly resembled his daughter in face, figure, and size.

When they came to the King's daughter, she had twelve suits of huntsmen's clothes made, all alike, and the eleven maidens had to put on the huntsmen's clothes, and she herself put on the twelfth suit. Thereupon she took leave of her father, and rode away with them, and rode to the court of her former betrothed, whom she loved so dearly. Then she asked if he required any huntsmen, and if he would take all of them into his service. The King looked at her and did not know her, but as they were such handsome fellows, he said: "Yes," and that he would willingly take them, and now they were the King's twelve huntsmen.

The King, however, had a lion which was a wondrous animal, for he knew all concealed and secret things. It came to pass that one evening he said to the King: "You think you have twelve huntsmen?" "Yes," said the King, "they are twelve huntsmen." The lion continued: "You are mistaken, they are twelve girls." The King said: "That cannot be true! How will you prove that to me?" "Oh, just let some peas be strewn in the ante-chamber," answered the lion, "and then you will soon see. Men have a firm step, and when they walk over peas none of them stir, but girls trip and skip, and drag their feet, and the peas roll about." The King was well pleased with the counsel, and caused the peas to be strewn.

There was, however, a servant of the King's who favoured the huntsmen, and when he heard that they were going to be put to this test he went to them and repeated everything, and said: "The lion wants to make the King believe that you are girls." Then the King's daughter thanked him, and said to her maidens: "Show some strength, and step firmly on the peas." So next morning when the King had the twelve huntsmen called before him, and they came into the ante-chamber where the peas were lying, they stepped so firmly on them, and had such a strong, sure walk, that not one of the peas either rolled or stirred. Then they went away again, and the King said to the lion: "You have lied to me, they walk just like men." The lion said: "They have been informed that they were going to be put to the test, and have assumed some strength. Just let twelve spinning-wheels be brought into the ante-chamber, and they will go to them and be pleased with them, and that is what no man would do." The King liked the advice, and had the spinning-wheels placed in the ante-chamber.

But the servant, who was well disposed to the huntsmen, went to them, and disclosed the project. So when they were alone the King's daughter said to her eleven girls: "Show some constraint, and do not look round at the spinning-wheels." And next morning when the King had his twelve huntsmen summoned, they went through the ante-chamber, and never once looked at the spinning wheels. Then the King again said to the lion: "You have deceived me, they are men, for they have not looked at the spinning-wheels." The lion replied: "They have learnt that they were going to be put to the test, and have restrained themselves." The King, however, would no longer believe the lion.

The twelve huntsmen always followed the King to the chase, and his liking for them continually increased. Now it came to pass that once when they were out hunting, news came that the King's bride was approaching. When the true bride heard that, it hurt her so much that her heart was almost broken, and she fell fainting to the ground. The King thought something had happened to his dear huntsman, ran up to him, wanted to help him, and drew his glove off. Then he saw the ring which he had given to his first bride, and when he looked in her face he recognized her. Then his heart was so touched that he kissed her, and when she opened her eyes he said: "You are mine, and I am yours, and no one in the world can alter that." He sent a messenger to the other bride, and entreated her to return to her own kingdom, for he had a wife already, and someone who had just found an old key did not require a new one. Thereupon the wedding was celebrated, and the lion was again taken into favour, because, after all, he had told the truth.

THE THIEF AND HIS MASTER

Hans wished to put his son to learn a trade, so he went into the church and prayed to our Lord God to know which would be the most suitable for him. Then the clerk got behind the altar, and said: "Thieving, thieving." On this Hans goes back to his son, and tells him he is to learn thieving, and that the Lord God had said so. So he goes with his son to seek a man who is acquainted with thieving. They walk a long time and come into a great forest, where stands a little house with an old woman in it. Hans says: "Do you know of a man who is acquainted with thieving?" "You can learn that here quite well," says the woman, "my son is a master of it." So he speaks with the son, and asks if he knows thieving really well. The master-thief says: "I will teach him well. Come back when a year is over, and then if you recognize your son, I will take no payment at all for teaching him; but if you don't know him, you must give me two hundred talers."

The father goes home again, and the son learns witchcraft and thieving, thoroughly. When the year is out, the father is full of anxiety to know how he shall recognize his son. As he is thus going about in his trouble, he meets a little dwarf, who says: "Man, what ails you, that you are always in such trouble?"

"Oh," says Hans, "a year ago I placed my son with a master-thief who told me I was to come back when the year was out, and that if I then did not know my son when I saw him, I was to pay two hundred talers; but if I did know him I was to pay nothing, and now I am afraid of not knowing him and can't tell where I am to get the money." Then the dwarf tells him to take a crust of bread with him, and to stand beneath the chimney. "There on the cross-beam is a basket, out of which a little bird is peeping, and that is your son."

Hans goes thither, and throws a crust of black bread in front of the basket with the bird in it, and the little bird comes out, and looks up. "Hello, my son, are you here?" says the father, and the son is delighted to see his father, but the master-thief says: "The devil must have prompted you, or how could you have known your son?" "Father, let us go," said the youth.

Then the father and son set out homeward. On the way a carriage comes driving by. Hereupon the son says to his father: "I will change myself into a large greyhound, and then you can earn a great deal of money by me." Then the gentleman calls from the carriage: "My man, will you sell your dog?" "Yes," says the father. "How much do you want for it?" "Thirty talers." "Well, man, that is a great deal, but as it is such a very fine dog I will have it." The gentleman takes it into his carriage, but when they have driven a little farther the dog springs out of the carriage through the window, and goes back to his father, and is no longer a greyhound.

They go home together. Next day there is a fair in the neighbouring town, so the youth says to his father: "I will now change myself into a beautiful horse, and you can sell me; but when you have sold me, you must take off my bridle, or I cannot become a man again." Then the father goes with the horse to the fair, and the master-thief comes and buys the horse for a hundred talers, but the father forgets, and does not take off the bridle. So the man goes home with the horse, and puts it in the stable. When the maid crosses the threshold, the horse says: "Take off my bridle, take off my bridle." Then the maid stands still, and says: "What, can you speak?" So she goes and takes the bridle off, and the horse becomes a sparrow, and flies out at the door, and the master-thief becomes a sparrow also, and flies after him. Then they come together and cast lots, but the master loses, and betakes himself to the water and is a fish. Then the youth also becomes a fish, and they cast lots again, and the master loses. So the master changes himself into a cock, and the youth becomes a fox, and bites the master's head off, and he died and has remained dead to this day.

JORINDA AND JORINGEL

There was once an old castle in the midst of a large and dense forest, and in it an old woman who was a witch dwelt all alone. In the day-time she changed herself into a cat or a screech-owl, but in the evening she took her proper shape again as a human being. She could lure wild beasts and birds to her, and then she killed and boiled and roasted them. If anyone came within one hundred paces of the castle he was obliged to stand still, and could not stir from the place until she bade him be free. But whenever an innocent maiden came within this circle, she changed her into a bird, and shut her up in a wicker-work cage, and carried the cage into a room in the castle. She had about seven thousand cages of rare birds in the castle.

Now, there was once a maiden who was called Jorinda, who was fairer than all other girls. She and a handsome youth named Joringel had promised to marry each other. They were still in the days of betrothal, and their greatest happiness was being together. One day in order that they might be able to talk together in peace they went for a walk in the forest. "Take care," said Joringel, "that you do not go too near the castle."

It was a beautiful evening; the sun shone brightly between the trunks of the trees into the dark green of the forest, and the turtle-doves sang mournfully upon the beech trees.

Jorinda wept now and then: she sat down in the sunshine and was sorrowful. Joringel was sorrowful too; they were as sad as if they were about to die. Then they looked around them, and were quite at a loss, for they did not know by which way they should go home. The sun was still half above the mountain and half under.

Joringel looked through the bushes, and saw the old walls of the castle close at hand. He was horror-stricken and filled with deadly fear. Jorinda was singing:

> "My little bird, with the necklace red,
> Sings sorrow, sorrow, sorrow,
> He sings that the dove must soon be dead,
> Sings sorrow, sor——jug, jug, jug."

Joringel looked for Jorinda. She was changed into a nightingale, and sang "jug, jug, jug." A screech-owl with glowing eyes flew three times round about her, and three times cried "to-whoo, to-whoo, to-whoo!"

Joringel could not move: he stood there like a stone, and could neither weep nor speak, nor move hand or foot.

The sun had now set. The owl flew into the thicket, and directly afterwards there came out of it a crooked old woman, yellow and lean, with large red eyes and a hooked nose, the point of which reached to her chin. She muttered to herself, caught the nightingale, and took it away in her hand.

Joringel could neither speak nor move from the spot; the nightingale was gone. At last the woman came back, and said in a hollow voice: "Greet you, Zachiel. If the moon shines on the cage, Zachiel, let him loose at once." Then Joringel was freed. He fell on his knees before the woman and begged that she would give him back his Jorinda, but she said that he should never have her again, and went away. He called, he wept, he lamented, but all in vain: "Hooh, what is to become of me?"

Joringel went away, and at last came to a strange village; there he kept sheep for a long time. He often walked round and round the castle, but not too near to it. At last he dreamt one night that he found a blood-red flower, in the middle of which was a beautiful large pearl; that he picked the flower and went with it to the castle, and that everything he touched with the flower was freed from enchantment; he also dreamt that by means of it he recovered his Jorinda.

In the morning, when he awoke, he began to seek over hill and dale for such a flower. He sought until the ninth day, and then, early in the morning, he found the blood-red flower. In the middle of it there was a large dew-drop, as big as the finest pearl.

Day and night he journeyed with this flower to the castle. When he was within a hundred paces of it he was not held fast, but walked on to the door. Joringel was full of joy; he touched the door with the flower, and it sprang open. He walked in through the courtyard, and listened for the sound of the birds. At last he heard it. He went on and found the room from whence it came, and there the witch was feeding the birds in the seven thousand cages.

When she saw Joringel she was angry, very angry, and scolded and spat poison and gall at him, but she could not come within two paces of him. He did not take any notice of her, but went and looked at the cages with the birds; but there were many hundred nightingales, how was he to find his Jorinda again?

Just then he saw the old woman quietly take away a cage with a bird in it, and go towards the door.

Swiftly he sprang towards her, touched the cage with the flower, and also the old woman. She could now no longer bewitch anyone; and Jorinda was standing there, clasping him round the neck, and she was as beautiful as ever. Then all the other birds were turned into maidens again, and he went home with his Jorinda, and they lived happily together for a long time.

THE THREE SONS OF FORTUNE

A father once called his three sons before him, and he gave to the first a cock, to the second a scythe, and to the third a cat. "I am already aged," said he, "my death is night, and I have wished to provide for you before my end; money I have not, and what I now give you seems of little worth, but all depends on your making a sensible use of it. Only seek out of country where such things are still unknown, and fortune is made."

After the father's death the eldest went away with his cock, but wherever he came the cock was already known; in the towns he saw him from a long distance, sitting upon the steeples and turning round with the wind, and in the villages he heard more than one crowing; no one would show any wonder at the creature, so that it did not look as if he would make his fortune by it.

At last, however, it happened that he came to an island where the people knew nothing about cocks, and did not even understand how to divide their time. They certainly knew when it was morning or evening, but at night, if they did not sleep through it, not one of them knew how to find out the time.

"Look!" said he, "what proud creature! It has a ruby-red crown upon its head, and wears spurs like a knight; it calls you three times during the night, at fixed hours, and when it calls for the last time, the sun soon rises. But if it crows by broad daylight, then take notice, for there will certainly be a change of weather."

The people were well pleased; for a whole night they did not sleep, and listened with great delight as the cock at two, four, and six o'clock, loudly and clearly proclaimed the time. They asked if the creature were for sale, and how much he wanted for it. "About as much gold as an ass can carry," answered he. "A ridiculously small price for such a precious creature!" they cried unanimously, and willingly gave him what he had asked.

When he came home with his wealth his brothers were astonished, and the second said: "Well, I will go forth and see whether I cannot get rid of my scythe as profitably." But it did not look as if he would, for labourers met him everywhere, and they had scythes upon their shoulders as well as he.

At last, however, he chanced upon an island where the people knew nothing of scythes. When the corn was ripe there, they took cannon out to the fields and shot it down. Now this was rather an uncertain affair; many shot right over it, others hit the ears instead of the stems, and shot them away, whereby much was lost, and besides all this, it made a terrible noise. So the man set to work and mowed it down so quietly and quickly that the people opened their mouths with astonishment. They agreed to give him what he wanted for the scythe, and he received a horse laden with as much gold as it could carry.

And now the third brother wanted to take his cat to the right man. He fared just like the other; so long as he stayed on the mainland there was nothing to be done. Every place had cats, and there were so many of them that new-born kittens were generally drowned in the ponds.

At last he sailed over to an island, and it luckily happened that no cats had ever yet been seen there, and that the mice had got the upper hand so much that they danced upon the tables and benches whether the master were at home or not. The people complained bitterly of the plague; the King himself in his palace did not know how to protect himself against them; mice squeaked in every corner, and gnawed whatever they could lay hold of with their teeth. But now the cat began her chase, and soon cleared a couple of rooms, and the people begged the King to buy the wonderful beast for the country. The King willingly gave what was asked, which was a mule laden with gold, and the third brother came home with the greatest treasure of all.

The cat made herself merry with the mice in the royal palace, and killed so many that they could not be counted. At last she grew warm with the work and thirsty, so she stood still, lifted up her head and cried: "Mew! mew!" When they heard this strange cry, the King and all his people were frightened, and in their terror ran all at once out of the palace. Then the King took counsel what was best to be done; at last it was determined to send a herald to the cat, and demand that she should leave the palace, or if not, she was to expect that force would be used against her. The councillors said: "Rather will we let ourselves be plagued with the mice, for to that misfortune we are accustomed, than give up our lives to such a monster as this." A noble youth, therefore, was sent to ask the cat whether she would peaceably quit the castle? But the cat, whose thirst had become still greater, merely answered: "Mew!

mew!" The youth understood her to say: "Most certainly not! most certainly not!" and took this answer to the King. "Then," said the councillors, "she shall yield to force." Cannon were brought out, and the palace was soon in flames. When the fire reached the room where the cat was sitting, she sprang safely out of the window; but the besiegers did not leave off until the whole palace was shot down to the ground.

HOW SIX MEN GOT ON IN THE WORLD

There was once a man who understood all kinds of arts; he served in war, and behaved well and bravely, but when the war was over he received his dismissal, and three farthings for his expenses on the way. "Wait," said he, "I shall not be content with this. If I can only meet with the right people, the King will yet have to give me all the treasure of the country." Then full of anger he went into the forest, and saw a man standing therein who had plucked up six trees as if they were blades of corn. He said to him: "Will you be my servant and go with me?" "Yes," he answered, "but, first, I will take this little bundle of sticks home to my mother," and he took one of the trees, and wrapped it round the five others, lifted the bundle on his back, and carried it away. Then he returned and went with his master, who said: "We two ought to be able to get through the world very well," and when they had walked on for a short while they found a huntsman who was kneeling, had shouldered his gun, and was about to fire. The master said to him: "Huntsman, what are you going to shoot?" He answered: "Two miles from here a fly is sitting on the branch of an oak-tree, and I want to shoot its left eye out." "Oh, come with me," said the man, "if we three are together, we certainly ought to be able to get on in the world!" The huntsman was ready, and went with him, and they came to seven windmills whose sails were turning round with great speed, and yet no wind was blowing either on the right or the left, and no leaf was stirring. Then said the man: "I know not what is driving the windmills, not a breath of air is stirring," and he went onwards with his servants, and when they had walked two miles they saw a man sitting on a tree who was shutting one nostril, and blowing out of the other. "Good gracious! what are you doing up there?" He answered: "Two miles from here are seven windmills; look, I am blowing them till they turn round." "Oh, come with me," said the man. "If we four are together, we shall carry the whole world before us!" Then the blower came down and went with him, and after a while they saw a man who was standing on one leg and had taken off the other, and laid it beside him. Then the master said: "You have arranged things very comfortably to have a rest." "I am a runner," he replied, "and to stop myself running far too fast, I have taken off one of my legs, for if I run with both, I go quicker than any bird can fly." "Oh, go with me. If we five are together, we shall carry the whole world before us." So he went with them, and it was not long before they met a man who wore a cap, but wore it entirely over one ear. Then the master said to him: "Gracefully, gracefully, don't stick your cap on one ear, you look just like a tom-fool!" "I must not wear it otherwise," said he, "for if I set my hat straight, a terrible frost comes on, and all the birds in the air are frozen, and drop dead on the ground." "Oh, come with me," said the master. "If we six are together, we can carry the whole world before us."

Now the six came to a town where the King had proclaimed that whosoever ran a race with his daughter and won the victory, should be her husband, but whosoever lost it, must lose his head. Then the man presented himself and said: "I will, however, let my servant run for me." The King replied: "Then his life also must be staked, so that his head and yours are both set on the victory." When that was settled and made secure, the man buckled the other leg on the runner, and said to him: "Now be nimble, and help us to win." It was fixed that the one who was the first to bring some water from a far distant well was to be the victor. The runner received a pitcher, and the King's daughter one too, and they began to run at the same time, but in an instant, when the King's daughter had got a very little way, the people who were looking on could see no more of the runner, and it was just as if the wind had whistled by. In a short time he reached the well, filled his pitcher with water, and turned back. Half-way home, however, he was overcome with fatigue, and set his pitcher down, lay down himself, and fell asleep. But he had made a pillow of a horse's skull which was lying on the ground, in order that he might lie uncomfortably, and soon wake up again. In the meantime the King's daughter, who could also run very well—quite as well as any ordinary mortal can—had reached the well, and was hurrying back with her pitcher full of water, and when she saw the runner lying there asleep, she was glad and said: "My enemy is delivered over into my hands," emptied his pitcher, and ran on. And now all would have been lost if by good luck the huntsman had not been standing at the top of the castle, and had not seen everything with his sharp eyes. Then said he: "The King's daughter shall still not prevail against us; and he loaded his gun, and shot so cleverly, that he shot the horse's skull away from under the runner's head without hurting him. Then the runner awoke, leapt up, and saw that his pitcher was empty, and that the King's daughter was already far in advance. He did not lose heart, however, but ran back to the well with his pitcher, again drew some water, and was at home again even ten minutes before the King's daughter. "Behold!" said he, "only now have I begun to use my legs; what I did before did not deserve to be called running."

But it pained the King, and still more his daughter, that she should be carried off by a common discharged soldier like that; so they took counsel with each other how to get rid of him and his companions. Then said the King to her: "I have thought of a way; don't be afraid, they shall not come back again." And he said to them: "You shall now make merry together, and eat and drink," and he conducted them to a room which had a floor of iron, and the doors also were of iron, and the windows were guarded with iron bars. There was a table in the room covered with delicious food, and the King said to them: "Go in, and enjoy yourselves." And when they were inside, he ordered the doors to be shut and bolted. Then he sent for the cook, and commanded him to make a fire under the room until the iron became red-hot. This the cook did, and the six who were sitting at table began to feel quite warm, and they thought the heat was caused by the food; but as it became still greater, and they wanted to get out, and found that the doors and windows were bolted, they became aware that the King must have an evil intention, and wanted to suffocate them. "He shall not succeed, however," said the one with the cap. "I will cause a frost to come, before which the fire shall be ashamed, and creep away." Then he put his cap on straight, and immediately there came such a frost that all heat disappeared, and the food on the dishes began to freeze. When an hour or two had passed by, and the King believed that they had perished in the heat, he had the doors opened to behold them himself. But when the doors were opened, all six were standing there, alive and well, and said that they should very much like to get out to warm themselves, for the very food was fast frozen to the dishes with the cold. Then, full of anger, the King went down to the cook, scolded him, and asked why he had not done what he had been ordered to do. But the cook replied: "There is heat enough there, just look yourself." Then the King saw that a fierce fire was burning under the iron room, and perceived that there was no getting the better of the six in this way.

Again the King considered how to get rid of his unpleasant guests, and caused their chief to be brought and said: "If you will take gold and renounce my daughter, you shall have as much as you will."

"Oh, yes, Lord King," he answered, "give me as much as my servant can carry, and I will not ask for your daughter."

On this the King was satisfied, and the other continued: "In fourteen days, I will come and fetch it." Thereupon he summoned together all the tailors in the whole kingdom, and they were to sit for fourteen days and sew a sack. And when it was ready, the strong one who could tear up trees had to take it on his back, and go with it to the King. Then said the King: "Who can that strong fellow be who is carrying a bundle of linen on his back that is as big as a house?" and he was alarmed and said: "What a lot of gold he can carry away!" Then he commanded a ton of gold to be brought, which took sixteen of his strongest men to carry, but the strong one snatched it up in one hand, put it in his sack, and said: "Why don't you bring more at the same time?—that hardly covers the bottom!" Then, little by little, the King caused all his treasure to be brought thither, and the strong one pushed it into the sack, and still the sack was not half full with it." "Bring more," cried he, "these few crumbs don't fill it." Then seven thousand carts with gold had to be gathered together in the whole kingdom, and the strong one thrust them and the oxen harnessed to them into his sack. "I will examine it no longer," said he, "but will just take what comes, so long as the sack is but full." When all that was inside, there was still room for a great deal more; then he said: "I will just make an end of the thing; people do sometimes tie up a sack even when it is not full." So he took it on his back, and went away with his comrades. When the King now saw how one single man was carrying away the entire wealth of the country, he became enraged, and bade his horsemen mount and pursue the six, and ordered them to take the sack away from the strong one. Two regiments speedily overtook the six, and called out: "You are prisoners, put down the sack with the gold, or you will all be cut to pieces!" "What say you?" cried the blower, "that we are prisoners! Rather than that should happen, all of you shall dance about in the air." And he closed one nostril, and with the other blew on the two regiments. Then they were driven away from each other, and carried into the blue sky over all the mountains—one here, the other there. One sergeant cried for mercy; he had nine wounds, and was a brave fellow who did not deserve ill-treatment. The blower stopped a little so that he came down without injury, and then the blower said to him: "Now go home to your King, and tell him he had better send some more horsemen, and I will blow them all into the air." When the King was informed of this he said: "Let the rascals go. There is magic in them." Then the six conveyed the riches home, divided it amongst them, and lived in content until their death.

THE WOLF AND THE MAN

Once upon a time the fox was talking to the wolf of the strength of man; how no animal could withstand him, and how all were obliged to employ cunning in order to protect themselves from him. Then the wolf answered: "If I had but the chance of seeing a man for once, I would set on him not-withstanding." "I can help you to do that," said the fox. "Come to me early to-morrow morning, and I will show you one." The wolf presented himself betimes, and the fox took him out on the road by which the huntsmen went daily. First came an old discharged soldier. "Is that a man?" inquired the wolf. "No," answered the fox, "that was one." Afterwards came a little boy who was going to school. "Is that a man?" "No, that will be one." At length came a hunter with his double-barrelled gun at his back, and hanger by his side. Said the fox to the wolf: "Look, there comes a man, you must attack him, but I will take myself off to my hole." The wolf then rushed on the man. When the huntsman saw him he said: "It is a pity that I have not loaded with a bullet," aimed, and fired his small shot in his face. The wolf pulled a very wry grimace, but did not let himself be frightened, and attacked him again, on which the huntsman gave him the second barrel. The wolf swallowed his pain, and rushed on the huntsman, but he drew out his bright hanger, and gave him a few cuts with it right and left, so that, bleeding everywhere, he ran howling back to the fox. "Well, brother wolf," said the fox, "how have you got on with man?" "Ah!" replied the wolf, "I never imagined the strength of man to be what it is! First, he took a stick from his shoulder, and blew into it, and then something flew into my face which tickled me terribly; then he breathed once more into the stick, and it flew into my nose like lightning and hail; when I was quite close, he drew a white rib out of his body, and he beat me so with it that I was all but left lying dead." "See what a braggart you are!" said the fox. "You throw your hatchet so far that you cannot fetch it back again!"

THE WOLF AND THE FOX

The wolf had the fox with him, and whatsoever the wolf wished, that the fox was compelled to do, for he was the weaker, and he would gladly have been rid of his master. It chanced that once as they were going through the forest, the wolf said: "Red-fox, get me something to eat, or else I will eat you yourself." Then the fox answered: "I know a farm-yard where there are two young lambs; if you are inclined, we will fetch one of them." That suited the wolf, and they went thither, and the fox stole the little lamb, took it to the wolf, and went away. The wolf devoured it, but was not satisfied with one; he wanted the other as well, and went to get it. But as he did it so clumsily, the mother of the little lamb heard him, and began to cry out terribly, and to bleat so that the farmers came running there. They found the wolf, and beat him so mercilessly, that he went to the fox limping and howling. "You have misled me finely," said he; "I wanted to fetch the other lamb, and the country folks surprised me, and have beaten me to a jelly." The fox replied, "Why are you such a glutton?"

Next day they again went into the country, and the greedy wolf once more said: "Red-fox, get me something to eat, or I will eat you yourself." Then answered the fox: "I know a farm-house where the wife is baking pancakes to-night; we will get some of them for ourselves." They went there, and the fox slipped round the house, and peeped and sniffed about until he discovered where the dish was, and then snatched six pancakes and carried them to the wolf. "There is something for you to eat," said he to him, and then went his way. The wolf swallowed down the pancakes in an instant, and said: "They make one want more," and went thither and tore the whole dish down so that it broke in pieces. This made such a great noise that the woman came out, and when she saw the wolf she called the people, who hurried there, and beat him as long as their sticks would hold together, till with two lame legs, and howling loudly, he returned to the fox in the forest. "How abominably you have misled me!" cried he, "the peasants caught me, and tanned my skin for me." But the fox replied: "Why are you such a glutton?"

On the third day, when they were out together, and the wolf could

only limp along painfully, he again said: "Red-fox, get me something
to eat, or I will eat you yourself." The fox answered: "I know a man
who has been killing, and the salted meat is lying in a barrel in the
cellar; we will get that." Said the wolf: "I will go when you do, that you
may help me if I am not able to get away." "I am willing," said the fox,
and showed him the by-paths and ways by which at length they
reached the cellar. There was meat in abundance, and the wolf attacked
it instantly and thought: "There is plenty of time before I need leave
off!" The fox liked it also, but looked about everywhere, and often ran
to the hole by which they had come in, to find out if his body was still
thin enough to slip through it. The wolf said: "Dear fox, tell me why
you are running here and there so much, and jumping in and out?"

"I must see that no one is coming," replied the crafty fellow. "Don't
eat too much!" Then said the wolf: "I shall not leave until the barrel is

empty." In the meantime the farmer, who had heard the noise of the fox's jumping, came into the cellar. When the fox saw him he was out of the hole at one bound. The wolf wanted to follow him, but he had made himself so fat with eating that he could no longer get through, but stuck fast. Then came the farmer with a cudgel and struck him dead, but the fox bounded into the forest, glad to be rid of the old glutton.

GOSSIP WOLF AND THE FOX

The she-wolf brought into the world a young one, and invited the fox to be godfather. "After all, he is a near relative of ours," said she, "he has a good understanding, and much talent; he can instruct my little son, and help him forward in the world." The fox, too, appeared quite honest, and said: "Worthy Mrs. Gossip, I thank you for the honour which you are doing me; I will, however, conduct myself in such a way that you shall be repaid for it." He enjoyed himself at the feast, and made merry; afterwards he said: "Dear Mrs. Gossip, it is our duty to take care of the child, it must have good food that it may be strong. I know a sheep-fold from which we might fetch a nice morsel." The wolf was pleased with the idea, and she went out with the fox to the farm-yard. He pointed out the fold from afar, and said: "You will be able to creep in there without being seen, and in the meantime I will look about on the other side to see if I can pick up a chicken." He, however, did not go there, but sat down at the entrance to the forest, stretched his legs and rested. The she-wolf crept into the stable. A dog was lying there, and it made such a noise that the peasants came running out, caught Gossip Wolf, and poured a strong burning mixture, which had been prepared for washing, over her skin. At last she escaped, and dragged herself outside. There lay the fox, who pretended to be full of complaints, and said: "Ah, dear Mrs. Gossip, how ill I have fared, the peasants have fallen on me, and have broken every limb I have; if you do not want me to lie where I am and perish, you must carry me away." The she-wolf herself was only able to walk slowly, but she was in such concern about the fox that she took him on her back, and slowly carried him who was perfectly safe and sound to her house. Then the fox cried to her: "Farewell, dear Mrs. Gossip, may the roasting you have had do you good," laughed heartily at her, and bounded off.

THE FOX AND THE CAT

It happened that the cat met the fox in a forest, and as she thought to herself: "He is clever and full of experience, and much esteemed in the world," she spoke to him in a friendly way. "Good-day, dear Mr. Fox, how are you? How is all with you? How are you getting on in these hard times?" The fox, full of all kinds of arrogance, looked at the cat from head to foot, and for a long time did not know whether he would give any answer or not. At last he said: "Oh, you wretched beard-cleaner, you piebald fool, you hungry mouse-hunter, what can you be thinking of? Have you the cheek to ask how I am getting on? What have you learnt? How many arts do you understand?" "I understand but one," replied the cat, modestly. "What art is that?" asked the fox. "When the hounds are following me, I can spring into a tree and save myself." "Is that all?" said the fox. "I am master of a hundred arts, and have into the bargain a sackful of cunning. You make me sorry for you; come with me, I will teach you how people get away from the hounds." Just then came a hunter with four dogs. The cat sprang nimbly up a tree, and sat down at the top of it, where the branches and foliage quite concealed her. "Open your sack, Mr. Fox, open your sack," cried the cat to him, but the dogs had already seized him, and were holding him fast. "Ah, Mr. Fox," cried the cat. "You with your hundred arts are left in the lurch! Had you been able to climb like me, you would not have lost your life."

THE PINK

There was once upon a time a Queen to whom God had given no children. Every morning she went into the garden and prayed to God in heaven to bestow on her a son or a daughter. Then an angel from heaven came to her and said: "Be at rest, you shall have a son with the power of wishing, so that whatsoever in the world he wishes for, that shall he have." Then she went to the King, and told him the joyful tidings, and when the time was come she gave birth to a son, and the King was filled with gladness.

Every morning she went with the child to the garden where the wild beasts were kept, and washed herself there in a clear stream. It happened once when the child was a little older, that it was lying in her arms and she fell asleep. Then came the old cook, who knew that the child had the power of wishing, and stole it away, and he took a hen, and cut it in pieces, and dropped some of its blood on the Queen's apron and on her dress. Then he carried the child away to a secret place, where a nurse was obliged to suckle it, and he ran to the King and accused the Queen of having allowed her child to be taken from her by the wild beasts. When the King saw the blood on her apron, he believed this, fell into such a passion that he ordered a high tower to be built, in which neither sun nor moon could be seen, and had his wife put into it, and walled up. Here she was to stay for seven years without meat or drink, and die of hunger. But God sent two angels from heaven in the shape of white doves, which flew to her twice a day, and carried her food until the seven years were over.

The cook, however, thought to himself: "If the child has the power of wishing, and I am here, he might very easily get me into trouble." So he left the palace and went to the boy, who was already big enough to speak, and said to him: "Wish for a beautiful palace for yourself with a garden, and all else that pertains to it." Scarcely were the words out of the boy's mouth, when everything was there that he had wished for. After a while the cook said to him: "It is not well for you to be so alone, wish for a pretty girl as a companion." Then the King's son wished for one, and she immediately stood before him, and was more beautiful than any painter could have painted her. The two played together, and loved each other with all their hearts, and the old cook went out hunting like a nobleman. The thought occurred to him, however, that the King's son might some day wish to be with his father, and thus bring him into great peril. So he went out and took the maiden aside, and said: "To-night when the boy is asleep, go to his bed and plunge

this knife into his heart, and bring me his heart and tongue, and if you do not do it, you shall lose your life." Thereupon he went away, and when he returned next day she had not done it, and said: "Why should I shed the blood of an innocent boy who has never harmed anyone?" The cook once more said: "If you do not do it, it shall cost you your own life." When he had gone away, she had a little hind brought to her, and ordered her to be killed, and took her heart and tongue, and laid them on a plate, and when she saw the old man coming, she said to the boy: "Lie down in your bed, and draw the clothes over you." Then the wicked wretch came in and said: "Where are the boy's heart and tongue?" The girl reached the plate to him, but the King's son threw off the quilt, and said: "You old sinner, why did you want to kill me? Now will I pronounce thy sentence. You shall become a black poodle and have a gold collar round your neck, and shall eat burning coals, till the flames burst forth from your throat." And when he had spoken these words, the old man was changed into a poodle dog, and had a gold collar round his neck, and the cooks were ordered to bring up some live coals, and these he ate, until the flames broke forth from his throat. The King's son remained there a short while longer, and he thought of his mother, and wondered if she were still alive. At length he said to the maiden: "I will go home to my own country; if you will go with me, I will provide for you." "Ah," she replied, "the way is so long, and what shall I do in a strange land where I am unknown?" As she did not seem quite willing, and as they could not be parted from each other, he wished that she might be changed into a beautiful pink, and took her with him. Then he went away to his own country, and the poodle had to run after him. He went to the tower in which his mother was confined, and as it was so high, he wished for a ladder which would reach up to the very top. Then he mounted up and looked inside, and cried: "Beloved mother, Lady Queen, are you still alive, or are you dead?" She answered: "I have just eaten, and am still satisfied," for she thought the angels were there. Said he: "I am your dear son, whom the wild beasts were said to have torn from your arms; but I am alive still, and will soon set you free." Then he descended again, and went to his father, and caused himself to be announced as a strange huntsman, and asked if he could offer him service. The King said yes, if he was skilful and could get game for him, he should come to him, but that deer had never taken up their quarters in any part of the district or country. Then the huntsman promised to procure as much game for him as he could possibly use at the royal table. So he summoned all the huntsmen together, and bade them go out into the forest with him. And he went with them and made them form a great circle, open at one end where he stationed himself, and began to wish. Two hundred deer and more came running inside the circle at once, and the huntsmen shot them. Then they were all placed on sixty country carts, and driven home to the King, and for once he was able to deck his table with game, after having had none at all for years.

Now the King felt great joy at this, and commanded that his entire household should eat with him next day, and made a great feast. When they were all assembled together, he said to the huntsmen: "As you are so clever, you shall sit by me." He replied: "Lord King, your majesty must excuse me, I am a poor huntsman." But the King insisted on it, and said: "You shall sit by me," until he did it. Whilst he was sitting there, he thought of his dearest mother, and wished that one of the King's principal servants would begin to speak of her, and would ask how it was faring with the Queen in the tower, and if she were alive still, or had perished. Hardly had he formed the wish than the marshal began, and said: "Your majesty, we live joyously here, but how is the Queen living in the tower? Is she still alive, or has she died?" But the King replied: "She let my dear son be torn to pieces by wild beasts; I will not have her named." Then the huntsman arose and said: "Gracious lord father, she is alive still, and I am her son, and I was not carried away by wild beasts, but by that wretch the old cook, who tore me from her arms when she was asleep, and sprinkled her apron with the blood of a chicken." Thereupon he took the dog with the golden collar, and said: "That is the wretch!" and caused live coals to be brought, and these the dog was compelled to devour before the sight of all, until flames burst forth from its throat. On this the huntsman asked the King if he would like to see the dog in his true shape, and wished him back into the form of the cook, in the which he stood immediately, with his white apron, and his knife by his side. When the King saw him he fell into a passion, and ordered him to be cast into the deepest dungeon. Then the huntsman spoke further and said: "Father, will you see the maiden who brought me up so tenderly and who was afterwards to murder me, but did not do it, though her own life depended on it?" The King replied: "Yes, I would like to see her." The son said: "Most gracious father, I will show her to you in the form of a beautiful flower," and he thrust his hand into his pocket and brought forth the pink, and placed it on the royal table, and it was so beautiful that the King had never seen one to equal it. Then the son said: "Now will I show her to you in her own form," and wished that she might become a maiden, and she stood there looking so beautiful that no painter could have made her look more so.

And the King sent two waiting-maids and two attendants into the tower, to fetch the Queen and bring her to the royal table. But when she was led in she ate nothing, and said: "The gracious and merciful God who has supported me in the tower, will soon set me free." She lived three days more, and then died happily, and when she was buried, the two white doves which had brought her food to the tower, and were angels of heaven, followed her body and seated themselves on her grave. The aged King ordered the cook to be torn in four pieces, but grief consumed the King's own heart, and he soon died. His son married the beautiful maiden whom he had brought with him as a flower in his pocket, and whether they are still alive or not, is known to God.

CLEVER GRETEL

There was once a cook named Gretel, who wore shoes with red heels, and when she walked out with them on, she turned herself this way and that, was quite happy and thought: "You certainly are a pretty girl!" And when she came home she drank, in her gladness of heart, a draught of wine, and as wine excites a desire to eat, she tasted the best of whatever she was cooking until she was satisfied, and said: "The cook must know what the food is like."

It came to pass that the master one day said to her: "Gretel, there is a guest coming this evening; prepare me two fowls very daintily." "I will see to it, master," answered Gretel. She killed two fowls, scalded them, plucked them, put them on the spit, and towards evening set them before the fire, that they might roast. The fowls began to turn brown,

and were nearly ready, but the guest had not yet arrived. Then Gretel called out to her master: "If the guest does not come, I must take the fowls away from the fire, but it will be a sin and a shame if they are not eaten the moment they are at their juiciest." The master said: "I will run myself, and fetch the guest." When the master had turned his back, Gretel laid the spit with the fowls on one side, and thought: "Standing so long by the fire there, makes one sweat and thirsty; who knows when they will come? Meanwhile, I will run into the cellar, and take a drink." She ran down, set a jug, said: "God bless it for you, Gretel," and took a good drink, and thought that wine should flow on, and should not be interrupted, and took yet another hearty draught.

Then she went and put the fowls down again to the fire, basted them, and drove the spit merrily round. But as the roast meat smelt so good, Gretel thought: "Something might be wrong, it ought to be tasted!" She touched it with her finger, and said: "Ah! how good fowls are! It certainly is a sin and a shame that they are not eaten at the right time!" She ran to the window, to see if the master was not coming with his guest, but she saw no one, and went back to the fowls and thought: "One of the wings is burning! I had better take it off and eat it." So she cut it off, ate it, and enjoyed it, and when she had done, she thought: "The other must go down too, or else master will observe that something is missing." When the two wings were eaten, she went and looked for her master, and did not see him. It suddenly occurred to her: "Who knows? They are perhaps not coming at all, and have turned in somewhere." Then she said: "Well, Gretel, enjoy yourself, one fowl has been cut into, take another drink, and eat it up entirely; when it is eaten you will have some peace, why should God's good gifts be spoilt?" So she ran into the cellar again, took an enormous drink and ate up the one chicken in great glee. When one of the chickens was swallowed down, and still her master did not come, Gretel looked at the other and said: "Where one is, the other should be likewise, the two go together; what's right for the one is right for the other; I think if I were to take another draught it would do me no harm." So she took another hearty drink, and let the second chicken follow the first.

While she was making the most of it, her master came and cried: "Hurry up, Gretel, the guest is coming directly after me!" "Yes, sir, I will soon serve up," answered Gretel. Meantime the master looked to see that the table was properly laid, and took the great knife, wherewith he was going to carve the chickens, and sharpened it on the steps. Presently the guest came, and knocked politely and courteously at the house-door. Gretel ran, and looked to see who was there, and when she saw the guest, she put her finger to her lips and said: "Hush! hush! go away as quickly as you can, if my master catches you it will be the worse for you; he certainly did ask you to supper, but his intention is to cut off your two ears. Just listen how he is sharpening the knife for it!" The guest heard the sharpening, and hurried down the steps again as fast as he could. Gretel was not idle; she ran screaming to her master, and cried: "You have invited a fine guest!" "Why, Gretel? What do you mean by that?" "Yes," said she, "he has taken the chickens which I was just going to serve up, off the dish, and has run away with them!" "That's a nice trick!" said her master, and lamented the fine chickens. "If he had but left me one, so that something remained for me to eat." He called to him to stop, but the guest pretended not to hear. Then he ran after him with the knife still in his hand, crying: "Just one, just one," meaning that the guest should leave him just one chicken, and not take both. The guest, however, thought no otherwise than that he was to give up one of his ears, and ran as if fire were burning under him, in order to take them both home with him.

THE OLD MAN AND HIS GRANDSON

There was once a very old man, whose eyes had become dim, his ears
dull of hearing, his knees trembled, and when he sat at table he could
hardly hold the spoon, and spilt the broth upon the table-cloth or let it
run out of his mouth. His son and his son's wife were disgusted at this,
so the old grandfather at last had to sit in the corner behind the stove,
and they gave him his food in an earthenware bowl, and not even
enough of it. And he used to look towards the table with his eyes full of
tears. Once, too, his trembling hands could not hold the bowl, and it
fell to the ground and broke. The young wife scolded him, but he said
nothing and only sighed. Then they bought him a wooden bowl for a
few half-pence, out of which he had to eat.

They were once sitting thus when the little grandson of four years
old began to gather together some bits of wood upon the ground.
"What are you doing there?" asked the father. "I am making a little
trough," answered the child, "for father and mother to eat out of when
I am big."

The man and his wife looked at each other for a while, and presently
began to cry. Then they took the old grandfather to the table, and

henceforth always let him eat with them, and likewise said nothing if he did spill a little of anything.

THE WATER-NIXIE

A little brother and sister were once playing by a well, and while they were thus playing, they both fell in. A water-nixie lived down below, who said: "Now I have got you, now you shall work hard for me!" and carried them off with her. She gave the girl dirty tangled flax to spin, and she had to fetch water in a bucket with a hole in it, and the boy had to hew down a tree with a blunt axe, and they got nothing to eat but dumplings as hard as stones. Then at last the children became so impatient, that they waited until one Sunday, when the nixie was at church, and ran away. But when church was over, the nixie saw that the birds were flown, and followed them with great strides. The children saw her from afar, and the girl threw a brush behind her which formed an immense hill of bristles, with thousands and thousands of spikes, over which the nixie was forced to scramble with great difficulty; at last, however, she got over. When the children saw this, the boy threw behind him a comb which made a great ridge with a thousand times a thousand teeth, but the nixie managed to keep herself steady on them, and at last crossed over. Then the girl threw behind her a looking-glass which formed a hill of mirrors, and was so slippery that it was impossible for the nixie to cross it. Then she thought: "I will go home quickly and fetch my axe, and cut the hill of glass in half." Long before she returned, however, and had hewn through the glass, the children had escaped to a great distance, and the water-nixie was obliged to trundle back to her well again.

THE DEATH OF THE LITTLE HEN

Once upon a time the little hen went with the little cock to the nut-hill, and they agreed together that whichsoever of them found a kernel of a nut should share it with the other. Then the hen found a large, large nut, but said nothing about it, intending to eat the kernel herself. The kernel, however, was so large that she could not swallow it, and it remained sticking in her throat, so that she was alarmed lest she should be choked. Then she cried: "Cock, I entreat you to run as fast as you can and fetch me some water, or I shall choke." The little cock did run as fast as he could to the spring, and said: "Stream, you are to give me some water; the little hen is lying on the nut-hill, and she has swallowed a large nut, and is choking." The well answered: "First run to the bride, and get her to give you some red silk." The little cock ran to the bride and said: "Bride, you are to give me some red silk; I want to give red silk to the well, the well is to give me some water, I am to take the water to the little hen who is lying on the nut-hill and has swallowed a great nut-kernel, and is choking with it." The bride answered: "First run and bring me my little wreath which is hanging to a willow." So the little cock ran to the willow, and drew the wreath from the branch and took it to the bride, and the bride gave him some red silk for it, which he took to the well, who gave him some water for it. Then the little cock took the water to the hen, but when he got there the hen had choked in the meantime, and lay there dead and did not move. Then the cock was so distressed that he cried aloud, and every animal came

to lament the little hen, and six mice built a little carriage to carry her to her grave, and when the carriage was ready they harnessed themselves to it, and the cock drove. On the way, however, they met the fox, who said: "Where are you going, little cock?" "I am going to bury my little hen." "May I drive with you?" "Yes, but seat yourself at the back of the carriage, for in the front my little horses could not drag you." Then the fox seated himself at the back, and after that the wolf, the bear, the stag, the lion, and all the beasts of the forest did the same. Then the procession went onwards, and they reached a stream. "How are we to cross over?" said the little cock. A straw was lying by the stream and it said: "I will lay myself straight across, and then you can drive over me." But when the six mice came to the bridge, the straw slipped and fell into the water, and the six mice all fell in and were drowned. Then they were again in difficulty, and a coal came and said: "I am large enough, I will lay myself across, and you shall drive over me." So the coal also laid itself across the water, but unhappily just touched it, at which the coal hissed, was extinguished and died. When a stone saw that, it took pity on the little cock, wished to help him, and laid itself over the water. Then the cock drew the carriage himself, but when he got it over and reached the shore with the dead hen, and was about to draw over the others who were sitting behind as well, there were too many of them, the carriage ran back, and they all fell into the water together, and were drowned. Then the little cock was left alone with the dead hen, and dug a grave for her and laid her in it, and made a mound above it, on which he sat down and fretted until he died too, and then everyone was dead.

BROTHER LUSTIG

There was once upon a time a great war, and when it came to an end, many soldiers were discharged. Then Brother Lustig also received his dismissal, and with it nothing but a small loaf of ammunition-bread, and four kreuzers in money, with which he departed. St. Peter, however, had placed himself in his way in the form of a poor beggar, and when Brother Lustig came up, he begged alms of him. Brother Lustig replied: "Dear beggar-man, what am I to give you? I have been a soldier, and have received my dismissal, and have nothing but this little loaf of ammunition-bread, and four kreuzers of money; when that is gone, I shall have to beg as well as you. Still I will give you something." Thereupon he divided the loaf into four parts, and gave the apostle one of them, and a kreuzer likewise. St. Peter thanked him, went onwards, and threw himself again in the soldier's way as a beggar, but in another shape; and when he came up begged a gift of him as before. Brother Lustig spoke as he had done before, and again gave him a quarter of the loaf and one kreuzer. St. Peter thanked him, and went onwards, but for the third time placed himself in another shape as a beggar on the road, and spoke to Brother Lustig. Brother Lustig gave him also the third quarter of bread and the third kreuzer. St. Peter thanked him, and Brother Lustig went onwards, and had but a quarter of the loaf, and one kreuzer. With that he went into an inn, ate the bread, and ordered one kreuzer's worth of beer. When he had had it, he journeyed onwards, and then St. Peter, who had assumed the appearance of a discharged soldier, met and spoke to him thus: "Good day, comrade, can you not give me a bit of bread, and a kreuzer to get a drink?" "Where am I to procure it?" answered Brother Lustig: "I have been discharged, and I got nothing but a loaf of ammunition-bread and four kreuzers in money. I met three beggars on the road, and I gave each of them a quarter of my bread, and one kreuzer. The last quarter I ate in the inn, and had a drink with the last kreuzer. Now my pockets are empty, and if you also have nothing we can go a-begging together." "No," answered St. Peter, "we need not quite do that. I know a little about medicine, and I will soon earn as much as I require by that." "Indeed," said Brother Lustig, "I know nothing of that, so I must go and beg alone." "Just come with me," said St. Peter, "and if I earn anything, you shall have half of it." "All right," said Brother Lustig, and they went away together.

Then they came to a peasant's house inside which they heard loud lamentations and cries; so they went in, and there the husband was lying sick unto death, and very near his end, and his wife was crying and weeping quite loudly. "Stop that howling and crying," said St. Peter, "I will make the man well again," and he took a salve out of his pocket, and healed the sick man in a moment, so that he could get up, and was in perfect health. In great delight the man and his wife said: "How can we reward you? What shall we give you?" But St. Peter would take nothing, and the more the peasant folks offered him, the more he refused. Brother Lustig, however, nudged St. Peter, and said: "Take something; most surely we are in need of it." At length the woman brought a lamb and said to St. Peter that he really must take that, but he would not. Then Brother Lustig gave him a poke in the side, and said: "Pray take it; we are certainly in great want of it!" Then St. Peter said at last: "Well, I will take the lamb, but I won't carry it; if you insist on having it, you must carry it." "That is nothing," said Brother Lustig, "I will easily carry it," and took it on his shoulder. Then they departed and came to a wood, but Brother Lustig had begun to feel the lamb heavy, and he was hungry, so he said to St. Peter: "Look, that's a good place, we might cook the lamb there, and eat it." "As you like," answered St. Peter, "but I can't have anything to do with the cooking; if you will cook, there is a kettle for you, and in the meantime I will walk about a little until it is ready. But you must not begin to eat until I have come back; I will come at the right time." "Well, go, then," said Brother Lustig, "I understand cookery, I will manage it." Then St. Peter went away, and Brother Lustig killed the lamb, lighted a fire, threw the meat into the kettle, and boiled it. When the lamb, however, was quite ready, and the apostle Peter had not come back, Brother Lustig took it out of the kettle, cut it up, and found the heart. "That is said to be the best part," said he, and tasted it, but at last he ate it all up. At length St. Peter returned and said: "You may eat the whole of the lamb yourself, I will only have the heart, give me that." Then Brother Lustig took a knife and fork, and pretended to look anxiously about amongst the lamb's flesh, but not to be able to find the heart, and at last he said abruptly: "There is none here." "But where can it be?" said the apostle. "I don't know," replied Brother Lustig, "but look, what fools we both are, to seek for the lamb's heart, and neither of us to remember that a lamb has no heart!" "Oh," said St. Peter, "that is something quite new! Every animal has a heart, why is a lamb to have none?" "No, be assured, my brother," said Brother Lustig, "that a lamb has no heart; just consider it seriously, and then you will see that it really has none." "Well, it is all right," said St. Peter, "if there is no heart, then I want none of the lamb; you may eat it alone." "What I can't eat now, I will carry away in my knapsack," said Brother Lustig, and he ate half the lamb, and put the rest in his knapsack.

They went farther, and then St. Peter caused a great stream of water to flow right across their path, and they were obliged to pass through it. Said St. Peter: "Do you go first." "No," answered Brother Lustig, "you must go first," and he thought: "if the water is too deep I will stay behind." Then St. Peter strode through it, and the water just reached to his knee. So Brother Lustig began to go through also, but the water grew deeper and reached to his throat. Then he cried: "Brother, help me!" St. Peter said: "Then will you confess that you have eaten the lamb's heart?" "No," said he, "I have not eaten it." Then the water grew deeper still and rose to his mouth. "Help me, brother," cried the soldier. St. Peter said: "Then will you confess that you have eaten the lamb's heart?" "No," he replied, "I have not eaten it." St. Peter, however, would not let him be drowned, but made the water sink and helped him through it.

Then they journeyed onwards, and came to a kingdom where they heard that the King's daughter lay sick unto death. "Hi, there, brother!" said the soldier to St. Peter, "this is a chance for us; if we can heal her we shall be provided for, for life!" But St. Peter was not half quick enough for him: "Come, lift your legs, my dear brother," said he, "that we may get there in time." But St. Peter walked slower and slower, though Brother Lustig did all he could to drive and push him on, and at last they heard that the princess was dead. "Now we are done for!" said Brother Lustig; "that comes of your sleepy way of walking!" "Just be quiet," answered St. Peter, "I can do more than cure sick people; I can bring dead ones to life again." "Well, if you can do that," said Brother Lustig, "it's all right, but you should earn at least half the kingdom for us by that." Then they went to the royal palace, where everyone was in great grief, but St. Peter told the King that he would restore his daughter to life. He was taken to her, and said: "Bring me a kettle and some water," and when that was brought, he bade everyone go out, and allowed no one to remain with him but Brother Lustig. Then he cut off all the dead girl's limbs, and threw them in the water, lighted a fire beneath the kettle, and boiled them. And when the flesh had fallen away from the bones, he took out the beautiful white bones, and laid them on a table, and arranged them together in their natural order.

When he had done that, he stepped forward and said three times: "In the name of the holy Trinity, dead woman, arise." And at the third time, the princess arose, living, healthy and beautiful. Then the King was in the greatest joy, and said to St. Peter: "Ask for your reward; even if it were half my kingdom, I would give it." But St. Peter said: "I want nothing for it." "Oh, you tomfool!" thought Brother Lustig to himself, and nudged his comrade's side, and said: "Don't be so stupid! If you have no need of anything, I have." St. Peter, however, would have nothing, but as the King saw that the other would very much like to have something, he ordered his treasurer to fill Brother Lustig's knapsack with gold. Then they went on their way, and when they came to a forest, St. Peter said to Brother Lustig: "Now, we will divide the gold." "Yes," he replied, "we will." So St. Peter divided the gold, and divided it into three heaps. Brother Lustig thought to himself: "What crazy idea has he got in his head now? He is making three shares, and there are only two of us!" But St. Peter said: "I have divided it exactly; there is one share for me, one for you and one for him who ate the lamb's heart."

"Oh, I ate that!" replied Brother Lustig, and hastily swept up the gold. "You may trust what I say." "But how can that be true," said St. Peter, "when a lamb has no heart?" "Eh, what, brother, what can you be thinking of? Lambs have hearts like other animals, why should only they have none?" "Well, so be it," said St. Peter, "keep the gold to yourself, but I will stay with you no longer; I will go my way alone." "As you like, dear brother," answered Brother Lustig. "Farewell."

Then St. Peter went a different road, but Brother Lustig thought: "It is a good thing that he has taken himself off, he is certainly a strange saint." Then he had money enough, but did not know how to manage it, squandered it, gave it away, and when some time had gone by, once more had nothing. Then he arrived in a certain country where he heard that the King's daughter was dead. "Oh, ho!" thought he, "that may be a good thing for me; I will bring her to life again, and see that I am paid as I ought to be." So he went to the King, and offered to raise the dead girl to life again. Now the King had heard that a discharged soldier was travelling about and bringing dead persons to life again, and thought that Brother Lustig was the man; but as he had no confidence in him, he consulted his councillors first, who said that he might give it a trial as his daughter was dead. Then Brother Lustig ordered water to be brought to him in a kettle, bade every one go out, cut the limbs off, threw them in the water and lighted a fire beneath, just as he had seen St. Peter do. The water began to boil, the flesh fell off, and then he took the bones out and laid them on the table, but he did not know the order in which to lay them, and placed them all wrong and in confusion. Then he stood before them and said: "In the name of the most holy Trinity, dead maiden, I bid you arise," and he said this thrice, but the bones did not stir. So he said it thrice more, but also in vain: "Confounded girl that you are, get up!" cried he, "get up, or it shall be all the worse for you!" When he had said that, St. Peter suddenly appeared in his former shape as a discharged soldier; he entered by the window and said: "Godless man, what are you doing? How can the dead maiden arise, when you have thrown about her bones in such confusion?" "Dear brother, I have done everything to the best of my ability," he answered. "This once, I will help you out of your difficulty, but one thing I tell you, and that is that if ever you undertake anything of the kind again, it will be the worse for you, and also that you must neither demand nor accept the smallest thing from the King for this!" Thereupon St. Peter laid the bones in their right order, said to the maiden three times: "In the name of the most holy Trinity, dead maiden, arise," and the King's daughter arose, healthy and beautiful as before. Then St. Peter went away again by the window, and Brother Lustig was rejoiced to find that all had passed off so well, but was very much vexed to think that after all he was not to take anything for it. "I should just like to know," thought he, "what fancy that fellow has got in his head, for what he gives with one hand he takes away with the other—there is no sense whatever in it!" Then the King offered Brother Lustig whatsoever he wished to have, but he did not dare to take anything; however, by hints and cunning, he contrived to make the King order his knapsack to be filled with gold for him, and with that he departed. When he got out, St. Peter was standing by the door, and said: "Just look what a man you are; did I not forbid you to take anything, and there you have your knapsack full of gold!" "How can I help that," answered Brother Lustig, "if people will put it in for me?" "Well, I tell you this, that if ever you set about anything of this kind again you shall suffer for it!" "All right, brother, have no fear, now I have money, why

should I trouble myself with washing bones?" "Faith," said St. Peter, "a long time that gold will last! In order that after this you may never tread in forbidden paths, I will bestow on your knapsack this property, namely, that whatsoever you wish to have inside it, shall be there. Farewell, you will now never see me more." "Good-bye," said Brother Lustig, and thought to himself: "I am very glad that you have taken yourself off, you strange fellow; I shall certainly not follow you." But of the magical power which had been bestowed on his knapsack, he thought no more.

Brother Lustig travelled about with his money, and squandered and wasted what he had as before. When at last he had no more than four kreuzers, he passed by an inn and thought: "The money must go," and ordered three kreuzers' worth of wine and one kreuzer's worth of bread for himself. As he was sitting there drinking, the smell of roast goose made its way to his nose. Brother Lustig looked about and peeped, and saw that the host had two geese roasting in the oven. Then he remembered that his comrade had said that whatsoever he wished to have in his knapsack should be there, so he said: "Oh, ho! I must try that with the geese." So he went out, and when he was outside the door, he said: "I wish those two roasted geese out of the oven and in my knapsack," and when he had said that, he unbuckled it and looked in, and there they were inside it. "Ah, that's right!" said he, "now I am a made man!" and went away to a meadow and took out the roast meat. When he was in the midst of his meal, two journeymen came up and looked at the second goose, which was not yet touched, with hungry eyes. Brother Lustig thought to himself: "One is enough for me," and called the two men up and said: "Take the goose, and eat it to my health." They thanked him, and went with it to the inn, ordered themselves a half bottle of wine and a loaf, took out the goose which had been given them, and began to eat. The hostess saw them and said to her husband: "Those two are eating a goose; just look and see if it is not one of ours, out of the oven." The landlord ran thither, and behold the oven was empty! "What!" cried he, "you thievish crew, you want to eat goose as cheap as that? Pay for it this moment; or I will wash you well with green hazel-sap." The two said: "We are no thieves, a discharged soldier gave us the goose, outside there in the meadow." "You shall not throw dust in my eyes that way! the soldier was here—but he went out by the door, like an honest fellow. I looked after him myself; you are the thieves and shall pay!" But as they could not pay, he took a stick, and cudgeled them out of the house.

Brother Lustig went his way and came to a place where there was a magnificent castle, and not far from it a wretched inn. He went to the inn and asked for a night's lodging, but the landlord turned him away, and said: "There is no more room here, the house is full of noble guests." "It surprises me that they should come to you and not go to that splendid castle," said Brother Lustig. "Ah, indeed," replied the host, "but it is no slight matter to sleep there for a night; no one who has tried it so far, has ever come out of it alive."

"If others have tried it," said Brother Lustig, "I will try it too."

"Leave it alone," said the host, "it will cost you your neck." "It won't kill me at once," said Brother Lustig, "just give me the key, and some good food and wine." So the host gave him the key, and food and wine, and with this Brother Lustig went into the castle, enjoyed his supper, and at length, as he was sleepy, he lay down on the ground, for there was no bed. He soon fell asleep, but during the night was disturbed by a great noise, and when he awoke, he saw nine ugly devils in the room, who had made a circle, and were dancing around him. Brother Lustig said: "Well, dance as long as you like, but none of you must come too close." But the devils pressed continually nearer to him, and almost stepped on his face with their hideous feet. "Stop, you devils' ghosts," said he, but they behaved still worse. Then Brother Lustig grew angry, and cried: "Stop! You'll soon see how I can make you quiet!" and got the leg of a chair and struck out into the midst of them with it. But nine devils against one soldier were still too many, and when he struck those in front of him, the others seized him behind by the hair, and tore it unmercifully. "Devils' crew," cried he, "this is too much, but just wait. Into my knapsack, all nine of you!" In an instant they were in it, and then he buckled it up and threw it into a corner. After this all was suddenly quiet, and Brother Lustig lay down again, and slept till it was bright day. Then came the inn-keeper, and the nobleman to whom the castle belonged, to see how he had fared; but when they perceived that he was merry and well they were astonished, and asked: "Have the spirits done you no harm, then?" "The reason why they have not," answered Brother Lustig, "is because I have got the whole nine of them in my knapsack! You may once more inhabit your castle quite tranquilly, none of them will ever haunt it again." The nobleman thanked him, made him rich presents, and begged him to remain in his service, and he would provide for him as long as he lived. "No," replied Brother Lustig, "I am used to wandering about, I will travel farther." Then he went away, and entered into a smithy, laid the knapsack, which contained the nine devils on the anvil, and asked the smith and his apprentices to strike it. So they smote with their great hammers with all their strength, and the devils uttered howls which were quite pitiable. When he opened the knapsack after this, eight of them were dead, but one which had been lying in a fold of it, was still alive, slipped out, and went back again to hell.

Thereupon Brother Lustig travelled a long time about the world, and those who know, can tell many a story about him. But at last he grew old, and thought of his end, so he went to a hermit who was known to be a pious man, and said to him: "I am tired of wandering about, and want now to behave in such a manner that I shall enter into the kingdom of Heaven." The hermit replied: "There are two roads, one is broad and pleasant, and leads to hell, the other is narrow and rough, and leads to heaven." "I should be a fool," thought Brother Lustig, "if I were to take the narrow, rough road." So he set out and took the broad and pleasant road, and at length came to a great black door, which was the door of Hell. Brother Lustig knocked, and the door-keeper peeped out to see who was there. But when he saw Brother Lustig, he was terrified, for he was the very same ninth devil who had been shut up in the knapsack, and had escaped from it with a black eye. So he pushed the bolt in again as quickly as he could, ran to the highest devil, and said: "There is a fellow outside with a knapsack, who wants to come in, but as you value your lives don't allow him to enter, or he will wish the whole of hell into his knapsack. He once gave me a frightful hammering when I was inside it." So they called out to Brother Lustig that he was to go away again, for he should not get in there! "If they won't have me here," thought he, "I will see if I can find a place for myself in Heaven, for I must stay somewhere." So he turned about and went onwards until he came to the door of Heaven, where he knocked. St. Peter was sitting hard by as door-keeper. Brother Lustig recognized him at once, and thought: "Here I find an old friend, I shall get on better."

But St. Peter said: "I can hardly believe that you want to come into Heaven." "Let me in, brother; I must get in somewhere; if they would have taken me into Hell, I should not have come here." "No," said St. Peter, "you shall not enter." "Then if you will not let me in, take your knapsack back, for I will have nothing at all from you." "Give it here, then," said St. Peter. Then Brother Lustig gave him the knapsack into Heaven through the bars, and St. Peter took it, and hung it up beside his seat. Then said Brother Lustig: "And now I wish myself inside my knapsack," and in a second he was in it, and in Heaven, and St. Peter was forced to let him stay there.

GAMBLING HANSEL

Once upon a time there was a man who did nothing but gamble, and for that reason people never called him anything but Gambling Hansel, and as he never ceased to gamble, he played away his house and all that he had. Now the very day before his creditors were to take his house from him, came the Lord and St. Peter, and asked him to give them shelter for the night. Then Gambling Hansel said: "For my part, you may stay the night, but I cannot give you a bed or anything to eat." So the Lord said he was just to take them in, and they themselves would buy something to eat, to which Gambling Hansel made no objection. Thereupon St. Peter gave him three groschen, and said he was to go to the baker's and fetch some bread. So Gambling Hansel went, but when he reached the house where the other gambling vagabonds were gathered together, they, although they had won all that he had, greeted him clamorously, and said: "Hansel, do come in." "Oh," said he, "do you want to win the three groschen, too?" On this they would not let him go. So he went in, and played away the three groschen also. Meanwhile St. Peter and the Lord were waiting, and as he was so long in coming, they set out to meet him. When Gambling Hansel came, however, he pretended that the money had fallen into the gutter, and kept raking about in it all the while to find it, but our Lord already knew that he had lost it in play. St. Peter again gave him three groschen, and now he did not allow himself to be led away once more, but fetched them the loaf. Our Lord then inquired if he had no wine, and he said: "Alack, sir, the casks are all empty!" But the Lord said he was to go down into the cellar, for the best wine was still there. For a long time he would not believe this, but at length he said: "Well, I will go down, but I know that there is none there." When he turned the tap, however, lo and behold, the best of wine ran out! So he took it to them, and the two passed the night there. Early next day our Lord told Gambling Hansel that he might beg three favours. The Lord expected that he would ask to go to Heaven; but Gambling Hansel asked for a pack of cards with which he could win everything, for dice with which he would win everything, and for a tree whereon every kind of fruit would grow, and from which no one who had climbed up, could descend until he bade him do so. The Lord gave him all that he had asked, and departed with St. Peter.

And now Gambling Hansel at once set about gambling in real earnest, and before long he had gained half the world. Upon this St. Peter said to the Lord: "Lord, this thing must not go on; at last he will win the whole world. We must send Death to him." And they sent Death to him. When Death appeared, Gambling Hansel had just seated himself at the gaming-table, and Death said: "Hansel, come out a while." But Gambling Hansel said: "Just wait a little until the game is done, and in the meantime get up into that tree out there, and gather a little fruit that we may have something to munch on our way." Thereupon Death climbed up, but when he wanted to come down again, he could not, and Gambling Hansel left him up there for seven years, during which time no one died.

So St. Peter said to the Lord: "Lord, this thing must not go on. People no longer die; we must go ourselves." And they went themselves, and the Lord commanded Hansel to let Death come down. So Hansel went at once to Death and said to him: "Come down," and Death took him directly and put an end to him. They went away together and came to the next world, and then Gambling Hansel made straight for the door of Heaven, and knocked at it. "Who is there?" "Gambling Hansel." "Ah, we will have nothing to do with him! Begone!" So he went to the door of Purgatory, and knocked once more. "Who is there?" "Gambling Hansel." "Ah, there is quite enough weeping and wailing here without him. We do not want to gamble, just go away again." Then he went to the door of Hell, and there they let him in. There was, however, no one at home but old Lucifer and the crooked devils (the straight ones were just busy in the world). And no sooner was Hansel there than he sat down to gamble again. Lucifer, however, had nothing to lose, but his mis-shapen devils, and Gambling Hansel won them from him, as with his cards he could not fail to do. And now he was off again with his crooked devils, and they went to Hohenfurt and pulled up a hop-pole, and with it went to Heaven and began to thrust the pole against it, and Heaven began to crack. So again St. Peter said: "Lord, this thing cannot go on, we must let him in, or he will overthrow the whole Heaven." And they let him in. But Gambling Hansel instantly began to play again, and there was such a noise and confusion that there was no hearing what they themselves were saying. Therefore St. Peter once more said: "Lord, this cannot go on, we must throw him down, or he will make all Heaven rebellious." So they went to him at once, and threw him down, and his soul broke into fragments, and went into the gambling vagabonds who are living this very day.

HANS IN LUCK

Hans had served his master for seven years, so he said to him: "Master, my time is up; now I should be glad to go back home to my mother; give me my wages." The master answered: "You have served me faithfully and honestly; as the service was so shall the reward be"; and he gave Hans a piece of gold as big as his head. Hans pulled his handkerchief out of his pocket, wrapped up the lump in it, put it on his shoulder, and set out on the way home.

As he went on, always putting one foot before the other, he saw a horseman trotting quickly and merrily by on a lively horse. "Ah!" said Hans quite loud, "what a fine thing it is to ride! There you sit as on a chair; you stumble over no stones, you save your shoes, and cover the ground, you don't know how."

The rider, who had heard him, stopped and called out: "Hi, there, Hans! why do you go on foot, then?"

"I must," answered he, "for I have this lump to carry home; it is true that it is gold, but I cannot hold my head straight for it, and it hurts my shoulder."

"I will tell you what," said the rider, "we will exchange: I will give you my horse, and you can give me your lump."

"With all my heart," said Hans, "but I can tell you, you will have to crawl along with it."

The rider got down, took the gold, and helped Hans up; then gave him the bridle tight in his hands and said: "If you want to go at a really good pace, you must click your tongue and call out: 'Jup! Jup!'"

Hans was heartily delighted as he sat upon the horse and rode away so bold and free. After a little while he thought that it ought to go faster, and he began to click with his tongue and call out: "Jup! Jup!" The horse put himself into a sharp trot, and before Hans knew where he was, he was thrown off and lying in a ditch which separated the field from the highway. The horse would have gone off too if it had not been stopped by a countryman, who was coming along the road and driving a cow before him.

Hans pulled himself together and stood up on his legs again, but he was vexed, and said to the countryman: "It is a poor joke, this riding, especially when one gets hold of a mare like this, that kicks and throws one off, so that one has a chance of breaking one's neck. Never again will I mount it. Now I like your cow, for one can walk quietly behind her, and have, over and above, one's milk, butter and cheese every day without fail. What would I not give to have such a cow." "Well," said the countryman, "if it would give you so much pleasure, I do not mind giving the cow for the horse." Hans agreed with the greatest delight; the countryman jumped upon the horse, and rode quickly away.

Hans drove his cow quietly before him, and thought over his lucky bargain. "If only I have a morsel of bread—and that can hardly fail me—I can eat butter and cheese with it as often as I like; if I am thirsty, I can milk my cow and drink the milk. My goodness, what more can I want?"

When he came to an inn he made a halt, and in his great content ate up what he had with him—his dinner and supper—and all he had, and with his last few farthings had half a glass of beer. Then he drove his cow onwards along the road to his mother's village.

As it drew nearer mid-day, the heat was more oppressive, and Hans found himself upon a moor which it took about an hour to cross. He felt it very hot and his tongue clave to the roof of his mouth with thirst. "I can find a cure for this," thought Hans; "I will milk the cow now and refresh myself with the milk." He tied her to a withered tree, and as he had no pail he put his leather cap underneath; but try as he would, not a drop of milk came. And as he set himself to work in a clumsy way, the impatient beast at last gave him such a blow on his head with its hind foot, that he fell on the ground, and for a long time could not think where he was.

By good fortune a butcher just then came along the road with a wheel-barrow, in which lay a young pig. "What sort of a trick is this?" cried he, and helped the good Hans up. Hans told him what had happened. The butcher gave him his flask and said: "Take a drink and refresh yourself. The cow will certainly give no milk, it is an old beast; at the best it is only fit for the plough, or for the butcher." "Well, well," said Hans, as he stroked his hair down on his head, "who would have thought it? Certainly it is a fine thing when one can kill a beast like that at home; what meat one has! But I do not care much for beef, it is not juicy enough for me. A young pig like that now is the thing to have; it tastes quite different; and then there are the sausages!"

"Listen, Hans," said the butcher, "out of love for you I will exchange, and will let you have the pig for the cow." "Heaven repay you for your kindness!" said Hans as he gave up the cow, whilst the pig was unbound from the barrow, and the cord by which it was tied was put in his hand.

Hans went on, and thought to himself how everything was going just as he wished; if he did meet with any vexation it was immediately set right. Presently there joined him a lad who was carrying a fine white goose under his arm. They said good morning to each other, and Hans began to tell of his good luck, and how he had always made such good bargains. The boy told him that he was taking the goose to a christening-feast. "Just lift her," added he, and laid hold of her by the wings; "how heavy she is—she has been fattened up for the last eight weeks. Whoever has a bit of her when she is roasted will have to wipe the fat from both sides of his mouth." "Yes," said Hans, as he weighed her in one hand, "she is a good weight, but my pig is no bad one."

Meanwhile the lad looked suspiciously from one side to the other, and shook his head. "Look here," he said at length, "it may not be all right with your pig. In the village through which I passed, the Mayor himself had just had one stolen out of its sty. I fear—I fear that you have got hold of it there. They have sent out some people and it would be a bad business if they caught you with the pig; at the very least, you would be shut up in the dark hole."

The good Hans was terrified. "Goodness!" he said, "help me out of this fix; you know more about this place than I do, take my pig and leave me your goose." "I shall risk something at that game," answered the lad, "but I will not be the cause of your getting into trouble." So he took the cord in his hand, and drove away the pig quickly along a by-path.

The good Hans, free from care, went homewards with the goose under his arm. "When I think over it properly," said he to himself, "I have even gained by the exchange: first there is the good roastmeat, then the quantity of fat which will drip from it, and which will give me dripping for my bread for a quarter of a year, and lastly the beautiful white feathers; I will have my pillow stuffed with them, and then indeed I shall go to sleep without rocking. How glad my mother will be!"

As he was going through the last village, there stood a scissors-grinder with his barrow; as his wheel whirred he sang:

"I sharpen scissors and quickly grind,
My coat blows out in the wind behind."

Hans stood still and looked at him; at last he spoke to him and said: "All's well with you, as you are so merry with your grinding." "Yes," answered the scissors-grinder, "the trade has a golden foundation. A real grinder is a man who as often as he puts his hand into his pocket finds gold in it. But where did you buy that fine goose?"

"I did not buy it, but exchanged my pig for it."

"And the pig?"

"That I got for a cow."

"And the cow?"

"I took that instead of a horse."

"And the horse?"

"For that I gave a lump of gold as big as my head."

"And the gold?"

"Well, that was my wages for seven years' service."

"You have known how to look after yourself each time," said the grinder. "If you can only get on so far as to hear the money jingle in your pocket whenever you stand up, you will have made your fortune."

"How shall I manage that?" said Hans. "You must be a grinder, as I am; nothing particular is wanted for it but a grindstone, the rest finds itself. I have one here; it is certainly a little worn, but you need not give me anything for it but your goose; will you do it?"

"How can you ask?" answered Hans. "I shall be the luckiest fellow on earth; if I have money whenever I put my hand in my pocket, why should I ever worry again?" and he handed him the goose and received the grindstone in exchange. "Now," said the grinder, as he took up an ordinary heavy stone that lay by him, "here is a strong stone for you into the bargain; you can hammer well upon it, and straighten your old nails. Take it with you and keep it carefully."

Hans loaded himself with the stones, and went on with a contented heart, his eyes shining with joy. "I must have been born with a caul," he cried; "everything I want happens to me just as if I were a Sunday-child."

Meanwhile, as he had been on his legs since daybreak, he began to feel tired. Hunger also tormented him, for in his joy at the bargain by which he got the cow he had eaten up all his store of food at once. At last he could only go on with great trouble, and was forced to stop every minute; the stones, too, weighed him down dreadfully. Then he could not help thinking how nice it would be if he had not to carry them just then.

He crept like a snail to a well in a field, and there he thought that he would rest and refresh himself with a cool draught of water, but in order that he might not injure the stones in sitting down, he laid them carefully by his side on the edge of the well. Then he sat down on it, and was to stoop and drink, when he made a slip, pushed against the stones, and both of them fell into the water. When Hans saw them with his own eyes sinking to the bottom, he jumped for joy, and then knelt down, and with tears in his eyes thanked God for having shown him this favour also, and delivered him in so good a way, and without his having any need to reproach himself, from those heavy stones which had been the only things that troubled him.

"There is no man under the sun so fortunate as I," he cried out. With a light heart and free from every burden he now ran on until he was with his mother at home.

HANS MARRIED

There was once upon a time a young peasant named Hans, whose uncle wanted to find him a rich wife. He therefore seated Hans behind the stove, and had it made very hot. Then he fetched a pot of milk and plenty of white bread, gave him a bright newly-coined farthing in his hand, and said: "Hans, hold that farthing fast, crumble the white bread into the milk, and stay where you are, and do not stir from that spot till I come back." "Yes," said Hans, "I will do all that." Then the uncle put on a pair of old patched trousers, went to a rich peasant's daughter in the next village, and said: "Won't you marry my nephew Hans?—you will get an honest and sensible man who will suit you." The covetous father asked: "How is it with regard to his means? Has he bread to break?" "Dear friend," replied the uncle, "my young nephew has a snug berth, a nice bit of money in hand, and plenty of bread to break, besides he has quite as many patches as I have," (and as he spoke, he slapped the patches on his trousers, but in that district small pieces of land were called patches also). "If you will give yourself the trouble to go home with me, you shall see at once that all is as I have said." Then the miser did not want to lose this good opportunity, and said: "If that is the case, I have nothing further to say against the marriage."

So the wedding was celebrated on the appointed day, and when the young wife went out of doors to see the bridegroom's property, Hans took off his Sunday coat and put on his patched smock and said: "I might spoil my good coat." Then together they went out and wherever a vineyard came in sight, or fields and meadows were divided from each other, Hans pointed with his finger and then slapped either a large or a small patch on his smock, and said: "That patch is mine, and that too, my dearest, just look at it," meaning thereby that his wife should not stare at the broad land, but look at his garment, which was his own.

"Were you at the wedding too?" "Yes, indeed I was there, and in full dress. My head-dress was of snow; then the sun came out, and it was melted. My coat was of cobwebs, and I had to pass by some thorns which tore it off me; my shoes were of glass, and I trod on a stone and they said, 'Klink', and broke in two."

THE GOLD-CHILDREN

There was once a poor man and a poor woman who had nothing but a little cottage, and who earned their bread by fishing, and always lived from hand to mouth. But it came to pass one day when the man was sitting by the water-side, and casting his net, that he drew out a fish entirely of gold. As he was looking at the fish, full of astonishment, it began to speak and said: "Listen, fisherman, if you will throw me back again into the water, I will change your little hut into a splendid castle." Then the fisherman answered: "Of what use is a castle to me, if I have nothing to eat?" The gold fish continued: "That shall be taken care of, there will be a cupboard in the castle in which, when you open it, shall be dishes of the most delicate meats, and as many of them as you can desire." "If that be true," said the man, "then I can well do you a favour." "Yes," said the fish, "there is, however, the condition that you shall disclose to no one in the world, whosoever he may be, whence your good luck has come, if you speak but one single word, all will be over." Then the man threw the wonderful fish back again into the water, and went home.

But where his hovel had formerly stood, now stood a great castle. He opened wide his eyes, entered, and saw his wife dressed in beautiful clothes, sitting in a splendid room, and she was quite delighted, and said: "Husband, how has all this come to pass? It suits me very well." "Yes," said the man, "it suits me too, but I am frightfully hungry, just give me something to eat." Said the wife: "But I have got nothing and don't know where to find anything in this new house." "There is no need of your knowing," said the man, "for I see yonder a great cupboard, just unlock it." When she opened it, there stood cakes, meat, fruit, wine, quite a bright prospect.

Then the woman cried joyfully: "What more can you want, my dear?" and they sat down, and ate and drank together. When they had had enough, the woman said: "But, husband, whence come all these riches?" "Alas," answered he, "do not question me about it, for I dare not tell you anything; if I disclose it to anyone, then all our good fortune will disappear." "Very good," said she, "if I am not to know anything, then I do not want to know anything." However, she was not in earnest; she never rested day or night, and she goaded her husband until in his impatience he revealed that all was owing to a wonderful golden fish which he had caught, and to which in return he had given its liberty. And as soon as the secret was out, the splendid castle with the cupboard immediately disappeared, they were once more in the old fisherman's hut, and the man was obliged to follow his former trade and fish. But fortune would so have it, that he once more drew out the golden fish. "Listen," said the fish, "if you will throw me back into the water again, I will once more give you the castle with the cupboard full of roast and boiled meats; only be firm, for your life's sake don't reveal from whom you have it, or you will lose it all again!" "I will take good care," answered the fisherman, and threw the fish back into the water. Now at home everything was once more in its former magnificence, and the wife was overjoyed at their good fortune, but curiosity left her no peace, so that after a couple of days she began to ask again how it had come to pass, and how he had managed to secure it. The man kept silence for a short time, but at last she made him so angry that he broke out, and betrayed the secret. In an instant the castle disappeared, and they were back again in their old hut. "Now you have got what you want," said he; "and we can gnaw at a bare bone again." "Ah," said the woman, "I had rather not have riches if I am not to know from whom they come, for then I have no peace."

The man went back to fish, and after a while he chanced to draw out the gold fish for a third time. "Listen," said the fish, "I see very well that I am fated to fall into your hands, take me home and cut me into six pieces; give your wife two of them to eat, two to your horse and bury two of them in the ground, then they will bring you a blessing." The fisherman took the fish home with him, and did as it had bidden him. It came to pass, however, that from the two pieces that were buried in the ground two golden lilies sprang up, that the horse had two golden foals, and the fisherman's wife bore two children who were made entirely of gold. The children grew up, became tall and handsome, and the lilies and horses grew likewise. Then they said: "Father, we want to mount our golden steeds and travel out in the world." But he answered sorrowfully: "How shall I bear it if you go away, and I know not how it fares with you?" Then they said: "The two golden lilies remain here. By them you can see how it is with us; if they are fresh, then we are in health; if they are withered, we are ill; if they perish, then we are dead." So they rode forth and came to an inn, in which were many people, and when they perceived the gold-children they began to laugh, and jeer. When one of them heard the mocking he felt ashamed and would not go out into the world, but turned back and went home again to his father. But the other rode forward and reached a great forest. As he was about to enter it, the people said: "It is not safe for you to ride through, the wood is full of robbers who would treat you badly. You will fare ill, and when they see that you are all of gold, and your horse likewise, they will assuredly kill you."

But he would not allow himself to be frightened, and said: "I must and will ride through it." Then he took bear-skins and covered himself and his horse with them, so that the gold was no more to be seen, and

rode fearlessly into the forest. When he had ridden onward a little he heard a rustling in the bushes, and heard voices speaking together. From one side came cries of: "There is one," but from the other: "Let him go, 'tis a bearskin, as poor and bare as a church-mouse, what should we gain from him?" So the gold-child rode joyfully through the forest, and no evil befell him.

One day he entered a village wherein he saw a maiden, who was so beautiful that he did not believe that any more beautiful than she existed in the world. And as such a mighty love took possession of him, he went up to her and said: "I love you with my whole heart, will you be my wife?" He, too, pleased the maiden so much that she agreed and said: "Yes, I will be your wife, and be true to you my whole life long." Then they were married, and just as they were in the greatest happiness, home came the father of the bride, and when he saw that his daughter's wedding was being celebrated, he was astonished, and said: "Where is the bridegroom?" They showed him the gold-child, who, however, still wore his bear-skins. Then the father said wrathfully: "A bearskin shall never have my daughter!" and was about to kill him. Then the bride begged as hard as she could, and said: "He is my husband, and I love him with all my heart!" until at last he allowed himself to be appeased. Nevertheless the idea never left his thoughts, so that next morning he rose early, wishing to see whether his daughter's husband was a common ragged beggar. But when he peeped in, he saw a magnificent golden man in the bed, and the cast-off bear-skins lying on the ground. Then he went back and thought: "What a good thing it was that I restrained my anger! I would have committed a great crime." But the gold-child dreamed that he rode out to hunt a splendid stag, and when he awoke in the morning, he said to his wife: "I must go out hunting." She was uneasy, and begged him to stay there, and said: "You might easily meet with a great misfortune," but he answered: "I must and will go."

Thereupon he got up, and rode forth into the forest, and it was not long before a fine stag crossed his path exactly according to his dream. He aimed and was about to shoot it, when the stag ran away. He gave chase over hedges and ditches for the whole day without feeling tired, but in the evening the stag vanished from his sight, and when the gold-child looked round him, he was standing before a little house, wherein sat a witch. He knocked, and a little old woman came out and asked: "What are you doing so late in the midst of the great forest?" "Have you not seen a stag?" "Yes," answered she, "I know the stag well," and thereupon a little dog which had come out of the house with her, barked at the man violently. "Will you be silent, you odious toad," said he, "or I will shoot you dead." Then the witch cried out in a passion: "What! will you slay my little dog?" and immediately transformed him, so that he lay like a stone, and his bride awaited him in vain, and thought: "That which I so greatly dreaded, which lay so heavily on my heart, has come upon him!" But at home the other brother was standing by the gold-lilies, when one of them suddenly drooped. "Good heavens!" said he, "my brother has met with some great misfortune! I must go away to see if I can possibly rescue him." Then the father said: "Stay here, if I lose you also, what shall I do?" But he answered: "I must and will go forth!"

Then he mounted his golden horse, and rode forth and entered the great forest, where his brother lay turned to stone. The old witch came out of her house and called him, wishing to entrap him also, but he did not go near her, and said: "I will shoot you, if you will not bring my brother to life again." She touched the stone, though very unwillingly, with her forefinger, and he was immediately restored to his human shape. And the two gold-children rejoiced, when they saw each other again, kissed and caressed each other, and rode away together out of the forest, the one home to his bride, and the other to his father. The father then said: "I knew well that you had rescued your brother, for the golden lily suddenly rose up and blossomed out again." Then they lived happily, and they prospered until their death.

THE FOX AND THE GEESE

The fox once came to a meadow in which sat a flock of fine fat geese, on which he smiled and said: "I come in the nick of time, you are sitting together quite beautifully, so that I can eat you up one after the other." The geese cackled with terror, sprang up, and began to wail and beg piteously for their lives. But the fox would listen to nothing, and said: "There is no mercy to be had! You must die." At length one of them took heart and said: "If we poor geese are to yield up our vigorous young lives, show us the only possible favour and allow us one more prayer, that we may not die in our sins, and then we will place ourselves in a row, so that you can always pick yourself out the fattest." "Yes," said the fox, "that is reasonable, and a pious request. Pray away, I will wait till you are done." Then the first began a good long prayer, for ever saying: "Ga! Ga!" and as she would make no end, the second did not wait until her turn came, but began also: "Ga! Ga!" The third and fourth followed her, and soon they were all cackling together.

When they have done praying, the story shall be continued further, but at present they are still praying unceasingly.

THE POOR MAN AND THE RICH MAN

In olden times, when the Lord himself still used to walk about on this earth amongst men, it once happened that he was tired and overtaken by the darkness before he could reach an inn. Now there stood on the road before him two houses facing each other; the one large and beautiful, the other small and poor. The large one belonged to a rich man, and the small one to a poor man.

Then the Lord thought: "I shall be no burden to the rich man, I will stay the night with him." When the rich man heard someone knocking at his door, he opened the window and asked the stranger what he wanted. The Lord answered: "I only ask for a night's lodging."

Then the rich man looked at the traveller from head to foot and as the Lord was wearing common clothes, and did not look like one who had much money in his pocket, he shook his head, and said: "No, I cannot take you in, my rooms are full of herbs and seeds; and if I were to lodge everyone who knocked at my door, I might very soon go begging myself. Go somewhere else for a lodging," and with this he shut down the window and left the Lord standing there.

So the Lord turned his back on the rich man, and went across to the small house and knocked. He had hardly done so when the poor man opened the little door and bade the traveller come in. "Pass the night with me, it is already dark," said he; "you cannot go any further to-night." This pleased the Lord, and he went in. The poor man's wife shook hands with him, and welcomed him, and said he was to make himself at home and put up with what they had got; they had not much to offer him, but what they had they would give him with all their hearts. Then she put the potatoes on the fire, and while they were boiling, she milked the goat, that they might have a little milk with them. When the cloth was laid, the Lord sat down with the man and his wife, and he enjoyed their coarse food, for there were happy faces at the table. When they had had supper and it was bed-time, the woman called her husband apart and said: "Listen, dear husband, let us make up a bed of straw for ourselves to-night, and then the poor traveller can sleep in our bed and have a good rest, for he has been walking the whole day through, and that makes one weary." "With all my heart," he answered. "I will go and offer it to him;" and he went to the stranger and invited him, if he had no objection, to sleep in their bed and rest his limbs properly. But the Lord was unwilling to take their bed from the two old folks; however, they would not be satisfied, until at length he did it and lay down in their bed, while they themselves lay on some straw on the ground.

Next morning they got up before daybreak, and made as good a breakfast as they could for the guest. When the sun shone in through the little window, and the Lord had got up, he again ate with them, and then prepared to set out on his journey.

But as he was standing at the door he turned round and said: "As you are so kind and good, you may wish three things for yourselves and I will grant them." Then the man said: "What else should I wish for but eternal happiness, and that we two, as long as we live, may be healthy and have every day our daily bread; for the third wish, I do not know what to have." And the Lord said to him: "Will you wish for a new house instead of this old one?" "Oh, yes," said the man; "if I can have that, too, I should like it very much." And the Lord fulfilled his wish, and changed their old house into a new one, again gave them his blessing, and went on.

The sun was high when the rich man got up and leaned out of his window and saw, on the opposite side of the way, a new clean-looking house with red tiles and bright windows where the old hut used to be. He was very much astonished, and called his wife and said to her: "Tell me, what can have happened? Last night there was a miserable little hut standing there, and to-day there is a beautiful new house. Run over and see how that has come to pass."

So his wife went and asked the poor man, and he said to her: "Yesterday evening a traveller came here and asked for a night's lodging, and this morning when he took leave of us he granted us three wishes—eternal happiness, health during this life and our daily bread as well, and, besides this, a beautiful new house instead of our old hut."

When the rich man's wife heard this, she ran back in haste and told her husband how it had happened. The man said: "I could tear myself to pieces! If I had but known that! The traveller came to our house too, and wanted to sleep here, and I sent him away." "Quick!" said his wife, "get on your horse. You can still catch the man up, and then you must ask to have three wishes granted to you also."

The rich man followed the good counsel and galloped away on his horse, and soon came up with the Lord. He spoke to him softly and pleasantly, and begged him not to take it amiss that he had not let him in directly; he was looking for the front-door key, and in the meantime the stranger had gone away; if he returned the same way he must come and stay with him. "Yes," said the Lord; "if I ever come back again, I will do so." Then the rich man asked if he might not wish for three things too, as his neighbour had done. "Yes," said the Lord, he might, but it would not be to his advantage, and he had better not wish for anything; but the rich man thought that he could easily ask for something which would add to his happiness, if he only knew that it would be granted. So the Lord said to him: "Ride home, then, and three wishes which you shall make, shall be fulfilled."

The rich man had now gained what he wanted, so he rode home, and began to consider what he should wish for. As he was thus thinking he let the bridle fall, and the horse began to caper about, so that he was continually disturbed in his meditations, and could not collect his thoughts at all. He patted its neck, and said: "Gently, Lisa," but the horse only began new tricks. Then at last he was angry, and cried quite impatiently: "I wish your neck was broken!" Directly he had said the words, down the horse fell on the ground, and there it lay dead and never moved again. And thus was his first wish fulfilled. As he was miserly by nature, he did not like to leave the harness lying there; so he cut it off, and put it on his back; and now he had to go on foot. "I have still two wishes left," said he, and comforted himself with that thought.

And now as he was walking slowly through the sand, and the sun was burning hot at noon-day, he grew quite bad-tempered and angry. The saddle hurt his back, and he had not yet any idea what to wish for. "If I were to wish for all the riches and treasures in the world," said he to himself, "I should still think of all kinds of other things later on. I know that, beforehand. But I will manage so that there is nothing at all left me to wish for afterwards." Then he sighed and said: "Ah, if I were but that Bavarian peasant, who likewise had three wishes granted to him, and knew quite well what to do, and in the first place wished for a great deal of beer, and in the second for as much beer as he was able to drink, and in the third for a barrel of beer into the bargain."

Many a time he thought he had found it, but then it seemed to him to be, after all, too little. Then it came into his mind, what an easy life his wife had, for she stayed at home in a cool room and enjoyed herself. This really did vex him, and before he was aware, he said: "I just wish she was sitting there on this saddle, and could not get off it, instead of

my having to drag it along on my back." And as the last word was spoken, the saddle disappeared from his back, and he saw that his second wish had been fulfilled. Then he really did feel hot. He began to run and wanted to be quite alone in his own room at home, to think of something really big for his last wish. But when he arrived there and opened the parlour-door, he saw his wife sitting in the middle of the room on the saddle, crying and complaining, and quite unable to get off it. So he said: "Do bear it, and I will wish for all the riches on earth for you, only stay where you are." She, however, called him a fool, and said: "What good will all the riches on earth do me, if I am to sit on this saddle? You have wished me on it, so you must help me off." So whether he would or not, he was forced to let his third wish be that she should be quit of the saddle, and able to get off it, and immediately the wish was fulfilled. So he got nothing by it but vexation, trouble, abuse, and the loss of his horse; but the poor people lived contentedly, quietly, and piously until their happy death.

THE SINGING, SOARING LARK

There was once upon a time a man who was about to set out on a long journey, and on parting he asked his three daughters what he should bring back with him for them. Whereupon the eldest wished for pearls, the second wished for diamonds, but the third said: "Dear father, I should like a singing, soaring lark." The father said: "Yes, if I can get it, you shall have it," kissed all three, and set out. Now when the time had come for him to be on his way home again, he had brought pearls and diamonds for the two eldest, but he had sought everywhere in vain for a singing, soaring lark for the youngest, and he was very unhappy about it, for she was his favourite child. Then his road lay through a forest, and in the midst of it was a splendid castle, and near the castle stood a tree, but quite on the top of the tree, he saw a singing, soaring lark. "Aha, you come just at the right moment!" he said, quite delighted, and called to his servant to climb up and catch the little creature. But as he approached the tree, a lion leapt from beneath it, shook himself, and roared till the leaves on the trees trembled. "He who tries to steal my singing, soaring lark," he cried, "will I devour." Then the man said: "I did not know that the bird belonged to you. I will make amends for the wrong I have done and ransom myself with a large sum of money, only spare my life." The lion said: "Nothing can save you, unless you will promise to give me for my own what first meets you on your return home; and if you will do that, I will grant you your life, and you shall have the bird for your daughter, into the bargain." But the man hesitated and said: "That might be my youngest daughter, she loves me best, and always runs to meet me on my return home." The servant, however, was terrified and said: "Why should your daughter be the very one to meet you, it might as easily be a cat, or dog?" Then the man allowed himself to be persuaded, took the singing, soaring lark, and promised to give the lion whatsoever should first meet him on his return home.

When he reached home and entered his house, the first who met him was no other than his youngest and dearest daughter, who came running up, kissed and embraced him, and when she saw that he had brought with him a singing, soaring lark, she was beside herself with joy. The father, however, could not rejoice, but began to weep, and said: "My dearest child, I have bought the little bird dear. In return for it, I have been obliged to promise you to a savage lion, and when he has you he will tear you in pieces and devour you," and he told her all, just as it had happened, and begged her not to go there, come what might. But she consoled him and said: "Dearest father, indeed your promise must be fulfilled. I will go thither and soften the lion, so that I may return to you safely." Next morning she had the road pointed out to her, took leave, and went fearlessly out into the forest. The lion, however, was an enchanted prince and was by day a lion, and all his people were lions with him, but in the night they resumed their natural human shapes. On her arrival she was kindly received and led into the castle. When night came, the lion turned into a handsome man, and their wedding was celebrated with great magnificence. They lived happily together, remained awake at night, and slept in the daytime. One day he came and said: "To-morrow there is a feast in your father's house, because your eldest sister is to be married, and if you are inclined to go there, my lions shall conduct you." She said: "Yes, I should very much like to see my father again," and went thither, accompanied by the lions. There was great joy when she arrived, for they had all believed that she had been torn in pieces by the lion, and had long ceased to live. But she told them what a handsome husband she had, and how well off she was, remained with them while the wedding-feast lasted, and then went back again to the forest. When the second daughter was about to be married, and she was again invited to the wedding, she said to the lion: "This time I will not be alone, you must come with me." The lion, however, said that it was too dangerous for him, for if when there a ray from a burning candle fell on him, he would be changed into a dove, and for seven years long would have to fly about with the doves. She said: "Ah, but do come with me, I will take great care of you, and guard you from all light." So they went away together, and took with them their little child as well. She had a room built there, so strong and thick that no ray could pierce through it; in this he was to shut himself up when the candles were lit for the wedding-feast. But the door was made of green wood which warped and left a little crack which no one noticed. The wedding was celebrated with magnificence, but when the procession with all its candles and torches came back from church, and passed by this apartment, a ray about the breadth of a hair fell on the King's son, and when this ray touched him, he was transformed in an instant, and when she came in and looked for him, she did not see him, but a white dove was sitting there. The dove said to her: "For seven years must I fly about the world, but at every seventh step that you take I will let fall a drop of red blood and a white feather, and these will show you the way, and if you follow the trace you can release me." Thereupon the dove flew out at the door, and she followed him, and at every seventh step a red drop of blood and a little white feather fell down and showed her the way.

So she went continually further and further in the wide world, never looking about her or resting, and the seven years were almost past; then she rejoiced and thought that they would soon be saved, and yet they were so far from it! Once when they were thus moving onwards, no little feather and no drop of red blood fell, and when she raised her eyes the dove had disappeared. And as she thought to herself: "In this no man can help you," she climbed up to the sun, and said to him: "You shine into every crevice, and over every peak, have you not seen a white dove flying?" "No," said the sun, "I have seen none, but I present you with a casket, open it when you are in sorest need." Then she thanked the sun, and went on until evening came and the moon appeared; she then asked her: "You shine the whole night through, and on every field and forest, have you not seen a white dove flying?" "No," said the moon, "I have seen no dove, but here I give you an egg, break it when you are in great need." She thanked the moon, and went on until the night wind came up and blew on her, then she said to it: "You blow over every tree and under every leaf, have you not seen a white dove flying?" "No," said the night wind, "I have seen none, but I will ask the three other winds, perhaps they have seen it." The east wind and the west wind came, and had seen nothing, but the south wind said: "I have seen the white dove, it has flown to the Red Sea, where it has become a lion again, for the seven years are over, and the lion is there fighting with a dragon; the dragon, however, is an enchanted princess." The night wind then said to her: "I will advise you; go to the Red Sea, on the right bank are some tall reeds, count them, break off the eleventh, and strike the dragon with it, then the lion will be able to subdue it, and both then will regain their human form. After that, look round and you will see the griffin which is by the Red Sea; swing yourself, with your beloved, on to his back, and the bird will carry you over the sea to your own home. Here is a nut for you, when you are above the center of the sea, let the nut fall, it will immediately shoot up, and a tall nut-tree will grow out of the water on which the griffin may rest; for if he cannot rest, he will not be strong enough to carry you across, and if you forget to throw down the nut, he will let you fall into the sea."

Then she went thither, and found everything as the night wind had said. She counted the reeds by the sea, and cut off the eleventh, struck the dragon therewith, whereupon the lion conquered it, and immediately both of them regained their human shapes. But when the princess, who hitherto had been the dragon, was released from enchantment, she took the youth by the arm, seated herself on the griffin, and carried him off with her. There stood the poor maiden who had wandered so far and was again forsaken. She sat down and cried, but at last she took courage and said: "Stil I will go as far as the wind blows and as long as the cock crows, until I find him," and she went forth by long, long roads, until at last she came to the castle where both of them were living together; there she heard that soon a feast was to be held, in which they would celebrate their wedding, but she said: "God still helps me," and opened the casket that the sun had given her. A dress lay therein as brilliant as the sun itself. So she took it out and put it on, and went up into the castle, and everyone, even the bride herself, looked at her with astonishment. The dress pleased the bride so well that she thought it might do for her wedding-dress, and asked if it was for sale. "Not for money or land," answered she, "but for flesh and blood." The bride asked her what she meant by that, so she said: "Let me sleep a night in the chamber where the bridegroom sleeps." The bride would not, yet wanted very much to have the dress; at last she consented, but the page was to give the prince a sleeping-draught. When it was night, therefore, and the youth was already asleep, she was led into the chamber; she seated herself on the bed and said: "I have followed after you for seven years. I have been to the sun and the moon, and the four winds, and have enquired for you, and have helped you against the dragon; will you, then, quite forget me?" But the prince slept so soundly that it only seemed to him as if the wind were whistling outside in the fir-trees. When therefore day broke, she was led out again, and had to give up the golden dress. And as that even had been of no avail, she was sad, went out into a meadow, sat down there, and wept. While she was sitting there, she thought of the egg which the moon had given her; she opened it, and there came out a clucking hen with twelve chickens all of gold, and they ran about chirping, and crept again under the old hen's wings; nothing more beautiful was ever seen in the world! Then she arose, and drove them through the meadow before her, until the bride looked out of the window. The little chickens pleased her so much that she immediately came down and asked if they were for sale. "Not for money or land, but for flesh and blood; let me sleep another night in the chamber where the bridegroom sleeps." The bride said: "Yes," intending to cheat her as on the former evening. But when the prince went to bed he asked the page what the murmuring and rustling in the night had been. On this the page told all; that he had been forced to give him a sleeping-draught, because a poor girl had slept secretly in the chamber, and that he was to give him another that night. The prince said: "Pour out the draught by the bed-side." At night, she was again led in, and when she began to relate how ill all had fared with her, he immediately recognized his beloved wife by her voice, sprang up and cried: "Now I really am released! I have been as it were in a dream, for the strange princess has bewitched me so that I have been compelled to forget you, but God has delivered me from the spell at the right time." Then they both left the castle secretly in the night, for they feared the father of the princess, who was a sorcerer, and they seated themselves on the griffin which bore them across the Red Sea, and when they were in the midst of it, she let fall the nut. Immediately a tall nut-tree grew up, whereon the bird rested, and then carried them home, where they found their child, who had grown tall and beautiful, and they lived thenceforth happily until their death.

THE GOOSE-GIRL

There was once upon a time an old Queen whose husband had been dead for many years, and she had a beautiful daughter. When the princess grew up she was betrothed to a prince who lived at a great distance. When the time came for her to be married, and she had to journey forth into the distant kingdom, the aged Queen packed up for her many costly vessels of silver and gold, and trinkets also of gold and silver; and cups and jewels, in short, everything which appertained to a royal dowry, for she loved her child with all her heart. She likewise sent her maid-in-waiting, who was to ride with her, and hand her over to the bridegroom, and each had a horse for the journey, but the horse of the King's daughter was called Falada, and could speak. So when the hour of parting had come, the aged mother went into her bedroom, took a small knife and cut her finger with it until it bled. Then she held a white handkerchief to it into which she let three drops of blood fall, gave it to her daughter and said: "Dear child, preserve this carefully, it will be of service to you on your way."

So they took a sorrowful leave of each other; the princess put the piece of cloth in her bosom, mounted her horse, and then went away to her bridegroom. After she had ridden for a while she felt a burning thirst, and said to her waiting-maid: "Dismount, and take my cup which you have brought with you for me, and get me some water from the stream, for I should like to drink." "If you are thirsty," said the waiting-maid, "get off your horse yourself, and lie down and drink out of the water, I don't choose to be your servant." So in her great thirst the princess alighted, bent down over the water in the stream and drank, and was not allowed to drink out of the golden cup. Then she said: "Ah, Heaven!" and the three drops of blood answered: "If this your mother knew, her heart would break in two." But the King's daughter was humble, said nothing, and mounted her horse again. She rode some miles further, but the day was warm, the sun scorched her, and she was thirsty once more, and when they came to a stream of water, she again cried to her waiting-maid: "Dismount, and give me some water in my golden cup," for she had long ago forgotten the girl's ill words. But the waiting-maid said still more haughtily: "If you wish to drink, get it yourself, I don't choose to be your maid." Then in her great thirst the King's daughter alighted, bent over the flowing stream, wept and said: "Ah, Heaven!" and the drops of blood again replied: "If this your mother knew, her heart would break in two." And as she was thus drinking and leaning right over the stream, the handkerchief with the three drops of blood fell out of her bosom, and floated away with the water without her observing it, so great was her trouble. The waiting-maid, however, had seen it, and she rejoiced to think that she had now power over the bride, for since the princess had lost the drops of blood, she had become weak and powerless. So now when she wanted to mount her horse again, the one that was called Falada, the waiting-maid said: "Falada is more suitable for me, and my nag will do for you," and the princess had to be content with that. Then the waiting-maid, with many hard words, bade the princess exchange her royal apparel for her own shabby clothes; and at length she was compelled to swear by the clear sky above her, that she would not say one word of this to anyone at the royal court, and if she had not taken this oath she would have been killed on the spot. But Falada saw all this, and observed it well.

The waiting-maid now mounted Falada, and the true bride the bad horse, and thus they travelled onwards, until at length they entered the royal palace. There were great rejoicings over her arrival, and the prince sprang forward to meet her, lifted the waiting-maid from her horse, and thought she was his consort. She was conducted upstairs, but the real princess was left standing below. Then the old King looked out of the window and saw her standing in the courtyard, and noticed how dainty and delicate and beautiful she was, and instantly went to the royal apartment, and asked the bride about the girl she had with her who was standing down below in the courtyard, and who she was. "I picked her up on my way for a companion; give the girl something to work at, that she may not stand idle. But the old King had no work for her, and knew of none, so he said: "I have a little boy who tends the geese, she may help him." The boy was called Conrad, and the true bride had to help him to tend the geese. Soon afterwards the false bride said to the young King: "Dearest husband, I beg you to do me a favour." He answered: "I will do so most willingly." "Then send for the knacker, and have the head of the horse on which I rode here cut off,

for it vexed me on the way." In reality, she was afraid that the horse might tell how she had behaved to the King's daughter. Then she succeeded in making the King promise that it should be done, and the faithful Falada was to die; this came to the ears of the real princess, and she secretly promised to pay the knacker a piece of gold if he would perform a small service for her. There was a great dark-looking gateway in the town, through which morning and evening she had to pass with the geese: would he be so good as to nail up Falada's head on it, so that she might see him again, more than once. The knacker's man promised to do that, and cut off the head, and nailed it fast beneath the dark gateway.

Early in the morning, when she and Conrad drove out their flock beneath this gateway, she said in passing:

"Alas, Falada, hanging there!"

Then the head answered:

"Alas, young Queen, how ill you fare!
If this your mother knew,
Her heart would break in two."

Then they went still further out of the town, and drove their geese into the country. And when they had come to the meadow, she sat down and unbound her hair which was like pure gold, and Conrad saw it and delighted in its brightness, and wanted to pluck out a few hairs. Then she said:

"Blow, blow, thou gentle wind, I say,
Blow Conrad's little hat away,
And make him chase it here and there,
Until I have braided all my hair,
And bound it up again."

And there came such a violent wind that it blew Conrad's hat far away across country, and he was forced to run after it. When he came back she had finished combing her hair and was putting it up again, and he could not get any of it. Then Conrad was angry, and would not speak to her, and thus they watched the geese until the evening, and then they went home.

Next day when they were driving the geese out through the dark gateway, the maiden said:

"Alas, Falada, hanging there!"

Falada answered:

"Alas, young Queen, how ill you fare!
If this your mother knew,
Her heart would break in two."

And she sat down again in the field and began to comb out her hair, and Conrad ran and tried to clutch it, so she said in haste:

"Blow, blow, thou gentle wind, I say,
Blow Conrad's little hat away,
And make him chase it here and there,
Until I have braided all my hair,
And bound it up again."

Then the wind blew, and blew his little hat off his head and far away, and Conrad was forced to run after it, and when he came back, her hair had been put up a long time, and he could get none of it, and so they looked after their geese till evening came.

But in the evening after they had got home, Conrad went to the old King, and said: "I won't tend the geese with that girl any longer!" "Why not?" inquired the aged King. "Oh, because she vexes me the whole day long." Then the aged King commanded him to relate what it was that she did to him. And Conrad said: "In the morning when we pass beneath the dark gateway with the flock, there is a horse's head on the wall, and she says to it:

'Alas, Falada, hanging there!'

And the head replies:

'Alas, young Queen how ill you fare!
If this your mother knew,
Her heart would break in two.' "

And Conrad went on to relate what happened on the goose pasture,
and how when there he had to chase his hat.

The aged King commanded him to drive his flock out again next
day, and as soon as morning came, he placed himself behind the dark
gateway, and heard how the maiden spoke to the head of Falada, and
then he too went into the country, and hid himself in the thicket in the
meadow. There he soon saw with his own eyes the goose-girl and the
goose-boy bringing their flock, and how after a while she sat down and
unplaited her hair, which shone with radiance. And soon she said:

"Blow, blow, thou gentle wind, I say,
Blow Conrad's little hat away,
And make him chase it here and there,
Until I have braided all my hair,
And bound it up again."

Then came a blast of wind and carried off Conrad's hat, so that he had
to run far away, while the maiden quietly went on combing and plait-
ing her hair, all of which the King observed. Then, quite unseen, he
went away, and when the goose-girl came home in the evening, he
called her aside, and asked why she did all these things. "I may not tell
that, and I dare not lament my sorrows to any human being, for I have
sworn not to do so by the heaven which is above me; if I had not done
that, I should have lost my life." He urged her and left her no peace, but
he could draw nothing from her. Then said he: "If you will not tell me
anything, tell your sorrows to the iron-stove there," and he went away.
Then she crept into the iron-stove, and began to weep and lament, and
emptied her whole heart, and said: "Here am I deserted by the whole
world, and yet I am a King's daughter, and a false waiting-maid has by
force brought me to such a pass that I have been compelled to put off
my royal apparel, and she has taken my place with my bridegroom, and
I have to perform menial service as a goose-girl. If this my mother
knew, her heart would break in two."

The aged King, however, was standing outside by the pipe of the stove, and was listening to what she said, and heard it. Then he came back again, and bade her come out of the stove. And royal garments were placed on her, and it was marvellous how beautiful she was! The aged King summoned his son, and revealed to him that he had got the false bride who was only a waiting-maid, but that the true one was standing there, as the former goose-girl. The young King rejoiced with all his heart when he saw her beauty and youth, and a great feast was made ready to which all the people and all good friends were invited. At the head of the table sat the bridegroom with the King's daughter at one side of him, and the waiting-maid on the other, but the waiting-maid was blinded, and did not recognize the princess in her dazzling array. When they had eaten and drunk, and were merry, the aged King asked the waiting-maid as a riddle, what punishment a person deserved who had behaved in such and such a way to her master, and at the same time related the whole story, and asked what sentence such a person merited. Then the false bride said: "She deserves no better fate than to be stripped entirely naked, and put in a barrel which is studded inside with pointed nails, and two white horses should be harnessed to it, which will drag her along through one street after another, till she is dead." "It is you," said the aged King, "and you have pronounced your own sentence, and thus shall it be done unto you." And when the sentence had been carried out, the young King married his true bride, and both of them reigned over their kingdom in peace and happiness.

THE YOUNG GIANT

Once upon a time a countryman had a son who was as big as a thumb, and did not become any bigger, and during several years did not grow one hair's breadth. Once when the father was going out to plough, the little one said: "Father, I will go out with you." "You would go out with me?" said the father. "Stay here, you will be of no use out there, besides you might get lost!" Then Thumbling began to cry, and for the sake of peace his father put him in his pocket, and took him with him. When he was outside in the field, he took him out again, and set him in a freshly-cut furrow. Whilst he sat there, a great giant came over the hill. "Do you see that great bogie?" said the father, for he wanted to frighten the little fellow to make him behave well; "he is coming to fetch you." The giant, however, had scarcely taken two steps with his long legs before he was in the furrow. He took up little Thumbling carefully with two fingers, examined him, and without saying one word went away with him. His father stood by, but could not utter a sound for terror, and he thought nothing else but that his child was lost, and that as long as he lived he should never set eyes on him again.

But the giant carried him home, let him suckle at his breast, and Thumbling grew and became tall and strong after the manner of giants. When two years had passed, the old giant took him into the forest, wanted to test him, and said: "Pull up a stick for yourself." Then the boy was already so strong that he tore up a young tree out of the earth by the roots. But the giant thought: "We must do better than that," took him back again, and suckled him two years longer. When he tested him, his strength had increased so much that he could tear an old tree out of the ground. That was still not enough for the giant; he again suckled him for two years, and when he then went with him into the forest and said: "Now, just tear up a real stick," the boy tore up the biggest oak-tree from the earth, so that it cracked, and that was a mere trifle to him. "Now that will do," said the giant, "you are perfect," and took him back to the field from whence he had brought him. His father was there following the plough. The young giant went up to him, and said: "Does my father see what a fine man his son has grown into?"

The farmer was alarmed, and said: "No, you are not my son; I don't want you—leave me!" "Truly I am your son; allow me to do your work, I can plough as well as you, nay better." "No, no, you are not my son, and you cannot plough—go away!" However, as he was afraid of this great man, he let go of the plough, stepped back and sat down at the side of the land. Then the youth took the plough, and just grasped it with one hand, but his pressure was so strong that the plough went deep into the earth. The farmer could not bear to see that, and called to him: "If you are determined to plough, you must not press so hard on it, that makes bad work." The youth, however, unharnessed the horses, and drew the plough himself, saying: "Just go home, father, and bid my mother make ready a large dish of food, and in the meantime I will go over the field." Then the farmer went home, and ordered his wife to prepare the food; but the youth ploughed the field which was two acres large, quite alone, and then he harnessed himself to the harrow, and harrowed the whole of the land, using two harrows at once. When he had done it, he went into the forest, and pulled up two oak-trees, laid them across his shoulders, and hung on them one harrow behind and one before, and also one horse behind and one before, and carried all as if it had been a bundle of straw, to his parents' house. When he entered the yard, his mother did not recognize him, and asked: "Who is that horrible tall man?" The farmer said: "That is our son." She said: "No, that cannot be our son, we never had such a tall one, ours was a little thing." She called to him: "Go away, we do not want you!" The youth was silent, but led his horses to the stable, gave them some oats and hay, and all that they wanted. When he had done this, he went into the parlour, sat down on the bench and said: "Mother, now I should like something to eat, will it soon be ready?" She said: "Yes," and brought in two immense dishes full of food, which would have been enough to satisfy herself and her husband for a week. The youth, however, ate the whole of it himself, and asked if she had nothing more to set before him. "No," she replied, "that is all we have." "But that was only a taste, I must have more." She did not dare to oppose him, and went and put a huge pig's trough full of food on the fire, and when it was ready, carried it in. "At length come a few crumbs," said he, and gobbled all there was, but it was still not sufficient to appease his hunger. Then said he: "Father, I see well that with you I shall never have food enough; if you will get me an iron staff which is strong, and

which I cannot break against my knees, I will go out into the world."
The farmer was glad, put his two horses in his cart, and fetched from
the smith a staff so large and thick that the two horses could only just
bring it away. The youth laid it across his knees, and snap! he broke it
in two in the middle like a bean-stalk, and threw it away. The father
then harnessed four horses, and brought a bar which was so long and
thick, that the four horses could only just drag it. The son snapped this
also in twain against his knees, threw it away, and said: "Father, this can
be of no use to me, you must harness more horses, and bring a
stronger staff." So the father harnessed eight horses, and brought one
which was so long and thick, that the eight horses could only just carry
it. When the son took it in his hand, he immediately snapped off the
end of it, and said: "Father, I see that you will not be able to procure me
any such staff as I want, I will remain no longer with you."

So he went away, and gave out that he was a smith's apprentice. He
arrived at a village, wherein lived a smith who was a stingy fellow, who
never did a kindness to any one, but wanted everything for himself. The
youth went into the smithy and asked if he needed a journeyman.
"Yes," said the smith, and looked at him, and thought: "That is a strong
fellow who will strike out well, and earn his bread." So he asked: "How
much wages do you want?" "I don't want any at all," he replied, "only
every fortnight, when the other journeymen are paid, I will give you
two blows, and you must bear them." The miser was heartily satisfied,
and thought he would thus save much money. Next morning, the
strange journeyman was to begin to work, but when the master
brought the glowing bar, and the youth struck his first blow, the iron
flew asunder, and the anvil sank so deep into the earth, that there was
no bringing it out again. Then the miser grew angry, and said: "Oh,
but I can't make any use of you, you strike far too powerfully; how
much will you have for the one blow?"

Then said he: "I will give you only quite a small blow, that's all."
And he raised his foot, and gave him such a kick that he flew away over
four loads of hay. Then he sought out the thickest iron bar in the
smithy for himself, took it as a stick in his hand, and went onwards.

When he had walked for some time, he came to a small farm, and
asked the bailiff if he did not require a head-man. "Yes," said the
bailiff, "I can make use of one; you look a capable fellow who can do

something, how much a year do you want as wages?" He again replied
that he wanted no wages at all, but that every year he would give him
three blows, which he must bear. Then the bailiff was satisfied, for he,
too, was a covetous fellow. Next morning all the servants were to go
into the wood, and the others were already up, but the head-man was
still in bed. Then one of them called to him: "Get up, it is time; we are
going into the wood, and you must go with us." "Ah," said he quite
roughly and surlily, "you may just go, then; I shall be back again before
any of you." Then the others went to the bailiff, and told him that the
head-man was still lying in bed, and would not go into the wood with
them. The bailiff said they were to awake him again, and tell him to
harness the horses. The head-man, however, said as before: "Just go
there, I shall be back again before any of you." And then he stayed in
bed two hours longer. At length he arose from the feathers, but first he
got himself two bushels of peas from the loft, made himself some
broth, ate it at his leisure, and when that was done, went and harnessed
the horses, and drove into the wood. Not far from the wood was a
ravine through which he had to pass, so he first drove the horses on,
and then stopped them, and went behind the cart, took trees and
brushwood, and made a great barricade, so that no horse could get
through. When he was entering the wood, the others were just driving
out of it with their loaded carts to go home; then said he to them:
"Drive on, I will still get home before you do." He did not drive far
into the wood, but at once tore two of the very largest trees of all out of
the earth, threw them on his cart, and turned round. When he came to
the barricade, the others were still standing there, not able to get
through. "Don't you see," said he, "That if you had stayed with me,
you would have got home just as quickly, and would have had another
hour's sleep?" He now wanted to drive on, but his horses could not
work their way through, so he unharnessed them, laid them on the top
of the cart, took the shafts in his own hands, and pulled it all through,
and he did this just as easily as if it had been laden with feathers. When
he was over, he said to the others: "There, you see, I have got over
quicker than you," and drove on, and the others had to stay where they
were. In the yard, however, he took a tree in his hand, showed it to the
bailiff, and said: "Isn't that a fine cord of wood?" Then said the bailiff
to his wife: "The servant is a good one—even if he does sleep long, he

is still home before the others." So he served the bailiff for a year, and when that was over, and the other servants were getting their wages, he said it was time for him to take his too. The bailiff, however, was afraid of the blows which he was to receive, and earnestly entreated him to excuse him from having them; for rather than that, he himself would be head-man, and the youth should be bailiff. "No," said he, "I will not be a bailiff, I am head-man, and will remain so, but I will administer that which we agreed on." The bailiff was willing to give him what-soever he demanded, but it was of no use, the head-man said no to everything. Then the bailiff did not know what to do, and begged for a fortnight's delay, for he wanted to find some way of escape. The head-man consented to this delay. The bailiff summoned all his clerks together, and they were to think the matter over, and give him advice. The clerks pondered for a long time, but at last they said that no one was sure of his life with the head-man, for he could kill a man as easily as a midge, and that the bailiff ought to make him get into the well and clean it, and when he was down below, they would roll up one of the mill-stones which was lying there, and throw it on his head; and then he would never return to daylight. The advice pleased the bailiff, and the head-man was quite willing to go down the well. When he was standing down below at the bottom, they rolled down the largest mill-stone and thought they had broken his skull, but he cried: "Chase away those hens from the well, they are scratching in the sand up there, and throwing the grains into my eyes, so that I can't see." So the bailiff cried: "Sh-sh,"—and pretended to frighten the hens away. When the head-man had finished his work, he climbed up and said: "Just look what a beautiful neck-tie I have on," and behold it was the mill-stone which he was wearing round his neck. The head-man now wanted to take his reward, but the bailiff again begged for a fortnight's delay. The clerks met together and advised him to send the head-man to the haunted mill to grind corn by night, for from thence as yet no man had ever returned in the morning alive. The proposal pleased the bailiff, he called the head-man that very evening, and ordered him to take eight bushels of corn to the mill, and grind it that night, for it was wanted. So the head-man went to the loft, and put two bushels in his right pocket, and two in his left, and took four in a wallet, half on his back, and half on his breast, and thus laden went to the haunted mill. The miller told

him that he could grind there very well by day, but not by night, for the mill was haunted, and that up to the present time whosoever had gone into it at night had been found in the morning lying dead inside. He said: "I will manage it, just you go and put your head on the pillow." Then he went into the mill, and poured out the corn. About eleven o'clock he went into the miller's room, and sat down on the bench. When he had sat there a while, a door suddenly opened, and a large table came in, and on the table, wine and roasted meats placed themselves, and much good food besides, but everything came of itself, for no one was there to carry it. After this the chairs pushed themselves up, but no people came, until all at once he beheld fingers, which handled knives and forks, and laid food on the plates, but with this exception he saw nothing. As he was hungry, and saw the food, he, too, placed himself at the table, ate with those who were eating, and enjoyed it. When he had had enough, and the others also had quite emptied their dishes, he distinctly heard all the candles being suddenly snuffed out, and as it was now pitch dark, he felt something like a box on the ear. Then he said: "If anything of that kind comes again, I shall strike out in return." And when he had received a second box on the ear, he, too, struck out. And so it continued the whole night. He took nothing without returning it, but repaid everything with interest, and did not slay about him in vain. At daybreak, however, everything ceased. When the miller had got up, he wanted to look after him, and wondered if he were still alive. Then the youth said: "I have eaten my fill, have received some boxes on the ear, but I have given some in return." The miller rejoiced, and said that the mill was now released from the spell, and wanted to give him much money as a reward. But he said: "Money, I will not have, I have enough of it." So he took his meal on his back, went home, and told the bailiff that he had done what he had been told to do, and would now have the reward agreed on. When the bailiff heard that, he was seriously alarmed and quite beside himself; he walked to and fro in the room, and drops of sweat ran down from his forehead. Then he opened the window to get some fresh air, but before he was aware, the head-man had given him such a kick that he flew through the window out into the air, and so far away that no one ever saw him again. Then said the head-man to the bailiff's wife: "If he does not come back, you must take the other blow." She cried: "No, no, I cannot bear it," and opened the other window, because drops of sweat were running down her forehead. Then he gave her such a kick that she, too, flew out, and as she was lighter she went much higher than her husband. Her husband cried: "Do come to me," but she replied: "Come you to me, I cannot come to you." And they hovered about there in the air, and could not get to each other, and whether they are still hovering about, or not, I do not know, but the young giant took up his iron bar, and went on his way.

THE GNOME

There was once upon a time a rich King who had three daughters, who daily went to walk in the palace garden, and the King was a great lover of all kinds of fine trees, but there was one for which he had such an affection, that if anyone gathered an apple from it he wished him a hundred fathoms underground. And when harvest time came, the apples on this tree were all as red as blood. The three daughters went every day beneath the tree, and looked to see if the wind had not blown down an apple, but they never by any chance found one, and the tree was so loaded with them that it was almost breaking, and the branches hung down to the ground. Then the King's youngest child had a great desire for an apple, and said to her sisters: "Our father loves us far too much to wish us underground, it is my belief that he would only do that to people who were strangers." And while she was speaking, the child plucked off quite a large apple, and ran to her sisters, saying: "Just taste, my dear little sisters, for never in my life have I tasted anything so delightful." Then the two other sisters also ate some of the apple, whereupon all three sank deep down into the earth, where they could hear no cock crow.

When mid-day came, the King wished to call them to come to dinner, but they were nowhere to be found. He sought them everywhere in the palace and garden, but could not find them. Then he was much troubled, and made known to the whole land that whosoever brought his daughters back again should have one of them to wife. Hereupon so many young men went about the country in search, that there was no counting them, for everyone loved the three children because they were so kind to all, and so fair of face. Three young huntsmen also went out, and when they had traveled about for eight days, they arrived at a great castle, in which were beautiful apartments, and in one room a table was laid on which were delicate dishes which were still so warm that they were smoking, but in the whole of the

castle no human being was either to be seen or heard. They waited there for half a day, and the food still remained warm and smoking, and at length they were so hungry that they sat down and ate, and agreed with each other that they would stay and live in that castle, and that one of them, who should be chosen by casting lots, should remain in the house, and the two others seek the King's daughters. They cast lots, and the lot fell on the eldest; so next day the two younger went out to seek, and the eldest had to stay at home. At mid-day came a small, small mannikin and begged for a piece of bread; then the huntsman took the bread which he had found there, and cut a round off the loaf and was about to give it to him, but while he was giving it to the mannikin, the latter let it fall, and asked the huntsman to be so good as to give him that piece again. The huntsman was about to do so and stooped, on which the mannikin took a stick, seized him by the hair, and gave him a good beating. Next day, the second stayed at home, and he fared no better. When the two others returned in the evening, the eldest said: "Well, how have you got on?"

"Oh, very badly," said he, and then they lamented their misfortune together, but they said nothing about it to the youngest, for they did not like him at all, and always called him Stupid Hans, because he did not know the ways of the world. On the third day, the youngest stayed at home, and again the little mannikin came and begged for a piece of bread. When the youth gave it to him, the elf let it fall as before, and asked him to be so good as to give him that piece again. Then said Hans to the little mannikin, "What! can you not pick up that piece yourself? If you will not take as much trouble as that for your daily bread, you do not deserve to have it." Then the mannikin grew very angry and said he was to do it, but the huntsman would not, and took my dear mannikin, and gave him a thorough beating. Then the mannikin screamed terribly, and cried: "Stop, stop, and let me go, and I will tell you where the King's daughters are." When Hans heard that, he left off beating him and the mannikin told him that he was a gnome, and that there were more than a thousand like him, and that if he would go with him he would show him where the King's daughters were. Then he showed him a deep well, but there was no water in it. And the elf said that he knew well that the companions Hans had with him did not intend to deal honorably with him, therefore if he wished to deliver the King's children, he must do it alone. The two other brothers would also be very glad to recover the King's daughters, but they did not want to have any trouble or danger. Hans was therefore to take a large basket, and he must seat himself in it with his hunting knife and a bell, and be let down. Below were three rooms, and in each of them was a princess, who was lousing a dragon with many heads, which he must cut off. And having said all this, the elf vanished. When it was evening the two brothers came and asked how he had got on, and he said: "Pretty well so far," and that he had seen no one except at mid-day when a little mannikin had come and begged for a piece of bread, that he had given some to him, but that the mannikin had let it fall and had asked him to pick it up again; but as he did not choose to do that, the elf had begun to scold, and that he had lost his temper, and had given the elf a beating, at which he had told him where the King's daughters were. Then the two were so angry at this that they grew green and yellow. Next morning they went to the well together, and drew lots who should first seat himself in the basket, and again the lot fell on the eldest, and he was to seat himself in it, and take the bell with him. Then he said: "If I ring, you must draw me up again immediately." When he had gone down for a short distance, he rang, and they at once drew him up again. Then the second seated himself in the basket, but he did just the same as the first, and then it was the turn of the youngest, but he let himself be lowered quite to the bottom. When he had got out of the basket, he took his knife, and went and stood outside the first door and listened, and heard the dragon snoring quite loudly. He opened the door slowly, and one of the princesses was sitting there, and had nine dragon's heads lying upon her lap, and was lousing them. Then he took his knife and hewed at them, and the nine fell off. The princess sprang up, threw her arms round his neck, embraced and kissed him repeatedly, and took her stomacher, which was made of pure gold, and hung it round his neck. Then he went to the second princess, who had a dragon with five heads to louse, and delivered her also, and to the youngest, who had a dragon with four heads, he went likewise. And they all rejoiced, and embraced him and kissed him without stopping. Then he rang very loud, so that those above heard him, and he placed the princesses one after the other in the basket, and had them all drawn up, but when it came to his own turn he remembered the words of the elf, who had told him that his comrades did not mean well by him. So he took a great stone which was lying there, and placed it in the basket, and when it was about half way up, his false brothers above cut the rope, so that the basket with the stone fell to the ground, and they thought that he was dead, and ran away with the three princesses, making them promise to tell their father that it was they who had delivered them. Then they went to the King, and each demanded a princess in marriage.

In the meantime the youngest huntsman was wandering about the three chambers in great trouble, fully expecting to have to end his days there, when he saw, hanging on the wall, a flute; then said he: "Why do you hang there? No one can be merry here." He looked at the dragons' heads likewise and said: "You too cannot help me now." He walked to and fro for such a long time that he made the surface of the ground quite smooth. But at last other thoughts came to his mind, and he took the flute from the wall, and played a few notes on it, and suddenly a number of elves appeared, and with every note that he sounded one more came. Then he played until the room was entirely filled. They all asked what he desired, so he said he wished to get above ground back to day-light, on which they seized him by every hair that grew on his head, and thus they flew with him onto the earth again. When he was above ground, he at once went to the King's palace, just as the wedding of one princess was about to be celebrated, and he went to the room where the King and his three daughters were. When the princesses saw him they fainted. Hereupon the King was angry, and ordered him to be put in prison at once, because he thought he must have done some injury to the children. When the princesses came to themselves, however, they entreated the King to set him free again. The King asked why, and they said that they were not allowed to tell that, but their father said that they were to tell it to the stove. And he went out, listened at the door, and heard everything. Then he caused the two brothers to be hanged on the gallows, and to the third he gave his youngest daughter, and on that occasion I wore a pair of glass shoes, and I struck them against a stone, and they said "Klink," and were broken.

THE KING OF THE GOLDEN MOUNTAIN

There was a certain merchant who had two children, a boy and a girl; they were both young, and could not walk. And two richly-laden ships of his sailed forth to sea with all his property on board, and just as he was expecting to win much money by them, news came that they had gone to the bottom, and now instead of being a rich man he was a poor one, and had nothing left but one field outside the town. In order to drive his misfortune a little out of his thoughts, he went out to this field, and as he was walking to and fro in it, a little black mannikin stood suddenly by his side, and asked why he was so sad, and what he was taking so much to heart. Then said the merchant: "If you could help me I would willingly tell you." "Who knows?" replied the black dwarf. "Perhaps, I can help you." Then the merchant told him that all he possessed had gone to the bottom of the sea, and that he had nothing left but this field. "Do not trouble yourself," said the dwarf. "If you will promise to give me the first thing that rubs itself against your leg when you are at home again, and to bring it here to this place in twelve years' time, you shall have as much money as you will." The merchant thought: "What can that be but my dog?" and did not remember his little boy, so he said yes, gave the black man a written and sealed promise, and went home.

When he reached home, his little boy was so delighted that he held himself by a bench, trotted up to him and seized him fast by the legs. The father was shocked, for he remembered his promise, and now knew what he had pledged himself to do; as, however, he still found no money in his chest, he thought the dwarf had only been jesting. A month afterwards he went up to the garret, intending to gather together some old tin and to sell it, and saw lying there a great heap of money. Then he was happy again, made purchases, became a greater merchant than before, and felt that God was good to him. In the meantime the boy grew tall, and at the same time bright and clever. But the nearer the twelfth year approached the more anxious grew the merchant, so that his distress might be seen in his face. One day his son asked what ailed him, but the father would not say. The boy, however, persisted so long, that at last he told him that without being aware of what he was doing, he had promised him to a black dwarf, and had received much money for doing so. He said likewise that he had set his hand and seal to this, and that now when twelve years had gone by he would have to give him up. Then said the son: "Oh, father, do not be uneasy, all will go well. The black man has no power over me." The son had himself blessed by the priest, and when the time came, father and son went together to the field, and the son made a circle and placed himself inside it with his father. Then came the black dwarf and said to the old man: "Have you brought with you that which you have promised me?" He was silent, but the son asked: "What do you want here?" Then said the black dwarf: "I have to speak with your father, and not with you." The son replied: "You have betrayed and misled my father, give back the writing." "No," said the black dwarf, "I will not give up my rights." They spoke together for a long time after this, but at last they agreed that the son, as he did not belong to the enemy of mankind, nor yet to his father, should seat himself in a small boat, which should lie on water which was flowing away from them, and that the father should push it off with his own foot, and then the son should remain given up to the water. So he took leave of his father, placed himself in a little boat, and the father had to push it off with his own foot. The boat capsized so that the keel was uppermost and the deck under water, and the father believed his son was lost, and went home and mourned for him.

The boat, however, did not sink, but floated quietly away, and the boy sat safely inside it, and it floated thus for a long time, until at last it ran into an unknown shore. Then he landed and saw a beautiful castle before him, and set out to go to it. But when he entered it, he found that it was bewitched. He went through every room, but all were empty until he reached the last, where a snake lay coiled in a ring. The snake, however, was an enchanted maiden, who rejoiced to see him, and said: "Have you come, oh, my deliverer? I have already waited twelve years for you; this kingdom is bewitched, and you must set it free." "How can I do that?" he inquired. "To-night come twelve black men, covered with chains who will ask what you are doing here; but be silent; give them no answer, and let them do what they will with you; they will torment you, beat you, stab you; let everything pass, only do not speak; at twelve o'clock, they must go away again. On the second night twelve others will come; on the third, four-and-twenty, who will cut off your head, but at twelve o'clock their power will be over, and then if you have endured all, and have not spoken the slightest word, I shall be released. I will come to you, and will have, in a bottle, some of the water of life. I will rub you with that, and then you will come to life again, and be as healthy as before." Then said he: "I will gladly set you free." And everything happened just as she had said; the black men could not force a single word from him, and on the third night the snake became a beautiful princess, who came with the water of life and brought him back to life again. So she threw herself into his arms and kissed him, and there was joy and gladness in the whole castle. After this their marriage was celebrated, and he was King of the Golden Mountain.

They lived very happily together, and the Queen bore a fine boy. Eight years had already gone by, when the King bethought him of his father; his heart was moved, and he wished to visit him. The Queen, however, would not let him go away, and said: "I know beforehand that it will cause my unhappiness"; but he suffered her to have no rest until she consented. At their parting she gave him a wishing-ring, and said: "Take this ring and put it on your finger, and then you will immediately be transported whithersoever you would be, only you must promise me not to use it in wishing me away from this place and with thy father." That he promised her, put the ring on his finger, and wished himself at home, just outside the town where his father lived. Instantly he found himself there, and made for the town, but when he came to the gate, the sentries would not let him in, because he wore such strange and yet such rich and magnificent clothing. Then he went to a hill where a shepherd was watching his sheep, changed clothes with him, put on his old shepherd's-coat, and then entered the town without hindrance. When he came to his father, he made himself known to him, but he did not at all believe that the shepherd was his son, and said he certainly had had a son, but that he was dead long ago; however, as he saw he was a poor, needy shepherd, he would give him something to eat. Then the shepherd said to his parents: "I am verily your son. Do you know of no mark on my body by which you could recognize me?" "Yes," said his mother, "our son had a raspberry mark under his right arm." He slipped back his shirt, and they saw the raspberry under his right arm, and no longer doubted that he was their son. Then he told them that he was King of the Golden Mountain, and a king's daughter was his wife, and that they had a fine son of seven years old. Then said the father: "That is certainly not true; it is a fine kind of king who goes about in a ragged shepherd's-coat." On this the son fell in a passion, and without thinking of his promise, turned his ring round, and wished both his wife and child with him. They were there in a second, but the Queen wept, and reproached him, and said that he had broken his word, and had brought misfortune upon her. He said: "I have done it thoughtlessly, and not with evil intention," and tried to calm her, and she pretended to believe this; but she had mischief in her mind.

Then he led her out of the town into the field, and showed her the stream where the little boat had been pushed off, and then he said: "I am tired; sit down, I will sleep awhile on your lap." And he laid his head on her lap, and she picked his lice for a while until he fell asleep. When he was asleep, she first drew the ring from his finger, then she drew away the foot which was under him, leaving only the slipper behind her, and she took her child in her arms, and wished herself back in her own kingdom. When he awoke, there he lay quite deserted, and his wife and child were gone, and so was the ring from his finger, the slipper only was still there as a token. "Home to your parents you cannot return," thought he, "they would say that you were a wizard; you must be off, and walk on until you arrive in your own kingdom." So he went away and came at length to a hill by which three giants were standing, disputing with each other because they did not know how to divide their father's property. When they saw him passing by, they called to him and said little men had quick wits, and that he was to divide their inheritance for them. The inheritance, however, consisted of a sword, which, if anyone took it in his hand, and said: "All heads off but mine," every head would lie on the ground; secondly, of a cloak which made any one who put it on invisible; thirdly, of a pair of boots which could transport the wearer to any place he wished in a moment. He said: "Give me the three things that I may see if they are still in good condition." They gave him the cloak, and when he had put it on, he was invisible and changed into a fly. Then he resumed his own form and said: "The cloak is a good one, now give me the sword." They said: "No, we will not give you that; if you were to say, 'All heads off but mine', all our heads would be off, and you alone would be left with yours." Nevertheless they gave it to him on the condition that he was only to try it against a tree. This he did, and the sword cut in two the trunk of a tree as if it had been a blade of straw. Then he wanted to have the boots likewise, but they said: "No, we will not give them; if you had them on your feet and were to wish yourself at the top of the hill, we should be left down here with nothing." "Oh, no," said he, "I will not do that." So they gave him the boots as well. And now when he had got all these things, he thought of nothing but his wife and his child, and said as though to himself: "Oh, if I were but on the Golden Mountain," and at the same moment he vanished from the sight of the giants, and thus their inheritance was divided. When he was near his palace, he heard sounds of joy, and fiddles, and flutes, and the people told him that his wife was celebrating her wedding with another. Then

he fell into a rage, and said: "False woman, she betrayed and deserted me whilst I was asleep!" So he put on his cloak, and unseen by all went into the palace. When he entered the dining-hall a great table was spread with delicious food, and the guests were eating and drinking, and laughing, and jesting. She sat on a royal seat in the midst of them in splendid apparel, with a crown on her head. He placed himself behind her, and no one saw him. When she put a piece of meat on a plate for herself, he took it away and ate it, and when she poured out a glass of wine for herself, he took it away and drank it. She was always helping herself to something, and yet she never got anything, for plate and glass disappeared immediately. Then dismayed and ashamed, she arose and went to her chamber and wept, but he followed her there. She said: "Has the devil power over me, or did my deliverer never come?" Then he struck her in the face, and said: "Did your deliverer never come? It is he who has you in his power, you traitor. Have I deserved this from you?" Then he made himself visible, went into the hall, and cried: "The wedding is at an end, the true King has returned." The kings, princes, and councillors who were assembled there, ridiculed and mocked him, but he did not trouble to answer them, and said: "Will you go away, or not?" On this they tried to seize him and pressed upon him, but he drew his sword and said: "All heads off but mine," and all the heads rolled on the ground, and he alone was master, and once more King of the Golden Mountain.

THE RAVEN

There was once upon a time a Queen who had a little daughter who was still so young that she had to be carried. One day the child was naughty, and the mother might say what she liked, but the child would not be quiet. Then she became impatient, and as the ravens were flying about the palace, she opened the window and said: "I wish you were a raven and would fly away, and then I should have some rest." Scarcely had she spoken the words, before the child was changed into a raven, and flew from her arms out of the window. It flew into a dark forest, and stayed in it a long time, and the parents heard nothing of their child. Then one day a man was on his way through this forest and heard the raven crying, and followed the voice, and when he came nearer, the bird said: "I am a King's daughter by birth, and am bewitched, but you can set me free." "What am I to do?" asked he. She said: "Go further into the forest, and you will find a house, wherein sits an aged woman, who will offer you meat and drink, but you must accept nothing; for if you eat and drink anything, you will fall into a sleep, and then you will not be able to set me free. In the garden behind the house there is a great heap of tan, and on this you shall stand and wait for me. For three days I will come every afternoon at two o'clock in a carriage. On the first day four white horses will be harnessed to it, then four chestnut horses, and lastly four black ones; but if you are not awake, but sleeping, I shall not be set free." The man promised to do everything that she desired, but the raven said: "Alas! I know already that you will not set me free; you will accept something from the woman." Then the man once more promised that he would certainly not touch anything either to eat or to drink. But when he entered the house the old woman came to him and said: "Poor man, how faint you are; come and refresh yourself; eat and drink." "No," said the man, "I will not eat or drink." She, however, let him have no peace, and said: "If you will not eat, take one drink out of the glass; one is nothing." Then he let himself be persuaded, and drank. Shortly before two o'clock in the afternoon he went into the garden to the tan heap to wait for the raven. As he was standing there, his weariness all at once became so great that he could not struggle against it, and lay down for a short time, but he was determined not to go to sleep. Hardly, however, had he lain down, than his eyes closed of their own accord, and he fell asleep and slept so soundly that nothing in the world could have aroused him. At two o'clock the raven came driving up with four white horses, but she was already in deep grief and said: "I know he is asleep." And when she came into the garden, he was indeed lying there asleep on the heap of tan. She alighted from the carriage, went to him, shook him, and called him, but he did not awake. Next day about noon, the old woman came again and brought him food and drink, but he would not take any of it. But she let him have no rest and persuaded him until at length he again took one drink out of the glass. Towards two o'clock he went into the garden to the tan heap to wait for the raven, but all at once felt such a great weariness that his limbs would no longer support him. He could not help himself, and was forced to lie down, and fell into a heavy sleep. When the raven drove up with four brown horses, she was already full of grief, and said: "I know he is asleep." She went to him, but there he lay sleeping, and there was no wakening him. Next day the old woman asked what was the meaning of this? He was neither eating nor drinking anything; did he want to die? He replied: "I am not allowed to eat or drink, and will not do so." But she set a dish with food, and a glass with wine before him, and when he smelt it he could not resist, and swallowed a deep draught. When the time came, he went out into the garden to the heap of tan, and waited for the King's daughter; but he became still more weary than on the day before, and lay down and slept as soundly as if he had been a stone. At two o'clock the raven came with four black horses, and the coachman and everything else was black. She was already in the deepest grief, and said: "I know that he is asleep and cannot set me free. When she came to him, there he was lying fast asleep. She shook him and called him, but she could not waken him. Then she laid a loaf beside him, and after that a piece of meat, and thirdly a bottle of wine, and he might consume as much of all of them as he liked, but they would never grow less. After this she took a gold ring from her finger, and put it on his, and her name was graven on it. Lastly, she laid a letter beside him wherein was written what she had given him, and that none of the things would ever grow less; and in it was also written: "I see right well that here you will never be able to set me free, but if you are still willing to do so, come to the golden castle of Stromberg; it lies in your power, of that I am certain." And when she had given him all these things, she seated herself in her carriage, and drove to the golden castle of Stromberg.

When the man awoke and saw that he had slept, he was sad at heart, and said: "She has certainly driven by, and I have not set her free." Then he perceived the things which were lying beside him, and read the letter wherein was written how everything had happened. So he arose and went away, intending to go to the golden castle of Stromberg, but he did not know where it was. After he had walked about the world for a long time, he entered into a dark forest, and walked for fourteen days, and still could not find his way out. Then it was once more evening, and he was so tired that he lay down in a thicket and fell asleep. Next day he went onwards, and in the evening, as he was again about to lie down beneath some bushes, he heard such a howling and crying that he could not go to sleep. And at the time when people light the candles, he saw one glimmering, and arose and went towards it. Then he came to a house which seemed very small, for in front of it a great giant was standing. He thought to himself: "If I go in, and the giant sees me, it will very likely cost me my life."

At length he ventured it and went in. When the giant saw him, he said: "It is well that you come, for it is long since I have eaten; I will at once devour you for my supper." "I'd rather you did not," said the man, "I do not like to be eaten; but if you have any desire to eat, I have quite enough here to satisfy you." "If that be true," said the giant, "you may be easy, I was only going to devour you because I had nothing else." Then they went, and sat down to the table, and the man took out the bread, wine, and meat which would never come to an end. "This pleases me well," said the giant, and ate to his heart's content. Then the man said to him: "Can you tell me where the golden castle of Stromberg is?" The giant said: "I will look at my map; all the towns, and villages, and houses are to be found on it." He brought out the map which he had in the room and looked for the castle, but it was not to be found on it. "It's no matter!" said he, "I have some still larger maps in my cupboard upstairs, and we will look at them." But there, too, it was in vain. The man now wanted to set out again, but the giant begged him to wait a few days longer until his brother, who had gone

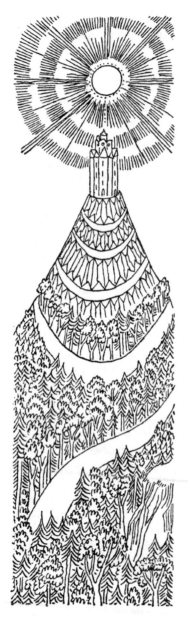

out to bring some provisions, came home. When the brother came home they inquired about the golden castle of Stromberg. He replied: "When I have eaten and have had enough, I will look at the map." Then he went with them up to his chamber, and they searched on his map, but could not find it. Then he brought out still older maps, and they never rested until they found the golden castle of Stromberg, but it was many thousand miles away. "How am I to get there?" asked the man. The giant said: "I have two hours' time, during which I will carry you into the neighborhood, but after that I must be at home to suckle the child that we have." So the giant carried the man to about a hundred leagues from the castle, and said: "You can very well walk the rest of the way alone." And he turned back, but the man went onwards day and night, until at length he came to the golden castle of Stromberg. It stood on a glass-mountain, and the bewitched maiden was driving in her carriage round the castle, and then went inside it. He rejoiced when he saw her and wanted to climb up to her, but when he began to do so he always slipped down the glass again. And when he saw that he could not reach her, he was very worried, and said to himself: "I will stay down here below, and wait for her." So he built himself a hut and stayed in it for a whole year, and every day saw the King's daughter driving about above, but never could reach her.

Then one day he saw from his hut three robbers who were beating each other, and cried to them: "God be with you!" They stopped when they heard the cry, but as they saw no one, they once more began to beat each other, and that too most dangerously. So he again cried: "God be with you." Again they stopped, looked round about, but as they saw no one they went on beating each other. Then he cried for the third time: "God be with you," and thought: "I must see what these three are about," and went thither and asked why they were beating each other so furiously. One of them said that he had found a stick, and that when he struck a door with it, that door would spring open. The next said that he had found a mantle, and that whenever he put it on, he was invisible, but the third said he had found a horse on which a man could ride everywhere, even up the glass-mountain. And now they did not know whether they ought to have these things in common, or whether they ought to divide them. Then the man said: "I will give you something in exchange for these three things. Money indeed have I not, but I have other things of more value; but first I must make an experiment to see if you have told the truth." Then they put him on the horse, threw the mantle round him, and gave him the stick in his hand, and when he had all these things they were no longer able to see him. So he gave them some vigorous blows and cried: "Now, vagabonds, you have got what you deserve: are you satisfied?" And he rode up the glass-mountain, but when he came in front of the castle at the top, it was shut. Then he struck the door with his stick, and it sprang open immediately. He went in and ascended the stairs until he came to the hall where the maiden was sitting with a golden goblet of wine before her. She, however, could not see him because he had the mantle on. And when he came up to her, he drew from his finger the ring which she had given him, and threw it into the goblet so that it rang. Then she cried: "That is my ring, so the man who is to set me free must be here." They searched the whole castle and did not find him, but he had gone out, and had seated himself on the horse and thrown off the mantle. When they came to the door, they saw him and cried aloud in their delight. Then he alighted and took the King's daughter in his arms, but she kissed him and said: "Now have you set me free, and to-morrow we will celebrate our wedding."

THE PEASANT'S WISE DAUGHTER

There was once a poor peasant who had no land, but only a small house, and one daughter. Then said the daughter: "We ought to ask our lord the King for a bit of newly-cleared land." When the King heard of their poverty, he presented them with a piece of land, which she and her father dug up, and intended to sow with a little corn and grain of that kind. When they had dug nearly the whole of the field, they found in the earth a mortar made of pure gold. "Listen," said the father to the girl, "as our lord the King has been so gracious and presented us with the field, we ought to give him this mortar in return for it." The daughter, however, would not consent to this, and said: "Father, if we have the mortar without having the pestle as well, we shall have to get the pestle, so you had much better say nothing about it." But he would not obey her, and took the mortar and carried it to the King, said that he had found it in the cleared land, and asked if he would accept it as a present. The King took the mortar, and asked if he had found nothing besides that? "No," answered the countryman. Then the King said that he must now bring him the pestle. The peasant said they had not found that, but he might just as well have spoken to the wind; he was put in prison, and was to stay there until he produced the pestle. The servants had daily to carry him bread and water, which is what people get in prison, and they heard how the man cried out continually: "Ah! if I had but listened to my daughter! Alas, alas, if I had but listened to my daughter!" Then the servants went to the King and told him how the prisoner was always crying: "Ah! if I had but listened to my daughter!" and would neither eat nor drink. So he commanded the servants to bring the prisoner before him, and then the King asked the peasant why he was always crying: "Ah! if I had but listened to my daughter!" and what it was that his daughter had said. "She told me that I ought not to take the mortar to you, for I should have to produce the pestle as well." "If you have a daughter who is as wise as that, let her come here." She was therefore obliged to appear before the King, who asked her if she really was so wise, and said he would set her a riddle, and if she could guess that, he would marry her. She at once said yes, she would guess it. Then said the King: "Come to me not clothed, not naked, not riding, not walking, not in the road, and not off the road, and if you can do that I will marry you." So she went away, put off everything she had on, and then she was not clothed, and took a great fishing net, and seated herself in it and wrapped it entirely round and round her, so that she was not naked, and she hired an ass, and tied the fisherman's net to its tail, so that it was forced to drag her along, and that was neither riding nor walking. The ass had also to drag her in the ruts, so that she only touched the ground with her big toe, and that was neither being in the road nor off the road. And when she arrived in that fashion, the King said she had guessed the riddle and fulfilled all the conditions. Then he ordered her father to be released from the prison, took her to wife, and gave into her care all the royal possessions.

Now when some years had passed, the King was once reviewing his troops on parade, when it happened that some peasants who had been selling wood stopped with their waggons before the palace; some of them had oxen yoked to them, and some horses. There was one peasant who had three horses, one of which was delivered of a young foal, and it ran away and lay down between two oxen which were in front of the waggon. When the peasants came together, they began to dispute, to beat each other and make a disturbance, and the peasant with the oxen wanted to keep the foal, and said one of the oxen had given birth to it, and the other said his horse had had it, and that it was his. The quarrel came before the King, and he gave the verdict that the foal should stay where it had been found, and so the peasant with the oxen, to whom it did not belong, got it. Then the other went away, and wept and lamented over his foal. Now he had heard how gracious his lady the Queen was because she herself had sprung from poor peasant folks, so he went to her and begged her to see if she could not help him to get his foal back again. Said she: "Yes, I will tell you what to do, if you will promise me not to betray me. Early to-morrow morning, when the King parades the guard, place yourself there in the middle of the road by which he must pass, take a great fishing-net and pretend to be fishing; go on fishing, and empty out the net as if you had got it full"—and then she told him also what he was to say if he was questioned by the King. The next day, therefore, the peasant stood there, and fished on dry ground. When the King passed by, and saw that, he sent his messenger to ask what the stupid man was about. He answered: "I am fishing." The messenger asked how he could fish when there was no water there. The peasant said: "It is as easy for me to fish on dry land as it is for an ox to have a foal." The messenger went back and took the answer to the King, who ordered the peasant to be brought to him and told him that this was not his own idea, and he wanted to know whose it was. The peasant, said the King, must confess this at once. The peasant, however, would not do so, and said always, God forbid he should! the idea was his own. So they laid him on a heap of straw, and beat him and tormented him so long that at last he admitted that he had got the idea from the Queen.

When the King reached home again, he said to his wife: "Why have you behaved so falsely to me? I will not have you any longer for a wife; your time is up, go back to the place from whence you came—to your peasant's hut." One favor, however, he granted her; she might take with her the one thing that was dearest and best in her eyes; and thus was she dismissed. She said: "Yes, my dear husband, if you command this, I will do it," and she embraced him and kissed him, and said she would take leave of him. Then she ordered a powerful sleeping draught to be brought, to drink farewell to him; the King took a long draught, but she took only a little. He soon fell into a deep sleep, and when she perceived that, she called a servant and took a fair white linen cloth and wrapped the King in it, and the servant was forced to carry him into a carriage that stood before the door, and she drove with him to her own little house. She laid him in her own little bed, and he slept one day and one night without awakening, and when he awoke he looked round and said: "Good God! where am I?" He called his attendants, but none of them were there. At length his wife came to his bedside and said: "My dear lord and King, you told me I might bring away with me from the palace that which was dearest and most precious in my eyes—I have nothing more precious and dear than yourself, so I have brought you with me." Tears rose to the King's eyes and he said: "Dear wife, you shall be mine and I will be yours," and he took her back with him to the royal palace and was married again to her, and at the present time they are very likely still living.

OLD HILDEBRAND

Once upon a time lived a peasant and his wife, and the parson of the village had a fancy for the wife, and had wished for a long while to spend a whole day happily with her. The peasant woman, too, was quite willing. One day, therefore, he said to the woman: "Listen, my dear friend, I have now thought of a way by which we can for once spend a whole day happily together. I'll tell you what; on Wednesday, you must take to your bed, and tell your husband you are ill, and as long as you complain and act being ill properly, and go on doing so until Sunday when I have to preach, I will then say in my sermon that whosoever has at home a sick child, a sick husband, a sick wife, a sick father, a sick mother, a sick brother or whosoever else it may be, and makes a pilgrimage to the Göckerli hill in Italy, where you can get a peck of laurel-leaves for a kreuzer, the sick child, the sick husband, the sick wife, the sick father, or sick mother, the sick sister, or whosoever else it may be, will be restored to health immediately."

"I will manage it," said the woman promptly. On the Wednesday, therefore, the peasant woman took to her bed, and complained and lamented as agreed on, and her husband did everything for her that he could think of, but nothing did her any good, and when Sunday came the woman said: "I feel as ill as if I were going to die at once, but there is one thing I should like to do before my end—I should like to hear the parson's sermon that he is going to preach to-day." On that the peasant said: "Ah, my child, do not do it—you might make yourself worse if you were to get up. Look, I will hear the sermon, and will attend to it very carefully, and will tell you everything the parson says."

"Well," said the woman, "go, then, and pay great attention, and repeat to me all that you hear." So the peasant heard the sermon, and the parson said, if any one had at home a sick child, a sick husband, a sick wife, a sick father, a sick mother, a sick sister, brother or any one else, and would make a pilgrimage to the Göckerli hill in Italy, where a peck of laurel-leaves costs a kreuzer, the sick child, sick husband, sick wife, sick father, sick mother, sick sister, brother, or whosoever else it might be, would be restored to health instantly, and whosoever wished to undertake the journey was to go to him after the service was over, and he would give him the sack for the laurel-leaves and the kreuzer. Then no one was more rejoiced than the peasant, and after the service was over, he went at once to the parson, who gave him the bag for the laurel-leaves and the kreuzer. After that he went home, and even at the house door he cried: "Hurrah! dear wife, it is now almost the same thing as if you were well! The parson has preached to-day that whosoever had at home a sick child, a sick husband, a sick wife, a sick father, a sick mother, a sick sister, brother or whoever it might be, and would make a pilgrimage to the Göckerli hill in Italy, where a peck of laurel-leaves costs a kreuzer, the sick child, sick husband, sick wife, sick father, sick mother, sick sister, brother, or whosoever else it was, would be cured immediately, and now I have already got the bag and the kreuzer from the parson, and will at once begin my journey so that you may get well the faster," and thereupon he went away. He was hardly gone however before the woman got up, and the parson was there immediately.

But now we will leave these two for a while, and follow the peasant, who walked on quickly without stopping, in order to get the sooner to the Göckerli hill, and on his way he met his gossip. His gossip was an egg-merchant, and was just coming from the market, where he had sold his eggs. "May you be blessed," said the gossip, "where are you off to so fast?"

"To all eternity, my friend," said the peasant, "my wife is ill, and I have been to-day to hear the parson's sermon, and he preached that if any one had in his house a sick child, a sick husband, a sick wife, a sick father, a sick mother, a sick sister, brother or any one else, and made a pilgrimage to the Göckerli hill in Italy, where a peck of laurel-leaves costs a kreuzer, the sick child, the sick husband, the sick wife, the sick father, the sick mother, the sick sister, brother, or whosoever else it was, would be cured immediately, and so I have got the bag for the laurel-leaves and the kreuzer from the parson, and now I am beginning my pilgrimage." "But listen, gossip," said the egg-merchant to the peasant, "are you, then, stupid enough to believe such a thing as that? Don't you know what it means? The parson wants to spend a whole day alone with your wife in peace, so he has given you this job to do to get you out of the way."

"My word!" said the peasant. "How I'd like to know if that's true!"

"Come, then," said the gossip, "I'll tell you what to do. Get into my egg-basket and I will carry you home, and then you will see for yourself." So that was settled, and the gossip put the peasant into his egg-basket, and carried him home.

When they got to the house, hurrah! everything was already very merry there! The woman had already had nearly everything killed that was in the farmyard, and had made pancakes, and the parson was there, and had brought his fiddle with him. The gossip knocked at the door, and the woman asked who was there. "It is I, gossip," said the egg-merchant, "give me shelter this night; I have not sold my eggs at the market, so now I have to carry them home again, and they are so heavy that I shall never be able to do it, for it is dark already."

"Indeed, my friend," said the woman, "you come at a very inconvenient time for me, but as you are here it can't be helped. Come in, and take a seat there on the bench by the stove." Then she placed the gossip and the basket which he carried on his back on the bench by the stove. The parson and the woman, however, were as merry as could be. At length the parson said: "Listen, my dear friend, you can sing beautifully; sing something to me." "Oh," said the woman, "I cannot sing now. In my young days indeed I could sing well enough, but that's all over now."

"Come," said the parson once more, "do sing some little song." On that the woman began and sang:

> "I've sent my husband away from me
> To the Göckerli hill in Italy."

Thereupon the parson sang,

> "I wish 'twas a year before he came back,
> I'd never ask him for the laurel-leaf sack.
>   Hallelujah."

Then the gossip who was in the background began to sing (but I ought to tell you the peasant was called Hildebrand), so the gossip sang:

"What are you doing, my Hildebrand dear,
There on the bench by the stove so near?
                    Hallelujah."

And then the peasant sang from his basket:

"All singing I ever shall hate from this day,
And here in this basket no longer I'll stay.
                    Hallelujah."

And he climbed out of the basket, and flogged the parson out of the house.

THE THREE LITTLE BIRDS

About a thousand or more years ago, there were in this country nothing but small kings, and one of them who lived on the Keuterberg was very fond of hunting. Once on a time when he was riding forth from his castle with his huntsmen, three girls were watching their cows upon the mountain, and when they saw the King with all his followers, the eldest girl pointed to him, and called to the two other girls: "Hullo! Hullo! If I do not get that one, I will have none." Then the second girl answered from the other side of the hill, and pointed to the one who was on the King's right hand: "Hullo! Hullo! If I do not get that one, I will have none." And then the youngest pointed to the one who was on the left hand, and cried: "Hullo! Hullo! If I do not get him, I will have no one." These, however, were the two ministers. The King heard all this, and when he had come back from the chase, he caused the three girls to be brought to him, and asked them what they had said yesterday on the mountain. This they would not tell him, so the King asked the eldest if she really would take him for her husband. Then she said: "Yes," and the two ministers married the two sisters, for they were all three fair and beautiful of face, especially the Queen, who had hair like flax.

But the two sisters had no children, and once when the King was obliged to go from home he invited them to come to the Queen in order to cheer her, for she was about to bear a child. She had a little boy who brought a bright red star into the world with him. Then the two sisters said to each other that they would throw the beautiful boy into the water. When they had thrown him in (I believe it was into the Weser), a little bird flew up into the air, which sang:

"To thy death art thou sped
Until God's word be said.
In the white lily bloom,
Brave boy, is thy tomb."

When the two heard that, they were frightened to death, and ran away in great haste. When the King came home they told him that the Queen had been delivered of a dog. Then the King said: "What God does, is well done!" But a fisherman who dwelt near the water fished the little boy out again while he was still alive, and as his wife had no children, they reared him. When a year had gone by, the King again went away, and the Queen had another little boy, whom the false sisters likewise took and threw into the water. Then up flew a little bird again and sang:

> "To thy death art thou sped
> Until God's word be said.
> In the white lily bloom,
> Brave boy, is thy tomb."

And when the King came back, they told him that the Queen had once more given birth to a dog, and he again said: "What God does, is well done." The fisherman, however, fished this one also out of the water, and reared him.

Then the King again journeyed forth, and the Queen had a little girl, whom also the false sisters threw into the water. Then again a little bird flew up on high and sang:

> "To thy death art thou sped
> Until God's word be said.
> In the white lily bloom,
> Bonny girl, is thy tomb."

And when the King came home they told him that the Queen had been delivered of a cat. Then the King grew angry, and ordered his wife to be cast into prison, and therein was she shut up for many long years.

When the children had grown up, the eldest once went out with some other boys to fish, but the other boys would not have him with them, and said: "Go your way, foundling."

Hereupon he was much troubled, and asked the old fisherman if that was true. The fisherman told him that once when he was fishing he had drawn him out of the water. So the boy said he would go forth and seek his father. The fisherman, however, entreated him to stay, but he would not let himself be hindered, and at last the fisherman consented. Then the boy went on his way and walked for many days, and at last he came to a great stretch of water by the side of which stood an old woman fishing. "Good day, mother," said the boy.

"Many thanks," said she.

"You will fish long enough before you catch anything."

"And you will seek long enough before you find your father. How will you get over the water?" said the woman.

"God knows."

Then the old woman took him up on her back and carried him through it, and he sought for a long time, but could not find his father.

When a year had gone by, the second boy set out to seek his brother. He came to the water, and all fared with him just as with his brother. And now there was no one at home but the daughter, and she mourned for her brothers so much that at last she also begged the fisherman to let her set forth, for she wished to go in search of her brothers. Then she likewise came to the great stretch of water, and she said to the old woman: "Good day, mother."

"Many thanks," replied the old woman.

"May God help you with your fishing," said the maiden. When the old woman heard that, she became quite friendly, and carried her over the water, gave her a wand, and said to her: "Go, my daughter, ever onwards by this road, and when you come to a great black dog, you must pass it silently and boldly, without either laughing or looking at it. Then you will come to a great high castle, on the threshold of which you must let the wand fall, and go straight through the castle, and out again on the other side. There you will see an old fountain out of which a large tree has grown, whereon hangs a bird in a cage which you must take down. Take likewise a glass of water out of the fountain, and with these two things go back by the same way. Pick up the wand again from the threshold and take it with you, and when you again pass by the dog, strike him in the face with it, but be sure that you hit him, and then just come back here to me." The maiden found everything exactly as the old woman had said, and on her way back she found her two brothers who had sought each other over half the world. They went together to the place where the black dog was lying on the road; she struck it in the face, and it turned into a handsome prince who went with them to the river. There the old woman was still standing. She rejoiced much to see them again, and carried them all over the water, and then she too went away, for now she was freed. The others, however, went to the old fisherman, and all were glad that they had found each other again, but they hung the bird on the wall.

But the second son could not settle at home, and took his crossbow and went a-hunting. When he was tired he took his flute, and made music. The King was hunting too, and heard that and went thither, and when he met the youth, he said: "Who has given you leave to hunt here?"

"Oh, no one."

"To whom do you belong, then?"

"I am the fisherman's son."

"But he has no children."

"If you will not believe, come with me."

That the King did, and questioned the fisherman, who told him everything, and the little bird on the wall began to sing:

> "The mother sits alone
> There in the prison small,
> O King of royal blood,
> These are thy children all.
> The sisters twain so false,
> They wrought the children woe,
> There in the waters deep
> Where the fishermen come and go."

Then they were all terrified, and the King took the bird, the fisherman and the three children back with him to the castle, and ordered the prison to be opened and brought his wife out again. She had grown quite ill and weak, so the daughter gave her some of the water of the fountain to drink, and she became strong and healthy. But the two false sisters were burnt, and the daughter married the prince.

THE WATER OF LIFE

There was once a King who had an illness, and no one believed that he would come out of it with his life. He had three sons who were much distressed about it, and went down into the palace-garden and wept. There they met an old man who inquired as to the cause of their grief. They told him that their father was so ill that he would most certainly die, for nothing seemed to cure him. Then the old man said: "I know of one more remedy, and that is the water of life; if he drinks of it he will become well again; but it is hard to find." The eldest said: "I will manage to find it," and went to the sick King, and begged to be allowed to go forth in search of the water of life, for that alone could save him. "No," said the King, "the danger of it is too great. I would rather die." But he begged so long that the King consented. The prince thought in his heart: "If I bring the water, then I shall be best beloved of my father, and shall inherit the kingdom." So he set out, and when he had ridden forth a little distance, a dwarf stood there in the road who called to him and said: "Whither away so fast?" "Silly shrimp," said the prince, very haughtily, "it is nothing to do with you," and rode on. But the little dwarf had grown angry, and had wished an evil wish. Soon after this the prince entered a ravine, and the further he rode the closer the mountains drew together, and at last the road became so narrow that he could not advance a step further; it was impossible either to turn his horse or to dismount from the saddle, and he was shut in there as if in prison. The sick King waited long for him, but he came not. Then the second son said: "Father, let me go forth to seek the water," and thought to himself: "If my brother is dead, then the kingdom will fall to me." At first the King would not allow him to go either, but at last he yielded, so the prince set out on the same road that his brother had taken, and he too met the dwarf, who stopped him to ask, whither he was going in such haste. "Little shrimp," said the prince, "that is nothing to do with you," and rode on without giving him another look. But the dwarf bewitched him, and he, like the other, rode into a ravine, and could neither go forwards nor backwards. So fare haughty people.

As the second son also remained away, the youngest begged to be allowed to go forth to fetch the water, and at last the King was obliged to let him go. When he met the dwarf and the latter asked him whither he was going in such haste, he stopped, gave him an explanation, and said: "I am seeking the water of life, for my father is sick unto death." "Do you know, then, where that is to be found?" "No," said the prince. "As you have borne yourself as is seemly, and not haughtily like your false brothers, I will give you the information and tell you how you may obtain the water of life. It springs from a fountain in the courtyard of an enchanted castle, but you will not be able to make your way to it, if I do not give you an iron wand and two small loaves of bread. Strike thrice with the wand on the iron door of the castle, and it will spring open: inside lie two lions with gaping jaws, but if you throw a loaf to each of them, they will be quieted. Then hasten to fetch some of the water of life before the clock strikes twelve, else the door will shut again, and you will be imprisoned." The prince thanked him, took the wand and the bread, and set out on his way. When he arrived, everything was as the dwarf had said. The door sprang open at the third stroke of the wand, and when he had appeased the lions with the bread, he entered the castle, and came to a large and splendid hall, wherein sat some enchanted princes whose rings he drew off their fingers. A sword and a loaf of bread were lying there, which he carried away. After this, he entered a chamber, in which was a beautiful maiden who rejoiced when she saw him, kissed him, and told him that he had set her free, and should have the whole of her kingdom, and that if he would return in a year their wedding should be celebrated; likewise she told him where the spring of the water of life was, and that he was to hasten and draw some of it before the clock struck twelve. Then he went onwards, and at last entered a room where there was a beautiful newly-made bed, and as he was very weary, he felt inclined to rest a little. So he lay down and fell asleep. When he awoke, it was striking a quarter to twelve. He sprang up in a fright, ran to the spring, drew some water in a cup which stood near, and hastened away. But just as he was passing through the iron door, the clock struck twelve, and the door fell to with such violence that it carried away a piece of his heel.

He, however, rejoicing at having obtained the water of life, went homewards, and again passed the dwarf. When the latter saw the sword and the loaf, he said: "With these you have won great wealth; with the sword you can slay whole armies, and the bread will never come to an end." But the prince would not go home to his father without his brothers, and said: "Dear dwarf, can you not tell me where my two brothers are? They went out before I did in search of the water of life, and have not returned." "They are imprisoned between two mountains," said the dwarf. "I have condemned them to stay there, because they were so haughty." Then the prince begged until the dwarf

released them, but he warned him and said: "Beware of them, for they have bad hearts." When his brothers came, he rejoiced, and told them how things had gone with him, that he had found the water of life, and had brought a cupful away with him, and had rescued a beautiful princess, who was willing to wait a year for him, and then their wedding was to be celebrated, and he would obtain a great kingdom. After that they rode on together, and chanced upon a land where war and famine reigned, and the King already thought he must perish, for the scarcity was so great. Then the prince went to him and gave him the loaf, wherewith he fed and satisfied the whole of his kingdom, and then the prince gave him the sword also, wherewith he slew the hosts of his enemies, and could now live in rest and peace. The prince then took back his loaf and his sword, and the three brothers rode on. But after this they entered two more countries where war and famine reigned, and each time the prince gave his loaf and his sword to the Kings, and had now delivered three kingdoms, and after that they went on board a ship and sailed over the sea. During the passage, the two eldest conversed apart and said: "The youngest has found the water of life and not we, for that our father will give him the kingdom,—the kingdom which belongs to us, and he will rob us of all our fortune." They then began to seek revenge, and plotted with each other to destroy him. They waited until they found him fast asleep, then they poured the water of life out of the cup, and took it for themselves, but into the cup they poured salt sea-water.

Now therefore, when they arrived home, the youngest took his cup to the sick King in order that he might drink out of it, and be cured. But scarcely had he drunk a very little of the salt sea-water than he became still worse than before. And as he was lamenting over this, the two eldest brothers came, and accused the youngest of having intended to poison him, and said that they had brought him the true water of life, and handed it to him. He had scarcely tasted it, when he felt his sickness departing, and became strong and healthy as in the days of his youth. After that they both went to the youngest, mocked him, and said: "You certainly found the water of life, but you have had the pain, and we the gain; you should have been cleverer, and should have kept your eyes open. We took it from you whilst you were asleep at sea, and when a year is over, one of us will go and fetch the beautiful princess.

But beware that you do not disclose aught of this to our father; indeed he does not trust you, and if you say a single word, you shall lose your life into the bargain, but if you keep silent, you shall have it as a gift."

The old King was angry with his youngest son, and thought he had plotted against his life. So he summoned the court together, and had sentence pronounced upon his son, that he should be secretly shot. And once when the prince was riding forth to the chase, suspecting no evil, the King's huntsman was told to go with him, and when they were quite alone in the forest, the huntsman looked so sorrowful that the prince said to him: "Dear huntsman, what ails you?" The huntsman said: "I cannot tell you, and yet I ought." Then the prince said: "Say openly what it is, I will pardon you." "Alas!" said the huntsman, "I am to shoot you dead, the King has ordered me to do it." Then the prince was shocked, and said: "Dear huntsman, let me live; there, I give you my royal garments; give me your common ones in their stead." The huntsman said: "I will willingly do that, indeed I would not have been able to shoot you." Then they exchanged clothes, and the huntsman returned home, while the prince went further into the forest. After a time three waggons of gold and precious stones came to the King for his youngest son, which were sent by the three Kings who had slain their enemies with the prince's sword, and maintained their people with his bread, and who wished to show their gratitude for it. The old King then thought: "Can my son have been innocent?" and said to his people: "Would that he were still alive, how it grieves me that I have suffered him to be killed!" "He still lives," said the huntsman, "I could not find it in my heart to carry out your command," and told the King how it had happened. Then a stone fell from the King's heart, and he had it proclaimed in every country that his son might return and be taken into favour again.

The princess, however, had a road made up to her palace which was quite bright and golden, and told her people that whosoever came riding straight along it to her, would be the right one and was to be admitted, and whoever rode by the side of it, was not the right one, and was not to be admitted. As the time was now close at hand, the eldest thought he would hasten to go to the King's daughter, and give himself out as her rescuer, and thus win her for his bride, and the kingdom to boot. Therefore he rode forth, and when he arrived in front of the palace, and saw the splendid golden road, he thought: "It would be a sin and a shame if I were to ride over that," and turned aside, and rode on the right side of it. But when he came to the door, the servants told him that he was not the right one, and was to go away again. Soon after this the second prince set out, and when he came to the golden road, and his horse had put one foot on it, he thought: "It would be a sin and a shame, a piece might be trodden off," and he turned aside and rode on the left side of it, and when he reached the door, the attendants told him he was not the right one, and he was to go away again. When at last the year had entirely expired, the third son likewise wished to ride out of the forest to his beloved, and with her forget his sorrows. So he set out and thought of her so incessantly, and wished to be with her so much, that he never noticed the golden road at all. So his horse rode onwards up the middle of it, and when he came to the door, it was opened and the princess received him with joy, and said he was her saviour, and lord of the kingdom, and their wedding was celebrated with great rejoicing. When it was over she told him that his father invited him to come to him, and had forgiven him. So he rode thither, and told him everything; how his brothers had betrayed him, and how he had nevertheless kept silence. The old King wished to punish them, but they had put to sea, and never came back as long as they lived.

DOCTOR KNOWALL

There was once upon a time a poor peasant called Crabb, who drove with two oxen a load of wood to the town, and sold it to a doctor for two talers. When the money was being counted out to him, it so happened that the doctor was sitting at table, and when the peasant saw how well he ate and drank, his heart desired what he saw, and he would willingly have been a doctor too. So he remained standing a while, and at length inquired if he too could not be a doctor. "Oh, yes," said the doctor, "that is soon managed." "What must I do?" asked the peasant. "In the first place buy yourself an A B C book of the kind which has a cock on the frontispiece; in the second, turn your cart and your two oxen into money, and get yourself some clothes, and whatsoever else pertains to medicine; thirdly, have a sign painted for yourself with the words: 'I am Doctor Knowall', and have that nailed up above your house-door." The peasant did everything that he had been told to do. When he had doctored people awhile, but not long, a rich and great lord had some money stolen. Then he was told about Doctor Knowall who lived in such and such a village, and must know what had become of the money. So the lord had the horses harnessed to his carriage, drove out to the village, and asked Crabb if he were Doctor Knowall,

Yes, he was, he said. Then he was to go with him and bring back the stolen money. "Oh, yes, but Grete, my wife, must go too." The lord was willing, and let both of them have a seat in the carriage, and they all drove away together. When they came to the nobleman's castle, the table was spread, and Crabb was told to sit down and eat. "Yes, but my wife, Grete, too," said he, and he seated himself with her at the table. And when the first servant came with a dish of delicate fare, the peasant nudged his wife, and said: "Grete, that was the first," meaning that was the servant who brought the first dish. The servant, however, thought he intended by that to say: "That is the first thief," and as he actually was so, he was terrified, and said to his comrade outside: "The doctor knows all: we shall fare ill, he said I was the first." The second did not want to go in at all, but was forced. So when he went in with his dish, the peasant nudged his wife, and said: "Grete, that is the second." This servant was equally alarmed, and he got out as fast as he could. The third fared no better, for the peasant again said: "Grete, that is the third." The fourth had to carry in a dish that was covered, and the lord told the doctor that he was to show his skill, and guess what was beneath the cover. Actually, there were crabs. The doctor looked at the dish, had no idea what to say, and cried: "Ah, poor Crabb." When the lord heard that, he cried: "There! he knows it; he must also know who has the money!"

On this the servants looked terribly uneasy, and made a sign to the doctor that they wished him to step outside for a moment. When therefore he went out, all four of them confessed to him that they had stolen the money, and said that they would willingly restore it and give him a heavy sum into the bargain, if he would not denounce them, for if he did they would be hanged. They led him to the spot where the money was concealed. With this the doctor was satisfied, and returned to the hall, sat down to the table, and said: "My lord, now will I search in my book where the gold is hidden." The fifth servant, however, crept into the stove to hear if the doctor knew still more. But the doctor sat still and opened his A B C book, turned the pages backwards and forwards, and looked for the cock. As he could not find it immediately he said: "I know you are there, so you had better come out!" Then the fellow in the stove thought that the doctor meant him, and full of terror, sprang out, crying: "That man knows everything!" Then Doctor Knowall showed the lord where the money was, but did not say who had stolen it, and received from both sides much money in reward, and became a renowned man.

THE SPIRIT IN THE BOTTLE

There was once a poor woodcutter who toiled from early morning till late at night. When at last he had laid by some money he said to his boy: "You are my only child, I will spend the money which I have earned with the sweat of my brow on your education; if you learn some honest trade you can support me in my old age, when my limbs have grown stiff and I am obliged to stay at home." Then the boy went to a High School and learned diligently so that his masters praised him, and he remained there a long time. When he had worked through two classes, but was still not yet perfect in everything, the little pittance which the father had earned was all spent, and the boy was obliged to return home to him. "Ah," said the father, sorrowfully, "I can give you no more, and in these hard times I cannot earn a farthing more than will suffice for our daily bread." "Dear father," answered the son, "don't trouble yourself about it, if it is God's will, it will turn to my advantage. I shall soon accustom myself to it." When the father wanted to go into the forest to earn money by helping to chop and stack wood, the son said: "I will go with you and help you." "Nay, my son," said the father, "that would be hard for you; you are not accustomed to rough work, and will not be able to bear it. Besides, I have only one axe and no money left wherewith to buy another." "Just go to the neighbour," answered the son, "he will lend you his axe until I have earned one for myself."

The father then borrowed an axe of the neighbour, and next morning at break of day they went out into the forest together. The son helped his father and was quite merry and brisk about it. But when the sun was right over their heads, the father said: "We will rest, and have our dinner, and then we shall work twice as well." The son took his bread in his hands, and said: "Just you rest, father, I am not tired; I will walk up and down a little in the forest, and look for birds' nests." "Oh, you fool," said the father, "why should you want to run about there? Afterwards you will be tired, and no longer able to raise your arm; stay here, and sit down beside me."

The son, however, went into the forest, ate his bread, was very merry and peered in among the green branches to see if he could discover a bird's nest anywhere. So he walked to and fro until at last he came to a great dangerous-looking oak, which certainly was already many hundred years old, and which five men could not have spanned. He stood still and looked at it, and thought: "Many a bird must have built its nest in that." Then all at once it seemed to him that he heard a voice. He listened and became aware that someone was crying in a very smothered voice: "Let me out, let me out!" He looked around, but could discover nothing; then he fancied that the voice came out of the ground. So he cried: "Where are you?" The voice answered: "I am down here amongst the roots of the oak-tree. Let me out! Let me out!"

The schoolboy began to loosen the earth under the tree, and search among the roots, until at last he found a glass bottle in a little hollow. He lifted it up and held it against the light, and then saw a creature shaped like a frog, springing up and down in it. "Let me out! Let me out!" it cried anew, and the boy, thinking no evil, drew the cork out of the bottle. Immediately a spirit ascended from it, and began to grow, and grew so fast that in a very few moments he stood before the boy, a terrible fellow as big as half the tree. "Do you know," he

cried in an awful voice, "what your reward is for having let me out?" "No," replied the boy fearlessly, "how should I know that?" "Then I will tell you," cried the spirit; "I must strangle you for it." "You should have told me that sooner," said the boy, "for I should then have left you shut up, but my head shall stand fast for all you can do; more persons than one must be consulted about that." "More persons here, more persons there," said the spirit. "You shall have the reward you have earned. Do you think that I was shut up there for such a long time as a favour? No, it was a punishment for me. I am the mighty Mercurius. Whoso releases me, him must I strangle." "Slowly," answered the boy, "not so fast. I must first know that you really were shut up in that little bottle, and that you are the right spirit. If, indeed, you can get in again, I will believe, and then you may do as you will with me." The spirit said haughtily: "That is a very trifling feat," drew himself together, and made himself as small and slender as he had been at first, so that he crept through the same opening, and right through the neck of the bottle in again. Scarcely was he within than the boy thrust the cork he had drawn back into the bottle, and threw it among the roots of the oak into its old place, and the spirit was deceived.

And now the schoolboy was about to return to his father, but the spirit cried very piteously: "Ah, do let me out! ah, do let me out!" "No," answered the boy, "not a second time! He who has once tried to take my life shall not be set free by me, now that I have caught him again." "If you will set me free," said the spirit, "I will give you so much that you will have plenty all the days of your life." "No," answered the boy, "you would cheat me as you did the first time." "You are spurning your own good luck." said the spirit; "I will do you no harm, but will reward you richly." The boy thought: "I will venture it, perhaps he will keep his word, and anyhow he shall not get the better of me." Then he took out the cork, and the spirit rose up from the bottle as he had done before, stretched himself out and became as big as a giant. "Now you shall have your reward," said he, and handed the boy a little rag just like sticking-plaster, and said: "If you spread one end of this over a wound it will heal, and if you rub steel or iron with the other end it will be changed into silver." "I must just try that," said the boy, and went to a tree, tore off the bark with his axe, and rubbed it with one end of the plaster. It immediately closed together and was healed. "Now, it is all right," he said to the spirit, "and we can part." The spirit thanked him for his release, and the boy thanked the spirit for his present, and went back to his father.

"Where have you been racing about?" said the father; "why have you forgotten your work? I always said that you would never come to anything." "Be easy, father, I will make it up." "Make it up indeed," said the father angrily, "that's no use." "Take care, father, I will soon hew that tree there, so that it will split." Then he took his plaster, rubbed the axe with it, and dealt a mighty blow, but as the iron had changed into silver, the edge bent: "Hi, father, just look what a bad axe you've given me, it has become quite crooked." The father was shocked and said: "Ah, what have you done? now I shall have to pay for that, and have not the wherewithal, and that is all the good I have got by your work." "Don't get angry," said the son, "I will soon pay for the axe." "Oh, you blockhead," cried the father, "wherewith will you pay for it? You have nothing but what I give you. These are students' tricks that are sticking in your head, you have no idea of woodcutting."

After a while the boy said: "Father, I can really work no more, we had better take a holiday." "Eh, what!" answered he. "Do you think I will sit with my hands lying in my lap like you? I must go on working, but you may take yourself off home." "Father, I am here in this wood for the first time, I don't know my way alone. Do go with me." As his anger had now abated, the father at last let himself be persuaded and went home with him. Then he said to the son: "Go and sell your damaged axe, and see what you can get for it, and I must earn the difference, in order to pay the neighbour." The son took the axe, and carried it into town to a goldsmith, who tested it, laid it in the scales, and said: "It is worth four hundred talers, I have not so much as that by me." The son said: "Give me what you have, I will lend you the rest." The goldsmith gave him three hundred talers, and remained a hundred in his debt. The son thereupon went home and said: "Father, I have got the money, go and ask the neighbour what he wants for the axe." "I know that already," answered the old man, "one taler, six groschen." "Then give him two talers, twelve groschen, that is double and enough; see, I have money in plenty," and he gave the father a hundred talers, and said: "You shall never know want, live as comfortably as you like." "Good heavens!" said the father, "how have you come by these riches?" The boy then told how all had come to pass, and how he, trusting in his luck, had made such a packet. But with the money that was left, he went back to the High School and went on learning more, and as he could heal all wounds with his plaster, he became the most famous doctor in the whole world.

THE DEVIL'S SOOTY BROTHER

A discharged soldier had nothing to live on, and did not know how to make his way. So he went out into the forest, and when he had walked for a short time, he met a little man who turned out to be the Devil. The little man said to him: "What ails you, you seem so very sorrowful?" Then the soldier said: "I am hungry, but have no money." The Devil said: "If you will hire yourself to me, and be my serving-man, you shall have enough for all your life. You shall serve me for seven years,

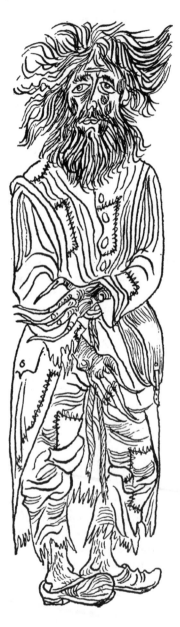

and after that you shall again be free. But one thing I must tell you, and that is, you must not wash, comb, or trim yourself, or cut your hair or nails, or wipe the water from your eyes." The soldier said: "All right, if there is no help for it," and went off with the little man, who straightway led him down into hell. Then he told him what he had to do: he was to poke the fire under the kettles wherein the hell-broth was stewing, keep the house clean, drive all the sweepings behind the doors, and see that everything was in order, but if he once peeped into the kettles, it would go ill with him. The soldier said: "Good, I will take care." And then the old Devil went out again on his wanderings, and the soldier entered upon his new duties, made the fire, and swept the dirt well behind the doors, just as he had been bidden. When the old Devil came back again, he looked to see if all had been done, appeared satisfied, and went forth a second time. The soldier now took a good look on every side; the kettles were standing all round hell with a mighty fire below them, and inside they were boiling and sputtering. He would have given anything to look inside them, if the Devil had not so particularly forbidden him: at last, he could no longer restrain himself, slightly raised the lid of the first kettle, and peeped in, and there he saw his former corporal sitting. "Aha, old bird!" said he. "Do I meet you here? You once had me in your power, now I have you," and he quickly let the lid fall, poked the fire, and added a fresh log. After that, he went to the second kettle, raised its lid also a little, and peeped in and there sat his former ensign. "Aha, old bird, so I find you here! you once had me in your power, now I have you." He closed the lid again, and fetched yet another log to make it really hot. Then he wanted to see who might be sitting up in the third kettle—and who should it be but his general. "Aha, old bird, do I meet you here? Once you had me in your power, now I have you," and he fetched the bellows and made hell-fire blaze right under him. So he did his work seven years in hell, did not wash, comb, or trim himself, or cut his hair or nails, or wash the water out of his eyes, and the seven years seemed so short to him that he thought he had only been half a year. Now when the time had fully gone by, the Devil came and said: "Well Hans, what have you done?" "I poked the fire under the kettles, and I have swept all the dirt well behind the doors."

"But you have peeped into the kettles as well; it is lucky for you that you added fresh logs to them, or else your life would have been forfeited; now that your time is up, will you go home again?" "Yes," said the soldier, "I should very much like to see what my father is doing at home." The Devil said: "In order that you may receive the wages you have earned, go and fill your knapsack full of the sweepings, and take it home with you. You must also go unwashed and uncombed, with long hair on your head and beard, and with uncut nails and dim eyes, and when you are asked whence you come, you must say: 'From hell', and when you are asked who you are, you are to say: 'The Devil's sooty brother, and my King as well'." The soldier held his peace, and did as the Devil bade him, but he was not at all satisfied with his wages.

Then as soon as he was up in the forest again, he took his knapsack from his back, to empty it, but on opening it, the sweepings had become pure gold. "I should never have expected that," said he, and was well pleased, and entered the town. The landlord was standing in front of the inn, and when he saw the soldier approaching, he was terrified, because Hans looked such a horrible sight, worse than a

scare-crow. He called to him and asked: "Whence do you come?"
"From hell." "Who are you?" "The Devil's sooty brother, and my King
as well." Then the host would not let him enter, but when Hans
showed him the gold, he came and unlatched the door himself. Hans
then ordered the best room and attendance, ate, and drank his fill, but
neither washed nor combed himself as the Devil had bidden him, and
at last lay down to sleep. But the knapsack full of gold remained before
the eyes of the landlord, and left him no peace, and during the night he
crept in and stole it away. Next morning, however, when Hans got up
and wanted to pay the landlord and travel further, behold, his knapsack
was gone! But he soon composed himself and thought: "You have been
unfortunate from no fault of your own," and straightway went back
again to hell, complained of his misfortune to the old Devil, and
begged for his help. The Devil said: "Seat yourself, I will wash, comb,
and trim you, cut your hair and nails, and wash your eyes for you,"
and when he had done with him, he gave him the knapsack back again
full of sweepings, and said: "Go and tell the landlord that he must
return you your money, or else I will come and fetch him, and he shall
poke the fire in your place." Hans went up and said to the landlord:
"You have stolen my money; if you do not return it, you shall go down
to hell in my place, and will look as horrible as I." Then the landlord
gave him the money, and more besides, only begging him to keep it
secret. And Hans was now a rich man.

He set out on his way home to his father, bought himself a shabby
smock to wear, and strolled about making music, for he had learned to
do that while he was with the Devil in hell. There was, however, an old
King in that country, before whom he had to play, and the King was so
delighted with his playing, that he promised him his eldest daughter in

marriage. But when she heard that she was to be married to a common fellow in a smock, she said: "Rather than do that, I would go into the deepest water." Then the King gave him the youngest, who was quite willing to do it to please her father; and thus the Devil's sooty brother got the King's daughter, and when the aged King died, the whole kingdom likewise.

BEARSKIN

There was once a young fellow who enlisted as a soldier, conducted himself bravely, and was always the foremost when it rained bullets. So long as the war lasted, all went well, but when peace was made, he received his dismissal, and the captain said he might go where he liked. His parents were dead, and he had no longer a home, so he went to his brothers and begged them to take him in, and keep him until war broke out again. The brothers, however, were hard-hearted and said: "What can we do with you? You are of no use to us; go and make a living for yourself." The soldier had nothing left but his gun; so he took that on his shoulder, and went forth into the world. He came to a wide heath, on which nothing was to be seen but a circle of trees; under these he sat sorrowfully down, and began to think over his fate. "I have no money," thought he, "I have learnt no trade but that of fighting, and now that they have made peace they don't want me any longer; so I see before-hand that I shall have to starve." All at once he heard a rustling, and when he looked round, a strange man stood before him, who wore a green coat and looked right stately, but had a hideous cloven foot. "I know already what you are in need of," said the man; "gold and possessions shall you have, as much as you can make away with, do what you will, but first I must know if you are fearless, that I may not bestow my money in vain." "A soldier and fear—how can those two things go together?" he answered; "you can put me to the proof." "Very well, then," answered the man, "look behind you." The soldier turned round, and saw a large bear, which came growling towards him. "Oho!" cried the soldier, "I will tickle your nose for you, so that you shall soon lose your fancy for growling," and he aimed at the bear and shot it through the muzzle; it fell down and never stirred again. "I see quite well," said the stranger, "that you are not wanting in courage, but there is still another condition which you will have to fulfil." "If it does not endanger my salvation," replied the soldier, who knew very well who was standing by him. "If it does, I'll have nothing to do with it." "You will look to that for yourself," answered Green-coat; "you shall for the next seven years neither wash yourself, nor comb your beard, nor your hair, nor cut your nails, nor once say the Lord's prayer. I will give you a coat and a cloak, which during this time you must wear. If you die during these seven years, you are mine; if you remain alive, you are free, and rich to boot, for all the rest of your life." The soldier thought of the great extremity in which he now found himself, and as he so often had gone to meet death, he resolved to risk it now also, and agreed to the terms. The Devil took off his green coat, and gave it to the soldier, and said: "If you have this coat on your back and put your hand into the pocket, you will always find it full of money." Then he pulled the skin off the bear and said: "This shall be your cloak, and your bed also, for thereon shall you sleep, and in no other bed shall you lie, and because of this apparel shall you be called Bearskin." Whereupon the Devil vanished.

The soldier put the coat on, felt at once in the pocket, and found that the thing was really true. Then he put on the bearskin and went forth into the world, and enjoyed himself, refraining from nothing that did him good and his money harm. During the first year his appearance was passable, but during the second he began to look like a monster. His hair covered nearly the whole of his face, his beard was like a piece of coarse felt, his fingers had claws, and his face was so covered with dirt that if cress had been sown on it, it would have come up. Whosoever saw him, ran away, but as he everywhere gave the poor money to pray that he might not die during the seven years, and as he paid well for everything he still always found shelter. In the fourth year, he entered an inn where the landlord would not receive him, and would not even let him have a place in the stable, because he was afraid the horses would be scared. But as Bearskin thrust his hand into his pocket and pulled out a handful of ducats, the host let himself be persuaded and gave him a room in an outhouse. Bearskin, however, was obliged to promise not to let himself be seen lest the inn should get a bad name.

As Bearskin was sitting alone in the evening, and wishing from the bottom of his heart that the seven years were over, he heard a loud lamenting in a neighbouring room. He had a compassionate heart, so he opened the door, and saw an old man weeping bitterly, and wringing his hands. Bearskin went nearer, but the man sprang to his feet and tried to escape from him. At last when the man perceived that Bearskin's voice was human he let himself be prevailed upon, and by kind words Bearskin succeeded so far that the old man revealed the cause of his grief. His property had dwindled away by degrees, he and his daughters would have to starve, and he was so poor that he could not pay the innkeeper, and was to be put in prison. "If that is your only trouble," said Bearskin, "I have plenty of money." He caused the innkeeper to be brought thither, paid him and even put a purse full of gold into the poor old man's pocket.

When the old man saw himself set free from all his troubles he did not know how to show his gratitude. "Come with me," said he to Bearskin; "my daughters are all miracles of beauty, choose one of them for yourself as a wife. When she hears what you have done for me, she will not refuse you. You do in truth look a little strange, but she will soon put you to rights again." This pleased Bearskin well, and he went.

When the eldest saw him she was so terribly alarmed at his face that she screamed and ran away. The second stood still and looked at him from head to foot, but then she said: "How can I accept a husband who no longer has a human form? The shaven bear that once was here and passed itself off for a man pleased me far better, for at any rate it wore a hussar's dress and white gloves. If he were only ugly, I might get used to that." The youngest, however, said: "Dear father, that must be a good man to have helped you out of your trouble, so if you have promised him a bride for doing it, your promise must be kept." It was a pity that Bearskin's face was covered with dirt and with hair, for if not they might have seen how delighted he was when he heard these words. He took a ring from his finger, broke it in two, and gave her one half, the other he kept for himself. Then he wrote his name on her half, and hers on his, and begged her to keep her piece carefully. Then he took his leave and said: "I must still wander about for three years, and if I do not return then, you are free, for I shall be dead. But pray to God to preserve my life."

The poor betrothed bride dressed herself entirely in black, and when she thought of her future bridegroom, tears came into her eyes. Nothing but contempt and mockery fell to her lot from her sisters. "Take care," said the eldest, "if you give him your hand, he will strike his claws into it." "Beware!" said the second. "Bears like sweet things, and if he takes a fancy to you, he will eat you up." "You must always do as he likes," began the elder again, "or else he will growl." And the second continued: "But the wedding will be a merry one, for bears dance well." The bride was silent, and did not let them vex her. Bearskin, however, travelled about the world from one place to another, did good where he was able, and gave generously to the poor that they might pray for him.

At length, as the last day of the seven years dawned, he went once more out on to the heath, and seated himself beneath the circle of trees. It was not long before the wind whistled, and the Devil stood before him and looked angrily at him; then he threw Bearskin his old coat, and asked for his own green one back. "We have not got so far as that yet," answered Bearskin, "you must first make me clean." Whether the Devil liked it or not, he was forced to fetch water, and wash Bearskin, comb his hair, and cut his nails. After this, he looked like a brave soldier, and was much handsomer than he had ever been before.

When the Devil had gone away, Bearskin was quite light-hearted. He went into the town, put on a magnificent velvet coat, seated himself in a carriage drawn by four white horses, and drove to his bride's house. No one recognized him. The father took him for a distinguished general, and led him into the room where his daughters were sitting. He was forced to place himself between the two eldest, who helped him to wine, gave him the best pieces of meat, and thought that in all the world they had never seen a handsomer man. The bride, however, sat opposite to him in her black dress, and never raised her eyes, nor spoke a word. When at length he asked the father if he would give him one of his daughters to wife, the two eldest jumped up, ran into their bedrooms to put on splendid dresses, for each of them fancied she was the chosen one. The stranger, as soon as he was alone with his bride, brought out his half of the ring, and threw it in a glass of wine which he handed across the table to her. She took the wine, but when she had drunk it, and found the half ring lying at the bottom, her heart began to beat. She got the other half, which she wore on a ribbon round her neck, joined them, and saw that the two pieces fitted exactly together. Then said he: "I am your betrothed bridegroom, whom you saw as Bearskin, but through God's grace I have again received my human form, and have once more become clean." He went up to her, embraced her, and gave her a kiss. In the meantime the two sisters came back in full dress, and when they saw that the handsome man had fallen to the share of the youngest, and heard that he was Bearskin, they ran out full of anger and rage. One of them drowned herself in the well, the other hanged herself on a tree. In the evening, some one knocked at the door, and when the bridegroom opened it, it was the devil in his green coat, who said: "You see, I have now got two souls in the place of your one!"

THE WILLOW-WREN AND THE BEAR

Once in summer-time the bear and the wolf were walking in the forest, and the bear heard a bird singing so beautifully that he said: "Brother wolf, what bird is it that sings so well?" "That is the King of birds," said the wolf, "before whom we must bow down." In reality the bird was the willow-wren. "If that's the case," said the bear, "I should very much like to see his royal palace; come, take me thither." "That is not done quite as you seem to think," said the wolf; "you must wait until the Queen comes." Soon afterwards, the Queen arrived with some food in her beak, and the lord King came too, and they began to feed their young ones. The bear would have liked to go at once, but the wolf held him back by the sleeve, and said: "No, you must wait until the lord and lady Queen have gone away again." So they took stock of the hole where the nest lay, and trotted away. The bear, however, could not rest until he had seen the royal palace, and when a short time had passed, went to it again. The King and Queen had just flown out, so he peeped in and saw five or six young ones lying there. "Is that the royal palace?" cried the bear; "it is a wretched palace, and you are not King's children, you are disreputable children!" When the young wrens heard that, they were frightfully angry, and screamed: "No, that we are not! Our parents are honest people! Bear, you will have to pay for that!"

The bear and the wolf grew uneasy, and turned back and went into their holes. The young willow-wrens, however, continued to cry and scream, and when their parents again brought food they said: "We will not so much as touch one fly's leg, no, not if we were dying of hunger, until you have settled whether we are respectable children or not; the bear has been here and has insulted us!" Then the old King said: "Be easy, he shall be punished," and he at once flew with the Queen to the bear's cave, and called in: "Old Growler, why have you insulted my children? You shall suffer for it—we will punish you by a bloody war." Thus war was announced to the Bear, and all four-footed animals were

summoned to take part in it, oxen, asses, cows, deer, and every other animal the earth contained. And the willow-wren summoned everything which flew in the air, not only birds, large and small, but midges, and hornets, bees and flies had to come.

When the time came for the war to begin, the willow-wren sent out spies to discover who was the enemy's commander-in-chief. The gnat, who was the most crafty, flew into the forest where the enemy was assembled, and hid herself beneath a leaf of the tree where the password was to be announced. There stood the bear, and he called the fox before him and said: "Fox, you are the most cunning of all animals, you shall be general and lead us." "Good," said the fox, "but what signal shall we agree upon?" No one knew that, so the fox said: "I have a fine long bushy tail, which almost looks like a plume of red feathers. When I lift my tail up quite high, all is going well, and you must charge; but if I let it hang down, run away as fast as you can." When the gnat had heard that, she flew away again, and revealed everything, down to the minutest detail, to the willow-wren. When day broke, and the battle was to begin, all the four-footed animals came running up with such a noise that the earth trembled. The willow-wren with his army also came flying through the air with such a humming, and whirring, and swarming that every one was uneasy and afraid, and on both sides they advanced against each other. But the willow-wren sent down the hornet, with orders to settle beneath the fox's tail, and sting with all his might. When the fox felt the first sting, he started so that he lifted one leg, from pain, but he bore it, and still kept his tail high in the air; at the second sting, he was forced to put it down for a moment; at the third, he could hold out no longer, screamed, and put his tail between his legs. When the animals saw that, they thought all was lost, and began to flee, each into his hole, and the birds had won the battle.

Then the King and Queen flew home to their children and cried: "Children, rejoice, eat and drink to your heart's content, we have won the battle!" But the young wrens said: "We will not eat yet, the bear must come to the nest, and beg for pardon and say that we are honourable children, before we will do that." Then the willow-wren flew to the bear's hole and cried: "Growler, you are to come to the nest to my children, and beg their pardon, or else every rib of your body shall be broken." So the bear crept thither in the greatest fear, and begged their pardon. And now at last the young wrens were satisfied, and sat down together and ate and drank, and made merry till quite late into the night.

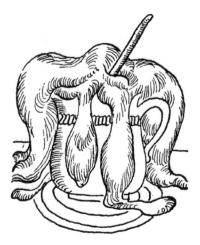

SWEET PORRIDGE

There was a poor but good little girl who lived alone with her mother, and they no longer had anything to eat. So the child went into the forest, and there an aged woman met her who was aware of her sorrow, and presented her with a little pot, which when she said: "Cook, little pot, cook," would cook good, sweet porridge, and when she said: "Stop, little pot," it ceased to cook. The girl took the pot home to her mother, and now they were freed from their poverty and hunger, and ate sweet porridge as often as they chose. Once on a time when the girl had gone out, her mother said: "Cook, little pot, cook." And it did cook and she ate till she was satisfied, and then she wanted the pot to stop cooking, but did not know the word. So it went on cooking and the porridge rose over the edge, and still it cooked on until the kitchen and whole house were full, and then the next house, and then the whole street, just as if it wanted to satisfy the hunger of the whole world, and there was the greatest distress, but no one knew how to stop it. At last when only one single house remained, the child came home and just said: "Stop, little pot," and it stopped and gave up cooking, and whosoever wished to return to the town had to eat his way back.

WISE FOLKS

One day a peasant took his good hazel-stick out of the corner and said to his wife: "Trina, I am going across country, and shall not return for three days. If during that time the cattle-dealer should happen to call and want to buy our three cows, you may strike a bargain at once, but not unless you can get two hundred talers for them; nothing less, do you hear?" "For heaven's sake, just go in peace," answered the woman, "I will manage that." "You, indeed," said the man. "You once fell on your head when you were a little child, and that affects you even now; but let me tell you this, if you do anything foolish, I will make your back black and blue, and not with paint, I assure you, but with the stick which I have in my hand, and the colouring shall last a whole year, you may rely on that." And having said that, the man went on his way.

Next morning the cattle-dealer came, and the woman had no need to say many words to him. When he had seen the cows and heard the price, he said: "I am quite willing to give that. Honestly speaking, they are worth it. I will take the beasts away with me at once." He unfastened their chains and drove them out of the byre, but just as he was going out of the yard-door, the woman clutched him by the sleeve and said: "You must give me the two hundred talers now, or I cannot let the cows go." "True," answered the man, "but I have forgotten to buckle on my money-belt. Have no fear, however, you shall have security for my paying. I will take two cows with me and leave one, and then you will have a good pledge." The woman saw the force of this, and let the man go away with the cows, and thought to herself: "How pleased Hans will be when he finds how cleverly I have managed it!" The peasant came home on the third day as he had said he would, and at

once inquired if the cows were sold. "Yes, indeed, dear Hans," answered the woman, "and as you said, for two hundred talers. They are scarcely worth so much, but the man took them without making any objection." "Where is the money?" asked the peasant. "Oh, I have not got the money," replied the woman; "he had happened to forget his money-belt, but he will soon bring it, and he left good security behind him." "What kind of security?" asked the man. "One of the three cows, which he shall not have until he has paid for the other two. I have managed very cunningly, for I have kept the smallest, which eats the least." The man was enraged and lifted up his stick, and was just going to give her the beating he had promised her, when suddenly he let the stick fail and said: "You are the stupidest goose that ever waddled on God's earth, but I am sorry for you. I will go out into the highways and wait for three days to see if I find anyone who is still stupider than you. If I succeed in doing so, you shall go scot-free, but if I do not find him, you shall receive your well-deserved reward without any discount."

He went out into the great highways, sat down on a stone, and waited for what would happen. Then he saw a peasant's waggon coming towards him, and a woman was standing upright in the middle of it, instead of sitting on the bundle of straw which was lying beside her, or walking near the oxen and leading them. The man thought to himself: "That is certainly one of the kind I am in search of," and jumped up and ran backwards and forwards in front of the waggon like one who is not in his right mind. "What do you want, my friend?" said the woman to him; "I don't know you, where do you come from?" "I have fallen down from Heaven," replied the man, "and don't know how to get back again, couldn't you drive me up?" "No," said the woman, "I don't know the way, but if you come from Heaven you can surely tell me how my husband is, who has been there these three years. You must have seen him?" "Oh, yes, I have seen him, but all men can't get on well. He keeps sheep, and the sheep give him a great deal to do. They run up the mountains and lose their way in the wilderness, and he has to run after them and drive them together again. His clothes are all torn to pieces too, and will soon fall off his body. There is no tailor there, for Saint Peter won't let any of them in, as you know by the story." "Who would have thought it?" cried the woman, "I tell you what, I will fetch his Sunday coat which is still hanging at home in the cupboard. He can wear that and look respectable. You will be so kind as to take it with you." "That won't do very well," answered the peasant; "people are not allowed to take clothes into Heaven, they are taken away at the gate." "Then listen," said the woman, "I sold my fine wheat yesterday and got a good lot of money for it, I will send that to him. If you hide the purse in your pocket, no one will know that you have it." "If you can't manage it any other way," said the peasant," I will do you that favour." "Just sit still where you are," said she, "and I will drive home and fetch the purse, I shall soon be back again. I do not sit down on the bundle of straw, but stand up in the waggon, because it makes it lighter for the cattle." She drove her oxen away, and the peasant thought: "That woman has a perfect talent for folly, if she really brings the money, my wife may think herself fortunate, for she will get no beating." It was not long before she came in a great hurry with the money, and with her own hands put it in his pocket. Before she went away, she thanked him again a thousand times for his courtesy.

When the woman got home again, she found her son who had come in from the field. She told him what unexpected things had befallen her, and then added: "I am truly delighted at having found an opportunity of sending something to my poor husband. Who would ever have imagined that he could be suffering for want of anything up in Heaven?" The son was full of astonishment. "Mother," said he, "it is not every day that a man comes from Heaven in this way, I will go out immediately, and see if he is still to be found; he must tell me what it is like up there, and how the work is done." He saddled the horse and rode off with all speed. He found the peasant who was sitting under a willow-tree, and was about to count the money in the purse. "Have you seen the man who has fallen down from Heaven?" cried the youth to him. "Yes," answered the peasant, "he has set out on his way back there, and has gone up that hill, from whence it will be rather nearer; you could still catch him up, if you were to ride fast" "Alas," said the youth, "I have been doing tiring work all day, and the ride here has completely worn me out; you know the man, be so kind as to get on my horse, and go and persuade him to come here." "Aha!" thought the peasant, "here is another who has not a brain in his head!" "Why should I not do you this favour?" said he, and mounted the horse and rode off at a quick trot. The youth remained sitting there till night fell, but the peasant never came back. "The man from Heaven must certainly have been in a great hurry, and would not turn back," thought he, "and the peasant has no doubt given him the horse to take to my father." He went home and told his mother what had happened, and that he had sent his father the horse so that he might not have to be always running about. "You have done well," answered she, "your legs are younger than his, and you can go on foot."

When the peasant got home, he put the horse in the stable beside the cow which he had as a pledge, and then went to this wife and said: "Trina, as your luck would have it, I have found two who are still sillier fools than you; this time you escape without a beating. I will store it up for another occasion." Then he lighted his pipe, sat down in his grandfather's chair, and said: "It was a good stroke of business to get a sleek horse and a great purse full of money into the bargain, for two lean cows. If stupidity always brought in as much as that, I would be quite willing to hold it in honour." So thought the peasant, but you no doubt prefer simpletons.

TALES OF THE PADDOCK

I

There was once a little child whose mother gave her every afternoon a small bowl of milk and bread, and the child seated herself in the yard with it. But when she began to eat, a paddock came creeping out of a crevice in the wall, dipped its little head in the dish, and ate with her. The child took pleasure in this, and when she was sitting there with her little dish and the paddock did not come at once, she cried:

> "Paddock, paddock, come swiftly
> Hither come, thou tiny thing,
> Thou shalt have thy crumbs of bread,
> Thou shalt refresh thyself with milk."

Then the paddock came in haste, and enjoyed its food. It even showed gratitude, for it brought the child all kinds of pretty things from its hidden treasures, bright stones, pearls, and golden playthings. The paddock, however, drank only the milk, and left the bread-crumbs alone. Then one day the child took its little spoon and struck the paddock gently on its head, and said: "Eat the bread-crumbs as well, little thing." The mother, who was standing in the kitchen, heard the child talking to someone, and when she saw that she was striking a paddock with her spoon, ran out with a log of wood, and killed the good little creature.

From that time forth, a change came over the child. As long as the paddock had eaten with her, she had grown tall and strong, but now she lost her pretty rosy cheeks and wasted away. It was not long before the funeral bird began to cry in the night, and the redbreast to collect little branches and leaves for a funeral wreath, and soon afterwards the child lay on her bier.

II

An orphan child was sitting by the town walls spinning, when she saw a paddock coming out of a hole low down in the wall. Swiftly she spread out beside it one of the blue silk handkerchiefs for which paddocks have such a strong liking, and which are the only things they will creep on. As soon as the paddock saw it, it went back, then returned, bringing with it a small golden crown, laid it on the handkerchief, and then went away again. The girl took up the crown, which glittered and was of delicate golden filagree work. It was not long before the paddock came back for the second time, but when it did not see the crown any more, it crept up to the wall, and in its grief smote its little head against it as long as it had strength to do so, until at last it lay there dead. If the girl had but left the crown where it was, the paddock would certainly have brought still more of its treasures out of the hole.

III

The paddock cries: "Huhu, huhu." The child says: "Come out." The paddock comes out, whereupon the child inquires about her little sister: "Have you not seen little Red-stockings?" The paddock says: "No, I have not. Have you? Huhu, huhu, huhu."

THE POOR MILLER'S BOY AND THE CAT

In a certain mill lived an old miller who had neither wife nor child, and three apprentices served under him. As they had been with him several years, he one day said to them: "I am old, and want to sit behind the stove. Go out, and whichsoever of you brings me the best horse home, to him will I give the mill, and in return for it he shall take care of me till my death." The third of the boys, however, was the dunce, who was looked on as foolish by the others; they begrudged the mill to him; and afterwards he would not even have it. Then all three went out together, and when they came to the village, the two said to stupid Hans: "You may just as well stay here, as long as you live you will never get a horse." Hans, however, went with them, and when it was night they came to a cave in which they lay down to sleep. The two smart ones waited until Hans had fallen asleep, then they got up, and went away leaving him where he was. And they thought they had done a very clever thing, but it was certain to turn out ill for them. When the sun rose, and Hans woke up, he was lying in a deep cavern. He looked around on every side and exclaimed: "Oh, heavens, where am I?" Then he got up and clambered out of the cave, went into the forest, and thought: "Here I am quite alone and deserted, how shall I obtain a horse now?" Whilst he was thus walking full of thought, he met a small tabby-cat which said quite kindly: "Hans, where are you going?" "Alas, you can not help me." "I well know your desire," said the cat. "You wish to have a beautiful horse. Come with me, and be my faithful servant for seven years long, and then I will give you one more beautiful than any you have ever seen in your whole life." "Well, this is a strange cat!" thought Hans, "but I am determined to see if she is telling the truth." So she took him with her into her enchanted castle, where there were nothing but kittens who were her servants. They leapt nimbly upstairs and downstairs, and were merry and happy. In the evening when they sat down to dinner, three of them had to make music. One played the bass viol, the other the fiddle, and the third put the trumpet to his lips, and blew out his cheeks as much as he possibly could. When they had dined, the table was carried away, and the cat said: "Now, Hans, come and dance with me." "No," said he, "I won't dance with a pussy cat. I have never done that yet." "Then take him to bed," said she to the cats. So one of them lighted him to his bed-room, one pulled his shoes off, one his stockings, and at last one of them blew out the candle. Next morning they returned and helped him out of bed, one put his stockings on for him, one tied his garters, one brought his shoes, one washed him, and one dried his face with her tail. "That feels very soft!" said Hans. He, however, had to serve the cat, and chop some wood every day, and to do that, he had an axe of silver, and the wedge and saw were of silver and the mallet of copper. So he chopped the wood small; stayed there in the house and had good meat and drink, but never saw anyone but the tabby-cat and her servants. Once she said to him: "Go and mow my meadow, and dry the grass," and gave him a scythe of silver, and a whetstone of gold, but bade him deliver them up again carefully. So Hans went thither, and did what he was bidden, and when he had finished the work, he carried the scythe, whetstone, and hay to the house, and asked if it was not yet time for her to give him his reward. "No," said the cat, "you must first do something more for me of the same kind. There is timber of silver, carpenter's axe, square, and everything that is needful, all of silver—with these build me a small house." Then Hans built the small house, and said that he had now done everything, and still he had no horse. Nevertheless, the seven years had gone by with him as if they were six months. The cat asked him if he would like to see her horses. "Yes," said Hans. Then she opened the door of the small house, and when she had opened it, there stood twelve horses,—such horses, so bright and shining, that his heart rejoiced at the sight of them. And now she gave him to eat and to drink, and said: "Go home, I will not give you your horse now; but in three days' time I will follow you and bring it." So Hans set out, and she showed him the way to the mill. She, however, had never once given him a new coat, and he had been obliged to keep on his dirty old smock, which he had brought with him, and which during the seven years had everywhere become too small for him. When he reached home, the two other apprentices were there again as well, and each of them certainly had brought a horse with him, but one of them was a blind one, and the other lame. They asked Hans where his horse was. "It will follow me in three days' time." Then they laughed and said: "Indeed, stupid Hans, where will you get a horse? It will be a fine one!" Hans went into the parlour, but the miller said he should not sit down to table, for he was so ragged and torn, that they would all be ashamed of him if any one came in. So they gave him a mouthful of food outside, and at night, when they went to rest, the two others would not let him have a bed, and at last he was forced to creep into the goose-house, and lie down on a little hard straw. In the morning when he awoke, the three days had passed, and a coach came with six horses and they shone so bright that it was delightful to see them!—and a servant brought a seventh as well, which was for the poor miller's boy. And a magnificent princess alighted from the coach and went into the mill, and this princess was the little tabby-cat whom poor Hans had served for seven years. She asked the miller where the miller's boy and dunce was. Then the miller said: "We cannot have him here in the mill, for he is so ragged; he is lying in the goose-house." Then the King's daughter said that they were to bring him immediately. So they brought him out, and he had to hold his little smock together to cover himself. The servants unpacked splendid garments, and washed him and dressed him, and when that was done, no King could have looked more handsome. Then the maiden desired to see the horses which the other apprentices had brought home with them, and one of them was blind and the other lame. So she ordered the servant to bring the seventh horse, and when the miller saw it, he said that such a horse as that had never yet entered his yard. "And that is for the third miller's-boy," said she. "Then he must have the mill," said the miller, but the King's daughter said that the horse was there, and that he was to keep his mill as well, and took her faithful Hans and set him in the coach, and drove away with him. They first drove to the little house which he had built with the silver tools, and behold it was a great castle, and everything inside it was of silver and gold; and then she married him, and he was rich, so rich that he had enough for all the rest of his life. After this, let no one ever say that anyone who is silly can never become a person of importance.

THE TWO TRAVELLERS

Hill and vale do not meet, but the children of men do, good and bad. In this way a shoemaker and a tailor once met on their travels. The tailor was a handsome little fellow who was always merry and full of enjoyment. He saw the shoemaker coming towards him from the other side, and as he observed by his bag what kind of a trade he plied, he sang a little mocking song to him:

"Sew me the seam,
Draw me the thread,
Spread it over with pitch,
Knock the nail on the head."

The shoemaker, however, could not bear a joke; he pulled a face as if he had drunk vinegar, and made a gesture as if he were about to seize the tailor by the throat. But the little fellow began to laugh, reached him his bottle, and said: "No harm was meant, take a drink, and swallow your anger down." The shoemaker took a very hearty drink, and the storm on his face began to clear away. He gave the bottle back to the tailor, and said: "I took a hearty gulp; they say it comes from much drinking, but not from great thirst. Shall we travel together?" "All right," answered the tailor, "if only it suits you to go into a big town where there is no lack of work." "That is just where I want to go," answered the shoemaker. "In a small hamlet there is nothing to earn, and in the country, people like to go barefoot." They travelled therefore onwards together, and always set one foot before the other like a weasel in the snow.

Both of them had time enough, but little to bite and to break. When they reached a town they went about and paid their respects to the tradesmen, and because the tailor looked so lively and merry, and had such fine red cheeks, every one gave him work willingly, and when luck was good the master's daughters gave him a kiss beneath the porch, as well. When he again fell in with the shoemaker, the tailor had always the most in his bundle. The ill-tempered shoemaker made a wry face, and thought: "The greater the rascal the more the luck," but the tailor began to laugh and to sing, and shared all he got with his comrade. If a couple of pence jingled in his pockets, he ordered good cheer, and thumped the table in his joy till the glasses danced, and it was lightly come, lightly go, with him.

When they had travelled for some time, they came to a great forest through which passed the road to the capital. Two foot-paths, however, led through it, one of which was a seven days' journey, and the other only two, but neither of the travellers knew which way was the short one. They seated themselves beneath an oak-tree, and took counsel together how they should forecast, and for how many days they should provide themselves with bread. The shoemaker said: "One must look before one leaps, I will take with me bread for a week." "What!" said the tailor, "drag bread for seven days on one's back like a beast of burden, and not be able to look about. I shall trust in God, and not trouble myself about anything! The money I have in my pocket is as good in summer as in winter, but in hot weather bread gets dry, and mouldy into the bargain; even my coat does not last as far as it might. Besides, why should we not find the right way? Bread for two days, and that's enough." Each, therefore, bought his own bread, and then they tried their luck in the forest.

It was as quiet there as in a church. No wind stirred, no brook murmured, no bird sang, and through the thickly-leaved branches no sunbeam forced its way. The shoemaker spoke never a word, the bread weighed so heavily on his back that the sweat streamed down his cross and gloomy face. The tailor, however, was quite merry, he jumped about, whistled on a leaf, or sang a song, and thought to himself: "God in Heaven must be pleased to see me so happy."

This lasted two days, but on the third the forest would not come to an end, and the tailor had eaten up all his bread, so after all his heart sank down a yard deeper. Nevertheless, he did not lose courage, but relied on God and on his luck. On the evening of the third day he lay down hungry under a tree, and rose again next morning hungry still; so also passed the fourth day, and when the shoemaker seated himself on a fallen tree and devoured his dinner, the tailor was only a spectator. If he begged for a little piece of bread, the other laughed mockingly, and said: "You have always been so merry, now you can see for once what it is to be sad: the birds which sing too early in the morning are struck by the hawk in the evening." In short, he was pitiless. But on the fifth morning the poor tailor could no longer stand up, and was hardly able to utter one word for weakness; his cheeks were white, and his eyes red. Then the shoemaker said to him: "I will give you a bit of bread to-day, but in return for it, I will put out your right eye. The unhappy tailor who still wished to save his life, had to submit; he wept once more with both eyes, and then held them out, and the shoemaker, who had a heart of stone, put out his right eye with a sharp knife. The tailor called to remembrance what his mother had formerly said to him when he had been eating secretly in the pantry. "Eat what one can, and suffer what one must." When he had consumed his dearly-bought bread, he got on his legs again, forgot his misery and comforted himself with the thought that he could always see enough with one eye. But on the sixth day, hunger made itself felt again, and gnawed him almost to the heart. In the evening he fell down by a tree, and on the seventh morning he could not raise himself up for faintness, and death was close at hand. Then said the shoemaker: "I will show mercy and give you bread once more, but you shall not have it for nothing, I shall put out your other eye for it." And now the tailor felt how thoughtless his life had been, prayed to God for forgiveness, and said: "Do what you will, I will bear what I must, but remember that our Lord God does not always look on passively, and that an hour will come when the evil deed which you have done to me, and which I have not deserved of you, will be requited. When times were good with me, I shared what I had with you. My trade is of that kind that each stitch must always be exactly like the other. If I no longer have my eyes and can sew no more I must go a-begging. At any rate do not leave me here alone when I am blind, or I shall die of hunger." The shoemaker, however, who had driven God out of his heart, took the knife and put out his left eye. Then he gave him a bit of bread to eat, held out a stick to him, and drew him on behind him.

When the sun went down, they got out of the forest, and before them in the open country stood the gallows. Thither the shoemaker guided the blind tailor, and then left him alone and went his way. Weariness, pain, and hunger made the wretched man fall asleep, and he slept the whole night. When day dawned he awoke, but knew not where he lay. Two poor sinners were hanging on the gallows, and a

crow sat on the head of each of them. Then one of the men who had been hanged began to speak, and said: "Brother, are you awake?" "Yes, I am awake," answered the second. "Then I will tell you something," said the first; "the dew which this night has fallen down over us from the gallows, gives every one who washes himself with it his eyes again. If blind people did but know this, how many would regain their sight who do not believe that to be possible."

When the tailor heard that, he took his pocket-handkerchief, pressed it on the grass, and when it was moist with dew, washed the sockets of his eyes with it. Immediately was fulfilled what the man on the gallows had said, and a couple of healthy new eyes filled the sockets. It was not long before the tailor saw the sun rise behind the mountains; in the plain before him lay the great royal city with its magnificent gates and hundred towers, and the golden balls and crosses which were on the spires began to shine. He could distinguish every leaf on the trees, saw the birds which flew past, and the midges which danced in the air. He took a needle out of his pocket, and as he could thread it as well as ever he had done, his heart danced with delight. He threw himself on his knees, thanked God for the mercy he had shown him, and said his morning prayer. Nor did he forget to pray for the poor sinners who were hanging there swinging against each other in the wind like the pendulums of clocks. Then he took his bundle on his back and soon forgot the pain of heart he had endured, and went on his way singing and whistling.

The first thing he met was a brown foal running about the fields at large. He caught it by the mane, and wanted to spring on it and ride into the town. The foal, however, begged to be set free. "I am still too young," it said, "even a light tailor such as you are would break my back in two—let me go till I have grown strong. A time may perhaps come when I may reward you for it."

"Run off," said the tailor, "I see you are still a giddy thing." He gave it a touch with a switch over its back, whereupon it kicked up its hind legs for joy, leapt over hedges and ditches, and galloped away into the open country.

But the little tailor had eaten nothing since the day before. "The sun to be sure fills my eyes," said he, "but the bread does not fill my mouth. The first thing that comes my way and is even half edible will have to suffer for it." In the meantime a stork stepped solemnly over the meadow towards him. "Halt, halt!" cried the tailor, and seized him by the leg: "I don't know if you are good to eat or not, but my hunger leaves me no great choice. I must cut your head off, and roast you." "Don't do that," replied the stork; "I am a sacred bird which brings mankind great profit, and no one does me an injury. Leave me my life, and I may do you good in some other way." "Well, be off, Cousin Longlegs," said the tailor. The stork rose up, let its long legs hang down, and flew gently away.

"What's to be the end of this?" said the tailor to himself at last, "my hunger grows greater and greater, and my stomach more and more empty. Whatsoever comes in my way now is lost." At this moment he saw a couple of young ducks which were on a pond come swimming towards him. "You come just at the right moment," said he, and laid hold of one of them and was about to wring its neck. On this an old duck which was hidden among the reeds, began to scream loudly, and swam to him with open beak, and begged him urgently to spare her dear children. "Can you not imagine," said she, "how your mother would mourn if any one wanted to carry you off, and give you your finishing stroke?" "Just be quiet," said the good-tempered tailor, "you shall keep your children," and put the prisoner back into the water.

When he turned round, he was standing in front of an old tree which was partly hollow, and saw some wild bees flying in and out of it. "There I shall at once find the reward of my good deed," said the tailor, "the honey will refresh me." But the Queen-bee came out, threatened him and said: "If you touch my people, and destroy my nest, our stings shall pierce your skin like ten thousand red-hot needles. But if you will leave us in peace and go your way, we will do you a service for it another time."

The little tailor saw that here also nothing was to be done. "Three dishes empty and nothing on the fourth is a bad dinner!" He dragged himself therefore with his starved-out stomach into the town, and as it was just striking twelve, all was ready-cooked for him in the inn, and he was able to sit down at once to dinner. When he was satisfied he said: "Now I will get to work." He went round the town, sought a master, and soon found a good situation. And as he had thoroughly learnt his trade, it was not long before he became famous, and every one wanted to have his new coat made by the little tailor, whose importance increased daily. "I can go no further in skill," said he, "and yet things improve every day." At last the King appointed him court-tailor.

But what odd things do happen in the world! On the very same day his former comrade the shoemaker also became court-shoemaker. When the latter caught sight of the tailor, and saw that he had once more two healthy eyes, his conscience troubled him. "Before he takes revenge on me," thought he to himself, "I must dig a pit for him." He, however, who digs a pit for another, falls into it himself. In the evening when work was over and it had grown dusk, he stole to the King and said: "Lord King, the tailor is an arrogant fellow and has boasted that he will get the gold crown back again which was lost in ancient times." "That would please me very much," said the King, and he caused the tailor to be brought before him next morning, and ordered him to get the crown back again, or to leave the town for ever. "Oho!" thought the tailor, "a rogue gives more than he has got. If the surly King wants me to do what can be done by no one, I will not wait till morning, but will go out of the town at once, to-day." He packed up his bundle, therefore, but when he was without the gate he could not help being sorry to give up his good fortune, and turn his back on the town in which all had gone so well with him. He came to the pond where he had made the acquaintance of the ducks; at that very moment the old one whose young ones he had spared, was sitting there by the shore, pluming herself with her beak. She knew him again instantly, and asked why he was hanging his head so. "You will not be surprised when you hear what has befallen me," replied the tailor, and told her his fate. "If that be all," said the duck, "we can help you. The crown fell into the water, and lies down below at the bottom; we will soon bring it up again for you. In the meantime just spread out your handkerchief on the bank." She dived down with her twelve young ones, and in five minutes she was up again and sat with the crown resting on her wings, and the twelve young ones were swimming round about and had put their beaks under it, and were helping to carry it. They swam to the shore and put the crown on the handkerchief. No one can imagine how magnificent the crown was; when the sun shone on it, it gleamed like a hundred thousand carbuncles. The tailor tied his handkerchief together by the four corners, and carried it to the King, who was full of joy, and put a gold chain round the tailor's neck.

When the shoemaker saw that one blow had failed, he contrived a second, and sent to the King and said: "Lord King, the tailor has become insolent again; he boasts that he will copy in wax the whole of the royal palace, with everything that pertains to it, loose or fast, inside and out." The King sent for the tailor and ordered him to copy in wax the whole of the royal palace, with everything that pertained to it, movable or immovable, within and without, and if he did not succeed in doing this, or if so much as one nail on the wall were wanting, he should be imprisoned for his whole life underground.

The tailor thought: "It gets worse and worse! No one can endure that!" and threw his bundle on his back, and went forth. When he came to the hollow tree, he sat down and hung his head. The bees came flying out, and the Queen-bee asked him if he had a stiff neck, since he hung his head so. "Alas, no," answered the tailor, "something quite different weighs me down," and he told her what the King had demanded of him. The bees began to buzz and hum amongst themselves, and the Queen-bee said: "Just go home again, but come back tomorrow at this time, and bring a large sheet with you, and then all will be well." So he turned back again, but the bees flew to the royal palace and straight into it through the open windows, crept round about into every corner, and inspected everything most carefully. Then they hurried back and modelled the palace in wax with such rapidity that any one looking on would have thought it was growing before his eyes. By the evening all was ready, and when the tailor came next morning, the whole of the splendid building was there, and not one nail in the wall or tile of the roof was wanting, and it was delicate withal, and white as snow, and smelt sweet as honey. The tailor wrapped it carefully in his cloth and took it to the King, who could not admire it enough, placed it in his largest hall, and in return for it presented the tailor with a large stone house.

The shoemaker, however, did not give up, but went for the third time to the King and said: "Lord King, it has come to the tailor's ears that no water will spring up in the court-yard of the castle, and he has boasted that it shall rise up in the midst of the court-yard to a man's height and be clear as crystal." Then the King ordered the tailor to be brought before him and said: "If a stream of water does not rise in my court-yard by to-morrow as you have promised, the executioner shall in that very place make you shorter by a head." The poor tailor did not take long to think about it, but hurried out to the gate, and because this time it was a matter of life and death to him, tears rolled down his face. Whilst he was thus going forth full of sorrow, the foal to which he had formerly given its liberty, and which had now become a beautiful chestnut horse, came leaping towards him. "The time has come," it said to the tailor, "when I can repay you for your good deed. I know already what is needful to you, but you shall soon have help; get on me, my back can carry two such as you." The tailor's courage came back to him; he jumped up in one bound, and the horse went full speed into the town, and right up to the court-yard of the castle. It galloped as quick as lightning thrice round it, and at the third time it fell violently down. At the same instant, however, there was a terrific clap of thunder, a fragment of earth in the middle of the courtyard sprang like a cannon-ball into the air, and over the castle, and directly after it a jet of water rose as high as a man on horseback, and the water was as pure as crystal, and the sunbeams began to dance on it. When the King saw this, he arose in amazement, and went and embraced the tailor in the sight of all men.

But good fortune did not last long. The King had daughters in plenty, one still prettier than the other, but he had no son. So the malicious shoemaker betook himself for the fourth time to the King, and said: "Lord King, the tailor has not given up his arrogance. He has now boasted that if he liked, he could cause a son to be brought to the Lord King through the air." The King commanded the tailor to be summoned, and said: "If you cause a son to be brought to me within nine days, you shall have my eldest daughter to wife." "The reward is indeed great," thought the little tailor; "one would willingly do some-thing for it, but the cherries grow too high for me, if I climb for them, the bough will break beneath me, and I shall fall."

He went home, seated himself cross-legged on his work-table, and thought over what was to be done. "It can't be managed," cried he at last, "I will go away; after all, I can't live in peace here." He tied up his bundle and hurried away to the gate. When he got to the meadow, he perceived his old friend the stork, who was walking backwards and forwards like a philosopher. Sometimes he stood still, took a frog into close consideration, and at length swallowed it down. The stork came to him and greeted him. "I see," he began, "that you have your pack on your back. Why are you leaving the town?" The tailor told him what the King had required of him, and how he could not perform it, and lamented his misfortune. "Don't let that turn your hair grey," said the stork, "I will help you out of your difficulty. For a long time now, I have carried the children in swaddling-clothes into the town, so for once in a way I can fetch a little prince out of the well. Go home and be easy. In nine days from this time repair to the royal palace, and there will I come." The little tailor went home, and at the appointed time was at the castle. It was not long before the stork came flying thither and tapped at the window. The tailor opened it, and Cousin Longlegs came carefully in, and walked with solemn steps over the smooth marble pavement. He had, moreover, a baby in his beak that was as lovely as an angel, and stretched out its little hands to the Queen. The stork laid it in her lap, and she caressed it and kissed it, and was beside herself with delight. Before the stork flew away, he took his travelling bag off his back and handed it over to the Queen. In it there were little paper parcels with coloured sweetmeats, and they were divided amongst the little princesses. The eldest, however, received none of them, but instead got the merry tailor for a husband. "It seems to me," said he, "just as if I had won the highest prize. My mother was right after all, she always said that whoever trusts in God and only has good luck, can never fail."

The shoemaker had to make the shoes in which the little tailor danced at the wedding festival, after which he was commanded to quit the town for ever. The road to the forest led him to the gallows. Worn out with anger, rage, and the heat of the day, he threw himself down. When he had closed his eyes and was about to sleep, the two crows flew down from the heads of the men who were hanging there, and pecked his eyes out. In his madness he ran into the forest and must have died there of hunger, for no one has ever either seen him or heard of him again.

HANS THE HEDGEHOG

There was once a country man who had money and land in plenty, but however rich he was, his happiness was still lacking in one respect—he had no children. Often when he went into the town with the other peasants they mocked him and asked why he had no children. At last he became angry, and when he got home he said: "I will have a child, even if it be a hedgehog." Then his wife had a child that was a hedgehog in the upper part of his body and a boy in the lower, and when she saw the child, she was terrified, and said: "See, there you have brought ill-luck on us." Then said the man: "What can be done now? The boy must be christened, but we shall not be able to get a godfather for him." The woman said: "And we cannot call him anything else but Hans the Hedgehog."

When he was christened, the parson said: "He cannot go into any ordinary bed because of his spikes." So a little straw was put behind the stove, and Hans the Hedgehog was laid on it. His mother could not suckle him, for he would have pricked her with his quills. So he lay there behind the stove for eight years, and his father was tired of him and thought: "If he would but die!" He did not die, however, but remained lying there. Now it happened that there was a fair in the town, and the peasant was about to go to it, and asked his wife what he should bring back with him for her. "A little meat and a couple of white rolls which are wanted for the house," said she. Then he asked the servant, and she wanted a pair of slippers and some stockings with clocks. At last he said also: "And what will you have, Hans my Hedgehog?" "Dear father," he said, "do bring me bagpipes." When, therefore, the father came home again, he gave his wife what he had bought for her, meat and white rolls; and then he gave the maid the slippers, and the stockings with clocks; and, lastly, he went behind the stove, and gave Hans the Hedgehog the bagpipes. And when Hans the Hedgehog had the bagpipes, he said: "Dear father, do go to the forge and get the cock shod, and then I will ride away, and never come back again." At this, the father was delighted to think that he was going to get rid of him, and had the cock shod for him, and when it was done, Hans the Hedgehog got on it, and rode away, but took swine and asses with him which he intended to keep in the forest. When they got there he made the cock fly on to a high tree with him, and there he sat for many a long year, and watched his asses and swine until the herd was quite large, and his father knew nothing about him. And while he was sitting in the tree, he played his bagpipes, and made music which was very beautiful. Once a King came travelling by who had lost his way and heard the music. He was astonished at it, and sent his servant forth to look all round and see from whence this music came. He spied about, but saw nothing but a little animal sitting up aloft on the tree, which looked like a cock with a hedgehog on it which made this music. Then the King told the servant he was to ask why he sat there, and if he knew the road which led to his kingdom. So Hans the Hedgehog descended from the tree, and said he would show the way if the King would write a bond and promise him whatever he first met in the royal courtyard as soon as he arrived at home. Then the King thought: "I can easily do that, Hans the Hedgehog understands nothing, and I can write what I like." So the King took pen and ink and wrote something, and when he had done it, Hans the Hedgehog showed him the way, and he got safely home. But his daughter, when she saw him from afar, was so overjoyed that she ran to meet him, and kissed him. Then he remembered Hans the Hedgehog, and told her what had happened, and that he had been forced to promise whatsoever first met him when he got home, to a very strange animal which sat on a cock as if it were a horse, and made beautiful music, but that instead of writing that he should have what he wanted, he had written that he should not have it. Thereupon the princess was glad, and said he had done well, for she never would have gone away with the Hedgehog.

Hans the Hedgehog, however, looked after his asses and pigs, and was always merry and sat on the tree and played his bagpipes.

Now it came to pass that another King came journeying by with his attendants and runners, and he also had lost his way, and did not know how to get home again because the forest was so large. He likewise heard the beautiful music from a distance, and asked his runner what that could be, and told him to go and see. Then the runner went under the tree, and saw the cock sitting at the top of it, and Hans the Hedgehog on the cock. The runner asked him what he was doing up there. "I am keeping my asses and my pigs; but what is your desire?" The messenger said that they had lost their way, and could not get back into their own kingdom, and asked if he would not show them the way. Then Hans the Hedgehog descended the tree with the cock, and told the aged King that he would show him the way, if he would give him for his own whatsoever first met him in front of his royal palace. The King said: "Yes," and wrote a promise to Hans the Hedgehog that he should have this. That done, Hans rode on before him on the cock, and pointed out the way, and the King reached his kingdom again in safety. When he got to the courtyard, there were great rejoicings. Now he had an only daughter who was very beautiful; she ran to meet him, threw her arms round his neck, and was delighted to have her old father back again. She asked him where in the world he had been so long. So he told her how he had lost his way, and had very nearly not come back at all, but that as he was travelling through a great forest, a creature, half hedgehog, half man, who was sitting astride a cock in a high tree, and making music, had shown him the way and helped him to get out, but that in return he had promised him whatsoever first met him in the royal court-yard, and how that was she herself, which made him unhappy now. But on this she promised that, for love of her father, she would willingly go with this Hans if he came.

Hans the Hedgehog, however, took care of his pigs, and the pigs became more pigs until there were so many in number that the whole forest was filled with them. Then Hans the Hedgehog resolved not to live in the forest any longer, and sent word to his father to have every stye in the village emptied, for he was coming with such a great herd that all might kill who wished to do so. When his father heard that, he was troubled, for he thought Hans the Hedgehog had died long ago. Hans the Hedgehog, however, seated himself on the cock, and drove the pigs before him into the village, and ordered the slaughter to begin. Ha!—then there was a butchery and a chopping that might have been heard two miles off! After this Hans the Hedgehog said: "Father, let me have the cock shod once more at the forge, and then I will ride away and never come back as long as I live." Then the father had the cock shod once more, and was pleased that Hans the Hedgehog would never return again.

Hans the Hedgehog rode away to the first kingdom. There the King had commanded that whosoever came mounted on a cock and had bagpipes with him should be shot at, cut down, or stabbed by everyone, so that he might not enter the palace. When, therefore, Hans the Hedgehog came riding thither, they all pressed forward against him with their pikes, but he spurred the cock and it flew up over the gate in front of the King's window and lighted there, and Hans cried that the King must give him what he had promised, or he would take both his life and his daughter's. Then the King began to speak to his daughter, and to beg her to go away with Hans in order to save her own life and her father's. So she dressed herself in white, and her father gave her a carriage with six horses and magnificent attendants together with gold and possessions. She seated herself in the carriage, and placed Hans the Hedgehog beside her with the cock and the bagpipes, and then they took leave and drove away, and the King thought he should never see her again. But he was deceived in his expectation, for when they were at a short distance from the town, Hans the Hedgehog took her pretty clothes off, and pierced her with his hedgehog's spikes until she bled all over. "That is the reward of your falseness," said he, "go your way, I will not have you!" and on that he chased her home again, and she was disgraced for the rest of her life.

Hans the Hedgehog, however, rode on further on the cock, with his bagpipes, to the dominions of the second King to whom he had shown the way. But this one had arranged that if any one resembling Hans the Hedgehog should come, they were to present arms, give him safe conduct, cry long life to him, and lead him to the royal palace.

But when the King's daughter saw him she was terrified, for he really looked too strange. Then she remembered that she could not change her mind, for she had given her promise to her father. So Hans the Hedgehog was welcomed by her, and married to her, and had to go with her to the royal table, and she seated herself by his side, and they ate and drank. When the evening came and they wanted to go to sleep, she was afraid of his quills, but he told her she was not to fear, for no harm would befall her, and he told the old King that he was to appoint four men to watch by the door of the chamber, and light a great fire, and when he entered the room and was about to get into bed, he would creep out of his hedgehog's skin and leave it lying there by the bedside, and that the men were to run nimbly to it, throw it in the fire, and stay by it until it was consumed. When the clock struck eleven, he went into the chamber, stripped off the hedgehog's skin, and left it lying by the bed. Then came the men and fetched it swiftly, and threw it in the fire; and when the fire had consumed it, he was saved, and lay there in bed in human form, but he was coal-black as if he had been burnt. The King sent for his physician who washed him with precious salves, and anointed him, and he became white, and was a handsome young man. When the King's daughter saw that she was glad, and the next morning they arose joyfully, ate and drank, and then the marriage was properly solemnized, and Hans the Hedgehog received the kingdom from the aged King.

When several years had passed he went with his wife to his father, and said that he was his son. The father, however, declared he had no son—he had never had but one, and he had been born like a hedgehog with spikes, and had gone forth into the world. Then Hans made himself known, and the old father rejoiced and went with him to his kingdom.

My tale is done,
And away it has run
To little Augusta's house.

THE SHROUD

There was once a mother who had a little boy of seven years old, who was so handsome and lovable that no one could look at him without liking him, and she herself worshipped him above everything in the world. Now it so happened that he suddenly became ill, and God took him to himself; and for this the mother could not be comforted, and wept both day and night. But soon afterwards, when the child had been buried, it appeared by night in the places where it had sat and played during its life, and if the mother wept, it wept also, and when morning came it disappeared. But as the mother would not stop crying, it came one night, in the little white shroud in which it had been laid in its coffin, and with its wreath of flowers round its head, and stood on the bed at her feet, and said: "Oh, mother, do stop crying, or I shall never fall asleep in my coffin, for my shroud will not dry because of all your tears, which fall upon it." The mother was afraid when she heard that, and wept no more. The next night the child came again, and held a little light in its hand, and said: "Look, mother, my shroud is nearly dry, and I can rest in my grave." Then the mother gave her sorrow into God's keeping, and bore it quietly and patiently, and the child came no more, but slept in its little bed beneath the earth.

THE JEW AMONG THORNS

There was once a rich man, who had a servant who served him diligently and honestly: he was every morning the first out of bed, and the
last to go to rest at night; and whenever there was a difficult job to be
done, which nobody cared to undertake, he was always the first to set
himself to it. Moreover, he never complained, but was contented with
everything, and always merry.

When a year was ended, his master gave him no wages, for he said to
himself: "That is the cleverest way; for I shall save something, and he
will not go away, but stay quietly in my service." The servant said
nothing, but did his work the second year as he had done it the first;
and when at the end of this, likewise, he received no wages, he submit-
ted and still stayed on.

When the third year also was past, the master considered, put his
hand in his pocket, but pulled nothing out. Then at last the servant said:
"Master, for three years I have served you honestly, be so good as to
give me what I ought to have; for I wish to leave, and look about me a
little more in the world."

"Yes, my good fellow," answered the old miser; "you have served me
industriously, and therefore you shall be graciously rewarded;" and he
put his hand into his pocket, but counted out only three farthings,
saying: "There, you have a farthing for each year; that is large and
liberal pay, such as you would have received from few masters."

The honest servant, who understood little about money, put his
fortune into his pocket, and thought: "Ah! now that I have my purse
full, why need I trouble and plague myself any longer with hard work!"
So on he went, up hill and down dale; and sang and jumped to his
heart's content. Now it came to pass that as he was going by a thicket a
little man stepped out, and called to him: "Whither away, merry
brother? I see you do not carry many cares." "Why should I be sad?"
answered the servant; "I have enough; three years' wages are jingling in
my pocket."

"How much is your treasure?" the dwarf asked him.

"How much? Three farthings sterling, all told."

"Look here," said the dwarf, "I am a poor needy man, give me your three farthings; I can work no longer, but you are young, and can easily earn your bread."

And as the servant had a good heart, and felt pity for the little man, he gave him the three farthings, saying: "Take them in the name of Heaven, I shall not be any the worse for it."

Then the little man said: "As I see you have a good heart I grant you three wishes, one for each farthing, they shall all be fulfilled."

"Aha?" said the servant, "you are one of those who can work wonders! Well, then, if it is to be so, I wish, first, for a gun, which shall hit everything that I aim at; secondly, for a fiddle, which when I play on it, shall compel all who hear it to dance; thirdly, that if I ask a favour of any one he shall not be able to refuse it."

"All that shall you have," said the dwarf; and put his hand into the bush, and just imagine, there lay a fiddle and gun, all ready, just as if they had been ordered. These he gave to the servant, and then said to him: "Whatever you may ask at any time, no man in the world shall be able to deny you."

"Heart alive! What more can one desire?" said the servant to himself, and went merrily onwards. Soon afterwards he met a Jew with a long goat's-beard, who was standing listening to the song of a bird which was sitting up at the top of a tree. "Good heavens," he was exclaiming, "that such a small creature should have such a fearfully loud voice! if it were but mine! if only some one would sprinkle some salt upon its tail!"

"If that is all," said the servant, "the bird shall soon be down here"; and taking aim he blew, and down fell the bird into the thorn-bushes. "Go, you rogue," he said to the Jew, "and fetch the bird out for yourself!"

"Oh!" said the Jew, "leave out the rogue, my master, and I will do it

at once. I will get the bird out for myself, now that you have hit it."
Then he lay down on the ground, and began to crawl into the thicket.

When he was fast among the thorns, the good servant's humour so
tempted him that he took up his fiddle and began to play. In a moment
the Jew's legs began to move, and to jump into the air, and the more
the servant fiddled the better went the dance. But the thorns tore his
shabby coat from him, combed his beard, and pricked and plucked
him all over the body. "Oh dear," cried the Jew, "what do I want with
your fiddling? leave the fiddle alone, master; I do not want to dance."

But the servant did not listen to him, and thought: "You have fleeced
people often enough, now the thorn-bushes shall do the same to you;"
and he began to play over again, so that the Jew had to jump higher
than ever, and scraps of his coat were left hanging on the thorns. "Oh,
woe's me!" cried the Jew; "I will give the gentleman whatsoever he
asks if only he leaves off fiddling—a whole purse full of gold." "If you
are so liberal," said the servant, "I will stop my music; but this I must
say to your credit, that you dance to it so well that one must really
admire it;" and having taken the purse he went his way.

The Jew stood still and watched the servant quietly until he was far
off and out of sight, and then he screamed out with all his might: "You
miserable musician, you beer-house fiddler! wait till I catch you alone,
I will hunt you till the soles of your shoes fall off! You ragamuffin! just
put six farthings in your mouth, that you may be worth three half-
pence!" and went on abusing him as fast as he could speak. As soon as
he had refreshed himself a little in this way, and got his breath again, he
ran into the town to the justice.

"My lord judge," he said, "I have come to make a complaint; see
how a rascal has robbed and ill-treated me on the public highway! a
stone on the ground might pity me; my clothes all torn, my body
pricked and scratched, my little all gone with my purse,—good ducats,
each piece better than the last; for God's sake let the man be thrown
into prison!"

"Was it a soldier," said the judge, "who cut you thus with his
sabre?" "Nothing of the sort!" said the Jew; "it was no sword that he
had, but a gun hanging at his back, and a fiddle at his neck; the wretch
may easily be recognized."

So the judge sent his people out after the man, and they found the good servant, who had been going quite slowly along, and they found, too, the purse with the money upon him. As soon as he was taken before the judge he said: "I did not touch the Jew, nor take his money; he gave it to me of his own free will, that I might leave off fiddling because he could not bear my music."

"Heaven defend us!" cried the Jew, "his lies are as thick as flies upon the wall."

But the judge also did not believe his tale, and said: "This is a bad defence, no Jew would do that." And because he had committed robbery on the public highway, he sentenced the good servant to be hanged. As he was being led away the Jew again screamed after him: "You vagabond! you dog of a fiddler! now you are going to receive your well-earned reward!" The servant walked quietly with the hangman up the ladder, but upon the last step he turned round and said to the judge: "Grant me just one request before I die."

"Yes, if you do not ask your life," said the judge.

"I do not ask for life," answered the servant, "but as a last favour let me play once more upon my fiddle."

The Jew raised a great cry of "Murder! murder! for goodness' sake do not allow it! Do not allow it!" But the judge said: "Why should I not let him have this short pleasure? it has been granted to him, and he shall have it." However, he could not have refused on account of the gift which had been bestowed on the servant.

Then the Jew cried: "Oh! woe's me! tie me, tie me fast!" while the good servant took his fiddle from his neck, and made ready. As he gave the first scrape, they all began to quiver and shake, the judge, his clerk, and the hangman and his men, and the cord fell out of the hand of the one who was going to tie the Jew fast. At the second scrape all raised their legs, and the hangman let go his hold of the good servant, and made himself ready to dance. At the third scrape they all leaped up and began to dance; the judge and the Jew being the best at jumping. Soon all who had gathered in the market-place out of curiosity were dancing with them; old and young, fat and lean, one with another. The dogs, likewise, which had run there, got up on their hind legs and capered about; and the longer he played, the higher sprang the dancers, so that they knocked against each other's heads, and began to shriek terribly.

At length the judge cried, quite out of breath: "I will give you your life if you will only stop fiddling." The good servant thereupon had compassion, took his fiddle and hung it round his neck again, and stepped down the ladder. Then he went up to the Jew, who was lying upon the ground panting for breath, and said: "You rascal, now confess, whence you got the money, or I will take my fiddle and begin to play again." "I stole it, I stole it!" cried he; "but you have honestly earned it." So the judge had the Jew taken to the gallows and hanged as a thief.

THE SKILFUL HUNTSMAN

There was once a young fellow who had learnt the trade of locksmith, and told his father he would now go out into the world and seek his fortune. "Very well," said the father, "I am quite content with that," and gave him some money for his journey. So he travelled about and looked for work. After a time he resolved not to follow the trade of locksmith any more, for he no longer liked it, but he took a fancy for hunting. Then there met him in his rambles a huntsman dressed in green, who asked whence he came and whither he was going. The youth said he was a locksmith's apprentice, but that the trade no longer pleased him, and he had a liking for huntsmanship, would he teach it to him. "Oh, yes," said the huntsman, "if you will go with me." Then the young fellow went with him, apprenticed himself to him for some years, and learnt the art of hunting. After this he wished to try his luck elsewhere, and the huntsman gave him nothing in the way of payment but an air-gun, which had, however, this property, that it hit its mark without fail whenever he shot with it. Then he set out and found himself in a very large forest, which he could not get to the end of in one day. When evening came he seated himself in a high tree in order to escape from the wild beasts. Towards midnight, it seemed to him as if a tiny little light glimmered in the distance. Then he looked down through the branches towards it, and kept well in his mind where it was. But in the first place he took off his hat and threw it down in the direction of the light, so that he might go to the hat as a mark when he had descended. He got down and went to his hat, put it on again and went straight forwards. The farther he went, the larger the light grew, and when he got close to it he saw that it was an enormous fire, and that three giants were sitting by it, who had an ox on the spit, and were roasting it. Presently one of them said: "I must just taste if the meat will soon be fit to eat," and pulled a piece off, and was about to put it in his mouth when the huntsman shot it out of his hand. "Well, really," said the giant, "if the wind has not blown the bit out of my hand!" and helped himself to another. But when he was just about to bite into it, the huntsman again shot it away from him. On this the giant gave the one who was sitting next to him a box on the ear, and cried angrily: "Why are you snatching my piece away from me?" "I have not snatched it away," said the other, "a sharpshooter must have shot it away from you." The giant took another piece, but again could not keep it in his hand, for the huntsman shot it out. Then the giant said: "That must be a good shot to shoot the bit out of one's very mouth, such an one would be useful to us." And he cried aloud: "Come here, you sharpshooter, seat yourself at the fire beside us and eat your fill, we

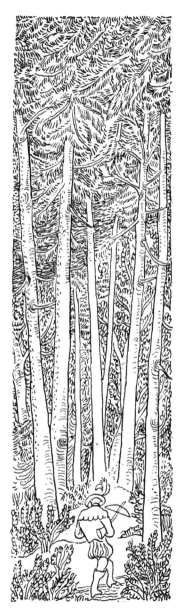

will not hurt you; but if you will not come, and we have to bring you
by force, you are a lost man!" On this the youth went up to them and
told them he was a skilled huntsman, and that whatever he aimed at
with his gun, he was certain to hit. Then they said if he would go with
them he should be well treated, and they told him that outside the
forest there was a great lake, behind which stood a tower, and in the
tower was imprisoned a lovely princess, whom they wished very much
to carry off. "Yes," said he, "I will soon get her for you." Then they
added: "But there is still something else, there is a tiny little dog, which
begins to bark directly any one goes near, and as soon as it barks every
one in the royal palace wakens up, and for this reason we cannot get
there; can you undertake to shoot it dead?" "Yes," said he, "that will be
quite fun for me." After this he got into a boat and rowed over the lake,
and as soon as he landed, the little dog came running out, and was
about to bark, but the huntsman took his airgun and shot it dead.
When the giants saw that, they rejoiced, and thought they already had
the King's daughter safe, but the huntsman wished first to see how
matters stood, and told them that they must stay outside until he called
them. Then he went into the castle, and all was perfectly quiet within,
and every one was asleep. When he opened the door of the first room, a
sword was hanging on the wall which was made of pure silver, and
there was a golden star on it, and the name of the King, and on a table
near it lay a sealed letter which he broke open, and inside it was written
that whosoever had the sword could kill everything which opposed
him. So he took the sword from the wall, hung it at his side and went
onwards: then he entered the room where the King's daughter was
lying sleeping, and she was so beautiful that he stood still and, holding
his breath, looked at her. He thought to himself: "How can I give an
innocent maiden into the power of the wild giants, who have evil in
their minds?" He looked about further, and under the bed stood a pair
of slippers, on the right one was her father's name with a star, and on
the left her own name with a star. She wore also a large scarf of silk
embroidered with gold, and on the right side was her father's name,
and on the left her own, all in golden letters. Then the huntsman took a
pair of scissors and cut the right corner off, and put it in his knapsack,
and then he also took the right slipper with the King's name, and thrust
that in. Now the maiden still lay sleeping, and she was quite sewn into

her night-dress, and he cut a morsel from this also, and thrust it in with the rest, but he did all without touching her. Then he went forth and left her lying asleep undisturbed, and when he came to the gate again, the giants were still standing outside waiting for him, and expecting that he was bringing the princess. But he cried to them that they were to come in, for the maiden was already in their power, that he could not open the gate to them, but there was a hole through which they must creep. Then the first approached, and the huntsman wound the giant's hair round his hand, pulled the head in, and cut it off at one stroke with his sword, and then drew the rest of him in. He called to the second and cut his head off likewise, and then he killed the third also, and he was well pleased that he had freed the beautiful maiden from her enemies, and he cut out their tongues and put them in his knapsack. Then thought he: "I will go home to my father and let him see what I have already done, and afterwards I will travel about the world; the luck which God is pleased to grant me will easily find me."

But when the King in the castle awoke, he saw the three giants lying there dead. So he went into the sleeping-room of his daughter, awoke her, and asked who could have killed the giants? Then said she: "Dear father, I know not, I have been asleep." But when she arose and would have put on her slippers, the right one was gone, and when she looked at her scarf it was cut, and the right corner was missing, and when she looked at her night-dress a piece was cut out of it. The King summoned his whole court together, soldiers and every one else who was there, and asked who had set his daughter at liberty, and killed the giants. Now it happened that he had a captain, who was one-eyed and a hideous man, and he said that he had done it. Then the old King said that as he had accomplished this, he should marry his daughter. But the maiden said: "Rather than marry him, dear father, I will go away into the world as far as my legs can carry me." But the King said that if she would not marry him she should take off her royal garments and wear peasant's clothing, and go forth, and that she should go to a potter, and begin a trade in earthen vessels. So she put off her royal apparel, and went to a potter and borrowed crockery enough for a stall, and she promised him also that if she had sold it by the evening, she would pay for it. Then the King said she was to seat herself in a corner with it and sell it, and he arranged with some peasants to drive over it with their carts, so that everything should be broken into a thousand pieces. When therefore the King's daughter had placed her stall in the street, by came the carts, and broke all she had into tiny fragments. She began to weep and said: "Alas, how shall I ever pay for the pots now?" The King, however, had wished by this to force her to marry the captain; but instead of that, she again went to the potter, and asked him if he would lend to her once more. He said, "No," she must first pay for what she already had. Then she went to her father and cried and lamented, and said she would go forth into the world. Then said he: "I will have a little hut built for you in the forest outside, and in it you shall stay all your life long and cook for every one, but you shall take no money for it." When the hut was ready, a sign was hung on the door whereon was written: "To-day given, to-morrow sold." There she remained a long time, and it was rumoured about the world that a maiden was there who cooked without asking for payment, and that this was set forth on a sign outside her door. The huntsman heard it likewise, and thought to himself: "That would suit you. You are poor, and have no money." So he took his air-gun and his knapsack, wherein all the things which he had formerly carried away with him from the castle as tokens of his truthfulness were still lying, and went into the forest, and found the hut with the sign: "To-day given, to-morrow sold." He had put on the sword with which he had cut off the heads of the three giants, and thus entered the hut, and ordered something to eat to be given to him. He was charmed with the beautiful maiden, who was indeed as lovely as any picture. She asked him whence he came and whither he was going, and he said: "I am roaming about the world." Then she asked him where he had got the sword, for that truly her father's name was on it. He asked her if she were the King's daughter. "Yes," answered she. "With this sword," said he, "did I cut off the heads of three giants." And he took their tongues out of his knapsack in proof. Then he also showed her the slipper, and the corner of the scarf, and the piece of the night-dress. Hereupon she was overjoyed, and said that he was the one who had delivered her. On this they went together to the old King, and fetched him to the hut, and she led him into her room, and told him that the huntsman was the man who had really set her free from the giants. And when the aged King saw all the proofs of this, he could no longer doubt, and said that he was very glad he knew how everything had happened, and that the huntsman should have her to wife, on which the maiden was glad at heart. Then she dressed the huntsman as if he were a foreign lord, and the King ordered a feast to be prepared. When they went to table, the captain sat on the left side of the King's daughter, but the huntsman was on the right, and the captain thought he was a foreign lord who had come on a visit. When they had eaten and drunk, the old King said to the captain that he would set before him something which he must guess. "Supposing someone said that he had killed the three giants and he were asked where the giants' tongues were, and he were forced to go and look, and there were none in their heads. How could that have happened?" The captain said: "Then they cannot have had any." "Not so," said the King. "Every animal has a tongue," and then he likewise asked what punishment should be meted out to anyone who made such an answer. The captain replied: "He ought to be torn in pieces." Then the King said he had pronounced his own sentence, and the captain was put in prison and then torn in four pieces; but the King's daughter was married to the huntsman. After this he brought his father and mother, and they lived with their son in happiness, and after the death of the old King he received the kingdom.

THE FLAIL FROM HEAVEN

A countryman was once going out to plough with a pair of oxen. When he got to the field, both the animals' horns began to grow, and went on growing, and when he wanted to go home they were so big that the oxen could not get through the gateway. By good luck a butcher came by just then, and he delivered them over to him, and made the bargain in this way, that he should bring the butcher a peck of rape-seed, and then the butcher was to count him out a Brabant taler for every seed. I call that well sold! The peasant now went home, and carried the peck of rape-seed to him on his back. On the way, however, he lost one seed out of the bag. The butcher paid him justly as agreed on, and if the peasant had not lost the seed, he would have had one taler more. By the time he returned, the seed had grown into a tree

which reached up to the sky. Then thought the peasant: "As you have the chance, you must just see what the angels are doing up there above. So he climbed up, and saw that the angels above were threshing oats, and he looked on. While he was thus watching them, he observed that the tree on which he was standing, was beginning to totter; he peeped down, and saw that someone was just going to cut it down. "If I were to fall down from hence it would be a bad thing," thought he, and in his extremity he did not know how to save himself better than by taking the chaff of the oats which lay there in heaps, and twisting a rope of it. He likewise snatched a hoe and a flail which were lying about in heaven, and let himself down by the rope. But he came down on the earth exactly in the middle of a deep, deep hole. So it was a real stroke of luck that he had brought the hoe, for he hoed himself a flight of steps with it, and mounted up, and took the flail with him as a token of his truth, so that no one could have any doubt of his story.

THE TWO KINGS' CHILDREN

There was once upon a time a King who had a little boy in whose stars it had been foretold that he should be killed by a stag when he was sixteen years of age, and when he had reached that age the huntsmen once went hunting with him. In the forest, the King's son was separated from the others, and all at once he saw a great stag which he wanted to shoot, but could not hit. At length he chased the stag so far that they were quite out of the forest, and then suddenly a great tall man was standing there instead of the stag, and said: "It is well that I have you. I have already ruined six pairs of glass skates with running after you, and have not been able to reach you." Then he took the King's son with him, and dragged him through a great lake to a great palace, and he had to sit down to table with him and eat something. When they had eaten something together the King said: "I have three daughters, you must keep watch over the eldest for one night, from nine in the evening till six in the morning, and every time the clock strikes, I will come myself and call, and if you then give me no answer, to-morrow morning you shall be put to death, but if you always give me an answer, you shall have her to wife."

When the young folks went to the bedroom there stood a stone image of St. Christopher, and the King's daughter said to it: "My father will come at nine o'clock, and every hour till it strikes three, when he calls, give him an answer instead of the King's son." Then the stone image of St. Christopher nodded its head quite quickly, and then more and more slowly till at last it again stood still. The next morning the King said to him: "You have done the business well, but I cannot give my daughter away. You must now watch a night by my second daughter, and then I will consider with myself, whether you can have my eldest daughter to wife, but I shall come every hour myself, and when I call you, answer me, and if I call you and you do not reply, your blood shall flow. Then they both went into the sleeping-room, and there stood a still larger stone image of St. Christopher, and the King's daughter said to it: "If my father calls, answer him." Then the great stone image of St. Christopher again nodded its head quite quickly and then more and more slowly, until at last it stood still again. And the King's son lay down on the threshold, put his hand under his head and slept. The next morning the King said to him: "You have done the business really well, but I cannot give my daughter away; you must now watch a night by the youngest princess, and then I will consider with myself whether you can have my second daughter to wife. But I shall come every hour myself, and when I call you answer me, and if I call you and you answer not, your blood shall flow for me."

Then they once more went to the sleeping-room together, and there was a much greater and much taller image of St. Christopher than the two first had been. The King's daughter said to it: "When my father calls, answer." Then the great tall stone image of St. Christopher

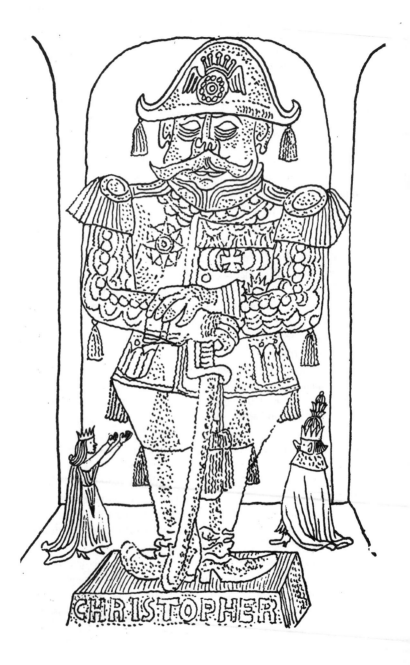

CHRISTOPHER

nodded quite half an hour with its head, until at length the head stood still again. And the King's son laid himself down on the threshold of the door and slept. The next morning the King said: "You have indeed watched well, but I cannot give you my daughter now; I have a great forest, if you cut it down for me between six o'clock this morning and six at night, I will think about it." Then he gave him a glass axe, a glass wedge, and a glass mallet. When he got into the wood, he began at once to cut, but the axe broke in two. Then he took the wedge, and struck it once with the mallet, and it became as short and as small as sand. Then he was much troubled and believed he would have to die, and sat down and wept.

Now when it was noon the King said: "One of you girls must take him something to eat." "No," said the two eldest, "we will not take it to him; the one by whom he last watched can take him something." Then the youngest was forced to go and take him something to eat. When she got into the forest, she asked him how he was getting on. "Oh," said he, "I am getting on very badly." Then she said he was to come and just eat a little. "Nay," said he, "I cannot do that, I have to die anyway, so I will eat no more." Then she spoke so kindly to him and begged him just to try, that he came and ate something. When he had eaten something she said: "I will pick your lice a while, and then you will feel happier."

So she loused him, and he became weary and fell asleep, and then she took her handkerchief and made a knot in it, and struck it three times on the earth, and said: "Earth-workers, come forth." In a moment, numbers of little earth-men came forth, and asked what the King's daughter commanded. Then said she: "In three hours' time the great forest must be cut down, and all the wood laid in heaps." So the little earth-men went about and got together the whole of their kindred to help them with the work. They began at once, and when the three hours were over, all was done, and they came back to the King's daughter and told her so. Then she took her white handkerchief again and said: "Earth-workers, go home." At this they all disappeared.

When the King's son awoke, he was delighted, and she said: "Come home when it has struck six o'clock." He did as she told him, and then the King asked: "Have you made away with the forest?" "Yes," said the King's son. When they were sitting at table, the King said: "I cannot yet give you my daughter to wife, you must still do something more for her sake." So he asked what it was to be. "I have a great fish-pond," said the King. "You must go to it to-morrow morning and clear it of all mud until it is as bright as a mirror, and fill it with every kind of fish." The next morning the King gave him a glass shovel and said: "The fish-pond must be done by six o'clock. So he went away, and when he came to the fish-pond he stuck his shovel in the mud and it broke in two. Then he stuck his hoe in the mud, and it broke also. Then he was much troubled. At noon the youngest daughter brought him something to eat, and asked him how he was getting on. So the King's son said everything was going very ill with him, and he would certainly have to lose his head. "My tools have broken to pieces again." "Oh," said she, "you must just come and eat something, and then you will be in another frame of mind." "No," said he, "I cannot eat, I am far too unhappy for that!" Then she gave him many good words until at last he came and ate something. Then she loused him again, and he fell asleep, so once more she took her handkerchief, tied a knot in it, and struck the ground thrice with the knot, and said: "Earth-workers, come forth." In a moment a great many little earth-men came and asked what she desired, and she told them that in three hours' time, they must have the fish-pond entirely cleaned out, and it must be so clear that people could see themselves reflected in it, and every kind of fish must be in it. The little earth-men went away and summoned all their kindred to help them, and in two hours it was done. Then they returned to her and said: "We have done as you have commanded." The King's daughter took the handkerchief and once more struck thrice on the ground with it, and said: "Earth-workers, go home again." Then they all went away.

When the King's son awoke the fish-pond was done. Then the King's daughter went away also, and told him that when it was six he was to come to the house. When he arrived at the house the King asked: "Have you got the fish-pond done?" "Yes," said the King's son. That was very good.

When they were again sitting at table the King said: "You have certainly done the fish-pond, but I cannot give you my daughter yet; you must just do one thing more." "What is that, then?" asked the King's son. The King said he had a great mountain on which there was nothing but briars which must all be cut down, and at the top of it the youth must build a great castle, which must be as strong as could be conceived, and all the furniture and fittings belonging to a castle must be inside it. And when he arose next morning the King gave him a glass axe and a glass gimlet, and he was to have all done by six o'clock. As he was cutting down the first briar with the axe, it broke off short, and so small that the pieces flew all round about, and he could not use the gimlet either. Then he was quite miserable, and waited for his dearest to see if she would not come and help him in his need. When it was mid-day she came and brought him something to eat. He went to meet her and told her all, and ate something, and let her louse him and fell asleep. Then she once more took the knot and struck the earth with it, and said: "Earth-workers, come forth!" Then came once again numbers of earth-men, and asked what her desire was. Then said she: "In the space of three hours you must cut down the whole of the briars, and a castle must be built on the top of the mountain that must be as strong as any one could conceive, and all the furniture that pertains to a castle must be inside it." They went away, and summoned their kindred to help them and when the time was come, all was ready. Then they came to the King's daughter and told her so, and the King's daughter took her handkerchief and struck thrice on the earth with it, and said: "Earth-workers, go home," on which they all disappeared. When therefore the King's son awoke and saw everything done, he was as happy as a bird in air.

When it had struck six, they went home together. Then said the King: "Is the castle ready?" "Yes," said the King's son. When they sat down to table, the King said: "I cannot give away my youngest daughter until the two eldest are married." Then the King's son and the King's daughter were quite troubled, and the King's son had no idea what to do. But he went by night to the King's daughter and ran away with her. When they had got a little distance away, the King's daughter peeped round and saw her father behind her. "Oh," said she, "what are we to do? My father is behind us, and will take us back with him. I will at once change you into a briar, and myself into a rose, and I will shelter myself in the midst of the bush." When the father reached the place, there stood a briar with one rose on it, and he was about to gather the rose, when the thorn pricked his finger so that he was forced to go home again. His wife asked why he had not brought their daughter back with him. So he said he had nearly got up to her, but that all at once he had lost sight of her, and a briar with one rose was growing on the spot.

Then said the Queen: "If you had but gathered the rose, the briar would have been forced to come too." So he went back again to fetch the rose, but in the meantime the two were already far over the plain, and the King ran after them. Then the daughter once more looked round and saw her father coming, and said: "Oh, what shall we do now? I will instantly change you into a church and myself into a priest, and I will stand up in the pulpit, and preach." When the King got to the place, there stood a church, and in the pulpit was a priest preaching. So he listened to the sermon, and then went home again.

Then the Queen asked why he had not brought their daughter with him, and he said: "Nay, I ran a long time after her, and just as I thought I should soon overtake her, a church was standing there and a priest was in the pulpit preaching." "You should just have brought the priest," said his wife, "and then the church would soon have come. It is no use to send you, I must go there myself." When she had walked for some time, and could see the two in the distance, the King's daughter peeped round and saw her mother coming, and said: "Now we are undone, for my mother is coming herself: I will immediately change you into a fish-pond and myself into a fish."

When the mother came to the place, there was a large fish-pond, and in the midst of it a fish was leaping about and peeping out of the water, and it was quite merry. She wanted to catch the fish, but she could not. Then she was very angry, and drank up the whole pond in order to catch the fish, but it made her so ill that she was forced to vomit, and vomited the whole pond out again. Then she cried: "I see very well that nothing can be done now," and asked them to come back to her. Then the King's daughter went back again, and the Queen gave her daughter three walnuts, and said: "With these you can help yourself when you are in your greatest need." So the young folks once more went away together. And when they had walked quite ten miles, they arrived at the castle from whence the King's son came, and near it was a village. When they reached it, the King's son said: "Stay here, my dearest, I will just go to the castle, and then will I come with a carriage and with attendants to fetch you."

When he got to the castle they all rejoiced greatly at having the

King's son back again, and he told them he had a bride who was now in the village, and they must go with the carriage to fetch her. Then they harnessed the horses at once, and many attendants seated themselves outside the carriage. When the King's son was about to get in, his mother gave him a kiss, and he forgot everything which had happened, and also what he was about to do. At this his mother ordered the horses to be taken out of the carriage again, and everyone went back into the house. But the maiden sat in the village and watched and watched, and thought he would come and fetch her, but no one came. Then the King's daughter took service in the mill which belonged to the castle, and was obliged to sit by the pond every afternoon and clean the tubs. And the Queen came one day on foot from the castle, and went walking by the pond and saw the well-grown maiden sitting there, and said: "What a fine strong girl that is! She pleases me well!" Then she and all with her looked at the maid, but no one knew her. So a long time passed by during which the maiden served the miller honourably and faithfully. In the meantime, the Queen had sought a wife for her son, who came from quite a distant part of the world. When the bride came, they were at once to be married. And many people hurried together, all of whom wanted to see everything. Then the girl said to the miller that he might be so good as to give her leave to go also. So the miller said: "Yes, do go there." When she was about to go, she opened one of the three walnuts, and a beautiful dress lay inside it. She put it on, and went into the church and stood by the altar. Suddenly came the bride and bridegroom, and seated themselves before the altar, and when the priest was just going to bless them, the bride peeped half round and saw the maiden standing there. Then she stood up again, and said she would not be given away until she also had as beautiful a dress as that lady there. So they went back to the house again, and sent to ask the lady if she would sell that dress. No, she would not sell it, but the bride might perhaps earn it. Then the bride asked her how she was to do this. Then the maiden said if she might sleep one night outside the King's son's door, the bride might have what she wanted. So the bride said, Yes, she was willing to do that. But the servants were ordered to give the King's son a sleeping draught, and then the maiden laid herself down on the threshold and lamented all night long. She had had the forest cut down for him, she had had the fish-pond cleaned out for him, she had had the castle built for him, she had changed him into a briar, and then into a church, and at last into a fish-pond, and yet he had forgotten her so quickly. The King's son did not hear one word of it, but the servants had been awakened, and had listened to it, and had not known what it could mean. The next morning when they were all up, the bride put on the dress, and went away to the church with the bridegroom. In the meantime the maiden opened the second walnut, and a still more beautiful dress was inside it. She put it on, and went and stood by the altar in the church, and everything happened as it had happened the time before. And the maiden again lay all night on the threshold which led to the chamber of the King's son, and the servant was once more to give him a sleeping draught. The servant, however, went to him and gave him something to keep him awake, and then the King's son went to bed, and the miller's maiden bemoaned herself as before on the threshold of the door, and told of all that she had done. All this the King's son heard, and was sore troubled, and what was past came back to him. Then he wanted to go to her, but his mother had locked the door. The next morning, however, he went at once to his beloved, and told her everything which had happened to him, and prayed her not to be angry with him for having forgotten her. Then the King's daughter opened the third walnut, and within it was a still more magnificent dress, which she put on, and went with her bridegroom to church, and numbers of children came who gave them flowers, and offered them gay ribbons to bind about their feet, and they were blessed by the priest, and had a merry wedding. But the false mother and the bride had to depart. And the mouth of the person who last told all this is still warm.

THE CUNNING LITTLE TAILOR

There was once upon a time a princess who was extremely proud. If a wooer came she gave him some riddle to guess, and if he could not guess it, he was sent contemptuously away. She let it be made known also that whosoever solved her riddle should marry her, let him be who he might. At length, three tailors fell in with each other, the two eldest of whom thought they had done so many dexterous jobs of work successfully that they could not fail to succeed in this also; the third was a little, useless harum-scarum, who did not even know his trade, but thought he must have some luck in this venture, for where else was it to come from? Then the two others said to him: "Just stay at home; you cannot do much with your little understanding." The little tailor, however, did not let himself be discouraged, and said he had set his mind to work on this for once, and he would manage well enough, and he went forth as if the whole world were his.

They all three announced themselves to the princess, and said she was to propound her riddle to them, and that the right persons were now come, who had understandings so fine that they could be threaded in a needle. Then said the princess: "I have two kinds of hair on my head, of what colour is it?" "If that be all," said the first, "it must be black and white, like the cloth which is called 'pepper and salt'." The princess said: "Wrongly guessed; let the second answer." Then said the second: "If it be not black and white, then it is brown and red, like my father's Sunday coat." "Wrongly guessed," said the princess, "let the third give the answer for I see very well he knows it for certain." Then the little tailor stepped boldly forth and said: "The princess has a silver and a golden hair on her head, and those are the two different colours. When the princess heard that, she turned pale and nearly fell down with terror, for the little tailor had guessed her riddle, and she had firmly believed that no man on earth could discover it. When her courage returned she said: "You have not won me yet by that; there is still something else that you must do. Below, in the stable, is a bear with which you shall pass the night, and when I get up in the morning if you are still alive, you shall marry me." She expected, however, she would thus get rid of the tailor, for the bear had never yet left anyone alive who had fallen into his

clutches. The little tailor did not let himself be frightened away, but was quite delighted, and said: "Boldly ventured is half won."

So when the evening came, our little tailor was taken down to the bear. The bear was about to set on the little fellow at once, and give him a hearty welcome with his paws. "Softly, softly," said the little tailor, "I will soon make you quiet." Then quite composedly, and as if he had no anxiety in the world, he took some nuts out of his pocket, cracked them, and ate the kernels. When the bear saw that, he was seized with a desire to have some nuts too. The tailor felt in his pockets, and reached him a handful; they were, however, not nuts, but pebbles. The bear put them in his mouth, but could get nothing out of them, let him bite as he would. "Eh!" thought he, "what a stupid blockhead am I! I cannot even crack a nut!" and then he said to the tailor: "Here, crack me the nuts." "There, see what a stupid fellow you are!" said the little tailor, "to have such a great mouth, and not be able to crack a small nut!" Then he took the pebble and nimbly put a nut in his mouth in the place of it, and crack, it was in two! "I must try the thing again," said the bear; "when I watch you, I then think I ought to be able to do it too." So the tailor once more gave him a pebble, and the bear tried and tried to bite into it with all the strength of his body. But even you do not believe that he managed it. When that was over, the tailor took out a violin from beneath his coat, and played something to himself. When the bear heard the music, he could not help beginning to dance, and when he had danced a while, the thing pleased him so well that he said to the little tailor: "Listen, is it difficult to fiddle?" "Easy enough for a child. Look, with the left hand I lay my fingers on it, and with the right I stroke it with the bow, and then it goes merrily, hop sa sa vivallalera!"

"So," said the bear; "fiddling is a thing I should like to learn too, that I might dance whenever I felt like it. What do you think of that? Will you give me lessons?" "With all my heart," said the tailor, "if you have a talent for it. But just let me see your claws, they are terribly long, I must cut your nails a little." Then a vice was brought, and the bear put his claws in it, and the little tailor screwed it tight, and said: "Now wait until I come with the scissors," and he let the bear growl as he liked, and lay down in the corner on a bundle of straw, and fell asleep.

When the princess heard the bear growling so fiercely during the night, she believed nothing else but that he was growling for joy, and had made an end of the tailor. In the morning she arose careless and happy, but when she peeped into the stable, the tailor stood gaily before her, and was as healthy as a fish in water. Now she could not say another word against the wedding because she had given a promise before everyone, and the King ordered a carriage to be brought in which she was to drive to church with the tailor, and there she was to be married. When they had climbed into the carriage, the two other tailors, who had false hearts and envied him his good fortune, went into the stable and unscrewed the bear again. The bear in great fury ran after the carriage. The princess heard him snorting and growling; she was terrified, and she cried: "Ah, the bear is behind us and wants to get you!" The tailor was quick and stood on his head, stuck his legs out of the window, and cried: "Do you see the vice? If you do not be off you shall be put into it again." When the bear saw that, he turned round and ran away. The tailor drove quietly to church, and the princess was married to him at once, and he lived with her as happy as a woodlark. Whosoever does not believe this, must pay a taler.

THE BRIGHT SUN BRINGS IT TO LIGHT

A tailor's apprentice was travelling about the world in search of work, and at one time he could find none, and his poverty was so great that he had not a farthing to live on. Presently he met a Jew on the road, and as he thought he would have a great deal of money about him, the tailor thrust God out of his heart, fell on the Jew, and said: "Give me your money, or I will strike you dead." Then said the Jew: "Grant me my life, I have no money but eight farthings." But the tailor said: "Money you have; and it shall be produced," and used violence and beat him until he was near death. And when the Jew was dying, the last words he said were: "The bright sun will bring it to light," and thereupon he died. The tailor's apprentice felt in his pockets and sought for money, but he found nothing but eight farthings, as the Jew had said. Then he took him up and carried him behind a clump of trees, and went onwards to seek work. After he had travelled about a long while, he found work in a town with a master who had a pretty daughter, with whom he fell in love, and he married her, and lived in good and happy wedlock.

After a long time when he and his wife had two children, the wife's father and mother died, and the young people kept house alone. One morning, when the husband was sitting on the table before the window, his wife brought him his coffee, and when he had poured it out into the saucer, and was just going to drink, the sun shone on it and the reflection gleamed hither and thither on the wall above, and made circles on it. Then the tailor looked up and said: "Yes, it would like very much to bring it to light, and cannot!" The woman said: "O, dear husband, and what is that, then? What do you mean by that?" He answered: "I must not tell you." But she said: "If you love me, you must tell me," and used her most affectionate words, and said that no one

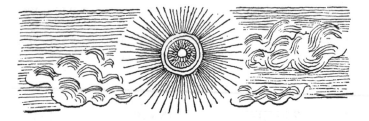

should ever know it, and left him no rest. Then he told her how years ago, when he was travelling about seeking work and quite worn out and penniless, he had killed a Jew, and that in the last agonies of death, the Jew had spoken the words: "The bright sun will bring it to light." And now, the sun had just wanted to bring it to light, and had gleamed and made circles on the wall, but had not been able to do it. After this, he again charged her particularly never to tell this, or he would lose his life, and she did promise. However, when he had sat down to work again, she went to her great friend and confided the story to her, and asked her never to repeat it to any human being, but before three days were over, the whole town knew it, and the tailor was brought to trial, and condemned. And thus, after all, the bright sun did bring it to light.

THE BLUE LIGHT

There was once on a time a soldier who for many years had served the King faithfully, but when the war came to an end could serve no longer because of the many wounds which he had received. The King said to him: "You may return to your home, I need you no longer, and you will not receive any more money, for he only receives wages who renders me service for them." Then the soldier did not know how to earn a living, went away greatly troubled, and walked the whole day, until in the evening he entered a forest. When darkness came on, he saw a light, which he went up to, and came to a house wherein lived a witch. "Do give me one night's lodging, and a little to eat and drink," said he to her, "or I shall starve." "Oho!" she answered, "who gives anything to a run-away soldier? Yet will I be compassionate, and take you in, if you will do what I wish." "What do you wish?" said the soldier. "That you should dig all round my garden for me, tomorrow." The soldier consented, and next day laboured with all his strength, but could not finish it by the evening. "I see well enough," said the witch, "that you can do no more today, but I will keep you yet another night, in payment for which you must tomorrow chop me a load of wood, and chop it small." The soldier spent the whole day in doing it, and in the evening the witch proposed that he should stay one night more. "Tomorrow, you shall only do me a very trifling piece of work. Behind my house, there is an old dry well, into which my light has fallen, it burns blue, and never goes out, and you shall bring it up again." Next day the old woman took him to the well, and let him down in a basket. He found the blue light, and made her a signal to draw him up again. She did draw him up, but when he came near the edge, she stretched down her hand and wanted to take the blue light away from him. "No," said he, perceiving her evil intention, "I will not give you the light until I am standing with both feet upon the ground." The witch fell into a passion, let him fall again into the well, and went away.

The poor soldier fell without injury on the moist ground, and the blue light went on burning, but of what use was that to him? He saw very well that he could not escape death. He sat for a while very sorrowfully, then suddenly he felt in his pocket and found his tobacco pipe, which was still half full. "This shall be my last pleasure," thought he, pulled it out, lit it at the blue light and began to smoke. When the smoke had circled about the cavern, suddenly a little black dwarf stood before him, and said: "Lord, what are your commands?" "What my commands are?" replied the soldier, quite astonished. "I must do everything you bid me," said the little man. "Good," said the soldier; "then in the first place help me out of this well." The little man took him by the hand, and led him through an underground passage, but he did not forget to take the blue light with him. On the way the dwarf showed him the treasures which the witch had collected and hidden there, and the soldier took as much gold as he could carry. When he was above, he said to the little man: "Now go and bind the old witch, and carry her before the judge." In a short time she came by like the wind, riding on a wild tom-cat and screaming frightfully. Nor was it long before the little man re-appeared. "It is all done," said he, "and the witch is already hanging on the gallows. What further commands has my lord?" inquired the dwarf. "At this moment, none," answered the soldier; "you can return home, only be at hand immediately, if I summon you." "Nothing more is needed than that you should light your pipe at the blue light, and I will appear before you at once." Thereupon he vanished from his sight.

The soldier returned to the town from which he had come. He went to the best inn, ordered himself handsome clothes, and then bade the landlord furnish him a room as handsome as possible. When it was ready and the soldier had taken possession of it, he summoned the little black mannikin and said: "I have served the King faithfully, but he has dismissed me, and left me to hunger, and now I want to take my revenge." "What am I to do?" asked the little man. "Late at night, when the King's daughter is in bed, bring her here in her sleep, she shall do servant's work for me." The mannikin said: "That is an easy thing for me to do, but a very dangerous thing for you, for if it is discovered, you will fare ill." When twelve o'clock had struck, the door sprang open, and the mannikin carried in the princess. "Aha! are you there?" cried the soldier, "get to your work at once! Fetch the broom and sweep the chamber." When she had done this, he ordered her to come to his chair, and then he stretched out his feet and said: "Pull off my boots," and then he threw them in her face, and made her pick them up again, and clean and brighten them. She, however, did everything he bade her, without opposition, silently and with halfshut eyes. When the first cock crowed, the mannikin carried her back to the royal palace, and laid her in her bed.

Next morning when the princess arose she went to her father, and told him that she had had a very strange dream. "I was carried through the streets with the rapidity of lightning," said she, "and taken into a soldier's room, and I had to wait upon him like a servant, sweep his room, clean his boots, and do all kinds of menial work. It was only a dream, and yet I am just as tired as if I really had done everything." "The dream may have been true," said the King, "I will give you a piece of advice. Fill your pocket full of peas, and make a small hole in the pocket, and then if you are carried away again, they will fall out and leave a track in the streets." But unseen by the King, the mannikin was standing beside him when he said that, and heard all. At night when the sleeping princess was again carried through the streets, some peas certainly did fall out of her pocket, but they made no track, for the crafty mannikin had just before scattered peas in every street there was. And again the princess was compelled to do servant's work until cock-crow.

Next morning the King sent his people out to seek the track, but it was all in vain, for in every street poor children were sitting, picking up peas, and saying: "It must have rained peas, last night." "We must think of something else," said the King; "keep your shoes on when you go to bed, and before you come back from the place where you are taken, hide one of them there, I will soon contrive to find it." The black mannikin heard this plot, and at night when the soldier again ordered him to bring the princess, revealed it to him, and told him that he knew of no expedient to counteract this stratagem, and that if the shoe were found in the soldier's house it would go badly with him. "Do what I bid you," replied the soldier, and again this third night the princess was obliged to work like a servant, but before she went away, she hid her shoe under the bed.

Next morning the King had the entire town searched for his daughter's shoe. It was found at the soldier's, and the soldier himself, who at the entreaty of the dwarf had gone outside the gate, was soon brought back, and thrown into prison. In his flight he had forgotten the most valuable things he had, the blue light and the gold, and had only one ducat in his pocket. And now loaded with chains, he was standing at the window of his dungeon, when he chanced to see one of his comrades passing by. The soldier tapped at the pane of glass, and when this man came up, said to him: "Be so kind as to fetch me the small bundle I have left lying in the inn, and I will give you a ducat for doing it." His comrade ran thither and brought him what he wanted. As soon as the soldier was alone again, he lighted his pipe and summoned the black mannikin. "Have no fear," said the latter to his master. "Go wheresoever they take you, and let them do what they will, only take the blue light with you." Next day the soldier was tried, and though he had done nothing wicked, the judge condemned him to death. When he was led forth to die, he begged a last favour of the King. "What is it?" asked the King. "That I may smoke one more pipe on my way." "You may smoke three," answered the King, "but do not imagine that I will spare your life." Then the soldier pulled out his pipe and lighted it at the blue light, and as soon as a few wreaths of smoke had ascended, the mannikin was there with a small cudgel in his hand, and said: "What does my lord command?" "Strike down to earth that false judge there, and his constable, and spare not the King who has treated me so ill."

Then the mannikin fell on them like lightning, darting this way and that way, and whosoever was so much as touched by his cudgel fell to earth, and did not venture to stir again. The King was terrified; he threw himself on the soldier's mercy, and merely to be allowed to live at all, gave him his kingdom for his own, and his daughter to wife.

THE WILFUL CHILD

Once upon a time there was a child who was wilful, and would not do what her mother wished. For this reason God had no pleasure in her, and let her become ill, and no doctor could do her any good, and in a short time she lay on her death-bed. When she had been lowered into

her grave, and the earth was spread over her, all at once her arm came out again, and stretched upwards, and when they had put it in and spread fresh earth over it, it was all to no purpose, for the arm always came out again. Then the mother herself was obliged to go to the grave, and strike the arm with a rod, and when she had done that, it was drawn in, and then at last the child had rest beneath the ground.

THE THREE ARMY SURGEONS

Three army surgeons who thought they knew their art perfectly, were travelling about the world, and they came to an inn where they wanted to pass the night. The host asked whence they came, and whither they were going. "We are roaming about the world and practising our art." "Show me just once what you can do," said the host. Then the first said he would cut off his hand, and put it on again early next morning; the second said he would tear out his heart, and replace it next morning; the third said he would gouge out his eyes and heal them again next morning. "If you can do that," said the innkeeper, "you have learnt everything." They, however, had a salve, with which they rubbed themselves, which joined parts together, and they constantly carried with them the little bottle in which it was. Then they cut the hand, heart and eyes from their bodies as they had said they would, and laid them all together on a plate, and gave it to the innkeeper. The innkeeper gave it to a servant-girl who was to set it in the cupboard, and take good care of it. Secretly, however, the girl had a lover, who was a soldier. When therefore the innkeeper, the three army surgeons, and everyone else in the house were asleep, the soldier came and wanted something to eat. The girl opened the cupboard and brought him some food, and in her love forgot to shut the cupboard-door again; she seated herself at the table by her lover, and they chatted away together. While she sat so contentedly there, thinking of no ill luck, the cat came creeping in, found the cupboard open, took the hand and heart and eyes of the three army surgeons, and ran off with them. When the soldier had done eating, and the girl was taking away the things and going to shut the cupboard, she saw that the plate which the innkeeper had given her to take care of, was empty. Then she said in a fright to her lover: "Ah, miserable girl, what shall I do? The hand is gone, the heart and the eyes are gone too, what will become of me in the morning?" "Be easy," said he, "I will help you out of your trouble—there is a thief hanging outside on the gallows, I will cut off his hand. Which hand was it?" "The right one." Then the girl gave him a sharp knife, and he went and cut the poor sinner's right hand off, and brought it to her. After this he caught the cat and gouged its eyes out, and now nothing but the heart was missing. "Have you not been slaughtering, and are not the dead pigs in the cellar?" said he. "Yes," said the girl. "That's fine," said the soldier, and he went down and fetched a pig's heart. The girl placed all together on the plate, and put it in the cupboard, and when after this her lover took leave of her, she went quietly to bed.

In the morning when the three army surgeons got up, they told the girl she was to bring them the plate on which the hand, heart, and eyes were lying. Then she brought it out of the cupboard, and the first fixed the thief's hand on and smeared it with his salve, and it promptly grew to his arm. The second took the cat's eyes and put them in his own head. The third fixed the pig's heart firm in the place where his own had been, and the innkeeper stood by, admired their skill, and said he had never yet seen such a thing as that done, and would sing their praises and recommend them to everyone. Then they paid their bill, and travelled farther.

As they were on their way, the one with the pig's heart did not stay with them at all, but wherever there was a corner he ran to it, and rooted about in it with his nose as pigs do. The others wanted to hold him back by the tail of his coat, but that did no good; he tore himself loose, and ran wherever the dirt was deepest. The second also behaved very strangely; he rubbed his eyes, and said to the others: "Comrades, what has happened? These are not my eyes! I don't see at all. Will one of you lead me, so that I do not fall." Then with difficulty they travelled on till evening, when they reached another inn. They went into the bar together, and there at a table in the corner sat a rich man counting money. The one with the thief's hand walked round about him, made a few jerky movements with his arm, and at last when the stranger

turned away, snatched at the pile of money, and took a handful from it. One of them saw this, and said: "Comrade, what are you about? You must not steal—shame on you!" "Eh," said he, "but what can I do? My hand twitches, and I am forced to snatch things whether I will or not."

After this, they lay down to sleep, and while they were lying there it was so dark that no one could see his own hand. All at once the one with the cat's eyes awoke, aroused the others, and said: "Brothers, just look up, do you see the white mice running about there?" The two sat up, but could see nothing. Then said he: "Things are not right with us, we have not got back again what is ours. We must return to the innkeeper, he has deceived us." So they went back the next morning, and told the host they had not received what was their own; that the first had a thief's hand, the second cat's eyes, and the third a pig's heart. The innkeeper said that the girl must be to blame for that, and was going to call her, but when she had seen the three coming, she had run out by the backdoor, and not come back. Then the three said he must give them a great deal of money, or they would set the red cock on his roof.* He gave them what he had, and whatever he could raise, and the three went away with it. It was enough for the rest of their lives, but they would rather have had their own rightful organs.

THE SEVEN SWABIANS

Seven Swabians were once together. The first was Master Schulz; the second, Jackli; the third, Marli; the fourth, Jergli; the fifth, Michal; the sixth, Hans; the seventh, Veitli: all seven had made up their minds to travel about the world to seek adventures and perform great deeds. But in order that they might go in safety and with arms in their hands, they thought it would be advisable that they should have one solitary, but very strong, and very long spear made for them. This spear all seven of them took in their hands at once; in front walked the boldest and bravest, and that was Master Schulz; all the others followed in a row, and Veitli was the last. Then it came to pass one day in the hay month,

---

* The symbol of a red cock for fire is of remote antiquity.

when they had walked a long distance, and still had a long way to go before they reached the village where they were to pass the night, that as they were in a meadow in the twilight a great beetle or hornet flew by them from behind a bush, and hummed in a menacing manner. Master Schulz was so terrified that he all but dropped the spear, and a cold sweat broke out over his whole body. "Hark! hark!" cried he to his comrades, "Good heavens! I hear a drum." Jackli, who was behind him holding the spear, and into whose nose some smell had risen, said: "Something is most certainly going on, for I smell the powder and the match." At these words Master Schulz began to take to flight, and in a trice jumped over a hedge, but as he just happened to jump on to the teeth of a rake which had been left lying there after the hay-making, the handle of it struck against his face and gave him a tremendous blow.

"O dear! O dear!" screamed Master Schulz. "Take me prisoner; I surrender! I surrender!" The other six all leapt over, one on the top of the other, crying: "If you surrender, I surrender too! If you surrender, I surrender too!" At length, as no enemy was there to bind and take them away, they saw that they had been mistaken, and in order that the story might not be known, and they be treated as fools and ridiculed, they all swore to each other to hold their peace about it until one of them should speak of it by mistake.

Then they journeyed onwards. The second danger which they survived cannot be compared with the first. Some days afterwards, their path led them through a fallow-field where a hare was sitting sleeping in the sun. Her ears were standing straight up, and her great glassy eyes were wide open. All of them were alarmed at the sight of the horrible wild beast, and they consulted together as to what it would be the least dangerous to do. For if they were to run away, they knew that the monster would pursue and swallow them whole. So they said: "We must go through a great and dangerous struggle. Boldly ventured, is half won," and all seven grasped the spear, Master Schulz in front, and Veitli behind. Master Schulz was always trying to keep the spear back, but Veitli had become quite brave while behind, and wanted to dash forward and cried:

"Strike home, in every Swabian's name,
Or else I wish you may be lame."

But Hans knew how to meet this, and said:

"Thunder and lightning, it's fine to prate,
But for dragon-hunting you are always late."

Michal cried:

"Nothing is missing, not even a hair,
Be sure the Devil himself is there."

Then it was Jergli's turn, and he said:

"If it be not he, it's at least his mother,
Or else the Devil's own step-brother."

And now Marli had a bright thought, and said to Veitli:

"Advance, Veitli, advance, advance,
And I behind will hold the lance."

Veitli, however, did not obey, and Jackli said:

"Tis Schulz's place the first to be,
No one deserves that honour but he."

Then Master Schulz plucked up his courage, and said, gravely:

"Then let us boldly advance to the fight,
Thus we shall show our valour and might."

Hereupon they all together set on the dragon. Master Schulz crossed himself and prayed for God's assistance, but as all this was of no avail, and he was getting nearer and nearer to the enemy, he screamed: "Oho! Oho! ho! ho! ho!" in the greatest anguish. This awakened the hare, which in great alarm darted swiftly away. When Master Schulz saw her thus flying from the field of battle, he cried in his joy:

"Quick, Veitli, quick, look there, look there,
The monster's nothing but a hare!"

But the Swabian allies went in search of further adventures, and came to the Moselle, a mossy, quiet, deep river, over which there are few bridges, and which in many places people have to cross in boats. As the seven Swabians did not know this, they called to a man who was working on the opposite side of the river, to know how people contrived to get across. The distance and their way of speaking made the man unable to understand what they wanted, and he said: "What? what?" in the way people speak in the neighbourhood of Treves. Master Schulz thought he was saying: "Wade, wade through the water," and as he was the first, began to set out and went into the Moselle. It was not long before he sank in the mud and the deep waves which drove against him, but his hat was blown on the opposite shore by the wind, and a frog sat down beside it, and croaked: "Wat, wat, wat." The other six on the opposite side heard that, and said: "Oho, comrades, Master Schulz is calling us; if he can wade across, why cannot we?" So they all jumped into the water together in a great hurry, and were drowned, and thus one frog took the lives of all six of them, and not one of the Swabian allies ever reached home again.

THE THREE APPRENTICES

There were once three apprentices, who had agreed to keep always together while travelling, and always to work in the same town. At one time, however, their masters

had no more work to give them, so that at last they were in rags, and had nothing to live on. Then one of them said: "What shall we do? We cannot stay here any longer, we will travel once more, and if we do not find any work in the town we go to, we will arrange with the innkeeper there, that we are to write and tell him where we are staying, so that we can always have news of each other, and then we will separate." And that seemed best to the others also. They went forth, and met on the way a richly-dressed man who asked who they were. "We are apprentices looking for work; up to this time we have kept together, but if we cannot find anything to do we are going to separate." "There is no need for that," said the man, "if you will do what I tell you, you shall not want for gold or for work;— nay, you shall become great lords, and drive in your carriages!" One of them said: "If our souls and salvation be not endangered, we will certainly do it." "They will not," replied the man, "I have no claim on you." One of the others, however, had looked at his feet, and when he saw a horse's foot and a man's foot, he did not want to have anything to do with him. Then the Devil said: "Be easy, I have no designs on you, but on another soul, which is half my own already, and whose measure shall but run full." As they were now secure, they consented, and the Devil told them what he wanted: the first was to answer: "All three of us," to every question; the second was to say: "For money," and the third: "And quite right too!" They were always to say this, one after the other, but they were not to say one word more, and if they disobeyed this order, all their money would disappear at once, but so long as they observed it, their pockets would always be full. As a beginning, he at once gave them as much as they could carry, and told them to go to such and such an inn when they got to the town. They went to it, and the innkeeper came to meet them, and asked if they wished for anything to eat? The first replied: "All three of us." "Yes," said the host, "that is what I mean." The second said: "For money." "Of course," said the host. The third said: "And quite right too!" "Certainly it is right," said the host.

Good meat and drink were now brought to them, and they were well waited on. After the dinner came the payment, and the innkeeper gave the bill to the one who said: "All three of us," the second said: "For money," and the third: "And quite right too!" "Indeed it is right," said the host, "all three pay, and without money I can give nothing." They, however, paid even more than he had asked. The lodgers, who were looking on, said: "These people must be mad." "Yes, indeed they are," said the host, "they are not very wise." So they stayed some time in the inn, and said nothing else but "All three of us," "For money," and "And quite right too!" But they saw and knew all that was going on. It so happened that a great merchant came with a large sum of money, and said: "Sir host, take care of my money for me, here are three crazy apprentices who might steal it from me." The host did as he was asked. As he was carrying the trunk into his room, he felt that it was heavy with gold. Thereupon he gave the three apprentices a lodging below, but the merchant received a separate apartment upstairs. When it was midnight, and the host thought that all were asleep, he came with his wife, and they had an axe and struck the rich merchant dead; and after they had murdered him they went to bed again. When it was day there was a great outcry; the merchant lay dead in bed bathed in blood. All the guests came running out, but the host said: "The three crazy apprentices have done this"; the lodgers confirmed it, and said: "It can have been no one else." The innkeeper, however, had them called, and said to them: "Have you killed the merchant?" "All three of us," said the first; "For money," said the second; and the third added: "And quite right too!" "There now, you hear," said the host, "they confess it themselves." They were taken to prison, therefore, and were to be tried. When they saw that things were going so seriously, they were after all afraid, but at night the Devil came and said: "Bear it just one day longer, and do not spurn your luck, not one hair of your head shall be hurt."

The next morning they were led to the bar, and the judge said: "Are you the murderers?" "All three of us." "Why did you kill the merchant?" "For money." "You wicked wretches, you have no horror of your sins?" "And quite right too!" "They have confessed, and are still stubborn" said the judge, "lead them to death instantly." So they were taken out, and the host had to go with them into the circle. When they were taken hold of by the executioner's men, and were just going to be led up to the scaffold where the hangman was standing with naked sword, a coach drawn by four chestnut horses came up suddenly, driving so fast that fire flashed from the stones, and someone made signs from the window with a white handkerchief. Then said the hangman: "It is a pardon coming," and "Pardon! pardon!" was called from the carriage also. Then the Devil stepped out as a very noble gentleman, beautifully dressed, and said: "You three are innocent; you may now speak, make known what you have seen and heard." Then said the eldest: "We did not kill the merchant, the murderer is standing there in the circle," and he pointed to the innkeeper. "In proof of this, go into his cellar, where many others whom he has killed are still hanging." Then the judge sent the executioner's men thither, and they found it was as the apprentices said, and when they had informed the judge of this, he caused the innkeeper to be led up, and his head was cut off. Then said the Devil to the three: "Now I have got the soul which I wanted to have, and you are free, and have money for the rest of your lives."

THE KING'S SON WHO FEARED NOTHING

There was once a king's son, who was no longer content to stay at home in his father's house, and as he had no fear of anything, he thought: "I will go forth into the wide world, there the time will not seem long to me, and I shall see wonders enough." So he took leave of his parents, and went forth, and on and on from morning till night, and whichever way his path led it was the same to him. It came to pass that he arrived at the house of a giant, and as he was so tired he sat down by the door and rested. And as he let his eyes roam here and there, he saw the giant's playthings lying in the yard. These were a couple of enormous balls, and nine-pins as tall as a man. After a while he had a fancy to set the nine-pins up and then rolled the balls at them, and screamed and cried out when the nine-pins fell, and had a merry time of it. The giant heard the noise, stretched his head out of the window, and saw a man who was not taller than other men, and yet played with his nine-pins. "Little worm," cried he, "why are you playing with my balls? Who gave you strength to do it?" The King's son looked up, saw the giant, and said: "Oh, you blockhead, you think indeed that you only have strong arms, I can do everything I want to do." The giant came down and watched the bowling with great admiration, and said: "Child of man, if you are one of that kind, go and bring me an apple of the tree of life." "What do you want with it?" said the King's son. "I do not want the apple for myself," answered the giant, "but I have a betrothed bride who wishes for it. I have travelled far about the world and cannot find the tree." "I will soon find it," said the King's son, "and I do not know what is to prevent me from getting the apple down." The giant said: "You really believe it to be so easy! The garden in which the tree stands is surrounded by an iron railing, and in front of the railing lie wild beasts, each close to the other, and they keep watch and let no man go in." "They will be sure to let me in," said the King's son. "Yes, but even if you do get into the garden, and see the apple hanging to the tree, it is still not yours; a ring hangs in front of it, through which any one who wants to reach the apple and break it off, must put his hand, and no one has yet had the luck to do it." "That luck will be mine," said the King's son.

Then he took leave of the giant, and went forth over mountain and

valley, and through plains and forests, until at length he came to the wondrous garden.

The beasts lay round about it, but they had put their heads down and were asleep. Moreover, they did not awake when he went up to them, so he stepped over them, climbed the fence, and got safely into the garden. There, in the very middle of it, stood the tree of life, and the red apples were shining upon the branches. He climbed up the trunk to the top, and as he was about to reach out for an apple, he saw a ring hanging before it; but he thrust his hand through that without any difficulty, and picked the apple. The ring closed tightly on his arm, and all at once he felt a prodigious strength flowing through his veins. When he had come down again from the tree with the apple, he would not climb over the fence, but grasped the great gate, and had no need to shake it more than once before it sprang open with a loud crash. Then he went out, and the lion which had been lying in front of the gate, was awake and sprang after him, not in rage and fierceness, but following him humbly as its master.

The King's son took the giant the apple he had promised him, and said: "You see, I have brought it without difficulty." The giant was glad that his desire had been so soon satisfied, hastened to his bride, and gave her the apple for which she had wished. She was a beautiful and wise maiden, and as she did not see the ring on his arm, she said: "I shall never believe that you have brought the apple, until I see the ring on your arm." The giant said: "I have nothing to do but go home and fetch it," and thought it would be easy to take away by force from the weak man, what he would not give of his own free will. He therefore demanded the ring from him, but the King's son refused it. "Where the apple is, the ring must be also," said the giant; "if you will not give it of your own accord, you must fight me for it."

They wrestled with each other for a long time, but the giant could not harm the King's son, who was strengthened by the magical power of the ring. Then the giant thought of a ruse, and said: "I have got warm with fighting, and so have you. We will bathe in the river, and cool ourselves before we begin again." The King's son, who knew nothing of falsehood, went with him to the water, and pulled off with his clothes the ring also from his arm, and sprang into the river. The giant instantly snatched the ring, and ran away with it, but the lion, which had observed the theft, pursued the giant, tore the ring out of his hand, and brought it back to its master. Then the giant placed himself behind an oak-tree, and while the King's son was busy putting on his clothes again, surprised him, and put both his eyes out.

And now the unhappy King's son stood there, and was blind and knew not how to help himself. Then the giant came back to him, took him by the hand as if he were someone who wanted to guide him, and led him to the top of a high rock. There he left him standing, and thought: "Just two steps more, and he will fall down and kill himself, and I can take the ring from him." But the faithful lion had not deserted its master; it held him fast by the clothes, and drew him gradually back again. When the giant came and wanted to rob the dead man, he saw that his cunning had been in vain. "Is there no way, then, of destroying a weak child of man like that?" said he angrily to himself, and seized the King's son and led him back again to the precipice by another way, but the lion which saw his evil design, helped its master out of danger here also. When they had come close to the edge, the giant let the blind man's hand drop, and was going to leave him behind alone, but the lion pushed the giant so that he was thrown down and fell, dashed to pieces, on the ground.

The faithful animal again drew its master back from the precipice, and guided him to a tree by which flowed a clear brook. The King's son sat down there, but the lion lay down, and sprinkled the water in his face with its paws. Scarcely had a couple of drops wetted the sockets of his eyes, than he was once more able to see something, and noticed a little bird flying quite close by, which hit itself against the trunk of a tree. So it went down to the water and bathed itself therein, and then it soared upwards and swept between the trees without touching them, as if it had recovered its sight. Then the King's son recognized a sign from God and stooped down to the water, and washed and bathed his face in it. And when he arose he had his eyes once more, brighter and clearer than they had ever been.

The King's son thanked God for his great mercy, and travelled with his lion onwards through the world. And it came to pass that he arrived before a castle which was enchanted. In the gateway stood a maiden of beautiful form and fine face, but she was quite black. She spoke to him and said: "Ah, if you could but deliver me from the evil spell which is thrown over me." "What shall I do?" said the King's son. The maiden answered: "You must pass three nights in the great hall of this enchanted castle, but you must let no fear enter your heart. When they are doing their worst to torment you, if you bear it without letting a sound escape you, I shall be free. Your life they dare not take." Then said the King's son: "I have no fear; with God's help I will try it." So he went gaily into the castle, and when it grew dark he seated himself in the large hall and waited. Everything was quiet, however, till midnight, when all at once a great tumult began, and out of every hole and corner came little devils. They behaved as if they did not see him, seated themselves in the middle of the room, lighted a fire, and began to gamble. When one of them lost, he said: "It is not right; some one is here who does not belong to us; it is his fault that I am losing." "Wait, you fellow behind the stove, I am coming," said another. The screaming became still louder, so that no one could have heard it without terror. The King's son stayed sitting quite calmly, and was not afraid; but at last the devils jumped up from the ground, and fell on him, and there were so many of them that he could not defend himself from them. They dragged him about on the floor, pinched him, pricked him, beat him, and tormented him, but no sound escaped from him. Towards morning they disappeared, and he was so exhausted that he could scarcely move his limbs, but when day dawned the black maiden came to him. She bore in her hand a little bottle wherein was the water of life wherewith she washed him, and he at once felt all pain depart and new strength flow through his veins. She said: "You have held out successfully for one night, but two more lie before you." Then she went away again, and as she was going, he observed that her feet had become white. The next night the devils came and began their gambling anew. They fell on the King's son, and beat him much more severely than the night before, until his body was covered with wounds. But as he bore all quietly, they were forced to leave him, and when dawn appeared, the maiden came and healed him with the water of life. And when she went away, he saw with joy that she had already become white to the tips of her fingers. And now he had only one night more to go through, but it was the worst. The devils came again: "Are you still there?" cried they, "you shall be tormented till your breath stops." They pricked him and beat him, and threw him here and there, and pulled him by the arms and legs as if they wanted to tear him to pieces, but he bore everything, and never uttered a cry. At last the devils vanished, but he lay fainting there, and did not stir, nor could he raise his eyes to look at the maiden who came in, and sprinkled and bathed him with the water of life. But suddenly he was freed from all pain, and felt fresh and healthy as if he had awakened from sleep, and when he opened his eyes he saw the maiden standing by him, snow-white, and fair as day. "Rise," said she, "and swing your sword three times over the stairs, and then all will be delivered." And when he had done that, the whole castle was released from enchantment, and the maiden was a rich King's daughter. The servants came and said that the table was set in the great hall, and dinner served up. Then they sat down and ate and drank together, and in the evening the wedding was solemnized with great rejoicings.

DONKEY CABBAGES

There was once a young hunstman who went into the forest to lie in wait. He had a fresh and joyous heart, and as he was going thither, whistling upon a leaf, an ugly old crone came up, who spoke to him and said: "Good-day, dear huntsman, truly you are merry and contented, but I am suffering from hunger and thirst, do give me an alms." The huntsman took pity on the poor old creature, felt in his pocket, and gave her what he could afford. He was then about to go further, but the old woman stopped him and said: "Listen, dear huntsman, to what I tell you; I will make you a present in return for your good heart. Go on your way now, but in a little while you will come to a tree, whereon nine birds are sitting which have a cloak in their claws, and are fighting for it; take your gun and shoot into the midst of them. They will let the cloak fall down to you, but one of the birds will be hurt, and will drop down dead. Carry away the cloak, it is a wishing-cloak; when you throw it over your shoulders, you only have to wish to be in a certain place, and you will be there in the twinkling of an eye. Take out the heart of the dead bird and swallow it whole, and every morning early, when you get up, you will find a gold piece under your pillow." The huntsman thanked the wise woman, and thought to himself: "Those are fine things that she has promised me, if all does but come true." And verily when he had walked about a hundred paces, he heard in the branches above him such a screaming and twittering that he looked up and saw there a swarm of birds who were tearing a piece of cloth about with their beaks and claws, and tugging and fighting as if each wanted to have it all to himself. "Well," said the huntsman, "this is amazing, it has really come to pass just as the old crone foretold!" and he took the gun from his shoulder, aimed and fired right into the midst of them, so that the feathers flew about. The birds instantly took to flight with loud outcries, but one dropped down dead, and the cloak fell at the same time. Then the huntsman did as the old woman had directed him, cut open the bird, sought the heart, swallowed it down, and took the cloak home with him.

Next morning, when he awoke, the promise occurred to him, and he wished to see if it also had been fulfilled. When he lifted up the pillow, the gold piece shone in his eyes, and next day he found another, and so it went on, every time he got up. He gathered together a heap of gold, but at last he thought: "Of what use is all my gold to me if I stay at home? I will go forth and see the world."

He then took leave of his parents, buckled on his huntsman's pouch and gun, and went out into the world. It came to pass, that one day he travelled through a dense forest, and when he came to the end of it, in the plain before him stood a fine castle. An old woman was standing with a wonderfully beautiful maiden, looking out of one of the windows. The old woman, however, was a witch and said to the maiden: "There comes one out of the forest, who has a wonderful treasure in his body. We must filch it from him, daughter of my heart, it is more suitable for us than for him. He has a bird's heart about him, by means of which a gold piece lies every morning under his pillow." She told her what she was to do to get it, and what part she had to play, and finally threatened her, and said with angry eyes: "And if you do not attend to what I say, it will be the worse for you." Now when the huntsman came nearer he noticed the maiden, and said to himself: "I have travelled about for such a long time, I will take a rest for once, and enter that beautiful castle. I have certainly money enough." Nevertheless, the real reason was that he had caught sight of the beautiful picture.

He entered the house, and was well received and courteously entertained. Before long he was so much in love with the young witch that he no longer thought of anything else, and only saw things as she saw them, and liked to do what she desired. The old woman then said: "Now we must have the bird's heart, he will never miss it." She brewed a potion, and when it was ready, poured it into a goblet and gave it to the maiden, who was to present it to the huntsman. She did so, saying: "Now, my dearest, drink to me." So he took the goblet, and when he had swallowed the draught, he brought up the heart of the bird. The girl had to take it away secretly and swallow it herself, for the old woman would have it so. Thenceforward he found no more gold under his pillow, but it lay instead under that of the maiden, from whence the old woman fetched it away every morning; but he was so much in love and so befooled, that he thought of nothing else but of passing his time with the girl.

Then the old witch said: "We have the bird's heart, but we must also take the wishing-cloak away from him." The girl answered: "We will leave him that, he has lost his wealth." The old woman was angry and said: "Such a mantle is a wonderful thing, and is seldom to be found in this world. I must and will have it!" She gave the girl several blows, and said that if she did not obey, it should fare ill with her. So she did the old woman's bidding, placed herself at the window and looked on the distant country, as if she were very sorrowful. The huntsman asked: "Why do you stand there so sorrowfully?" "Ah, my beloved," was her answer, "over yonder lies the Garnet Mountain, where the precious stones grow. I long for them so much that when I think of them, I feel quite sad, but who can get them? Only the birds; they fly and can reach them, but a man never." "Have you nothing else to complain of?" said the huntsman. "I will soon remove that burden from your heart." With that he drew her under his mantle, wished himself on the Garnet Mountain, and in the twinkling of an eye they were sitting on it together. Precious stones were glistening on every side so that it was a joy to see them, and together they gathered the finest and costliest of them. Now, the old woman had, through her sorceries, contrived that the eyes of the huntsman should become heavy. He said to the maiden: "We will sit down and rest awhile, I am so tired that I can no longer stand on my feet." Then they sat down, and he laid his head in her lap, and fell asleep. When he was asleep, she unfastened the mantle from his shoulders, and wrapped herself in it, picked up the garnets and stones, and wished herself back at home with them.

But when the huntsman had slept his fill and awoke, and perceived that his sweetheart had betrayed him, and left him alone on the wild mountain, he said: "Oh, what treachery there is in the world!" and sat down there in trouble and sorrow, not knowing what to do. But the mountain belonged to some wild and monstrous giants who dwelt thereon and lived their lives there, and he had not sat long before he saw three of them coming towards him, so he lay down as if he were sunk in a deep sleep. Then the giants came up, and the first kicked him with his foot and said: "What sort of an earth-worm is this, lying here contemplating his inside?" The second said: "Step upon him and kill him." But the third said, contemptuously: "That would indeed be worth your while; just let him live, he cannot remain here; and when he climbs higher, toward the summit of the mountain, the clouds will lay hold of him and bear him away." So saying they passed by. But the huntsman had paid heed to their words, and as soon as they were gone, he rose and climbed up to the summit of the mountain, and when he had sat there a while, a cloud floated towards him, caught him up, carried him away, and travelled about for a long time in the heavens. Then it sank lower, and let itself down on a great cabbage-garden, girt round by walls, so that he came softly to the ground on cabbages and vegetables.

Then the huntsman looked about him and said: "If I had but something to eat! I am so hungry, and to proceed on my way from here will be difficult; I see here neither apples nor pears, nor any other sort of fruit, everywhere nothing but cabbages," but at length he thought: "At a pinch I can eat some of the leaves, they do not taste particularly good, but they will refresh me." With that he picked himself out a fine head of cabbage, and ate it, but scarcely had he swallowed a couple of mouthfuls than he felt very strange and quite different.

Four legs grew on him, a thick head and two long ears, and he saw with horror that he was changed into an ass. Still as his hunger increased every minute, and as the juicy leaves were suitable to his present nature, he went on eating with great zest. At last he arrived at a different kind of cabbage, but as soon as he had swallowed it, he again felt a change, and resumed his former human shape.

Then the huntsman lay down and slept off his fatigue. When he awoke next morning, be broke off one head of the bad cabbages and another of the good ones, and thought to himself: "This shall help me to get my own again and punish treachery." Then he took the cabbages with him, climbed over the wall, and went forth to look for the castle of his sweetheart. After wandering about for a couple of days he was lucky enough to find it again. He dyed his face brown, so that his own mother would not have known him; and begged for shelter: "I am so tired," said he, "that I can go no further." The witch asked: "Who are you, countryman, and what is your business?" "I am a king's messenger, and was sent out to seek the most delicious salad which grows beneath the sun. I have even been so fortunate as to find it, and am carrying it about with me; but the heat of the sun is so intense that the delicate cabbage threatens to wither, and I do not know if I can carry it any further."

When the old woman heard of the exquisite salad, she was greedy, and said: "Dear countryman, let me just try this wonderful salad." "Why not?" answered he, "I have brought two heads with me, and will give you one of them," and he opened his pouch and handed her the bad cabbage. The witch suspected nothing amiss, and her mouth watered so for this new dish that she herself went into the kitchen and dressed it. When it was prepared she could not wait until it was set on

the table, but took a couple of leaves at once, and put them in her mouth, but hardly had she swallowed them than she was deprived of her human shape, and she ran out into the courtyard in the form of an ass. Presently the maid-servant entered the kitchen, saw the salad standing there ready prepared, and was about to carry it up; but on the way, according to habit, she was seized by the desire to taste, and she ate a couple of leaves. Instantly the magic power showed itself, and she likewise became an ass and ran out to the old woman, and the dish of salad fell to the ground. Meantime the messenger sat beside the beautiful girl, and as no one came with the salad and she also was longing for it, she said: "I don't know what has become of the salad." The huntsman thought: "The salad must have already taken effect," and said: "I will go to the kitchen and inquire about it." As he went down he saw the two asses running about in the courtyard; the salad, however, was lying on the ground. "All right," said he, "the two have taken their portion," and he picked up the other leaves, laid them on the dish, and carried them to the maiden. "I bring you the delicate food myself," said he, "in order that you may not have to wait longer." Then she ate of it, and was, like the others, immediately deprived of her human form, and ran out into the courtyard in the shape of an ass.

After the huntsman had washed his face, so that the transformed ones could recognize him, he went down into the courtyard, and said: "Now you shall receive the wages of your treachery," and bound them together, all three with one rope, and drove them along until he came to a mill. He knocked at the window, the miller put out his head, and asked what he wanted. "I have three unmanageable beasts," answered he, "which I don't want to keep any longer. Will you take them in, and give them food and stable room, and manage them as I tell you, and then I will pay you what you ask." The miller said: "Why not? but how am I to manage them?" The huntsman then said that he was to give three beatings and one meal daily to the old donkey, and that was the witch; one beating and three meals to the younger one, which was the servant-girl; and to the youngest, which was the maiden, no beatings and three meals, for he could not bring himself to have the maiden beaten. After that he went back into the castle, and found therein everything he needed.

After a couple of days, the miller came and said he must inform him that the old ass which had received three beatings and only one meal daily was dead; "the two others," he continued, "are certainly not dead, and are fed three times daily, but they are so sad that they cannot last much longer." The huntsman was moved to pity, put away his anger, and told the miller to drive them back again to him. And when they came, he gave them some of the good salad, so that they became human again. The beautiful girl fell on her knees before him, and said: "Ah, my beloved, forgive me for the evil I have done you; my mother drove me to it: it was done against my will, for I love you dearly. Your wishing-cloak hangs in a cupboard, and as for the bird's-heart I will take a vomiting potion." But he thought otherwise, and said: "Keep it; it is all the same, for I will take you for my true wife." So the wedding was celebrated, and they lived happily together until their death.

THE OLD WOMAN IN THE WOOD

A poor servant-girl was once travelling with the family with which she was in service, through a great forest, and when they were in the midst of it, robbers came out of the thicket, and murdered all they found. All perished together except the girl, who had jumped out of the carriage in a fright, and hidden herself behind a tree. When the robbers had gone away with their booty, she came out and beheld the great disaster. Then she began to weep bitterly, and said: "What can a poor girl like me do now? I do not know how to get out of the forest, no human being lives in it, so I must certainly starve." She walked about and looked for a road, but could find none. When it was evening she seated herself under a tree, gave herself into God's keeping, and resolved to sit waiting there and not go away, let happen what might. When she had sat there for a while, a white dove came flying to her with a little golden key in its beak. It put the little key in her hand, and said: "Do you see that great tree, therein is a little lock; open it with the tiny key, and you will find food enough, and suffer no more hunger." Then she went to the tree and opened it, and found milk in a little dish, and white bread to break into it, so that she could eat her fill. When she was satisfied, she said: "It is now the time when the hens at home go to roost, I am so tired I could go to bed too." Then the dove flew to her again, and brought another golden key in its bill, and said: "Open that tree there, and you will find a bed." So she opened it, and found a beautiful white bed, and she prayed God to protect her during the night, and lay down and slept. In the morning the dove came for the third time, and again brought a little key, and said: "Open that tree there, and you will find clothes." And when she opened it, she found garments beset with gold and with jewels, more splendid than those of any king's daughter. So she lived there for some time, and the dove came every day and provided her with all she needed, and it was a quiet good life.

Then one day the dove came and said: "Will you do something for my sake?" "With all my heart," said the girl. Then said the little dove: "I will guide you to a small house; enter it, and inside it, an old woman will be sitting by the fire and will say: 'Good-day.' But on your life give her no answer, let her do what she will, but pass by her on the right side; further on, there is a door, which open, and you will enter into a room where a quantity of rings of all kinds are lying, amongst which are some magnificent ones with shining stones; leave them, however, where they are, and seek out a plain one, which must likewise be amongst them, and bring it here to me as quickly as you can." The girl went to the little house, and came to the door. There sat an old woman who stared when she saw her, and said: "Good day, my child." The girl gave her no answer, and opened the door. "Whither away," cried the old woman, and seized her by the gown, and wanted to hold her fast, saying: "That is my house; no one can go in there if I choose not to allow it." But the girl was silent, got away from her, and went straight into the room. Now there lay on the table an enormous quantity of rings, which gleamed and glittered before her eyes. She turned them over and looked for the plain one, but could not find it. While she was seeking, she saw the old woman and how she was stealing away, and wanting to go off with a bird-cage which she had in her hand. So she went after her and took the cage out of her hand, and when she raised it up and looked into it, a bird was inside which had the plain ring in its bill. Then she took the ring, and ran quite joyously home with it, and thought the little white dove would come and get the ring, but it did not. Then she leant against a tree, determined to wait for the dove. As she thus stood, it seemed just as if the tree was soft and pliant, and was letting its branches down. And suddenly the branches twined around her, and were two arms, and when she looked around, the tree was a handsome man, who embraced and kissed her heartily, and said: "You have delivered me from the power of the old woman, who is a wicked witch. She had changed me into a tree, and every day for two hours I was a white dove, and so long as she possessed the ring I could not regain my human form." Then his servants and his horses, who had likewise been changed into trees, were freed from the enchantment also, and stood beside him. And he led them forth to his kingdom, for he was a King's son, and they married, and lived happily.

THE THREE BROTHERS

There was once a man who had three sons, and nothing else in the world but the house in which he lived. Now each of the sons wished to have the house after his father's death; but the father loved them all alike, and did not know what to do; he did not wish to sell the house, because it had belonged to his forefathers, else he might have divided the money amongst them. At last he conceived a plan, and he said to his sons: "Go into the world, and try each of you to learn a trade, and,

when you all come back, he who makes the best masterpiece shall have the house."

The sons were well content with this, and the eldest determined to be a blacksmith, the second a barber, and the third a fencing-master. They fixed a time when they should all come home again, and then each went his way.

It chanced that they all found skilful masters, who taught them their trades well. The blacksmith had to shoe the King's horses, and he thought to himself: "The house is mine, without doubt." The barber shaved only distinguished people, and he too already looked upon the house as his own. The fencing-master suffered many a blow, but he grit his teeth, and let nothing vex him; "for," said he to himself, "if you are afraid of a blow, you'll never win the house."

When the appointed time had gone by, the three brothers came back home to their father; but they did not know how to find the best opportunity for showing their skill, so they sat down and consulted together. As they were sitting thus, all at once a hare came running across the field. "Ah, ha, just in time!" said the barber. So he took his basin and soap, and lathered away until the hare drew near; then he soaped and shaved off the hare's whiskers whilst he was running at the top of his speed, and did not even cut his skin or injure a hair on his body. "Well done!" said the old man, "if the others do not make a great effort, the house is yours."

Soon after, up came a nobleman in his coach, dashing along at full speed. "Now you shall see what I can do, father," said the blacksmith; so away he ran after the coach, took all four shoes off the feet of one of the horses whilst he was galloping, and put on four new shoes without stopping him. "You are a fine fellow, and as clever as your brother," said his father; "I do not know to which I ought to give the house."

Then the third son said: "Father, let me have my turn, if you please;" and, as it was beginning to rain, he drew his sword, and flourished it backwards and forwards above his head so fast that not a drop fell upon him. It rained still harder and harder, till at last it came down in torrents; but he only flourished his sword faster and faster, and remained as dry as if he were sitting in a house. When his father saw this he was amazed, and said: "This is the masterpiece, the house is yours!"

His brothers were satisfied with this, as was agreed beforehand; and, as they loved one another very much, they all three stayed together in the house, followed their trades, and, as they had learnt them so well and were so clever, they earned a great deal of money. Thus they lived together happily until they grew old; and at last, when one of them fell sick and died, the two others grieved so sorely about it that they also fell ill, and soon after died. And because they had been so clever, and had loved one another so much, they were all laid in the same grave.

THE DEVIL AND HIS GRANDMOTHER

There was a great war, and the King had many soldiers, but gave them small pay, so small that they could not live upon it, so three of them agreed among themselves to desert. One of them said to the others: "If we are caught we shall be hanged on the gallows; how shall we manage it?" Another said: "Look at that great cornfield, if we were to hide ourselves there, no one could find us; the troops are not allowed to enter it, and to-morrow they are to march away." They crept into the corn, only the troops did not march away, but remained lying all round about it. They stayed in the corn for two days and two nights, and were so hungry that they all but died, but if they had come out, their death would have been certain. Then said they: "What is the use of our deserting if we have to perish miserably here?" But now a fiery dragon came flying through the air, and it came down to them, and asked why they had concealed themselves there. They answered: "We are three soldiers who have deserted because the pay was so bad, and now we

shall have to die of hunger if we stay here, or to dangle on the gallows if we go out." "If you will serve me for seven years," said the dragon, "I will convey you through the army so that no one shall seize you." "We have no choice and are compelled to accept," they replied. Then the dragon caught hold of them with his claws, and carried them away through the air over the army, and put them down again on the earth far from it; but the dragon was no other than the Devil. He gave them a small whip and said: "Whip with it and crack it, and then as much gold will spring up round about as you can wish for; then you can live like great lords, keep horses, and drive your carriages, but when the seven years have come to an end, you are my property." Then he put before them a book which they were all three forced to sign. "But first I will ask you a riddle," said he, "and if you can guess it, you shall be free, and released from my power." Then the dragon flew away from them, and they went away with their whip, had gold in plenty, ordered themselves rich apparel, and travelled about the world. Wherever they were they lived in pleasure and magnificence, rode on horseback, drove in carriages, ate and drank, but did nothing wicked. The time slipped quickly by, and when the seven years were coming to an end, two of them were terribly anxious and alarmed; but the third took the affair easily, and said: "Brothers, fear nothing, I still have my wits about me, I shall guess the riddle." They went out into the open country and sat down, and the two pulled sorrowful faces. Then an aged woman came up to them who inquired why they were so sad. "Well," said they, "what has that got to do with you? After all, you cannot help us." "Who knows?" said she, "just confide your trouble to me." So they told her that they had been the Devil's servants for nearly seven years, and that he had provided them with gold as though it were hay, but that they had sold themselves to him, and were forfeited to him, if at the end of the seven years they could not guess a riddle. The old woman said: "If you are to be saved, one of you must go into the forest, there he will come to a fallen rock which looks like a little house, he must enter that, and then he will obtain help." The two melancholy ones thought to themselves: "That will still not save us," and stayed where they were, but the third, the merry one, got up and walked on in the forest until he found the rock-house. In the little house a very aged woman was sitting, who was the Devil's grandmother, and asked the soldier where he came from, and what he wanted there. He told her everything that had happened, and as he pleased her well, she had pity on him, and said she would help him. She lifted up a great stone which lay above a cellar, and said: "Conceal yourself there, you can hear everything that is said here; only sit still, and do not stir. When the dragon comes, I will question him about the riddle, he tells everything to me, so listen carefully to his answer." At twelve o'clock at night, the dragon came flying thither, and asked for his dinner. The grandmother laid the table, and served up food and drink, so that he was pleased, and they ate and drank together. In the course of conversation, she asked him what kind of a day he had had, and how many souls he had got. "Nothing went very well to-day," he answered, "but I have laid hold of three soldiers,—I have them safe." "Indeed! three soldiers, they're clever, they may escape you yet." The Devil said mockingly: "They are mine! I will set them a riddle, which they will never be able to guess!" "What riddle is that?" she inquired. "I will tell you: in the great North Sea lies a dead dogfish, that shall be your roast meat, and the rib of a whale shall be your silver spoon, and a hollow old horse's hoof shall be your wineglass." When the Devil had gone to bed, the old grandmother raised up the stone, and let out the soldier. "Did you give heed to everything?" "Yes," said he, "I know enough, and will save myself." Then he had to go back another way, through the window, secretly and with all speed to his companions. He told them how the Devil had been outwitted by the old grandmother, and how he had learned the answer to the riddle from him. Then they were all delighted, and of good cheer, and took the whip and whipped so much gold for themselves that it ran all over the ground.

When the seven years had fully gone by, the Devil came with the book, showed the signatures, and said: "I will take you with me to hell. There you shall have a meal! If you can guess what kind of roast meat you will have to eat, you shall be free and released from your bargain, and may keep the whip as well." Then the first soldier began and said: "In the great North Sea lies a dead dogfish, that no doubt is the roast meat." The Devil was angry, and began to mutter "Hm! hm! hm!" and asked the second: "But what will your spoon be?" "The rib of a whale, that is to be our silver spoon." The Devil made a wry face, again growled "Hm! hm! hm" and said to the third: "And do you also know what your wineglass is to be?" "An old horse's hoof is to be our wineglass." Then the Devil flew away with a loud cry, and had no more power over them, but the three kept the whip, whipped as much money for themselves with it as they wanted, and lived happily to their end.

FERDINAND THE FAITHFUL AND FERDINAND THE UNFAITHFUL

Once upon a time lived a man and a woman who so long as they were rich had no children, but when they were poor they got a little boy. They could find no godfather for him, so the man said he would just go to another village to see if he could get one there. On his way he met a poor man, who asked him where he was going. He said he was going to see if he could get a godfather, because he was so poor that no one would stand as godfather for him. "Oh," said the poor man, "you are poor, and I am poor; I will be godfather for you, but I am so badly off I can give the child nothing. Go home and tell the midwife that she is to come to the church with the child."

When they all got to the church together, the beggar was already there, and he gave the child the name of Ferdinand the Faithful.

When he was going out of the church, the beggar said: "Now go home, I can give you nothing, and you likewise ought to give me nothing." But he gave a key to the midwife, and told her when she got home she was to give it to the father, who was to take care of it until the child was fourteen years old, and then he was to go on the heath where there was a castle which the key would fit, and that all which was

therein should belong to him. Now when the child was seven years old and had grown very big, he once went to play with some other boys, and each of them boasted that he had got more from his godfather than the other; but the child could say nothing, and was vexed, and went home and said to his father: "Did I get nothing at all, then, from my godfather?" "Oh, yes," said the father, "you have a key—if there is a castle standing on the heath, just go to it and open it." Then the boy went thither, but no castle was to be seen, or heard of.

After seven years more, when he was fourteen years old, he again went thither, and there stood the castle. When he had opened it, there was nothing within but a horse,—a white one. Then the boy was so full of joy because he had a horse, that he mounted on it and galloped back to his father. "Now I have a white horse, and I will travel," said he. So he set out, and as he was on his way, a pen was lying on the road. At first he thought he would pick it up, but then again he thought to himself: "You should leave it lying there; you will easily find a pen where you are going, if you have need of one." As he was thus riding away, a voice called after him: "Ferdinand the Faithful, take it with you." He looked around, but saw no one; so he went back again and picked it up. When he had ridden a little way farther, he passed by a lake, and a fish was lying on the bank, gasping and panting for breath, so he said: "Wait, my dear fish, I will help you to get into the water," and he took hold of it by the tail, and threw it into the lake. Then the fish put its head out of the water and said: "As you have helped me out of the mud I will give you a flute; when you are in any need, play on it, and then I will help you, and if ever you let anything fall in the water, just play and I will reach it out to you." Then he rode away, and there came to him a man who asked him where he was going. "Oh, to the next place." "What is your name?" "Ferdinand the Faithful." "So! then we have got almost the same name, I am called Ferdinand the Unfaithful." And they both set out to the inn in the nearest place.

Now it was unfortunate that Ferdinand the Unfaithful knew everything that the other had ever thought and everything he was about to do; he knew it by means of all kinds of wicked arts. There was in the inn an honest girl, who had a bright face and behaved very prettily. She fell in love with Ferdinand the Faithful because he was a handsome man, and she asked him whither he was going. "Oh, I am just travelling round about," said he. Then she said he ought to stay there, for the King of that country wanted an attendant or an outrider, and he ought to enter his service. He answered he could not very well go to any one like that and offer himself. Then said the maiden: "Oh, but I will soon do that for you." And so she went straight to the King, and told him that she knew of an excellent servant for him. He was well pleased with that, and had Ferdinand the Faithful brought to him, and wanted to make him his servant. He, however, liked better to be an outrider, for where his horse was, there he also wanted to be, so the King made him an outrider. When Ferdinand the Unfaithful learnt that, he said to the girl: "What! Do you help him and not me?" "Oh," said the girl, "I will help you too." She thought: "I must keep friends with that man, for he is not to be trusted." She went to the King, and offered him as a servant, and the King was willing.

Now when the King met his lords in the morning, he always lamented and said: "Oh, if I only had my love with me." Ferdinand the Unfaithful, however, was always hostile to Ferdinand the Faithful. So once, when the King was complaining thus, he said: "You have the outrider, send him away to get her, and if he does not do it, his head must be struck off." Then the King sent for Ferdinand the Faithful, and told him that there was, in this place or in that place, a girl he loved, and that he was to bring her to him, and if he did not do it he should die.

Ferdinand the Faithful went into the stable to his white horse, and complained and lamented: "Oh, what an unhappy man am I!" Then someone behind him cried: "Ferdinand the Faithful, why do you weep?" He looked round but saw no one, and went on lamenting: "Oh, my dear little white horse, now must I leave you; now must I die." Then someone cried once more: "Ferdinand the Faithful, why do you weep?" Then for the first time he was aware that it was his little white horse who was putting that question. "Do you speak, my little white horse; can you do that?" And again, he said: "I am to go to this place and to that, and am to bring the bride; can you tell me how I am to set about it?" Then answered the little white horse: "Go to the King, and say if he will give you what you must have, you will get her for him. If he will give you a ship full of meat, and a ship full of bread, it will succeed. Great giants dwell on the lake, and if you take no meat with you for them, they will tear you to pieces, and there are the large birds which would pluck the eyes out of your head if you had no bread for them." Then the King made all the butchers in the land kill, and all the bakers bake, that the ships might be filled. When they were full, the little white horse said to Ferdinand the Faithful: "Now mount me, and go with me into the ship, and then when the giants come, say:

'Peace, peace, my dear little giants,
I have had thought of ye,
Something I have brought for ye.'

And when the birds come, you shall again say:

'Peace, peace, my dear little birds,
I have had thought of ye,
Something I have brought for ye.'

Then they will do nothing to you, and when you come to the castle, the giants will help you. Then go up to the castle, and take a couple of giants with you. There the princess lies sleeping; you must, however, not awaken her, but the giants must lift her up, and carry her in her bed to the ship." And now everything took place as the little white horse had said, and Ferdinand the Faithful gave the giants and the birds what he had brought with him for them, and that made the giants willing, and they carried the princess in her bed to the King. And when she came to the King, she said she could not live, she must have her writings, they had been left in her castle. Then by the instigation of Ferdinand the Unfaithful, Ferdinand the Faithful was called, and the King told him he must fetch the writings from the castle, or he should die. Then he went once more into the stable, and bemoaned himself and said: "Oh, my dear little white horse, now I am to go away again, how am I to do it?" Then the little white horse said he was just to load the ships full again. So it happened again as it had happened before, and the giants and the birds were satisfied, and made gentle by the meat. When they came to the castle, the white horse told Ferdinand the Faithful that he must go in, and that on the table in the princess's bed-room lay the writings. And Ferdinand the Faithful went in, and fetched them. When they were on the lake, he let his pen fall into the water; then said the white horse: "Now I cannot help you at all." But he remembered his flute, and began to play on it, and the fish came with the pen in its mouth, and gave it to him. So he took the writings to the castle, where the wedding was celebrated.

The Queen, however, did not love the King because he had no nose, but she would have much liked to love Ferdinand the Faithful. Once, therefore, when all the lords of the court were together, the Queen said she could do feats of magic, that she could cut off anyone's head and put it on again, and that one of them ought just to try it. But none of them would be the first, so Ferdinand the Faithful, again at the instigation of Ferdinand the Unfaithful, undertook it and she hewed off his head, and put it on again for him, and it healed together directly, so that it looked as if he had a red thread round his throat. Then the King said to her: "My child, and where have you learnt that?" "Oh," she said, "I understand the art; shall I just try it on you also?" "Oh, yes," said he. So she cut off his head, but did not put it on again; and pretended that she could not get it on, and that it would not stay. Then the King was buried, but she married Ferdinand the Faithful.

He, however, always rode on his white horse, and once when he was seated on it, it told him that he was to go on to the heath which he knew, and gallop three times round it. And when he had done that, the white horse stood up on its hind legs, and was changed into a King's son.

THE IRON STOVE

In the days when wishing was still of some use, a King's son was bewitched by an old witch, and shut up in an iron stove in a forest. There he passed many years, and no one could rescue him. Then a King's daughter came into the forest, who had lost herself, and could not find her father's kingdom again. After she had wandered about for nine days, she at length came to the iron stove. Then a voice came forth from it, and asked her: "Whence do you come, and whither are you going?" She answered: "I have lost my father's kingdom, and cannot get home again." Then a voice inside the iron stove said: "I will help you to get home again, and that indeed most swiftly, if you will promise to do what I desire of you. I am the son of a far greater King than your father, and I will marry you."

Then was she afraid, and thought: "Good Heavens! What can I do with an iron stove?" But as she much wished to get home to her father, she promised to do as he desired. But he said: "You shall return here, and bring a knife with you, and scrape a hole in the iron." Then he gave her a companion who walked near her, but did not speak, and in two hours he took her home; there was great joy in the castle when the King's daughter came home, and the old King fell on her neck, and kissed her. She, however, was sorely troubled, and said: "Dear father, what I have suffered! I should never have got home again from the great wild forest, if I had not come to an iron stove, but I have been forced to give my word that I will go back to it, set it free, and marry it." Then the old King was so terrified that he all but fainted, for he had but this one daughter. They therefore resolved they would send, in her place, the miller's daughter, who was very beautiful. They took her there, gave her a knife, and said she was to scrape at the iron stove. So she scraped at it for four-and-twenty hours, but could not bring off the least morsel of it. When day dawned, a voice in the stove said: "It seems to me it is day outside." Then she answered: "It seems so to me too; I fancy I hear the noise of my father's mill."

"So you are a miller's daughter! Then go your way at once, and let the King's daughter come here." Then she went away at once, and told the old King that the man outside there would have none of her—he wanted the King's daughter. Then the old King grew frightened, and the daughter wept. But there was a swine-herd's daughter, who was even prettier than the miller's daughter, and they determined to give her a piece of gold to go to the iron stove instead of the King's daughter. So she was taken thither, and she also had to scrape for four-and-twenty hours. She, however, was no better at it. When day broke, a voice inside the stove cried: "It seems to me it is day outside!" Then answered she: "So it seems to me also; I fancy I hear my father's horn blowing."

"Then you are a swineherd's daughter! Go away at once, and tell the King's daughter to come, and tell her all must be done as was promised, and if she does not come, everything in the kingdom shall be ruined and destroyed, and not one stone be left standing on another." When the King's daughter heard that she began to weep, but now there was nothing for it but to keep her promise. So she took leave of her father, put a knife in her pocket, and went forth to the iron stove in the forest. When she got there, she began to scrape, and the iron gave way, and when two hours were over, she had already scraped a small hole. Then she peeped in, and saw a youth so handsome, and so brilliant with gold and with precious jewels, that her very soul was delighted. So she went on scraping, and made the hole so large that he was able to get out. Then said he: "You are mine, and I am yours; you are my bride, and have released me." He wanted to take her away with him to his kingdom, but she entreated him to let her go once again to her father, and the King's son allowed her to do so, but she was not to say more to her father than three words, and then she was to come back again. So she went home, but she spoke more than three words, and instantly the iron stove disappeared, and was taken far away over glass mountains and piercing swords; but the King's son was set free, and no longer shut up in it. After this she bade good-bye to her father, took some money with her, but not much, and went back to the great forest, and looked for the iron stove, but it was nowhere to be found. For nine days she sought it, and then her hunger grew so great that she did not know what to do, for she had nothing to live on. When it was evening, she seated herself in a small tree, and made up her mind to spend the night there, as she was afraid of wild beasts. When midnight drew near she saw in the distance a small light, and thought: "Ah, there I should be saved!" She got down from the tree, and went towards the light, but on the way she prayed. Then she came to a little old house, and much grass had grown all about it, and a small heap of wood lay in front of it. She thought: "Ah, whither have I come," and peeped in through the window, but she saw nothing inside but toads, big and little, except a table well covered with wine and roast meat, and the plates and glasses were of silver. Then she took courage, and knocked at the door, and immediately the fat toad cried:

> "Little green waiting-maid,
> Waiting-maid with the limping leg,
> Little dog of the limping leg,
> Hop hither and thither,
> And quickly see who is without."

And a small toad came walking by and opened the door to her. When she entered, they all bade her welcome, and she was forced to sit down. They asked: "Where have you come from, and whither are you going?" Then she related all that had befallen her, and how because she had transgressed the order which had been given her not to say more than three words, the stove, and the King's son also, had disappeared, and now she was about to seek him over hill and dale until she found him. Then the old fat one said:

> "Little green waiting-maid,
> Waiting-maid with the limping leg,
> Little dog of the limping leg,
> Hop hither and thither,
> And bring me the great box."

Then the little one went and brought the box. After this they gave her meat and drink, and took her to a well-made bed, which felt like silk and velvet, and she laid herself therein, in God's name, and slept. When morning came she arose, and the old toad gave her three needles out of the great box which she was to take with her; they would be needed by her, for she had to cross a high glass mountain, and go over three piercing swords and a great lake. If she did all this she would get her

lover back again. Then she gave her three things, which she was to take the greatest care of, namely, three large needles, a plough-wheel, and three nuts. With these she travelled onwards, and when she came to the glass mountain which was so slippery, she stuck the three needles first behind her feet and then before them, and so got over it, and when she was over it, she hid them in a place which she marked carefully. After this she came to the three piercing swords, and then she seated herself on her plough-wheel, and rolled over them. At last she arrived in front of a great lake, and when she had crossed it, she came to a large and beautiful castle. She went in and asked for a place; she was a poor girl, she said, and would like to be hired. She knew, however, that the King's son whom she had released from the iron stove in the great forest was in the castle. Then she was taken as a scullery-maid at low wages. But already the King's son had another maiden by his side whom he wanted to marry, for he thought that she had long been dead.

In the evening, when she had washed up and was done, she felt in her pocket and found the three nuts which the old toad had given her. She cracked one with her teeth, and was going to eat the kernel when lo and behold there was a stately royal garment in it! But when the bride heard of this she came and asked for the dress, and wanted to buy it, and said: "It is not a dress for a servant-girl." No, she said, she would not sell it, but if the bride would grant her one thing she should have it, and that was permission to sleep one night in her bridegroom's chamber. The bride gave her permission because the dress was so pretty, and she had never had one like it. When it was evening she said to her bridegroom: "That silly girl will sleep in your room." "If you are willing, so am I," said he. She, however, gave him a glass of wine in which she had poured a sleeping-draught. So the bridegroom and the scullery-maid went to sleep in the room, and he slept so soundly that she could not waken him.

She wept the whole night and cried: "I set you free when you were in an iron stove in the wild forest, I sought you, and walked over a glass mountain, and three sharp swords, and a great lake before I found you, and yet you will not hear me!"

The servants sat by the chamber-door, and heard how she thus wept the whole night through, and in the morning they told it to their lord. And the next evening when she had washed up, she opened the second nut, and a far more beautiful dress was within it, and when the bride beheld it, she wished to buy that also. But the girl would not take money, and begged that she might once again sleep in the bridegroom's chamber. The bride, however, gave him a sleeping-draught, and he slept so soundly that he could hear nothing. But the scullery-maid wept the whole night long, and cried: "I set you free when you were in an iron stove in the wild forest, I sought you, and walked over a glass mountain, and over three sharp swords and a great lake before I found you, and yet you will not hear me!" The servants sat by the chamber-door and heard her weeping the whole night through, and in the morning informed their lord of it. And on the third evening, when she had washed up, she opened the third nut, and within it was a still more beautiful dress which was stiff with pure gold. When the bride saw that she wanted to have it, but the maiden only gave it up on condition that she might for the third time sleep in the bridegroom's apartment. The King's son, however, was on his guard, and threw the sleeping-draught away. Now when she began to weep and to cry: "Dearest love, I set you free when you were in the iron stove in the terrible wild forest," the King's son leapt up and said: "You are the true one, you are mine, and I am yours." Thereupon, while it was still night, he got into a carriage with her, and they took away the false bride's clothes so that she could not get up. When they came to the great lake, they sailed across it, and when they reached the three sharp-cutting swords they seated themselves on the plough-wheel, and when they got to the glass mountain they thrust the three needles in it, and so at length they got to the little old house; but when they went inside, it was a great castle, and the toads were all disenchanted, and were King's children, and full of happiness. Then the wedding was celebrated, and the King's son and the princess remained in the castle, which was much larger than the castles of their fathers. But as the old King grieved at being left alone, they fetched him away, and brought him to live with them, and they had two kingdoms, and lived in happy wedlock.

> A mouse did run,
> The story is done.

THE LAZY SPINNER

In a certain village there once lived a man and his wife, and the wife was so lazy that she would never work at anything; whatever her husband gave her to spin, she did not get done, and what she did spin she did not wind, but let it all remain entangled in a heap. If the man scolded her, she was always ready with her tongue, and said: "Well, how should I wind it, when I have no reel? Just you go into the forest and get me one." "If that is all," said the man, "then I will go into the forest, and get some wood for making reels." Then the woman was afraid that if he had the wood he would make her a reel of it, and she would have to wind her yarn off, and then begin to spin again. She bethought herself a little, and then a lucky idea occurred to her, and she secretly followed the man into the forest, and when he had climbed into a tree to choose and cut the wood, she crept into the thicket below where he could not see her, and cried:

> "He who cuts wood for reels shall die,
> And he who winds, shall perish."

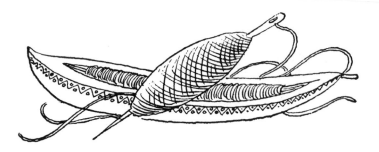

The man listened, laid down his axe for a moment, and began to consider what that could mean. "Well," he said at last, "what can that have been; my ears must have been singing, I won't alarm myself for nothing." So he once more seized the axe, and began to hew. Then again there came a cry from below:

> "He who cuts wood for reels shall die,
> And he who winds, shall perish."

He stopped, and felt afraid and alarmed, and pondered over the circumstance. But when a few moments had passed, he took heart again, and a third time he stretched out his hand for the axe, and began to cut. But someone called out a third time, and said loudly:

> "He who cuts wood for reels shall die,
> And he who winds, shall perish."

That was enough for him, and all inclination had departed from him, so he hastily descended the tree, and set out on his way home. The woman ran as fast as she could by byways so as to get home first. So when he entered the parlour, she put on an innocent look as if nothing had happened, and said: "Well, have you brought a nice piece of wood for reels?" "No," said he, "I see very well that winding won't do," and told her what had happened to him in the forest, and from that time forth left her in peace about it. Nevertheless after some time, the man again began to complain of the disorder in the house. "Wife," said he, "it is really a shame that the spun yarn should lie there all entangled!"

"I'll tell you what," said she, "as we still don't come by any reel, go you up into the loft, and I will stand down below, and will throw the yarn up to you, and you will throw it down to me, and so we shall get a skein after all." "Yes, that will do," said the man. So they did that, and when it was done, he said: "The yarn is in skeins, now it must be boiled." The woman was again distressed, and said: "Yes, we will boil it to-morrow morning early," but she was secretly contriving another trick.

Early in the morning she got up, lighted a fire, and put the kettle on, only instead of the yarn, she put in a lump of tow, and let it boil. After that she went to the man who was still lying in bed, and said to him: "I must just go out, you must get up and look after the yarn which is in the kettle on the fire, but you must be at hand at once; mind that, for if the cock should happen to crow, and you are not attending to the yarn, it will become tow." The man was willing and took good care not to loiter. He got up as quickly as he could, and went into the kitchen. But when he reached the kettle and peeped in, he saw, to his horror, nothing but a lump of tow. Then the poor man was as still as a mouse, thinking he had neglected it, and was to blame, and in future said no more about yarn and spinning. But you yourself must own she was an odious woman!

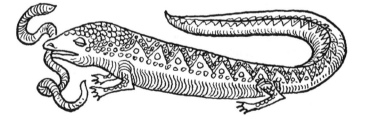

THE FOUR SKILFUL BROTHERS

There was once a poor man who had four sons, and when they were grown up, he said to them: "My dear children, you must now go out into the world, for I have nothing to give you, so set out, go abroad and learn a trade, and see how you can make your way." So the four brothers took their sticks, bade their father farewell, and went through the town-gate together. When they had travelled about for some time, they came to a cross-roads which branched off in four different directions. Then said the eldest: "Here we must separate, but on this day four years hence, we will meet each other again at this spot, and in the meantime we will seek our fortunes."

Then each of them went his way, and the eldest met a man who asked him where he was going, and what he was intending to do. "I want to learn a trade," he replied. Then the other said: "Come with me, and be a thief." "No," he answered, "that is no longer regarded as a reputable trade, and the end of it is that one has to swing on the gallows." "Oh," said the man, "you need not be afraid of the gallows; I will only teach you to get such things as no other man could ever lay hold of, and no one will ever detect you." So he allowed himself to be talked into it, and while with the man became an accomplished thief, and so dexterous that nothing was safe from him, if he once desired to have it. The second brother met a man who put the same question to him—what he wanted to learn in the world. "I don't know yet," he replied. "Then come with me, and be an astronomer; there is nothing better than that, for nothing is hid from you." He liked the idea, and became such a skilful astronomer that when he had learnt everything, and was about to travel onwards, his master gave him a telescope and said to him: "With that you can see whatsoever takes place either on earth or in heaven, and nothing can remain concealed from you." A huntsman took the third brother into training, and gave him such excellent instruction in everything which related to huntsmanship that he became an experienced hunter. When he went away, his master gave him a gun and said: "It will never fail you; whatsoever you aim at, you are certain to hit." The youngest brother also met a man who spoke to him, and inquired what his intentions were. "Would you not like to be a tailor?" said he. "Not that I know of," said the youth; "sitting doubled up from morning till night, driving the needle and the goose backwards and forwards, is not to my taste." "Oh, but you are speaking in ignorance," answered the man; "with me you would learn a very different kind of tailoring, which is respectable and proper, and for the most part very honourable." So he let himself be persuaded, and went with the man, and learnt his art from the very beginning. When they parted, the man gave the youth a needle, and said: "With this you can sew together whatever is given you, whether it is as soft as an egg or as hard as steel; and it will all become one piece of stuff, so that no seam will be visible."

When the appointed four years were over, the four brothers arrived at the same time at the cross-roads, embraced and kissed each other, and returned home to their father. "So now," said he, quite delighted, "the wind has blown you back again to me." They told him of all that had happened to them, and that each had learnt his own trade. Now they were sitting just in front of the house under a large tree, and the father said: "I will put you all to the test, and see what you can do." Then he looked up and said to his second son: "Between two branches up at the top of this tree, there is a chaffinch's nest, tell me how many eggs there are in it?" The astronomer took his glass, looked up, and said: "There are five." Then the father said to the eldest: "Fetch the eggs down without disturbing the bird which is sitting hatching them." The skilful thief climbed up, and took the five eggs from beneath the bird, which never observed what he was doing, and remained quietly sitting where she was, and brought them down to his father. The father took them, and put one of them on each corner of the table, and the fifth in the middle, and said to the huntsman: "With one shot you shall shoot me the five eggs in two, through the middle." The huntsman aimed, and shot the eggs, all five as the father had desired, and that at one shot. He certainly must have had some of the powder for shooting round corners! "Now it's your turn," said the father to the fourth son; "you shall sew the eggs together again, and the young birds that are inside them as well, and you must do it so that they are not hurt by the shot." The tailor brought his needle, and sewed them as his father wished. When he had done this the thief had to climb up the tree again, and carry them to the nest, and put them back again under the bird without her being aware of it. The bird sat her full time, and after a few days the young ones crept out, and they had a red line round their necks where they had been sewn together by the tailor.

"Well," said the old man to his sons, "you really ought to be praised to the skies; you have used your time well, and learnt something good.

I can't say which of you deserves the most praise. That will be proved if you have but an early opportunity of using your talents." Not long after this, there was a great uproar in the country, for the King's daughter was carried off by a dragon. The King was full of trouble about it, both by day and night, and caused it to be proclaimed that whosoever brought her back should have her to wife. The four brothers said to each other: "This would be a fine opportunity for us to show what we can do!" and resolved to go forth together and liberate the King's daughter. "I will soon know where she is," said the astronomer, and looked through his telescope and said: "I see her already, she is far away from here on a rock in the sea, and the dragon is beside her watching her." Then he went to the King, and asked for a ship for himself and his brothers, and sailed with them over the sea until they came to the rock. There the King's daughter was sitting, and the dragon was lying asleep on her lap. The huntsman said, "I dare not fire, I should kill the beautiful maiden at the same time." "Then I will try my art," said the thief, and he crept thither and stole her away from under the dragon, so quietly and dexterously, that the monster never noticed it, but went on snoring. Full of joy, they hurried off with her on board ship, and steered out into the open sea; but the dragon, who when he awoke had found no princess there, followed them, and came snorting angrily through the air. Just as he was circling above the ship, and about to descend on it, the huntsman shouldered his gun, and shot him to the heart. The monster fell down dead, but was so large and powerful that his fall shattered the whole ship. Fortunately, however, they laid hold of a couple of planks, and swam about the wide sea. Then again they were in great peril, but the tailor, who was not idle, took his wondrous needle, and with a few stitches sewed the planks together, and they seated themselves upon them, and collected together all the fragments of the vessel. Then he sewed these so skilfully together, that in a very short time the ship was once more seaworthy, and they could go home again in safety.

When the King once more saw his daughter, there were great rejoicings. He said to the four brothers: "One of you shall have her to wife, but which of you it is to be you must settle among yourselves." Then a heated argument arose among them, for each of them preferred his own claim. The astronomer said: "If I had not seen the princess, all your arts would have been useless, so she is mine." The thief said: "What would have been the use of your seeing, if I had not got her away from the dragon? so she is mine." The huntsman said: "You and the princess, and all of you, would have been torn to pieces by the dragon if my ball had not hit him, so she is mine." The tailor said: "And if I, by my art, had not sewn the ship together again, you would all of you have been miserably drowned, so she is mine." Then the King pronounced his verdict: "Each of you has an equal right, and as all of you cannot have the maiden, none of you shall have her, but I will give to each of you, as a reward, half a kingdom." The brothers were pleased with this decision, and said: "It is better thus than that we should be at variance with each other." Then each of them received half a kingdom, and they lived with their father in the greatest happiness as long as it pleased God.

ONE-EYE, TWO-EYES, AND THREE-EYES

There was once a woman who had three daughters, the eldest of whom was called One-eye, because she had only one eye in the middle of her forehead, and the second, Two-eyes, because she had two eyes like other folks, and the youngest, Three-eyes, because she had three eyes; and her third eye was also in the center of her forehead. However, as Two-eyes saw just as other human beings did, her sisters and her mother could not endure her. They said to her: "You, with your two eyes, are no better than the common people; you do not belong to us!" They pushed her about, and threw old clothes to her, and gave her nothing to eat but what they left, and did everything that they could to make her unhappy.

It came to pass that Two-eyes had to go out into the fields and tend the goat, but she was still quite hungry, because her sisters had given her so little to eat. So she sat down on a ridge and began to weep, and so bitterly that two streams ran down from her eyes. And once when she looked up in her grief, a woman was standing beside her, who said: "Why are you weeping, little Two-eyes?" Two-eyes answered: "Have I not reason to weep, when I have two eyes like other people, and my sisters and mother hate me for it, and push me from one corner to another, throw old clothes to me, and give me nothing to eat but the scraps they leave? To-day they have given me so little that I am still quite hungry." Then the wise woman said: "Wipe away your tears, Two-eyes, and I will tell you something to stop your ever suffering from hunger again; just say to your goat:

'Bleat, my little goat, bleat,
Cover the table with something to eat,'

and then a clean well-spread little table will stand before you, with the most delicious food upon it of which you may eat as much as you are inclined for, and when you have had enough, and have no more need of the little table, just say,

'Bleat, bleat, my little goat, I pray,
And take the table quite away,'

and then it will vanish again from your sight." Hereupon the wise woman departed. But Two-eyes thought: "I must instantly make a trial, and see if what she said is true, for I am far too hungry," and she said:

"Bleat, my little goat, bleat,
Cover the table with something to eat,"

and scarcely had she spoken the words than a little table, covered with a white cloth, was standing there, and on it was a plate with a knife and fork, and a silver spoon; and the most delicious food was there also, warm and smoking as if it had just come out of the kitchen. Then Two-eyes said the shortest prayer she knew: "Lord God, be our Guest for-ever, Amen," and helped herself to some food, and enjoyed it. And when she was satisfied, she said, as the wise woman had taught her:

"Bleat, bleat, my little goat, I pray,
And take the table quite away,"

and immediately the little table and everything on it was gone again.

"That is a delightful way of keeping house!" thought Two-eyes, and was quite glad and happy.

In the evening, when she went home with her goat, she found a small earthenware dish with some food, which her sisters had set ready for her, but she did not touch it. Next day she again went out with her goat, and left the few bits of broken bread which had been handed to her, lying untouched. The first and second time that she did this, her sisters did not notice it at all, but as it happened every time, they did observe it, and said: "There is something wrong about Two-eyes, she always leaves her food untasted, and she used to eat up everything that was given her; she must have discovered other ways of getting food." In order that they might learn the truth, they resolved to send One-eye with Two-eyes when she went to drive her goat to the pasture, to observe what Two-eyes did when she was there, and whether anyone brought her anything to eat and drink.

So when Two-eyes set out the next time, One-eye went to her and said: "I will go with you to the pasture, and see that the goat is well taken care of, and driven where there is food." But Two-eyes knew what was in One-eye's mind, and drove the goat into high grass and said: "Come, One-eye, we will sit down, and I will sing something to you." One-eye sat down and was tired with the unaccustomed walk and the heat of the sun, and Two-eyes sang constantly:

"One-eye, are you waking?
One-eye, are you sleeping?"

until One-eye shut her one eye, and fell asleep, and as soon as Two-eyes saw that One-eye was fast asleep, and could discover nothing, she said:

"Bleat, my little goat, bleat,
Cover the table with something to eat,"

and seated herself at her table, and ate and drank until she was satisfied, and then she again cried:

"Bleat, bleat, my little goat, I pray,
And take the table quite away,"

and in an instant all had vanished. Two-eyes now awakened One-eye, and said: "One-eye, you want to take care of the goat, and go to sleep while you are doing it, but in the meantime the goat might run all over the world. Come, let us go home again." So they went home, and again Two-eyes let her little dish stand untouched, and One-eye could not tell her mother why she would not eat it, and to excuse herself said: "I fell asleep when I was out."

Next day the mother said to Three-eyes: "This time you shall go and observe if Two-eyes eats anything when she is out, and if anyone fetches her food and drink, for she must eat and drink in secret." So Three-eyes went to Two-eyes, and said: "I will go with you and see if the goat is taken proper care of, and driven where there is food." But Two-eyes knew what was in Three-eyes' mind, and drove the goat into high grass and said: "We will sit down, and I will sing something to you, Three-eyes." Three-eyes sat down and was tired with the walk and with the heat of the sun, and Two-eyes began the same song as before, and sang:

"Three-eyes, are you waking?"

but then, instead of singing:

"Three-eyes, are you sleeping?"

as she ought to have done, she thoughtlessly sang:

"Two-eyes, are you sleeping?"

and sang all the time:

"Three-eyes, are you waking?
Two-eyes, are you sleeping?"

Then two of the eyes which Three-eyes had, shut and fell asleep, but the third, as it had not been named in the song, did not sleep. It is true that Three-eyes shut it, but only in her cunning, to pretend it was asleep too, but it blinked, and could see everything very well. And when Two-eyes thought that Three-eyes was fast asleep, she used her little charm:

"Bleat, my little goat, bleat,
Cover the table with something to eat,"

and ate and drank as much as her heart desired, and then ordered the table to go away again,

"Bleat, bleat, my little goat, I pray,
And take the table quite away,"

and Three-eyes had seen everything. Then Two-eyes came to her, waked her and said: "Have you been asleep, Three-eyes? You keep

watch very well! Come, we will go home." And when they got home, Two-eyes again did not eat, and Three-eyes said to the mother: "Now, I know why that haughty thing there does not eat. When she is out, she says to the goat:

'Bleat, my little goat, bleat,
Cover the table with something to eat,'

and then a little table appears before her covered with the best of food, much better than any we have here, and when she has eaten all she wants, she says:

'Bleat, bleat, my little goat, I pray,
And take the table quite away,'

and all disappears. I watched everything closely. She put two of my eyes to sleep by means of a charm, but luckily the one in my forehead kept awake." Then the envious mother cried: "Do you want to fare better than we do? The desire shall pass from you," and she fetched a butcher's knife, and thrust it into the heart of the goat, which fell down dead.

When Two-eyes saw that, she went out full of sadness, seated herself on the ridge of grass at the edge of the field, and wept bitter tears. Suddenly the wise woman once more stood by her side, and said: "Two-eyes, why are you weeping?" "Have I not reason to weep?" she answered. "The goat which covered the table for me every day when I spoke your charm, has been killed by my mother, and now I shall again have to bear hunger and want." The wise woman said: "Two-eyes, I will give you a piece of good advice; ask your sisters to give you the entrails of the slaughtered goat, and bury them in the ground in front of the house, and your fortune will be made." Then she vanished, and Two-eyes went home and said to her sisters: "Dear sisters, do give me some part of my goat; I don't wish for what is good, but give me the entrails." Then they laughed and said: "If that's all you want, you can have it." So Two-eyes took the entrails and buried them quietly in the evening, in front of the house-door, as the wise woman had counselled her to do.

Next morning, when they all awoke, and went to the house-door, there stood a strangely magnificent tree with leaves of silver, and fruit of gold hanging among them, so that in all the wide world there was nothing more beautiful or precious. They did not know how the tree could have come there during the night, but Two-eyes saw that it had grown up out of the entrails of the goat, for it was standing on the exact spot where she had buried them. Then the mother said to One-eye: "Climb up, my child, and gather some of the fruit of the tree for us." One-eye climbed up, but when she was about to get hold of one of the golden apples, the branch escaped from her hands, and that happened each time, so that she could not pluck a single apple, let her do what she might. Then said the mother: "Three-eyes, you climb up; you with your three eyes can look about you better than One-eye." One-eye slipped down, and Three-eyes climbed up. Three-eyes was not more skilful, and might try as she would, but the golden apples always escaped her. At length the mother grew impatient, and climbed up herself, but could get hold of the fruit no better than One-eye and Three-eyes, for she always clutched empty air. Then said Two-eyes: "Let me go up, perhaps I may succeed better." The sisters cried: "You indeed, with your two eyes, what can you do?" But Two-eyes climbed up, and the golden apples did not avoid her, but came into her hand of their own accord, so that she could pluck them one after the other, and brought a whole apronful down with her. The mother took them away from her, and instead of treating poor Two-eyes any better for this, she and One-eye and Three-eyes were only envious, because Two-eyes alone had been able to get the fruit, and they treated her still more cruelly.

It so befell that once when they were all standing together by the tree, a young knight came up. "Quick, Two-eyes," cried the two sisters, "creep under this, and don't disgrace us!" and with all speed they turned an empty barrel which was standing close by the tree over poor Two-eyes, and they swept the golden apples which she had been gathering, under it too. When the knight came nearer he was a handsome lord, who stopped and admired the magnificent gold and silver tree, and said to the two sisters: "To whom does this fine tree belong? Anyone who would bestow one branch of it on me might in return for it ask whatsoever he desired." Then One-eye and Three-eyes replied that the tree belonged to them, and that they would give him a branch. They both took great trouble, but they were not able to do it, for the branches and fruit both moved away from them every time. Then said the knight: "It is very strange that the tree should belong to you, and that you should not have the power to break a piece off." They again asserted that the tree was their property. Whilst they were saying so, Two-eyes rolled out a couple of golden apples from under the barrel to the feet of the knight, for she was vexed with One-eye and Three-eyes, for not speaking the truth. When the knight saw the apples he was astonished, and asked where they came from. One-eye and Three-eyes answered that they had another sister, who was not allowed to show herself, for she had only two eyes like any common person. The knight, however, desired to see her, and cried: "Two-eyes, come forth." Then Two-eyes, quite comforted, came from beneath the barrel, and the knight was surprised at her great beauty, and said: "You, Two-eyes, can certainly break off a branch from the tree for me." "Yes," replied Two-eyes, "that I certainly shall be able to do, for the tree belongs to me." And she climbed up, and with the greatest ease broke off a branch with beautiful silver leaves and golden fruit, and gave it to the knight. Then said the knight: "Two-eyes, what shall I give you for it?" "Alas!" answered Two-eyes, "I suffer from hunger and thirst, grief and want, from early morning till late night; if you would take me with you, and rescue me, I should be happy." So the knight lifted Two-eyes on to his horse, and took her home with him to his father's castle, and there he gave her beautiful clothes, and meat and drink to her heart's content, and as he loved her so much he married her, and the wedding was solemnized with great rejoicing.

When Two-eyes was thus carried away by the handsome knight, her two sisters grudged her good fortune in downright earnest. "The wonderful tree, however, still remains with us," thought they, "and even if we can gather no fruit from it, still every one will stand still and look at it, and come to us and admire it. Who knows what good things may be in store for us?" But next morning, the tree had vanished, and all their hopes were at an end. And when Two-eyes looked out of the window of her own little room, to her great delight it was standing in front of it, and so it had followed her.

Two-eyes lived a long time in happiness. Once two poor women came to her in her castle, and begged for alms. She looked in their faces, and recognized her sisters, One-eye, and Three-eyes, who had fallen into such poverty that they had to wander about and beg their bread from door to door. Two-eyes, however, made them welcome, and was kind to them, and took care of them, so that they both with all their hearts repented the evil that they had done their sister in their youth.

FAIR KATRINELJE AND PIF-PAF-POLTRIE

Good-day, Father Hollenthe." "Many thanks, Pif-paf-poltrie." "May I be allowed to have your daughter?" "Oh, yes, if Mother Malcho

(Milch-cow), Brother High-and-Mighty, Sister Käsetraut, and fair Katrinelje are willing, you can have her." "Where is Mother Malcho, then?" "She is in the cow-house, milking the cow."

"Good-day, Mother Malcho." "Many thanks, Pif-paf-poltrie." "May I be allowed to have your daughter?" "Oh, yes, if Father Hollenthe, Brother High-and-Mighty, Sister Käsetraut, and fair Katrinelje are willing, you can have her." "Where is Brother High-and-Mighty, then?" "He is in the room chopping some wood." "Good-day, Brother High-and-Mighty." "Many thanks, Pif-paf-poltrie." "May I be allowed to have your sister?" "Oh, yes, if Father Hollenthe, Mother Malcho, Sister Käsetraut, and fair Katrinelje are willing, you can have her." "Where is Sister Käsetraut, then?" "She is in the garden cutting cabbages." "Good-day, Sister Käsetraut." "Many thanks, Pif-paf-poltrie." "May I be allowed to have your sister?" "Oh, yes, if Father Hollenthe, Mother Malcho, Brother High-and-Mighty, and fair Katrinelje are willing, you may have her." "Where is fair Katrinelje, then?" "She is in the room counting out her farthings." "Good day, fair Katrinelje." "Many thanks, Pif-paf-poltrie." "Will you be my bride?" "Oh, yes, if Father Hollenthe, Mother Malcho, Brother High-and-Mighty, and Sister Käsetraut are willing, I am ready."

"Fair Katrinelje, how much dowry do you have?" "Fourteen farthings in ready money, three and a half groschen owing to me, half a pound of dried apples, a handful of pretzels, and a handful of roots.

And many other things are mine,
Have I not a dowry fine?

Pif-paf-poltrie, what is your trade? Are you a tailor?" "Something better." "A shoemaker?" "Something better." "A husbandman?"

"Something better." "A joiner?" "Something better." "A smith?" "Something better." "A miller?" "Something better." "Perhaps a broom-maker?" "Yes, that's what I am, is it not a fine trade?"

THE FOX AND THE HORSE

A peasant had a faithful horse which had grown old and could do no more work, so his master would no longer give him anything to eat and said: "I can certainly make no more use of you, but still I mean well by you; if you prove yourself still strong enough to bring me a lion here, I will maintain you, but now take yourself away out of my stable," and with that he chased him into the open country. The horse was sad, and went to the forest to seek a little protection there from the weather. Then the fox met him and said: "Why do you hang your head so, and go about all alone?" "Alas," replied the horse, "avarice and fidelity do not dwell together in one house. My master has forgotten what services I have performed for him for so many years, and because I can no longer plough well, he will give me no more food, and has driven me out." "Without giving you a chance?" asked the fox. "The chance was a bad one. He said, if I were still strong enough to bring him a lion, he would keep me, but he well knows that I cannot do that." The fox said: "I will help you, just lay yourself down, stretch yourself out, as if you were dead, and do not stir." The horse did as the fox desired, and the fox went to the lion, who had his den not far off, and said: "A dead horse is lying outside there, just come with me, you can have a rich meal." The lion went with him, and when they were both standing by the horse the fox said: "After all, it is not very convenient for you here—I tell you what—I will fasten it to you by the tail, and then you can drag it into your cave, and devour it in peace."

This advice pleased the lion: he lay down, and in order that the fox might tie the horse fast to him, he kept quite quiet. But the fox tied the lion's legs together with the horse's tail, and twisted and fastened all so well and so strongly that no strength could break it. When he had finished his work, he tapped the horse on the shoulder and said: "Pull, white horse, pull." Then up sprang the horse at once, and drew the lion away with him. The lion began to roar so that all the birds in the forest flew out in terror, but the horse let him roar, and drew him and dragged him over the country to his master's door. When the master saw the lion, he was of a better mind, and said to the horse: "You shall stay with me and fare well," and he gave him plenty to eat until he died.

THE SHOES THAT WERE DANCED TO PIECES

There was once upon a time a King who had twelve daughters, each one more beautiful than the other. They all slept together in one chamber, in which their beds stood side by side, and every night when they were in them the King locked the door, and bolted it. But in the morning when he unlocked the door, he saw that their shoes were worn out with dancing, and no one could find out how that had come to pass. Then the King caused it to be proclaimed that whosoever could discover where they danced at night, should choose one of them for his wife and be King after his death, but that whosoever came forward and had not discovered it within three days and nights, should have forfeited his life. It was not long before a King's son presented himself, and offered to undertake the enterprise. He was well received, and in the evening was led into a room adjoining the princesses' sleeping-chamber. His bed was placed there, and he was to observe where they went and danced, and in order that they might do nothing secretly or go away to some other place, the door of their room was left open.

But the eyelids of the prince grew heavy as lead, and he fell asleep, and when he awoke in the morning, all twelve had been to the dance, for their shoes were standing there with holes in the soles. On the second and third nights there was no difference, and then his head was struck off without mercy. Many others came after this and undertook the enterprise, but all forfeited their lives. Now it came to pass that a poor soldier, who had a wound, and could serve no longer, found himself on the road to the town where the King lived. There he met an old woman, who asked him where he was going. "I hardly know myself," answered he, and added in jest: "I had half a mind to discover where the princesses danced their shoes into holes, and thus become King." "That is not so difficult," said the old woman, "you must not drink the wine which will be brought to you at night, and must pretend to be sound asleep." With that she gave him a little cloak, and said: "If you wear this, you will be invisible, and then you can steal after the twelve." When the soldier had received this good advice, he fell to in earnest, took heart, went to the King, and announced himself as a suitor. He was as well received as the others, and royal garments were put upon him. He was conducted that evening at bed-time into the ante-chamber, and as he was about to go to bed, the eldest came and brought him a cup of wine, but he had tied a sponge under his chin, and let the wine run down into it, without drinking a drop. Then he lay down and when he had lain a while, he began to snore, as if in the deepest sleep. The twelve princesses heard that, and laughed, and the eldest said: "He, too, might as well have saved his life." With that they got up, opened wardrobes, presses, cupboards, and brought out pretty dresses; dressed themselves before the mirrors, sprang about, and rejoiced at the prospect of the dance. Only the youngest said: "I know not how it is; you are very happy, but I feel very strange; some misfortune is certainly about to befall us." "You are a goose, who are always frightened," said the eldest. "Have you forgotten how many Kings' sons have already come here in vain? I had hardly any need to give the soldier a sleeping-draught, the booby would not have awakened anyway." When they were all ready they looked carefully at the soldier, but he had closed his eyes and did not move or stir, so they felt themselves safe enough. The eldest then went to her bed and tapped it; whereupon it immediately sank into the earth, and one after the other they descended through the opening, the eldest going first. The soldier, who had watched everything, tarried no longer, put on his little cloak, and went down last with the youngest. Half-way down the steps, he just trod a little on her dress; she was terrified at that, and cried out: "What is that? who is pulling at my dress?" "Don't be so silly!" said the eldest, "you have caught it on a nail."

Then they went all the way down, and when they were at the bottom, they were standing in a wonderfully pretty avenue of trees, all the leaves of which were of silver, and shone and glistened. The soldier thought: "I must carry a token away with me," and broke off a twig from one of them, on which the tree cracked with a loud report. The youngest cried out again: "Something is wrong, did you hear the crack?" But the eldest said: "It is a gun fired for joy, because we have got rid of our prince so quickly." After that they came into an avenue where all the leaves were of gold, and lastly into a third where they were of bright diamonds; he broke off a twig from each, which made such a crack each time that the youngest started back in terror, but the eldest still maintained that they were salutes. They went on and came to a great lake whereon stood twelve little boats, and in every boat sat a handsome prince, all of whom were waiting for the twelve, and each took one of them with him, but the soldier seated himself by the youngest. Then her prince said: "I wonder why the boat is so much heavier to-day; I shall have to row with all my strength, if I am to get it across." "What should cause that," said the youngest, "but the warm weather? I feel very warm too." On the opposite side of the lake stood a splendid, brightly-lit castle, from whence resounded the joyous music of trumpets and kettle-drums. They rowed there, entered, and each prince danced with the girl he loved, but the soldier danced with them unseen, and when one of them had a cup of wine in her hand he drank it up, so that the cup was empty when she carried it to her mouth; the youngest was alarmed at this, but the eldest always silenced her. They danced there till three o'clock in the morning when all the shoes were danced into holes, and they were forced to leave off; the princes rowed them back again over the lake, and this time the soldier seated himself by the eldest. On the shore they took leave of their princes, and promised to return the following night. When they reached the stairs the soldier ran on in front and lay down in his bed, and when the twelve had come up slowly and wearily, he was already snoring so loudly that they could all hear him, and they said: "So far as he is concerned, we are safe." They took off their beautiful dresses, laid them away, put the worn-out shoes under the bed, and lay down. Next morning the soldier was resolved not to speak, but to watch the wonderful goings-on, and again went with them a second and a third night. Then everything was just as it had been the first time, and each time they danced until their shoes were worn to pieces. But the third time he took a cup away with him as a token. When the hour had arrived for him to give his answer, he took the three twigs and the cup, and went to the King, but the twelve stood behind the door, and listened for what he was going to say. When the King put the question: "Where have my twelve daughters danced their shoes to pieces in the night?" he answered: "In an underground castle with twelve princes," and related how it had come to pass, and brought out the tokens. The King then summoned his daughters, and asked them if the soldier had told the truth, and when they saw that they were betrayed, and that falsehood would be of no avail, they were obliged to confess all. Thereupon the King asked which of them he would have to wife? He answered: "I am no longer young, so give me the eldest." Then the wedding was celebrated on the self-same day, and the kingdom was promised him after the King's death. But the princes were bewitched for as many days as they had danced nights with the twelve.

THE SIX SERVANTS

In olden times there lived an aged Queen who was a sorceress, and her daughter was the most beautiful maiden under the sun. The old woman, however, had no other thought than how to lure mankind to destruction, and when a wooer appeared, she said that whosoever wished to have her daughter, must first perform a task, or die. Many had been dazzled by the daughter's beauty, and had actually risked this, but they never could accomplish what the old woman enjoined them to do, and then no mercy was shown; they had to kneel down, and their heads were struck off. A certain King's son who had also heard of the maiden's beauty, said to his father: "Let me go there, I want to demand her in marriage." "Never," answered the King; "if you were to go, it would be going to your death." On this the son lay down and was sick unto death, and for seven years he lay there, and no physician could heal him. When the father perceived that all hope was over, with a heavy heart he said to him: "Go thither, and try your luck, for I know no other means of curing you." When the son heard that, he rose from his bed and was well again, and joyfully set out on his way.

And it came to pass that as he was riding across a heath, he saw from afar something like a great heap of hay lying on the ground, and when he drew nearer, he could see that it was the stomach of a man, who had laid himself down there, but the stomach looked like a small mountain. When the fat man saw the traveller, he stood up and said: "If you are in need of any one, take me into your service." The prince answered: "What can I do with such a clumsy man?" "Oh," said the Stout One, "this is nothing, when I really puff myself up, I am three thousand times fatter." "If that's the case," said the prince, "I can make use of you, come with me." So the Stout One followed the prince, and after a while they found another man who was lying on the ground with his ear laid to the turf. "What are you doing there?" asked the King's son. "I am listening," replied the man. "What are you listening to so attentively?" "I am listening to what is just going on in the world, for nothing escapes my ears; I even hear the grass growing." "Tell me," said the prince, "what you hear at the court of the old Queen who has the beautiful daughter." Then he answered: "I hear the whizzing of the sword that is striking off a wooer's head." The King's son said: "I can make use of you, come with me." They went onwards, and then saw a pair of feet lying and part of a pair of legs, but could not see the rest of the body. When they had walked on for a great distance, they came to the body, and at last to the head also. "Why," said the prince, "what a tall rascal you are!" "Oh," replied the Tall One, "that is nothing at all yet; when I really stretch out my limbs, I am three thousand times as tall, and taller than the highest mountain on earth. I will gladly enter your service, if you will take me." "Come with me," said the prince, "I can make use of you." They went onwards and found a man sitting by the road who had bound up his eyes. The prince said to him: "Have you weak eyes, that you cannot look at the light?" "No," replied the man, "but I must not remove the bandage, for whatsoever I look at with my eyes, splits to pieces, so powerful is my glance. If you can use that, I shall be glad to serve you." "Come with me," replied the King's son, "I can make use of you." They journeyed onwards and found a man who was lying in the hot sunshine, trembling and shivering all over his body, so that not a limb was still. "How can you shiver when the sun is shining so warm?" said the King's son. "Alas," replied the man," I am of quite a different nature. The hotter it is, the colder I am, and the frost pierces through all my bones; and the colder it is, the hotter I am. In the midst of ice, I cannot endure the heat, nor in the midst of fire, the cold." "You are a strange fellow!" said the prince, "but if you will enter my service, follow me." They travelled onwards, and saw a man standing who made a long neck and looked about him, and could see over all the mountains. "What are you looking at so eagerly?" said the King's son. The man replied: "I have such sharp eyes that I can see into every forest and field, and hill and valley, all over the world." The prince said: "Come with me if you will, for I am still in want of such an one."

And now the King's son and his six servants came to the town where the aged Queen dwelt. He did not tell her who he was, but said: "If you will give me your beautiful daughter, I will perform any task you set me." The sorceress was delighted to get such a handsome youth as this into her net, and said: "I will set you three tasks, and if you are able to perform them all, you shall be husband and master of my daughter." What is the first to be?" "You shall fetch me my ring which I have dropped into the Red Sea." So the King's son went home to his servants and said: "The first task is not easy. A ring is to be got out of the Red Sea. Come, find some way of doing it." Then the man with the sharp sight said: "I will see where it is lying," and looked down into the water and said: "It is hanging there, on a pointed stone." The Tall One carried them thither, and said: "I would soon get it out, if I could only see it." "Oh, is that all!" cried the Stout One, and lay down and put his mouth to the water, on which all the waves fell into it just as if it had been a whirlpool, and he drank up the whole sea till it was as dry as a meadow. The Tall One stooped down a little, and brought out the ring with his hand. Then the King's son rejoiced when he had the ring, and took it to the old Queen. She was astonished, and said: "Yes, it is the right ring. You have safely performed the first task, but now comes the second. Do you see the meadow in front of my palace? Three hundred fat oxen are feeding there, and these must you eat, skin, hair, bones, horns and all, and down below in my cellar lie three hundred casks of wine, and these you must drink up as well, and if one hair of the oxen, or one little drop of the wine is left, your life will be forfeited to me." "May I invite no guests to this repast?" inquired the prince, "no dinner is good without some company." The old woman laughed maliciously, and replied: "You may invite one for the sake of companionship, but no more."

The King's son went to his servants and said to the Stout One: "You shall be my guest to-day, and shall eat your fill." Hereupon the Stout One puffed himself up and ate the three hundred oxen without leaving one single hair, and then he asked if he was to have nothing but his breakfast. Then he drank the wine straight from the casks without feeling any need of a glass, and drained them down to their dregs. When the meal was over, the prince went to the old woman, and told her that the second task also was performed. She wondered at this and said: "No one has ever done so much before, but one task still remains," and she thought to herself: "You shall not escape me, and will not keep your head on your shoulders! This night," said she, "I will bring my daughter to you in your chamber, and you shall put your arms around her, but when you are sitting there together, beware of falling asleep. When twelve o'clock is striking, I will come, and if she is then no longer in your arms, you are lost." The prince thought: "The task is easy, I will most certainly keep my eyes open." Nevertheless he called his servants, told them what the old woman had said, and remarked: "Who knows what treachery may lurk behind this. Foresight is a good thing—keep watch, and take care that the maiden does not go out of my room again." When night fell, the old woman came with her daughter, and gave her into the prince's arms, and then the Tall One wound himself round the two in a circle, and the Stout One placed himself by the door, so that no living creature could enter. There the two sat, and the maiden spoke never a word, but the moon shone through the window on her face, and the prince could behold her wondrous beauty. He did nothing but gaze at her, and was filled with love and happiness, and his eyes never felt weary. This lasted until eleven o'clock, when the old woman cast such a spell over all of them that they fell asleep, and at the self-same moment the maiden was carried away.

Then they all slept soundly until a quarter to twelve, when the magic lost its power, and all awoke again. "Oh, misery and misfortune!" cried the prince, "now I am lost!" The faithful servants also began to lament, but the Listener said: "Be quiet, I want to listen." Then he listened for an instant and said: "She is on a rock, three hundred leagues from hence, bewailing her fate. You alone, Tall One, can help her; If you will stand up, you will be there in a couple of steps."

"Yes," answered the Tall One, "but the one with the sharp eyes must go with me, that we may destroy the rock." Then the Tall One took the one with bandaged eyes on his back, and in the twinkling of an eye they were on the enchanted rock. The Tall One immediately took the bandage from the other's eyes, and he did but look round, and the rock shivered into a thousand pieces. Then the Tall One took the maiden in his arms, carried her back in a second, then fetched his companion with the same rapidity, and before it struck twelve they were all sitting as they had sat before, quite merrily and happily. When twelve struck, the aged sorceress came stealing in with a malicious face, as much as to say: "Now he is mine!" for she believed that her daughter was on the rock three hundred leagues off. But when she saw her in the prince's arms, she was alarmed, and said: "Here is one who knows more than I do!" She dared not make any opposition, and was forced to give him her daughter. But she whispered in her ear: "It is a disgrace to you to

have to obey common people, and that you are not allowed to choose a husband to your own liking."

On this the proud heart of the maiden was filled with anger, and she meditated revenge. Next morning she caused three hundred great bundles of wood to be got together, and said to the prince that though the three tasks were performed, she would still not be his wife until some one was ready to seat himself in the midst of the wood, and bear the fire. She thought that none of his servants would let themselves be burnt for him, and that out of love for her, he himself would place himself upon it, and then she would be free. But the servants said: "Every one of us had done something except the Frosty One, he must set to work," and they put him in the middle of the pile, and set fire to it. Then the fire began to burn, and burnt for three days until all the wood was consumed, and when the flames had burnt out, the Frosty One was standing amid the ashes, trembling like an aspen leaf, and saying: "I never felt such a frost during the whole course of my life; if it had lasted much longer, I should have been benumbed!"

As no other pretext was to be found, the beautiful maiden was now forced to take the unknown youth as a husband. But when they drove away to church, the old woman said: "I cannot endure the disgrace," and sent her warriors after them with orders to cut down all who opposed them, and bring back her daughter. But the Listener had sharpened his ears, and heard the secret discourse of the old woman. "What shall we do?" said he to the Stout One. But he knew what to do, and spat out once or twice behind the carriage some of the sea-water which he had drunk, and a great lake arose in which the warriors were caught and drowned. When the sorceress perceived that, she sent her mailed knights; but the Listener heard the rattling of their armour, and undid the bandage from one eye of Sharp-eyes, who looked for a while rather fixedly at the enemy's troops, on which they all sprang to pieces like glass. Then the youth and the maiden went on their way undisturbed, and when the two had been blessed in church, the six servants took leave, and said to their master: "Your wishes are now satisfied, you need us no longer, we will go our way and seek our fortunes."

Half a league from the palace of the prince's father was a village near which a swineherd tended his herd, and when they came thither the prince said to his wife: "Do you know who I really am? I am no prince, but a herder of swine, and the man who is there with that herd, is my father. We two shall have to set to work also, and help him." Then he alighted with her at the inn, and secretly told the innkeepers to take away her royal apparel during the night. So when she awoke in the morning, she had nothing to put on, and the innkeeper's wife gave her an old gown and a pair of worsted stockings, and at the same time seemed to consider it a great present, and said: "If it were not for the sake of your husband I should have given you nothing at all!" Then the princess believed that he really was a swineherd, and tended the herd with him, and thought to herself: "I have deserved this for my haughtiness and pride." This lasted for a week, and then she could endure it no longer, for she had sores on her feet. And now came a couple of people who asked if she knew who her husband was. "Yes," she answered, "he is a swineherd, and has just gone out with cords and ropes to try to drive a little bargain," But they said: "Just come with us, and we will take you to him," and they took her up to the palace, and when she entered the hall, there stood her husband in kingly raiment. But she did not recognize him until he took her in his arms, kissed her, and said: "I suffered so much for you that you, too, had to suffer for me." And then the wedding was celebrated, and he who has related this, wished that he, too, has been present at it.

THE WHITE BRIDE AND THE BLACK BRIDE

A woman was walking about the fields with her daughter and her step-daughter cutting fodder, when the Lord came towards them in the form of a poor man, and asked: "Which is the way into the village?" "If you want to know," said the mother, "seek it for yourself," and the daughter added: "If you are afraid you will not find it, take a guide with you," But the step-daughter said: "Poor man, I will take you there, come with me." Then God was angry with the mother and daughter, and turned his back on them, and wished that they should become as black as night and as ugly as sin. To the poor step-daughter, however, God was gracious, and went with her, and when they were near the village, he said a blessing over her, and spoke: "Choose three things for yourself, and I will grant them to you." Then said the maiden: "I should like to be as beautiful and fair as the sun," and instantly she was white and fair as day. "Then I should like to have a purse of money which would never grow empty." That the Lord gave her also, but he said: "Do not forget what is best of all." Said she: "For my third wish, I desire, after my death, to inhabit the eternal kingdom of Heaven." That also was granted unto her, and then the Lord left her. When the step-mother came home with her daughter, and they saw that they were both as black as coal and ugly, but that the step-daughter was white and beautiful, wickedness increased still more in their hearts, and they thought of nothing else but how they could do her an injury. The step-daughter, however, had a brother called Reginer, whom she loved much, and she told him all that had happened. And Reginer said to her: "Dear sister, I will paint your portrait, that I may continually see you before my eyes, for my love for you is so great that I should like always to look at you." Then she answered: "But, I pray you, let no one see the picture." So he painted his sister and hung up the picture in his room; he, however, dwelt in the King's palace, for he was his coachman. Every day he went and stood before the picture, and thanked God for the happiness of having such a dear sister. Now it happened that the King whom he served, had just lost his wife, who had been so beautiful that no one could be found to compare with her, and on this account the King was in deep grief. The attendants about the court, however, noticed that the coachman stood daily before this beautiful picture, and they were jealous of him, so they informed the King. Then the latter ordered the picture to be brought to him, and when he saw that it was like his lost wife in every respect, except that it was still more beautiful, he fell mortally in love with it. He caused the coachman to be brought before him, and asked whom the portrait represented. The coachman said it was his sister, so the King resolved to take no one but her as his wife, and gave him a carriage and horses and splendid garments of cloth of gold, and sent him forth to fetch his chosen bride. When Reginer came on this errand, his sister was glad, but the black maiden was jealous of her good fortune, and grew angry above all measure, and said to her mother: "Of what use are all your arts to us now when you cannot procure such a piece of luck for me?" "Be quiet," said the old woman, "I will soon divert it to you"—and by her arts of witchcraft, she so troubled the eyes of the coachman that he was half-blind, and she stopped the ears of the white maiden so that she was half-deaf. Then they got into the carriage, first the bride in her noble royal apparel, then the step-mother with her daughter, and Reginer sat on the box to drive. When they had been on the way for some time the coachman cried:

"Cover thee well, my sister dear,
That the rain may not wet thee,
That the wind may not load thee with dust,
That thou may'st be fair and beautiful
When thou appearest before the King."

The bride asked: "What is my dear brother saying?" "Ah," said the old woman, "he says that you ought to take off your golden dress and give it to your sister." Then she took it off, and put it on the black maiden, who gave her in exchange for it a shabby grey gown. They drove onwards, and a short time afterwards, the brother again cried:

"Cover thee well, my sister dear,
That the rain may not wet thee,
That the wind may not load thee with dust,
That thou may'st be fair and beautiful
When thou appearest before the King."

The bride asked: "What is my dear brother saying?" "Ah," said the old woman, "he says that you ought to take off your golden hood and give it to your sister." So she took off the hood and put it on her sister, and sat with her own head uncovered. And they drove on farther. After a while, the brother once more cried:

> "Cover thee well, my sister dear,
> That the rain may not wet thee,
> That the wind may not lead thee with dust,
> That thou may'st be fair and beautiful
> When thou appearest before the King."

The bride asked: "What is my dear brother saying?" "Ah," said the old woman, "he says you must look out of the carriage." They happened to be on a bridge, which crossed deep water. When the bride stood up and leant forward out of the carriage, they both pushed her out, and she fell into the middle of the water. At the same moment that she sank, a snow-white duck arose out of the mirror-smooth water, and swam down the river. The brother had observed nothing of it, and drove the carriage on until they reached the court. Then he took the black maiden to the King as his sister, and thought she really was so, because his eyes were dim, and he saw the golden garments glittering. When the King saw the boundless ugliness of his intended bride, he was very angry, and ordered the coachman to be thrown into a pit which was full of adders and nests of snakes. The old witch, however, knew so well how to flatter the King and deceive his eyes by her arts, that he kept her and her daughter until she appeared quite endurable to him, and he really married her.

One evening when the black bride was sitting on the King's knee, a white duck came swimming up the gutter to the kitchen, and said to the kitchen-boy: "Boy, light a fire, that I may warm my feather." The kitchen-boy did it, and lighted a fire on the hearth. Then came the duck and sat down by it, and shook herself and smoothed her feathers to rights with her bill. While she was thus sitting and enjoying herself, she asked: "What is my brother Reginer doing?" The scullery-boy replied: "He is imprisoned in the pit with adders and with snakes." The she asked: "What is the black witch doing in the house?" The boy answered: "She is loved by the King and happy."

"May God have mercy on him," said the duck, and swam forth by the gutter.

The next night she came again and put the same questions, and the third night also. Then the kitchen-boy could bear it no longer, and went to the King and revealed all to him. The King, however, wanted to see it for himself, and next evening went thither, and when the duck thrust her head in through the gutter, he took his sword and cut through her neck, and suddenly she changed into a most beautiful maiden, exactly like the picture which her brother had made of her. The King was full of joy, and as she stood there quite wet, he caused splendid apparel to be brought and had her clothed in it. Then she told how she had been betrayed by cunning and falsehood, and at last thrown down into the water, and her first request was that her brother should be brought forth from the pit of snakes, and when the King had fulfilled this request, he went into the chamber where the old witch was, and asked if she knew the punishment for one who does this and that, and related what had happened. Then was she so blinded that she was aware of nothing and said: "She deserves to be stripped naked, and put into a barrel with nails, and that a horse should be harnessed to the barrel, and the horse sent all over the world." All of which was done to her, and to her black daughter. But the King married the white and beautiful bride, and rewarded her faithful brother, and made him a rich and distinguished man.

IRON HANS

There was once upon a time a King who had a great forest near his palace, full of all kinds of wild animals. One day he sent out a huntsman to shoot him a roe, but he did not come back. "Perhaps some accident has befallen him," said the King, and the next day he sent out two more huntsmen who were to search for him, but they too stayed away. Then on the third day, he sent for all his huntsmen, said: "Scour the whole forest through, and do not give up until you have found all three." But

of these also, none came home again, and of the pack of hounds which they had taken with them, none were seen again. From that time forth, no one would any longer venture into the forest, and it lay there in deep stillness and solitude, and nothing was seen of it, but sometimes an eagle or a hawk flying over it. This lasted for many years, when an unknown huntsman announced himself to the King as seeking a situation, and offered to go into the dangerous forest. The King, however, would not give his consent, and said: "It is not safe in there; I fear it would fare with you no better than with the others, and you would never come out again." The huntsman replied: "Lord, I will venture it at my own risk, of fear I know nothing."

The huntsman therefore betook himself with his dog to the forest. It was not long before the dog fell in with some game on the way, and wanted to pursue it; but hardly had the dog run two steps when it stood before a deep pool, could go no farther, and a naked arm stretched itself out of the water, seized it, and drew it under. When the huntsman saw that, he went back and fetched three men to come with buckets and bale out the water. When they could see to the bottom there lay a wild man whose body was brown like rusty iron, and whose hair hung over his face down to his knees. They bound him with cords, and led him away to the castle. There was great astonishment over the wild man; the King, however, had him put in an iron cage in his court-yard, and forbade the door to be opened on pain of death, and the Queen herself was to take the key into her keeping. And from this time forth every one could again go into the forest with safety.

The King had a son of eight years, who was once playing in the court-yard, and while he was playing, his golden ball fell into the cage. The boy ran thither and said: "Give me my ball out." "Not till you have opened the door for me," answered the man. "No," said the boy, "I will not do that; the King has forbidden it," and ran away. The next day he again went and asked for his ball; the wild man said: "Open my door," but the boy would not. On the third day the King had ridden out hunting, and the boy went once more and said: "I cannot open the door even if I wished, for I have not the key." Then the wild man said: "It lies under your mother's pillow, you can get it there." The boy, who wanted to have his ball back, cast all thought to the winds, and brought the key. The door opened with difficulty, and the boy pinched his fingers. When it was open the wild man stepped out, gave him the golden ball, and hurried away. The boy had become afraid; he called and cried after him: "Oh, wild man, do not go away, or I shall be beaten!" The wild man turned back, took him up, set him on his shoulder, and went with hasty steps into the forest. When the King came home, he observed the empty cage, and asked the Queen how that had happened. She knew nothing about it, and sought the key, but it was gone. She called the boy, but no one answered. The King sent out people to seek for him in the fields, but they did not find him. Then he could easily guess what had happened, and much grief reigned in the royal court.

When the wild man had once more reached the dark forest, he took the boy down from his shoulder, and said to him: "You will never see your father and mother again, but I will keep you with me, for you have set me free, and I have compassion on you. If you do all I bid you, you shall fare well. Of treasure and gold have I enough, and more than anyone in the world." He made a bed of moss for the boy on which he slept, and the next morning the man took him to a well, and said: "Behold, the gold well is as bright and clear as crystal, you shall sit beside it, and take care that nothing falls into it, or it will be polluted. I will come every evening to see if you have obeyed my order." The boy placed himself by the brink of the well, and often saw a golden fish or a golden snake show itself therein, and took care that nothing fell in. As he was thus sitting, his finger hurt him so violently that he involuntarily put it in the water. He drew it quickly out again, but saw that it was quite gilded, and whatsoever pains he took to wash the gold off again, all was to no purpose. In the evening Iron Hans came back, looked at the boy, and said: "What has happened to the well?" "Nothing, nothing," he answered, and held his finger behind his back, that the man might not see it. But he said: "You have dipped your finger into the water, this time it may pass, but take care you do not again let anything go in." By daybreak the boy was already sitting by the well and watching it. His finger hurt him again and he passed it over his head, and then unhappily a hair fell down into the well. He took it quickly out, but it was already quite gilded. Iron Hans came, and already knew what had happened. "You have let a hair fall into the well," said he. "I will allow you to watch by it once more, but if this happens for the third time then the well is polluted, and you can no longer remain with me."

On the third day, the boy sat by the well, and did not stir his finger, however much it hurt him. But the time was long to him, and he looked at the reflection of his face on the surface of the water. And as he still bent down more and more while he was doing so, and trying to look straight into the eyes, his long hair fell down from his shoulders into the water. He raised himself up quickly, but the whole of the hair of his head was already golden and shone like the sun. You can imagine how terrified the poor boy was! He took his pocket-handkerchief and tied it round his head, in order that the man might not see it. When he came he already knew everything, and said: "Take the handkerchief off." Then the golden hair streamed forth, and let the boy excuse himself as he might, it was of no use. "You have not stood the trial, and can stay here no longer. Go forth into the world, there you will learn what poverty is. But as you have not a bad heart, and as I mean well by you, there is one thing I will grant you; if you fall into any difficulty, come to the forest and cry: 'Iron Hans,' and then I will come and help you. My power is great, greater than you think, and I have gold and silver in abundance."

Then the King's son left the forest, and walked by beaten and unbeaten paths ever onwards until at length he reached a great city. There he looked for work, but could find none, and he had learnt nothing by which he could help himself. At length he went to the palace, and asked if they would take him in. The people about court did not at all know what use they could make of him, but they liked him, and told him to stay. At length the cook took him into his service, and said he might carry wood and water, and rake the cinders together. Once when it so happened that no one else was at hand, the cook ordered him to carry the food to the royal table, but as he did not like to let his golden hair be seen, he kept his little cap on. Such a thing as that had never yet come under the King's notice, and he said: "When you come to the royal table you must take your hat off." He answered: "Ah, Lord, I cannot; I have a bad sore place on my head." Then the King had the cook called before him and scolded him, and asked how he could take such a boy as that into his service; and that he was to send him away at once. The cook, however, had pity on him, and exchanged him for the gardener's boy.

And now the boy had to plant and water the garden, hoe and dig, and bear the wind and bad weather. Once in summer when he was working alone in the garden, the day was so warm he took his little cap off that the air might cool him. As the sun shone on his hair it glittered and flashed so that the rays fell into the bed-room of the King's daughter, and up she sprang to see what that could be. Then she saw the boy, and cried to him: "Boy, bring me a wreath of flowers." He put his cap on with all haste, and gathered wild field-flowers and bound them together. When he was ascending the stairs with them, the gardener met him, and said: "How can you take the King's daughter a garland of such common flowers? Go quickly, and get another, and seek out the prettiest and rarest." "Oh, no," replied the boy, "the wild ones have more scent, and will please her better." When he got into the room, the King's daughter said: "Take your cap off, it is not seemly to keep it on in my presence." He again said: "I may not, I have a sore head." She, however, caught at his cap and pulled it off, and then his golden hair rolled down on his shoulders, and it was splendid to behold. He wanted to run out, but she held him by the arm, and gave him a handful of ducats. With these he departed, but he cared nothing for the gold pieces. He took them to the gardener, and said: "I present them to your children, they can play with them." The following day the King's daughter again called to him that he was to bring her a wreath of field-flowers, and when he went in with it, she instantly snatched at his cap, and wanted to take it away from him, but he held it fast with both hands. She again gave him a handful of ducats, but he would not keep them, and gave them to the gardener for play-things for his children. On the third day things went just the same; she could not get his cap away from him, and he would not have her money.

Not long afterwards, the country was overrun by war. The King gathered together his people, and did not know whether or not he could offer any opposition to the enemy, who was superior in strength and had a mighty army. Then said the gardener's boy: "I am grown up, and will go to the wars also, only give me a horse." The others laughed, and said: "Seek one for yourself when we are gone, we will leave one behind us in the stable for you." When they had gone forth, he went into the stable, and led the horse out; it was lame of one foot, and limped hobblety jig, hobblety jig; nevertheless he mounted it, and rode away to the dark forest. When he came to the outskirts, he called "Iron Hans" three times so loudly that it echoed through the trees. There-upon the wild man appeared immediately, and said: "What do you desire?" "I want a strong steed, for I am going to the wars." "That you shall have, and still more than you ask for." Then the wild man went back into the forest, and it was not long before a stable-boy came out of it, who led a horse that snorted with its nostrils, and could hardly be restrained, and behind them followed a great troop of warriors entirely equipped in iron, and their swords flashed in the sun. The youth made over his three-legged horse to the stable-boy, mounted the other, and rode at the head of the soldiers. When he got near the battle-field a great part of the King's men had already fallen, and little was wanting to make the rest give way. Then the youth galloped thither with his iron soldiers, broke like a hurricane over the enemy, and beat down all who opposed him. They began to flee, but the youth pursued, and never stopped, until there was not a single man left. Instead of returning to the King, however, he conducted his troop by byways back to the forest, and called forth Iron Hans. "What do you desire?" asked the wild man. "Take back your horse and your troops, and give me my three-legged horse again." All that he asked was done, and soon he was riding on his three-legged horse. When the King returned to his palace, his daughter went to meet him, and wished him joy of his victory. "I am not the one who carried away the victory," said he, "but a strange knight who came to my assistance with his soldiers." The daughter wanted to hear who the strange knight was, but the King did not know, and said: "He followed the enemy, and I did not see him again." She inquired of the gardener where his boy was, but he smiled, and said: "He has just come home on his three-legged horse, and the others have been mocking him, and crying: 'Here comes our hobblety jig back again!' They asked, too: 'Under what hedge have you been lying sleeping all the time?' So he said: 'I did the best of all, and it would have gone badly without me.' And then he was still more ridiculed."

The King said to his daughter: "I will proclaim a great feast that shall last for three days, and you shall throw a golden apple. Perhaps the unknown man will show himself." When the feast was announced, the youth went out to the forest, and called Iron Hans. "What do you desire?" asked he. "That I may catch the King's daughter's golden apple." "It is as safe as if you had it already," said Iron Hans. "You shall likewise have a suit of red armour for the occasion, and ride on a spirited chestnut-horse." When the day came, the youth galloped to the spot, took his place amongst the knights, and was recognized by no one. The King's daughter came forward, and threw a golden apple to the knights, but none of them caught it but he, only as soon as he had it he galloped away.

On the second day Iron Hans equipped him as a white knight, and gave him a white horse. Again he was the only one who caught the apple, and he did not linger an instant, but galloped off with it. The King grew angry, and said: "That is not allowed; he must appear before me and tell his name." He gave the order that if the knight who caught the apple, should go away again they should pursue him, and if he would not come back willingly, they were to cut him down and stab him.

On the third day, he received from Iron Hans a suit of black armour and a black horse, and again he caught the apple. But when he was riding off with it, the King's attendants pursued him, and one of them got so near him that he wounded the youth's leg with the point of his sword. The youth nevertheless escaped from them, but his horse leapt so violently that the helmet fell from the youth's head, and they could see that he had golden hair. They rode back and announced this to the King.

The following day the King's daughter asked the gardener about his boy. "He is at work in the garden; the queer creature has been at the festival too, and only came home yesterday evening; he has likewise shown my children three golden apples which he has won."

The King had him summoned into his presence, and he came and again had his little cap on his head. But the King's daughter went up to him and took it off, and then his golden hair fell down over his shoulders, and he was so handsome that all were amazed. "Are you the knight who came every day to the festival, always in different colours, and who caught the three golden apples?" asked the King. "Yes," answered he, "and here the apples are," and he took them out of his pocket, and returned them to the King. "If you desire further proof, you may see the wound which your people gave me when they followed me. But I am likewise the knight who helped you to your victory over your enemies." "If you can perform such deeds as that, you are no gardener's boy; tell me, who is your father?" "My father is a mighty King, and gold have I in plenty as great as I require." "I well see," said the King, "that I own thanks to you; can I do anything to please you?" "Yes," answered he, "that indeed you can. Give me your daughter to wife." The maiden laughed, and said: "He does not stand much on ceremony, but I have already seen by his golden hair that he was no gardener's boy," and then she went and kissed him. His father and mother came to the wedding, and were in great delight, for they had given up all hope of ever seeing their dear son again. And as they were sitting at the marriage-feast, the music suddenly stopped, the doors opened, and a stately King came in with a great retinue. He went up to the youth, embraced him and said: "I am Iron Hans, and was by enchantment a wild man, but you have set me free; all the treasures which I possess shall be your property."

THE THREE BLACK PRINCESSES

East India was besieged by an enemy who would not retire until he had received six hundred dollars. Then the townsfolk caused it to be proclaimed by beat of drum that whosoever was able to procure the money should be burgomaster. Now there was a poor fisherman who fished on the sea with his son, and the enemy came and took the son prisoner, and gave the father six hundred dollars for him. So the father went and gave them to the great men of the town, and the enemy departed, and the fisherman became burgomaster. Then it was proclaimed that whosoever did not say "Mr. Burgomaster," should be put to death on the gallows.

The son got away again from the enemy, and came to a great forest on a high mountain. The mountain opened, and he went into a great enchanted castle, wherein chairs, tables, and benches were all hung with black. Then came three young princesses who were dressed entirely in black, but had a little white on their faces; they told him he was not to be afraid, they would not hurt him, and that he could rescue them. He said he would gladly do that, if he did but know how. At this, they told him he must for a whole year not speak to them and also not look at them, and what he wanted to have he was just to ask for, and if they dared give him an answer they would do so. When he had been there for a long while he said he should like to go to his father, and they told him he might go. He was to take with him this purse with money, put on this coat, and in a week he must be back there again.

Then he was lifted up, and was instantly in East India. He could no longer find his father in the fisherman's hut, and asked the people where the poor fisherman could be, and they told him he must not say that, or he would come to the gallows. Then he went to his father and said: "Fisherman, how have you got here?" Then the father said: "You must not say that, if the great men of the town knew of that, you would come to the gallows." He, however, would not give in, and was brought to the gallows. When he was there, he said: "O, my masters, just give me leave to go to the old fisherman's hut." Then he put on his old smock, and came back to the great men, and said: "Do you not now see? Am I not the son of the poor fisherman? Did I not earn bread for my father and mother in this dress?" Hereupon his father knew him again, and begged his pardon, and took him home with him, and then he related all that had happened to him, and how he had got into a forest on a high mountain, and the mountain had opened and he had gone into an enchanted castle, where all was black, and three young princesses had come to him who were black except a little white on their faces. And they had told him not to fear, and that he could rescue them. Then his mother said that might very likely not be a good thing to do, and that he ought to take a blessed candle with him, and drop some boiling wax on their faces.

He went back again, and he was in great fear, and he dropped the wax on their faces as they were sleeping, and they all turned half-white. Then all the three princesses sprang up, and said: "You accursed dog, our blood shall cry for vengeance on you! Now there is no man born in the world, nor will any ever be born who can set us free! We have still three brothers who are bound by seven chains—they shall tear you to pieces." Then there was a loud shrieking all over the castle, and he sprang out of the window, and broke his leg, and the castle sank into the earth again, the mountain closed again, and no one knew where the castle had stood.

KNOIST AND HIS THREE SONS

Between Werrel and Soist there lived a man whose name was Knoist, and he had three sons. One was blind, the other lame, and the third stark-naked. Once on a time they went into a field, and there they saw a hare. The blind one shot it, the lame one caught it, the naked one put it in his pocket. Then they came to a mighty big lake, on which there were three boats, one sailed, one sank, the third had no bottom to it. They all three got into the one with no bottom to it. Then they came to a mighty big forest in which there was a mighty big tree; in the tree was a mighty big chapel—in the chapel was a sexton made of beech-wood and a box-wood parson, who dealt out holy water with cudgels.

"How truly happy is that one
Who can from holy water run!"

THE MAID OF BRAKEL

A girl from Brakel once went to St. Anne's Chapel at the foot of the Hinnenberg, and as she wanted to have a husband, and thought there was no one else in the chapel, she sang:

"Oh, holy Saint Anne!
Help me soon to a man.
Thou know'st him right well,
By Suttmer gate does he dwell,
His hair it is yellow,
Thou know'st him right well."

The clerk, however, was standing behind the altar and heard that, so he cried in a very gruff voice:

"You shall not have him! You shall not have him!"

The maiden thought that the child Mary who stood by her mother Anne had called out that to her, and was angry, and cried:

"Fiddle de dee, conceited thing, hold your tongue, and let your mother speak!"

MY HOUSEHOLD

Whither do you go?" "To Walpe." "I to Walpe, you to Walpe, so, so, together we'll go."

"Have you a man? What is his name?" "Cham." "My man Cham, your man Cham; I to Walpe, you to Walpe; so, so, together we'll go."

"Have you a child; how is he styled?" "Wild." "My child Wild, your child Wild; my man Cham, your man Cham; I to Walpe, you to Walpe, so, so, together we'll go."

"Have you a cradle? How do you call your cradle?" "Hippodadle." "My cradle Hippodadle, your cradle Hippodadle, my child Wild, your child Wild, my man Cham, your man Cham; I to Walpe, you to Walpe, so, so, together we'll go."

"Have you also a drudge? What name has your drudge?" "From-work-do-not-budge." "My drudge From-work-do-not-budge, your drudge From-work-do-not-budge; my cradle Hippodadle, your cradle Hippodadle; my child Wild, your child Wild; my man Cham, your man Cham; I to Walpe, you to Walpe, so, so, together we'll go."

THE LAMBKIN AND THE LITTLE FISH

There were once a little brother and a little sister, who loved each other with all their hearts. Their own mother, however, was dead, and they had a step-mother who was not kind to them, and secretly did everything she could to hurt them. It so happened that the two were playing with other children in a meadow before the house, and there was a pond in the meadow which came up to one side of the house. The children ran about it, and caught each other, and played at counting out.

"Eneke Beneke, let me live,
And I to you my bird will give.
The little bird, it straw shall seek,
The straw I'll give to the cow to eat.
The pretty cow shall give me milk,
The milk I'll to the baker take.
The baker he shall bake a cake,
The cake I'll give unto the cat.
The cat shall catch some mice for that,
The mice I'll hang up in the smoke,
And then you'll see the *snow*."

They stood in a circle while they played this, and the one to whom the word "snow" fell, had to run away and all the others ran after him and caught him. As they were running about so merrily the step-mother watched them from the window, and grew angry. And as she understood arts of witchcraft she bewitched them both, and changed the little brother into a fish, and the little sister into a lamb. Then the fish swam here and there about the pond and was very sad, and the lambkin walked up and down the meadow, and was miserable, and could not eat or touch one blade of grass. Thus passed a long time, and then strangers came as visitors to the castle. The false step-mother

thought: "This is a good opportunity," and called the cook and said to him: "Go and fetch the lamb from the meadow and kill it, we have nothing else for the visitors." Then the cook went away and got the lamb, and took it into the kitchen and tied its feet, and all this it bore patiently. When he had drawn out his knife and was whetting it on the door-step to kill the lamb, he noticed a little fish swimming backwards and forwards in the water, in front of the gutter-stone and looking up at him. This, however, was the brother, for when the fish saw the cook take the lamb away, it followed them and swam along the pond to the house; then the lamb cried down to it:

"Ah, brother, in the pond so deep,
How sad is my poor heart!
The cook he whets his knife
To take away my life."

The little fish answered:

"Ah, little sister, up on high
How sad is my poor heart
While in this pond I lie."

When the cook heard that the lambkin could speak and said such sad words to the fish down below, he was terrified and thought this could be no common lamb, but must be bewitched by the wicked woman in the house. Then said he: "Be easy, I will not kill you," and took another sheep and made it ready for the guests, and conveyed the lambkin to a good peasant woman, to whom he related all that he had seen and heard.

The peasant, however, was the very woman who had been foster-mother to the little sister, and she suspected at once who the lamb was, and went with it to a wise woman. Then the wise woman pronounced a blessing over the lambkin and the little fish, by means of which they regained their human forms, and after this she took them both into a little hut in a great forest, where they lived alone, but were contented and happy.

SEMSI MOUNTAIN

There were once two brothers, the one rich, the other poor. The rich one, however, gave nothing to the poor one, and he gained a scanty living by trading in corn, and often did so badly that he had no bread for his wife and children. Once when he was wheeling a barrow through the forest he saw, on one side of him, a great, bare, naked-looking mountain, and as he had never seen it before, he stood still and stared at it with amazement.

While he was thus standing he saw twelve great, wild men coming towards him, and as he believed they were robbers he pushed his barrow into the thicket, climbed up a tree, and waited to see what would happen. The twelve men, however, went to the mountain and cried: "Semsi mountain, Semsi mountain, open up," and immediately the barren mountain opened down the middle, and the twelve went into it, and as soon as they were within, it shut. After a short time, it opened again, and the men came forth carrying heavy sacks on their shoulders, and when they were all once more in the daylight they said: "Semsi mountain, Semsi mountain, shut yourself;" then the mountain closed together, and there was no longer any entrance to be seen to it, and the twelve went away.

When they were quite out of sight the poor man got down from the tree, and was curious to know what was secretly hidden in the mountain. So he went up to it and said: "Semsi mountain, Semsi mountain, open up," and the mountain opened to him also. Then he went inside, and the whole mountain was a cavern full of silver and gold, and behind lay great piles of pearls and sparkling jewels, heaped up like corn. The poor man hardly knew what to do, and whether he might take any of these treasures for himself or not; at last he filled his pockets with gold, but he left the pearls and precious stones where they were. When he came out again he also said: "Semsi mountain, Semsi mountain, shut yourself;" and the mountain closed itself, and he went home with his barrow.

And now he had no more cause for anxiety, but could buy bread for his wife and children with his gold, and wine into the bargain. He lived joyously and honourably, gave help to the poor, and did good to every

one. When the money came to an end, however, he went to his brother, borrowed a measure that held a bushel, and brought himself some more, but did not touch any of the most valuable things. When for the third time he wanted to fetch something, he again borrowed the measure of his brother. But the rich man had long been envious of his brother's possessions, and of the handsome household which he kept up, and could not understand from whence the riches came, and what his brother wanted with the measure. Then he thought of a cunning trick, and covered the bottom of the measure with pitch, and when he got the measure back a piece of gold was sticking to it. He at once went to his brother and asked him: "What have you been measuring in the bushel measure?" "Corn and barley," said the other. Then he showed him the piece of gold and threatened that if he did not tell the truth he would accuse him before a court of justice. The poor man then told him everything, just as it had happened. So the rich man ordered his carriage to be made ready, and drove away, resolved to use the opportunity better than his brother had done, and to bring back with him quite different treasures.

When he came to the mountain he cried: "Semsi mountain, Semsi mountain, open up." The mountain opened, and he went inside it. There lay the treasures all before him, and for a long time he did not know which to grab first. At length he loaded himself with as many precious stones as he could carry. He wished to carry his burden outside, but as his heart and soul were entirely full of the treasures, he had forgotten the name of the mountain, and cried: "Simeli mountain, Simeli mountain, open up." That, however, was not the right name, and the mountain never stirred, but remained shut. Then he was alarmed, and the longer he thought about it the more his thoughts confused themselves, and all his treasures were of no help to him. In the evening the mountain opened, and the twelve robbers came in, and when they saw him they laughed, and cried out: "Bird, have we caught you at last! Did you think we had never noticed that you had been in here twice? We could not catch you then; this third time you shall not get out again!" Then he cried: "It was not I, it was my brother," but let him beg for his life and say what he would, they cut off his head.

GOING A-TRAVELLING

There was once a poor woman who had a son, who much wished to travel, but his mother said: "How can you travel? We have no money at all for you to take away with you." Then said the son: "I will manage very well for myself; I will always say: 'Not much, not much, not much.'"

So he walked for a long time and always said: "Not much, not much, not much." Then he passed by a company of fishermen and said: "God speed you! not much, not much, not much." "What do you say, churl, 'not much?'" And when the net was drawn out they had not caught much fish. So one of them fell on the youth with a stick and said: "Have you never seen me threshing?" "What ought I to say, then?" asked the youth. "You must say: 'Get it full, get it full.'" After this he again walked a long time, and said: "Get it full, get it full," until he came to the gallows, where they had got a poor sinner whom they were about to hang. Then said he: "Good morning; get it full, get it full." "What do you say, knave, 'get it full?' Do you want to make out that there are still more wicked people in the world—is not this enough?" And he again got some blows on his back. "What am I to say, then?" said he. "You must say: 'May God have pity on the poor soul.'"

Again the youth walked on for a long while and said: "May God have pity on the poor soul!" Then he came to a pit by which stood a knacker who was cutting up a horse. The youth said: "Good morning; God have pity on the poor soul!" "What do you say, you ill-tempered knave?" and the knacker gave him such a box on the ear, that he could not see out of his eyes. "What am I to say, then?" "You must say: 'Let the carrion lie in the pit!'"

So he walked on, and always said: "Let the carrion lie in the pit, let the carrion lie in the pit." And he came to a cart full of people, so he said: "Good morning, let the carrion lie in the pit!" Then the cart fell into a pit, and the driver took his whip and cracked it upon the youth, till he was forced to crawl back to his mother, and as long as he lived he never went out a travelling again.

THE DONKEY

Once upon a time there lived a King and a Queen, who were rich, and had everything they wanted, but no children. The Queen lamented over this day and night, and said: "I am like a field on which nothing grows." At last God gave her her wish, but when the child came into the world, it did not look like a human child, but was a little donkey. When the mother saw that, her lamentations and outcries began in real earnest; she said she would far rather have had no child at all than have a donkey, and that they were to throw it into the water that the fishes might devour it. But the King said: "No, since God has sent him he shall be my son and heir, and after my death sit on the royal throne, and wear the kingly crown." The donkey, therefore, was brought up and grew bigger, and his ears grew up high and straight. And he was of a merry disposition, jumped about, played and took especial pleasure in music, so that he went to a celebrated musician and said: "Teach me your art, that I may play the lute as well as you do." "Ah, dear little master," answered the musician, "that would come very hard to you, your fingers are not quite suited to it, and are far too big. I am afraid the strings would not last." But no excuses were of any use—the donkey was determined to play the lute. And since he was persevering and industrious, he at last learnt to do it as well as the master himself. The young lordling once went out walking full of thought and came to a well; he looked into it and in the mirror-clear water saw his donkey's form. He was so distressed about it, that he went out into the wide world and only took with him one faithful companion. They travelled up and down, and at last they came into a kingdom where an old King reigned who had a single but wonderfully beautiful daughter. The

donkey said: "Here we will stay," knocked at the gate, and cried: "A guest is without—open, that he may enter." When the gate was not opened, he sat down, took his lute and played it in the most delightful manner with his two fore-feet. Then the door-keeper opened his eyes, and gaped, and ran to the King and said: "Outside by the gate sits a young donkey which plays the lute as well as an experienced master!" "Then let the musician come to me," said the King. But when a donkey came in, everyone began to laugh at the lute-player. And when the donkey was asked to sit down and eat with the servants, he was unwilling, and said: "I am no common stable-ass, I am a noble one." Then they said: "If that is what you are, seat yourself with the soldiers." "No," said he, "I will sit by the King." The King smiled, and said good-humoredly: "Yes, it shall be as you will, little ass, come here to me."

Then he asked: "Little ass, how does my daughter please you?" The donkey turned his head towards her, looked at her, nodded and said: "I like her above measure, I have never yet seen anyone so beautiful as she is." "Well, then, you shall sit next her too," said the King. "That is exactly what I wish," said the donkey, and he placed himself by her side, ate and drank, and knew how to behave himself daintily and cleanly. When the noble beast had stayed a long time at the King's court, he thought: "What good does all this do me, I shall still have to go home again," let his head hang sadly, and went to the King and asked for his dismissal. But the King had grown fond of him, and said: "Little ass, what ails you? You look as sour as a jug of vinegar, I will give you what you want. "Do you want gold?" "No," said the donkey, and shook his head. "Do you want jewels and rich dress?" "No." "Do you wish for half my kingdom?" "Indeed, no." Then said the King: "If I did but know what would make you content. Will you have my pretty daughter to wife?" "Ah, yes," said the ass, "I should indeed like her," and all at once he became quite merry and full of happiness, for that was exactly what he was wishing for. So a great and splendid wedding was held. In the evening, when the bride and bridegroom were led into their bed-room, the King wanted to know if the ass would behave well, and ordered a servant to hide himself there. When they were both within, the bridegroom bolted the door, looked around, and as he believed that they were quite alone, he suddenly threw off his ass's skin, and stood there in the form of a handsome royal youth. "Now," said he, "you see who I am, and see also that I am not unworthy of you." Then the bride was glad, and kissed him, and loved him dearly. When morning came, he jumped up, put his animal's skin on again, and no one could have guessed what kind of a form was hidden beneath it. Soon came the old King. "Ah," cried he, "so the little ass is already up! But surely you are sad," said he to his daughter, "that you have not got a proper man for your husband?" "Oh, no, dear father, I love him as well as if he were the handsomest in the world, and I will keep him as long as I live." The King was surprised, but the servant who had concealed himself came and revealed everything to him. The King said: "That cannot be true." "Then watch yourself the next night, and you will see it with your own eyes; and hark you, lord King, if you were to take his skin away and throw it in the fire, he would be forced to show himself in his true shape." "Your advice is good," said the King, and at night when they were asleep, he stole in, and when he got to the bed he saw by the light of the moon a noble-looking youth lying there, and the skin lay stretched on the ground. So he took it away, and had a great fire lighted outside, and threw the skin into it, and remained by it himself until it was all burnt to ashes. But since he was anxious to know how the robbed man would behave himself, he stayed awake the whole night and watched. When the youth had slept his fill, he got up by the first light of morning, and wanted to put on the ass's skin, but it was not to be found. At this he was alarmed, and, full of grief and anxiety, said: "Now I shall have to contrive to escape." But when he went out, there stood the King, who said: "My son, whither away in such haste? what have you in mind? Stay here, you are such a handsome man, you shall not go away from me. I will now give you half my kingdom, and after my death you shall have the whole of it." "Then I hope that what begins so well may end well, and I will stay with you," said the youth. And the old man gave him half the kingdom, and in a year's time, when he died, the youth had the whole, and after the death of his father he had another kingdom as well, and lived in all magnificence.

THE UNGRATEFUL SON

A man and his wife were once sitting by the door of their house, and they had a roasted chicken set before them, and were about to eat it together. Then the man saw that his aged father was coming, and hastily took the chicken and hid it, for he would not permit him to have any of it. The old man came, took a drink, and went away. Now the son wanted to put the roasted chicken on the table again, but when he took it up, it had become a great toad, which jumped into his face and sat there and never went away again, and if any one wanted to take it off, it looked venomously at him as if it would jump in his face, so that no one would venture to touch it. And the ungrateful son was forced to feed the toad every day, or else it fed itself on his face; and thus he went about the world knowing no rest.

THE TURNIP

There were once two brothers who both served as soldiers; one of them was rich, and the other poor. Then the poor one, to escape from his poverty, doffed his soldier's coat, and turned farmer. He dug and hoed his bit of land, and sowed it with turnip-seed. The seed came up, and one turnip grew there which became large and strong, and visibly grew bigger and bigger, and seemed as if it would never stop growing, so that it might have been called the princess of turnips, for never was such an one seen before, and never will such an one be seen again.

At length it was so enormous that by itself it filled a whole cart, and two oxen were required to draw it, and the farmer had not the least idea what he was to do with the turnip, or whether it would be a fortune to him or a misfortune. At last he thought: "If you sell it, what will you get for it that is of any importance, and if you eat it yourself, why, the small turnips would do you just as much good; it would be better to take it to the King, and make him a present of it."

So he placed it on a cart, harnessed two oxen, took it to the palace, and presented it to the King. "What strange thing is this?" said the King. "Many wonderful things have come before my eyes, but never such a monster as this! From what seed can this have sprung, or are you a favourite of good fortune and have met with it by chance?" "Ah, no!" said the farmer, "no favourite am I. I am a poor soldier, who because he could no longer support himself hung his soldier's coat on a nail and took to farming land. I have a brother who is rich and well known to you, Lord King, but I, because I have nothing, am forgotten by everyone."

Then the King felt compassion for him, and said: "You shall be raised from your poverty, and shall have such gifts from me that you shall be equal to your rich brother." Then he bestowed on him much gold, and lands, and meadows, and herds, and made him immensely rich, so that the wealth of the other brother could not be compared with his. When the rich brother heard what the poor one had gained for himself with one single turnip, he envied him, and thought in every way how he also could come by a similar piece of luck. He set about it in a much more cunning way, however, and took gold and horses and

carried them to the King, and made certain the King would give him a much larger present in return. If his brother had got so much for one turnip, what would he not carry away with him in return for such beautiful things as these? The King accepted his present, and said he had nothing to give him in return that was more rare and excellent than the great turnip. So the rich man was obliged to put his brother's turnip in a cart and have it taken to his home. There, he did not know on whom to vent his rage and anger, until bad thoughts came to him, and he resolved to kill his brother. He hired murderers, who were to lie in ambush, and then he went to his brother and said: "Dear brother, I know of a hidden treasure, we will dig it up together, and divide it between us." The other agreed to this, and accompanied him without suspicion. While they were on their way the murderers fell on him, bound him, and would have hanged him to a tree. But just as they were doing this, loud singing and the sound of a horse's feet were heard in the distance. On this their hearts were filled with terror, and they pushed their prisoner hastily into the sack, hung it on a branch, and took to flight. He, however, worked up there until he had made a hole in the sack through which he could put his head. The man who was coming by was no other than a travelling student, a young fellow who rode on his way through the wood joyously singing his song. When he who was aloft saw that someone was passing below him, he cried: "Good day! You have come at a lucky moment." The student looked round on every side, but did not know whence the voice came. At last he said: "Who calls me?" Then an answer came from the top of the tree: "Raise your eyes; here I sit aloft in the Sack of Wisdom. In a short time have I learnt great things; compared with this all schools are a jest; in a very short time I shall have learnt everything, and shall descend wiser than all other men. I understand the stars, and the signs of the zodiac, and the tracks of the winds, the sand of the sea, the healing of illness, and the virtues of all herbs, birds and stones. If you were once within it you would feel what noble things issue forth from the Sack of Knowledge."

The student, when he heard all this, was astonished, and said: "Blessed be the hour in which I have found you! May not I also enter the sack for a while?" He who was above replied as if unwillingly: "For a short time I will let you get into it, if you reward me and give me good words; but you must wait an hour longer, for one thing remains which I must learn before I do it." When the student had waited a while he became impatient, and begged to be allowed to get in at once, his thirst for knowledge was so very great. So he who was above pretended at last to yield, and said: "In order that I may come forth from the house of knowledge you must let it down by the rope, and then you shall enter it." So the student let the sack down, untied it, and set him free, and then cried: "Now draw me up at once," and was about to get into the sack. "Halt!" said the other, "that won't do," and took him by the head and put him upside down into the sack, fastened it, and drew the disciple of wisdom up the tree by the rope. Then he swung him in the air and said: "How goes it with you, my dear fellow? Behold, already you feel wisdom coming, and you are gaining valuable experience. Keep perfectly quiet until you become wiser." Thereupon he mounted the student's horse and rode away, but in an hour's time sent someone to let the student out again.

THE OLD MAN MADE YOUNG AGAIN

At the time when our Lord still walked this earth, he and St. Peter stopped one evening at a smith's and received free quarters. Then it came to pass that a poor beggar, hard pressed by age and infirmity, came to this house and begged alms of the smith. St. Peter had compassion on him and said: "Lord and master, if it please you, cure his torments that he may be able to win his own bread." The Lord said kindly: "Smith, lend me your forge, and put on some coals for me, and then I will make this ailing old man young again." The smith was quite willing, and St. Peter blew the bellows, and when the coal fire sparkled up large and high our Lord took the little old man, pushed him in the forge in the midst of the red-hot fire, so that he glowed like a rose-bush, and praised God with a loud voice. After that the Lord went to the quenching tub, put the glowing little man into it so that the water closed over him, and after he had carefully cooled him, gave him his blessing, when behold the little man sprang nimbly out, looking fresh, straight, healthy, and as if he were but twenty. The smith, who had watched everything closely and attentively, invited them all to supper. He, however, had an old half-blind crooked, mother-in-law who went

to the youth, and with great earnestness asked if the fire had burnt him much. He answered that he had never felt more comfortable, and that he had sat in the red heat as if he had been in cool dew. The youth's words echoed in the ears of the old woman all night long, and early next morning, when the Lord had gone on his way again and had heartily thanked the smith, the latter thought he might make his old mother-in-law young again likewise, as he had watched everything so carefully, and it lay in the province of his trade. So he called to ask her if she, too, would like to go bounding about like a girl of eighteen. She said: "With all my heart, as the youth has come out of it so well." So the smith made a great fire, and thrust the old woman into it, and she writhed about this way and that, and uttered terrible cries of murder. "Sit still; why are you screaming and jumping about so?" cried he, and as he spoke he blew the bellows again until all her rags were burnt. The old woman cried without ceasing, and the smith thought to himself: "I have not quite the right art," and took her out and threw her into the cooling-tub. Then she screamed so loudly that the smith's wife upstairs and her daughter-in-law heard it, and they both ran downstairs, and saw the old woman lying in a heap in the quenching-tub, howling and screaming, with her face wrinkled and shriveled and all out of shape. Thereupon the two, who were both with child, were so terrified that that very night two boys were born who were not made like men but apes, and they ran into the woods, and from them sprang the race of apes.

THE LORD'S ANIMALS AND THE DEVIL'S

The Lord God had created all animals, and had chosen out the wolf to be his dog, but he had forgotten the goat. Then the Devil made ready and began to create also, and created goats with fine long tails. Now when they went to pasture, they generally remained caught in the hedges by their tails, whereupon the Devil had to go and disentangle them, with a great deal of trouble. This enraged him at last, and he went and bit off the tail of every goat, as may be seen to this day by the stump.

Then he let them go to pasture alone, but it came to pass that the Lord God perceived how at one time they gnawed away at a fruitful tree, at another injured the noble vines, or destroyed other tender plants. This distressed him, so that in his goodness and mercy he summoned his wolves, who soon tore in pieces the goats that went there. When the Devil observed this, he went before the Lord and said: "Your creatures have destroyed mine." The Lord answered: "Why did you create things to do harm?" The Devil said: "I was compelled to do it: inasmuch as my thoughts run on evil. What I create can have no other nature, and you must pay me heavy damages." "I will pay you as soon as the oak leaves fall; come then, your money will then be ready counted out." When the oak-leaves had fallen, the Devil came and demanded what was due to him. But the Lord said: "In the church of Constantinople stands a tall oak-tree which still has all its leaves." With raging and curses, the Devil departed, and went to seek the oak, wandered in the wilderness for six months before he found it, and when he returned, all the oaks had in the meantime covered themselves again with green leaves. Then he had to forfeit his indemnity, and in his rage he put out the eyes of all the remaining goats, and put his own in instead.

This is why all goats have devil's eyes, and their tails bitten off, and why he likes to assume their shape.

THE BEAM

There was once a sorcerer who was standing in the midst of a great crowd of people performing his wonders. He had a cock brought in,

which lifted a heavy beam and carried it as if it were as light as a feather. But a girl was present who had just found a four-leaved clover, and had thus become so wise that no deception could stand out against her, and she saw that the beam was nothing but a straw. So she cried: "You people, do you not see that it is a straw that the cock is carrying, and no beam?" Immediately the enchantment vanished, and the people saw what it was, and drove the magician away in shame and disgrace. He, however, full of inward anger, said: "I will soon revenge myself."

After some time the girl's wedding-day came, and she was decked out, and went in a great procession over the fields to the place where the church was. All at once she came to a stream which was very much swollen, and there was no bridge and no plank to cross it. Then the bride nimbly took her clothes up, and wanted to wade through it. And just as she was thus standing in the water, a man, and it was the sorcerer, cried mockingly close beside her: "Aha! Where are your eyes that you take that for water?" Then her eyes were opened, and she saw that she was standing with her clothes lifted up in the middle of a field that was blue with the flowers of blue flax. Then all the people saw it likewise, and chased her away with ridicule and laughter.

THE OLD BEGGAR-WOMAN

There was once an old woman, but you have surely seen an old woman go a-begging before now? This woman begged likewise, and when she got anything she said: "May God reward you." The beggar-woman came to a door, and there by the fire a friendly rogue of a boy was standing warming himself. The boy said kindly to the poor old woman as she was standing shivering thus by the door: "Come, old mother, and warm yourself." She came in, but stood too near the fire, so that her old rags began to burn, and she was not aware of it. The boy stood and saw that, but he ought to have put the flames out. Is it not true that he ought to have put them out? And if he had not any water, then he should have wept all the water in his body out of his eyes, and that would have supplied two pretty streams with which to extinguish them.

THE THREE SLUGGARDS

A certain King had three sons who were all equally dear to him, and he did not know which of them to appoint as his successor after his own death. When the time came when he was about to die, he summoned them to his bedside and said: "Dear children, I have been thinking of something which I will declare unto you; whichsoever of you is the laziest shall have the kingdom." The eldest said: "Then, father, the kingdom is mine, for I am so idle that if I lie down to rest, and a drop falls in my eye, I will not open it that I may sleep." The second said: "Father, the kingdom belongs to me, for I am so idle that when I am sitting by the fire warming myself, I would rather let my heel be burnt off than draw back my leg." The third said: "Father, the kingdom is

mine, for I am so idle that if I were going to be hanged, and had the rope already round my neck, and any one put a sharp knife into my hand with which I might cut the rope, I would rather let myself be hanged than raise my hand to the rope." When the father heard that, he said: "You have carried it the farthest, and shall be King."

THE TWELVE IDLE SERVANTS

Twelve servants who had done nothing all the day would not exert themselves at night either, but laid themselves on the grass and boasted of their idleness. The first said: "What is your laziness to me, I have to concern myself about mine own. The care of my body is my principal work, I eat not a little and drink still more. When I have had four meals, I fast a short time until I feel hunger again, and that suits me best. To get up early is not for me; when it is getting near mid-day, I already seek out a resting-place for myself. If the master call, I do exactly as if I had not heard him, and if he call a second time, I wait awhile before I get up, and then go to him very slowly. In this way life is endurable."

The second said: "I have a horse to look after, but I leave the bit in his mouth, and if I do not want to, I give him no food, and I say he has had it already. I, instead, lay myself in the oat-chest and sleep for four hours. After this I stretch out one foot and move it a couple of times over the horse's body, and then he is combed and cleaned. Why should anyone go to much trouble about that? This job is irksome enough as it is."

The third said: "Why plague oneself with work? Nothing comes of it! I laid myself in the sun, and fell asleep. It began to rain a little, but why should I get up? I let it rain on in God's name. At last came a splashing shower, so heavy indeed, that it pulled the hair out of my head and washed it away, and I got a hole in the skull; I put a plaster on it, and then it was all right. I have already had several injuries of that kind."

The fourth said: "If I am to undertake some work, I first loiter about for an hour that I may save up my strength. After that I begin quite slowly, and ask if there isn't someone there who could help me. Then I let him do most of the work, and in reality only look on; but even that is still too much for me."

The fifth said: "That's nothing! Just think, I am to take away the manure from the horse's stable, and load the cart with it. I begin slowly, and if I have taken anything on the fork, I only half-raise it up, and then I rest just a quarter of an hour before I quite throw it in. It is more than enough if I take out a cartful in the day. I have no fancy for killing myself with work."

The sixth said: "Shame on you; I am afraid of no work, but I lie down for three weeks, and never once take my clothes off. What is the use of buckling your shoes on? For all I care they may fall off my feet, it makes no difference to me. If I am going up some steps, I drag one foot slowly after the other on to the first step, and then I count the rest of them that I may know where I must rest."

The seventh said: "I don't think much of that; my master looks after my work, only he is not at home the whole day. But I neglect nothing, I run as fast as it is possible to crawl. If I am to move at all, four sturdy men must push me with all their might. I came where six men were lying sleeping on a bed beside each other. I lay down by them and slept too. There was no wakening me again, and when they wanted to have me home, they had to carry me."

The eighth said: "I see plainly that I am the only active fellow; if a stone lie before me, I do not trouble to raise my legs and step over it. I lay myself down on the ground, and if I am wet and covered with mud and dirt, I stay lying until the sun has dried me again. At the very most, I only turn myself so that it can shine on me."

The ninth said: "That is the right way! To-day the bread was before me, but I was too idle to take it, and nearly died of hunger! Moreover a jug stood by it, but it was so big and heavy that I did not like to lift it up, and preferred bearing thirst. Just to turn myself round was too much for me, I remained lying like a log the whole day."

The tenth said: "Laziness has brought misfortune on me, a broken leg and swollen calves. Three of us were lying in the road, and I had my legs stretched out. Someone came with a cart, and the wheels went over me. I might indeed have drawn my legs back, but I did not hear the cart coming, for the midges were humming about my ears, and creeping in at my nose and out again at my mouth; who would take the trouble to drive the vermin away?"

The eleventh said: "I walked out of my job yesterday. I had no fancy for carrying heavy books to my master any longer or fetching them away again. There was no end of it all day long. But to tell the truth, he fired me, and would not keep me any longer, for his clothes, which I had left lying in the dust, were all moth-eaten, and a good thing, too."

The twelfth said: "To-day I had to drive the cart into the country, and made myself a bed of straw on it, and had a good sleep. The reins slipped out of my hand, and when I awoke, the horse had nearly torn itself loose, the harness was gone, the strap which fastened the horse to the shafts was gone, and so were the collar, the bridle and bit. Some one had come by, who had carried everything away. Besides this, the cart had got into a quagmire and stuck fast. I left it standing, and stretched myself on the straw again. At last the master himself came, and pushed the cart out, and if he had not come I should not be lying here but there, and sleeping in all tranquillity."

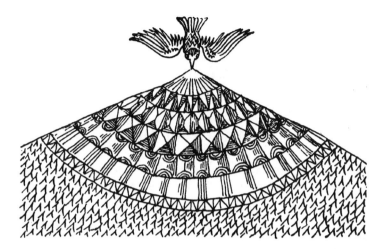

THE SHEPHERD BOY

There was once upon a time a shepherd boy whose fame spread far and wide because of the wise answers which he gave to every question. The King of the country heard of it likewise, but did not believe it, and sent for the boy. Then he said to him: "If you can give me an answer to three questions which I will ask you, I will look on you as my own child, and you shall dwell with me in my royal palace." The boy said: "What are the three questions?" The King said: "The first is, how many drops of water are there in the ocean?" The shepherd boy answered: "Lord King, if you will have all the rivers on earth dammed up so that not a single drop runs from them into the sea until I have counted it, I will tell you how many drops there are in the sea." The King said: "The next question is, how many stars are there in the sky?" The shepherd boy said: "Give me a great sheet of white paper," and then he made so many fine points on it with a pen that they could scarcely be seen, and it was all but impossible to count them; any one who looked at them would have lost his sight. Then he said: "There are as many stars in the sky as there are points on the paper; just count them." But no one was able to do it. The King said: "The third question is, how many seconds of time are there in eternity?" Then said the shepherd boy: "In Lower Pomerania is the Diamond Mountain, which is two miles high, two miles wide, and two miles deep; every hundred years a little bird comes and sharpens its beak on it, and when the whole mountain is worn away by this, then the first second of eternity will be over."

THE STAR MONEY

There was once upon a time a little girl whose father and mother were dead, and she was so poor that she no longer had a room to live in, or bed to sleep in, and at last she had nothing else but the clothes she was wearing and a little bit of bread in her hand which some charitable soul had given her. She was good and pious, however. And as she was thus forsaken by all the world, she went forth into the open country, trusting in the good God. Then a poor man met her, who said: "Ah, give me something to eat, I am so hungry!" She handed him the whole of her piece of bread, and said: "May God bless you," and went onwards. Then came a child who moaned and said: "My head is so cold, give me something to cover it with." So she took off her hood and gave it to him; and when she had walked a little farther, she met another child who had no jacket and was frozen with cold. Then she gave it her own; and a little farther on one begged for a frock, and she gave away that also. At length she got into a forest and it had already become dark, and there came yet another child, and asked for a shirt, and the good little girl thought to herself: "It is a dark night and no one sees you, you can very well give your shirt away," and took it off, and gave away that also. And as she so stood, and had not one single thing left, suddenly some stars from heaven fell down, and they were nothing else but hard smooth pieces of money, and although she had just given her shirt away, she had a new one which was of the very finest linen. Then she put the money into it, and was rich all the days of her life.

THE STOLEN FARTHINGS

A father was one day sitting at dinner with his wife and his children, and a good friend who had come on a visit ate with them. And as they thus sat, and it was striking twelve o'clock, the stranger saw the door open, and a very pale child dressed in snow-white clothes came in. It did not look around, and it did not speak; but went straight into the next room. Soon afterwards it came back, and went out at the door again in the same quiet manner. On the second and on the third day, it came also exactly in the same way. At last the stranger asked the father to whom the beautiful child that went into the next room every day at noon belonged. "I have never seen it," said he, neither did he know to whom it could belong. The next day when it again came, the stranger pointed it out to the father, who however did not see it, and the mother and the children also all saw nothing. At this the stranger got up, went to the room door, opened it a little, and peeped in. Then he saw the child sitting on

the ground, and busily digging and seeking about between the boards of the floor, but when it saw the stranger, it disappeared. He now told what he had seen and described the child exactly, and the mother recognized it, and said: "Ah, it is my dear child who died a month ago." They took up the boards and found two farthings which the child had once received from its mother that it might give them to a poor man; it, however, had thought: "You can buy yourself a biscuit for that," and had kept the farthings, and hidden them in the openings between the boards; and therefore it had had no rest in its grave, and had come every day at noon to seek for these farthings. The parents gave the money at once to a poor man, and after that the child was never seen again.

LOOKING FOR A BRIDE

There was once a young shepherd who wanted very much to marry, and was acquainted with three sisters who were all equally pretty, so that it was difficult for him to make a choice, and he could not decide to give the preference to any one of them. Then he asked his mother for advice, and she said: "Invite all three, and set some cheese before them, and watch how they eat it." The youth did so; the first swallowed the cheese with the rind on; the second hastily cut the rind off the cheese, but she cut it so quickly that she left much good cheese with it, and threw that away also; the third peeled the rind off carefully, and cut neither too much nor too little. The shepherd told all this to his mother, who said: "Take the third for your wife." This he did, and lived contentedly and happily with her.

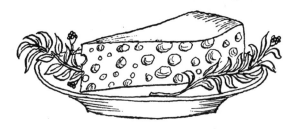

THE HURDS

There was once on a time a maiden who was pretty, but idle and negligent. When she had to spin she was so out of temper that if there was a little knot in the flax, she at once pulled out a whole heap of it, and strewed it about on the ground beside her. Now she had a servant who was industrious, and gathered together the bits of flax which were thrown away, cleaned them, spun them fine, and had a beautiful gown made out of them for herself. A young man had wooed the lazy girl, and the wedding was to take place. On the eve of the wedding, the industrious one was dancing merrily about in her pretty dress, and the bride said:

"Ah, how that girl does jump about, dressed in my hurds."

The bridegroom heard that, and asked the bride what she meant by it. Then she told him that the girl was wearing a dress made of the flax which she had thrown away. When the bridegroom heard that, and saw how idle she was, and how industrious the poor girl was, he gave her up and went to the other, and chose her as his wife.

THE SPARROW AND HIS FOUR CHILDREN

A sparrow had four young ones in a swallow's nest. When they were fledged, some naughty boys pulled out the nest, but fortunately all the birds got safely away in the high wind. Then the old bird was grieved that as his sons had all gone out into the world, he had not first warned them of every kind of danger, and given them good instruction how to deal with each.

In the autumn a great many sparrows assembled together in a wheatfield, and there the old bird met his four children again, and full of joy took them home with him. "Ah, my dear sons, how I have been worrying about you all through the summer, because you got away in the wind without my teaching; listen to my words, obey your father, and be well on your guard. Little birds have to encounter great dangers!" And then he asked the eldest where he had spent the summer, and how he had supported himself. "I stayed in the gardens, and looked for caterpillars and small worms, until the cherries were ripe." "Ah, my son," said the father, "tit-bits are not bad, but there is great risk about them; on that account take great care of yourself henceforth, and particularly when people are going about the gardens who carry long green poles which are hollow inside and have a little hole at the top." "Yes, father, but what if a little green leaf is stuck over the hole with wax?" said the son. "Where have you seen that?" "In a merchant's garden," said the youngster. "Oh, my son, merchant folks are smart folks," said the father. "If you have been among the children of the world, you have learned worldly craftiness enough, only see that you use it well, and do not be too confident."

Then he asked the next: "Where have you passed your time?" "At court," said the son. "Sparrows and silly little birds are of no use in that place—there one finds much gold, velvet, silk, armour, harnesses, sparrow-hawks, screech-owls and lanners; keep to the horses' stable where they winnow oats, or thresh, and then fortune may give you your daily grain of corn in peace." "Yes, father," said the son, "but when the stable-boys make traps and fix their gins and snares in the straw, many a one is caught." "Where have you seen that?" said the old bird. "At court, among the stable-boys." "Oh, my son, court boys are bad boys! If you have been to court and among the lords, and have left no feathers there, you have learnt a fair amount, and will know very well how to go about the world, but look around you and above you, for the wolves often devour the wisest dogs."

The father examined the third also: "Where did you seek your fortune?" "I have cast my tub and rope on the cart-roads and highways, and sometimes met with a grain of corn or barley." "That is indeed dainty fare," said the father, "but take care what you are about and look carefully around, especially when you see anyone stooping and about to pick up a stone, for then you have not much time to waste." "That is true," said the son, "but what if anyone should carry a bit of rock, or ore, ready beforehand in his breast or pocket?" "Where have you seen that?" "Among the miners, dear father; when they get out of the pit, they generally take little bits of ore with them." "Mining folks are

working folks, and clever folks. If you have been among mining lads, you have seen and learnt something, but when you go thither beware, for many a sparrow has been brought to a bad end by a mining boy throwing a piece of cobalt."

At length the father came to the youngest son: "You, my dear chirping nestling, were always the silliest and weakest; stay with me, the world has many rough, wicked birds which have crooked beaks and long claws, and lie in wait for poor little birds and swallow them. Keep with those of your own kind, and pick up little spiders and caterpillars from the trees, or the houses, and then you will live long in peace." "My dear father, he who feeds himself without injury to other people fares well, and no sparrow-hawk, eagle, or kite will hurt him if he commits himself and his lawful food, evening and morning, faithfully to God, who is the Creator and Preserver of all forest and village birds, who likewise heareth the cry and prayer of the young ravens, for no sparrow or wren ever falls to the ground except by his will." "Where have you learnt this?" The son answered: "When the great blast of wind tore me away from you I came to a church, and there during the summer I have picked up the flies and spiders from the windows, and heard this discourse preached. The Father of all sparrows fed me all the summer through, and kept me from all misfortune and from ferocious birds." "Indeed, my dear son, if you take refuge in the churches and help to clear away spiders and buzzing flies, and chirp unto God like the young ravens, and commend yourself to the eternal Creator, all will be well with you, and that even if the whole world were full of wild malicious birds.

> He who to God commits his ways,
> In silence suffers, waits, and prays,
> Preserves his faith and conscience pure,
> He is of God's protection sure."

THE STORY OF SCHLAURAFFEN LAND

In the time of Schlauraffen I went forth and saw Rome and the Lateran hanging by a small silken thread, and a man without feet who outran a swift horse, and a keen sharp sword that cut through a bridge. I saw a young ass with a silver nose which pursued two fleet hares, and a lime-tree that was very large, on which hot cakes were growing. I saw a lean old goat which carried about a hundred cart-loads of fat on his body, and sixty loads of salt. Have I not told enough lies? I saw a plough ploughing without horse or cow, and a child of one year threw four millstones from Ratisbon to Treves, and from Treves to Strasburg, and a hawk swam over the Rhine, which he had a perfect right to do. I heard some fishes begin to make such a disturbance with each other, that it resounded as far as heaven, and sweet honey flowed like water from a deep valley to the top of a high mountain, and these were strange things. There were two crows which were mowing a meadow, and I saw two gnats building a bridge, and two doves tore a wolf to pieces; two children brought forth two kids, and two frogs threshed corn together. I saw two mice consecrating a bishop, and two cats scratching out a bear's tongue. Then a snail came running up and killed two furious lions. There stood a barber and shaved a woman's beard off; and two sucking-children bade their mother hold her tongue. There I saw two greyhounds which brought a mill out of the water; and a broken-down old horse was beside it, and said it was right. And four horses were standing in the yard threshing corn with all their might, and two goats were heating the stove, and a red cow shot the bread into the oven. Then a hen crowed, Cock-a-doodle-doo! The story is all told—Cock-a-doodle-doo!

THE DITMARS TALE OF WONDERS

I will tell you something. I saw two roasted fowls flying; they flew quickly and had their breasts turned to heaven and their backs to hell, and an anvil and a mill-stone swam across the Rhine prettily, slowly, and gently, and a frog sat on the ice at Whitsuntide and ate a plough-share. There fellows who wanted to catch a hare, went on crutches and stilts; one of them was deaf, the second blind, the third dumb, and the fourth could not stir a step. Do you want to know how it was done?

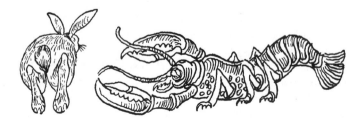

First, the blind man saw the hare running across the field, the dumb one called to the lame one, and the lame one seized it by the neck.

There were certain men who wished to sail on dry land, and they set their sails in the wind, and sailed away over great fields. Then they sailed over a high mountain, and there they were miserably drowned. A crab was chasing a hare which was running away at full speed, and high up on the roof lay a cow which had climbed up there. In that country the flies are as big as the goats are here. Open the window, that the lies may fly out.

A RIDDLING TALE

Three women were transformed into flowers which grew in the field, but one of them was allowed to be in her own home at night. Then once when day was drawing near, and she was forced to go back to her companions in the field and become a flower again, she said to her husband: "If you will come this afternoon and gather me, I shall be set free and henceforth stay with you." And he did so. Now the question is, how did her husband know her, for the flowers were exactly alike, and without any difference? Answer: as she was at her home during the night and not in the field, no dew fell on her as it did on the others, and by this her husband knew her.

SNOW WHITE AND ROSE RED

There was once a poor widow who lived in a lonely cottage. In front of the cottage was a garden wherein stood two rose-trees, one of which bore white and the other red roses. She had two children who were like the two rose-trees, and one was called Snow White, and the other Rose Red. They were as good and happy, as busy and cheerful as ever two children in the world were, only Snow White was more quiet and gentle than Rose Red. Rose Red liked better to run about in the meadows and fields seeking flowers and catching butterflies; but Snow White sat at home with her mother, and helped her with her house-work, or read to her when there was nothing to do.

The two children were so fond of one another that they always held each other by the hand when they went out together, and when Snow White said: "We will not leave each other," Rose Red answered: "Never so long as we live," and their mother would add: "What one has she must share with the other."

They often ran about the forest alone and gathered red berries, and no beasts did them any harm, but came close to them trustfully. The little hare would eat a cabbage-leaf out of their hands, the roe grazed by their side, the stag leapt merrily by them, and the birds sat still upon the boughs, and sang whatever they knew.

No mishap overtook them; if they had stayed too late in the forest, and night came on, they laid themselves down near one another upon the moss, and slept until morning came, and their mother knew this and did not worry on their account.

Once when they had spent the night in the wood and the dawn had roused them, they saw a beautiful child in a shining white dress sitting near their bed. He got up and looked quite kindly at them, but said nothing and went away into the forest. And when they looked round they found that they had been sleeping quite close to a precipice, and would certainly have fallen into it in the darkness if they had gone only a few paces further. And their mother told them that it must have been the angel who watches over good children.

Snow White and Rose Red kept their mother's little cottage so neat that it was a pleasure to look inside it. In the summer Rose Red took care of the house, and every morning laid a wreath of flowers by her mother's bed before she awoke, in which was a rose from each tree. In the winter Snow White lit the fire and hung the kettle on the hob. The kettle was of brass and shone like gold, so brightly was it polished. In the evening, when the snowflakes fell, the mother said: "Go, Snow White, and bolt the door," and then they sat round the hearth, and the mother took her spectacles and read aloud out of a large book, and the two girls listened as they sat and spun. And close by them lay a lamb upon the floor, and behind them upon a perch sat a white dove with its head hidden beneath its wings.

One evening, as they were thus sitting comfortably together, some-one knocked at the door as if he wished to be let in. The mother said: "Quick, Rose Red, open the door, it must be a traveller who is seeking shelter." Rose Red went and pushed back the bolt, thinking that it was a poor man, but it was not; it was a bear that stretched his broad, black head within the door.

Rose Red screamed and sprang back, the lamb bleated, the dove fluttered, and Snow White hid herself behind her mother's bed. But the bear began to speak and said: "Do not be afraid, I will do you no harm! I am half-frozen, and only want to warm myself a little beside you."

"Poor bear," said the mother, "lie down by the fire, only take care that you do not burn your coat." Then she cried: "Snow White, Rose Red, come out, the bear will do you no harm, he means well." So they both came out, and by-and-by the lamb and dove came nearer, and were not afraid of him. The bear said: "Here, children, knock the snow out of my coat a little;" so they brought the broom and swept the bear's hide clean; and he stretched himself by the fire and growled content-edly and comfortably. It was not long before they grew quite at home, and played tricks with their clumsy guest. They tugged his hair with their hands, put their feet upon his back and rolled him about, or they took a hazel-switch and beat him, and when he growled they laughed. But the bear took it all in good part, only when they were too rough he called out: "Leave me alive, children,

Snow White, Rose Red,
Will you beat your wooer dead?"

When it was bed-time, and the others went to bed, the mother said to the bear: "You can lie there by the hearth, and then you will be safe from the cold and the bad weather." As soon as day dawned the two children let him out, and he trotted across the snow into the forest.

Henceforth the bear came every evening at the same time, laid himself down by the hearth, and let the children amuse themselves with him as much as they liked; and they got so used to him that the doors were never fastened until their black friend had arrived.

When spring had come and all outside was green, the bear said one morning to Snow White: "Now I must go away, and cannot come back for the whole summer." "Where are you going, then, dear bear?" asked Snow White. "I must go into the forest and guard my treasures from the wicked dwarfs. In the winter, when the earth is frozen hard, they are obliged to stay below and cannot work their way through; but now, when the sun has thawed and warmed the earth, they break through it, and come out to pry and steal; and what once gets into their hands, and in their caves, does not easily see daylight again."

Snow White was quite sorry at his departure, and as she unbolted the door for him, and the bear was hurrying out, he caught against the bolt and a piece of his hairy coat was torn off, and it seemed to Snow White as if she had seen gold shining through it, but she was not sure about it. The bear ran away quickly, and was soon out of sight behind the trees.

A short time afterwards the mother sent her children into the forest to get fire-wood. There they found a big tree which lay felled on the ground, and close by the trunk something was jumping backwards and forwards in the grass, but they could not make out what it was. When they came nearer they saw a dwarf with an old withered face and a snow-white beard a yard long. The end of the beard was caught in a crevice of the tree, and the little fellow was jumping about like a dog tied to a rope, and did not know what to do.

He glared at the girls with his fiery red eyes and cried: "Why do you stand there? Can you not come here and help me?" "What are you up to, little man?" asked Rose Red. "You stupid, prying goose!" answered the dwarf; "I was going to split the tree to get a little wood for cooking. The little bit of food that we people get is immediately burnt up with heavy logs; we do not swallow so much as you coarse, greedy folk. I

had just driven the wedge safely in, and everything was going as I wished; but the cursed wedge was too smooth and suddenly sprang out, and the tree closed so quickly that I could not pull out my beautiful white beard; so now it is tight in and I cannot get away, and the silly, sleek, milk-faced things laugh! Ugh! how odious you are!"

The children tried very hard, but they could not pull the beard out, it was caught too fast. "I will run and fetch some one," said Rose Red. "You senseless goose!" snarled the dwarf; "why should you fetch some one? You are already two too many for me; can you not think of something better?" "Don't be impatient," said Snow White, "I will help you," and she pulled her scissors out of her pocket, and cut off the end of the beard.

As soon as the dwarf felt himself free he laid hold of a bag which lay amongst the roots of the tree, and which was full of gold, and lifted it up, grumbling to himself: "Uncouth people, to cut off a piece of my fine beard. Bad luck to you!" and then he swung the bag upon his back, and went off without even once looking at the children.

Some time afterwards Snow White and Rose Red went to catch a dish of fish. As they came near the brook they saw something like a large grasshopper jumping towards the water, as if it were going to leap in. They ran to it and found it was the dwarf. "Where are you going?" said Rose Red; "you surely don't want to go into the water?" "I am not such a fool!" cried the dwarf; "don't you see that the accursed fish wants to pull me in?" The little man had been sitting there fishing, and unluckily the wind had tangled up his beard with the fishing-line; a moment later a big fish made a bite and the feeble creature had not strength to pull it out; the fish kept the upper hand and pulled the dwarf towards him. He held on to all the reeds and rushes, but it was of little good, for he was forced to follow the movements of the fish, and was in urgent danger of being dragged into the water.

The girls came just in time; they held him fast and tried to free his beard from the line, but all in vain, beard and line were entangled fast together. There was nothing to do but to bring out the scissors and cut the beard, whereby a small part of it was lost. When the dwarf saw that he screamed out: "Is that civil, you toad-stool, to disfigure a man's face? Was it not enough to clip off the end of my beard? Now you have cut off the best part of it. I cannot let myself be seen by my people. I wish you had been made to run the soles off your shoes!" Then he took out a sack of pearls which lay in the rushes, and without another word he dragged it away and disappeared behind a stone.

It happened that soon afterwards the mother sent the two children to the town to buy needles and thread, and laces and ribbons. The road led them across a heath upon which huge pieces of rock lay strewn about. There they noticed a large bird hovering in the air, flying slowly round and round above them; it sank lower and lower, and at last settled near a rock not far away. Immediately they heard a loud, piteous cry. They ran up and saw with horror that the eagle had seized their old acquaintance the dwarf, and was going to carry him off.

The children, full of pity, at once took tight hold of the little man, and pulled against the eagle so long that at last he let his booty go. As soon as the dwarf had recovered from his first fright he cried with his shrill voice: "Could you not have done it more carefully! You dragged at my brown coat so that it is all torn and full of holes, you clumsy creatures!" Then he took up a sack full of precious stones, and slipped away again under the rock into his hole. The girls, who by this time were used to his ingratitude, went on their way and did their business in the town.

As they crossed the heath again on their way home they surprised the dwarf, who had emptied out his bag of precious stones in a clean spot, and had not thought that anyone would come there so late. The evening sun shone upon the brilliant stones; they glittered and sparkled with all colours so beautifully that the children stood still and stared at them. "Why do you stand gaping there?" cried the dwarf, and his ashen-gray face became copper-red with rage. He was still cursing when a loud growling was heard, and a black bear came trotting towards them out of the forest. The dwarf sprang up in a fright, but he could not reach his cave, for the bear was already close. Then in the dread of his heart he cried: "Dear Mr. Bear, spare me, I will give you all my treasures; look, the beautiful jewels lying there! Grant me my life; what do you want with such a slender little fellow as I? you would not feel me between your teeth. Come, take these two wicked girls, they are tender morsels for you, fat as young quails; for mercy's sake eat them!" The bear took no heed of his words, but gave the wicked creature a single blow with his paw, and he did not move again.

The girls had run away, but the bear called to them: "Snow White and Rose Red, do not be afraid; wait, I will come with you." Then they recognised his voice and waited, and when he came up to them suddenly his bearskin fell off, and he stood there a handsome man, clothed all in gold. "I am a King's son," he said, "and I was bewitched by that wicked dwarf, who had stolen my treasures; I have had to run about the forest as a savage bear until I was freed by his death. Now he has got his well-deserved punishment."

Snow White was married to him, and Rose Red to his brother, and they divided between them the great treasure which the dwarf had gathered together in his cave. The old mother lived peacefully and happily with her children for many years. She took the two rose-trees with her, and they stood before her window, and every year bore the most beautiful roses, white and red.

THE WISE SERVANT

How fortunate is the master, and how well all goes in his house, when he has a wise servant who listens to his orders and does not obey them, but prefers following his own wisdom. A clever Hans of this kind was

once sent out by his master to seek a lost cow. He stayed away a long time, and the master thought: "Faithful Hans does not spare any pains over his work!" But when he did not come back at all, the master was afraid lest some misfortune had befallen him, and set out himself to look for him. He had to search a long time, but at last he caught sight of the boy running up and down a large field. "Now, dear Hans," said the master when he had got up to him, "have you found the cow which I sent you to seek?" "No, master," he answered, "I have not found the cow, but then I have not looked for it." "Then what have you looked for, Hans?" "Something better, and that luckily I have found." "What is that, Hans?" "Three blackbirds," answered the boy. "And where are they?" asked the master. "I see one of them, I hear the other, and I am running after the third," answered the wise boy.

Take example by this, do not trouble yourselves about your masters or their orders, but rather do what comes into your head and pleases you, and then you will act just as wisely as clever Hans.

THE GLASS COFFIN

Let no one ever say that a poor tailor cannot do great things and win honours; all that is needed is that he should go to the right smithy, and what is of most consequence, that he should have good luck. A civil, smart tailor's apprentice once went out travelling, and came into a great forest, and, as he did not know the way, he lost himself. Night fell and nothing was left for him to do in this painful solitude, but to seek a bed. He might certainly have found a good bed on the soft moss, but the fear of wild beasts let him have no rest there, and at last he made up his mind to spend the night in a tree. He sought out a high oak, climbed up to the top of it, and thanked God that he had his goose with him, for otherwise the wind which blew over the top of the tree would have carried him away.

After he had spent some hours in the darkness, not without fear and trembling, he saw at a very short distance the glimmer of a light, and as he thought that a human habitation might be there, where he would be better off than on the branches of a tree, he got carefully down and went towards the light. It guided him to a small hut that was woven together of reeds and rushes. He knocked boldly, the door opened, and by the light which came forth he saw a little hoary old man who wore a coat made of bits of coloured stuff sewn together. "Who are you, and what do you want?" asked the man in a grumbling voice. "I am a poor tailor," he answered, "whom night has surprised here in the wilderness, and I earnestly beg you to take me into your hut until morning." "Go your way," replied the old man in a surly voice, "I will have nothing to do with tramps; seek for yourself a shelter elsewhere." Having said this, he was about to slip into his hut again, but the tailor held him so tightly by the corner of his coat, and pleaded so piteously, that the old man, who was not so ill-natured as he wished to appear, was at last softened, and took him into the hut with him where he gave him something to eat, and then offered him a very good bed in a corner.

The weary tailor needed no rocking; but slept sweetly till morning, but even then would not have thought of getting up, if he had not been aroused by a great noise. A violent sound of screaming and roaring forced its way through the thin walls of the hut. The tailor, full of unwonted courage, jumped up, put his clothes on in haste, and hurried out. Then close by the hut, he saw a great black bull and a beautiful stag, which were just preparing for a violent struggle. They rushed at each other with such extreme rage that the ground shook with their trampling, and the air resounded with their cries. For a long time it was uncertain which of the two would gain the victory; at length the stag thrust his horns into his adversary's body, whereupon the bull fell to the earth with a terrific roar, and was finished off by a few strokes from the stag.

The tailor, who had watched the fight with astonishment, was still standing there motionless, when the stag in full career bounded up to him, and before he could escape, caught him up on his great horns. He had not much time to collect his thoughts, for it went in a swift race over stock and stone, mountain and valley, wood and meadow. He held with both hands to the ends of the horns, and resigned himself to his fate. It seemed to him just as if he were flying away. At length the stag stopped in front of a wall of rock, and gently let the tailor down. The tailor, more dead than alive, required some time to come to himself. When he had in some degree recovered, the stag, which had remained standing by him, pushed its horns with such force against a door in the rock, that it sprang open. Flames of fire shot forth, after which followed a great smoke, which hid the stag from his sight. The tailor did not know what to do, or whither to turn, in order to get out of this desert and back to human beings again. Whilst he was standing thus undecided, a voice sounded out of the rock, which cried to him: "Enter without fear, no evil shall befall you." He hesitated, but driven by a mysterious force, he obeyed the voice and went through the iron-door into a large spacious hall, whose ceiling, walls and floor were made of shining polished square stones, on each of which were carved signs which were unknown to him. He looked at everything full of admiration, and was on the point of going out again, when he once more heard the voice which said to him: "Step on the stone which lies in the middle of the hall, and great good fortune awaits you."

His courage had already grown so great that he obeyed the order. The stone began to give way under his feet, and sank slowly down into the depths. When it was once more firm, and the tailor looked round, he found himself in a hall which in size resembled the former. Here, however, there was more to look at and to admire. Hollow places were cut in the walls, in which stood vases of transparent glass and filled with coloured spirit or with a bluish vapour. On the floor of the hall two great glass chests stood opposite to each other, which at once excited his curiosity. When he went to one of them he saw inside it a handsome structure like a castle surrounded by farm-buildings, stables and barns, and a quantity of other good things. Everything was small, but exceedingly carefully and delicately made, and seemed to be carved out by a dexterous hand with the greatest precision.

He might not have turned away his eyes from the consideration of this rarity for some time, had not the voice once more made itself heard. It ordered him to turn round and look at the glass chest which was standing opposite. How his admiration increased when he saw therein a maiden of the greatest beauty! She lay as if asleep, and was wrapped in her long fair hair as in a precious mantle. Her eyes were closely shut, but the brightness of her complexion and a ribbon which her breathing moved to and fro, left no doubt that she was alive. The tailor was looking at the beauty with beating heart, when she suddenly opened her eyes, and started up at the sight of him with a shock of joy. "Divine Providence!" cried she, "my deliverance is at hand! Quick, quick, help me out of my prison; if you push back the bolt of this glass coffin, then I shall be free." The tailor obeyed without delay, and she immediately raised up the glass lid, came out and hastened into the corner of the hall, where she covered herself with a large cloak. Then

she seated herself on a stone, ordered the young man to come to her, and after she had imprinted a friendly kiss on his lips, she said: "My long-desired deliverer, kind Heaven has guided you to me, and put an end to my sorrows. On the self-same day when they end, shall your happiness begin. You are the husband chosen for me by Heaven, and shall pass your life in unbroken joy, loved by me, and rich to overflowing in every earthly possession. Seat yourself, and listen to the story of my life:

"I am the daughter of a rich count. My parents died when I was still in my tender youth, and recommended me in their last will to my elder brother, by whom I was brought up. We loved each other so tenderly, and were so alike in our way of thinking and our inclinations, that we both embraced the resolution never to marry, but to stay together to the end of our lives. In our house there was no lack of company;

neighbours and friends visited us often, and we showed the greatest hospitality to every one. So it came to pass one evening that a stranger came riding to our castle and, under pretext of not being able to get on to the next place, begged for shelter for the night. We granted his request with ready courtesy, and he entertained us in the most agreeable manner during supper by conversation intermingled with stories. My brother liked the stranger so much that he begged him to spend a couple of days with us, to which, after some hesitation, he consented. We did not rise from table until late in the night, the stranger was shown to a room, and I hastened, as I was tired, to lay my limbs in my soft bed. Hardly had I fallen off to sleep, when the sound of faint and delightful music awoke me. As I could not conceive from whence it came, I wanted to summon my waiting-maid who slept in the next room, but to my astonishment I found that speech was taken away from me by an unknown force. I felt as if a nightmare were weighing down my breast, and was unable to make the very slightest sound. In the meantime, by the light of my night-lamp, I saw the stranger enter my room through two doors which were fast bolted. He came to me and said, that by magic arts which were at his command, he had caused the lovely music to sound in order to awaken me, and that he now forced his way through all fastenings with the intention of offering his hand and heart. My dislike of his magic arts was so great, however, that I refused to answer him. He remained for a time standing without moving, apparently with the idea of waiting for a favourable decision, but as I continued to keep silence, he angrily declared he would revenge himself and find means to punish my pride, and left the room. I passed the night in the greatest disquietude, and fell asleep only towards morning. When I awoke, I hurried to my brother, but did not find him in his room, and the attendants told me that he had ridden forth with the stranger to the chase at daybreak.

"I at once suspected nothing good. I dressed myself quickly, ordered my palfrey to be saddled, and accompanied only by one servant, rode full gallop to the forest. The servant fell with his horse, and could not follow me, for the horse had broken its foot. I pursued my way without halting, and in a few minutes I saw the stranger coming towards me with a beautiful stag which he led by a cord. I asked him where he had left my brother, and how he had come by this stag, out of whose great eyes I saw tears flowing. Instead of answering me, he began to laugh loudly. I fell into a great rage at this, pulled out a pistol and discharged it at the monster; but the ball rebounded from his breast and went into my horse's head. I fell to the ground, and the stranger muttered some words which deprived me of consciousness.

"When I came to my senses again I found myself in this underground cave in a glass coffin. The magician appeared once again, and said he had changed my brother into a stag, my castle with all that belonged to it, diminished in size by his arts, he had shut up in the other glass chest, and my people, who were all turned into smoke, he had confined in glass bottles. He told me that if I would now comply with his wish, it would be an easy thing for him to put everything back in its former state, as he had nothing to do but open the vessels, and everything would return once more to its natural form. I answered him as little as I had done the first time. He vanished and left me in my prison, in which a deep sleep came on me. Among the visions which passed before my eyes, the most comforting was that in which a young man came and set me free, and when I opened my eyes to-day I saw you, and beheld my dream fulfilled. Help me to accomplish the other things which happened in those visions. The first is that we lift the glass chest in which my castle is enclosed, on to that broad stone."

As soon as the stone was laden, it began to rise up on high with the maiden and the young man, and mounted through the opening of the ceiling into the upper hall, from whence they then could easily reach the open air. Here the maiden opened the lid, and it was marvellous to behold how the castle, the houses, and the farm buildings which were enclosed, stretched themselves out and grew to their natural size with the greatest rapidity. After this, the maiden and the tailor returned to the cave beneath the earth, and had the vessels which were filled with smoke carried up by the stone. The maiden had scarcely opened the bottles when the blue smoke rushed out and changed itself into living men, in whom she recognized her servants and her people. Her joy was still more increased when her brother, who had killed the magician in the form of the bull, came out of the forest towards them in his human form, and on the self-same day the maiden, in accordance with her promise, gave her hand at the altar to the lucky tailor.

LAZY HARRY

Harry was lazy, and although he had nothing else to do but drive his goat daily to pasture, he nevertheless groaned when he went home after his day's work was done. "It is indeed a heavy burden," said he, "and a wearisome employment to drive a goat into the field this way year after year, till late into the autumn! If one could but lie down and sleep, but no, one must have one's eyes open lest the goat hurts the young trees, or squeezes itself through the hedge into a garden, or runs away altogether. How can one have any rest, or enjoy one's life?" He seated himself, collected his thoughts, and considered how he could set his shoulders free from this burden. For a long time all thinking was to no purpose, but suddenly it was as if scales fell from his eyes. "I know what I will do," he cried, "I will marry fat Trina who has also a goat, and can take mine out with hers, and then I shall have no more need to trouble myself."

So Harry got up, set his weary legs in motion, and went right across the street, for it was no farther, to where the parents of fat Trina lived, and asked for their industrious and virtuous daughter in marriage. The parents did not reflect long. "Birds of a feather, flock together," they thought, and consented.

So fat Trina became Harry's wife, and led out both the goats. Harry had a good time of it, and had no work that he required to rest from but his own idleness. He went out with her only now and then, and said: "I merely do it that I may afterwards enjoy rest more, otherwise one loses all feeling for it."

But fat Trina was no less idle. "Dear Harry," said she one day, "why should we make our lives so toilsome when there is no need for it, and thus ruin the best days of our youth? Would it not be better for us to give the two goats which disturb us every morning in our sweetest sleep with their bleating, to our neighbour, and he will give us a beehive for them. We will put the beehive in a sunny place behind the house, and trouble ourselves no more about it. Bees do not require to be taken care of, or driven into the field; they fly out and find the way home again for themselves, and collect honey without giving the very least trouble." "You have spoken like a sensible woman," replied Harry.

"We will carry out your proposal without delay, and besides all that, honey tastes better and nourishes one better than goat's milk, and it can be kept longer too."

The neighbour willingly gave a beehive for the two goats. The bees flew in and out from early morning till late evening without ever tiring, and filled the hive with the most beautiful honey, so that in autumn Harry was able to take a whole pitcherful out of it.

They placed the jug on a board which was fixed to the wall of their bed-room, and as they were afraid that it might be stolen, or that the mice might find it, Trina brought in a stout hazel-stick and put it beside her bed, so that without unnecessary motion she might reach it with her hand, and drive away the uninvited guests.

Lazy Harry did not like to leave his bed before noon. "He who rises early," said he, "wastes his substance." One morning when he was still lying amongst the feathers in broad daylight, resting after his long sleep, he said to his wife: "Women are fond of sweet things, and you are always tasting the honey in private; it will be better for us to exchange it for a goose with a young gosling, before you eat up the whole of it." "But," answered Trina, "not before we have a child to take care of them! Am I to worry myself with the little geese, and spend all my strength on them to no purpose?" "Do you think," said Harry, "that the youngster will look after geese? Now-a-days children no longer obey, they do according to their own fancy, because they consider themselves cleverer than their parents, just like that lad who was sent to seek the cow and chased three blackbirds." "Oh," replied Trina, "this one shall fare badly if he does not do what I say! I will take a stick and belabour his skin with more blows than I can count. Look, Harry," cried she in her zeal, and seized the stick with which she used to drive the mice away, "look, this is the way I will fall on him!" She reached her arm out to strike, but unhappily hit the honey-pitcher above the bed. The pitcher struck against the wall and fell down in shards, and the fine honey streamed out on the ground. "There lie the goose and the young gosling," said Harry, "and want no looking after. But it is lucky that the pitcher did not fall on my head. We have all reason to be satisfied with our lot." And then as he saw that there was still some honey in one of the shards he stretched out his hand for it, and said quite gaily: "The remains, my wife, we will still eat with relish, and we will rest a little after the fright we have had. What does it matter if we do get up a little later—the day is always long enough." "Yes," answered Trina, "we shall always get to the end of it at the proper time. You know, the snail was once asked to a wedding and set out to go, but arrived at the christening. In front of the house it fell over the fence, and said: 'Speed does no good.'"

THE GRIFFIN

There was once upon a time a King, but where he reigned and what he was called, I do not know. He had no son, but an only daughter who had always been ill, and no doctor had been able to cure her. Then it was foretold to the King that his daughter would find her health by eating an apple. So he ordered it to be proclaimed throughout the whole of his kingdom, that whosoever brought his daughter an apple with which she could find her health, should have her to wife, and be King. This became known to a peasant who had three sons, and he said to the eldest: "Go out into the garden and take a basketful of those beautiful apples with the red cheeks and carry them to the court; perhaps the King's daughter will be able to find her health with them, and then you will marry her and be King." The lad did so, and set out. When he had gone a short way he met a hoary little man who asked him what he had there in the basket, to which replied Uele—for so was he named—: "Frogs' legs." At this the little man said: "Well, so shall it be, and remain," and went away. At length Uele arrived at the palace, and made it known that he had brought apples which would cure the King's daughter if she ate them. This delighted the King hugely, and he caused Uele to be brought before him; but, alas! when he opened the basket, instead of having apples in it he had frogs' legs which were still kicking about. On this the King grew angry, and had him driven out of the house. When he got home he told his father how it had fared with him. Then the father sent the next son, who was called Säme, but all went with him just as it had gone with Uele. He also met the hoary little man, who asked what he had there in the basket. Säme said: "Hogs' bristles," and the hoary man said: "Well, so shall it be, and remain." When Säme got to the King's palace and said he brought apples with which the King's daughter might find her health, they did not want to let him go in, and said that one fellow had already been there, and had treated them as if they were fools. Säme, however, maintained that he certainly had the apples, and that they ought to let him go in. At length they believed him, and led him to the King. But when he uncovered the basket, he had but hogs' bristles. This enraged the King most terribly, so he caused Säme to be whipped out of the house. When he got home he related all that had befallen him, whereupon the youngest boy, whose name was Hans, but who was always called Stupid Hans, came and asked his father if he might go with some apples. "Oh!" said the father, "you would be just the right fellow for such a thing! If the clever ones can't manage it, what can you do?" The boy, however, insisted, and said: "Indeed, father, I wish to go." "Just get away, you stupid fellow, you must wait till you are wiser," said the father to that, and turned his back. Hans, however, pulled at the back of his smock and said: "Indeed, father, I wish to go." "Well, then, so far as I am concerned you may go, but you will soon come home again!" replied the old man in a spiteful voice. The boy was tremendously delighted and jumped for joy. "Well, act like a fool! you grow more stupid every day!" said the father again. But Hans was not discouraged, and did not let it spoil his pleasure, but as it was then night, he thought he might as well wait until the morrow, for he could not get to court that day. All night long he could not sleep in his bed, and if he did doze for a moment, he dreamt of beautiful maidens, of palaces, of gold, and of silver, and all kinds of things of that sort. Early in the morning, he went forth on his way, and directly afterwards the little shabby-looking man in his icy clothes, came to him and asked what he was carrying in the basket. Hans gave him the answer that he was carrying apples with which the King's daughter was to find her health. "Then," said the little man, "so shall they be, and remain." But at the court they would none of them let Hans go in, for they said two had already been there who had told them that they were bringing apples, and one of them had frogs' legs, and the other hogs' bristles. Hans, however, resolutely maintained that he most certainly had no frogs' legs, but some of the most beautiful apples in the whole kingdom. As he spoke so pleasantly, the door-keeper thought he could not be telling a lie, and asked him to go in, and he was right, for when Hans uncovered his basket in the King's presence, golden-yellow apples came tumbling out. The King was delighted, and caused some of them to be taken to his daughter, and then waited in anxious expectation until news should be brought to him of the effect they had. But before much time had passed by, news was brought to him: and who do you think it was who came? it was the daughter herself! As soon as she had eaten of those apples, she was cured, and sprang out of her bed. The joy the King felt cannot be described! but now he did not want to give his daughter in marriage to Hans, and said he must first make him a boat which would go quicker on dry land than on water. Hans agreed to the condition, and went home, and related how it had fared with him. Then the father sent Uele into the forest to make a boat of that kind. He worked diligently, and whistled all the time. At mid-day, when the sun was at its highest, came the little icy man and asked what he was making. Uele gave him for answer: "Wooden bowls for the kitchen." The icy man said: "So it shall be, and remain." By evening Uele thought he had now made the boat, but when he wanted to get into it, he had nothing but wooden bowls. The next day Säme went into the forest, but everything went with him just as it had done with Uele. On the third day Stupid Hans went. He worked away most industriously, so that the whole forest resounded with the heavy blows, and all the while he sang and whistled right merrily. At mid-day, when it was the hottest, the little man came again, and asked what he was making. "A boat which will go quicker on dry land than on water," replied Hans, "and when I have finished it, I am to have the King's daughter for my wife." "Well," said the little man, "such an one shall it be, and remain." In the evening, when the sun had turned into gold, Hans finished his boat, and all that was wanted for it. He got into it and rowed to the palace. The boat went as swiftly as the wind. The King saw it from afar, but would not give his daughter to Hans yet, and said he must first take a hundred hares out to pasture from early morning until late evening, and if one of them got away, he should not have his daughter. Hans was contented with this, and the next day went with his flock to the pasture, and took great care that none of them ran away.

Before many hours had passed came a servant from the palace, and told Hans that he must give her a hare instantly, for some visitors had come unexpectedly. Hans, however, was very well aware what that meant, and said he would not give her one; the King might set some hare soup before his guests next day. The maid, however, would not accept his refusal, and at last she began to argue with him. Then Hans said that if the King's daughter came herself, he would give her a hare. The maid told this in the palace, and the daughter did go herself. In the meantime the little man came again to Hans, and asked him what he was doing there. He said he had to watch over a hundred hares and see that none of them ran away, and then he might marry the King's daughter and be King. "Good," said the little man, "there is a whistle for you, and if one of them runs away, just whistle with it, and then it will come back again." When the King's daughter came, Hans gave her a hare into her apron; but when she had gone about a hundred steps with it, he whistled, and the hare jumped out of the apron, and before she could turn round was back to the flock again. When the evening came the hare-herd whistled once more, and looked to see if all were there, and then drove them to the palace. The King wondered how Hans had been able to take a hundred hares to graze without losing any of them; but he still would not give him his daughter yet, and said he

must now bring him a feather from the Griffin's tail. Hans set out at once, and walked straight forwards. In the evening he came to a castle, and there he asked for a night's lodging, for at that time there were no inns. The lord of the castle promised him that with much pleasure, and asked where he was going. Hans answered: "To the Griffin." "Oh! to the Griffin! They tell me he knows everything, and I have lost the key of an iron money-chest; so you might be so good as to ask him where it is." "Yes, indeed," said Hans, "I will do that." Early the next morning he went onwards, and on his way arrived at another castle in which he again stayed the night. When the people who lived there learnt that he was going to the Griffin, they said they had in the house a daughter who was ill, and that they had already tried every means to cure her, but none of them had done her any good, and he might be so kind as to ask the Griffin what would make their daughter healthy again. Hans said he would willingly do that, and went onwards. Then he came to a lake, and instead of a ferry-boat, a tall, tall man was there who had to carry everybody across. The man asked Hans whither he was journeying. "To the Griffin," said Hans. "Then when you get to him," said the man, "just ask him why I am forced to carry everybody over the lake." "Yes, indeed, most certainly I'll do that," said Hans. Then the man took him up on his shoulders, and carried him across. At length Hans arrived at the Griffin's house, but the wife only was at home, and not the Griffin himself. Then the woman asked him what he wanted. Thereupon he told her everything;—that he had to get a feather out of the Griffin's tail, and that there was a castle where they had lost the key of their money-chest, and he was to ask the Griffin where it was—that in another castle the daughter was ill, and he was to learn what would cure her—and then not far from thence there was a lake and a man beside it, who was forced to carry people across it, and he was very anxious to learn why the man was obliged to do it. Then said the woman: "Look here, my good friend, no Christian can speak to the Griffin; he devours them all; but if you like, you can lie down under his bed, and in the night, when he is quite fast asleep, you can reach out and pull a feather out of his tail, and as for those things which you are to learn, I will ask about them myself." Hans was quite satisfied with this, and got under the bed. In the evening, the Griffin came home, and as soon as he entered the room, said: "Wife, I smell a Christian." "Yes," said the woman, "one was here to-day, but he went away again;" and on that the Griffin said no more.

In the middle of the night when the Griffin was snoring loudly, Hans reached out and plucked a feather from his tail. The Griffin woke up instantly, and said: "Wife, I smell a Christian, and it seems to me that somebody was pulling at my tail." His wife said: "You have certainly been dreaming, and I told you before that a Christian was here to-day, but that he went away again. He told me all kinds of things—that in one castle they had lost the key of their money-chest, and could find it nowhere." "Oh! the fools!" said the Griffin; "the key lies in the wood-house under a log of wood behind the door." "And then he said that in another castle the daughter was ill, and they knew no remedy that would cure her." "Oh! the fools!" said the Griffin; "under the cellar-steps a toad has made its nest of her hair, and if she got her hair back she would be well." "And then he also said that there was a place where there was a lake and a man beside it who was forced to carry everybody across." "Oh, the fool!" said the Griffin; "if he only put one man down in the middle, he would never have to carry another across." Early the next morning the Griffin got up and went out. Then Hans came forth from under the bed, and he had a beautiful feather, and had heard what the Griffin had said about the key, and the daughter, and the man. The Griffin's wife repeated it all once more to him that he might not forget it, and then he went home again. First he came to the man by the lake, who asked him what the Griffin had said, but Hans replied that he must first carry him across, and then he would tell him. So the man carried him across, and when he was over Hans told him that all he had to do was to set one person down in the middle of the lake, and then he would never have to carry over any more. The man was hugely delighted, and told Hans that out of gratitude he would take him once more across, and back again. But Hans said no, he would save him the trouble, he was quite satisfied already, and pursued his way. Then he came to the castle where the daughter was ill; he took her on his shoulders, for she could not walk, and carried her down the cellar-steps and pulled out the toad's nest from beneath the lowest step and gave it into her hand, and she sprang off his shoulder and up the steps before him, and was quite cured. Then were the father and mother beyond measure rejoiced, and they gave Hans gifts of gold and of silver, and whatsoever else he wished for, that they gave him. And when he got to the other castle he went at once into the wood-house, and found the key under the log of wood behind the door, and took it to the lord of the castle. He was not a little pleased, and gave Hans as a reward much of the gold that was in the chest, and all kinds of things besides, such as cows, and sheep, and goats. When Hans arrived before the King, with all these things—with the money, and the gold, and the silver and the cows, sheep and goats, the King asked him how he had come by them. Then Hans told him that the Griffin gave every one whatsoever he wanted. So the King thought he himself could make use of such things, and set out on his way to the Griffin; but when he got to the lake, it happened that he was the very first who arrived there after Hans, and the man put him down in the middle of it and went away, and the King was drowned. Hans, however, married the daughter, and became King.

STRONG HANS

There were once a man and a woman who had an only child, and lived quite alone in a solitary valley. It came to pass that the mother once went into the wood to gather branches of fir, and took with her little Hans, who was just two years old. As it was spring-time, and the child took pleasure in the many-coloured flowers, she went still further onwards with him into the forest. Suddenly two robbers sprang out of the thicket, seized the mother and child, and carried them far away into the black forest, where no one ever came from one year's end to another. The poor woman urgently begged the robbers to set her and her child free, but their hearts were made of stone, they would not listen to her prayers and entreaties, and drove her on farther by force. After they had worked their way through bushes and briars for about two miles, they came to a rock where there was a door, at which the robbers knocked and it opened at once. They had to go through a long dark passage, and at last came into a great cavern, which was lighted by a fire which burnt on the hearth. On the wall hung swords, sabres, and other deadly weapons which gleamed in the light, and in the midst stood a black table at which four other robbers were sitting gambling, and the captain sat at the head of it. As soon as he saw the woman he came and spoke to her, and told her to be at ease and have no fear, they would do nothing to hurt her, but she must look after the housekeeping, and if she kept everything in order, she should not fare ill with them. Thereupon they gave her something to eat, and showed her a bed where she might sleep with her child.

The woman stayed many years with the robbers, and Hans grew tall and strong. His mother told him stories, and taught him to read an old book of tales about knights which she found in the cave. When Hans was nine years old, he made himself a strong club out of a branch of fir, hid it behind the bed, and then went to his mother and said: "Dear mother, pray tell me who is my father; I must and will know." His mother was silent and would not tell him, that he might not become home-sick; moreover she knew that the godless robbers would not let him go away, but it almost broke her heart that Hans should not go to his father. In the night, when the robbers came home from their robbing expedition, Hans brought out his club, stood before the captain, and said: "I now wish to know who my father is, and if you do not tell me at once I will strike you down." Then the captain laughed, and gave Hans such a box on the ear that he rolled under the table. Hans got up again, held his tongue, and thought: "I will wait another year and then try again, perhaps I shall do better then." When the year was over, he brought out his club again, rubbed the dust off it, looked at it well, and said: "It is a stout strong club." At night the robbers came home, drank one jug of wine after another, and their heads began to be heavy. Then Hans brought out his club, placed himself before the captain, and asked him who his father was. But the captain again gave him such a vigorous box on the ear that Hans rolled under the table; however, it was not long before he was up again, and so beat the captain and the robbers with his club, that they could no longer move either their arms or their legs. His mother stood in a corner full of admiration for his bravery and strength. When Hans had done his work, he went to his mother, and said: "Now I have shown myself to be in earnest, but now I must also know who my father is." "Dear Hans," answered the mother, "come, we will go and seek him until we find him." She took from the captain the key to the entrance-door, and Hans fetched a great meal-sack and packed into it gold and silver, and whatsoever else he could find that was beautiful, until it was full, and then he took it on his back. They left the cave, but how Hans did open his eyes when he came out of the darkness into daylight, and saw the green forest, and the flowers, and the birds, and the morning sun in the sky. He stood there and wondered at everything just as if he were not quite right in the head. His mother looked for the way home, and when they had walked for a couple of hours, they got safely into their lonely valley and to their little house. The father was sitting in the doorway. He wept for joy when he recognized his wife and heard that Hans was his son, for he had long regarded them both as dead. But Hans, although he was not twelve years old, was a head taller than his father. They went into the little room together, but Hans had scarcely put his sack on the bench by the stove, than the whole house began to crack—the bench broke down and then the floor, and the heavy sack fell through into the cellar. "God save us!" cried the father, "what's that? Now you have broken our little house to pieces!" "Don't let that turn your hair grey, dear father," answered Hans; "there, in that sack, is more than is wanting for a new house." The father and Hans at once began to build a new house; to buy cattle and land, and to keep a farm. Hans ploughed the fields, and when he followed the plough and pushed it into the ground, the bullocks had scarcely any need to draw.

The next spring, Hans said: "Keep all the money and have made for me a walking stick that weighs a hundred-weight, that I may go a-travelling." When the stick was ready, he left his father's house, went forth, and came to a deep, dark forest. There he heard something crunching and cracking, looked round, and saw a fir-tree which was wound round like a rope from the bottom to the top, and when he looked upwards he saw a great fellow who had laid hold of the tree and was twisting it like a willow-wand. "Hullo!" cried Hans, "what are you doing up there?" The fellow replied: "I got some faggots together yesterday and am twisting a rope for them." "That is what I like," thought Hans, "he has some strength," and he called to him: "Leave that alone, and come with me." The fellow came down, and he was taller by a whole head than Hans, and Hans was not little. "Your name is now Fir-twister," said Hans to him. Thereupon they went further and heard something knocking and hammering with such force that the ground shook at every stroke. Shortly afterwards they came to a mighty rock, before which a giant was standing and striking great pieces of it away with his fist. When Hans asked what he was doing, he answered: "At night, when I want to sleep, bears, wolves, and other vermin of that kind come, which sniff and snuffle about me and won't let me rest; so I want to build myself a house and lay myself inside it, so that I may have some peace." "Oh indeed," thought Hans, "I can make use of this one also;" and said to him: "Leave your house-building alone, and go with me; you shall be called Rock-splitter." The man consented, and they all three roamed through the forest, and wherever they went the wild beasts were terrified, and ran away from them. In the evening they came to an old deserted castle, went up into it, and laid themselves down in the hall to sleep. The next morning Hans went into the garden. It had run quite wild, and was full of thorns and brambles. And as he was thus walking round about, a wild boar rushed at him; he, however, gave it such a blow with his club that it fell directly. He took it on his shoulders and carried it in, and they put it on a spit, roasted it, and enjoyed themselves. Then they arranged that each day, in turn, two should go out hunting, and one should stay at home, and cook nine pounds of meat for each of them. Fir-twister stayed at home the first, and Hans and Rock-splitter went out hunting. When Fir-twister was busy cooking, a little shrivelled-up old mannikin came to him in the castle, and asked for some meat. "Be off, you sneaking imp," he answered, "you need no meat." But how astonished Fir-twister was when the little insignificant dwarf sprang up at him, and belaboured him so with his fists that he could not defend himself, but fell on the ground and gasped for breath! The dwarf did not go away until he had thoroughly vented his anger on him. When the two others came home from hunting, Fir-twister said nothing to them of the old mannikin and of the blows which he himself had received, and thought: "When they stay at home, they may just try their chance with the little scrubbing-brush;" and the mere thought of that gave him pleasure already.

The next day Rock-splitter stayed at home, and he fared just as Fir-twister had done, being very ill-treated by the dwarf because he was not willing to give him any meat. When the others came home in the evening, Fir-twister saw clearly what he had suffered, but both kept silence, and thought: "Hans also must taste some of that soup."

Hans, who had to stay at home the next day, did his work in the kitchen as it had to be done, and as he was standing skimming the pan, the dwarf came and without more ado demanded a piece of meat. Then Hans thought: "He is a poor wretch, I will give him some of my share, that the others may not run short," and handed him a bit. When the dwarf had devoured it, he again asked for some meat, and good-natured Hans gave it to him, and told him it was a handsome piece, and that he was to be content with it. But the dwarf begged again for the third time. "You are shameless!" said Hans, and gave him none. Then the malicious dwarf wanted to spring on him and treat him as he had treated Fir-twister and Rock-splitter, but he had chosen the wrong

man. Hans, without exerting himself much, gave him a couple of blows which made him jump down the castle steps. Hans was about to run after him, but fell right over him, flat on his face. When he rose up again, the dwarf had got the start of him. Hans hurried after him as far as the forest, and saw him slip into a hole in the rock. Hans now went home, but he had marked the spot. When the two others came back, they were surprised that Hans was so well. He told them what had happened, and then they no longer concealed how it had fared with them. Hans laughed and said: "It served you quite right; why were you so mean with your meat? It is a disgrace that you who are so big should have let yourselves be beaten by the dwarf." Thereupon they took a basket and a rope, and all three went to the hole in the rock into which the dwarf had slipped, and let Hans and his club down in the basket.

When Hans had reached the bottom, he found a door, and when he opened it a maiden was sitting there who was lovely as any picture, nay, so beautiful that no words can express it, and by her side sat the dwarf and grinned at Hans like a sea-cat! She, however, was bound with chains, and looked so mournfully at him that Hans felt great pity for her, and thought to himself: "You must deliver her out of the power of the wicked dwarf," and gave him such a blow with his club that he fell down dead. Immediately the chains fell from the maiden, and Hans was enraptured with her beauty. She told him she was a King's daughter whom a savage count had stolen away from her home, and imprisoned there among the rocks, because she would have nothing to say to him. The count, however, had set the dwarf as a watchman, and he had made her suffer misery and vexation enough. And now Hans placed the maiden in the basket and had her drawn up; the basket came down again, but Hans did not trust his two companions, and thought: "They have already shown themselves to be false, and told me nothing about the dwarf; who knows what design they may have against me?" So he put his club in the basket, and it was lucky he did; for when the basket was half-way up, they let it fall again, and if Hans had really been sitting in it he would have been killed. But now he did not know how he was to work his way out of the depths, and when he turned it over and over in his mind he found no counsel. "It is indeed sad," said he to himself, "that I have to waste away down here," and as he was thus walking backwards and forwards, he once more came to the little chamber where the maiden had been sitting, and saw that the dwarf had a ring on his finger which shone and sparkled. Then he drew it off and put it on, and when he turned it round on his finger, he suddenly heard something rustle over his head. He looked up and saw spirits of the air hovering above, who told him he was their master, and asked what his desire might be. Hans was at first struck dumb, but afterwards he said that they were to carry him up again. They obeyed instantly, and it was just as if he had flown up himself. But when he had arrived there, he found no one in sight. Fir-twister and Rock-splitter had hurried away, and had taken the beautiful maiden with them. But Hans turned the ring, and the spirits of the air came and told him that the two were on the sea. Hans ran and ran without stopping, until he came to the sea-shore, and there far, far out on the water, he perceived a little boat in which his faithless comrades were sitting; and in fierce anger he leapt, without thinking what he was doing, club in hand into the water, and began to swim, but the club, which weighed a hundred-weight, dragged him deep down until he was all but drowned. Then in the very nick of time he turned his ring, and immediately the spirits of the air came and bore him as swift as lightning into the boat. He swung his club and gave his wicked comrades the reward they merited and threw them into the water, and then he sailed with the beautiful maiden, who had been in the greatest alarm, and whom be delivered for the second time, home to her father and mother, and married her, and all rejoiced exceedingly.

THE PEASANT IN HEAVEN

Once upon a time a poor pious peasant died, and arrived before the gate of heaven. At the same time a very rich, rich lord came there who also wanted to get into heaven. Then Saint Peter came with the key, and opened the door, and let the great man in, but apparently did not see the peasant, and shut the door again. And now the peasant outside heard how the great man was received in heaven with all kinds of rejoicing, and how they were making music, and singing within. At length all became quite again, and Saint Peter came and opened the gate of heaven, and let the peasant in. The peasant, however, expected that they would make music and sing when he went in also, but all remained quite quiet; he was received with great affection, it is true,

and the angels came to meet him, but no one sang. Then the peasant asked Saint Peter how it was that they did not sing for him as they had done when the rich man went in, and said that it seemed to him that there in heaven things were done with just as much partiality as on earth. Then said Saint Peter: "By no means, you are just as dear to us as anyone else, and will enjoy every heavenly delight that the rich man enjoys, but poor fellows like you come to heaven every day, but a rich man like this does not come more than once in a hundred years!"

LEAN LISA

Lean Lisa was of a very different way of thinking from lazy Harry and fat Trina, who never let anything disturb their peace. She slaved away from morning till evening, and burdened her husband, Long Laurence, with so much work that he had heavier weights to carry than an ass with three sacks. But it was all to no purpose, for they had nothing and came to nothing. One night as she lay in bed, and could hardly move one limb for weariness, she still did not allow her thoughts to go to sleep. She thrust her elbow into her husband's side, and said: "Listen, Lenz, to what I have been thinking: if I were to find one florin and one was given to me, I would borrow another to put to them, and you too should give me another, and then as soon as I had got the four florins together, I would buy a young cow." This pleased the husband right well. "It is true," said he, "that I do not know where I am to get the florin which you want as a gift from me; but, if you can get the money

together, and can buy a cow with it, you will do well to carry out your project. I shall be glad," he added, "if the cow has a calf, and then I shall often get a drink of milk to refresh me." "The milk is not for you," said the woman, "we must let the calf suck that it may become big and fat, and we may be able to sell it well." "Certainly," replied the man, "but still we will take a little milk; that will do no harm." "Who has taught you to manage cows?" said the woman; "whether it does harm or not, I will not allow it, and even if you were to stand on your head for it, you should not have a drop of the milk! Do you think, because there is no satisfying you, Long Laurence, that you are to eat up what I earn with so much difficulty?" "Wife," said the man, "be quiet, or I will give you a blow on your mouth!" "What!" cried she, "you threaten me, you glutton, you rascal, you lazy Harry!" She was just laying hold of his hair, but Long Laurence got up, seized both Lean Lisa's withered arms in one hand, and with the other he pressed down her head into the pillow, let her scold, and held her until she fell asleep for very weariness. Whether she continued to wrangle when she awoke next morning, or whether she went out to look for the florin which she wanted to find, that I know not.

THE HUT IN THE FOREST

A poor wood-cutter lived with his wife and three daughters in a little hut on the edge of a lonely forest. One morning as he was about to go to his work, he said to his wife: "Let our eldest daughter bring me my dinner into the forest, or I shall never get my work done, and in order that she may not miss her way," he added, "I will take a bag of millet with me and strew the seeds on the path." When, therefore, the sun was just above the centre of the forest, the girl set out on her way with a bowl of soup, but the field-sparrows, and wood-sparrows, larks and finches, blackbirds and siskins had picked up the millet long before, and the girl could not find the track. Trusting to chance, she went on and on, until the sun sank and night began to fall. The trees rustled in the darkness, the owls hooted, and she began to be afraid. Then in the distance she perceived a light which glimmered between the trees. "There ought to be some people living there, who can take me in for the night," thought she, and went up to the light. It was not long before she came to a house the windows of which were all lighted up. She knocked, and a rough voice from inside cried: "Come in." The girl stepped into the dark entrance, and knocked at the door of the room. "Just come in," cried the voice, and when she opened the door, an old gray-haired man was sitting at the table, supporting his face with both hands, and his white beard fell down over the table almost as far as the ground. By the stove lay three animals, a hen, a cock, and a brindled cow. The girl told her story to the old man, and begged for shelter for the night. The man said:

"My pretty hen,
My pretty cock,
My pretty brindled cow,
What are you saying now?"

"Duks," answered the animals, and that must have meant: "We are willing," for the old man said: "Here you shall have shelter and food, go to the fire, and cook us our supper." The girl found in the kitchen abundance of everything, and cooked a good supper, but had no thought of the animals. She carried the full bowl to the table, seated herself by the gray-haired man, ate and satisfied her hunger. When she had had enough, she said: "But now I am tired, where is there a bed in which I can lie down, and sleep?" The animals replied:

> "Thou hast eaten with him,
> Thou hast drunk with him,
> Thou hast had no thought for us,
> So find out for thyself where thou canst pass the night."

Then said the old man: "Just go upstairs, and you will find a room with two beds, shake them up, and put white linen on them, and then I, too, will come and lie down to sleep." The girl went up, and when she had shaken the beds and put clean sheets on, she lay down in one of them without waiting any longer for the old man. After some time the gray-haired man came, held his candle over the girl and shook his head. When he saw that she had fallen into a sound sleep, he opened a trap-door, and let her down into the cellar.

Late at night, the wood-cutter came home, and reproached his wife for leaving him to hunger all day. "It is not my fault," she replied, "the girl went out with your dinner, and must have lost herself, but surely she will come back to-morrow." The wood-cutter, however, arose before dawn to go into the forest, and requested that the second daughter should take him his dinner that day. "I will take a bag with lentils," said he; "the seeds are larger than millet, the girl will see them better, and can't lose her way." At dinner-time, therefore, the girl took out the food, but the lentils had disappeared. The birds of the forest had picked them up as they had done the day before, and had left none. The girl wandered about in the forest until night, and then she too reached the house of the old man, was told to go in, and begged for food and a bed. The man with the white beard again asked the animals:

"My pretty hen,
My pretty cock,
My pretty brindled cow,
What are you saying now?"

The animals again replied "Duks," and everything happened just as it had happened the day before. The girl cooked a good meal, ate and drank with the old man, and did not concern herself about the animals, and when she inquired about her bed they answered:

"Thou hast eaten with him,
Thou hast drunk with him,
Thou hast had no thought for us,
So find out for thyself where thou canst pass the night."

When she was asleep the old man came, looked at her, shook his head, and let her down into the cellar.

On the third morning the wood-cutter said to his wife: "Send our youngest child out with my dinner to-day, she has always been good and obedient, and will stay in the right path, and not rove about like her sisters, the wild bumble-bees." The mother did not want to do it, and said: "Am I to lose my dearest child, as well?" "Have no fear," he replied, "the girl will not go astray; she is too prudent and sensible; besides I will take some peas with me, and strew them about. They are still larger than lentils, and will show her the way." But when the girl went out with her basket on her arm, the wood-pigeons had already got all the peas in their crops, and she did not know which way she was to turn. She was full of sorrow and never ceased to think how hungry her father would be, and how her good mother would grieve, if she did not go home. At length when it grew dark, she saw the light and came to the house in the forest. She begged quite prettily to be allowed to spend the night there, and the man with the white beard again asked his animals:

"My pretty hen,
My pretty cock,
My pretty brindled cow,
What are you saying now?"

"Duks," said they. Then the girl went to the stove where the animals were lying, and petted the cock and hen, and stroked their smooth feathers with her hand, and caressed the brindled cow between her horns, and when, in obedience to the old man's orders, she had made ready some good soup, and the bowl was placed upon the table, she said: "Am I to eat as much as I want, and the good animals to have nothing? Outside is food in plenty, I will look after them first." So she went and brought some barley and stewed it for the cock and hen, and a whole armful of sweet-smelling hay for the cow. "I hope you will like it, dear animals," said she, "and you shall have a refreshing draught in case you are thirsty." Then she fetched a bucketful of water, and the cock and hen jumped on to the edge of it and dipped their beaks in, and then held up their heads as the birds do when they drink, and the brindled cow also took a hearty draught. When the animals were fed, the girl seated herself at the table by the old man, and ate what he had left. It was not long before the cock and the hen began to thrust their heads beneath their wings, and the eyes of the cow likewise began to blink.

Then said the girl: "Ought we not to go to bed?

> My pretty hen,
> My pretty cock,
> My pretty brindled cow,
> What are you saying now?"

The animals answered "Duks,

> Thou hast eaten with us,
> Thou hast drunk with us,
> Thou hast had kind thought for all of us,
> We wish thee good-night."

Then the maiden went upstairs, shook the feather-beds, and laid clean sheets on them, and when she had done it the old man came and lay down in one of the beds, and his white beard reached down to his feet. The girl lay down on the other, said her prayers, and fell asleep.

She slept quietly till midnight, and then there was such a noise in the

house that she awoke. There was a sound of cracking and splitting in every corner, and the doors sprang open, and beat against the walls. The beams groaned as if they were being torn out of their joints, it seemed as if the staircase were falling down, and at length there was a crash as if the entire roof had fallen in. When, however, all grew quiet once more, and the girl was not hurt, she stayed quietly lying where she was, and fell asleep again. But when she woke up in the morning with the brilliancy of the sunshine, what did her eyes behold? She was lying in a vast hall, and everything around her shone with royal splendour; on the wall, golden flowers grew up on a ground of green silk, the bed was of ivory, and the canopy of red velvet, and on a chair close by, was a pair of slippers embroidered with pearls. The girl believed that she was in a dream, but three richly clad attendants came in, and asked what orders she would like to give. "If you will go," she replied, "I will get up at once and make ready some soup for the old man, and then I will feed the pretty hen, and the pretty cock, and the pretty brindled cow." She thought the old man was up already, and looked round at his bed; he, however, was not lying in it, but a stranger. And while she was looking at him, and becoming aware that he was young and handsome, he awoke, sat up in bed, and said: "I am a King's son, and was bewitched by a wicked witch, and made to live in this forest, as an old gray-haired man; no one was allowed to be with me but my three attendants in the form of a cock, a hen, and a brindled cow. The spell was not to be broken until a girl came to us whose heart was so good that she showed herself full of love, not only towards mankind, but towards animals—and that you have done, and by you at midnight we were set free, and the old hut in the forest was changed back again into my royal palace." And when they had arisen, the King's son ordered the three attendants to set out and fetch the father and mother of the girl to the marriage feast. "But where are my two sisters?" inquired the maiden. "I have locked them in the cellar, and to-morrow they shall be led into the forest, and shall live as servants to a charcoal-burner, until they have grown kinder, and do not leave poor animals to suffer hunger."

SHARING JOY AND SORROW

There was once a tailor, who was a quarrelsome fellow, and his wife, who was good, industrious, and pious, never could please him. Whatever she did, he was not satisfied, but grumbled and scolded, and knocked her about and beat her. As the authorities at last heard of it, they had him summoned and put in prison in order to make him better. He was kept for a while on bread and water, and then set free again. He was forced, however, to promise not to beat his wife any more, but to live with her in peace, and share joy and sorrow with her, as married people ought to do. All went on well for a time, but then he fell into his old ways, and was surly and quarrelsome. And because he dared not beat her, he would seize her by the hair and tear it out. The woman escaped from him, and sprang out into the yard, but he ran after her with his yard-measure and scissors, and chased her about, and threw the yard-measure and scissors at her, and whatever else came his way. When he hit her he laughed, and when he missed her, he stormed and swore. This went on so long that the neighbours came to the wife's assistance. The tailor was again summoned before the magistrates, and reminded of his promise. "Dear gentlemen," said he, "I have kept my word, I have not beaten her, but have shared joy and sorrow with her." "How can that be," said the judge, "as she continues to bring such heavy complaints against you?" "I have not beaten her, but just because she looked so strange I wanted to comb her hair with my hand; she, however, got away from me, and left me quite spitefully. Then I hurried after her, and in order to bring her back to her duty, I threw at her as a well-meant reminder whatever came readily to hand. I have shared joy and sorrow with her also, for whenever I hit her I was full of joy, and she of sorrow, and if I missed her, then she was joyful, and I sorry." The judges were not satisfied with this answer, but gave him the reward he deserved.

THE WILLOW-WREN

In olden times every sound still had its meaning and significance. When the smith's hammer resounded, it cried: "Strike away! strike away." When the carpenter's plane grated, it said: "Here goes! here goes." If the mill wheel began to clack, it said: "Help, Lord God! help, Lord God!" and if the miller was a cheat and set the mill a-going, it spoke high German, and first asked slowly: "Who is there? who is there?" and then answered quickly: "The miller! the miller!" and at last quite in a hurry: "He steals bravely! he steals bravely! three pecks in a bushel."

At this time the birds also had their own language which every one understood; now it only sounds like chirping, screeching, and whistling, and sometimes like music without words. It came into the birds' mind, however, that they would no longer be without a ruler, and would choose one of themselves to be their King. One alone among them, the green plover, was opposed to this. He had lived free and would die free, and anxiously flying hither and thither, he cried: "Where shall I go? where shall I go?" He retired into a solitary and unfrequented marsh, and showed himself no more among his fellows.

The birds now wished to discuss the matter, and on a fine May morning they all gathered together from the woods and fields: eagles and chaffinches, owls and crows, larks and sparrows, how can I name them all? Even the cuckoo came, and the hoopoe, his clerk, who is so called because he is always heard a few days before him, and a very small bird which as yet had no name, mingled with the band. The hen, which by some accident had heard nothing of the whole matter, was astonished at the great assemblage. "What, what, what is going to be done?" She cackled; but the cock calmed his beloved hen, and said: "Only a lot of rich people," and told her what they had on hand. It was decided that the one who could fly the highest should be King. A tree-frog which was sitting among the bushes, when he heard that, cried a warning: "No, no, no! no!" because he thought that many tears would be shed because of this; but the crow said: "Caw, caw," and that all would pass off peaceably.

It was now determined that on this fine morning they should at once begin to ascend, so that hereafter no one should be able to say: "I could easily have flown much higher, but the evening came on, and I could do no more." On a given signal, therefore, the whole troop rose up in the air. The dust ascended from the land, and there was tremendous fluttering and whirring and beating of wings, and it looked as if a black cloud was rising up. The little birds were soon left behind. They could go no farther, and fell back to the ground. the larger birds held out longer, but none could equal the eagle, who mounted so high that he could have plucked the eyes out of the sun. And when he saw that the others could not get up to him, he thought: "Why should you fly still higher? You are the King," and began to let himself down again. The birds beneath him at once cried to him: "You must be our King, no one has flown so high as you." "Except me," screamed the little fellow without a name, who had crept into the breast-feathers of the eagle. And as he was not at all tired, he rose up and mounted so high that he reached heaven itself. However, when he had gone as far as this, he folded his wings together, and called down with clear and penetrating voice: "I am King! I am King."

"You, our King?" cried the birds angrily. "You have managed it by trick and cunning!" So they made another condition. He should be King who could go down lowest in the ground. How the goose did flap about with its broad breast when it was once more on land! How

quickly the cock scratched a hole! The duck came off the worst of all, for she leapt into a ditch, but sprained her legs, and waddled away to a neighbouring pond, crying: "Cheating, cheating!" The little bird without a name, however, sought out a mousehole, slipped down into it, and cried out of it with his small voice: "I am King! I am King!"

"You our King!" cried the birds still more angrily. "Do you think your cunning shall prevail?" They determined to keep him a prisoner in the hole and starve him out. The owl was placed as sentinel in front of it, and was not to let the rascal out if she had any value for her life. When evening was come and all the birds were feeling very tired after the exertion of so much flying, they went to bed with their wives and children. The owl alone remained standing by the mouse-hole, gazing steadfastly into it with her great eyes. Then she, too, grew tired and thought to herself: "You might certainly shut one eye, you will still watch with the other, and the little villain shall not come out of his hole." So she shut one eye, and with the other looked straight at the mouse-hole. The little fellow put his head out and peeped, and wanted to slip away, but the owl came forward immediately, and he drew his head back again. Then the owl opened the one eye again, and shut the other, intending to shut them in turn all through the night. But when she next shut the one eye, she forgot to open the other, and as soon as both her eyes were shut she fell asleep. The little fellow soon observed that, and slipped away.

From that day forth, the owl has never dared to show herself by daylight, for if she does the other birds chase her and pluck her feathers out. She flies out only by night, but hates and pursues mice because they make such ugly holes. The little bird, too, is very unwilling to let himself be seen, because he is afraid it will cost him his life if he is caught. He steals about in the hedges, and when he is quite safe, he sometimes cries: "I am King," and for this reason, the other birds call him in mockery: "King of the hedges." No one, however, was so happy as the lark at not having to obey the little King. As soon as the sun appears, she ascends high in the air and cries: "Ah, how beautiful that is! beautiful that is! beautiful, beautiful! ah, how beautiful that is!"

THE SOLE

The fishes had for a long time been discontented because no order prevailed in their kingdom. None of them turned aside for the others, but all swam to the right or the left as they fancied, or darted between those who wanted to stay together, or got into their way; and a strong one gave a weak one a blow with its tail, which drove it away, or else swallowed it up without more ado. "How delightful it would be," said they, "if we had a king who enforced law and justice among us!" and they met together to choose for their ruler the one who could cleave through the water most quickly, and give help to the weak ones.

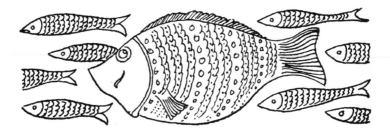

They placed themselves in rank and file by the shore, and the pike gave the signal with his tail, on which they all started. Like an arrow, the pike darted away, and with him the herring, the gudgeon, the perch, the carp, and all the rest of them. Even the sole swam with them, and hoped to win the race.

All at once, the cry was heard: "The herring is first! The herring is first!" "Who is first?" screamed angrily the flat envious sole, who had been left far behind, "who is first?" "The herring! The herring," was the answer. "The naked herring?" cried the jealous creature, "the naked herring?" Since that time the sole has been punished by having been given a mouth on one side.

THE BITTERN AND THE HOOPOE

Where do you like best to feed your flocks?" said a man to an old cowherd. "Here, sir, where the grass is neither too rich nor too poor, or else it is no use." "Why not?" asked the man. "Do you hear that melancholy cry from the meadow there?" answered the cowherd, "that is the bittern; he was once a cowherd, and so was the hoopoe also,—I will tell you the story: The bittern pastured his flocks on rich green meadows where flowers grew in abundance, so his cows became wild and unmanageable. The hoopoe drove his cattle on to high barren hills, where the wind plays with the sand, and his cows became thin, and got no strength. When it was evening, and the cowherds wanted to drive their cows homewards, the bittern could not get his together again; they were too high-spirited, and ran away from him. He called: 'Come, cows, come' but it was of no use; they took no notice of his calling. The hoopoe, however, could not even get his cows up on their legs, so faint and weak had they become. 'Up, up, up,' screamed he, but it was in vain, they remained lying on the sand. That is the way when one has no moderation. And to this day, though they have no flocks now to watch, the bittern cries: 'Come, cows, come,' and the hoopoe, 'Up, up, up.' "

THE OWL

Two or three hundred years ago, when people were far from being so crafty and cunning as they are nowadays, an extraordinary event took place in a little town. By some mischance one of the great owls, called horned owls, had come from the neighbouring woods into the barn of one of the townsfolk in the night-time, and when day broke did not dare to venture forth again from her retreat, for fear of the other birds, which raised a terrible outcry whenever she appeared. In the morning when the man-servant went into the barn to fetch some straw, he was so mightily alarmed at the sight of the owl sitting there in a corner, that he ran away and announced to his master that a monster, the like of which he had never set eyes on in his life, and which could devour a man without the slightest difficulty, was sitting in the barn, rolling its eyes about in its head. "I know your kind," said the master, "you have courage enough to chase a blackbird about the fields, but when you see a hen lying dead, you have to get a stick before you go near it. I must go and see for myself what kind of a monster it is," added the master, and went quite boldly into the granary and looked round him. When, however, he saw with his own eyes the strange grim creature, he was no less terrified than the servant had been. With two bounds he sprang out, ran to his neighbours, and begged them imploringly to lend him assistance against an unknown and dangerous beast, or else the whole town might be in danger if it were to break loose out of the barn, where it was shut up. A great noise and clamour arose in all the streets, the townsmen came armed with spears, hay-forks, scythes, and axes, as if they were going out against an enemy; finally the senators appeared with the burgomaster at their head. When they had drawn up in the market-place, they marched to the barn, and surrounded it on all sides. Thereupon one of the most courageous of them stepped forth and entered with his spear lowered, but came running out immediately afterwards with a shriek and as pale as death, and could not utter a single word. Yet two others ventured in, but they fared no better. At last one stepped forth; a great strong man who was famous for his warlike deeds, and said: "You will not drive away the monster by merely looking at him; we must be in earnest here, but I see that you have all turned into women, and not one of you dares to encounter the animal." He ordered them to give him some armour, had a sword and spear brought, and armed himself. All praised his courage, though many feared for his life. The two barn-doors were opened, and they saw the owl, which in the meantime had perched herself on the middle of a great cross-beam. He had a ladder brought, and when he raised it, and made ready to climb up, they all cried out to him that he was to bear himself bravely, and commended him to St. George, who slew the dragon. When he had just got to the top, and the owl perceived that he had designs on her, and was also bewildered by the crowd and the shouting, and knew not how to escape, she rolled her eyes, ruffled her feathers, flapped her wings, snapped her beak, and cried: "Tuwhit, tuwhoo," in a harsh voice. "Strike home! strike home!" screamed the crowd outside to the valiant hero. "Any one who was standing where I am standing," answered he, "would not cry: 'strike home!'" He certainly did plant his foot one rung higher on the ladder, but then he began to tremble, and half-fainting, went back again.

And now there was no one left who dared to place himself in such danger. "The monster," said they, "has poisoned and mortally wounded the very strongest man among us, by snapping at him and just breathing on him! Are we, too, to risk our lives?" They took counsel as to what they ought to do to prevent the whole town from being destroyed. For a long time everything seemed to be of no use, but at length the burgomaster found an expedient. "My opinion," said he, "is that we ought, out of the common purse, to pay for this barn,

and whatsoever corn, straw, or hay it contains, and thus indemnify the owner, and then burn down the whole building, and the terrible beast with it. Thus no one will have to endanger his life. This is no time for thinking of expense, and stinginess would be ill applied." All agreed with him. So they set fire to the barn at all four corners, and with it the owl was miserably burnt. Let any one who will not believe it, go thither and inquire for himself.

THE MOON

In days gone by there was a land where the nights were always dark, and the sky spread over it like a black cloth, for there the moon never rose, and no star shone in the gloom. At the creation of the world, the light at night had been sufficient. Three young fellows once went out of this country on a travelling expedition, and arrived in another kingdom, where, in the evening when the sun had disappeared behind the mountains, a shining globe was placed on an oak-tree, which shed a soft light far and wide. By means of this, everything could very well be seen and distinguished, even though it was not so brilliant as the sun. The travellers stopped and asked a countryman who was driving past with his cart, what kind of a light that was. "That is the moon," answered he; "our mayor bought it for three talers, and fastened it to the oak-tree. He has to pour oil into it daily, and to keep it clean, so that it may always burn clearly. He receives a taler a week from us for doing it."

When the countryman had driven away, one of them said: "We could make some use of this lamp, we have an oak-tree at home, which is just as big as this, and we could hang it on that. What a pleasure it would be not to have to feel about at night in the darkness!" "I'll tell you what we'll do," said the second; "we will fetch a cart and horses and carry away the moon. The people here may buy themselves another." "I'm a good climber," said the third, "I will bring it down." The fourth brought a cart and horses, and the third climbed the tree, bored a hole in the moon, passed a rope through it, and let it down. When the shining ball lay in the cart, they covered it over with a cloth, that no one might observe the theft. They conveyed it safely into their own country, and placed it on a high oak. Old and young rejoiced, when the new lamp let its light shine over the whole land, and bedrooms and sitting-rooms were filled with it. The dwarfs came forth from their caves in the rocks, and the tiny elves in their little red coats danced in rings on the meadows.

The four took care that the moon was provided with oil, cleaned the wick, and received their weekly taler, but they became old men, and when one of them grew ill, and saw that he was about to die, he appointed that one quarter of the moon, should, as his property, be laid in the grave with him. When he died, the mayor climbed up the tree, and cut off a quarter with the hedge-shears, and this was placed in his coffin. The light of the moon decreased, but still not visibly. When the second died, the second quarter was buried with him, and the light diminished. It grew weaker still after the death of the third, who likewise took his part of it away with him; and when the fourth was borne to his grave, the old state of darkness recommenced, and whenever the people went out at night without their lanterns they knocked their heads together in collision.

When, however, the pieces of the moon had united themselves together again in the world below, where darkness had always pre-

vailed, it came to pass that the dead became restless and awoke from their sleep. They were astonished when they were able to see again; the moonlight was quite sufficient for them, for their eyes had become so weak that they could not have borne the brilliance of the sun. They rose up and were merry, and fell into their former ways of living. Some of them went to the play and to dance, others hastened to the public-houses, where they asked for wine, got drunk, brawled, quarrelled, and at last took up cudgels, and belaboured each other. The noise became greater and greater, and at last reached even to heaven.

Saint Peter, who guards the gate of heaven, thought the lower world had broken out in revolt and gathered together the heavenly hosts, which were employed to drive back the Evil One when he and his associates storm the abode of the blessed. As these, however, did not come, he got on his horse and rode through the gate of heaven, down into the world below. There he reduced the dead to subjection, bade them lie down in their graves again, took the moon away with him, and hung it up in heaven.

THE DURATION OF LIFE

When God created the world and was about to fix the length of each creature's life, the ass came and asked: "Lord, how long shall I live?" "Thirty years," replied God; "does that content you?" "Ah, Lord," answered the ass, "that is a long time. Think of my painful existence! To carry heavy burdens from morning to night, to drag sacks of corn to the mill that others may eat bread, to be cheered and refreshed with nothing but blows and kicks. Relieve me of a portion of this long time." Then God had pity on him and relieved him of eighteen years. The ass went away comforted, and the dog appeared. "How long would you like to live?" said God to him; "thirty years are too many for the ass, but you will be satisfied with that." "Lord," answered the dog, "is that thy will? Consider how I shall have to run, my feet will never hold out so long, and when I have once lost my voice for barking, and my teeth for biting, what will be left for me to do but run from one corner to another and growl?" God saw that he was right, and released him

from twelve years of life. Then came the monkey: "You will certainly live thirty years willingly?" said the Lord to him; "you have no need to work as the ass and the dog have to, and will always enjoy yourself." "Ah! Lord," he answered, "it may seem as if that were the case, but it is quite different. When it rains millet-porridge I have no spoon. I am always to play merry pranks, and make faces which force people to laugh, and if they give me an apple, and I bite into it, why, it is sour! How often sadness hides itself behind mirth! I shall never be able to hold out for thirty years." God was gracious and took off ten.

At last man appeared, joyous, healthy and vigorous, and begged God to appoint his time for him. "Thirty years shall you live," said the Lord. "Is that enough for you?" "What a short time," cried man, "when I have built my house and my fire burns on my own hearth; when I have planted trees which blossom and bear fruit, and am just intending to enjoy my life, I am to die! O Lord, lengthen my time." "I will add to it the ass's eighteen years," said God. "That is not enough," replied the man. "You shall also have the dog's twelve years." "Still too little!" "Well, then," said God, "I will give you the monkey's ten years also, but more you shall not have." The man went away, but was not satisfied.

So man lives seventy years. The first thirty are his human years, which are soon gone; then is he healthy, merry, works with pleasure, and is glad of his life. Then follow the ass's eighteen years, when one burden after another is laid on him, he has to carry the corn which feeds others, and blows and kicks are the reward of his faithful services. Then come the dog's twelve years, when he lies in the corner, and growls and has no longer any teeth to bite with, and when this time is over the monkey's ten years form the end. Then man is weak-headed and foolish, does silly things, and becomes the jest of children.

DEATH'S MESSENGERS

In ancient times a giant was once travelling on a great highway, when suddenly an unknown man sprang up before him, and said: "Halt, not one step farther!" "What!" cried the giant, "a creature whom I can crush between my fingers, wants to block my way? Who are you that you dare to speak so boldly?" "I am Death," answered the other. "No one resists me, and you also must obey my commands." But the giant refused, and began to struggle with Death. It was a long, violent battle, in which at last the giant got the upper hand, and struck Death down with his fist, so that he collapsed by a stone. The giant went his way, and Death lay there conquered, and so weak that he could not get up again. "What will be done now," said he, "if I stay lying here in a corner? No one will die in the world, and it will get so full of people that they won't have room to stand beside each other." In the meantime a young man came along the road, who was strong and healthy, singing a song, and glancing around on every side. When he saw the half-fainting one, he went compassionately to him, raised him up, poured a strengthening draught out of his flask for him, and waited till he regained some strength. "Do you know," said the stranger, whilst he was getting up, "who I am, and who it is whom you have helped on his legs again?" "No," answered the youth, "I do not know you." "I am Death," said he. "I spare no one, and can make no exception with you,—but that you may see that I am grateful, I promise you that I will not fall on you unexpectedly, but will send my messengers to you

before I come and take you away." "Well," said the youth, "it is something gained that I shall know when you come, and at any rate be safe from you for so long." Then he went on his way, and was light-hearted, and enjoyed himself, and lived without thought. But youth and health did not last long. Soon came sicknesses and sorrows, which tormented him by day, and took away his rest by night. "Die, I shall not," said he to himself, "for Death will send his messengers before that, but I do wish these wretched days of sickness were over." As soon as he felt himself well again he began once more to live merrily. Then one day someone tapped him on the shoulder. He looked round, and Death stood behind him, and said: "Follow me, the hour of your departure from this world has come." "What," replied the man, "will you break your word? Did you not promise me that you would send your messengers to me before coming yourself? I have seen none!" "Silence!" answered Death. "Have I not sent one messenger to you, after another? Did not fever come and smite you, and shake you, and cast you down? Has dizziness not bewildered your head? Has not gout twitched you in all your limbs? Did not your ears sing? Did not tooth-ache bite into your cheeks? Was it not dark before your eyes? And besides all that, has not my own brother Sleep reminded you every night of me? Did you not lie by night as if you were already dead?" The man could make no answer; he yielded to his fate, and went away with Death.

MASTER PFRIEM*

Master Pfriem was a short, thin, but lively man, who never rested a moment. His face, of which his turned-up nose was the only prominent feature, was marked with small-pox and pale as death; his hair was gray and shaggy, his eyes small, but they glanced perpetually about on all sides. He saw everything, criticized everything, knew everything best, and was always in the right. When he went into the streets, he moved his arms about as if he were rowing; and once he struck the pail

* Pfriem: a cobbler's awl.

of a girl so high in the air that he himself was wetted all over by the water she was carrying. "Idiot!" cried he to her, shaking himself, "could you not see that I was coming behind you?" By trade he was a shoemaker, and when he worked he pulled his thread out with such force that he drove his fist into everyone who did not keep far enough off. No apprentice stayed more than a month with him, for he had always some fault to find with the very best work. At one time it was that the stitches were not even, at another that one shoe was too long, or one heel higher than the other, or the leather not cut large enough. "Wait," said he to his apprentice, "I will soon show you how we make skins soft," and he brought a strap and gave him a couple of lashes across the back. He called them all sluggards. He himself did not turn much work out of his hands, for he never sat still for a quarter of an hour. If his wife got up very early in the morning and lighted the fire, he jumped out of bed, and ran barefooted into the kitchen, crying: "Will you burn my house down for me? That is a fire one could roast an ox by! Does wood cost nothing?" If the servants were standing by their wash-tubs and laughing, and telling each other what they knew, he scolded them, and said: "There stand the geese cackling, and forgetting their work, to gossip! And why fresh soap? Disgraceful extravagance and shameful idleness into the bargain! They want to save their hands, and not rub the things properly!" And out he would run and knock a pail full of soap and water over, so that the whole kitchen was flooded. Someone was building a new house, so he hurried to the window to look on. "There, they are using that red sand-stone again that never dries!" cried he. "No one will ever be healthy in that house! and just look how badly the fellows are laying the stones! Besides, the mortar is good for nothing! It ought to have gravel in it, not sand. I shall live to see that house tumble down on the people who are in it." He sat down, put a couple of stitches in, and then jumped up again, unfastened his leather-apron, and cried: "I will just go out, and appeal to those men's consciences." He stumbled on the carpenters. "What's this?" cried he, "you are not working by the line! Do you expect the beams to be straight?—one wrong will put all wrong." He snatched an axe out of a carpenter's hand and wanted to show him how he ought to cut; but as a cart loaded with clay came by, he threw the axe away, and hastened to the peasant who was walking by the side of it: "You are not in your right mind," said he; "who yokes young horses to a heavily-laden cart? The poor beasts will die on the spot." The peasant did not give him an answer, and Pfriem in a rage ran back into his workshop. When he was setting himself to work again, the apprentice reached him a shoe. "Well, what's that again?" screamed he, "haven't I told you you ought not to cut shoes so broad? Who would buy a shoe like this, which is hardly anything else but a sole? I insist on my orders being followed exactly." "Master," answered the apprentice, "you may easily be quite right about the shoe being a bad one, but it is the one which you yourself cut out, and yourself set to work at. When you jumped up a while ago, you knocked it off the table, and I have only just picked it up. An angel from heaven, however, would never make you believe that."

One night Master Pfriem dreamed he was dead, and on his way to heaven. When he got there, he knocked loudly at the door. "I wonder," said he to himself, "that they have no knocker on the door,—one knocks one's knuckles sore." The apostle Peter opened the door, and wanted to see who demanded admission so noisily. "Ah, it's you, Master Pfriem," said he; "well, I'll let you in, but I warn you that you must give up that habit of yours, and find fault with nothing you see in heaven, or you may fare ill." "You might have spared your warning," answered Pfriem. "I know already what is seemly, and here, God be thanked, everything is perfect, and there is nothing to blame as there is on earth." So he went in, and walked up and down the wide expanses of heaven. He looked around him, to the left and to the right, but sometimes shook his head, or muttered something to himself. Then he saw two angels who were carrying away a beam. It was the beam which someone had had in his own eye whilst he was looking for the splinter in the eye of another. They did not carry the beam lengthways, however, but obliquely. "Did anyone ever see such a piece of stupidity?" thought Master Pfriem; but he said nothing, and seemed satisfied with it. "It comes to the same thing after all, whichever way they carry the beam, straight or athwart, if they only get along with it, and truly I do not see them knock against anything." Soon after this he saw two angels who were drawing water out of a well into a bucket, but at the same time he observed that the bucket was full of holes, and that the water was running out of it on every side. They were watering the earth with rain. "Hang it," he exclaimed; but happily recollected himself, and thought: "Perhaps it is only a pastime. If it is an amusement, then it seems they can do useless things of this kind especially here in heaven, where people, as I have already noticed, do nothing but idle about." He went farther and saw a cart which had stuck fast in a deep hole. "It's no wonder," said he to the man who stood by it; "who would load so unreasonably? what have you there?" "Good wishes," replied the man. "I could not get on the right way with it, but still I have pushed it safely up here, and here they won't leave me stuck." In fact an angel did come and harness two horses to it. "That's quite right," thought Pfriem, "but two horses won't get that cart out, it must at least have four to it." Another angel came and brought two more horses; she did not harness them in front of it, however, but behind. That was too much for Master Pfriem: "Clumsy creature," he burst out, "what are you doing there? Has any one ever since the world began seen a cart drawn in that way? But you, in your conceited arrogance, think that you know everything best." He was going to say more, but one of the inhabitants of heaven seized him by the throat and pushed him forth with irresistible strength. Beneath the gateway Master Pfriem turned his head round to take one more look at the cart, and saw that it was being raised into the air by four winged horses.

At this moment Master Pfriem awoke. "Things are certainly arranged in heaven otherwise than they are on earth," said he to himself, "and that excuses much; but who can see horses harnessed both behind and before with patience; to be sure they had wings, but who could know that? It is, besides, great folly to fix a pair of wings to a horse that has four legs to run with already! But I must get up, or else they will make nothing but mistakes in my house. It is a lucky thing though, that I am not really dead."

THE GOOSE-GIRL AT THE WELL

There was once upon a time a very old woman, who lived with her flock of geese in a remote clearing in the mountains, and there had a little house. The clearing was surrounded by a large forest, and every morning the old woman took her crutch and hobbled into it. There, however, she was quite active, more so than any one would have thought, considering her age, and collected grass for her geese, picked all the wild fruit she could reach, and carried everything home on her back. Anyone would have thought that the heavy load would have weighed her to the ground, but she always brought it safely home. If anyone met her, she greeted him quite courteously. "Good day, dear countryman, it is a fine day. Ah! you wonder that I should drag grass about, but everyone must take his burden on his back." Nevertheless, people did not like to meet her if they could help it, and took by preference a round-about way, and when a father with his boys passed her, he whispered to them: "Beware of the old woman. She has claws beneath her gloves; she is a witch."

One morning, a handsome young man was going through the forest. The sun shone bright, the birds sang, a cool breeze crept through the leaves, and he was full of joy and gladness. He had as yet met no one, when he suddenly perceived the old witch kneeling on the ground cutting grass with a sickle. She had already thrust a whole load into her bundle, and near it stood two baskets, which were filled with wild apples and pears. "But, good little mother," said he, "how can you carry all that away?" "I must carry it, dear sir," answered she, "rich folk's children have no need to do such things, but with the peasant folk the saying goes: 'Don't look behind you, you will only see how crooked your back is!'

"Will you help me?" she said, as he remained standing by her. "You have still a straight back and young legs, it would be a trifle to you. Besides, my house is not so very far from here, it stands there on the heath behind the hill. How soon you would bound up thither." The young man took compassion on the old woman. "My father is certainly no peasant," replied he, "but a rich count; nevertheless, that you may see that it is not only peasants who can carry things, I will take your bundle." "If you will try it," said she, "I shall be very glad. You will certainly have to walk for an hour, but what will that matter to you; only you must carry the apples and pears as well." The young man felt somewhat uneasy when he heard of an hour's walk, but the old woman would not let him off, packed the bundle on his back, and hung the two baskets on his arm. "See, it is quite light," said she. "No, it is not light," answered the count, and pulled a rueful face. "Verily, the bundle weighs as heavily as if it were full of cobblestones, and the apples and pears are as heavy as lead! I can scarcely breathe." He had a mind to put everything down again, but the old woman would not allow it. "Just look," said she mockingly, "the young gentleman will not carry what I, an old woman, have so often dragged along. You are ready with fine words, but when it comes to be earnest, you want to take to your heels. Why are you standing loitering there?" she continued; "step out. No one will take the bundle off again." As long as he walked on level ground, it was still bearable, but when they came to the hill and had to climb, and the stones rolled down under his feet as if they were alive, it was beyond his strength. Drops of sweat stood on his forehead, and ran, hot and cold, down his back. "Mother," said he, "I can go no farther. I want to rest a little." "Not here," answered the old woman, "when we have arrived at our journey's end, you can rest; but now you must go forward. Who knows what good it may do you?" "Old woman, you are becoming shameless!" said the count, and tried to throw off the bundle, but he laboured in vain; it stuck as fast to his back as if it grew there. He turned and twisted, but he could not get rid of it. The old woman laughed at this, and sprang about quite delighted on her crutch. "Don't get angry, dear sir," said she, "you are growing as red in the face as a turkey-cock! Carry your bundle patiently. I will give you a good present when we get home."

What could he do? He was obliged to submit to his fate, and crawl along patiently behind the old woman. She seemed to grow more and

more nimble, and his burden still heavier. All at once she made a bound, jumped on to the bundle and seated herself on the top of it; and however withered she might be, she was yet heavier than the stoutest country lass. The youth's knees trembled, but when he did not go on, the old woman hit him about the legs with a switch and with stinging-nettles. Groaning continually, he climbed the mountain, and at length reached the old woman's house, when he was just about to drop. When the geese perceived the old woman, they flapped their wings, stretched out their necks, ran to meet her, cackling all the while. Behind the flock walked, stick in hand, an old wench, strong and big, but ugly as night. "Good mother," said she to the old woman, "has anything happened to you, you have stayed away so long?" "By no means, my dear daughter," answered she, "I have met with nothing bad, but, on the contrary, with this kind gentleman, who has carried my burden for me; only think, he even took me on his back when I was tired. The way, too, has not seemed long to us; we have been merry, and have been cracking jokes with each other all the time." At last the old woman slid down, took the bundle off the young man's back, and the baskets from his arm, looked at him quite kindly, and said: "Now seat yourself on the bench before the door, and rest. You have fairly earned your wages, and they shall not be wanting." Then she said to the goose-girl: "Go into the house, my dear daughter, it is not becoming for you to be alone with a young gentleman; one must not pour oil on to the fire, he might fall in love with you." The count knew not whether to laugh or to cry. "Such a sweetheart as that," thought he, "could not touch my heart, even if she were thirty years younger." In the meantime the old woman stroked and fondled her geese as if they were children, and then went into the house with her daughter. The youth lay down on the bench, under a wild apple-tree. The air was warm and mild; on all sides stretched a green meadow, which was set with cowslips, wild thyme, and a thousand other flowers; through the midst of it rippled a clear brook on which the sun sparkled, and the white geese went walking backwards and forwards, or paddled in the water. "It is quite delightful here," said he, "but I am so tired that I cannot keep my eyes open; I will sleep a little. If only a gust of wind does not come and blow my legs off my body, for they are as rotten as tinder."

When he had slept a little while, the old woman came and shook him till he awoke. "Sit up," said she, "you can not stay here; I have certainly treated you ill enough, still it has not cost you your life. Of money and land you have no need, here is something else for you." Thereupon she thrust a little box into his hand, which was cut out of a single emerald. "Take great care of it," said she, "it will bring you good fortune." The count sprang up, and as he felt that he was quite fresh, and had recovered his vigour, he thanked the old woman for her present, and set off without even once looking back at the beautiful daughter. When he was already some way off, he still heard in the distance the noisy cry of the geese.

For three days the count had to wander in the wilderness before he could find his way out. He then reached a large town, and as no one knew him, he was led into the royal palace, where the King and Queen were sitting on their throne. The count fell on one knee, drew the emerald box out of his pocket, and laid it at the Queen's feet. She bade him rise and hand her the little box. Hardly, however, had she opened it, and looked therein, than she fell as if dead to the ground. The count was seized by the King's servants, and was being led to prison, when the Queen opened her eyes, and ordered them to release him, and every one was to go out, as she wished to speak with him in private.

When the Queen was alone, she began to weep bitterly, and said: "Of what use to me are the splendour and honours with which I am surrounded; every morning I awake in pain and sorrow. I had three daughters, the youngest of whom was so beautiful that the whole world looked on her as a wonder. She was as white as snow, as rosy as apple-blossom, and her hair as radiant as sun-beams. When she cried, not tears fell from her eyes, but pearls and jewels only. When she was fifteen years old, the King summoned all three sisters to come before his throne. You should have seen how all the people gazed when the youngest entered, it was just as if the sun were rising! Then the King spoke: 'My daughters, I know not when my last day may arrive; I will to-day decide what each shall receive at my death. You all love me, but the one of you who loves me best, shall fare the best.' Each of them said she loved him best. 'Can you not express to me,' said the King, 'how much you do love me, and thus I shall see what you mean?' The eldest spoke: 'I love my father as dearly as the sweetest sugar.' The second: 'I love my father as dearly as my prettiest dress.' But the youngest was silent. Then the father said: 'And you, my dearest child, how much do you love me?' 'I do not know, and can compare my love with nothing.' But her father insisted that she should name something. So she said at last: 'The best food does not please me without salt, therefore I love my father like salt.' When the King heard that, he fell into a passion, and said: 'If you love me like salt, your love shall also be repaid you with salt.' Then he divided the kingdom between the two elder, but caused a sack of salt to be bound on the back of the youngest, and two servants had to lead her forth into the wild forest. We all begged and prayed for her," said the Queen, "but the King's anger was not to be appeased. How she cried when she had to leave us! The whole road was strewn with the pearls which flowed from her eyes. The King soon afterwards repented of his great severity, and had the whole forest searched for the poor child, but no one could find her. When I think that the wild beasts have devoured her, I know not how to contain myself for sorrow; many a time I console myself with the hope that she is still alive, and may have hidden herself in a cave, or has found shelter with compassionate people. But picture to yourself, when I opened your little emerald box, a pearl lay therein, of exactly the same kind as those which used to fall from my daughter's eyes; and then you can also imagine how the sight of it stirred my heart. You must tell me how you came by that pearl." The count told her that he had received it from the old woman in the forest, who had appeared very strange to him, and must be a witch, but he had neither seen nor heard anything of the Queen's child. The King and the Queen resolved to seek out the old woman. They thought that there where the pearl had been, they would obtain news of their daughter.

The old woman was sitting in that lonely place at her spinning-wheel, spinning. It was already dusk, and a log which was burning on the hearth gave a scanty light. All at once there was a noise outside, the geese were coming home from the pasture, and uttering their hoarse cries. Soon afterwards the daughter also entered. But the old woman scarcely thanked her, and only shook her head a little. The daughter sat down beside her, took her spinning-wheel, and twisted the threads as nimbly as a young girl. Thus they both sat for two hours, and exchanged never a word. At last something rustled at the window and two fiery eyes peered in. It was an old night-owl, which cried "Uhu" three times. The old woman looked up just a little, then she said: "Now, my little daughter, it is time for you to go out and do your work." She rose and went out, and where did she go? Over the meadows ever onward into the valley. At last she came to a well, with three old oak-trees standing beside it; meanwhile the moon had risen large and round over the mountain, and it was so light that one could have found a needle. She removed a skin which covered her face, then bent down to the well, and began to wash herself. When she had finished, she dipped the skin also in the water, and then laid it on the meadow, so that it should bleach in the moonlight, and dry again. But how the maiden was changed! Such a change as that was never seen before! When the gray mask fell off, her golden hair broke forth like sun-beams, and spread about like a mantle over her whole form. Her eyes shone out as brightly as the stars in heaven, and her cheeks bloomed a soft red like apple-blossom.

But the fair maiden was sad. She sat down and wept bitterly. One tear after another forced itself out of her eyes, and rolled through her long hair to the ground. There she sat, and would have remained sitting a long time, if there had not been a rustling and cracking in the boughs of the neighbouring tree. She sprang up like a roe which has been overtaken by the shot of the hunter. Just then the moon was obscured by a dark cloud, and in an instant the maiden had put on the old skin and vanished, like a light blown out by the wind.

She ran back home, trembling like an aspen-leaf. The old woman was standing on the threshold, and the girl was about to relate what had befallen her, but the old woman laughed kindly, and said: "I already know all." She led her into the room and lighted a new log. She did not, however, sit down to her spinning again, but fetched a broom and began to sweep and scour. "All must be clean and sweet," she said to the girl. "But, mother," said the maiden, "why do you begin work at so late an hour? What do you expect?" "Do you know then what time it is?" asked the old woman. "Not yet midnight," answered the maiden, "but already past eleven o'clock." "Do you not remember," continued the old woman, "that it is three years to-day since you came to me? Your time is up, we can no longer remain together." The girl was terrified, and said: "Alas! dear mother, will you cast me off? Where shall I go? I have no friends, and no home to which I can go. I have always done as you bade me, and you have always been satisfied with me; do not send me away." The old woman would not tell the maiden what lay before her. "My stay here is over," she said to her, "but when I depart, house and parlour must be clean: therefore do not hinder me in my work. Have no care for yourself, you shall find a roof to shelter you, and the wages which I will give you shall also content you." "But tell me what is about to happen," the maiden continued to entreat. "I tell you again, do not hinder me in my work. Do not say a word more, go to your chamber, take the skin off your face, and put on the silken gown which you had on when you came to me, and then wait in your chamber until I call you."

But I must once more tell of the King and Queen, who had journeyed forth with the count in order to seek out the old woman in the wilderness. The count had strayed away from them in the wood by night, and had to walk onwards alone. Next day it seemed to him that he was on the right track. He still went forward, until darkness came on, then he climbed a tree, intending to pass the night there, for he feared that he might lose his way. When the moon illumined the surrounding country he perceived a figure coming down the mountain. She had no stick in her hand, but yet he could see that it was the goose-girl, whom he had seen before in the house of the old woman. "Oho," cried he, "there she comes, and if I once get hold of one of the witches, the other shall not escape me!" But how astonished he was, when she went to the well, took off the skin and washed herself, when her golden hair fell down all about her, and she was more beautiful than anyone whom he had ever seen in the whole world. He hardly dared to breathe, but stretched his head as far forward through the leaves as he could, and stared at her. Either he bent over too far, or whatever the cause might be, the bough suddenly cracked, and that very moment the maiden slipped into the skin, sprang away like a roe, and as the moon was suddenly covered, disappeared from his sight. Hardly had she disappeared, before the count descended from the tree, and hastened after her with nimble steps. He had not been gone long before he saw, in the twilight, two figures coming over the meadow. It was the King and Queen, who had perceived from a distance the light shining in the old woman's little house, and were going to it. The count told them what wonderful things he had seen by the well, and they did not doubt that it had been their lost daughter. They walked onwards full of joy, and soon came to the little house. The geese were sitting all round it, and had thrust their heads under their wings and were sleeping, and not one of them moved. The King and Queen looked in at the window, where the old woman was sitting quite quietly spinning, nodding her head and never looking round. The room was perfectly clean, as if the little mist men, who carry no dust on their feet, lived there. Their daughter, however, they did not see. They gazed at all this for a long time, until at last they took heart, and knocked softly at the window. The old woman appeared to have been expecting them; she rose, and called out quite kindly: "Come in,—I know you already." When they had entered the room, the old woman said: "You might have spared yourself the long walk, if you had not three years ago unjustly driven away your child, who is so good and lovable. No harm has come to her; for three years she has had to tend the geese; with them she has learnt no evil, but has preserved her purity of heart. You, however, have been sufficiently punished by the misery in which you have lived." Then she went to the chamber and called: "Come out, my little daughter." Thereupon the door opened, and the princess stepped out in her silken garments, with her golden hair and her shining eyes, and it was as if an angel from heaven had entered.

She went up to her father and mother, fell on their necks and kissed them; there was no help for it, they all had to weep for joy. The young count stood near them, and when she perceived him she became as red in the face as a moss-rose, she herself did not know why. The King said: "My dear child, I have given away my kingdom, what shall I give you?" "She needs nothing," said the old woman. "I give her the tears that she has wept on your account; they are precious pearls, finer than those that are found in the sea, and worth more than your whole kingdom, and I give her my little house as payment for her services." When the old woman had said that, she disappeared from their sight. The walls rattled a little, and when the King and Queen looked round, the little house had changed into a splendid palace, a royal table had been spread, and the servants were running hither and thither.

The story goes still further, but my grandmother, who related it to me, had partly lost her memory, and had forgotten the rest. I shall always believe that the beautiful princess married the count, and that they remained together in the palace, and lived there in all happiness so long as God willed it. Whether the snow-white geese, which were kept near the little hut, were verily young maidens (no one need take offence), whom the old woman had taken under her protection, and whether they now received their human form again, and stayed as handmaids to the young Queen, I do not exactly know, but I suspect it. This much is certain, that the old woman was no witch, as people thought, but a wise woman, who meant well. Very likely it was she who, at the princess's birth, gave her the gift of weeping pearls instead of tears. That does not happen nowadays, or else the poor would soon become rich.

EVE'S VARIOUS CHILDREN

When Adam and Eve were driven out of Paradise, they were compelled to build a house for themselves on barren ground, and eat their bread in the sweat of their brow. Adam dug up the land, and Eve spun. Every year Eve brought a child into the world; but the children were unlike each other, some pretty, and some ugly. After a considerable time had gone by, God sent an angel to them, to announce that he was coming to inspect their household. Eve, delighted that the Lord should be so gracious, cleaned her house diligently, decked it with flowers, and strewed rushes on the floor. Then she brought in her children, but only the beautiful ones. She washed and bathed them, combed their hair, put clean raiment on them, and cautioned them to conduct themselves decorously and modestly in the presence of the Lord. They were to bow down before him civilly, hold out their hands, and to answer his questions modestly and sensibly. The ugly children, however, were not to let themselves be seen. One hid himself beneath the hay, another under the roof, a third in the straw, the fourth in the stove, the fifth in the cellar, the sixth under a tub, the seventh beneath the wine-cask, the eighth under an old fur cloak, the ninth and tenth beneath the cloth out of which she always made their clothes, and the eleventh and twelfth under the leather out of which she cut their shoes. She had

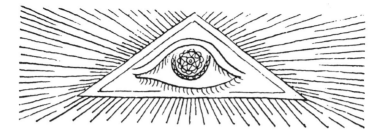

scarcely got ready, before there was a knock at the house-door. Adam looked through a chink, and saw that it was the Lord. Adam opened the door respectfully, and the Heavenly Father entered. There, in a row, stood the pretty children, and bowed before him, held out their hands, and knelt down. The Lord, however, began to bless them, laid his hands on the first, and said: "Thou shalt be a powerful king;" and to the second: "Thou a prince," to the third: "Thou a count," to the fourth: "Thou a knight," to the fifth: "Thou a nobleman," to the sixth: "Thou a burgher," to the seventh: "Thou a merchant," to the eighth: "Thou a learned man." He bestowed upon them also all his richest blessings. When Eve saw that the Lord was so mild and gracious, she thought: "I will bring hither my ill-favoured children also, it may be that he will bestow his blessing on them likewise." So she ran and brought them out of the hay, the straw, the stove, and wherever else she had concealed them. Then came the whole coarse, dirty, scabby, sooty band. The Lord smiled, looked at them all, and said: "I will bless these also." He laid his hands on the first, and said to him: "Thou shalt be a peasant," to the second: "Thou a fisherman," to the third: "Thou a smith," to the fourth: "Thou a tanner," to the fifth: "Thou a weaver," to the sixth: "Thou a shoemaker," to the seventh: "Thou a tailor," to the eighth: "Thou a potter," to the ninth: "Thou a waggoner," to the tenth: "Thou a sailor," to the eleventh: "Thou a messenger," to the twelfth: "Thou a scullion all the days of thy life."

When Eve had heard all this she said: "Lord, how unequally thou dividest thy gifts! After all they are all of them my children, whom I have brought into the world, thy favours should be given to all alike." But God answered: "Eve, thou dost not understand. It is right and necessary that the entire world should be supplied from thy children;

if they were all princes and lords, who would grow corn, thresh it, grind and bake it? Who would be blacksmiths, weavers, carpenters, masons, labourers, tailors and seamstresses? Each shall have his own place, so that one shall support the other, and all shall be fed like the limbs of one body." Then Eve answered: "Ah, Lord, forgive me, I was too quick in speaking to thee. Have thy divine will with my children."

THE NIXIE OF THE MILL-POND

There was once upon a time a miller who lived with his wife in great contentment. They had money and land, and their prosperity increased year by year more and more. But ill luck comes like a thief in the night: as their wealth had increased so did it again decrease, year by year, and at last the miller could hardly call the mill in which he lived, his own. He was in great distress, and when he lay down after his day's work, found no rest, but tossed about in his bed, sorely troubled. One morning he rose before daybreak and went out into the open air, thinking that perhaps there his heart might become lighter. As he was stepping over the mill-dam the first sunbeam was just breaking forth, and he heard a rippling sound in the pond. He turned round and perceived a beautiful woman, rising slowly out of the water. Her long hair, which she was holding off her shoulders with her soft hands, fell down on both sides, and covered her white body. He soon saw that she was the nixie of the mill-pond, and in his fright did not know whether he should run away or stay where he was. But the nixie made her sweet voice heard, called him by his name, and asked him why he was so sad. The miller was at first struck dumb, but when he heard her speak so kindly, he took heart, and told her how he had formerly lived in wealth and happiness, but that now he was so poor that he did not know what to do. "Be easy," answered the nixie, "I will make you richer and happier than you have ever been before, only you must promise to give me the young thing which has just been born in your house." "What else can that be," thought the miller, "but a puppy or a kitten?" and he promised her what she desired. The nixie descended into the water again, and he hurried back to his mill, consoled and in good spirits. He had not yet reached it, when the maid-servant came out of the house, and cried to him to rejoice, for his wife had given birth to a little boy. The miller stood as if struck by lightning; he saw very well that the cunning nixie had been aware of it, and had cheated him. Hanging his head, he went up to his wife's bedside and when she said: "Why do you not rejoice over the fine boy?" he told her what had befallen him, and what kind of a promise he had given to the nixie. "Of what use to me are riches and prosperity?" he added, "if I am to lose my child; but what can I do?" Even the relatives, who had come thither to wish them joy, did not know what to say. In the meantime prosperity again returned to the miller's house. All that he undertook succeeded. It was as if presses and coffers filled themselves of their own accord, and as if money multiplied nightly in the cupboards. It was not long before his wealth was greater than it had ever been before. But he could not rejoice over it untroubled, for the bargain which he had made with the nixie tormented his soul. Whenever he passed the mill-pond, he feared she might ascend and remind him of his debt. He never let the boy himself go near the water. "Beware," he said to him, "if you do but touch the water, a hand will rise, seize you, and draw you down." But as year after year went by and the nixie did not show herself again, the miller began to feel at ease. The boy grew up to be a youth and was apprenticed to a huntsman. When he had learnt everything, and had become an excellent huntsman, the lord of the village took him into his service. In the village lived a beautiful and true-hearted maiden, who pleased the huntsman, and when his master perceived that, he gave him a little house, the two were married, lived peacefully and happily, and loved each other with all their hearts.

One day the huntsman was chasing a roe; and when the animal turned aside from the forest into the open country, he pursued it and at last shot it. He did not notice that he was now in the neighborhood of the dangerous mill-pond, and went, after he had disembowelled the roe, to the water, in order to wash his blood-stained hands. Scarcely, however, had he dipped them in than the nixie ascended, smilingly wound her dripping arms around him, and drew him quickly down under the waves, which closed over him. When it was evening, and the huntsman did not return home, his wife became alarmed. She went out to seek him, and as he had often told her that he had to be on his guard against the snares of the nixie, and dared not venture into the neighbourhood of the mill-pond, she already suspected what had happened. She hastened to the water, and when she found his hunting-pouch lying on the shore, she could no longer have any doubt of the misfortune. Lamenting her sorrow, and wringing her hands, she called on her beloved by name, but in vain. She hurried across to the other side of the pond, and called him anew; she reviled the nixie with harsh words, but no answer greeted her. The surface of the water remained calm, only the crescent moon stared steadily back at her. The poor woman did not leave the pond. With hasty steps, she paced round and round it, without resting a moment, sometimes in silence, sometimes uttering a loud cry, sometimes softly sobbing. At last her strength came to an end, she sank down to the ground and fell into a heavy sleep. Presently a dream took possession of her.

She was anxiously climbing upwards between great masses of rock; thorns and briars caught her feet, the rain beat in her face, and the wind tossed her long hair about. When she had reached the summit, quite a different sight presented itself to her; the sky was blue, the air soft, the ground sloped gently downwards, and on a green meadow, gay with flowers of every colour, stood a pretty cottage. She went up to it and opened the door; there sat an old woman with white hair, who beckoned to her kindly. At that very moment, the poor woman awoke, day had already dawned, and she at once resolved to act in accordance with her dream. She laboriously climbed the mountain; everything was exactly as she had seen it in the night. The old woman received her kindly, and pointed out a chair on which she might sit. "You must have met with a misfortune," she said, "since you have sought out my lonely cottage." With tears, the woman related what had befallen her. "Be comforted," said the old woman, "I will help you. Here is a golden comb for you. Tarry till the full moon has risen, then go to the millpond, seat yourself on the shore, and comb your long black hair with this comb. When you have done, lay it down on the bank, and you will see what will happen." The woman returned home, but the time till the full moon came, passed slowly. When at last the shining disc appeared in the heavens, she went out to the mill-pond, sat down and combed her long black hair with the golden comb, and when she had finished, she laid it down at the water's edge. It was not long before

there was a movement in the depths, a wave rose, rolled to the shore, and bore the comb away with it. In not more than the time necessary for the comb to sink to the bottom, the surface of the water parted, and the head of the huntsman arose. He did not speak, but looked at his wife with sorrowful glances. At the same instant, a second wave came rushing up, and covered the man's head. All had vanished, the mill-pond lay peaceful as before, and nothing but the face of the full moon shone on it.

Full of sorrow, the woman went back, but again the dream showed her the cottage of the old woman. Next morning she again set out and complained of her woes to the wise woman. The old woman gave her a golden flute, and said: "Tarry till the full moon comes again, then take this flute; play a beautiful air on it, and when you have finished, lay it on the sand; then you will see what will happen." The wife did as the old woman told her. No sooner was the flute lying on the sand than there was a stirring in the depths, and a wave rushed up and bore the flute away with it. Immediately afterwards the water parted, and not only the head of the man, but half of his body also arose. He stretched out his arms longingly towards her, but a second wave came up, covered him, and drew him down again. "Alas, what does it help me," said the unhappy woman, "that I should see my beloved, only to lose him again?" Despair filled her heart anew, but the dream led her a third time to the house of the old woman. She set out, and the wise woman gave her a golden spinning-wheel, consoled her and said: "All is not yet fulfilled, tarry until the time of the full moon, then take the spinning-wheel, seat yourself on the shore, and spin the spool full, and when you have done that, place the spinning-wheel near the water, and you will see what will happen." The woman obeyed all she said exactly; as soon as the full moon showed itself, she carried the golden spinning-wheel to the shore, and span industriously until the flax came to an end, and the spool was quite filled with the threads. No sooner was the wheel standing on the shore than there was a more violent movement than before in the depths of the pond, and a mighty wave rushed up, and bore the wheel away with it. Immediately the head and the whole body of the man rose into the air, in a water-spout. He quickly sprang to the shore, caught his wife by the hand and fled. But they had scarcely gone a very little distance, when the whole pond rose with a frightful roar, and streamed out over the open country. The fugitives already saw death before their eyes, when the woman in her terror implored the help of the old woman, and in an instant they were transformed, she into a toad, he into a frog. The flood which had overtaken them could not destroy them, but it tore them apart and carried them far away.

When the water had dispersed and they both touched dry land again, they regained their human form, but neither knew where the other was; they found themselves among strange people, who did not know their native land. High mountains and deep valleys lay between them. In order to keep themselves alive, they were both obliged to tend sheep. For many long years they drove their flocks through field and forest and were full of sorrow and longing.

When spring had once more broken forth on the earth, they both went out one day with their flocks, and as chance would have it, they drew near each other. They met in a valley, but did not recognize each other; yet they rejoiced that they were no longer so lonely. Henceforth they each day drove their flocks to the same place; they did not speak much, but they felt comforted. One evening when the full moon was shining in the sky, and the sheep were already at rest, the shepherd pulled the flute out of his pocket, and played on it a beautiful but sorrowful air. When he had finished he saw that the shepherdess was weeping bitterly. "Why are you weeping?" he asked. "Alas," answered she, "thus shone the full moon when I played this air on the flute for the last time, and the head of my beloved rose out of the water." He looked at her, and it seemed as if a veil fell from his eyes, and he recognized his dear wife, and when she looked at him, and the moon shone in his face she knew him also. They embraced and kissed each other, and no one need ask if they were happy.

THE LITTLE FOLKS' PRESENTS

A tailor and a goldsmith were travelling together, and one evening when the sun had sunk behind the mountains, they heard the sound of distant music, which became more and more distinct. It sounded strange, but so pleasant that they forgot all their weariness and stepped quickly onwards. The moon had already arisen when they reached a hill on which they saw a crowd of little men and women, who had taken each other's hands, and were whirling round in the dance with the greatest pleasure and delight.

They sang to it most charmingly, and that was the music which the travellers had heard. In the midst of them sat an old man who was rather taller than the rest. He wore a parti-coloured coat, and his hoary beard hung down over his breast. The two remained standing full of astonishment, and watched the dance. The old man made a sign that they should enter, and the little folks willingly opened their circle. The goldsmith, who had a hump, and like all hunchbacks was daring enough, stepped in; the tailor felt a little afraid at first, and held back, but when he saw how merrily all was going, he plucked up his courage, and followed. The circle closed again directly, and the little folks went on singing and dancing with the wildest leaps. The old man, however, took a large knife which hung to his girdle, whetted it, and when it was sufficiently sharpened, he looked round at the strangers. They were terrified, but they had not much time for reflection, for the old man seized the goldsmith and with the greatest speed, shaved the hair of his head clean off, and then the same thing happened to the tailor. But their fear left them when, after he had finished his work, the old man clapped them both on the shoulder in a friendly manner, as much as to say, they had behaved well to let all that be done to them willingly, and without any struggle. He pointed with his finger to a heap of coals which lay at one side, and signified to the travellers by his gestures that they were to fill their pockets with them. Both of them obeyed, although they did not know of what use the coals would be to them, and then they went on their way to seek a shelter for the night. When they had got into the valley, the clock of the neighbouring monastery struck twelve, and the song ceased. In a moment all had vanished, and the hill lay in solitude in the moonlight.

The two travellers found an inn, and covered themselves up on their straw-beds with their coats, but in their weariness forgot to take the coals out of them before doing so. A heavy weight on their limbs awakened them earlier than usual. They felt in the pockets, and could not believe their eyes when they saw that they were not filled with coals, but with pure gold; happily, too, the hair of their heads and beards was there again as thick as ever.

They had now become rich folks, but the goldsmith, who, in accordance with his greedy disposition, had filled his pockets better, was twice as rich as the tailor. A greedy man, even if he has much, still wishes to have more, so the goldsmith proposed to the tailor that they should wait another day, go out again in the evening in order to bring back still greater treasures from the old man on the hill. The tailor refused, and said: "I have enough and am content; now I shall be a master, and marry my dear object (for so he called his sweetheart), and I am a happy man." But he stayed another day to please him. In the evening the goldsmith hung a couple of bags over his shoulders that he might be able to stow away a great deal, and took the road to the hill.

He found, as on the night before, the little folks at their singing and dancing, and the old man again shaved him clean, and made signs to him to take some coal. He was not slow about stuffing as much into his bags as would go, went back quite delighted, and covered himself over with his coat. "Even if the gold does weigh heavily," said he, "I will gladly bear that," and at last he fell asleep with the sweet anticipation of waking in the morning an enormously rich man.

When he opened his eyes, he got up in haste to examine his pockets, but how amazed he was when he drew nothing out of them but black coals, and that howsoever often he put his hands in them. "The gold I got the night before is still there for me," thought he, and went and brought it out, but how shocked he was when he saw that it likewise had again turned into coal. He smote his forehead with his dusty black

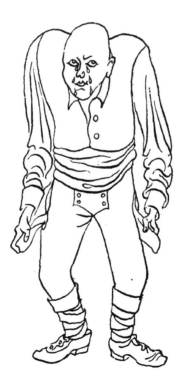

hand, and then he felt that his whole head was bald and smooth, as was also the place where his beard should have been. But his misfortunes were not yet over; he now remarked for the first time that in addition to the hump on his back, a second, just as large, had grown in front on his breast. Then he recognized the punishment of his greediness, and began to weep aloud. The good tailor, who was awakened by this, comforted the unhappy fellow as well as he could, and said: "You have been my comrade in my travelling time; you shall stay with me and share in my wealth." He kept his word, but the poor goldsmith was obliged to carry the two humps as long as he lived, and to cover his bald head with a cap.

THE GIANT AND THE TAILOR

A certain tailor who was great at boasting but ill at doing, took it into his head to go abroad for a while, and look about the world. As soon as he could manage it, he left his workshop, and wandered on his way, over hill and dale, sometimes hither, sometimes thither, but ever on and on. Once on his way he perceived in the blue distance a steep hill, and behind it a tower reaching to the clouds, which rose up out of a wild dark forest. "Thunder and lightning," cried the tailor, "what is that?" and as he was strongly goaded by curiosity, he went boldly towards it. But how he did gaze and gape when he came near it, for the tower had legs, and leapt in one bound over the steep hill, and was now standing as an all-powerful giant before him. "What do you want here, you tiny fly's leg?" cried the giant, with a voice as if it were thundering on every side. The tailor whimpered: "I want just to look about and see if I can earn a bit of bread for myself, in this forest." "If that is what you are after," said the giant, "you may have a place with me." "If it must be, why not? What wages shall I receive?" "You shall hear what wages you shall have. Every year three hundred and sixty-five days, and when it is leap-year, one more into the bargain. Does that suit you?" "All right," replied the tailor, and thought, in his own mind, "a man must cut his coat according to his cloth; I will try to get away as fast as I can."

At this the giant said to him: "Go, little ragamuffin, and fetch me a jug of water." "Had I not better bring the well itself at once, and the spring too?" asked the boaster, and went with the pitcher to the water. "What! the well and the spring too," growled the giant in his beard, for he was somewhat of a silly dolt, and began to be afraid. "That knave is not a fool, he has a mandrake in his body. Be on your guard, old Hans, this is no serving-man for you." When the tailor had brought the water, the giant bade him go into the forest, and cut a couple of blocks of wood and bring them back. "Why not the whole forest, at once, with one stroke. The whole forest, young and old, with all that is there, both gnarled and smooth?" asked the little tailor, and went to cut the wood. "What! the whole forest, young and old, with all that is there, both gnarled and smooth, and the well and its spring too," growled the credulous giant in his beard, and was still more terrified. "The knave can do much more than bake apples, and has a mandrake in his body. Be on your guard, old Hans, this is no serving-man for you!" When the tailor had brought the

wood, the giant commanded him to shoot two or three wild boars for supper. "Why not rather a thousand at one shot, and bring them all here?" inquired the insolent tailor. "What!" cried the timid giant in great terror; "let well alone to-night, and lie down to rest."

The giant was so terribly alarmed that he could not close an eye all night long for thinking what would be the best way to get rid of this accursed sorcerer of a servant. Time brings counsel. Next morning the giant and the tailor went to a marsh, round which stood a number of willow-trees. Then said the giant: "Listen, tailor, seat yourself on one of the willow-branches; I long of all things to see if you are big enough to bend it down." All at once the tailor was sitting on it, holding his breath, and making himself heavy, so heavy that the bough bent down. When, however, he was compelled to draw breath, it hurled him (for unfortunately he had not put his goose in his pocket) so high into the air that he never was seen again, and this to the great delight of the giant. If the tailor has not fallen down again, he must still be hovering about in the air.

THE NAIL

A merchant had done good business at the fair; he had sold his wares, and lined his money-bags with gold and silver. Then he wanted to travel homewards, and be in his own house before nightfall. So he packed his trunk with the money on his horse, and rode away.

At noon he rested in a town, and when he wanted to go farther the stable-boy brought out his horse and said: "A nail is wanting, sir, in the shoe of its near hind foot." "Let it be wanting," answered the merchant; "the shoe will certainly stay on for the six miles I have still to go. I am in a hurry."

In the afternoon, when he once more alighted and had his horse fed, the stable-boy went into the room to him and said: "Sir, a shoe is missing from your horse's near hind foot. Shall I take him to the blacksmith?" "Let it be wanting," answered the man; "the horse can very well hold out for the couple of miles which remain. I am in haste."

He rode forth, but before long the horse began to limp. It had not limped long before it began to stumble, and it had not stumbled long before it fell down and broke its leg. The merchant was forced to leave the horse where it was, and unbuckle the trunk, take it on his back, and go home on foot. And there he did not arrive until quite late at night. "And that cursed nail," said he to himself, "has caused all this disaster."

The more haste the less speed.

THE POOR BOY IN THE GRAVE

There was once a poor shepherd-boy whose father and mother were dead, and he was placed by the authorities in the house of a rich man, who was to feed him and bring him up. The man and his wife, however, had bad hearts, and were greedy and jealous of their riches, and vexed whenever anyone put a morsel of their bread in his mouth. The poor young fellow might do what he liked, he got little to eat, but only so many blows the more.

One day he had to watch a hen and her chickens, but she escaped through a hedge with them, and a hawk darted down instantly, and carried her off through the air. The boy called: "Thief! thief! rascal!" with all the strength of his body. But what good did that do? The hawk did not bring its prey back again. The man heard the noise, and ran to the spot, and as soon as he saw that his hen was gone, he fell in a rage, and gave the boy such a beating that he could not stir for two days. Then he had to take care of the chickens without the hen, but now his difficulty was greater, for one ran here and the other there. He thought he was doing a very wise thing when he tied them all together with a string, because then the hawk would not be able to steal any of them away from him. But he was very much mistaken. After two days, worn out with running about and hunger, he fell asleep; the bird of prey came, and seized one of the chickens, and as the others were tied fast to it, it carried them all off together, perched itself on a tree, and devoured them. The farmer was just coming home, and when he saw the misfortune, he got angry and beat the boy so unmercifully that he was forced to lie in bed for several days.

When he was on his legs again, the farmer said to him: "You are too stupid for me, I cannot make a herdsman of you, you must go as errand-boy." Then he sent him to the judge, to whom he was to carry a basketful of grapes, and he gave him a letter as well. On the way hunger and thirst tormented the unhappy boy so violently that he ate two grapes. He took the basket to the judge, but when the judge had read the letter, and counted the grapes he said: "Two are missing." The boy confessed quite honestly that, driven by hunger and thirst, he had devoured the two which were missing. The judge wrote a letter to the farmer, and asked for the same number of grapes again. These also the boy had to take to him with a letter. As he again was so extremely hungry and thirsty, he could not help it, and again ate two grapes. But first he took the letter out of the basket, put it under a stone and seated himself thereon in order that the letter might not see and betray him. The judge, however, again made him give an explanation about the missing grapes. "Ah," said the boy, "how have you learnt that? The letter could not know about it, for I put it under a stone before I did it." The judge could not help laughing at the boy's simplicity, and sent the man a letter wherein he cautioned him to look after the poor boy better, and not let him want for meat and drink, and also that he was to teach him what was right and what was wrong.

"I will soon show you the difference," said the hard man, "if you will eat, you must work, and if you do anything wrong, you shall be quite sufficiently taught by blows."

The next day he set him a hard task. He was to chop two bundles of hay for food for the horses, and then the man threatened: "In five hours," said he, "I shall be back again, and if the hay is not chopped by that time, I will beat you until you can not move a limb." The farmer went with his wife, the man-servant and the girl, to the yearly fair, and left nothing behind for the boy but a small bit of bread. The boy seated himself on the bench, and began to work with all his might. As he got warm over it he put his little coat off and threw it on the hay. In his terror lest he should not get done in time he kept constantly cutting, and in his haste, without noticing it, he chopped his little coat as well as the hay. He became aware of the misfortune too late; there was no repairing it. "Ah," cried he, "now all is over with me! The wicked man did not threaten me for nothing; if he comes back and sees what I have done, he will kill me. Rather than that I will take my own life."

The boy had once heard the farmer's wife say: "I have a pot with poison in it under my bed." She, however, had only said that to keep away greedy people, for there was honey in it. The boy crept under the bed, brought out the pot, and ate all that was in it. "I do not know," said he, "folks say death is bitter, but it tastes very sweet to me. It is no wonder that the farmer's wife has so often longed for death." He seated himself in a little chair, and was prepared to die. But instead of becoming weaker he felt himself strengthened by the nourishing food. "It cannot have been poison," thought he, "but the farmer once said there

was a small bottle of poison for flies in the closet in which he keeps his clothes; that, no doubt, will be the true poison, and bring death to me." It was, however, no poison for flies, but Hungarian wine. The boy got out the bottle, and emptied it. "This death tastes sweet too," said he, but shortly after when the wine began to mount into his brain and stupefy him, he thought his end was drawing near. "I feel that I must die," said he, "I will go away to the churchyard, and seek a grave." He staggered out, reached the churchyard, and laid himself in a newly-dug grave. He lost his senses more and more. In the neighborhood was an inn where a wedding was being held; when he heard the music, he fancied he was already in Paradise, until at length he lost all consciousness. The poor boy never awoke again; the heat of the strong wine and the cold night-dew deprived him of life, and he remained in the grave in which he had laid himself.

When the farmer heard the news of the boy's death he was terrified, and afraid of being brought to justice—indeed, his distress took such a powerful hold of him that he fell fainting to the ground. His wife, who was standing by the hearth with a pan of hot fat, ran to him to help him. But the flames enveloped the pan, the whole house caught fire, in a few hours it lay in ashes, and the rest of the years they had to live they passed in poverty and misery, tormented by the pangs of conscience.

THE TRUE BRIDE

There was once upon a time a girl who was young and beautiful, but she had lost her mother when she was quite a child, and her stepmother did all she could to make the girl's life wretched. Whenever this woman gave her anything to do, she worked at it indefatigably, and did everything that lay in her power. Still she could not touch the heart of the wicked woman; she was never satisfied; it was never enough. The harder the girl worked, the more work was put upon her, and all that the woman thought of was how to weigh her down with still heavier burdens, and make her life still more miserable.

One day she said to her: "Here are twelve pounds of feathers which you must pick, and if they are not done this evening, you may expect a

good beating. Do you imagine you are to idle away the whole day?"
The poor girl sat down to the work, but tears ran down her cheeks as
she did so, for she saw plainly enough that it was quite impossible to
finish the work in one day. Whenever she had a little heap of feathers
lying before her, and she sighed or smote her hands together in her
anguish, they flew away, and she had to pick them up again, and begin
her work anew. Then she put her elbows on the table, laid her face in
her two hands, and cried: "Is there no one, then, on God's earth to have
pity on me?" Then she heard a low voice which said: "Be comforted,
my child, I have come to help you." The maiden looked up, and an old
woman was by her side. She took the girl kindly by the hand, and said:
"Only tell me what is troubling you." As she spoke so kindly, the girl
told her of her miserable life, and how one burden after another was
laid upon her, and she never could get to the end of the work which
was given to her. "If I have not done these feathers by this evening, my
step-mother will beat me; she has threatened she will, and I know she
keeps her word." Her tears began to flow again, but the good old
woman said: "Do not be afraid, my child; rest a while, and in the
meantime I will look to your work." The girl lay down on her bed, and
soon fell asleep. The old woman seated herself at the table with the
feathers, and how they did fly off the quills, which she scarcely
touched with her withered hands! The twelve pounds were soon finished, and when the girl awoke, great snow-white heaps were lying,
piled up, and everything in the room was neatly cleared away, but the
old woman had vanished. The maiden thanked God, and sat still till
evening came, when the step-mother came in and marvelled to see the
work completed. "Just look, you awkward creature," said she, "what
can be done when people are industrious; and why could you not set
about something else? There you sit with your hands crossed." When
she went out she said: "The creature is worth more than her salt. I must
give her some work that is still harder."

Next morning she called the girl, and said: "There is a spoon for
you; with that you must empty out the great pond which is beside the
garden, and if it is not done by night, you know what will happen."
The girl took the spoon, and saw that it was full of holes; but even if it
had not been, she never could have emptied the pond with it. She set to
work at once, knelt down by the water, into which her tears were

falling, and began to empty it. But the good old woman appeared again, and when she learnt the cause of her grief, she said: "Be of good cheer, my child. Go into the thicket and lie down and sleep; I will soon do your work." As soon as the old woman was alone, she barely touched the pond, and a vapour rose up on high from the water, and mingled itself with the clouds. Gradually the pond was emptied, and when the maiden awoke before sunset and came thither, she saw nothing but the fishes which were struggling in the mud. She went to her step-mother, and showed her that the work was done. "It ought to have been done long before this," said she, and grew white with anger, but she meditated something new.

On the third morning she said to the girl: "You must build me a castle on the plain there, and it must be ready by the evening." The maiden was dismayed, and said: "How can I complete such a great work?" "I will endure no opposition," screamed the step-mother. "If you can empty a pond with a spoon that is full of holes, you can build a castle too. I will take possession of it this very day, and if anything is wanting, even if it be the most trifling thing in the kitchen or cellar, you know what lies before you!" She drove the girl out, and when she entered the valley, the rocks were there, piled up one above the other, and all her strength would not have enabled her even to move the very smallest of them. She sat down and wept, and still she hoped the old woman would help her. The old woman was not long in coming; she comforted her and said: "Lie down there in the shade and sleep, and I will soon build the castle for you. If it would be a pleasure to you, you can live in it yourself." When the maiden had gone away, the old woman touched the gray rocks. They began to rise, moved together and stood there as if giants had built the walls; and on these the building arose, and it seemed as if countless hands were working invisibly, and placing one stone upon another. There was a dull heavy noise from the ground; pillars arose of their own accord on high, and placed themselves in order near each other. The tiles laid themselves in order on the roof, and when noon-day came, the great weather-cock was already turning itself on the summit of the tower, like a golden maid with fluttering garments. The inside of the castle was being finished while evening was drawing near. How the old woman managed it, I know not; but the walls of the rooms were hung with silk and velvet;

embroidered chairs were there, and richly ornamented arm-chairs by marble tables; crystal chandeliers hung down from the ceilings, and mirrored themselves in the smooth floor; green parrots were there in gilt cages, and so were strange birds which sang most beautifully, and there was on all sides as much magnificence as if a king were going to live there. The sun was just setting when the girl awoke, and the brightness of a thousand lights flashed in her face. She hurried to the castle, and entered by the open door. The steps were spread with red cloth, and the golden balustrade beset with flowering trees. When she saw the splendour of the rooms, she stood as if turned to stone. Who knows how long she might have stood there if she had not remembered the step-mother? "Alas!" she said to herself, "if she could but be satisfied at last, and would give up making my life a misery to me." The girl went and told her that the castle was ready. "I will move into it at once," said she, and rose from her seat. When they entered the castle, she was forced to hold her hand before her eyes, the brilliancy of everything was so dazzling. "You see," said she to the girl, "how easy it has been for you to do this; I ought to have given you something harder." She went through all the rooms, and examined every corner to see if anything was wanting or defective; but she could discover nothing. "Now we will go down below," said she, looking at the girl with malicious eyes. "The kitchen and the cellar still have to be examined and if you have forgotten anything you shall not escape your punishment." But the fire was burning on the hearth, and the meat was cooking in the pans, the tongs and shovel were leaning against the wall, and the shining brazen utensils all arranged in sight. Nothing was missing, not even a coal-box and a water-pail. "Which is the way to the cellar?" she cried. "If that is not abundantly filled with wine casks it shall go ill with you." She herself raised up the trap-door and descended; but she had hardly made two steps before the heavy trap-door which was only laid back, fell down. The girl heard a scream, lifted up the door very quickly to go to her aid, but she had fallen down, and the girl found her lying lifeless at the bottom.

And now the magnificent castle belonged to the girl alone. She at first did not know how to reconcile herself to her good fortune. Beautiful dresses were hanging in the wardrobes, the chests were filled with gold and silver, or with pearls and jewels, and she never felt a desire that she was not able to gratify. And soon the fame of the beauty and riches of the maiden went over all the world. Wooers presented themselves daily, but none pleased her. At length the son of the King came and he knew how to touch her heart, and she betrothed herself to him. In the garden of the castle was a lime-tree, under which they were one day sitting together, when he said to her: "I will go home and obtain my father's consent to our marriage. I entreat you to wait for me here under this lime-tree, I shall be back with you in a few hours." The maiden kissed him on his left cheek, and said: "Keep true to me, and never let any one else kiss you on this cheek. I will wait here under the lime-tree until you return."

The maid stayed beneath the lime-tree until sunset, but he did not return. She sat there three days from morning till evening, waiting for him, but in vain. As he still was not there by the fourth day, she said: "Some accident has assuredly befallen him. I will go out and seek him, and will not come back until I have found him." She packed up three of her most beautiful dresses, one embroidered with bright stars, the second with silver moons, the third with golden suns, tied up a handful of jewels in her handkerchief, and set out. She inquired everywhere for her betrothed, but no one had seen him; no one knew anything about him. Far and wide did she wander through the world, but she found him not. At last she hired herself to a farmer as a cowherd, and buried her dresses and jewels beneath a stone.

And now she lived as a herdswoman, guarded her herd, and was very sad and full of longing for her beloved; she had a little calf which she taught to know her, and fed it out of her own hand, and when she said:

> "Little calf, little calf, kneel by my side,
> And do not forget your cowherd-maid,
> As the prince forgot his betrothed bride,
> Who waited for him 'neath the lime-tree's shade."

the little calf knelt down, and she stroked it.

And when she had lived for a couple of years alone and full of grief, a report was spread over all the land that the King's daughter was about to celebrate her marriage. The road to the town passed through the

village where the maiden was living, and it came to pass that once when the maiden was driving out her herd, the bridegroom travelled by. He was sitting proudly on his horse, and never looked round, but when she saw him she recognized her beloved, and it was just as if a sharp knife had pierced her heart. "Alas!" said she, "I believed him true to me, but he has forgotten me."

Next day he again came along the road. When he was near her she said to the little calf:

"Little calf, little calf, kneel by my side,
And do not forget your cowherd-maid,
As the prince forgot his betrothed bride,
Who waited for him 'neath the lime-tree's shade."

When he was aware of the voice, he looked down and reined in his horse. He looked into the girl's face and then put his hands before his eyes as if he were trying to remember something, but he soon rode onwards and was out of sight. "Alas!" said she, "he no longer knows me," and her grief was ever greater.

Soon after this a great festival three days long was to be held at the King's court, and the whole country was invited to it.

"Now will I try my last chance," thought the maiden, and when evening came she went to the stone under which she had buried her treasures. She took out the dress with the golden suns, put it on, and adorned herself with the jewels. She let down her hair, which she had concealed under a handkerchief, and it fell down in long curls about her, and thus she went into the town, and in the darkness was observed by no one. When she entered the brightly-lighted hall, every one started back in amazement, but no one knew who she was. The King's son went to meet her, but he did not recognize her. He led her out to dance, and was so enchanted with her beauty, that he thought no more of the other bride. When the feast was over, she vanished in the crowd, and hastened before daybreak to the village, where she once more put on her herd's dress.

Next evening she took out the dress with the silver moons, and put a half-moon made of precious stones in her hair. When she appeared at the festival, all eyes were turned upon her, but the King's son hastened to meet her, and filled with love for her, danced with her alone, and no longer so much as glanced at anyone else. Before she went away she was forced to promise him to come again to the festival on the last evening.

When she appeared for the third time, she wore the star-dress which sparkled at every step she took, and her hair-ribbon and girdle were starred with jewels. The prince had already been waiting for her for a long time, and forced his way up to her. "Do but tell who you are," said he, "I feel just as if I had already known you a long time." "Do you not know what I did when you left me?" Then she stepped up to him, and kissed him on his left cheek, and in a moment it was as if scales fell from his eyes, and he recognized the true bride. "Come," said he to her, "here I stay no longer," gave her his hand, and led her down to the carriage. The horses hurried away to the magic castle as if the wind had been harnessed to the carriage. The illuminated windows already shone in the distance. When they drove past the lime-tree, countless glow-worms were swarming about it. It shook its branches, and sent forth their fragrance. On the steps flowers were blooming, and the rooms echoed with the song of strange birds, but in the hall the entire court was assembled, and the priest was waiting to marry the bridegroom to the true bride.

THE HARE AND THE HEDGEHOG

This story, my dear young folks, seems to be false, but it really is true, for my grandfather, from whom I have it, used always, when relating it, to say: "It must be true, my son, or else no one could tell it to you." The story is as follows. One Sunday morning about harvest time, just as the buckwheat was in bloom, the sun was shining brightly in heaven, the cast wind was blowing warmly over the stubble-fields, the larks were singing in the air, the bees buzzing among the buckwheat, the people in their Sunday clothes were all going to church, and all creatures were happy, and the hedgehog was happy too.

The hedgehog, however, was standing by his door with his arms akimbo, enjoying the morning breezes, and slowly trilling a little song to himself, which was neither better nor worse than the songs which hedgehogs are in the habit of singing on a blessed Sunday morning. Whilst he was thus singing half aloud to himself, it suddenly occured to him that, while his wife was washing and drying the children, he might very well take a walk into the field, and see how his turnips were getting on. The turnips, in fact, were close beside his house, and he and his family were accustomed to eat them, for which reason he looked upon them as his own. No sooner said than done. The hedgehog shut the house-door behind him, and took the path to the field. He had not gone very far from home, and was just turning round the sloe-bush which stands there outside the field, to go up into the turnip-field, when he observed the hare who had gone out on business of the same kind, namely, to visit his cabbages. When the hedgehog caught sight of the hare, he bade him a friendly good morning. But the hare, who was in his own way a distinguished gentleman, and frightfully haughty, did not return the hedgehog's greeting, but said to him, assuming at the same time a very contemptuous manner: "How do you happen to be running about here in the field so early in the morning?" "I am taking a walk," said the hedgehog. "A walk!" said the hare, with a smile. "It seems to me that you might use your legs for a better purpose." This answer made the hedgehog furiously angry, for he can bear anything but a reference to his legs, just because they are crooked by nature. So now the hedgehog said to the hare: "You seem to imagine that you can do more with your legs than I with mine." "That is just what I do think," said the hare. "That can be put to the test," said the hedgehog. "I wager that if we run a race, I will outstrip you." "That is ridiculous! You with your short legs!" said the hare, "but for my part I am willing, if you have such a monstrous fancy for it. What shall we wager?" "A golden louis-d'or and a bottle of brandy," said the hedgehog. "Done," said the hare. "Shake hands on it, and then we may as well begin at once." "Nay," said the hedgehog, "there is no such great hurry! I am still fasting, I will go home first, and have a little breakfast. In half-an-hour I will be back again at this place."

Hereupon the hedgehog departed, for the hare was quite satisfied with this. On his way the hedgehog thought to himself: "The hare relies on his long legs, but I will contrive to get the better of him. He may be a great man, but he is a very silly fellow, and he shall pay for what he has said." So when the hedgehog reached home, he said to his wife: "Wife, dress yourself quickly, you must go out to the field with me." "What is going on, then?" said his wife. "I have made a wager with the hare, for a gold louis-d'or and a bottle of brandy. I am to run a race with him, and you must be present." "Good heavens, husband," the wife now cried, "are you not right in your mind, have you completely lost your wits? What can make you want to run a race with the hare?" "Hold your tongue, woman," said the hedgehog, "that is my affair. Don't begin to discuss things which are matters for men. Be off, dress yourself, and come with me." What could the hedgehog's wife do? She was forced to obey him, whether she liked it or not.

So when they had set out on their way together, the hedgehog said to his wife: "Now pay attention to what I am going to say. Look you, I will make the long field our race-course. The hare shall run in one furrow, and I in another, and we will begin to run from the top. Now all that you have to do is to place yourself here below in the furrow, and when the hare arrives at the end of the furrow on the other side of you, you must cry out to him: 'I am here already!'"

Then they reached the field, and the hedgehog showed his wife her place, and then walked up the field. When he reached the top, the hare was already there. "Shall we start?" said the hare. "Certainly," said the hedgehog. "Then both at once." So saying, each placed himself in his own furrow. The hare counted: "Once, twice, thrice, and away!" and went off like a whirlwind down the field. The hedgehog, however, only ran about three paces, and then he crouched down in the furrow, and stayed quietly where he was.

When the hare therefore arrived at full speed at the lower end of the field, the hedgehog's wife met him with the cry: "I am here already!" The hare was shocked and wondered not a little, he thought no other than that it was the hedgehog himself who was calling to him, for the hedgehog's wife looked just like her husband. The hare, however, thought to himself: "That has not been done fairly," and cried: "It must be run again, let us have it again." And once more he went off like the wind in a storm, so that he seemed to fly. But the hedgehog's wife stayed quietly in her place. So when the hare reached the top of the field, the hedgehog himself cried out to him: "I am here already." The hare, however, quite beside himself with anger, cried: "It must be run again, we must have it again." "All right," answered the hedgehog, "for my part we'll run as often as you choose." So the hare ran seventy-three times more, and the hedgehog always held out against him, and every time the hare reached either the top or the bottom, either the hedgehog or his wife said: "I am here already."

At the seventy-fourth time, however, the hare could no longer reach the end. In the middle of the field he fell to the ground, blood streamed out of his mouth, and he lay dead on the spot. But the hedgehog took the louis-d'or which he had won and the bottle of brandy, called his wife out of the furrow, and both went home together in great delight, and if they are not dead, they are living there still.

This is how it happened that the hedgehog made the hare run races with him on the Heath of Buxtehude* till he died, and since that time

* Buxtehude is a village near Hamburg.

no hare has ever had any fancy for running races with a Buxtehude hedgehog.

The moral of this story is, firstly, that no one, however great he may be, should permit himself to jest at any one beneath him, even if he be only a hedgehog. And, secondly, it teaches, that when a man marries, he should take a wife in his own position, who looks just as he himself looks. So whosoever is a hedgehog let him see to it that his wife is a hedgehog also, and so forth.

THE SPINDLE, THE SHUTTLE, AND THE NEEDLE

There was once a girl whose father and mother died while she was still a little child. All alone, in a small house at the end of the village, dwelt her godmother, who supported herself by spinning, weaving, and sewing. The old woman took the forlorn child to live with her, kept her to her work, and educated her in all that is good. When the girl was fifteen years old, the old woman became ill, called the child to her bedside, and said: "Dear daughter, I feel my end drawing near. I leave you the little house, which will protect you from wind and weather, and my spindle, shuttle, and needle, with which you can earn your bread." Then she laid her hands on the girl's head, blessed her, and said: "Only preserve the love of God in your heart, and all will go well with you." Thereupon she closed her eyes, and when she was laid in the earth, the maiden followed the coffin, weeping bitterly, and paid her the last mark of respect.

And now the maiden lived quite alone in the little house, and was industrious, and spun, wove, and sewed, and the blessing of the good old woman was on all that she did. It seemed as if the flax in the room increased of its own accord, and whenever she wove a piece of cloth or carpet, or had made a shirt, she at once found a buyer who paid her amply for it, so that she was in want of nothing, and even had something to share with others.

About this time, the son of the King was travelling about the country

looking for a bride. He was not to choose a poor one, and did not want to have a rich one. So he said: "She shall be my wife who is the poorest, and at the same time the richest." When he came to the village where the maiden dwelt, he inquired, as he did wherever he went, who was the richest and also the poorest girl in the place. They first named the richest; the poorest, they said, was the girl who lived in the small house quite at the end of the village. The rich girl was sitting in all her splendour before the door of her house, and when the prince approached her, she got up, went to meet him, and made him a low curtsy. He looked at her, said nothing, and rode on. When he came to the house of the poor girl, she was not standing at the door, but sitting in her little room. He stopped his horse, and saw through the window, on which the bright sun was shining, the girl sitting at her spinning-wheel, busily spinning. She looked up, and when she saw that the prince was looking in, she blushed all over her face, let her eyes fall, and went on spinning. I do not know whether, just at that moment, the thread was quite even; but she went on spinning until the King's son had ridden away again. Then she went to the window, opened it, and said: "It is so warm in this room!" and she looked after him as long as she could distinguish the white feathers in his hat. Then she sat down to work again in her room and went on with her spinning, and a saying which the old woman had often repeated when she was sitting at her work, came into her mind, and she sang these words to herself:

"Spindle, my spindle, haste, haste thee away,
And here to my house bring the wooer, I pray."

And what do you think happened? The spindle sprang out of her hand in an instant, and out of the door, and when, in her astonishment, she got up and looked after it, she saw that it was dancing out merrily into the open country, and drawing a shining golden thread after it. Before long, it had entirely vanished from her sight. As she had now no spindle, the girl took the weaver's shuttle in her hand, sat down to her loom, and began to weave.

The spindle, however, danced continually onwards, and just as the thread came to an end, reached the prince. "What do I see?" he cried; "the spindle certainly wants to show me the way!" turned his horse about, and rode back with the golden thread. The girl, however, was sitting at her work singing:

"Shuttle, my shuttle, weave well this day,
And guide the wooer to me, I pray."

Immediately the shuttle sprang out of her hand and out by the door. Before the threshold, however, it began to weave a carpet which was more beautiful than the eyes of man had ever yet beheld. Lilies and roses blossomed on both sides of it, and on a golden ground in the center green branches ascended, under which bounded hares and rabbits, stags and deer stretched their heads in between them, brightly-coloured birds were sitting in the branches above; they lacked nothing but the gift of song. The shuttle leapt hither and thither, and everything seemed to grow of its own accord.

As the shuttle had run away, the girl sat down to sew. She held the needle in her hand and sang:

"Needle, my needle, sharp-pointed and fine,
Prepare for the wooer this house of mine."

Then the needle leapt out of her fingers, and flew everywhere about the room as quick as lightning. It was just as if invisible spirits were working; it covered tables and benches with green cloth in an instant, and the chairs with velvet, and hung the windows with silken curtains. Hardly had the needle put in the last stitch than the maiden saw through the window the white feathers of the prince, whom the spindle had brought thither by the golden thread. He alighted, stepped over the carpet into the house, and when he entered the room, there stood the maiden in her poor garments, but she shone out from within them like a rose surrounded by leaves. "You are the poorest and also the richest," said he to her. "Come with me, you shall be my bride." She did not speak, but she gave him her hand. Then he gave her a kiss, led her forth, lifted her on to his horse, and took her to the royal castle, where the wedding was solemnized with great rejoicings. The spindle, shuttle, and needle were preserved in the treasure-chamber, and held in great honour.

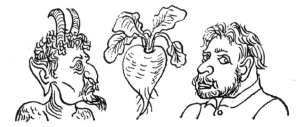

THE PEASANT AND THE DEVIL

There was once upon a time a far-sighted, crafty peasant whose tricks were much talked about. The best story, however, is how he once got hold of the Devil, and made a fool of him.

The peasant had one day been working in his field, and as twilight had set in, was making ready for the journey home, when he saw a heap of burning coals in the middle of his field, and when, full of astonishment, he went up to it, a little black Devil was sitting on the live coals. "Are you sitting upon a treasure?" said the peasant. "Yes, in truth," replied the Devil, "on a treasure which contains more gold and silver than you have ever seen in your life!" "The treasure lies in my field and belongs to me," said the peasant. "It is yours," answered the Devil, "if you will for two years give me one half of everything your field produces. Money I have enough, but I have a desire for the fruits of the earth." The peasant agreed to the bargain. "In order, however, that no dispute may arise about the division," said he, "everything that is above ground shall belong to you, and what is under the earth to me." The Devil was quite satisfied with that, but the cunning peasant had sown turnips.

Now when the time for harvest came, the Devil appeared and wanted to take away his crop; but he found nothing but the yellow withered leaves, while the peasant, full of delight, was digging up his turnips. "You have had the best of it for once," said the Devil, "but the next time that won't do. What grows above ground shall be yours, and what is under it, mine." "I am willing," replied the peasant; but when the time came to sow, he did not again sow turnips, but wheat. The grain became ripe, and the peasant went into the field and cut the full stalks down to the ground. When the Devil came, he found nothing but the stubble, and went away in a fury down into a cleft in the rocks. "That is the way to cheat the Devil," said the peasant, and went and fetched away the treasure.

THE CRUMBS ON THE TABLE

George one day said to his little chickens: "Come into the parlour and enjoy yourselves, and pick up the bread-crumbs on the table; your mistress has gone out to pay some visits." Then the chickens said: "No, no, we will not go. If the mistress gets to know it, she will beat us." George said: "She will know nothing about it. Do come; after all, she never

gives you anything good." Then the chickens again said: "Nay, nay, we must let it alone; we must not go." But George let them have no peace until at last they went, and got on the table, and ate up the bread-crumbs with all their might. But at that very moment the mistress came, and seized the stick in great haste, and beat them and treated them very harshly. And when they were outside the house, the chickens said to George: "Do, do, do, do, do you see?" Then George laughed and said: "Didn't, didn't, didn't I expect it?" So they just had to run away.

THE SEA-HARE

There was once upon a time a princess, who, high under the battlements in her castle, had an apartment with twelve windows, which looked out in every possible direction, and when she climbed up to it and looked around her, she could inspect her whole kingdom. When she looked out of the first, her sight was more keen than that of any other human being; from the second she could see still better, from the third more distinctly still, and so it went on, until the twelfth, from which she saw everything above the earth and under the earth, and nothing at all could be kept secret from her. Moreover, as she was haughty, and would be subject to no one, but wished to keep the dominion for herself alone, she caused it to be proclaimed that no one should ever be her husband who could not conceal himself from her so effectively, that it should be quite impossible for her to find him. He who tried this, however, and was discovered by her, was to have his head struck off, and stuck on a post. Ninety-seven posts with the heads of dead men were already standing before the castle, and no one had come forward for a long time. The princess was delighted, and thought to herself: "Now I shall be free as long as I live." Then three brothers appeared before her, and announced to her that they were desirous of trying their luck. The eldest believed he would be quite safe if he crept into a lime-pit, but she saw him from the first window, made him come out, and had his head cut off. The second crept into the cellar of the palace, but she perceived him also from the first window, and his fate was sealed. His head was placed on the nine and ninetieth post. Then the youngest came to her and entreated her to give him a day for consideration, and also to be so gracious as to overlook it if she should happen to discover him twice, but if he failed the third time, he would look on his life as over. As he was so handsome, and begged so earnestly, she said: "Yes, I will grant you that, but you will not succeed."

Next day he meditated for a long time how he should hide himself, but all in vain. Then he seized his gun and went out hunting. He saw a raven, took a good aim at him, and was just going to fire, when the bird cried, "Don't shoot; I will reward you!" He put his gun down, went on, and came to a lake where he surprised a large fish which had come up from the depths below to the surface of the water. When he had aimed at it, the fish cried: "Don't shoot, and I will reward you!" He allowed it to dive down again, went onwards, and met a fox which was lame. He fired and missed it, and the fox cried: "You had much better come here and draw the thorn out of my foot for me." He did this; but when he wanted to kill the fox and skin it, the fox said: "Stop, and I will reward you!" The youth let him go, and then as it was evening, returned home.

Next day he was to hide himself; but no matter how he puzzled his brains over it, he did not know where. He went into the forest to the raven and said: "I let you live on, so now tell me where I am to hide myself, so that the King's daughter shall not see me." The raven hung his head and thought it over for a long time. At length he croaked: "I have it." He fetched an egg out of his nest, cut it into two parts, and shut the youth inside it; then made it whole again, and seated himself on it. When the King's daughter went to the first window she could not discover him, nor could she from the others, and she began to be uneasy, but from the eleventh she saw him. She ordered the raven to be shot, and the egg to be brought and broken, and the youth was forced to come out. She said: "For once you are excused, but if you do not better than this, you are lost!"

Next day he went to the lake, called the fish to him and said: "I suffered you to live, now tell me where to hide myself so that the King's daughter may not see me." The fish thought for a while, and at last cried: "I have it! I will shut you up in my stomach." He swallowed him, and went down to the bottom of the lake. The King's

daughter looked through her windows, and even from the eleventh did not see him, and was alarmed; but at lenght from the twelfth she saw him. She ordered the fish to be caught and killed, and then the youth appeared. It is easy to imagine the state of mind he was in. She said: "Twice you are forgiven, but be sure that your head will be set on the hundredth post."

On the last day, he went with a heavy heart into the country, and met the fox. "You know how to find all kinds of hiding-places," said he; "I let you live, now advise me where I shall hide myself so that the King's daughter shall not discover me." "That's a hard task," answered the fox, looking very thoughtful. At length he cried: "I have it!" and went with him to a spring, dipped himself in it, and came out as a stall-keeper in the market, and dealer in animals. The youth had to dip himself in the water also, and was changed into a small sea-hare. The merchant went into the town, and showed the pretty little animal, and many persons gathered together to see it. At length the King's daughter came likewise, and as she liked it very much, she bought it, and gave the merchant a good deal of money for it. Before he gave it over to her, he said to it: "When the King's daughter goes to the window, creep quickly under the braids of her hair." And now the time arrived when she was to search for him. She went to one window after another in turn, from the first to the eleventh, and did not see him. When she did not see him from the twelfth either, she was full of anxiety and anger, and shut it down with such violence that the glass in every window shivered into a thousand pieces, and the whole castle shook.

She went back and felt the sea-hare beneath the braids of her hair. Then she seized it, and threw it on the ground exclaiming: "Away with you, get out of my sight!" It ran to the merchant, and both of them hurried to the spring, wherein they plunged, and received back their true forms. The youth thanked the fox, and said: "The raven and the fish are idiots compared with you; you know the right tune to play, there is no denying that!"

The youth went straight to the palace. The princess was already expecting him, and abandoned herself to her fate. The wedding was solemnized, and now he was king, and lord of all the kingdom. He never told her where he had concealed himself for the third time, and who had helped him, so she believed that he had done everything by his own skill, and she had a great respect for him, for she thought to herself: "He is able to do more than I."

THE MASTER-THIEF

One day an old man and his wife were sitting in front of a miserable house resting a while from their work. Suddenly a splendid carriage with four black horses came driving up, and a richly-dressed man descended from it. The peasant stood up, went to the great man, and asked what he wanted, and in what way he could serve him. The stranger stretched out his hand to the old man, and said: "I want nothing but to enjoy for once a country dish; cook me some potatoes, in the way you always have them, and then I will sit down at your table and eat them with pleasure." The peasant smiled and said: "You are a count or a prince, or perhaps even a duke; noble gentlemen often have such fancies, but you shall have your wish." The wife went into the kitchen, and began to wash and rub the potatoes, and to make them into balls, as they are eaten by the country-folks. Whilst she was busy with this work, the peasant said to the stranger: "Come into my garden with me for a while, I have still something to do there." He had dug some holes in the garden, and now wanted to plant trees in them. "Have you no children," asked the stranger, "who could help you with your work?" "No," answered the peasant, "I had a son, it is true, but it is long since he went out into the world. He was a ne'er-do-well; clever and knowing, but he would learn nothing and was full of bad tricks.

At last he ran away from me, and since then I have heard nothing of him."

The old man took a young tree, put it in a hole, drove in a post beside it, and when he had shovelled in some earth and had trampled it firmly down, he tied the stem of the tree above, below, and in the middle, fast to the post by a rope of straw. "But tell me," said the stranger, "why you don't tie that crooked knotted tree, which is lying in the corner there, bent down almost to the ground, to a post also that it may grow straight, as well as these?" The old man smiled and said: "Sir, you speak according to your knowledge, it is easy to see that you are not familiar with gardening. That tree there is old, and mis-shapen, no one can make it straight now. Trees must be trained while they are young." "That is how it was with your son," said the stranger, "if you had trained him while he was still young, he would not have run away; now he too must have grown hard and mis-shapen." "Truly it is a long time since he went away," replied the old man, "he must have changed." "Would you know him again if he were to come to you?" asked the stranger. "Hardly by his face," replied the peasant, "but he has a mark about him, a birth-mark on his shoulder, that looks like a bean." When he had said that the stranger pulled off his coat, bared his shoulder, and showed the peasant the bean. "Good God!" cried the old man, "you are really my son!" and love for his child stirred in his heart. "But," he added, "how can you be my son, you have become a great lord and live in wealth and luxury? How have you contrived to do that?" "Ah, father," answered the son, "the young tree was bound to no post and has grown crooked. Now it is too old, it will never be straight again. How have I come by all this? I have become a thief, but do not be alarmed, I am a master-thief. For me there are neither locks nor bolts, whatsoever I desire is mine. Do not imagine that I steal like a common thief, I only take some of the superfluity of the rich. Poor people are safe, I would rather give to them than take anything from them. It is the same with anything which I can have without trouble, cunning and dexterity—I never touch it." "Alas, my son," said the father, "it still does not please me, a thief is still a thief, I tell you it will end badly." He took him to his mother, and when she heard that was her son, she wept for joy, but when he told her that he had become a master-thief, two streams flowed down over her face. At length she said: "Even if he has become a thief, he is still my son, and my eyes have beheld him once more."

They sat down to table, and once again he ate with his parents the wretched food which he had not eaten for so long. The father said: "If our lord, the count up there in the castle, learns who you are, and what trade you follow, he will not take you in his arms and cradle you in them as he did when he held you at the font, but will cause you to swing from a halter." "Be easy, father, he will do me no harm, for I understand my trade. I will go to him myself this very day." When evening drew near, the master-thief seated himself in his carriage, and drove to the castle. The count received him civilly, for he took him for a distinguished man. When, however, the stranger made himself known, the count turned pale and was quite silent for some time. At length he said: "You are my godson, and on that account mercy shall take the place of justice, and I will deal leniently with you. Since you pride yourself on being a master-thief, I will put your art to the proof, but if you do not stand the test, you must marry the rope-maker's daughter, and the croaking of the raven must be your music on the occasion." "Lord Count," answered the master-thief, "think of three things, as difficult as you like, and if I do not perform your tasks, do with me what you will." The count reflected for some minutes, and then said: "Well, then, in the first place, you shall steal the horse I keep for my own riding, out of the stable; in the next, you shall steal the sheet from beneath the bodies of my wife and myself when we are asleep, without our observing it, and the wedding-ring of my wife as well; thirdly and lastly, you shall steal away out of the church, the parson and clerk. Mark what I am saying, for your life depends on it."

The master-thief went to the nearest town; there he bought the clothes of an old peasant woman, and put them on. Then he stained his face brown, and painted wrinkles on it as well, so that no one could have recognized him. Then he filled a small cask with old Hungary wine in which was mixed a powerful sleeping-drink. He put the cask in a basket, which he took on his back, and walked with slow and tottering steps to the count's castle. It was already dark when he arrived. He sat down on a stone in the court-yard and began to cough, like an asthmatic old woman, and to rub his hands as if he were cold. In front of the door of the stable some soldiers were lying round a fire;

one of them observed the woman, and called out to her: "Come nearer, old mother, and warm yourself beside us. After all, you have no bed for the night, and must take one where you can find it." The old woman tottered up to them, begged them to lift the basket from her back, and sat down beside them at the fire. "What have you got in your little cask, old hag?" asked one. "A good mouthful of wine," she answered. "I live by trade, for money and fair words I am quite ready to let you have a glass." "Let us have it here, then," said the soldier, and when he had tasted one glass he said: "When wine is good, I like another glass," and had another poured out for himself, and the rest followed his example. "Hallo, comrades," cried one of them to those who were in the stable, "here is an old girl who has wine that is as old as herself; take a draught, it will warm your stomachs far better than our fire." The old woman carried her cask into the stable. One of the soldiers had seated himself on the saddled riding-horse, another held its bridle in his hand, a third had laid hold of its tail. She poured out as much as they wanted until the spring ran dry. It was not long before the bridle fell from the hand of the one, and he fell down and began to snore, the other left hold of the tail, lay down and snored still louder. The one who was sitting in the saddle, did remain sitting, but bent his head almost down to the horse's neck, and slept and blew with his mouth like the bellows of a forge. The soldiers outside had already been asleep for a long time, and were lying on the ground motionless, as if dead. When the master-thief saw that he had succeeded, he gave the first a rope in his hand instead of the bridle, and the other who had been holding the tail, a wisp of straw, but what was he to do with the one who was sitting on the horse's back? He did not want to throw him down, for he might have awakened and have uttered a cry. He had a good idea, he unbuckled the girths of the saddle, tied a couple of ropes which were hanging to a ring on the wall fast to the saddle, and drew the sleeping rider up into the air on it, then he twisted the rope round the posts, and made it fast. He soon unloosed the horse from the chain, but if he had ridden over the stony pavement of the yard they would have heard the noise in the castle. So he wrapped the horse's hoofs in old rags, led him carefully out, leapt upon him, and galloped off.

When day broke, the master galloped to the castle on the stolen horse. The count had just got up, and was looking out of the window.

"Good morning, Sir Count," he cried to him, "here is the horse, which I have got safely out of the stable! Just look, how beautifully your soldiers are lying there sleeping; and if you will but go into the stable, you will see how comfortable your watchers have made it for themselves." The count could not help laughing. Then he said: "For once you have succeeded, but things won't go so well the second time, and I warn you that if you come before me as a thief, I will handle you as I would a thief."

When the countess went to bed that night, she closed her hand with the wedding-ring tightly together, and the count said: "All the doors are locked and bolted, I will keep awake and wait for the thief, but if he gets in by the window, I will shoot him." The master-thief, however, went in the dark to the gallows, cut a poor sinner who was hanging there down from the halter, and carried him on his back to the castle.

Then he set a ladder up to the bedroom, put the dead body on his shoulders, and began to climb up. When he had got so high that the head of the dead man showed at the window, the count, who was watching in his bed, fired a pistol at him, and immediately the master let the poor sinner fall down, descended the ladder, and hid himself in one corner. The night was sufficiently lighted by the moon, for the master to see distinctly how the count got out of the window on to the ladder, came down, carried the dead body into the garden, and began to dig a hole in which to lay it. "Now," thought the thief, "the favourable moment has come," stole nimbly out of his corner, and climbed up the ladder straight into the countess's bedroom. "Dear wife," he began in the count's voice, "the thief is dead, but, after all, he is my godson, and has been more of a scape-grace than a villain. I will not put him to open shame; besides, I am sorry for the parents. I will bury him myself before daybreak in the garden, that the thing may not be known. So give me the sheet, I will wrap up the body in it, and not bury him like a dog." The countess gave him the sheet. "I tell you what," continued the thief, "I have a fit of magnanimity, give me the ring, too—the unhappy man risked his life for it, so he may take it with him into his grave." She would not gainsay the count, and although she did it unwillingly she drew the ring from her finger, and gave it to him. The thief made off with both these things, and reached home safely before the count in the garden had finished his work of burying.

What a long face the count did pull when the master came next morning, and brought him the sheet and the ring. "Are you a wizard?" said he. "Who has fetched you out of the grave in which I myself laid you, and brought you to life again?" "You did not bury me," said the thief, "but the poor sinner on the gallows," and he told him exactly how everything had happened, and the count was forced to own to him that he was a clever, crafty thief. "But you have not reached the end yet," he added, "you have still to perform the third task, and if you do not succeed in that, all is of no use." The master smiled and returned no answer.

When night had fallen he went with a long sack on his back, a bundle under his arms, and a lantern in his hand to the village-church. In the sack he had some crabs, and in the bundle short wax-candles. He sat down in the churchyard, took out a crab, and stuck a wax-candle on his back. Then he lighted the little light, put the crab on the ground, and let it creep about. He took a second out of the sack, and treated it in the same way, and so on until the last was out of the sack. Hereupon he put on a long black garment that looked like a monk's cowl, and stuck a gray beard on his chin. When at last he was quite unrecognizable, he took the sack in which the crabs had been, went into the church, and ascended the pulpit. The clock in the tower was just striking twelve; when the last stroke had sounded, he cried with a loud and piercing voice: "Hearken, sinful men, the end of all things has come! The last day is at hand! Hearken! Hearken! Whosoever wishes to go to heaven with me must creep into the sack. I am Peter, who opens and shuts the gate of heaven. Behold how the dead outside there in the churchyard are wandering about collecting their bones. Come, come, and creep into the sack; the world is about to be destroyed!" The cry echoed through the whole village. The parson and clerk who lived nearest to the church, heard it first, and when they saw the lights which were moving about the churchyard, they observed that something unusual was going on, and went into the church. They listened to the sermon for a while, and then the clerk nudged the parson and said: "It would not be amiss if we were to use the opportunity together, and before the dawning of the last day, find an easy way of getting to heaven." "To tell the truth," answered the parson, "that is what I myself have been thinking, so if you are inclined, we will set out on our way." "Yes," answered the clerk, "but you, the pastor, have the precedence, I will follow." So the parson went first, and ascended the pulpit where the master opened his sack. The parson crept in first, and then the clerk. The master immediately tied up the sack tightly, seized it by the middle, and dragged it down the pulpit-steps, and whenever the heads of the two fools bumped against the steps, he cried: "We are going over the mountains." Then he drew them through the village in the same way, and when they were passing through puddles, he cried: "Now we are going through wet clouds," and when at last he was dragging them up the steps of the castle, he cried: "Now we are on the steps of heaven, and will soon be in the outer court." When he had got to the top, he pushed the sack into the pigeon-house, and when the pigeons fluttered about, he said: "Hark how glad the angels are, and how they are flapping their wings!" Then he bolted the door upon them, and went away.

Next morning he went to the count, and told him that he had performed the third task also, and had carried the parson and clerk out of the church. "Where have you left them?" asked the lord. "They are lying upstairs in a sack in the pigeon-house, and imagine that they are in heaven." The count went up himself, and convinced himself that the master had told the truth. When he had delivered the parson and clerk from their captivity, he said: "You are an arch-thief, and have won your wager. For once you escape with a whole skin, but see that you leave my land, for if ever you set foot on it again, you may count on your elevation to the gallows." The arch-thief took leave of his parents, once more went forth into the wide world, and no one has ever heard of him since.

THE DRUMMER

A young drummer went out quite alone one evening into the country, and came to a lake on the shore of which he perceived lying there three pieces of white linen. "What fine linen," said he, and put one piece in his pocket. He returned home, thought no more of what he had found, and went to bed. Just as he was going to sleep, it seemed to him as if someone was calling his name. He listened, and was aware of a soft voice which cried to him: "Drummer, drummer, wake up!" As it was a dark night he could see no one, but it appeared to him that a figure was hovering about his bed. "What do you want?" he asked. "Give me back my shift," answered the voice, "that you took away from me last evening by the lake." "You shall have it back again," said the drummer, "if you will tell me who you are." "Ah," replied the voice, "I am the daughter of a mighty King; but I have fallen into the power of a witch, and am shut up on the glass-mountain. I have to bathe in the lake every day with my two sisters, but I cannot fly back again without my shift. My sisters have gone away, but I have been forced to stay behind. I entreat you to give me my shift back." "Don't worry, poor child," said the drummer. "I will willingly give it back to you." He took it out of his pocket, and reached it to her in the dark. She snatched it in haste, and wanted to go away with it. "Stop a moment, perhaps I can help you." "You can only help me by ascending the glass-mountain, and freeing me from the power of the witch. But you cannot come to the glass mountain, and indeed if you were quite close to it you could not ascend it." "When I want to do a thing I always can do it," said the drummer; "I am sorry for you, and have no fear of anything. But I do not know the way which leads to the glass-mountain." "The road goes through the great forest, in which the man-eaters live," she answered, "and more than that, I dare not tell you." And then he heard her wings as she flew away.

By daybreak the drummer arose, buckled on his drum, and went without fear straight into the forest. After he had walked for a while without seeing any giants, he thought to himself: "I must waken up the sluggards," and he hung his drum before him, and beat such a roll that the birds flew out of the trees with loud cries. It was not long before a giant who had been lying sleeping among the grass, rose up, and was as tall as a fir-tree. "Wretch!" cried he; "what are you drumming here for, and wakening me out of my best sleep?" "I am drumming," he replied, "because I want to show the way to many thousands who are following me." "What do they want in my forest?" demanded the giant. "They want to put an end to you, and cleanse the forest of such a monster as you!" "Oho!" said the giant, "I will trample you all to death like so many ants." "Do you think you can do anything against us?" said the drummer; "if you stoop to take hold of one, he will jump away and hide himself; but when you are lying down and sleeping, they will come forth from every thicket, and creep up to you. Every one of them has a hammer of steel in his belt, and with that they will beat in your skull." The giant grew angry and thought: "If I meddle with the crafty

folk, it might turn out badly for me. I can strangle wolves and bears, but I cannot protect myself from these earth-worms." "Listen, little fellow," said he; "go back again, and I will promise you that for the future I will leave you and your comrades in peace, and if there is anything else you wish for, tell me, for I am quite willing to do something to please you." "You have long legs," said the drummer, "and can run quicker than I; carry me to the glass-mountain, and I will give my followers a signal to go back, and they shall leave you in peace this time." "Come here, worm," said the giant; "seat yourself on my shoulder, I will carry you where you wish to be." The giant lifted him up, and the drummer began to beat his drum up aloft to his heart's delight. The giant thought: "That is the signal for the other people to turn back."

After a while, a second giant was standing in the road, who took the drummer from the first, and stuck him in his button-hole. The drummer laid hold of the button, which was as large as a dish, held on by it, and looked merrily around. Then they came to a third giant, who took him out of the button-hole, and set him on the rim of his hat. Up there the drummer walked backwards and forwards, and looked over the trees, and when he perceived a mountain in the blue distance, he thought: "That must be the glass-mountain," and so it was. The giant only made two more steps, and they reached the foot of the mountain, where the giant put him down. The drummer demanded to be put on the summit of the glass-mountain, but the giant shook his head, growled something in his beard, and went back into the forest.

And now the poor drummer was standing before the mountain, which was as high as if three mountains were piled on each other, and at the same time as smooth as a looking-glass, and did not know how to get up it. He began to climb, but that was useless, for he always slipped back again. "If one was a bird now," thought he; but what was the good of wishing, no wings grew for him.

Whilst he was standing thus, not knowing what to do, he saw, not far from him, two men who were struggling fiercely together. He went up to them and saw that they were disputing about a saddle which was lying on the ground before them, and which both of them wanted to have. "What fools you are," said he, "to quarrel about a saddle, when you have not a horse for it!" "The saddle is worth fighting about," answered one of the men; "whosoever sits on it, and wishes himself in any place, even if it should be the very end of the earth, gets there the instant he has uttered the wish. The saddle belongs to us in common. It is my turn to ride on it, but that other man will not let me do it." "I will soon decide the quarrel," said the drummer, and he went to a short distance and stuck a white rod in the ground. Then he came back and said: "Now run to the goal, and whoever gets there first, shall ride first." Both set out at a trot; but hardly had they gone a couple of steps before the drummer swung himself on the saddle, wished himself on the glass-mountain, and before any one could turn round, he was there. On the top of the mountain was a plain; there stood an old stone house, and in front of the house lay a great fish-pond, but behind it was a dark forest. He saw neither men nor animals, everything was quiet; only the wind rustled amongst the trees, and the clouds moved by quite close above his head. He went to the door and knocked. When he had knocked for the third time, an old woman with a brown face and red eyes opened the door. She had spectacles on her long nose, and looked sharply at him; then she asked what he wanted. "Entrance, food, and a bed for the night," replied the drummer. "That you shall have," said the old woman, "if you will perform three services in return." "Why not?" he answered, "I am not afraid of any kind of work, however hard it may be." The old woman let him go in, and gave him some food and a good bed at night. The next morning when he had slept his fill, she took a thimble from her wrinkled finger, reached it to the drummer, and said: "Go to work now, and empty out the pond with this thimble; but you must have it done before night, and must have sought out all the fishes which are in the water and laid them side by side, according to their kind and size." "That is strange work," said the drummer, but he went to the pond, and began to empty it. He baled the whole morning; but what can anyone do to a great lake with a thimble, even if he were to bale for a thousand years?

When it was noon, he thought: "It is all useless, and whether I work or not it will come to the same thing." So he gave it up and sat down. Then came a maiden out of the house who set a little basket with food before him, and said: "What ails you, that you sit so sadly here?" He looked at her, and saw that she was wondrously beautiful. "Ah," said he, "I cannot finish the first piece of work, how will it be with the others? I came forth to seek a king's daughter who is said to dwell here, but I have not found her, and I will go farther." "Stay here," said the maiden, "I will help you out of your difficulty. You are tired, lay your head in my lap, and sleep. When you awake again, your work will be done." The drummer did not need to be told that twice. As soon as his eyes were shut, she turned a wishing-ring and said: "Rise, water. Fishes, come out." Instantly the water rose on high like a white mist, and moved away with the other clouds, and the fishes sprang on the shore and laid themselves side by side each according to his size and kind. When the drummer awoke, he saw with amazement that all was done. But the maiden said: "One of the fish is not lying with those of its own kind, but quite alone; when the old woman comes to-night and sees that all she demanded has been done, she will ask you: 'What is this fish lying alone for?' Then throw the fish in her face, and say: 'This one shall be for you, old witch.'" In the evening the witch came, and when she had put this question, he threw the fish in her face. She behaved as if she did not notice it, and said nothing, but looked at him with malicious eyes. Next morning she said: "Yesterday it was too easy for you, I must give you harder work. To-day you must hew down the whole of the forest, split the wood into logs, and pile them up, and everything must be finished by the evening." She gave him an axe, a mallet, and two wedges. But the axe was made of lead, and the mallet and wedges were of tin. When he began to cut, the edge of the axe was blunted, and the mallet and wedges were beaten out of shape. He did not know how to manage, but at mid-day the maiden came once more with his dinner and comforted him. "Lay your head on my lap," said she, "and sleep; when you awake, your work will be done." She turned her wishing-ring, and in an instant the whole forest fell down with a crash, the wood split, and arranged itself in heaps, and it seemed just as if unseen giants were finishing the work. When he awoke, the maiden said: "Do you see that the wood is piled up and arranged, one bough alone remains; but when the old woman comes this evening and asks you about that bough, give her a blow with it, and say: 'That is for you, you witch.'"

The old woman came: "There you see how easy the work was!" said she; "but for whom have you left that bough?" "For you, you witch," he replied, and gave her a blow with it. But she pretended not to feel it, laughed scornfully, and said: "Early to-morrow morning you shall arrange all the wood in one heap, set fire to it, and burn it." He rose at break of day, and began to pick up the wood, but how can a single man get a whole forest together? The work made no progress. The maiden, however, did not desert him in his need. She brought him his food at noon, and when he had eaten, he laid his head on her lap, and went to sleep. When he awoke, the entire pile of wood was burning in one enormous flame, which stretched its tongues out into the sky. "Listen to me," said the maiden, "when the witch comes, she will give you all kinds of orders; do whatever she asks you without fear, and then she will not be able to get the better of you, but if you are afraid, the fire will lay hold of you, and consume you. At last when you have done everything, seize her with both your hands, and throw her into the midst of the fire." The maiden departed, and the old woman came sneaking up to him. "Oh, I am cold," said she, "but that is a fire that burns; it warms my old bones, and does me good! But I see a log lying there which won't burn, bring it out for me. When you have done that, you are free, and may go where you like. Now, jump in!"

The drummer did not reflect long; he sprang into the midst of the flames, but they did not hurt him, and could not even singe a hair of his head. He carried the log out, and laid it down. Hardly, however, had the wood touched the earth than it was transformed, and the beautiful maiden who had helped him in his need stood before him, and by the silken and shining golden garments which she wore, he knew right well that she was the King's daughter. But the old woman laughed venomously, and said: "You think you have her safe, but you have not got her yet!" Just as she was about to fall on the maiden and take her away, the youth seized the old woman with both his hands, raised her up on high, and threw her into the jaws of the fire, which closed over her as if it were delighted that an old witch was to be burnt.

Then the King's daughter looked at the drummer, and when she saw that he was a handsome youth and remembered how he had risked his life to deliver her, she gave him her hand, and said: "You have ventured everything for my sake, but I also will do everything for yours. Promise to be true to me, and you shall be my husband. We shall not want for riches, we shall have enough with what the witch has gathered together here." She led him into the house, where there were chests and coffers crammed with the old woman's treasures. The maiden left the gold and silver where it was, and took only the precious stones. She would not stay any longer on the glass-mountain, so the drummer said to her: "Seat yourself by me on my saddle, and then we will fly down like birds." "I do not like the old saddle," said she, "I need only turn my wishing-ring and we shall be at home." "Very well, then," answered the drummer, "then wish us in front of the town-gate." In the twinkling of an eye they were there, but the drummer said: "I will just go to my parents and tell them the news. Wait for me outside here, I shall soon be back." "Ah," said the King's daughter, "I beg you to be careful. On your arrival do not kiss your parents on the right cheek, or else you will forget everything, and I shall stay behind here outside, alone and deserted." "How can I forget you?" said he, and promised her to come back very soon, and gave his hand upon it. When he went into his father's house, he had changed so much that no one knew who he was, for the three days which he had passed on the glass-mountain had been three years. Then he made himself known, and his parents fell on his neck with joy, and his heart was so moved that he forgot what the maiden had said, and kissed them on both cheeks. But when he had given them the kiss on the right cheek, every thought of the King's daughter vanished from him. He emptied out his pockets, and laid handfuls of the largest jewels on the table. The parents had not the least idea what to do with the riches. Then the father built a magnificent castle all surrounded by gardens, woods, and meadows as if a prince were going to live in it, and when it was ready, the mother said: "I have found a maiden for you and the wedding shall be in three days." The son was content to do as his parents desired.

The poor King's daughter had stood for a long time outside the town waiting for the return of the young man. When evening came, she said: "He must certainly have kissed his parents on the right cheek, and has forgotten me." Her heart was full of sorrow, she wished herself into a solitary little hut in a forest, and would not return to her father's court. Every evening she went into the town and passed the young man's house; he often saw her, but he no longer knew her. At length she heard the people saying: "The wedding will take place to-morrow." Then she said: "I will try if I can win back his heart."

On the first day of the wedding ceremonies, she turned her wishing-ring, and said: "A dress as bright as the sun." Instantly the dress lay before her, and it was as bright as if it had been woven of real sunbeams. When all the guests were assembled, she entered the hall. Every one was amazed at the beautiful dress, and the bride most of all, and as pretty dresses were the things she had most delight in, she went to the stranger and asked if she would sell it to her. "Not for money," she answered, "but if I may pass the first night outside the door of the room where your betrothed sleeps, I will give it up to you." The bride could not overcome her desire and consented, but she mixed a sleeping-draught with the wine her betrothed took at night, which made him fall into a deep sleep. When all had become still, the King's daughter crouched down by the door of the bedroom, opened it just a little, and cried:

> "Drummer, drummer, I pray you hear!
> Have you forgotten you held me dear?
> That on the glass-mountain we sat hour by hour?
> That I rescued your life from the witch's power?
> Did you not plight your troth to me?
> Drummer, drummer, hearken to me!"

But it was all in vain, for the drummer did not awake, and when morning dawned, the King's daughter was forced to go back again as she came. On the second evening she turned her wishing-ring and said: "A dress as silvery as the moon." When she appeared at the feast in the dress which was as soft as moonbeams, it again excited the desire of the bride, and the King's daughter gave it to her for permission to pass the second night also outside the door of the bedroom. Then in the stillness of the night, she cried:

> "Drummer, drummer, I pray you hear!
> Have you forgotten you held me dear?
> That on the glass-mountain we sat hour by hour?
> That I rescued your life from the witch's power?
> Did you not plight your troth to me?
> Drummer, drummer, hearken to me!"

But the drummer, who was stupefied with the sleeping-draught, could not be aroused. Sadly next morning she went back to her hut in the forest. But the people in the house had heard the lamentation of the unknown maiden, and told the bridegroom about it. They told him also that it was impossible that he could hear anything of it, because the maiden he was going to marry had poured a sleeping-draught into his wine.

On the third evening, the King's daughter turned her wishing-ring, and said: "A dress glittering like the stars." When she showed herself therein at the feast, the bride was quite beside herself with the splendor of the dress, which far surpassed the others, and she said: "I must, and will have it." The maiden gave it as she had given the others for permission to spend the night outside the bridegroom's door. The bridegroom, however, did not drink the wine which was handed to him before he went to bed, but poured it behind the bed, and when everything was quiet, he heard a sweet voice which called to him:

> "Drummer, drummer, I pray you hear!
> Have you forgotten you held me dear?
> That on the glass-mountain we sat hour by hour?
> That I rescued your life from the witch's power?
> Did you not plight your troth to me?
> Drummer, drummer, hearken to me!"

Suddenly his memory returned to him. "Ah," cried he, "how can I have acted so unfaithfully; but the kiss which in the joy of my heart I gave my parents, on the right cheek, that is to blame for it all. That is what stupefied me!" He sprang up, took the King's daughter by the hand, and led her to his parents' bed. "This is my true bride," said he; "if I marry the other, I shall do a great wrong." The parents, when they heard how everything had happened, gave their consent. Then the lights in the hall were lighted again, drums and trumpets were brought, friends and relations were invited to come, and the real wedding was solemnized with great rejoicing. The first bride received the beautiful dresses as a compensation, and declared herself satisfied.

THE EAR OF CORN

In former times, when God himself still walked the earth, the fruitfulness of the soil was much greater than it is now; then, the ears of corn did not bear fifty or sixty, but four or five hundred-fold. Then the corn grew from the bottom to the very top of the stalk, and according to the length of the stalk was the length of the ear. Men however are so made, that when they are too well off they no longer value the blessings which come from God, but grow indifferent and careless. One day a woman was passing by a corn-field when her little child, who was running beside her, fell into a puddle, and dirtied her frock. On this the mother tore up a handful of the beautiful ears of corn, and cleaned the frock with them.

When the Lord, who just then came by, saw that, he was angry, and said: "Henceforth shall the stalks of corn bear no more ears; men are no longer worthy of heavenly gifts." The by-standers who heard this, were terrified, and fell on their knees and prayed that he would still leave something on the stalks, even if the people were undeserving of it, for the sake of the innocent chickens which would otherwise have to starve. The Lord, who foresaw their suffering, had pity on them, and granted the request. So the ears were left as they now grow.

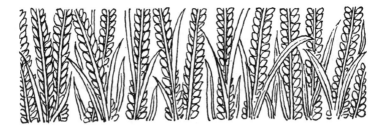

THE GRAVE-MOUND

A rich farmer was one day standing in his yard inspecting his fields and gardens. The corn was growing up vigorously and the fruit-trees were heavily laden with fruit. The grain of the year before still lay in such immense heaps in the loft that the rafters could hardly bear it. Then he went into the stable, where were well-fed oxen, fat cows, and horses bright as looking-glass. At length he went back into his sitting-room, and cast a glance at the iron chest in which his money lay.

Whilst he was thus standing surveying his riches, all at once there was a loud knock close by him. The knock was not at the door of his room, but at the door of his heart. It opened, and he heard a voice which said to him: "Have you done good to your family with it? Have you considered the necessities of the poor? Have you shared your bread with the hungry? Have you been contented with what you have, or did you always desire to have more?" The heart was not slow in answering: "I have been hard and pitiless, and have never shown any kindness to my own family. If a beggar came, I turned away my eyes from him. I have not troubled myself about God, but have thought only of increasing my wealth. If everything which the sky covers had been mine own, I should still not have had enough."

When he was aware of this answer he was greatly alarmed, his knees began to tremble, and he was forced to sit down.

Then there was another knock, but the knock was at the door of his room. It was his neighbour, a poor man who had a number of children whom he could no longer satisfy with food. "I know," thought the poor man, "that my neighbour is rich, but he is as hard as he is rich. I don't believe he will help me, but my children are crying for bread, so I will venture it." He said to the rich man: "You do not readily give away anything that is yours, but I stand here like one who feels the water rising above his head. My children are starving, lend me four measures of corn." The rich man looked at him long, and then the first sunbeam of mercy began to melt away a drop of the ice of greediness. "I will not lend you four measures," he answered. "I will make you a present of eight, but you must fulfil one condition." "What am I to do?" said the poor man. "When I am dead, you shall watch for three nights by my grave." The peasant was disturbed in his mind at this request, but in the need in which he was, he would have consented to anything; he accepted, therefore, and carried the corn home with him.

It seemed as if the rich man had foreseen what was about to happen, for when three days were gone by, he suddenly dropped down dead. No one knew exactly how it came to pass, but no one grieved for him. When he was buried, the poor man remembered his promise; he would willingly have been released from it, but he thought: "After all, he acted kindly by me. I have fed my hungry children with his corn, and even if that were not the case, where I have once given my promise I must keep it." At nightfall he went into the churchyard, and seated himself on the grave-mound. Everything was quiet, only the moon appeared above the grave, and frequently an owl flew past and uttered her melancholy cry. When the sun rose, the poor man betook himself in safety to his home, and in the same manner the second night passed quietly by. On the evening of the third day he felt a strange uneasiness, it seemed to him that something was about to happen. When he went out he saw, by the churchyard-wall, a man whom he had never seen before. He was no longer young, had scars on his face, and his eyes looked sharply and eagerly around. He was entirely covered with an old cloak, and nothing was visible but his great riding-boots. "What are you looking for here?" the peasant asked. "Are you not afraid of the lonely churchyard?"

"I am looking for nothing," he answered, "and I am afraid of nothing! I am like the youngster who went forth to learn how to shudder, and had his labour for his pains, but got the King's daughter to wife and great wealth with her, only I have remained poor. I am nothing but a paid-off soldier, and I mean to pass the night here, because I have no other shelter." "If you are without fear," said the peasant, "stay with me, and help me to watch that grave there."

"To keep watch is a soldier's business," he replied, "whatever we fall in with here, whether it be good or bad, we will share it between us." The peasant agreed to this, and they seated themselves on the grave together.

All was quiet until midnight, when suddenly a shrill whistling was heard in the air, and the two watchers perceived the Evil One standing bodily before them. "Be off, you scoundrels!" cried he to them, "the man who lies in that grave belongs to me; I want to take him, and if you don't go away I will wring your necks!" "Sir with the red feather," said the soldier, "you are not my captain, I have no need to obey you, and I have not yet learned what fear is. Go away, we shall stay sitting here."

The Devil thought to himself: "Money is the best means with which to lay hold of these two vagabonds." So he began to play a softer tune, and asked quite kindly, if they would not accept a bag of money, and go home with it. "That is worth listening to," answered the soldier, "but one bag of gold won't serve us, if you will give as much as will go into one of my boots, we will quit the field for you and go away."

"I have not so much as that about me," said the Devil, "but I will fetch it. In the neighbouring town lives a money-changer who is a good friend of mine, and will readily advance it to me." When the Devil had vanished the soldier took his left boot off, and said: "We will soon pull the charcoal-burner's nose for him, just give me your knife, comrade." He cut the sole off the boot, and put it in the high grass near the grave on the edge of a hole that was half over-grown. "That will do," said he; "now the chimney-sweep may come."

They both sat down and waited, and it was not long before the Devil returned with a small bag of gold in his hand. "Just pour it in," said the soldier, raising up the boot a little, "but that won't be enough."

The Black One shook out all that was in the bag; the gold fell through, and the boot remained empty. "Scoundrel," cried the soldier, "it won't do! Didn't I say so at once? Go back again, and bring more." The Devil shook his head, went, and in an hour's time came with a much larger bag under his arm. "Now pour it in," cried the soldier, "but I doubt the boot will be full." The gold clinked as it fell, but the boot remained empty. The Devil looked in himself with his burning eyes, and convinced himself of the truth. "You have shamefully big calves to your legs!" cried he, and made a wry face. "Did you think," replied the soldier, "that I had a cloven foot like you? Since when have you been so stingy? See that you get more gold together, or our bargain will come to nothing!" The Wicked One went off again. This time he stayed away longer, and when at length he appeared he was panting under the weight of a sack which lay on his shoulders. He emptied it into the boot, which was just as far from being filled as before. He

became furious, and was just going to tear the boot out of the soldier's hands, but at that moment the first ray of the rising sun broke forth from the sky, and the Evil Spirit fled away with loud shrieks. The poor soul was saved.

The peasant wished to divide the gold, but the soldier said: "Give what falls to my lot to the poor, I will come with you to your cottage, and together we will live in rest and peace on what remains, as long as God is pleased to permit."

OLD RINKRANK

There was once upon a time a King who had a daughter, and he caused a glass mountain to be made, and said that whosoever could cross to the other side of it without falling should have his daughter to wife. Then there was one who loved the King's daughter, and he asked the King if he might have her. "Yes," said the King; "if you can cross the mountain without falling, you shall have her." And the princess said she would go over it with him, and would hold him if he were about to fall. So they set out together to go over it, and when they were half way up the princess slipped and fell, and the glass mountain opened and shut her up inside it, and her betrothed could not see where she had gone, for the mountain closed immediately. Then he wept and lamented much, and the King was miserable too, and ordered the mountain to be broken open where she had been lost, and thought he would be able to get her out again, but they could not find the place into which she had fallen.

Meanwhile the King's daughter had fallen quite deep down into the earth into a great cave. An old fellow with a very long gray beard came to meet her, and told her that if she would be his servant and do everything he bade her, she might live, if not he would kill her. So she did all he bade her. In the mornings he took his ladder out of his pocket, and set it up against the mountain and climbed to the top by its help, and then he drew up the ladder after him. The princess had to cook his dinner, make his bed, and do all his work, and when he came home again he always brought with him a heap of gold and silver. When she had lived with him for many years, and had grown quite old, he called her Mother Mansrot, and she had to call him Old Rinkrank. Then once when he was out, and she had made his bed and washed his dishes, she shut the doors and windows all fast, and there was one little window through which the light shone in, and this she left open. When Old Rinkrank came home, he knocked at his door, and cried: "Mother Mansrot, open the door for me." "No," said she, "Old Rinkrank, I will not open the door for you." Then he said:

"Here stand I, poor Rinkrank,
On my seventeen long shanks,
On my weary, worn-out foot,
Wash my dishes, Mother Mansrot."

"I have washed your dishes already," said she. Then again he said:

"Here stand I, poor Rinkrank,
On my seventeen long shanks,
On my weary, worn-out foot,
Make me my bed, Mother Mansrot."

"I have made your bed already," said she. Then again he said:

> "Here stand I, poor Rinkrank,
> On my seventeen long shanks,
> On my weary, worn-out foot,
> Open the door, Mother Mansrot."

Then he ran all round his house, and saw that the little window was open, and thought: "I will look in and see what she can be about, and why she will not open the door for me." He tried to peep in, but could not get his head through because of his long beard. So he first put his beard through the open window, but just as he had got it through, Mother Mansrot came by and pulled the window down with a cord which she had tied to it, and his beard was shut fast in it. Then he began to cry most piteously, for it hurt him very much, and to entreat her to release him again. But she said not until he gave her the ladder with which he ascended the mountain. Then, whether he would or not, he had to tell her where the ladder was. And she fastened a very long ribbon to the window, and then she set up the ladder, and ascended the mountain, and when she was at the top of it she opened the window. She went to her father, and told him all that had happened to her. The King rejoiced greatly, and her betrothed was still there, and they went and dug up the mountain, and found Old Rinkrank inside it with all his gold and silver. Then the King had Old Rinkrank put to death, and took all his gold and silver. The princess married her betrothed, and lived right happily in great magnificence and joy.

THE CRYSTAL BALL

There was once an enchantress, who had three sons who loved each other as brothers, but the old woman did not trust them, and thought they wanted to steal her power from her. So she changed the eldest into an eagle, which was forced to dwell in the rocky mountains, and was often seen flying in great circles in the sky. The second, she changed into a whale, which lived in the deep sea, and all that was seen of it was that it sometimes spouted up a great jet of water in the air. Each of them bore his human form for only two hours daily. The third son, who was afraid she might change him into a raging wild beast—a bear perhaps, or a wolf, went secretly away. He had heard that a King's daughter who was bewitched, was imprisoned in the Castle of the Golden Sun, and was waiting to be set free. Those, however, who tried to free her risked their lives; three-and-twenty youths had already died a miserable death, and now only one other might make the attempt, after which no more must come. And as his heart was without fear, he made up his mind to seek out the Castle of the Golden Sun. He had already travelled about for a long time without being able to find it, when he came by chance into a great forest, and did not know the way out of it. All at once he saw in the distance two giants, who made a sign to him with their hands, and when he came to them they said: "We are quarreling about a cap, and which of us it is to belong to, and as we are equally strong, neither of us can get the better of the other. The small men are cleverer than we are, so we will leave the decision to you." "How can you dispute about an old cap?" said the youth. "You do not know what properties it has! It is a wishing-cap; whosoever puts it on, can wish himself away wherever he likes, and in an instant he will be there." "Give me the cap," said the youth, "I will go a short distance off, and when I call you, you must run a race, and the cap shall belong to the one who gets first to me." He put it on and went away, and thought of the King's daughter, forgot the giants, and walked continually onward. At length he sighed from the very bottom of his heart, and cried: "Ah, if I were but at the Castle of the Golden Sun," and hardly had the words passed his lips than he was standing on a high mountain before the gate of the castle.

He entered and went through all the rooms, until in the last he found the King's daughter. But how shocked he was when he saw her. She had an ashen-gray face full of wrinkles, bleary eyes, and red hair. "Are you the King's daughter, whose beauty the whole world praises?" cried he. "Ah," she answered, "this is not my form; human eyes can only see me in this state of ugliness, but that you may know what I am like, look in the mirror—it does not let itself be misled—it will show you my image as it is in truth." She gave him the mirror in his hand, and he saw therein the likeness of the most beautiful maiden on earth,

and saw, too, how the tears were rolling down her cheeks with grief. Then said he: "How can you be set free? I fear no danger." She said: "He who gets the crystal ball, and holds it before the enchanter, will destroy his power with it, and I shall resume my true shape. Ah," she added, "so many have already gone to meet death for this, and you are so young; I grieve that you should encounter such great danger." "Nothing can keep me from doing it," said he, "but tell me what I must do." "You shall know everything," said the King's daughter; "when you descend the mountain on which the castle stands, a wild bull will stand below by a spring, and you must fight with it, and if you have the luck to kill it, a fiery bird will spring out of it, which bears in its body a red-hot egg, and in the egg the crystal ball lies as its yolk. The bird, however, will not let the egg fall until forced to do so, and if it falls on the ground, it will flame up and burn everything that is near, and even the egg itself will melt, and with it the crystal ball, and then all your trouble will have been in vain.

The youth went down to the spring, where the bull snorted and bellowed at him. After a long struggle he plunged his sword in the animal's body, and it fell down. Instantly a fiery bird arose from it, and was about to fly away, but the young man's brother, the eagle, who was passing between the clouds, swooped down, hunted it away to the sea, and struck it with his beak until, in its extremity, it let the egg fall. The egg, however, did not fall into the sea, but on a fisherman's hut which stood on the shore and the hut began at once to smoke and was about to break out in flames. Then arose in the sea waves as high as a house, which streamed over the hut, and subdued the fire. The other brother, the whale, had come swimming to them, and had driven the water up on high. When the fire was extinguished, the youth sought for the egg and happily found it; it was not yet melted, but the shell was broken by being so suddenly cooled with the water, and he could take out the crystal ball unhurt.

When the youth went to the enchanter and held it before him, the latter said: "My power is destroyed, and from this time forth you are the King of the Castle of the Golden Sun. With this can you likewise give back to your brothers their human form." Then the youth hastened to the King's daughter, and when he entered the room, she was standing there in the full splendour of her beauty, and joyfully they exchanged rings with each other.

MAID MALEEN

There was once a King who had a son who asked in marriage the daughter of a mighty King; she was called Maid Maleen, and was very beautiful. As her father wished to give her to another, the prince was rejected; but as they both loved each other with all their hearts, they would not give each other up, and Maid Maleen said to her father: "I can and will take no other for my husband." Then the King flew into a passion, and ordered a dark tower to be built, into which no ray of sunlight or moonlight should enter. When it was finished, he said: "Therein shall you be imprisoned for seven years, and then I will come and see if your perverse spirit is broken." Meat and drink for the seven years were carried into the tower, and then she and her maid-in-waiting were led into it and walled up, and thus cut off from the sky and from the earth. There they sat in the darkness, and knew not when day or night began. The King's son often went round and round the tower, and called their names, but no sound from without pierced through the thick walls. What else could they do but lament and complain?

Meanwhile the time passed, and by the decline of food and drink they knew that the seven years were coming to an end. They thought the moment of their deliverance was come; but no stroke of the hammer was heard, no stone fell out of the wall, and it seemed to Maid Maleen that her father had forgotten her. As they had food only for a short time longer, and saw a miserable death awaiting them, Maid Maleen said: "We must try our last chance, and see if we can break through the wall." She took the bread-knife, and picked and bored at the mortar of a stone, and when she was tired, the waiting-maid took her turn. With great labour they succeeded in getting out one stone, and then a second, and a third, and when three days were over the first ray of light fell on their darkness, and at last the opening was so large that they could look out. The sky was blue, and a fresh breeze played on their faces; but how melancholy everything looked all around! Her father's castle lay in ruins, the town and the villages were, so far as could be seen, destroyed by fire, the fields far and wide laid to waste, and no human being was visible. When the opening in the wall was large enough for them to slip through, the waiting-maid sprang down first, and then Maid Maleen followed. But where were they to go? The enemy had ravaged the whole kingdom, driven away the King, and slain all the inhabitants. They wandered forth to seek another country, but nowhere did they find a shelter, or a human being to give them a mouthful of bread, and their need was so great that they were forced to appease their hunger with nettles. When, after long journeying, they came into another country, they tried to get work everywhere; but wherever they knocked they were turned away, and no one would have pity on them. At last they arrived in a large city and went to the royal palace. There also they were ordered to go away, but at last the cook said that they might stay in the kitchen and be scullions.

The son of the King in whose kingdom they were, however, was the very man who had been betrothed to Maid Maleen. His father had chosen another bride for him, whose face was as ugly as her heart was wicked. The wedding was fixed, and the maiden had already arrived; but because of her great ugliness she shut herself in her room, and allowed no one to see her, and Maid Maleen had to take her her meals from the kitchen. When the day came for the bride and the bridegroom to go to church, she was ashamed of her ugliness, and afraid that if she showed herself in the streets, she would be mocked and laughed at by the people. Then said she to Maid Maleen: "A great piece of luck has befallen you. I have sprained my foot, and cannot well walk through the streets; you shall put on my wedding-clothes and take my place; a greater honour than that you cannot have!" Maid Maleen, however, refused it, and said: "I wish for no honour which is not suitable for me." It was in vain, too, that the bride offered her gold. At last she said angrily: "If you do not obey me, it shall cost you your life. I have but to speak the word, and your head will lie at your feet." Then she was forced to obey, and put on the bride's magnificent clothes and all her jewels. When she entered the royal hall, every one was amazed at her great beauty, and the King said to his son: "This is the bride whom I have chosen for you, and whom you must lead to church." The bridegroom was astonished, and thought: "She is like my Maid Maleen, and I should believe that it was she herself, but she has

long been shut up in the tower, or dead." He took her by the hand and led her to church. On the way was a nettle-plant, and she said:

"Oh, nettle-plant,
Little nettle-plant,
What dost thou here alone?
I have known the time
When I ate thee unboiled,
When I ate thee unroasted."

"What are you saying?" asked the King's son. "Nothing," she replied, "I was only thinking of Maid Maleen." He was surprised that she knew about her, but kept silence. When they came to the foot-plank into the churchyard, she said:

"Foot-bridge, do not break,
I am not the true bride."

"What are you saying there?" asked the King's son. "Nothing," she replied, "I was only thinking of Maid Maleen." "Do you know Maid Maleen?" "No," she answered, "how should I know her; I have only heard of her." When they came to the church-door, she said once more:

"Church-door, break not,
I am not the true bride."

"What are you saying there?" asked he. "Ah," she answered, "I was only thinking of Maid Maleen." Then he took out a precious chain, put it round her neck, and fastened the clasp. Thereupon they entered the church, and the priest joined their hands together before the altar, and married them. He led her home, but she did not speak a single word the whole way. When they got back to the royal palace, she hurried into the bride's chamber, put off the magnificent clothes and the jewels, dressed herself in her gray gown, and kept nothing but the jewel on her neck, which she had received from the bridegroom.

When the night came, and the bride was to be led into the prince's apartment, she let her veil fall over her face, that he might not observe the deception. As soon as everyone had gone away, he said to her: "What did you say to the nettle-plant which was growing by the wayside?"

"To which nettle-plant?" asked she; "I don't talk to nettle-plants." "If you did not do it, then you are not the true bride," said he. So she bethought herself, and said:

"I must go out unto my maid,
Who keeps my thoughts for me."

She went out and sought Maid Maleen. "Girl, what have you been saying to the nettle?" "I said nothing but:

'Oh, nettle-plant,
Little nettle-plant,
What dost thou here alone?
I have known the time
When I ate thee unboiled,
When I ate thee unroasted.'"

The bride ran back into the chamber, and said: "I know now what I said to the nettle," and she repeated the words which she had just heard. "But what did you say to the foot-bridge when we went over it?" asked the King's son. "To the foot-bridge?" she answered. "I don't talk to foot-bridges." "Then you are not the true bride."

She again said:

"I must go out unto my maid,
Who keeps my thoughts for me."

and ran out and scolded Maid Maleen: "Girl, what did you say to the foot-bridge?"

"I said nothing but:

'Foot-bridge, do not break,
I am not the true bride.'"

"That costs you your life!" cried the bride, but she hurried into the room, and said: "I know now what I said to the foot-bridge," and she repeated the words. "But what did you say to the church-door?" "To the church-door?" she replied; "I don't talk to church-doors." "Then you are not the true bride."

She went out and scolded Maid Maleen, and said: "Girl, what did you say to the church-door?" "I said nothing but:

'Church-door, break not,
I am not the true bride.'"

"That will break your neck for you!" cried the bride, and flew into a terrible passion, but she hastened back into the room, and said: "I know now what I said to the church-door," and she repeated the words. "But where have you the jewel which I gave you at the church-door?" "What jewel?" she answered; "you did not give me any jewel." "I myself put it round your neck, and I myself fastened it; if you do not know that, you are not the true bride." He drew the veil from her face, and when he saw her immeasurable ugliness, he sprang back terrified, and said: "How do you come here? Who are you?" "I am your betrothed bride, but because I feared lest the people should mock me when they saw me out of doors, I commanded the scullery-maid to dress herself in my clothes, and to go to church instead of me." "Where is the girl?" said he; "I want to see her, go and bring her here." She went out and told the servants that the scullery-maid was an impostor, and that they must take her out into the court-yard and strike off her head. The servants laid hold of Maid Maleen and wanted to drag her out, but she screamed so loudly for help, that the King's son heard her voice, hurried out of his chamber and ordered them to set the maiden free instantly. Lights were brought, and then he saw on her neck the gold chain which he had given her at the church-door. "You are the true bride," said he, "who went with me to church; come with me now to my room." When they were both alone, he said: "On the way to the church you did name Maid Maleen, who was my betrothed bride; if I could believe it possible, I should think she was standing before me—you are like her in every respect." She answered: "I am Maid Maleen, who for your sake was imprisoned seven years in the darkness, who suffered hunger and thirst, and has lived so long in want and poverty. Today, however, the sun is shining on me once more. I was married to you in the church, and I am your lawful wife." Then they kissed each other, and were happy all the days of their lives. The false bride was rewarded for what she had done by having her head cut off.

The tower in which Maid Maleen had been imprisoned remained standing for a long time, and when the children passed by it they sang:

"Kling, klang, gloria.
Who sits within this tower?
A King's daughter, she sits within,
A sight of her I cannot win,
The wall it will not break,
The stone cannot be pierced.
Little Hans, with your coat so gay,
Follow me, follow me, fast as you may."

THE BOOTS OF BUFFALO-LEATHER

A soldier who is afraid of nothing, troubles himself about nothing. One of this kind had received his discharge, and as he had learnt no trade and could earn nothing, he travelled about and begged alms of kind people. He had an old raincoat on his back, and a pair of riding-boots of buffalo-leather which were still left to him. One day he was walking he knew not where, straight out into the open country, and at length came to a forest. He did not know where he was, but saw sitting on the trunk of a tree, which had been cut down, a man who was well dressed and wore a green shooting-coat. The soldier shook hands with him, sat down on the grass by his side, and stretched out his legs. "I see you have good boots on, which are well blacked," said he to the huntsman: "but if you had to travel about as I have, they would not last long. Look at mine, they are of buffalo-leather, and have been worn for a long time, but in them I can go through thick and thin." After a while the soldier got up and said: "I can stay no longer, hunger drives me onwards; but, Brother Brightboots, where does this road lead to?" "I

don't know that myself," answered the huntsman, "I have lost my way in the forest." "Then you are in the same plight as I," said the soldier; "birds of a feather flock together, let us remain together, and seek our way." The huntsman smiled a little, and they walked on further and further, until night fell. "We do not get out of the forest," said the soldier, "but there in the distance I see a light shining; there we might find something to eat." They found a stone house, knocked at the door, and an old woman opened it. "We are looking for quarters for the night," said the soldier, "and some lining for our stomachs, for mine is as empty as an old knapsack." "You cannot stay here," answered the old woman; "this is a robbers' house, and you would do wisely to get away before they come home, or you will be lost." "It won't be so bad as that," answered the soldier, "I have not had a mouthful for two days, and whether I am murdered here or die of hunger in the forest is all the same to me. I shall come in." The huntsman would not follow, but the soldier drew him in with him by the sleeve. "Come, my dear brother, we shall not come to an end so quickly as that!" The old woman had pity on them and said: "Creep in here behind the stove, and if they leave anything, I will give it to you on the sly when they are asleep." Scarcely were they in the corner before twelve robbers came bursting in, seated themselves at the table which was already laid, and vehemently demanded some food. The old woman brought in some great dishes of roast meat, and the robbers enjoyed that thoroughly. When the soldier smelled the food, he said to the huntsman: "I cannot hold out any longer, I shall seat myself at the table, and eat with them." "You will bring us to destruction," said the huntsman, and held him back by the arm. But the soldier began to cough loudly. When the robbers heard that, they threw away their knives and forks, leapt up, and discovered the two who were behind the stove. "Aha, gentlemen, are you in the corner?" cried they. "What are you doing here? Have you been sent as spies? Wait a while, and you shall learn how to fly on a dry bough." "But do be civil," said the soldier, "I am hungry, give me something to eat, and then you can do what you like with me." The robbers were astonished, and the captain said: "I see that you have no fear; well, you shall have some food, but after that you must die." "We shall see," said the soldier, and seated himself at the table, and began to cut away valiantly at the roast meat. "Brother Brightboots, come and eat," cried he to the huntsman; "you must be as hungry as I am, and cannot have better roast meat at home," but the huntsman would not eat. The robbers looked at the soldier in astonishment, and said: "The rascal uses no ceremony." After a while he said: "I have had enough food, now get me something good to drink." The chief of the robbers was in the mood to humour him in this also, and called to the old woman: "Bring a bottle out of the cellar, and mind it be of the best." The soldier drew the cork out with a loud noise, and then went with the bottle to the huntsman and said: "Watch this, brother, and you shall see something that will surprise you; I am now going to drink the health of the whole clan." Then he brandished the bottle over the heads of the robbers, and cried: "Long life to you all, but with your mouths open and your right hands lifted up," and then he drank a hearty draught. Scarcely were the words said than they all sat motionless as if made of stone, and their mouths were open and their right hands stretched up in the air. The huntsman said to the soldier: "I see that you are acquainted with tricks of another kind, but now come and let us go home." "Oho, my dear brother, but that would be marching away far too soon; we have conquered the enemy, and must first take the booty. Those men there are sitting fast, and are opening their mouths with astonishment, but they will not be allowed to move until I permit them. Come, eat and drink." The old woman had to bring another bottle of the best wine, and the soldier would not stir until he had eaten enough to last for three days. At last when day came, he said: "Now it is time to strike our tents, and in order that our march may be a short one, the old woman shall show us the nearest way to the town."

When they had arrived there, he went to his old comrades, and said: "Out in the forest I have found a nest full of gallows' birds. Come with me and we will take it." The soldier led them, and said to the huntsman: "You must go back again with me to see how they flutter when we seize them by the feet." He placed the men round about the robbers, and then he took the bottle, drank a mouthful, brandished it above them, and cried: "Long life to you all." Instantly they all regained the power of movement, but were thrown down and bound hand and foot with cords. Then the soldier ordered them to be thrown into a cart as if they had been so many sacks, and said: "Now drive them straight to prison." The huntsman, however, took one of the men aside and gave him another commission as well.

"Brother Brightboots," said the soldier, "we have safely routed the enemy and been well fed, now we will quietly walk behind them as if we were stragglers!" When they approached the town, the soldier saw a crowd of people pouring through the gate of the town who were raising loud cries of joy, and waving green boughs in the air. The he saw that the entire body-guard was coming up. "What can this mean?" said he to the huntsman. "Don't you know," he replied, "that the King has for a long time been absent from his kingdom, and that today he is returning, and every one is going to meet him." "But where is the King?" said the soldier; "I do not see him." "Here he is," answered the huntsman, "I am the King, and have announced my arrival." Then he opened his huntingcoat, and his royal garments were visible. The soldier was alarmed, and fell on his knees and begged him to forgive him for having in his ignorance treated him as an equal, and spoken to him by such a name. But the King shook hands with him, and said: "You are a brave soldier, and have saved my life. You shall never again be in want, I will take care of you. And if ever you would like to eat a piece of roast meat, as good as that in the robber's house, come to the royal kitchen. But if you would drink a health, you must first ask my permission."

THE GOLDEN KEY

In the winter time, when deep snow lay on the ground, a poor boy was forced to go out on a sledge to fetch wood. When he had gathered it together, and packed it, he wished, as he was so frozen with cold, not to go home at once, but to light a fire and warm himself a little. So he scraped away the snow, and as he was thus clearing the ground, he found a tiny, golden key. Hereupon he thought that where the key was, the lock must be also, and dug in the ground and found an iron chest. "If the key does but fit it!" thought he; "no doubt there are precious things in that little box." He searched, but no keyhole was there. At last he discovered one, but so small that it was hardly visible. He tried it, and the key fitted it exactly. Then he turned it once round, and now we must wait until he has quite unlocked it and opened the lid, and then we shall learn what wonderful things were lying in that box.

The Children's Legends

ST. JOSEPH IN THE FOREST

There was once upon a time a mother who had three daughters, the eldest of whom was rude and wicked, the second much better, although she had her faults, but the youngest was a pious, good child. The mother, however, was so strange, that it was just the eldest daughter whom she most loved, and she could not bear the youngest. On this account, she often sent the poor girl out into the great forest in order to get rid of her, for she thought she would lose herself and never come back again. But the guardian-angel which every good child has, did not forsake her, but always brought her into the right path again. Once, however, the guardian-angel behaved as if he were not there, and the child could not find her way out of the forest again. She walked on constantly until evening came, and then she saw a tiny light burning in the distance, ran up to it at once, and came to a little hut. She knocked, the door opened, and she came to a second door, where she knocked again. An old man, who had a snow-white beard and looked venerable, opened it for her; and he was no other than St. Joseph. He said quite kindly: "Come, dear child, seat yourself on my little chair by the fire, and warm yourself; I will fetch you clear water if you are thirsty; but here in the forest, I have nothing for you to eat but a couple of little roots, which you must first scrape and boil."

St. Joseph gave her the roots. The girl scraped them clean, then she brought a piece of pancake and the bread that her mother had given her to take with her; mixed all together in a pan, and cooked herself a thick soup. When it was ready, St. Joseph said: "I am so hungry; give me some of your food." The child was quite willing, and gave him more than she kept for herself, but God's blessing was with her, so that she was satisfied. When they had eaten, St. Joseph said: "Now we will go to bed; I have, however, only one bed, lay your self in it. I will lie on the ground on the straw." "No," answered she, "stay in your own bed, the straw is soft enough for me." But St. Joseph took the child in his arms, and carried her into the little bed, and there she said her prayers, and fell asleep. Next morning when she awoke, she wanted to say good morning to St. Joseph, but she did not see him. Then she got up and looked for him, but could not find him anywhere; at last she perceived, behind the door, a bag with money so heavy that she could just carry it, and on it was written that it was for the child who had slept there that night. On this she took the bag, bounded away with it, and got safely to her mother, and as she gave her mother all the money, she could not help being satisfied with her.

The next day, the second child also took a fancy to go into the forest. Her mother gave her a much larger piece of pancake and bread. It happened with her just as with the first child. In the evening she came to St. Joseph's little hut, who gave her roots for a thick soup. When it was ready, he likewise said to her: "I am so hungry, give me some of your food." Then the child said. "You may have your share." Afterwards, when St. Joseph offered her his bed and wanted to lie on the straw, she replied, "No, lie down in the bed, there is plenty of room for both of us." St. Joseph took her in his arms and put her in the bed, and laid himself on the straw.

In the morning when the child awoke and looked for St. Joseph, he had vanished, but behind the door she found a little sack of money that was about as long as a hand, and on it was written that it was for the child who had slept there last night. So she took the little bag and ran home with it, and took it to her mother, but she secretly kept two pieces for herself.

The eldest daughter had by this time grown inquisitive, and the next morning also insisted on going out into the forest. Her mother gave her pancakes—as many as she wanted, and bread and cheese as well. In the evening she found St. Joseph in his little hut, just as the two others had found him. When the soup was ready and St. Joseph said: "I am so hungry, give me some of the food," the girl answered: "Wait until I am satisfied; then if there is anything left you shall have it." But she ate nearly the whole of it, and St. Joseph had to scrape the dish. Afterwards, the good old man offered her his bed, and wanted to lie on the straw. She took it without making any opposition, laid herself down in the little bed, and left the hard straw to the white-haired man. Next morning when she awoke, St. Joseph was not to be found, but she did not trouble herself about that. She looked behind the door for a money-bag. She fancied something was lying on the ground, but as she could not very well distinguish what it was, she stooped down, so that she touched it with her nose, where it remained hanging, and when she

got up again, she saw, to her horror, that it was a second nose, which was hanging fast to her own. Then she began to scream and howl, but that did no good; she always had to look at her nose, for it stretched out so far. Then she ran out and screamed without stopping till she met St. Joseph, at whose feet she fell and begged until, out of pity, he took the nose off her again, even gave her two farthings. When she got home, her mother was standing before the door, and asked: "What have you had given to you?" Then she lied and said: "A great bag of money, but I have lost it on the way." "Lost it!" cried the mother; "oh, but we will soon find it again," and took her by the hand, and wanted to seek it with her. At first she began to cry, and did not wish to go, but at last she went. On the way, however, so many lizards and snakes broke loose on both of them, that they did not know how to save themselves. At last they stung the wicked child to death, and they stung the mother in the foot, because she had not brought her up better.

THE TWELVE APOSTLES

Three hundred years before the birth of the Lord Christ, there lived a mother who had twelve sons, but was so poor and needy that she no longer knew how she was to keep them alive. She prayed to God daily that he would grant that all her sons might be on the earth with Redeemer who was promised. When her necessity became still greater she sent one of them after the other out into the world to seek their bread. The eldest was called Peter, and he went out and had already walked a long way, a whole day's journey, when he came into a great forest. He sought for a way out, but could find none, and went farther and farther astray, and at the same time felt such great hunger that he could scarcely stand. At length he became so weak that he was forced to lie down, and he believed death to be at hand. Suddenly there stood beside him a small boy who shone with brightness, and was as beautiful and kind as an angel. The child smote his little hands together, until Peter was forced to look up and see him. Then the child said: "Why are you sitting there in such trouble?" "Alas!" answered Peter, "I am going about the world seeking bread, that I may yet see the dear Saviour who is promised, that is my greatest desire." The child said: "Come with me, and your wish shall be fulfilled." He took poor Peter by the hand, and led him between some cliffs to a great cavern. When they entered it, everything was shining with gold, silver, and crystal, and in the midst of it twelve cradles were standing side by side. Then said the little angel; "Lie down in the first, and sleep a while, I will rock you." Peter did so, and the angel sang to him and rocked him until he was asleep. And when he was asleep, the second brother came

also, guided thither by his guardian angel, and he was rocked to sleep like the first, and thus came the others, one after the other, until all twelve lay there sleeping in the golden cradles. They slept, however, three hundred years, until the night when the Saviour of the world was born. Then they awoke, and were with him on earth, and were called the twelve apostles.

THE ROSE

There was once a poor woman who had two children. The youngest had to go every day into the forest to fetch wood. Once when she had gone a long way to seek it, a little child, who was quite strong, came and helped her industriously to pick up the wood and carry it home, and then before a moment had passed the strange child disappeared. The child told her mother this, but at first she would not believe it. At length she brought a rose home, and told her mother that the beautiful child had given her this rose, and had told her that when it was in full bloom, he would return. The mother put the rose in water. One morning her child could not get out of bed. The mother went to the bed and found her dead, but she lay looking very happy. On the same morning, the rose was in full bloom.

POVERTY AND HUMILITY LEAD TO HEAVEN

There was once a King's son who went out into the world, and he was full of thought and sad. He looked at the sky, which was so beautifully pure and blue, then he sighed, and said: "How well must all be with one up there in heaven!" Then he saw a poor gray-haired man who was coming along the road towards him, and he spoke to him, and asked: "How can I get to heaven?" The man answered: "By poverty and humility. Put on my ragged clothes, wander about the world for seven years, and get to know what misery is, take no money, but if you are hungry ask compassionate hearts for a bit of bread; in this way you will reach heaven."

Then the King's son took off his magnificent coat, and wore in its place the beggar's garment, went out into the wide world, and suffered great misery. He took nothing but a little food, said nothing, but prayed to the Lord to take him into his heaven. When the seven years were over, he returned to his father's palace, but no one recognized him. He said to the servants: "Go and tell my parents that I have come back again." But the servants did not believe it, and laughed and left him standing there. Then said he: "Go and tell it to my brothers that they may come down, for I should so like to see them again." The servants would not do that either, but at last one of them went, and told it to the King's children, but these did not believe it, and did not trouble themselves about it. Then he wrote a letter to his mother, and described to her all his misery, but he did not say that he was her son. So, out of pity, the Queen had a place under the stairs assigned to him, and food taken to him daily by two servants. But one of them was ill-natured and said: "Why should the beggar have the good food?" and kept it for himself, or gave it to the dogs, and took the weak, emaciated beggar nothing but water; the other, however, was honest, and took the beggar what was sent to him. It was little, but he could live on it for a while, and all the time he was quite patient, but he grew continually weaker. As his illness increased, he desired to receive the last sacrament. When the mass was being celebrated, all the bells in the town and neighbourhood began to ring of their own accord. After mass the priest went to the poor man under the stairs, and there he lay dead. In one hand he had a rose, in the other a lily, and beside him was a paper on which was written his history.

When he was buried, a rose grew on one side of his grave, and a lily on the other.

GOD'S FOOD

There were once upon a time two sisters, one of whom had no children and was rich, and the other had five and was a widow, and so poor that she no longer had food enough to satisfy herself and her children. In her need, therefore, she went to her sister, and said: "My children and I are suffering the greatest hunger; you are rich, give me a mouthful of bread." The very rich sister was as hard as a stone, and said: "I myself have nothing in the house," and drove away the poor creature with harsh words. After some time the husband of the rich sister came home, and was just going to cut himself a piece of bread, but when he

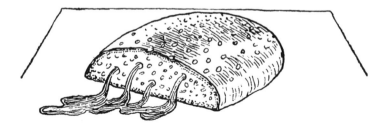

made the first cut into the loaf, out flowed red blood. When the woman saw that she was terrified and told him what had occurred. He hurried away to help the widow and her children, but when he entered her room, he found her praying. She had her two youngest children in her arms, and the three eldest were lying dead. He offered her food, but she answered: "For earthly food have we no longer any desire. God has already satisfied the hunger of three of us, and he will hearken to our supplications likewise." Scarcely had she uttered these words than the two little ones drew their last breath, whereupon her heart broke, and she sank down dead.

THE THREE GREEN TWIGS

There was once upon a time a hermit who lived in a forest at the foot of a mountain, and passed his time in prayer and good works, and every evening he carried, to the glory of God, two pails of water up the mountain. Many a beast drank of it, and many a plant was refreshed by it, for on the heights above, a strong wind blew continually, which dried the air and the ground, and the wild birds which dread mankind wheel about there, and with their sharp eyes search for a drink. And because the hermit was so pious, an angel of God, visible to his eyes, went up with him, counted his steps, and when the work was completed, brought him his food, even as the prophet of old was by God's command fed by the raven. When the hermit in his piety had already reached a great age, it happened that he once saw from afar a poor sinner being taken to the gallows. He said carelessly to himself: "There, that one is getting his deserts!" In the evening, when he was carrying the water up the mountain, the angel who usually accompanied him did not appear, and also brought him no food. Then he was terrified, and searched his heart, and tried to think how he could have sinned, as God was so angry, but he did not discover it. Then he neither ate nor drank, threw himself down on the ground, and prayed day and night. And as he was one day thus bitterly weeping in the forest, he heard a little bird singing beautifully and delightfully, and then he was still more troubled and said: "How joyously you sing, the Lord is not angry with you. Ah, if you could but tell me how I can have offended him, that I might do penance, and then my heart also would be glad again." Then the bird began to speak and said: "You have done injustice, in that you have condemned a poor sinner who was being led to the gallows, and for that the Lord is angry with you. He alone sits in judgment. However, if you will do penance and repent your sins, he will forgive you." Then the angel stood beside him with a dry branch in his hand and said: "You shall carry this dry branch until three green twigs sprout out of it, but at night when you will sleep, you shall lay it under your head. You shall beg your bread from door to door, and not tarry more than one night in the same house. That is the penance which the Lord lays on you."

Then the hermit took the piece of wood, and went back into the world, which he had not seen for so long. He ate and drank nothing but what was given him at the doors; many petitions, however, were not listened to, and many doors remained shut to him, so that he often did not get a crumb of bread.

Once when he had gone from door to door from morning till night, and no one had given him anything, and no one would shelter him for the night, he went forth into a forest, and at last found a cave which someone had made, and an old woman was sitting in it. Then said he: "Good woman, keep me with you in your house for this night;" but she said: "No, I dare not, even if I wished, I have three sons who are wicked and wild, if they come home from their robbing expedition, and find you, they would kill us both." The hermit said: "Let me stay, they will do no injury either to you or to me," and the woman was compassionate, and let herself be persuaded. Then the man lay down beneath the stairs, and put the bit of wood under his head. When the old woman saw him do that, she asked the reason of it, on which he told her that he carried the bit of wood about with him for a penance, and used it at night for a pillow, and that he had offended the Lord, because, when he had seen a poor sinner on the way to the gallows, he had said he was getting his deserts. Then the woman began to weep and cried: "If the Lord thus punishes one single word, how will it fare with my sons when they appear before him in judgment?"

At midnight the robbers came home and blustered and stormed. They made a fire, and when it had lighted up the cave and they saw a

man lying under the stairs, they fell in a rage and cried to their mother: "Who is the man? Have we not forbidden anyone whomsoever to be taken in?" Then said the mother: "Let him alone, it is a poor sinner who is expiating his crime." The robbers asked: "What has he done?" "Old man," cried they, "tell us your sins." The old man raised himself and told them how he, by one single word, had so sinned that God was angry with him, and how he was now expiating this crime. The robbers were so powerfully touched in their hearts by this story, that they were shocked with their life up to this time, reflected, and began with hearty repentance to do penance for it. The hermit, after he had converted the three sinners, lay down to sleep again under the stairs. In the morning, however, they found him dead, and out of the dry wood on which his head lay, three green twigs had grown up on high. Thus the Lord had once more received him into his favour.

OUR LADY'S LITTLE GLASS

Once upon a time a waggoner's cart which was heavily laden with wine had stuck so fast that in spite of all that he could do, he could not get it to move again. Then it chanced that Our Lady just happened to come by that way, and when she perceived the poor man's distress, she said to him: "I am tired and thirsty, give me a glass of wine, and I will set your cart free for you." "Willingly," answered the waggoner, "but I have no glass in which I can give you the wine." Then Our Lady plucked a little white flower with red stripes, called field bindweed,

which looks very like a glass, and gave it to the waggoner. He filled it with wine, and then Our Lady drank it, and in the self-same instant the cart was set free, and the waggoner could drive onwards. The little flower is still always called Our Lady's Little Glass.

THE AGED MOTHER

In a large town there was an old woman who sat in the evening alone in her room thinking how she had lost first her husband, then both her children, then one by one all her relatives, and at length, that very day, her last friend, and now she was quite alone and desolate. She was very sad at heart, and heaviest of all her losses to her was that of her sons; and in her pain she blamed God for it. She was still sitting lost in thought, when all at once she heard the bells ringing for early prayer. She was surprised that she had thus in her sorrow watched through the whole night, and lighted her lantern and went to church. It was already lighted up when she arrived, but not as it usually was with wax candles, but with a dim light. It was also crowded already with people, and all the seats were filled; and when the old woman got to her usual place it also was not empty, but the whole bench was entirely full. And when she looked at the people, they were none other than her dead relatives who were sitting there in their old-fashioned garments, but with pale faces. They neither spoke nor sang; but a soft humming and whispering was heard all over the church. Then an aunt of hers stood up, stepped forward, and said to the poor old woman: "Look there beside the altar, and you will see your sons." The old woman looked there, and saw her two children, one hanging on the gallows, the other bound to the wheel. Then said the aunt: "Behold, so would it have been with them if they had lived, and if the good God had not taken them to himself when they were innocent children." The old woman went trembling home, and on her knees thanked God for having dealt with her more kindly than she had been able to understand, and on the third day she lay down and died.

THE HEAVENLY WEDDING

A poor peasant-boy one day heard the priest say in church that whosoever desired to enter into the kingdom of heaven must always go straight onward. So he set out, and walked continually straight onwards over hill and valley without ever turning aside. At length his way led him into a great town, and into the midst of a church, where just at that time God's service was being performed. Now when he beheld all the magnificence of this, he thought he had reached heaven, sat down, and rejoiced with his whole heart. When the service was over, and the clerk bade him go out, he replied: "No, I will not go out again, I am glad to be in heaven at last." So the clerk went to the priest, and told him that there was a child in the church who would not go out again, because he believed he was in heaven. The priest said: "If he believes that, we will leave him inside." So he went to him, and asked if he had any inclination to work. "Yes," the little fellow replied, "I am accustomed to work, but I will not go out of heaven again." So he stayed in the church, and when he saw how the people came and knelt and prayed to Our Lady with the blessed child Jesus which was carved in wood, he thought: "That is the good God," and said: "Dear God, how thin you are! The people must certainly let you starve; but every day I will give you half my dinner." From this time forth, he every day took half his dinner to the image, and the image began to enjoy the food. When a few weeks had gone by, people remarked that the image was growing larger and stout and strong, and wondered much. The priest also could not understand it, but stayed in the church, and followed the little boy about, and then he saw how he shared his food with the Virgin Mary, and how she accepted it.

After some time the boy became ill, and for eight days could not leave his bed; but as soon as he could get up again, the first thing he did was to take his food to Our Lady. The priest followed him, and heard him say: "Dear God, do not take it amiss that I have not brought you anything for such a long time, for I have been ill and could not get up." Then the image answered him and said: "I have seen your good-will, and that is enough for me. Next Sunday you shall go with me to the wedding." The boy rejoiced at this, and repeated it to the priest, who begged him to go and ask the image if he, too, might be permitted to go. "No," answered the image, "you alone." The priest wished to prepare him first, and give him the holy communion and the child was willing, and next Sunday, when the host came to him, he fell down and died, and was at the eternal wedding.

THE HAZEL-BRANCH

One afternoon the Christ-child had laid himself in his cradle-bed and had fallen asleep. Then his mother came to him, looked at him full of gladness, and said: "Have you laid yourself down to sleep, my child? Sleep sweetly, and in the meantime I will go into the wood, and fetch you a handful of strawberries, for I know that you will be pleased with them when you awake." In the wood outside, she found a spot with the most beautiful strawberries; but as she was stooping down to gather one, an adder sprang up out of the grass. She was alarmed, left the strawberries where they were, and hastened away. The adder darted after her; but Our Lady, as you can readily understand, knew what it was best to do. She hid herself behind a hazel-bush, and stood there until the adder had crept away again. Then she gathered the strawberries, and as she set out on her way home she said: "As the hazel-bush has been my protection this time, it shall in future protect others also." Therfore, from the most remote times, a green hazel-branch has been the safest protection against adders, snakes, and everything else which creeps on the earth.

Folkloristic Commentary

1

THE WORK OF THE BROTHERS GRIMM

Frau Katherina Viehmann (1755–1815) was about fifty-five when the young Grimm brothers discovered her. She had married in 1777 a tailor of Niederzwehren, a village near Kassel, and was now a mother and a grandmother. "This woman," Wilhelm Grimm wrote in the preface to the first edition of the second volume (1815), ". . . has a strong and pleasant face and a clear, sharp look in her eyes; in her youth she must have been beautiful. She retains fast in mind these old sagas—which talent, as she says, is not granted to everyone; for there be many that cannot keep in their heads anything at all. She recounts her stories thoughtfully, accurately, with uncommon vividness and evident delight—first quite easily, but then, if required, over again, slowly, so that with a bit of practice it is possible to take down her dictation, word for word. Much was recorded in this way, and its fidelity is unmistakable. Anyone believing that traditional materials are easily falsified and carelessly preserved, and hence cannot survive over a long period, should hear how close she always keeps to her story and how zealous she is for its accuracy; never does she alter any part in repetition, and she corrects a mistake herself, immediately she notices it. Among people who follow the old ways of life without change, attachment to inherited patterns is stronger than we, impatient for variety, can realise."[1]

It was from such people that Jacob and Wilhelm collected, through a period of years, the materials for their book: simple folk of the farms and villages round about, and in the spinning rooms and beer halls of Kassel. Many stories were received, too, from friends. In the notes it is set down frequently, "From Dortchen Wild in Kassel," or "From Dortchen, in the garden house." Dorothea Wild—later Wilhelm's wife—supplied over a dozen of the stories. Together with her five sisters, she had been versed in fairylore by an old nurse, *die alte Marie*.[2] Another family were the Hassenpflugs, who had arrived with a store of tales from Hanau;[3] still another, the von Haxthausens, who resided in Westphalia.[4] The brothers searched for materials also in medieval German manuscripts, and in the Folk Books and collections from the time of Luther.

The special distinction of the work of Jacob and Wilhelm Grimm (1785–1863 and 1786–1859) was its scholarly regard for the sources. Earlier collectors had felt free to manipulate folk materials; the Grimms were concerned to let the speech of the people break directly into print. Among the Romantics of the generation just preceding, folk poetry had been venerated profoundly. Novalis had pronounced the folk tale, the

---

[1] Johannes Bolte and George Polívka, *Anmerkungen zu den Kinder- und Hausmärchen der Brüder Grimm*, Leipzig, 1912–1932, Vol. IV, pp. 443–444. To the "story-wife of Niederzwehren" we owe nineteen of the finest tales: 6. 9. 22. 29. 34. 58. 59. 61. 63. 71. 76. 89. 94. 98. 100. 102. 106. 108. 111. Some four years after the brothers had come to know her, she abruptly fell into poverty and sickness, and in another few months had died.

[2] The Wilds were six daughters and one son, the Grimms five sons and one daughter. Frau Wild gave stories 18. 30. Lisette gave variants of 41. 55. 105. Gretchen gave 2. 3. 154., Dortchen 13. 15. 24. 39. 46. 49. 56. 65. 88. 103. 105. parts of 52. 55. 60. and a variant of 34. *Die alte Marie* herself supplied 11. 26. 31. 44. 50. and a variant of 53.

[3] Ludwig Hassenpflug later married Lotte Grimm. His sisters, Jeannette and Amalie, gave stories 13. 14. 17. 20. 29. 41. 42. 53. part of 26. and variants of 61. 67. 76.

[4] A family of eight sons and six daughters. Their contributions began only after publication of the first edition of volume one (1812), but in the later editions some of their tales replaced earlier numbers. From their village of Bökendorf, near Brakel, come stories 7. 10. 16. 27. 60. 70. 72. 86. 91. 99. 101. 112. 113. 121. 123. 126. 129. 131. 134. 135. 139. and parts of 52. 97. The von Haxthausens gave also 133. and 143. from Münsterland, as well as some half dozen others from various parts of the country. (Cf. Bolte and Polívka, *op. cit.*, IV, pp. 437 ff.)

primary and highest poetical creation of man. Schiller had written extravagantly:

Tiefere Bedeutung
Liegt in dem Märchen meiner Kinderjahre
Als in der Wahrheit, die das Leben lehrt.[5]

Sir Walter Scott had collected and studied the balladry of the Scottish border. Wordsworth had sung of the Reaper. Yet no one before the Grimms had really acquiesced to the irregularities, the boorishness, the simplicity, of the folk talk. Anothologists had arranged, restored, and tempered; poets had built new masterpieces out of the rich raw material. But an essentially ethnographical approach, no one had so much as conceived.

The remarkable fact is that the Grimm brothers never *developed* their idea; they began with it full blown, as young students hardly out of law school. Jacob, browsing in the library of their favourite professor, the jurist Friedrich Karl von Savigny, had chanced on a selection of the German Minnesingers, and almost immediately their life careers had stood before them. Two friends, Clemens Brentano and Ludwig Achim von Arnim, who in 1805 had published, in the Romantic manner, the first volume of a collection of folk song, *Des Knaben Wunderhorn*, gave the brothers valuable encouragement. Jacob and Wilhelm assisted with the later volumes of the *Wunderhorn*, and began collecting from their friends. But at the same time, they were seeking out, decipehering, and beginning to edit, manuscripts from the Middle Ages. The book of fairy tales represented only a fraction of their immediate project. It would be, as it were, the popular exhibition hall of an ethnological museum: in the offices upstairs research would be going forward, which the larger public would hardly wish, or know how, to follow.

The programme proceeded against odds. In 1806 the armies of Napoleon overran Kassel. "Those days," wrote Wilhelm "of the collapse of all hitherto existing establishments will remain forever before

---

[5] Deeper meaning lies in the fairytale of my childhood than in the truth that is taught by life. (*Die Piccolomini*, III. 4.)

my eyes. . . . The ardour with which the studies in Old German were pursued helped overcome the spiritual depression. . . . Undoubtedly the world situation and the necessity to draw into the peacefulness of scholarship contributed to the reawakening of the long forgotten literature; but not only did we seek something of consolation in the past, our hope, naturally, was that this course of ours should contribute somewhat to the return of a better day." While "foreign persons, foreign manners, and a foreign, loudly spoken language" promenaded the thoroughfares, "and poor people staggered along the streets being led away to death," the brothers stuck to their work tables, to resurrect the present through the past.

Jacob in 1805 had visited the libraries of Paris; his ability to speak French now helped him to a small clerkship in the War Office. Two of his brothers were in the field with the hussars. Just after his mother's death, in 1808, he was appointed auditor to the state council and superintendent of the private library of Jerome Buonoparte, the puppet king of Westphalia. Thus he was freed from economic worry, but had considerable to do. Volume one of the *Nursery and Household Tales* appeared the winter of Napoleon's retreat from Moscow (1812); two years later, in the midst of the work on volume two, Jacob was suddenly dispatched to Paris to demand restitution of his city's library, which had been carried away by the French. Then in 1816, after attending the congress of Vienna as secretary of legation, he was again dispatched, to reclaim another treasure of books. He found the predicament not a little awkward. The librarian, Langlès, seeing him studying manuscripts in the *Bibliothèque*, prostested with indignation: "*Nous ne devons plus souffrir ce Monsieur Grimm, qui vient tous les jours travailler ici et qui nous enlève pourtant nos manuscrits.*"

Wilhelm was never as vigorous and positive as Jacob, but the more gay and gentle. During the years of the collection he suffered from a severe heart disorder, which for days riveted him to his room. The two were together all their lives. As children they had slept in the same bed and worked at the same table; as students they had had two beds and tables in the same room. Even after Wilhelm's marriage to Dortchen Wild, in 1825, Uncle Jacob shared the house, "and in such harmony and community that one might almost imagine the children were common property."[6] Thus it is difficult to say, with respect to their work, where Jacob ended and Wilhelm began.

The engraved portraits of the brothers reveal two very good looking youths, clear eyed, with delicately modelled features. Wilhelm's forhead is the larger, his chin, the sharper, his eyes look out from arched, slightly nettled brows. With firmer jaw Jacob watches, and a sturdier, more relaxed poise. His hair is a shade the darker, the less curled and tousled. Their mouths, well shaped, are identical. Both are shown with the soft, flaring, highly-stocked collars and the wind-blown hair-style of the period. They are alert, sharp nosed, sensitive nostrilled, and immediately interest the eye.

In the labour on the fairy tales Jacob supplied, apparently, the greater initiative, the stricter demands for scholarly precision, and a tireless zeal for collecting. Wilhelm toiled over the tales with sympathetic devotion, and with exquisite judgment in the patient task of selecting, piecing together, and arranging. As late as 1809, they had considered the advisability of turning over the manuscripts to Brentano. But Jacob mistrusted their friend's habit of reworking traditional materials— making them full of personal fantasy, cutting, amplifying, recombining brilliantly, and always flavouring to the contemporary palate. He complained of the mishandling of the text of the *Wunderhorn*. The poet, however, thought the scholar a little dull, and exhibited no interest whatsoever in the ideal of the chaste historical record. Achim von Arnim, on the other hand, aided and advised. Though he strove to persuade Jacob to relent a little, here and there, he did not reject the brothers when they insisted on their programme. It was he, who found a printer for the collection, Georg Andreas Reimer, in Berlin.

Volume one came out at Christmas time, with a dedication to Bettina, the wife of Achim von Arnim, for her little son, Johannes Freimund. In Vienna the book was banned as a work of superstition; but elsewhere, in spite of the political tension of the times, it was eagerly received. Clemens Brentano declared that he found the unimproved materials slovenly and often very boring; others complained of the impropriety of certain of the tales; newspaper reviews were few and cold. Nevertheless, the book enjoyed immediate success, and

[6] Richard Cleasby, *An Icelandic-English Dictionary*, Oxford, 1874, Introduction, p. lxix.

prospered. The Brothers Grimm had produced, in an unpredicted way, the masterpiece which the whole Romantic movement in Germany had been intending.

Von Arnim wrote to Wilhelm with quiet satisfaction: "You have collected propitiously, and have sometimes right propitiously helped; which, of course, you don't let Jacob know. . . ." Not all the tales had come from such talented heads as that of the story-wife of Niederzwehren. Some had been rather garbled. Many had been relayed by friends, and had lost flavour. A few had been found in fragments, and these had had to be matched. But Wilhelm had kept note of his adjustments; and their end had been, not to embellish, but to bring out the lines of the story which the inferior informant had obscured. Furthermore, throughout the later editions, which appeared from year to year, the work of the careful, loving, improving hand could be increasingly discerned. Wilhelm's method, as contrasted with the procedures of the Romantics, was inspired by his increasing familiarity with the popular modes of speech. He noted carefully the words that the people preferred to use and their typical manners of descriptive narrative, and then very carefully going over the story-texts, as taken from this or that raconteur, he chiselled away the more abstract, literary, or colourless turns and fitted in such characteristic, rich phrases, as he had gathered from the highways and the byways. Jacob at first demurred. But it was clear that the stories were gaining immensely by the patient devotion of the younger brother; and since Jacob, anyhow, was becoming involved in his grammatical studies, he gradually released to Wilhelm the whole responsibility. Even the first edition of volume two was largely in the hands of Wilhelm; thereafter the work was completely his.

Volume two appeared in January, 1815, the brothers having received assistance from all sides. "The two of us gathered the first volume alone," Wilhelm wrote to a friend, "quite by ourselves and hence very slowly, over a period of six years; now things are going much better and more rapidly." The second edition was issued, 1819, improved and considerably enlarged, and with an introduction by Wilhelm, "On the Nature of Folk Tales." Then, in 1822, appeared a third volume—a work of commentary, compiled partly from the notes of the earlier editions, but containing additional matter, as well as a most thorough comparative-historical study.[7] The brothers published a selection of fifty favourites in 1825, and in 1837 released a third edition of the two volume original, again amplified and improved. Still further improvements were to be noted in the editions of 1840, 1843, 1850, 1857. Translations in Danish, Swedish, and French came almost immediately; presently in Dutch, English, Italian, Spanish, Czech, Polish, Russian, Bulgarian, Hungarian, Finnish, Esthonian, Hebrew, Armenian, and Esperanto. Tales borrowed from the Grimm collection have since been recorded among the natives of Africa, Mexico, and the South Seas.

[7] This volume underwent revision for its final edition in 1856. It has recently been wholly renovated, and increased to five study volumes, under the editorship of Professors Johannes Bolte and George Polívka (cf. op. cit.).

2

THE TYPES OF STORY

The first effect of the work was a transformation throughout the world of the scholarly attitude toward the productions of the folk. A new humility before the informant becomes everywhere perceptible after the date, 1812. Exactitude, not beautification, becomes thereafter the first requirement, "touching up" the unforgivable sin. Furthermore, the number and competence of the collectors greatly and rapidly increased. Field-workers armed with pad and pencil marched forth to every corner of the earth. Solid volumes today stand ranged along the shelf from Switzerland, Frisia, Holland, Denmark, Sweden, Norway, Iceland and the Faroes, England, Scotland, Wales, Ireland, France, Italy, Corsica, Malta, Portugal and Spain, the Basques, the Rhaeto-Romanic mountaineers, the modern Greeks, Rumanians, Albanians, Slovenes, Serb-Croatians, Bulgarians, Macedonians, Czechs, Slovacs, Serbs and Poles, Great, White and Little Russians, Lithuanians, Latvians, Finns, Lapps and Esthonians, Cheremiss, Mordvinians, Votyaks and Syryenians, Gipsies and Hungarians, Turks, Kasan-Tatars, Chuvash and Bashkirs, Kalmuks, Buryats, Voguls and Ostyaks, Yakuts, Siberian Tatars, the peoples of the Caucasus, the populations of India and Iran, Mesopotamia, Syria, the Arabian desert, Tibet, Turkestan, Java and Sumatra, Borneo, the Celebes, the Philippines, Burma, Siam, Annam, China, Korea and Japan, Australia, Melanesia, Micronesia, Polynesia, the continent of

Africa, South, Middle and North America. Still unpublished archives accumulate in provincial, national, and international institutes. Where there was a lack, there is now such abundance that the problem is how to deal with it, how to get the mind around it, and what to think.

In this ocean of story, a number of kinds of narrative are encompassed. Many of the collections of so-called primitive materials include Myths; that is to say, religious recitations conceived as symbolic of the play of Eternity in Time. These are rehearsed, not for diversion, but for the spiritual welfare of the individual or community. Legends also appear; i.e. reviews of a traditional history (or of episodes from such a history) so rendered as to permit mythological symbolism to inform human event and circumstance. Whereas myths present in pictorial form cosmogonic and ontological intuitions, legends refer to the more immediate life and setting of the given society.[1] Something of the religious power of myth may be regarded as effective in legend, in which case, the native narrator must be careful concerning the circumstances of his recitation, lest the power break astray. Myths and legends may furnish entertainment incidentally, but they are essentially tutorial.

Tales, on the other hand, are frankly pastime: fireside tales, winternights' tales, nursery tales, coffee-house tales, sailor yarns, pilgrimage and caravan tales to pass the endless nights and days. The most ancient written records and the most primitive tribal circles attest alike to man's hunger for the good story. And every kind of thing has served. Myths and legends of an earlier period, now discredited or no longer understood, their former power broken (yet still potent to charm), have supplied much of the raw material for what now passes simply as Animal Tale, Fairy Tale, and Heroic or Romantic Adventure. The giants, and

---

[1] In German criticism the terms Sage and Legende are commonly distinguished. Sage designates any little, local story, associated with this or that specific hill or grove, pond or river. By a people inhabiting a spirit-haunted and memory-haunted landscape, the Sage is conceived to be a recitation of fact. The Sage may be developed into the Kunstsage, or "Literary Saga." Legende, on the other hand, denotes the religious tale associated with some specific shrine or relic. It is a later and more elaborate form than the Sage. The "Children's Legends" of the Grimm collection bring fairytale motifs to play around elements of Christian belief.—But the term "Legend," as used above, is more general. It includes both Sage and Legende, but also the materials of Chronicle and Epic.

gnomes of the Germans, the "little people" of the Irish, the dragons, knights, and ladies of Arthurian Romance, were once the gods and demons of the Green Isle and the European continent. Similarly, the divinities of the primitive Arabians appear as Jinn in the story-world of Islam. Tales of such origin are regarded with differing degrees of seriousness by the various people who recount them; and they can be received by the sundry members of the audience, severally, with superstitious awe, nostalgia for the days of belief, ironic amusement, or simple delight in the marvels of imagination and intricacies of plot. But no matter what the atmosphere of belief, the stories, in so far as they now are "Tales," are composed primarily for amusement. They are reshaped in terms of dramatic contrast, narrative suspense, repetition,[2] and resolution.

Certain characteristic opening and closing formulas set apart from the common world the timeless, placeless realm of faërie: "Once upon a time;" "In the days of good King Arthur;" "A thousand years ago tomorrow;" "Long, long ago, when Brahmadatta was the ruler of Benares"—"And so they lived happily ever after;" "That's all;" "A mouse did run, the story is done;" "So there they remain, happy and contented, while we stand barefoot as packasses and lick our teeth;" "Bo bow bended, my story's ended; if you don't like it, you may mend it." A handsome conclusion is attributed to the Zanzibar Swahili: "If the story was beautiful, the beauty belongs to us all; if it was bad, the fault is mine only, who told it."[3]

Prose is the normal vehicle of story, but at critical points little rhymes commonly appear:

Looking-glass, Looking-glass, on the wall,
Who in this land is the fairest of all?

Turn back, turn back, young maiden dear,
'Tis a murderer's house you enter here.

Peace, peace, my dear little giants,
I have had a thought of ye,
Something I have brought for ye.

---

[2] Throughout the Old World, repetition is commonly in threes; in America, fours.

[3] From Bolte and Polívka, op. cit., Vol. IV, p. 34.

> Little duck, little duck, dost thou see,
> Hänsel and Gretel are waiting for thee?
> There's never a plank, or bridge in sight,
> Take us across on thy back so white.

In Arabian tales, and less commonly European, the prose of the text slips momentarily into rhyme: "Thereupon sat a lady bright of blee, with brow beaming brilliantly, the dream of philosophy, whose eyes were fraught with Babel's gramarye and her eyebrows were arched as for archery;" "They all lived happy and died happy, and never drank out of a dry cappy;" "Now I had an army of a thousand thousand bridles, men of warrior mien with forearms strong and keen, armed with spears and mail-coats sheen and swords that gleam."

In the lovely French medieval chante-fable, *Aucassin et Nicolette*, verse passages regularly alternate with prose. In the *Bardic Lays* that served to entertain the heroes in the mead-hall, in the long *Epics* woven in later times, and in the *Ballads* of the folk, narrative goes into verse entirely. The spell of rhythm and rhyme is the spell of "once upon a time."[4]

"And as the cup went round merrily, quoth the Porter to the Kalandars: 'And you, O brothers mine, have ye no story or rare adventure to amuse use withal?' "—The empty hour is as gladly filled with a good personal adventure as with a fragment of traditional wonder. Hence, the world of actual life as caught in *Anecdote*, paced and timed to fix and justify attention, has contributed to the great category of the Tale. The anecdote may range from the ostensibly truthful, or only slightly exaggerated, to the frankly unbelievable. In the latter range it mingles readily with sheer *Invention*: the Joke, Merry Tale, and Ghost Adventure. Again, it can unite with the mythological stuff of traditional romance, and thus acquire some of the traits of legend.

A distinct and relatively recently developed category is the *Fable*. The best examples are the Greek and Medieval collections attributed to

---

[4] The literary folk tale can be rendered in either verse or prose. The huge Hindu collection of the *Kathāsaritsāgara*, "Ocean of the Streams of Story" (c. 1063–1081), is entirely in verse; the Arabian *Thousand Nights and One Night* (eleventh to fifteenth centuries) is in prose.

"Aesop," and the Oriental of the Brahmins, Buddhists, and Jains. The Fable is didactic. It is not, like Myth, a revelation of transcendental mysteries, but a clever illustration of a political or ethical point. Fables are witty, and not to be believed but understood.[5]

Under the single heading, *Märchen*, the Germans popularly comprehend the whole range of the Folk Tale. The Brothers Grimm, therefore, included in their collection folk stories of every available variety. Scholars since their day have analyzed the assortment and classified the tales according to type. The following listing is based on the standard index of story-types, prepared by the Finnish folklorist, Antti Aarne.[6]

I. *Animal Tales*: Wild Animals, 2. 23. 38. 73. 74. 132: Wild Animals and Domestic, 5. 27. 48. 75. Man and Wild Animals, 8. 72. 157. Domestic Animals, 10. 41. (compare 18.). Birds, 58. 86. 102. 171. Fish, 172. Other Animals and Objects, 105. i. 187.

II. *Ordinary Folk Tales*: A. *Tales of Magic*:[7] Supernatural Adversaries, 4. 5. 12. 15. 26. 42. 44. 46. 51. 56. 60. 66. 79. 81. 82. 85. 91. 99. 101. 106. 111. 113. 120. 121. 133. 181. 186. 191. 193. 197. (compare 163.). Supernatural or Enchanted Husband (Wife) or Other Relatives, 1. 9. 11. (compare 141.) 13. 25. 49. 50. 63. 69. 88. 92. 93. 106. 108. 123. 127. 135. 144. 160. 161. 169. 193. Supernatural Tasks, 24. 29. 100. Supernatural Helpers, 6. 14. 17. 19. 21. 55. 57. 62. 65. 71. 89. 97. 126. 130. 134. 136. Magic Objects, 16. 36. 54. 60. 64. 103. 107. 110. 116. 122. 165. 188. Supernatural Power or Knowledge, 16. 33. 76. 90. 118. 124. 129. 142. 149. Other Tales of the Supernatural, 3. 31. 37. 45. 47. 53. 96. B. *Religious Tales*: 28. 35. 81. 87. 92. 125. 145. 147. 167. 178. 194. 195. 206. C. *Novelle* (*Romantic Tales*): 22. 40. 52. 67. 94. 112. 114. 115.

---

[5] Some of the *Jātakas*, or tales of the early lives of the Buddha, are fables that half pretend to be little legends. Buddhist and Jain fables teach religious lore, Aesop and the Brahminical *Panchatantra* teach the wisdom of life.

[6] Antti Aarne, *Verzeichnis der Märchentypen*, Folklore Fellows Communications, Vol. I, No. 3, Helsinki, 1911. Johannes Bolte notes that the following are missing from Aarne's listing: *Animal Tales*: 30. 80. 173. 190.—*Ordinary Folk Tales*: 39. 43. 78. 109. 117. 137. 150. 154. 175. 177. 180. 182. 184. 196. 201–205. 208–210.—*Jokes and Anecdotes*: 77. 95. 119. 131. 162. 170. 200. (Bolte and Polívka, *op. cit.*, Vol. IV, pp. 467–470).

[7] Albert Wesselski (*Versuch einer Theorie des Märchens*, 1931, pp. 12, 32, etc.) is of the opinion that the term *Märchen* should be reserved for this category, II. A.

152. 179. 198. 199. D. *Tales of the Stupid Ogre*: 20. 183. 189. (compare 148.).

III. *Jokes and Anecdotes*: Numskull Stories, 70. 174. Stories about Married Couples, 34. 59. 83. 104. 128. 164. 168. Stories about a Woman (Girl), 34. 139. 155. 156. Stories about a Man (Boy), 61. and 192. (the Clever Man); 7.20. 59. 70. 98. and 104. (Lucky Accidents); 32. 120. and 143. (the Stupid Man). Tales of Lying, 146. 151. 158. 159. 185.

3

THE HISTORY OF THE TALES

The patterns of the folk tale are much the same throughout the world. This circumstance has given rise to a long and intricate learned discussion.[1] By and large, it is now fairly agreed that the general continuity, and an occasional correspondence to the detail, can be referred to the psychological unity of the human species, but that over this ground a profuse and continuous passing along of tales from mouth to ear—and by book—has been taking place, not for centuries only, but millenniums, and over immense reaches of the globe. Hence the folklore of each area must be studied for its peculiar history. Every story—every motif, in fact—has had its adventurous career.

The Grimm brothers regarded European folklore as the detritus of Old Germanic belief: the myths of ancient time had disintegrated, first into heroic legend and romance, last into these charming treasures of the nursery. But in 1859, the year of Wilhelm's death, a Sanskrit scholar, Theodore Benfey, demonstrated that a great portion of the lore of Europe had come, through Arabic, Hebrew and Latin translations, directly from India—and this as late as the thirteenth century

---

[1] A review by Dr. Ruth Benedict will be found in *The Encyclopedia of the Social Sciences*, article, "Folklore;" one by Professor William H. Halliday, under the same heading in *The Encyclopaedia Britannica*. A more detailed account with complete bibliography appears in Bolte and Polívka, *op. cit.*, Vol. V, pp. 239–264.

A.D.[2] Since Benfey's time, the evidence for a late, polygenetic development of the folk tale of Christian Europe has become abundant and detailed.

The scholars of the English Anthropological School at the close of the nineteenth century (E. B. Tylor, Andrew Lang, E. S. Hartland, and others), believed that the irrational elements of fairylore were grounded in savage superstition. Totemism, cannibalism, taboo, and the external soul, they discovered on every page. But to-day it is clear that such irrationalities are as familiar to modern European dream-life as to society on the Congo, and so we are no longer disposed to run a tale back to the paleolithic caves simply because the heroine marries a gazelle or eats her mother. Yet in a few of the stories of the Grimm collection actual vestiges of primitive ways can be identified with reasonable assurance;[3] and in perhaps half a dozen other signs persist from the barbaric period of the Migrations.[4]

A crisis in the history of the European folk tradition becomes apparent, about the tenth century A.D. A quantity of Late Classical matter was being imported from the Mediterranean by the itinerant entertainers, minstrels and jesters, who came swarming from the sunny south to infest the pilgrim routes and present themselves at castle doors.[5] And not only minstrels, missionaries too were at work. The fierce, warrior

---

[2] Theodore Benfey, *Pantschatantra: Fünf Bücher indischer Fabeln, Märchen und Erzählungen. Aus dem Sanskrit übersetzt mit Einleitung und Ammerkungen*, Leipzig, 1859.

[3] For examples, see the classification of tales at the conclusion of the present section, pp. 763–764, *infra*.

[4] Magic formulae betraying features of the early Germanic verse-style stand to this day in the Grimm collection:

> Rapúnzel, Rapúnzel,
> Lass dein Haár herúnter (No. 12.)

> Éntchen, Éntchen,
> Da steht Grétel und Háensel
> Kein Stég und keíne Brúecke
> Nimm úns auf deínen weíssen Rúecken. (No. 15.)

[5] How much Hellenistic and Roman material had infected the German tribal mythologies during earlier centuries, before and after the fall of Rome, remains a question; it is certain that much of the Balder and Woden imagery is by no means "primitive Aryan." (Cf. Franz Rolf Schröder, *Germanentum und Hellenismus*, Heidelberg, 1924; *Altgermanische Kulturprobleme*, Berlin and Leipzig, 1929.)

ideals of earlier story were submitting to a new piety and sentimental didactic: Slandered Virtue is triumphant, Patience is rewarded, Love endures.

There seems to have prevailed a comparative poverty of invention until the twelfth century, when the matter of India and the matter of Ireland found their ways to the fields of Europe. This was the period of the Crusades and the Chivalrous Romance, the former opening Europe wide to the civilization of the Orient, the latter conjuring from the realm of Celtic faërie a wild wonderworld of princesses enchanted in sleep, castles solitary in the forest adventurous, dragons steaming in rimy caverns, Merlin-magic, Morgan le Fay, cackling hags transmuted by a kiss into the damsel of the world. Europe inherited nearly everything of its fairyland from the imagination of the Celt.[6]

Shortly after this time came the Hindu *Panchatantra*. The work had been translated from Sanskrit into Persian in the sixth century A.D., from Persian into Arabic in the eighth, and from Arabic into Hebrew, around the middle of the thirteenth. About 1270, John of Capua turned the Hebrew into Latin, and from this Latin version the book passed into German and Italian. A Spanish translation had been made from the Arabic in 1251; an English was later drawn from the Italian. Individual stories became popular in Europe, and were then rapidly assimilated. "Out of the literary works," wrote Benfey, "the tales went to the people, and from the people they returned, transformed, to literary collections, then back they went to the people again, etc., and it was principally through this cooperative action that they achieved national and individual spirit—that quality of national validity and individual unity which contributes to not a few of them their high poetical worth."[7]

---

[6] The Youth of Siegfried, Brynhild's sleep, the sword in the tree and the broken sword, are motifs adopted from the Celtic tradition. The Icelandic Sagas and Eddas were powerfully influenced by the bards of Ireland. In the classification at the conclusion of the present section the tales under heading IV, *Chivalrous Work of the Middle Ages*, represent this body of matter as it was reworked under the influence of twelfth century Romance.

[7] Benfey, *op. cit.*, p. XXVI. On the basis of a garbled story from the East, the Buddha was canonized by the medieval Church as Saints Barlaam and Josaphat, Abbots; Feastday, November 27. Following the work of the nineteenth century folklorists, these names were expunged from the calendar.

A wonderful period opened in the thirteenth century. With the passing of the gallant days of the great crusades, the aristocratic taste for verse romance declined, and the lusty prose of the late medieval towns moved into its own. Prose compendiums of traditional lore began appearing, filled with every kind of gathered anecdote and history of wonder—vast, immeasurable compilations, which the modern scholar has hardly explored. A tumbling, broad, inexhaustible flood of popular merry tales, misadventures, hero, saint, and devil legends, animal fables, mock heroics, slap-stick jokes, riddles, pious allegories and popular ballads burst abruptly into manuscript and carried everything before it. Compounded with themes from the Cloister and the Castle, mixed with elements from the Bible and from the heathenness of the Orient, as well as the deep pre-Christian past, the wonderful hurly-burly broke into the stonework of the cathedrals, grinned from the stained glass, twisted and curled in humorous grotesque in and out of the letters of illuminated manuscripts, appeared in tapestries, on saddles and weapons, on trinket-caskets, mirrors and combs.[8] This was the first major flourishing in Europe of a literature of the people. From right and left the materials came, to left and right they were flung forth again, sealed with the sign of the late Gothic; so that no matter what the origin, they were now the re-creation of the European folk.

Much of this matter found its way into the literary works of the late Middle Ages, the Reformation and Renaissance (Boccaccio, Chaucer, Hans Sachs, Les cent nouvelles nouvelles, etc.) and then back, reshaped, to the people. The period of abundance continued to the time of the Thirty Years' War (1618–1648).

Finally, in France, at the court of Louis XIV, a vogue commenced for the delicate refashioning of fairy tales and fables—inspired, in part by a new French translation of a late Persian rendering of the Panchatantra, part by Antoine Galland's rendition of the Arabian Thousand Nights and One Night. The pastime yielded a plentiful harvest of freshly wrought, delicate pieces (La Fontaine, Perrault, the forty-one volumes of the Cabinet des Fées). Many were taken over by the people and crossed the Rhine.

So that by the time the Grimm brothers arrived to begin their

[8] Friedrich von der Leyen, Das Märchen, Leipzig, 3rd edition, 1925, pp. 147–148.

collection, much material had overlain the remote mythology of the early tribes. Tales from the four quarters, inventions from every level of society and all stages of Western history were commingled. Nevertheless, as they observed, a homogeneity of style and character pervades the total inheritance. A continuous process of re-creation, a kind of spiritual metabolism, has so broken the original structures in assimilating them to the living civilization, that only the most meticulous and skilful observation, analysis and comparative research can discover their provenience and earlier state. The Grimm brothers regarded this rich composition as a living unit and sought to probe its past; the modern scientist, on the other hand, searches the unit for its elements, then ferrets these to their remote sources. From the contemporary work we receive a more complex impression of the processes of culture than was possible in the period of the Grimms.

Let us turn, therefore, to the problem of the individual tale—the migratory element that enters our system and becomes adapted to our style of existence. What is its history? What can happen to it during the course of its career?

Passing from Orient to Occident, surviving the revolutions of history and the long attrition of time, traversing the familiar bounds of language and belief—the favourite now of a Saracen king, now of a hard warrior, now of a Capucian monk, now of old Marie—the tale undergoes kaleidoscopical mutations. The first problem of research is to identify, fix, and characterize the key-complex, the formal principle of the story's entity, that without which the story would not be. As the story then is followed throughout its peregrination, it is observed to assimilate to itself the materials offered from land to land. It changes, like a chameleon; puts on the colours of its background; lives and shapes itself to the requirements of the moment. "Such a tale," writes an American authority, "is at the same time a definite entity and an abstraction. It is an entity in the particular form in which it happens to be recorded at any moment; it is an abstraction in the sense that no two versions ever exactly agree and that consequently the tale lives only in endless mutations."[9]

---

[9] Archer Taylor, The Black Ox, Folklore Fellows Communications, Vol. XXIII, No. 70, Helsinki, 1927, p. 4.

In the life-course of any given version of a tale, a number of typical accidents may occur. A detail may be forgotten. A foreign trait may become naturalized, an obsolete modernized. A general term (animal) may become specialized (mouse), or, vice versa, a special generalized. The order of events may be rearranged. The personages may become confused, or the acts confused, or in some other way the traits of the story may cross-influence each other. Persons and things may become multiplied (particularly by the numbers 3, 5, and 7). Many animals may replace one (polyzoism). Animals may assume human shape (anthropomorphism), or vice versa. Animals may become demons, or vice versa. The narrator can appear as hero (egomorphism). Further: the story may be amplified with new materials. Such materials are generally derived from other folk tales. The expansion may take place at any point, but the beginning and end are the most likely to be amplified. Several tales can be joined into one. Finally: the inventiveness of an individual narrator may lead to intentional variations—for better or for worse.[10]

The serious study of popular story began, in Europe, with the Romantics. With the Grimm brothers the science came of age. With the foundation in Helsingfors, in 1907, of the Finnish society of the "Folklore Fellows," the now colossal subject was co-ordinated for systematic research over the entire world. The technique of the Geographic-Historical Method perfected by the associates of this pivotal group,[11] enables the modern scholar to trace the invisible path of the spoken tale practically to the doorstep of the inventor—over the bounds of states, languages, continents, even across oceans and around the globe. The work has required the co-operation of the scholars of the five continents; the international distribution of the materials has demanded an international research. Yet the work started in the usual way of folklore studies, as a labour of local, patriotic pride.

[10] Adapted from Antti Aarne, *Leitfaden der vergleichenden Märchenforschung*, FFC, II, 13, 1913, pp. 23–29. Cf. also, Taylor, *op. cit.*, p. 9, for a translation of the original list as given by Kaarle Krohn in *Mann und Fuchs*, Helsingfors, 1891, pp. 8–9.

[11] The technique was perfected by the Finnish School, but was independently developed by scholars in several quarters; for example, in America, Franz Boas, in Denmark, Axel Olrik, in France, Gaston Paris, E. Cosquin, in Germany, Johannes Bolte, Wilhelm Herz, Ernst Kuhn, Theodor Zachatiae, in Russia L. Kolmachevski.

About the middle of the nineteenth century, a strong nationalist movement had begun to mature in Finland. Buffeted for five hundred years between Sweden and Russia, the little nation had been annexed in 1809, by Czar Alexander I. Since the close of the eighteenth century, Swedish had been the official academic language. A group of young patriots now began to agitate for the restoration of the native spirit and the native tongue.

Elias Lönnrot (1802–1884), a country physician and student of Finnish philology, collected ballads and folk tales among the people. His work was a northern echo of the labours of the Brothers Grimm. Having gathered a considerable body of folk poetry around the legendary heroes, Väinämöinen, Ilmarinen, Lemminkainen, and Kullervo, he composed these in co-ordinated sequence and cast them in a uniform verse. 1835 he thus published the first edition of what has since become known as the folk-epic of Finland, the Kalevala, "The Land of Heroes."[12]

Julius Krohn (1835–1888), the first student at the university to presume to present his graduate thesis in Finnish, devoted himself to the study of the folk tradition, and in particular to the materials gathered by Lönnrot in the Kalevala. He discovered that among the ballads and popular stories of the Swedes, Russians, Germans, Tatars, etc., many of the motifs of Lönnrot's epic reappeared, but in variant combinations. The Kalevala, therefore, could not be studied all of a piece; its elements had to be traced down separately. With this discovery he took the first step toward the development of the Finnish geographic-historical method.

Julius Krohn next found that not all the Finnish examples of a given theme could be compared trait for trait with the foreign versions; only what seemed to him to be the oldest of the Finnish forms closely resembled those of the neighbouring lands. He concluded that the materials of the native epic had entered Finland from without and had undergone within the country gradual modification.

---

[12] A second edition, improved and enlarged, appeared in 1849. Translated into German (1852), it came under the eyes of Henry Wadsworth Longfellow, who was inspired to attempt a similar deed in the same metre for the American Indian; result: "The Song of Hiawatha."

Furthermore and finally, Julius Krohn perceived that each of the native modifications seemed to be limited in its geographical distribution. He took care, therefore, to keep precise note of the geographical sources as well as chronological relationships of his materials. In this way he was enabled to study the transformation of the motifs of a tale in its passage from mouth to mouth over the land and through the years. "First I sift and arrange the different variants according to chronology and topography," he wrote to the Hungarian philologist, P. Hunfalvy in 1884; "because I have discovered that only in this way is it possible to distinguish the original elements from the later additions."[13]

With respect to the *Kalevala*, Julius Krohn concluded that neither was it a very old legend nor were its materials originally Finnish. The narrative elements had arrived on the waves of a culture tide that had streamed over Europe through the centuries. Stemming from the gardens of the East and the fertile valleys of Antiquity, they had crossed southern Europe—largely by word of mouth—, then turned eastward again to the regions of the Slavs and Tatars, whence they had passed to the peoples of the north.[14] And as each folk had received, it had developed, reinterpreted and amplified, and then handed along the inheritance to the neighbour.

Thus in Finland, as in Germany, what had begun as the study of a national, developed inevitably into the review of an international tradition. And the scholarship that had started in patriotic fervour opened immediately into a world-wide collaboration. The son of Julius Krohn, Kaarle Krohn, applied the geographical method developed by his father to the special problem of the folk tale,[15] and it was he who in 1907, in collaboration with German and Scandinavian scholars, founded the research society that since his time has co-ordinated the work of many regions.

To illustrate the manner in which the research has been carried on:

---

[13] Kaarle Krohn, *Die folkloristische Arbeitsmethode*, Instituttet for Semmenlignende Kulturforskning, Oslo, 1926, pp. 13–14.

[14] Ibid., p. 13.

[15] Cf. Kaarle Krohn, *Bär (Wolf) und Fuchs*, Helsingfors, 1888; also, *Mann und Fuchs*, Helsingfors, 1891.

An index of folk tale types was issued in 1911 by Antti Aarne.[16] (The types distinguished in this basic study are those indicated above, pp. 752–753, for the varieties of story in the Grimm collection.) Each class was subdivided, and under each head appeared a directory of examples. Co-ordinated to Aarne's index then were published a series of special catalogues for a number of folk traditions: Finnish, Esthonian, Finnish-Swedish, Flemish, Norwegian, Lapp, Livonian, Rumanian, Hungarian, Icelandic, Spanish, and Prussian. For each culture all the available tales from the various published and unpublished archives were classified according to the principles of Aarne's index. Thus an order was beginning to be brought into fluid chaos.

Another type of work undertaken was that of the monograph. A monograph is a special study devoted to the tracing of a single tale through its twists and turns, disappearances and reappearances, over the globe and through the corridors of time. The technique for the preparation of such a work has been described as follows:

"1) The scholar undertaking to write a monograph on any folk narrative (folk tale, saga, legend, anecdote), must know all the extant versions ('variants') of this narrative, whether printed or unprinted, and no matter what the language in which they appear.

"2) He must compare all these versions, carefully, trait by trait, and without any previously formed opinion.

"3) During the investigation, he must always keep in mind the place and time of the rendering of each of the variants."[17]

"The homeland of any given folk tale can generally be judged to be the region in which the richest harvest of variants appears; furthermore, where the structure of the tale is most consistent, and where

[16] Antti Aarne, *Verzeichnis der Märchentypen*, Folklore Fellows Communications, Vol. I, No. 3, Helsingfors, 1910. This work was re-edited and brought up to date in 1928 by the American folklorist, Stith Thompson (Aarne and Thompson, *The Types of the Folk-Tale*, FFC., XXV, 74, 1928), and in 1929 by the Russian, N. P. Andrejev (*Ukazateli skazochnych syuzhetov po sistem Aarne*, 1929). Professor Thompson has since prepared a gigantic index of motifs, *Motif-Index of Folk-Literature*, Indiana University Studies, Vols. XIX-XXIII, Bloomington, Ind., 1932–1936.

[17] Walter Anderson, in Lutz Mackensen, *Handwörterbuch des deutschen Märchens*, Berlin and Leipzig, 1934 ff., Vol. II, article: "Geographisch-historische Methode."—A good example of such a monograph is the above noticed work of Archer Taylor, *The Black Ox*, FFC., XXIII, 70.

customs and beliefs may serve to illuminate the meaning of the tale. The farther a folk tale wanders from its home, the greater the damage to its configurations."[18]

The researches of the Finnish folklore school were supported and extended by an originally independent enterprise in Germany. In 1898 Professor Herman Grimm, the son of Wilhelm, turned over to Johannes Bolte (1858–1937) the unpublished materials of his father and his uncle, with the hope that a new edition might be prepared of the *Commentaries to the Nursery and Household Tales*. These commentaries had first appeared as appendices to the volumes of 1812 and 1815, then as a special volume in 1822, and finally in a third edition, 1856. Professor Bolte collated, trait by trait, with all the tales and variants gathered by the Grimms everything that could be drawn from the modern archives. He enlisted in the enterprise Professor George Polívka of Prague, who assisted in the analysis of the Slavic analogues. During the course of the next thirty-four years the opus grew to five closely printed volumes. The original work of the Grimms, which had opened a rich century of folk studies, collection and interpretation, was brought by this labour to stand securely in the mid-point of the modern field. The *Nursery and Household Tales* are to-day, as they were the first moment they left the press, the beginning and the middle, if in no way the end, of the study of the literature of the people.

The following classification of the stories according to the above described stages of development[19] is adapted from that supplied by Friedrich von der Leyen to his edition of the *Nursery and Household Tales* (Jena, 1912). The listing enables the reader to study for himself the stratifications of the inexhaustible text.

I. *Primitive Belief*: 28. 39. 55. 60. 85. 105, i. ii. 109. 154.—II. *Hero Sagas from the Period of the Migrations*: 47. 52. 89. 111. 198.—III. *Minstrel Work of the Tenth Century*: 8. 18. 20. 33. 37. 45. 61. 64. 90. 91. 103. 112. 114. 146. *151. 166. 183.—IV. *Chivalrous Work of the Middle Ages*: 1. 3. 4. 9. 11. 12. 13. 15. 19. 21. 24. 25. 31. 42. 43. 46. 49. 53. 57. 62. 63. 65. 67. 76. 88. 97. 106. 108. 113. 121. 123. 126. 127. 130. 135. 136. 137. 144. 169. 186. 192. 193. 201–210.—V. *Oriental Influences*: 6. 16. 29. 36. 51. 54. 56.

[18] Friedrich von der Leyen, *op. cit.*, p. 36.
[19] P. 846 ff. *supra*.

68. 71. 79. 92. 93. 94. 98. 107. 122. 129. 134. 143. 152. 165. 182.—
VI. *Animal Stories:* 2. 17. 23. 27. 48. 58. 72. 73. 74. 75. 102. 132. 148.
157. 171. 173. 177. 187.—VII. *Work of the Townsmen of the Fourteenth to
Sixteenth Centuries:* 7. 4. 32. 34. 35. 44. 59. 70. 77. 81. 82. 83. 84. 87. 95.
100. 101. 104. 110. 115. 116. 118. 119. 120. 124. 125. 128. 147. 149.
153. 162. 164. 167. 168. 170. 174. 175. 176. 177. 178. 180. 183. 184.
189. 194. 195. 199.—VIII. *From the Seventeenth and Eighteenth Centuries:* 5. 22.
26. 40. 50. 69. 78. 96. 99. 117. 133. 141. 142. 145. 150. 155. 156.
160. 161. 163. 179. 181. 188. 191. 197.—IX. *Jokes and Anecdotes:* 10. 30.
38. 41. 66. 80. 86. 105, iii. 131. 138. 139. 140. 158. 159. 190. 196.
200.

4

THE QUESTION OF MEANING

The Grimm brothers, Max Müller, Andrew Lang, and others, have pointed out that folk tales are "monstrous, irrational and unnatural," both as to the elements of which they are composed, and as to the plots that unify these elements. Since a tale may have a different origin from its elements, two questions propose themselves: What is the origin and meaning of the motifs? What is the origin and meaning of the tales?

a)The Motifs.

Many of the incidents of the merry tales, jokes, yarns, tall stories and anecdotes are simply comical and clever inventions spun from life. These offer no problem.

The "monstrous, irrational and unnatural" incidents, however, are of a kind with those of myth; indeed, they are frequently derived from myth. They must be explained as myth is explained. But then, how is myth explained?

The reply varies according to the authority:

Euhemerus, a Greek writer of the fourth century B.C., noting that Alexander the Great, shortly after his death, was already appearing in legend as a demi-god, propounded the view that the gods are only great mortals, deified. Snorri Sturleson (1179–1241), in the preface to his *Prose Edda*, explained in the same way the pagan divinities of the Norse. This theory, called "Euhemerism," has its advocates to this day.

Among the Indo-Germanic philologists in the period of the ascendancy of Max Müller, it was believed that myths were originally sentimental descriptions of nature. Man half consciously read the tragedy of his own life in the birth of the sun, its "kissing of the dew to death," its culmination, descent, and disappearance into the arms of night. Due to the fact that Indo-European nouns are either masculine or feminine, the descriptions tended to personify their objects. And due to the fact that the language was evolving, the original references of the personifying nouns were presently forgotten, so that the words were finally taken to be personal names.[1] For example, such a metaphorical name for the sun as Kephalos, the "Head" (of light), presently lost its meaning and was thought to refer to a human youth; and correspondingly, the fading dew, Prokris, bride of the "Head," became a mortal girl of tragical demise. One more step: the names might become confused with those of actual historical heroes, whereupon the myth would be transformed into a legend.[2]

Müller's theory was the most elaborate attempt to account for the mechanics of personification. Among the "Anthropologists" it was, more easily, simply assumed that savages and poets tend to attribute souls to things and to personify.[3] The childlike fantasy of primitive man, his poetic feeling and morbid, dream-ridden imagination, played into his attempts to describe and explain the world around him, and thus produced a phantasmagoric counter-world. But the savage's effort, at the core, was to discover the causes of things, and then, through spells, prayer, sacrifice, and sacrament, to control them. Mythology, therefore, was only a false etiology; ceremonial a misguided technology. With the gradual, unmethodical, but nevertheless inevitable recognition

[1] Müller always stressed descriptions of the sunset and sunrise. Other scholars, following his lead, cogitated on the lunar phases and the interplay of sun and moon (E. Siecke, *Die Liebesgeschichte des Himmels*, 1892; *Die Urreligion der Indogermanen*, 1897), or on the terror of storms and winds (A. Kuhn, *Die Herabkunft des Feuers und des Göttertranks*, 1859, 1886; W. Schwarz, *Die poetischen Naturerscheinungen der Griechen, Römer und Deutschen*, 1864–1879), or on the wonder of the stars (E. Stucken, *Astralmythen der Hebräer, Babylonier und Aegypter*, 1896–1907). For Müller's celebrated interpretation of "The Frog-King," (Grimm I.) as a sun-personification, see *Chips from a German Workshop*, London, 1880, Vol. II, pp. 249–252.

[2] F. Max Müller, *op. cit.*, Vol. II, pp. 1–146 ("Comparative Mythology," 1856).

[3] Cf. Edward B. Tylor, *Primitive Culture*, London, 1920, Chapters VIII-X.

of error upon error, man progressed through the labyrinth of wonder to the clearer headed stand of to-day.[4]

Another view (and it rather supplemented than contradicted the descriptive-etiological theory) represented primitive man as terrified by the presences of the grave, hence ever anxious to propitiate and turn them away. The roots of myth and ritual went down to the black subsoil of the grave-cult and fear of death.[5]

A fourth viewpoint was propounded by the French sociologist, Emile Durkheim. He argued that the collective superexcitation (*surexcitation*) of clan, tribal, and intertribal gatherings was experienced by every participating member of the group as an impersonal, infectious power (*mana*); and this power would be thought to emanate from the clan or tribal emblem (*totem*); and this emblem, therefore, would be set apart from all other objects as filled with *mana* (sacred vs. profane). This *totem*, this first cult object, would then infect with *mana* all associated objects, and through this contagion there would come into being a system of beliefs and practices relative to sacred things, uniting in a single moral community all believers.[6] The great contribution of Durkheim's theory, and what set it apart from all that had gone before, was that it represented religion not as a morbid exaggeration, false hypothesis, or unenlightened fear, but as a truth emotionally experienced, the truth of the relationship of the individual to the group.

This recognition by Durkheim of a kind of truth at the root of the image-world of myth is supported, expanded, and deepened, by the demonstration of the psychoanalysts that dreams are precipitations of unconscious desires, ideals, and fears, and furthermore, that the images of dream resemble—broadly, but then frequently to the detail—the

[4] "Reflection and enquiry should satisfy us that to our [savage] predecessors we are indebted for much of what we thought most of our own, and that their errors were not wilful extravagances or the ravings of insanity, but simply hypotheses, justifiable as such at the time when they were propounded, but which a further experience has proved to be inadequate. It is only by the successive testing of hypotheses and rejection of the false that truth is at last elicited." (Sir James G. Frazer, *The Golden Bough*, one volume edition, New York and London, 1922, etc., p. 264)

[5] Cf. Jane Ellen Harrison, *Prolegomena to the Study of Greek Religion*, Cambridge University Press, 3rd edition, 1922.

[6] Emile Durkheim, *Les Formes élémentaires de la vie religieuse*, Paris, 1912; English translation, New York and London, 1915, Book I, chapter I; Book II, chapters 5–6.

motifs of folk tale and myth. Having selected for their study the symbol-inventing, myth-motif-producing level of the psyche—source of all those universal themes ("Elementary Ideas") which men have read into the phenomena of nature, into the shadows of the tomb, the lives of the heroes, and the emblems of society—, the psychoanalysts have undoubtedly touched the central moment of the multifarious problem. In the light of their discussion, theories which before seemed mutually contradictory become easily co-ordinated. Man, nature, death, society—these have served simply as fields into which dream-meanings have been projected. Hence the references of the wild motifs are not really (no matter what the rationalizing consciousness may believe) to the sun, the moon, the stars—the wind and thunder—the grave—the hero—or even the power of the group, but through these, back again to a state of the psyche. Mytholgoy is psychology, misread as cosmology, history, and biography.

A still further step can and must be taken, however, before we shall have reached the bounds of the problem. Myth, as the psychoanalysts declare, is not a mess of errors; myth is a picture language. But the language has to be studied to be read. In the first place, this language is the native speech of dream. But in the second place, it has been studied, clarified, and enriched by the poets, prophets, and visionaries of untold millenniums. Dante, Aquinas and Augustine, al-Ghazali and Mahomet, Zarathustra, Shankārachārya, Nāgārjuna, and T'ai Tsung, were not bad scientists making mis-statements about the weather, or neurotics reading dreams into the stars, but masters of the human spirit teaching a wisdom of death and life. And the thesaurus of the myth-motifs was their vocabulary. They brooded on the state and way of man, and through their broodings came to wisdom; then teaching, with the aid of the picture-language of myth, they worked changes on the pattern of their inherited iconographies.

But not only in the higher cultures, even among the so-called primitives, priests, wizards, and visionaries interpret and re-interpret myth as symbolic of "the Way": "the Pollen Path of Beauty," as it is called, for example, among the Navaho. And this Way, congenial to the wholeness of man, is understood as the little portion of the great Way that binds the cosmos; for, as among the Babylonians, so everywhere, the crux of mythological teaching has always been that "an everlasting reiteration of unchanging principles and events takes place both in space and in time, in large as in small."[7] The Way of the individual is the microcosmic reiteration of the Way of the All and of each. In this sense the reasonings of the sages are not only psychological but metaphysical. They are not easily grasped. And yet they are the subtle arguments that inform the iconographies of the world.

Myths, therefore, as they now come to us, and as they break up to let their pregnant motifs scatter and settle into the materials of popular tale, are the purveyors of a wisdom that has borne the race of man through the long vicissitudes of his career. "The content of folklore," writes Ananda K. Coomaraswamy, "is metaphysics. Our inability to see this is due primarily to our abysmal ignorance of metaphysics and its technical terms."[8]

Therefore, in sum: The "monstrous, irrational and unnatural" motifs of folk tale and myth are derived from the reservoirs of dream and vision. On the dream level such images represent the total state of the individual dreaming psyche. But clarified of personal distortions and profounded—by poets, prophets, visionaries—, they become symbolic of the spiritual norm for Man the Microcosm. They are thus phrases from an image-language, expressive of metaphysical, psychological, and sociological truth. And in the primitive, oriental, archaic, and medieval societies this vocabulary was pondered and more or less understood. Only in the wake of the Enlightenment has it suddenly lost its meaning and been pronounced insane.

b) The Tales.

The folk tale, in contrast to the myth, is a form of entertainment. The story teller fails or succeeds in proportion to the amusement he affords. His motifs may be plucked from the tree of myth, but his craft is never precisely of the mythological order. His productions have to be judged, at last, not as science, sociology, psychology, or metaphysics, but as art—and specifically, art produced by individuals at discoverable

[7] Hugo Winckler, *Himmels- und Weltenbild der Babylonier, als Grundlage der Weltanschauung und Mythologie aller Völker*, Leipzig, 1901, p. 49.—The Babylonian astrological mythology, as described by Hugo Winckler, is a local specification, amplification, and application of themes that are of the essence of mythology everywhere.

[8] Ananda K. Coomaraswamy, "De la 'Mentalité Primitive,'" *Etudes traditionnelles*, 44e Année, Nos. 236–237–238, Paris, 1939, p. 278.

periods, in discoverable lands. We have to ask: What principles of craftsmanship inspired the narrators who gave shape to these stories in the long reaches of the past?

The Indian, Celtic, Arabian, and Medieval masters of narrative to whom we owe the most exquisite of our European tales were the practitioners of a craft that strove to reveal through mortal things the brilliance of eternal forms.[9] The quality of their work was not a naturalistic, but a spiritual precision, and their power, "Instructive Wonder." To us there may seem to be little distinction between such a craft and metaphysics; for we have enlarged the connotation of our term, "metaphysical," to include everything untranslatable into positivistic discourse. But peoples of the pre-modern type, whether gothic, oriental, archaic, totemistic, or primitive, typically took for granted the operation of a transcendent energy in the forms of space and time. It was required of every artist, no matter what his craft, that his product should show its sign of the spirit, as well as serve its mechanical end. The function of the craft of the tale, therefore, was not simply to fill the vacant hour, but to fill it with symbolic fare. And since symbolization is the characteristic pleasure of the human mind, the fascination of the tale increased in proportion to the richness of its symbolic content.

By an ironic paradox of time, the playful symbolism of the folk tale—a product of the vacant hour—today seems to us more true, more powerful to survive, than the might and weight of myth. For, whereas the symbolic figures of mythology were regarded (by all except the most sophisticated of the metaphysicians) not as symbolic figures at all but as actual divinities to be invoked, placated, loved and feared, the personages of the tale were comparatively unsubstantial. They were cherished primarily for their fascination. Hence, when the acids of the modern spirit dissolved the kingdoms of the gods, the tales in their essence were hardly touched. The elves were less real than before; but the tales, by the same token, the more alive. So that we may say that out of the whole symbol-building achievement of the past,

---

[9] Cf. Jacques Maritain, *Art and Scholasticism*, New York, 1930; Ananda K. Coomaraswamy, *The Transformation of Nature in Art*, Cambridge, Mass., 1934; Heinrich Zimmer, *Kunstform und Yoga*, Berlin, 1936.

what survives to us today (hardly altered in efficiency or in function) is the tale of wonder.

The tale survives, furthermore, not simply as a quaint relic of days childlike in belief. Its world of magic is symptomatic of fevers deeply burning in the psyche: permanent presences, desires, fears, ideals, potentialities, that have glowed in the nerves, hummed in the blood, baffled the senses, since the beginning. The one psyche is operative in both the figments of this vision-world and the deeds of human life. In some manner, then, the latter must stand prefigured in the former. History is the promise of *Märchen* realized through, and against the obstacles of, space and time. Playful and unpretentious as the archetypes of fairy tale may appear to be, they are the heroes and villains who have built the world for us. The debutante combing her hair before the glass, the mother pondering the future of a son, the labourers in the mines, the merchant vessel full of cargo, the ambassador with portfolio, the soldier in the field of war—all are working in order that the ungainsayable specifications of effective fantasy, the permanent patterns of the tale of wonder, shall be clothed in flesh and known as life.

And so we find that in those masterworks of the modern day which are of a visionary, rather than of a descriptive order, the forms long known from the nursery tale reappear, but now in adult maturity. While the Frazers and the Müllers were scratching their necks to invent some rational explanation for the irrational patterns of fairy lore, Wagner was composing his *Ring of the Nibelung*, Strindberg and Ibsen their symbolical plays, Nietzsche his *Zarathustra*, Melville his *Moby Dick*. Goethe had long completed the *Faust*, Spenser his *Faerie Queene*. To-day the novels of James Joyce, Franz Kafka, Thomas Mann, and many another, as well as the poems of every season, tell us that the gastric fires of human fantasy still are potent to digest raw experience and assimilate it to the creative genius of man. In these productions again, as in the story world of the past which they continue and in essence duplicate, the denotation of the symbols is human destiny: destiny recognized, for all its cannibal horrors, as a marvellous, wild, "monstrous, irrational and unnatural" wondertale to fill the void. This is the story our spirit asked for; this is the story we receive.

Through the vogues of literary history, the folk tale has survived.

Told and retold, losing here a detail, gaining there a new hero, disintegrating gradually in outline, but re-created occassionally by some narrator of the folk, the little masterpiece transports into the living present a long inheritance of story-skill, coming down from the romancers of the Middle Ages, the strictly disciplined poets of the Celts, the professional story-men of Islam, and the exquisite, fertile, brilliant fabulists of Hindu and Buddhist India. This little mare that we are reading has the touch on it of Somadeva, Shahrazad, Taliesin and Boccaccio, as well as the accent of the story-wife of Niederzwehren. If ever there was an art on which the whole community of mankind has worked—seasoned with the philosophy of the codger on the wharf and singing with the music of the spheres—it is this of the ageless tale.

The folk tale is the primer of the picture-language of the soul.

JOSEPH CAMPBELL

Routledge Classics
Get inside a great mind

British Folk Tales and Legends
A Sampler

Katharine Briggs

'Katharine Briggs has done a wonderful job of bringing all these old stories together.'
Daily Telegraph

Katharine Briggs was the most important folklorist this island has ever produced. In 1970 she published the monumental *Dictionary of British Folktales and Legends* to wide acclaim. It was a massive and authoritative four-volume set. This edition comprises the very best of those tales and legends. Gathered within are an extravaganza of beautiful princesses and stout stable boys, sour-faced witches and kings with hearts of gold. Each tale is a masterpiece of storytelling, from the hilarious 'Three Sillies' to the delightfully macabre 'Sammle's Ghost'.

Pb: 0–415–28602–6

A Book of Nonsense

Edward Lear

'I really don't know any author to whom I am half so grateful for my idle self as Edward Lear. I shall put him first of my hundred authors.'
John Ruskin

From the benighted Old Man with a Beard to the erudite Perpendicular Purple Polly, Edward Lear's world was inhabited by a bewildering variety of oddities. Pelicans, parrots, seals and rhinoceroses cavorted gaily with Dongs and Pobbles, not to mention the Quangle-Wangles! One of the world's most beloved writers, Lear's verse has delighted whole generations of readers. Available once again from its original publisher, *A Book of Nonsense* is a rarity, a feast of delightful playfulness that deserves to be on everyone's bookshelf.

Hb: 0–415–28599–2   Pb: 0–415–28600–X

For these and other classic titles from Routledge, visit
www.routledgeclassics.com

Routledge Classics
Get inside a great mind

Stories and Tales
Hans Christian Andersen

'These fairy tales . . . are of the nature of imperishable things.'
Hermann Hesse

A true classic of Western literature, *Stories and Tales* has delighted young and old for generations. This unique collection features more than eighty of Andersen's best-loved tales – from 'The Ugly Duckling' to 'The Red Shoes' and the thrilling, if chilling, 'Snow Queen'. The tales have a gently contemporary feel to them, despite having been written well over a century ago. Complete with the original, beautiful illustrations by A. W. Bayes, this marvellous book will be a welcome addition to anyone's bookshelf.

Hb: 0–415–28597–6   Pb: 0–415–28598–4

The Fairies in Tradition and Literature
Katharine Briggs

'Katharine Briggs is the magic mirror on the wall.'
Richard Adams

Who can forget the Cottingley fairies – and those grainy pictures of fairies cavorting on the hands of an awe-struck little girl? From each part of history and from every country, poets and writers have delighted in describing a magical world inhabited by elfin spirits. This remarkable book explores the history in literature and tradition of these wondrous creatures, the Little People. Capricious and vengeful, or beautiful and generous, these denizens of enchanted places have held us in thrall for generations.

Pb: 0–415–28601–8

For these and other classic titles from Routledge, visit
www.routledgeclassics.com